JA, WE ARE HIT. CURSE THESE MAD, COURAGEOUS ENGLANDERS!

EVEN AS JOHN FIRED THE TORPEDO, AN AVALANCHE OF FIRE ENGULFE JOHN, BERT AND TED BARCLAY WERE FLUNG INTO THE WATER AS THE TO SINK.

SHE'S GOING!

REFORMED AROUND TERRY AS THE L
E ENORMITY OF THE EXPLOSION.

GREAT SHOW — WELL DONE!

THE TRAPPED ENEMY WRE FINISHED ALMOST AT ONCE. BRAVELY THEY FOUGHT ON.

WATCH LADS, TH TOUG

AAGH!

Commando

FOR ACTION AND ADVENTURE

TRUE BRIT

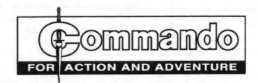

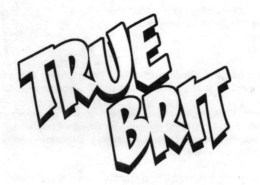

For Dan

Published in 2006 by Carlton Books Limited
An imprint of the Carlton Publishing Group
20 Mortimer Street
London W1T 3JW

A catalogue record for this book is available from the British Library.

ISBN 10: 1 84442 121 X
ISBN 13: 978 184442 121 3

Printed and bound in India
10 9 8 7 6 5 4 3 2 1

Commando
FOR ACTION AND ADVENTURE

THE TOUGHEST 12 COMMANDO COMIC BOOKS EVER!

EDITED BY GEORGE LOW, EDITOR OF COMMANDO

CARLTON
BOOKS

Contents

Introduction

First of all, many thanks to all of you out there who showed so much enthusiasm for *The Dirty Dozen*, the first bumper Commando book which displayed some of our earlier stories in all their glory. So it was back to the archives to seek out another collection of classic war yarns in the *True Brit* style to keep all you fans out there happy. Was it any easier to make this second selection? Well, no, it wasn't, but it was a lot of fun.

EXHAUSTED, BILL STARED IN DISBELIEF AS MASTRONI AIMED THE PISTOL STRAIGHT AT HIM.

I TOLD YOU BEFORE WHO WAS THE MASTER RACE. IF YOU HAD LISTENED, THEN PERHAPS YOU WOULDN'T HAVE TO DIE NOW.

More research led to further material that called out to be included. Looking over the files, it became clear that a script writer's phrase here or an artist's angle there had not lost any of their magic. Often, too, some new detail caught the eye. It says a lot for the writers and illustrators that their touch lives on so vibrantly after so many years.

THE SIGHT OF THE KILLER HURRICANES CHILLED THE NAZIS' BLOOD.

KEEP AT 'EM!

FIRING BACK AT THE DIVING HURRIS, THE HEINKELS FLEW STEADILY ON.

I personally find it difficult to pick out favourites. I know how hard our writers, past and present, strive to come up with a good idea for a plot and then battle to get a character right or include as much action as possible into our limited number of pictures. As for the artists, they take up the challenge to depict the stories in the best way they know how.

That is not easy at times, as one artist pointed out when he was asked to depict a massed cavalry charge … with elephants following at the rear. The sound of the mighty advance was nothing in comparison to the poor illustrator's wails of anguish. It clearly calls for determination and discipline on the part of all involved to publish even just one story.

What I have also learned after this second dig into the past is something we always knew and appreciated, but which we need to be reminded of at times. A brilliant band of writers and artists came together to let many, many people enjoy Commando.

Where did they get the ideas? Sometimes we fed them a morsel of information and that became a full-blown saga of adventure and action. More often, the fertile brains of our writers produced their own startling ideas. The best start to my week as an editor is to read through a plot outline and be won over by a cunning idea snaking across the page.

And any of our artists will tell you that they react best to the stories which catch their imagination. They can't resist adding their own little touches to emphasise a point. One memorable instance involved a very authentic Royal Air Force control tower room with an American Civil War Confederate soldier, complete with musket, just in view through the window.

All I have to say now is that I hope you enjoy thumbing through these pages and savouring what's on offer. If you already have *The Dirty Dozen*, then you know you're in for a good read … so enjoy. And that's an order!

George Low,
EDITOR, COMMANDO

BRITISH 3.7 INCH SCREW HOWITZER

Screw guns were so called because their barrels could be split in two for transport (along with the other parts) on mules. They were designed for the British army in India, and the earlier 2.75-inch model was used during the First World War. The later 3.7-inch gun saw service during the Second World War in the hilly areas of countries like Ethiopia, Norway, Italy and Burma. In fact, some were still in service in the late 1950s.

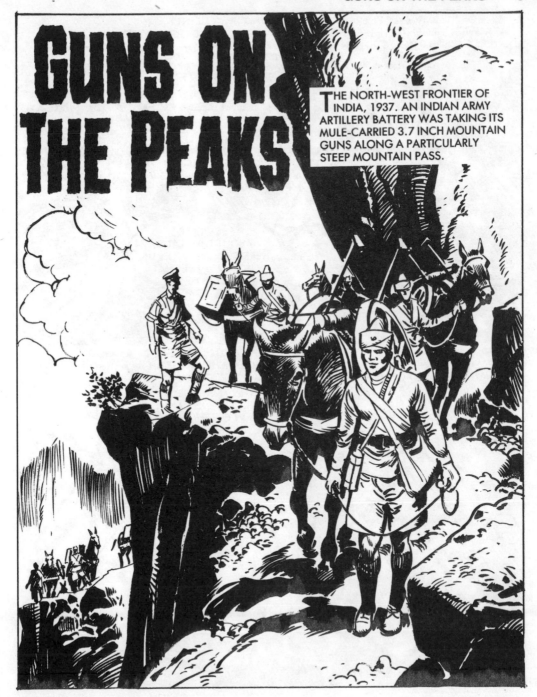

GUNS ON THE PEAKS

THE NORTH-WEST FRONTIER OF INDIA, 1937. AN INDIAN ARMY ARTILLERY BATTERY WAS TAKING ITS MULE-CARRIED 3.7 INCH MOUNTAIN GUNS ALONG A PARTICULARLY STEEP MOUNTAIN PASS.

ONE OF THE BRITISH OFFICERS COMMANDING THIS UNIT, LIEUTENANT BILL WARWICK, URGENTLY HELPED HIS SEPOYS TO ASSEMBLE THE GUNS WHICH WERE CARRIED INTO ACTION IN PIECES BY THE MULES.

LET'S BE QUICK ABOUT THIS, LADS. THERE'S AN INFANTRY UNIT DOWN THERE THAT NEEDS HELP!

IN THE TIME HE'D BEEN WITH THE BATTERY, BILL HAD PROVED HIMSELF TO BE A GOOD OFFICER, WHO DIDN'T MIND GETTING HIS HANDS DIRTY OR HELPING OUT IN A TIGHT SPOT, EARNING THE RESPECT OF HIS MEN.

ONCE THIS AMMO'S UP FRONT, WE CAN START ON THOSE PATHANS.

YES, SAHIB!

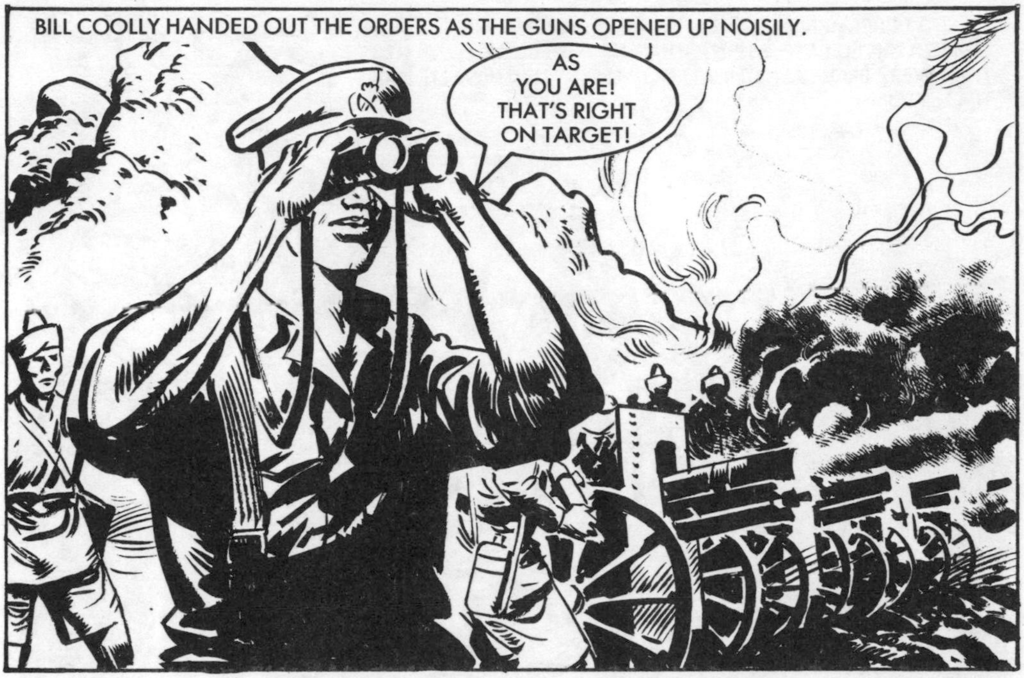
BILL COOLLY HANDED OUT THE ORDERS AS THE GUNS OPENED UP NOISILY.
AS YOU ARE! THAT'S RIGHT ON TARGET!

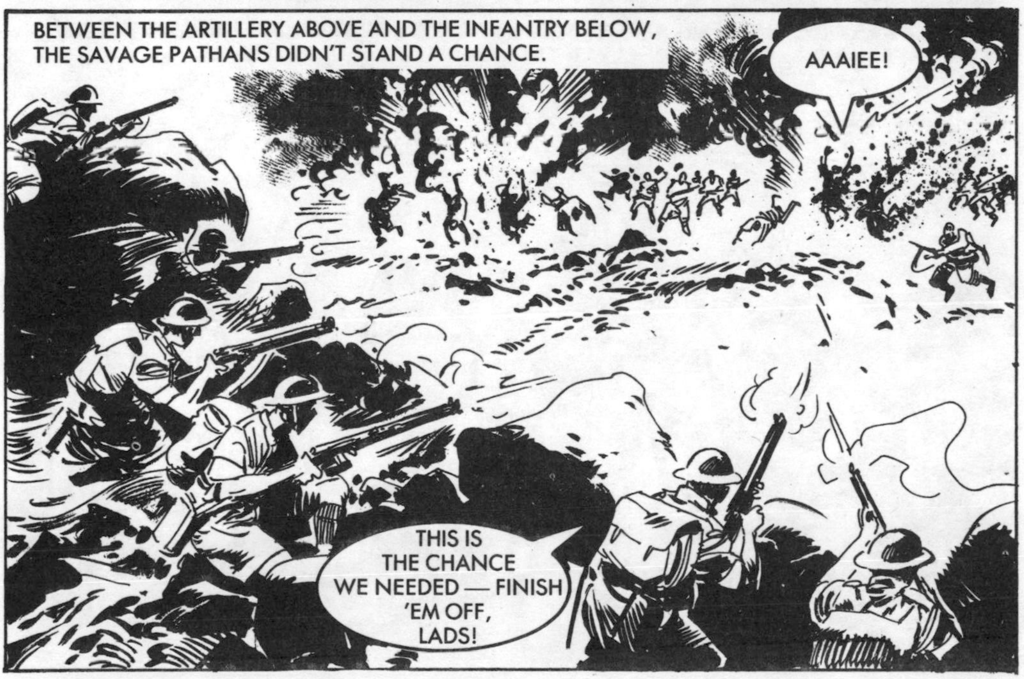
BETWEEN THE ARTILLERY ABOVE AND THE INFANTRY BELOW, THE SAVAGE PATHANS DIDN'T STAND A CHANCE.
AAAIEE!
THIS IS THE CHANCE WE NEEDED — FINISH 'EM OFF, LADS!

AS THE TRIBESMEN BEGAN TO RETREAT, TWO MORE GUNS ARRIVED LATE, STRUGGLING UP THE HILLSIDE. THEY WERE FROM ANOTHER TROOP LED BY LIEUTENANT TIM LEYTON.

C'MON, YOU LOT. THIS ISN'T A PICNIC, YOU KNOW!

LEYTON WAS OLDER THAN BILL AND HAD BEEN IN THE BATTERY LONGER. HE WAS THE TYPE OF OFFICER WHO SHOUTED ORDERS RATHER THAN HELP.

WE'RE ALREADY LATE, SO HURRY IT UP!

I KNOW WHAT I'D LIKE TO DO WITH HIM AND HIS GUNS, BROTHER.

TRULY HE IS NOT A PLEASANT SAHIB.

THE INDIAN TROOPS HAD NO RESPECT FOR LEYTON, TALKING SARCASTICALLY ABOUT HIM UNDER THEIR BREATH.

AS SOON AS LEYTON ARRIVED, HE STATED THAT HE WAS TAKING COMMAND. BILL DIDN'T LIKE HIS TONE AND TOTALLY DISAGREED.

OKAY, WARWICK. I'LL TAKE OVER FROM HERE, SEEING AS I HAVE MORE EXPERIENCE.

I DON'T THINK SO! THIS IS MY TROOP AND THEY'LL FOLLOW MY ORDERS!

BILL ORDERED THE MEN TO KEEP FIRING, AND THEY COMPLIED INSTANTLY WITH A DEAFENING SALVO.

FIRE AT WILL!

BILL'S SHOW OF COMMAND DISGRUNTLED LEYTON. HE STORMED OVER TO HIS MEN TO TAKE IT OUT ON THEM.

EVERYONE QUICKLY TOOK COVER AS SNIPER FIRE FROM PATHAN MARKSMEN BEGAN TO RICOCHET CRUELLY AMONGST THE ROCKS.

WITHOUT BREAKING FROM COVER, LEYTON ORDERED THE TWO NEAREST GUNS TO RETURN FIRE. BUT BILL INTERRUPTED, DRAWING HIS REVOLVER AND ORDERING THE CREWS TO CARRY ON AS THEY WERE.

BILL TOOK A YOUNG TROOPER, SHAMI NASTRI, AND THEY QUICKLY MADE THEIR WAY UP THROUGH THE ROCKS, CRAWLING AROUND TO OUTFLANK THE SNIPERS.

WHILE THE SNIPERS WERE CONCENTRATING THEIR FIRE ON THE GUNS, BILL AND SHAMI RAN DOWN THE MOUNTAINSIDE BEHIND THEM, TAKING THEM BY SURPRISE.

ONE PATHAN WAS ONLY WOUNDED AND FEIGNED DEATH UNTIL THE TWO MEN DREW CLOSER THEN FIRED AT SHAMI.

BILL QUICKLY TURNED AND DISPATCHED THE WILY TRIBESMAN.

SHAMI ONLY HAD A FLESH WOUND AND BILL HELPED HIM BACK DOWN TOWARDS THE GUNS, WELCOMED BY CHEERS FROM THE MEN. LEYTON WAS MORE THAN A LITTLE UNHAPPY WITH THE SITUATION.

WELL DONE!

I'LL NEVER GET A GRIP ON THE COMMAND NOW. BLAST WARWICK! I'LL GET MY REVENGE ONE DAY.

THE DEVASTATING FIRE FROM THE GUNS AND THE ROUTING OF THEIR SNIPERS WAS TOO MUCH FOR THE PATHANS. SILENTLY THE REMAINDER DISAPPEARED INTO THE HIGH MOUNTAINS.

BILL HELD NO HARD FEELINGS AGAINST LEYTON FOR HIS OVERBEARING MANNER AND, A FEW DAYS LATER BACK AT BASE, INVITED HIM TO JOIN A CLIMBING EXPEDITION IN EUROPE WITH OTHER OFFICERS WHILE THEY WERE ON LEAVE. BUT LEYTON STILL BORE A GRUDGE.

HOW ABOUT IT, TIM? FANCY SOME CLIMBING IN THE ALPS?

LET'S GET ONE THING CLEAR, WARWICK. YOU INSULTED ME ON THE MOUNTAINSIDE THAT DAY — AND I'LL NEVER FORGET IT!

AND SO THE TWO OFFICERS PARTED WITH BAD FEELINGS.

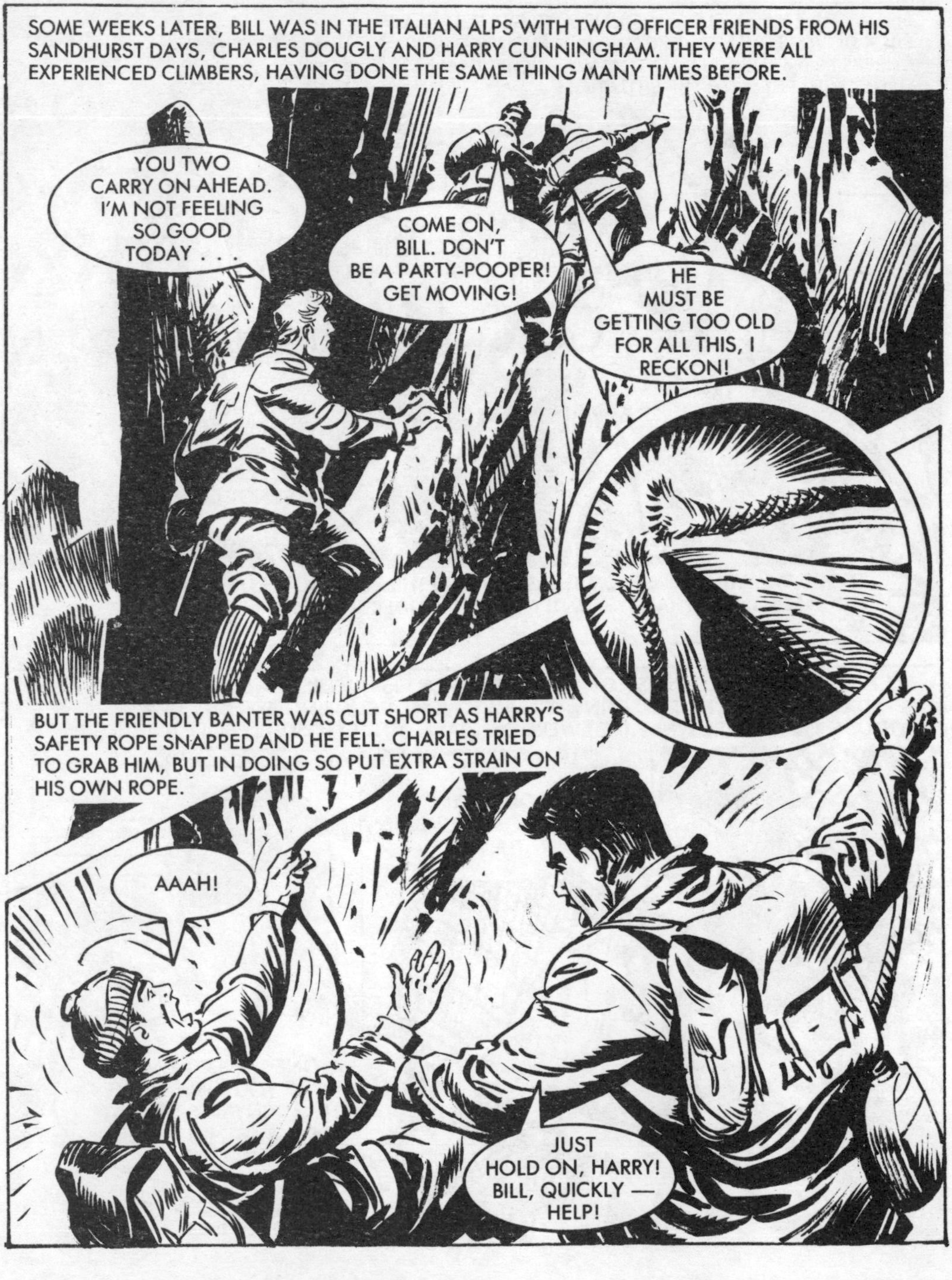
SOME WEEKS LATER, BILL WAS IN THE ITALIAN ALPS WITH TWO OFFICER FRIENDS FROM HIS SANDHURST DAYS, CHARLES DOUGLY AND HARRY CUNNINGHAM. THEY WERE ALL EXPERIENCED CLIMBERS, HAVING DONE THE SAME THING MANY TIMES BEFORE.
YOU TWO CARRY ON AHEAD. I'M NOT FEELING SO GOOD TODAY . . .
COME ON, BILL. DON'T BE A PARTY-POOPER! GET MOVING!
HE MUST BE GETTING TOO OLD FOR ALL THIS, I RECKON!
BUT THE FRIENDLY BANTER WAS CUT SHORT AS HARRY'S SAFETY ROPE SNAPPED AND HE FELL. CHARLES TRIED TO GRAB HIM, BUT IN DOING SO PUT EXTRA STRAIN ON HIS OWN ROPE.
AAAH!
JUST HOLD ON, HARRY! BILL, QUICKLY — HELP!

BUT BILL, FEELING ILL, DIDN'T MAKE IT. THE EXTRA STRAIN CAUSED CHARLES' ROPE TO BREAK AND THE TWO MEN FELL OFF THE FACE IN A SMALL AVALANCHE OF ROCKS AND RUBBLE. BILL WAS FORCED TO SCRAMBLE UNDER A ROCKY OUTCROP.

CHARLES AND HARRY'S SCREAMS SEEMED TO ECHO AROUND THE MOUNTAINS FOR EVER. SUDDENLY BILL WAS ALONE, SHOCKED, FROZEN TO THE ROCK FACE AND UNABLE TO MOVE.

LUCKILY, SOME ITALIAN MOUNTAIN TROOPS WERE ON EXERCISES IN THE AREA NEARBY. THEY WERE ALERTED BY THE NOISE OF THE AVALANCHE AND MADE THEIR WAY TOWARDS BILL'S CRIES FOR HELP. SERGEANT ENRICO TABARDI VOLUNTEERED TO GO DOWN AND RESCUE HIM.

HELP! HELP!

YOU WOULD RISK YOUR LIFE TO GO DOWN THERE, ENRICO? FOR SOME ENGLISHMAN?

IF IT WERE ONE OF YOU, WOULD YOU QUESTION MY ACTIONS? I DON'T THINK SO! WE OF THE MOUNTAINS SHOULD STICK TOGETHER COME WHAT MAY.

ENRICO CLIMBED DOWN TILL HE REACHED BILL AND TRIED TO COAX HIM TO LET GO.

YOU MUST HOLD ON TO ME. IT IS THE ONLY WAY WE WILL GET YOU TO THE TOP, SIGNOR.

I CAN'T . . . TOO SCARED!

THE ITALIAN GOT HOLD OF BILL.

THEN THERE IS ONLY ONE THING I CAN DO.

BEFORE BILL REALISED WHAT WAS HAPPENING, ENRICO TIGHTENED HIS HOLD ON HIM. THIS PUSHED THEM BOTH OFF THE CLIFF TILL THEY WERE DANGLING IN MID-AIR.

ENRICO KNEW THAT THERE WAS NOT TOO MUCH RISK IN WHAT HE HAD DONE AS THE ROPES WERE WELL ANCHORED AND HIS MEN WERE READY.

WITHIN MINUTES, THE OTHER ITALIANS WERE PULLING THEM TO THE TOP.

BILL WAS GIVEN A CANTEEN AND GULPED FROM IT AS THE UNIT'S C.O. INTRODUCED HIMSELF.

I AM CAPTAIN RICCI MASTRONI, COMMANDER OF THE MOUNTAIN TROOPS THAT SAVED YOU.

I THINK HE NEEDS A MOMENT TO DRINK AND REGAIN HIS SENSES, SIR.

BILL SALUTED THE CAPTAIN AS A MARK OF HIS RESPECT FOR THE OFFICER. BUT THE ITALIAN JUST SMILED, SMUGLY.

I'M LIEUTENANT BILL WARWICK, SIR. AND I OWE YOUR SERGEANT MY LIFE.

WELL, LIEUTENANT. LET THIS BE A LESSON FOR YOU TO REMEMBER AS AN EXAMPLE OF THE SUPERIOR AXIS FORCES.

THE POMPOUS CAPTAIN STRUTTED AWAY, LEAVING ENRICO TO APOLOGISE FOR HIS OFFICER'S ATTITUDE TO A SHOCKED BILL.

IGNORE HIM! I HAVE ALWAYS HAD A GREAT RESPECT FOR THE BRITISH ARMY.

THE WAY THINGS ARE GOING, YOU MAY BE FIGHTING AGAINST THE BRITISH SOON . . .

THE TROUBLE BREWING IN EUROPE WITH THE RISE OF THE FASCISTS WAS A WORRY, BUT BILL AND THE ITALIAN N.C.O. PARTED AS FRIENDS.

HARRY AND CHARLES HAD IMPORTANT FATHERS. ONE WAS AN M.P. AND THE OTHER A COLONEL. THESE PEOPLE AND THEIR FRIENDS WEREN'T HAPPY ABOUT THE INCIDENT IN THE ALPS BUT DIDN'T HAVE THE GUTS TO CONFRONT BILL ABOUT IT. INSTEAD, WHEN HE GOT BACK, HE FOUND HIMSELF INCREASINGLY SNUBBED AND IGNORED UNTIL ONE EVENING IN THE MESS HE FINALLY SNAPPED.

ALL RIGHT, YOU LOT. THERE'S NO NEED TO TALK ABOUT ME BEHIND MY BACK ANYMORE. I'M RESIGNING TOMORROW, AND YOU CAN GET LOST!

RESIGNING BECAUSE YOU DID NOTHING TO SAVE YOUR FELLOW OFFICERS, EH, WARWICK?

BUT BILL CONTAINED HIS ANGER AND REFRAINED FROM ANSWERING THE WICKED QUESTION, OR STARTING ANY TROUBLE.

WHEN WAR WAS DECLARED IN 1939, BILL WAS BORED WITH LIFE ON CIVVY STREET. MEMORIES OF HIS BAD DAYS AND FEARS WERE FORGOTTEN. DESPITE SOME SNEAKING DOUBTS, BILL RE-ENLISTED AND FOUND HIMSELF POSTED TO NORTH AFRICA IN 1940 TO FIGHT THE ITALIANS.

BACK WITH THE GUNS, THIS IS WHERE I BELONG. NOT PENCIL-PUSHING BEHIND SOME DESK BACK HOME.

THE ITALIANS WERE DESPISED BY THE BRITISH TROOPS. BILL LISTENED IN TO THE COMMENTS FROM THE CREW OF ONE OF HIS 18-POUNDER GUNS.

WE'LL GIVE THOSE STUPID EYETIES WHAT FOR!

KILL THE LOT OF 'EM — IT'S ALL THEY DESERVE! BUNCH OF COWARDLY SPAGHETTI-EATERS!

THEY'RE NOT ALL COWARDS. I CAN STILL REMEMBER THE BRAVE SERGEANT WHO SAVED MY LIFE.

BUT THE ITALIANS WEREN'T ALL STUPID. ONE TANK REGIMENT WITH ITS INFANTRY SUPPORT HAD OUTFLANKED THE POSITION HELD BY BILL'S BATTERY.

CLOSE IN AND FINISH THEM ALL OFF. WE HAVE THEM SURROUNDED!

BILL KEPT A COOL HEAD UNDER FIRE. HE HANDED OUT THE ORDERS TO THE TROOPS STEADILY. THE BATTLE TRULY BEGAN AS THE ITALIANS DREW NEARER.

BUT SERGEANT DAN DAVIS QUESTIONED THE ORDERS. FOR SOME REASON OR ANOTHER HE SEEMED TO HAVE TAKEN AN INSTANT DISLIKE TO THE LIEUTENANT.

THERE WAS NO TIME FOR THEM TO WITHDRAW AND BILL KNEW IT. HE HELPED THE GUN CREWS TO FRANTICALLY PULL THE GUNS INTO A CIRCLE AS THE ITALIANS CLOSED IN.

THEY'RE ALMOST ON TOP OF US, SIR.

THIS IS THE LAST GUN IN POSITION. NOW WE'LL SEE 'EM ALL OFF!

THE PLUCKY LIEUTENANT'S PREDICTION WAS CORRECT. FORMING THE CIRCLE HAD TO STRENGTHEN THEIR POSITION AND THE TANK CHARGE WAS BROUGHT TO AN ABRUPT HALT BY THEIR CONCENTRATED FIRE.

AAIEE!

THE ITALIANS LOST HEART AT THIS AND STARTED TO SURRENDER. DAVIS, STILL ANGRY AT HAVING BEEN BRUSHED ASIDE BY BILL EARLIER, TOOK OUT HIS FRUSTRATION ON ONE OF THE PRISONERS.

THAT'LL TEACH YOU TO TAKE US ON, EH? BUNCH OF BLACK-SHIRTED FANATICS!

UUUH!

BILL SAW WHAT DAVIS WAS DOING AND TOOK ACTION. BUT THE SERGEANT WASN'T THE TYPE TO TAKE A DRESSING-DOWN IN FRONT OF THE MEN LIGHTLY.

THEY'RE NOT ALL FANATICS, DAVIS! AND ONE SAVED MY LIFE!

OH, YEAH? I HEARD THAT YOUR LOVE OF ITALIANS LED TO YOUR RESIGNATION A FEW YEARS AGO — IS THAT RIGHT?

DAVIS HAD OBVIOUSLY DONE HIS HOMEWORK ON HIS NEW OFFICER. IT LEFT BILL SPEECHLESS.

I COULD SORT DAVIS OUT, BUT IT WOULD RESURRECT ALL THE OLD STORIES. I THINK I'LL LET THE MATTER DROP.

THE RUMOURS OF THE ACCIDENT WERE SPREAD BY DAVIS WHO MADE SURE THE LIEUTENANT OVERHEARD THEIR COMMENTS AT EVERY OCCASION. SO, DESPITE HAVING DONE WELL WITH THE UNIT, HE STILL HEARD THE WHISPERS OF THE INCIDENT BEING HIS FAULT.

DID THE LIEUTENANT RESIGN BEFORE THE WAR BECAUSE HE KNEW HE'D BE FIGHTING ITALIANS, SARGE?

THIS IS GETTING RIDICULOUS! DAVIS HAS GOT TOO MUCH OF A HOLD OVER THE MEN. I'LL HAVE TO DO SOMETHING ABOUT HIM.

BUT BEFORE BILL COULD TAKE ANY ACTION AGAINST THE SERGEANT, HE WAS ORDERED TO REPORT TO THE C.O., COLONEL REG MORRIS.

WARWICK, YOU'VE DONE A GOOD JOB HERE AND I'M SORRY TO LOSE YOU. BUT PEOPLE WITH YOUR EXPERIENCE ARE BADLY NEEDED IN ERITREA.

ERITREA, EH? WELL THAT'S FAR ENOUGH AWAY. MAYBE NOBODY WILL HAVE HEARD OF ME THERE.

HE ARRIVED AT A FORWARD TRANSIT CAMP IN ERITREA, A PROVINCE OF ETHIOPIA, TO BE MET BY A HARASSED MOVEMENTS OFFICER.

WARWICK, THANK GOODNESS YOU'RE HERE AT LAST. YOUR BATTERY'S CAPTAIN, JOE BRIGGS, WAS KILLED A COUPLE OF DAYS AGO. YOU'RE PROMOTED CAPTAIN AND WILL ASSUME COMMAND.

BUT . . . WHERE ARE THEY? WHO'S IN CHARGE JUST NOW?

WITHOUT BOTHERING TO ANSWER BILL'S QUESTION, THE MAJOR HURRIED OFF, LEAVING A BEWILDERED, NEWLY-PROMOTED CAPTAIN BEHIND HIM.

A SECTION OF INDIAN TROOPS FROM BILL'S BATTERY DULY ARRIVED AND, ONCE THEIR MULES WERE LOADED WITH SUPPLIES, BILL SET OFF WITH THEM FOR THE FRONT. AS THEY BEGAN TO CLIMB HIGHER AND HIGHER, THE CAPTAIN'S FEARS BEGAN TO RISE TO THE SURFACE.

I HOPE I CAN COPE WITH THIS. I HAVEN'T BEEN IN THE MOUNTAINS AT ALL SINCE CHARLES' AND HARRY'S ACCIDENT.

AT LEAST HE WAS BACK WITH THE 3.7 INCH MOUNTAIN GUNS, AND THEIR TASK TO SEEK OUT AND HARRY THE ITALIAN FORCES IN THE REGION GAVE HIM PLENTY SCOPE.

ONCE AT THE MOUNTAIN-TOP POSITION, HE REALISED THAT IT WAS HIS OLD BATTERY. AND THEN LEYTON WALTZED OVER, SMILING SMUGLY.

WELCOME TO OUR LITTLE WAR, WARWICK. YOU'LL BE UNDER MY COMMAND UNTIL THE NEW C.O. ARRIVES.

HE THINKS I'M STILL A LIEUTENANT. WITHOUT MY EXTRA PIP UP, HE DOESN'T REALISE THAT I'M A CAPTAIN NOW — AND THE NEW C.O.

BILL DIDN'T WANT TO CAUSE TROUBLE WITH THE VOLATILE LIEUTENANT, BUT HE KNEW THAT HE WOULD HAVE TO SORT THINGS OUT.

THERE'S NO EASY WAY TO TELL YOU THIS, LEYTON. BUT I'M A CAPTAIN NOW — AND I'M THE NEW C.O.

WHAT? YOU? I DON'T BELIEVE IT!

SOURLY LEYTON RADIOED H.Q. WHO CONFIRMED BILL'S PROMOTION.

. . . BILL WARWICK IS C.O. UNDERSTOOD, YES, SIR.

NOW THAT WE'VE GOT THAT SORTED OUT. WHAT'S THE EXACT POSITION HERE?

NOT WANTING TO HAVE A STAND-OFF SITUATION WITH LEYTON, HE ASKED HIS ADVICE FOR THE BEST ROUTE ACROSS THE MOUNTAINS. KNOWING THAT BILL HAD HAD THE BAD EXPERIENCE IN THE HIGH MOUNTAINS, THE LIEUTENANT CHOSE THE STEEPEST, ROCKIEST TERRAIN TO TRAVERSE.

THAT'S THE QUICKEST, MOST DIRECT ROUTE. HIGH UP THERE!

OH NO! EVEN HIGHER INTO THE MOUNTAINS! WILL I COPE?

THERE IS AN EASIER WAY AROUND, BUT IT'S A BIT LONGER, HE DOESN'T KNOW THAT THOUGH. HE'LL CRACK UP AND I'LL GET THE COMMAND.

SHAMI NASTRI, NOW A SERGEANT, APPROACHED LEYTON AS BILL HEADED OFF TO FIND HIS GEAR AND ASKED WHY THE OFFICER HAD CHOSEN THE HARDEST ROUTE.

I KNOW IT'S THE SHORTEST WAY, BUT WE HAVE A LOT OF EQUIPMENT, SAHIB.

DON'T QUESTION MY ORDERS, SERGEANT. JUST FOLLOW THEM! UNDERSTOOD? NOW GET THE MEN READY. WE MOVE OUT IN AN HOUR!

A FEW HOURS LATER, THEY WERE HALF-WAY ACROSS THE PASS WHEN SHAMI NOTICED A HEAVILY-BREATHING, SWEATING BILL SITTING AGAINST SOME ROCKS.

THE CAPTAIN DOESN'T LOOK WELL AT ALL. I MUST SEE IF HE'S ALL RIGHT.

I'LL JUST KEEP MY EYES SHUT FOR A LITTLE WHILE . . .

SHAMI WENT OVER, BUT BILL DIDN'T RECOGNISE HIM AT FIRST UNTIL HE REALISED THAT IT WAS HIS OLD FRIEND FROM HIS DAYS IN INDIA.

ARE YOU SURE YOU ARE ALL RIGHT, SAHIB?

WELL, I'VE CERTAINLY BEEN BETTER, SHAMI — OR SHOULD I SAY SERGEANT NASTRI NOW?

AFTER SOME WATER, BILL DECIDED TO GET SOME OF HIS FEARS OFF HIS CHEST TO THE MAN HE HAD FOUGHT WITH BEFORE.

OLD FRIEND, IT'S NOT THE PHYSICAL EFFORT THAT'S TAKING THE TOLL. IT'S THE BAD MEMORIES OF A MOUNTAIN ACCIDENT.

ONCE BILL HAD TOLD HIS STORY, SHAMI KNEW WHY LEYTON HAD CHOSEN SUCH A HARD ROUTE ACROSS THE MOUNTAINS.

THERE'S A MUCH EASIER PATH TO TRAVEL, A LITTLE LONGER, BUT A LOT EASIER GOING . . .

SO LEYTON KNOWS MY FEARS! I'M NOT GOING TO GIVE HIM ANY SATISFACTION, THOUGH. I'M THE C.O. AND I'VE GOT TO SET A GOOD EXAMPLE TO THE MEN.

BILL'S THOUGHTS WERE DISTURBED SUDDENLY WHEN BULLETS CRASHED DOWN AROUND THEM FROM ATTACKING ITALIAN C.R.32 FIGHTERS. THE MEN DIVED FOR COVER.

AAARGH!

THEY ARE GETTING TOO CLOSE TO OUR POSITIONS. WE MUST STOP THEM!

EVERYONE KNEW THAT THE MULES COULDN'T BE LEFT EXPOSED TO THE BULLETS. LEYTON HAD NO INTENTION OF BREAKING COVER TO RESCUE THEM HIMSELF — BUT THAT DIDN'T STOP HIM BARKING A THOUGHTLESS ORDER.

AS THE LIEUTENANT ANGRILY YELLED AT THE TROOPS TO OBEY, BILL WENT TO HELP THE UNFORTUNATE SEPOYS AFTER ORDERING SHAMI TO OPEN UP WITH HIS BREN.

SHAMI TARGETTED A PLANE AND IT TURNED INTO A FIREBALL WHEN HIS BULLETS CONNECTED WITH ITS FUEL TANK.

HURRY UP WHILE THE OTHER PLANES ARE RECOVERING FROM THAT!

BILL CALLED SOME OF HIS MEN TO HELP HIM WITH THE PLANES AS THE OTHER TROOPS DRAGGED THE MULES UNDER A NEARBY OVERHANG.

C'MON, LADS! WE'VE GOT TO SAVE THESE MULES OR THE MISSION IS OVER BEFORE IT'S BEGUN!

THEIR AMMUNITION SPENT, THE REMAINING PLANES FLEW OFF AND THE MEN CHEERED WITH RELIEF. SHAMI SHOOK A DEFIANT FIST AT THE RETREATING PLANES.

RUN FOR HOME, COWARDS!

SHAMI HAD SOME QUIET WORDS FOR BILL, WHICH ANGERED LEYTON AS HE EAVESDROPPED.

IT IS GOOD TO HAVE YOU BACK, SAHIB! YOUR KIND OF LEADERSHIP IS WHAT WE HAVE BEEN SADLY LACKING.

I'LL REMEMBER THAT REMARK, SERGEANT. YOU'LL PAY FOR THAT.

THE MEN WERE SOON ORGANISED AGAIN AND SET OFF. A FEW HOURS LATER THEY HEARD THE SOUNDS OF BATTLE AHEAD AND BILL WENT FORWARD TO INVESTIGATE.

BLIMEY! THE EYETIES HAVE GOT OUR BOYS WELL AND TRULY PINNED DOWN. BETTER TELL THE LADS TO HURRY IT UP!

THE CAPTAIN SCANNED AROUND A BIT MORE THROUGH HIS BINOCULARS AND WAS SHOCKED WHEN HE SAW WHO WAS IN CHARGE OF THE ITALIANS.

IT'S MASTRONI! IT WON'T BE A PUSHOVER AGAINST THOSE TOUGH MOUNTAIN TROOPS. THEY'RE WELL-TRAINED FOR THE CONDITIONS.

LEYTON CAME UP AND SURVEYED THE SCENE. HE WAS EXTREMELY PLEASED WITH HIMSELF WHEN HE REALISED THE BEST PLACE FOR THE GUNS.

THAT HIGH PLATEAU OVER THAT WAY IS OUR BEST OPTION, SIR.

AGREED!

I'M GETTING DIZZY JUST THINKING ABOUT CLIMBING UP THERE. BUT IT OFFERS THE BEST FIELD OF FIRE FOR THE GUNS AND I CAN'T SACRIFICE OTHER MEN'S LIVES BECAUSE OF MY FEARS!

EVEN THE MULES COULDN'T GO WHERE THEY WERE GOING AND THE GUNS WERE UNLOADED TO BE MANHANDLED UP. USING HEAVY ROPES, BILL HELPED THE OTHERS. BUT ABOUT HALF-WAY UP, HE GLANCED OVER THE EDGE AND SLACKENED HIS GRIP FOR A SECOND.

CAN'T CONCENTRATE! ALL I CAN THINK OF IS THE ACCIDENT EVERY TIME I LOOK DOWN . . .

WATCH OUT — IT'S SLIPPING!

SHAMI QUICKLY DROPPED THE AMMUNITION CRATE HE WAS CARRYING TO TAKE A HOLD OF THE ROPE AS BILL NEARLY COLLAPSED.

BILL KNEW HE HAD TO KEEP GOING AND FORCED HIMSELF ON. ONCE INTO POSITION, HE HELPED THE GUN CREWS TO ASSEMBLE THE GUNS. HE THREW HIMSELF AT THE TASK, WHICH HELPED TO TAKE HIS MIND OFF OF HIS FEARS. THEN A LOUD CRACK ECHOED THROUGH THE MOUNTAINS.

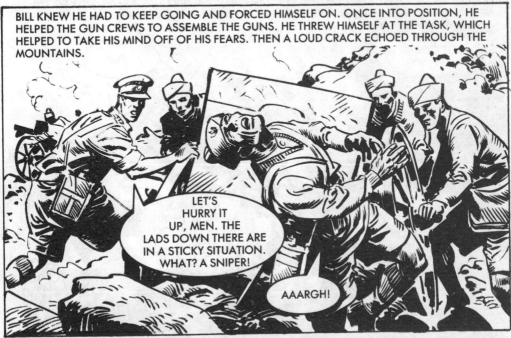

TWO MORE MEN WERE SHOT IN QUICK SUCCESSION AS BILL AND THE OTHERS DUCKED BEHIND COVER.

LEYTON WAS WITH A GROUP OF MEN HOISTING UP THE WHEELS OF A GUN. ONE OF THE MEN WITH HIM WAS SHOT AND LEYTON IMMEDIATELY DIVED FOR COVER.

WITHOUT LEYTON, THE BURDEN WAS TOO MUCH FOR THE MEN AND THE WHEELS PLUNGED DOWN. BECAUSE OF THE LIEUTENANT'S COWARDICE, THE BATTERY WAS TO BE A GUN SHORT.

HAVING WITNESSED THIS INCIDENT, BILL PUT IT ASIDE AS HE CALLED OVER TO SHAMI AFTER HE HAD CAREFULLY CHECKED THE AREA AHEAD.

IT'S ONLY ONE SNIPER — UP THERE SOMEWHERE! WE'VE GOT TO GET RID OF HIM OR WE'RE STUCK HERE.

I HAVEN'T SPOTTED HIM SO FAR.

LEYTON HAD TAKEN COVER BEHIND THE GUN-SCREEN NEXT TO BILL WHO WAS ALREADY ANGRY AT THE LIEUTENANT'S BEHAVIOUR, BUT WHAT THE MAN SAID NEXT IRRITATED BILL EVEN MORE.

WE'LL NEVER GET THAT SNIPER OUT. HE'S TOO WELL DUG IN!

YOU JUST KEEP YOUR HEAD DOWN — THAT'S WHAT YOU'RE GOOD AT! I'LL DRAW HIS FIRE.

BILL TOLD SHAMI TO LOCATE THE SNIPER AS HE ACTED AS A DECOY, DASHING FROM GUN TO GUN, BULLETS FOLLOWING HIS EVERY MOVE, ONLY INCHES AWAY.

HURRY IT UP, SERGEANT! FIND HIM — HE'S GETTING TOO CLOSE FOR COMFORT.

AFTER A FEW SHOTS, BILL TOOK COVER AGAIN AND LOOKED OVER AT HIS OLD FRIEND.

IT'S OKAY, SIR. WE'VE SEEN HIM!

IF YOU HADN'T, I WOULD'VE SENT YOU OUT NEXT, SHAMI!

UNDER SHAMI'S EAGLE EYE, A GUN WAS LAID AND THE SNIPER BLASTED OUT OF HIS POSITION.

AAAGH!

NOW THAT THE IMMEDIATE DANGER WAS OVER, LEYTON WAS THE FIRST TO JUMP OUT FROM BEHIND COVER AND ORDER THE MEN TO START THEIR ATTACK ON THE ITALIANS.

COME ON — GET THESE GUNS INTO ACTION. QUICKLY NOW!

THE MEN SAW LEYTON DIVE FOR COVER AFTER THE FIRST COUPLE OF SHOTS — AND WE LOST A GUN BECAUSE OF HIM. IF HE THROWS HIS WEIGHT AROUND LIKE THIS, WE'LL HAVE TROUBLE.

BILL IMMEDIATELY TOOK OVER, REALISING THAT THE MEN HAD LOST ALL RESPECT FOR LEYTON.

RIGHT, I'LL GIVE THE ORDERS. LET'S GIVE THOSE EYETIES A GOOD SENDING OFF!

I'M QUITE CAPABLE OF GIVING THE ORDERS. WHY DID WARWICK HAVE TO STEP IN?

THE GUNS' BARRAGE WASN'T A SURPRISE TO CAPTAIN MASTRONI, BUT THE FEROCITY AND ACCURACY WAS.

QUICKLY — IF WE STAY HERE, WE DIE. FALL BACK!

AS THE ITALIANS PULLED BACK, THE BRITISH INFANTRY FORCE LEFT BEHIND STARTED TO LOOK AFTER THE WOUNDED AND RE-ORGANISE.

I THOUGHT WE WERE GONERS FOR SURE UNTIL THOSE MOUNTAIN GUN BOYS SHOWED UP . . .

SOON MASTRONI AND HIS MEN WERE OUT OF SIGHT. BILL GAVE THE ORDER FOR THE MOUNTAIN GUNS TO STOP FIRING.

CEASE FIRE! WE'RE ONLY BLOWING UP ROCK NOW!

BILL WENT DOWN TO SEE THE INFANTRY C.O. — HE KNEW THAT THEY HAD TO PURSUE THE ITALIANS QUICKLY AS THEY WOULD SIMPLY DIG IN FURTHER ON.

JUST THOUGHT I'D CHECK EVERYTHING WAS ALL RIGHT WITH YOU LOT TO CARRY ON AFTER THE EYETIES.

WE'LL SOON BE FIT TO MOVE. JUST BE READY WITH THE GUNS ONCE WE'VE FLUSHED THEM OUT!

THE FOOT SLOGGERS PUSHED ON BUT RAN RIGHT INTO A WELL-PLACED AMBUSH. MASTRONI HAD POSITIONED MACHINE-GUNS TO GIVE A DEADLY CROSS-FIRE.

AARGH!

AMBUSH — TAKE COVER. CALL IN THE ARTILLERY!

HALF OF THE MEN WERE INSTANTLY CUT DOWN, WHILE THE OTHERS SCRAMBLED FOR WHATEVER MEAGRE COVER THEY COULD FIND. THE COLONEL REALISED HE WAS IN DEEP TROUBLE.

BACK AT THE GUNS, LEYTON SURVEYED THE SCENE AND ORDERED THE MEN TO OPEN FIRE. HE WAS EAGER TO IMPRESS THEM, TRYING TO REGAIN THEIR FAVOUR, BUT BILL SUDDENLY CALLED OUT.

DON'T FIRE! WHY?

IF WE SHOOT AT THE ITALIANS, WE'LL BRING A ROCK FALL DOWN ON THE REMAINING TROOPS. IT'S JUST WHAT THE EYETIES WANT.

BEING OUT-THOUGHT AGAIN ANGERED LEYTON. AS HE GAVE THE CAPTAIN ANOTHER BLACK LOOK, THE SHOOTING DOWN IN THE PASS SUDDENLY CAME TO A STANDSTILL.

OUR TROOPS ARE SURRENDERING. THE ITALIANS ARE TAKING WHAT'S LEFT OF THE MEN PRISONER!

CAPTAIN MASTRONI GLOATED OVER THE SCENE AS HIS SERGEANT, ENRICO TABARDI, SHOUTED OUT FOR FURTHER ORDERS REGARDING THEIR PRISONERS.

WHAT NOW, CAPTAIN? WHERE WILL WE PUT THEM?

THE VICIOUS ITALIAN OFFICER LOOKED DOWN GRIMLY, AND LIKE AN OLD ROMAN EMPEROR GAVE A THUMBS DOWN SIGNAL TO ENRICO.

KILL THEM! WE DO NOT HAVE TIME FOR PRISONERS.

THE PRISONERS, SEEING MASTRONI'S GESTURE, AND KNOWING A LITTLE ITALIAN, STARTED TO BECOME NERVOUS. ENRICO TRIED TO CALM THEM DOWN.

DON'T PANIC, I MAY BE YOUR ENEMY, BUT I'M NO MURDERER.

WE DON'T BELIEVE IT! LOOK AT YOUR CAPTAIN.

TELLING HIS MEN TO HOLD THEIR FIRE, ENRICO CLIMBED UP TO HAVE A WORD WITH THE CAPTAIN, ONLY TO FIND HIS OWN COMRADES HAD HIM COVERED.

STOP THERE — OR THEY'LL SHOOT! YOU SHOULDN'T DISOBEY MY DIRECT ORDERS.

MASTRONI AGAIN STRETCHED OUT HIS HAND AND THE SOLDIERS BELOW OPENED FIRE ON THE PRISONERS.

WHY ARE YOU DOING THIS? AARGH!

FROM HIS VANTAGE POINT, BILL COULD DO NOTHING TO STOP THE MASSACRE BUT IMMEDIATELY ORDERED THE GUNS INTO ACTION.

OPEN FIRE! WIPE OUT THOSE MURDERING SCUM!

THE GUNS WERE SPOT ON BUT MASTRONI DIDN'T CARE. HE HAD SACRIFICED MANY OF HIS OWN MEN TO MAKE HIS OWN ESCAPE EASIER.

HA! THE GUNS HAVE NOW BLOCKED THE PASS, JUST AS I'D PLANNED. THIS WILL SLOW DOWN THEIR PURSUIT. NOW WE MOVE ON TO OUR NEXT POSITION.

BILL WAS SHOCKED, HAVING SEEN THE ENTIRE UNIT HE PROMISED TO PROTECT DIE AT THE HANDS OF MASTRONI. BUT HE WAS DETERMINED TO CARRY ON.

WE'VE GOT TO GO AFTER THEM STRAIGHT AWAY. IF WE WASTE TOO MUCH TIME, THEY'LL GET DUG IN AGAIN AND HAVE TIME TO PLAN.

THEN WE MUST GO HIGH UP THE SLOPES OVER THAT WAY. THE PASS IS BLOCKED, SIR.

BILL FELT SICK WHEN HE LOOKED UP TOWARDS THE PATH THEY MUST TAKE.

I CAN'T SEEM TO SHAKE THIS FEAR LIKE I'D HOPED. BUT I'VE GOT TO PUSH ON. I OWE IT TO THOSE MEN WHO DIED.

SEEING BILL'S DISTRESS, LEYTON CAME FORWARD AND VOLUNTEERED TO JOIN HIM GOING AHEAD AFTER THE ITALIANS.

THIS COULD BE MY CHANCE TO SHOW UP WARWICK'S WEAKNESS AND GET BACK ON THE RIGHT SIDE OF THE MEN.

OKAY, LEYTON, YOU COME WITH ME. WE'LL TAKE TWO GUNS. SERGEANT — YOU AND THE OTHERS WILL HAVE TO TAKE THE LONGER ROUTE.

YES, SAHIB!

LOADING UP THE MULES WITH TWO OF THE GUNS, BILL GAVE A HUGE SIGH THEN THE ORDER TO MOVE OUT.

OKAY, MEN, LET'S GO! SERGEANT NASTRI IS TAKING THE OTHER ROUTE AND WE SHOULD CATCH THESE MURDERING ITALIANS BETWEEN US.

AS THEY CLIMBED HIGHER AND HIGHER, BILL BECAME MORE AND MORE TENSE AND UNEASY. HE SLOWED DOWN, MUCH TO LEYTON'S AMUSEMENT.

C'MON, CAPTAIN! CAN'T YOU HANDLE THESE MOUNTAINS? IF YOU WANT, I'LL TAKE OVER!

THE LIEUTENANT'S SMILE TURNED TO A SNEER AS BILL HAD TO SIT DOWN AND HAVE SOME WATER.

I FEEL SO HELPLESS! I CAN'T STOP SWEATING, AND MY HEART IS POUNDING.

A COMMOTION AMONGST THE MEN BROUGHT BILL TO HIS FEET. HE WENT TO INVESTIGATE, AND ONE OF THE MEN SHOWED HIM AN ASTONISHING SIGHT.

LOOK, SIR! ONE OF THE ITALIANS SURVIVED THE BOMBARDMENT. IT'S THE ONE WE SPOTTED CLIMBING UP BEFORE THEY SHOT THE PRISONERS.

ENRICO WAS JUST BARELY CLINGING ON, CALLING FOR HELP. LEYTON SHOWED NO PITY FOR HIM.

I RECKON WE SHOULD LEAVE HIM THERE TO DIE. IT'LL SAVE US SHOOTING HIM!

BILL TURNED ON LEYTON WHO SMILED TO HIMSELF AS HE REALISED HE HAD THE CAPTAIN JUST WHERE HE WANTED HIM.

IF WE DO THAT WE'RE NO BETTER THAN THEM. AND WE'RE NOT MURDERERS!

WELL THEN, SIR. SEEING AS HOW YOU'RE SUCH AN ACCOMPLISHED CLIMBER, YOU'D BETTER GO AND RESCUE HIM!

BILL GLANCED OVER THE EDGE OF THE CLIFF THEY WERE ON AND FELT DIZZY. HE TURNED TO THE MEN TO ASK ONE OF THEM TO DO IT. LEYTON ASKED WHY, WITH A SMUG GRIN THAT MADE BILL ANGRY.

YOU KNOW WELL I CAN'T AND WHY, LEYTON!

WELL THEN, WE'LL JUST HAVE TO LEAVE THAT EYETIE TO DIE.

AT LEYTON'S SNEERING REMARK, BILL FINALLY LOST HIS TEMPER. HE STORMED OVER TO A MULE AND GRABBED A LONG ROPE.

NO, HE WON'T DIE! I'LL MAKE SURE OF THAT.

I'VE GOT HIM! HE'LL EITHER CRACK UP COMPLETELY — OR FALL TO HIS DEATH!

TYING ONE END OF THE ROPE SECURELY, THE CAPTAIN THREW THE OTHER END OVER THE CLIFF AND PREPARED TO CLIMB DOWN TO THE STRANDED MAN.

I'VE GOT TO DO THIS OR I'M FINISHED. FOR MY SAKE AND THAT ITALIAN'S, I HOPE I CAN GET OVER MY FEARS.

BECAUSE OF AN OVERHANG IT WAS IMPOSSIBLE TO DROP THE ROPE STRAIGHT DOWN TO ENRICO.

CAUTIOUSLY, INCH BY INCH, HE MADE HIS WAY DOWN TILL HE WAS ALMOST AT THE STRANDED MAN.

THIS IS CERTAINLY KILL OR CURE! THE TRICKY PART IS GOING TO BE PASSING OVER THE ROPE.

BILL PASSED THE ROPE OVER TO THE ITALIAN, BARELY LOOKING AT HIM AS THEY BOTH CLUNG FEARFULLY TO THE CLIFF FACE.

HERE GRASP THIS! MY MEN WILL PULL YOU TO SAFETY.

GRACIAS, SIGNOR! YOU'RE A VERY BRAVE AND HONOURABLE MAN.

A QUICK SHOUT TO THE TOP AND ENRICO WAS ON HIS WAY TO SAFETY, AS BILL CLUNG GRIMLY ON. STANDING ON THE NARROW LEDGE WITH NO ROPE WAS THE ULTIMATE TEST.

GOT TO HANG ON — GOT TO! IF I DON'T I'M DEAD!

ONCE ENRICO WAS UP, HE HELPED THE SEPOYS PULL THEIR OFFICER UP. IT WAS A GREAT STRUGGLE, AND BILL SLIPPED A COUPLE OF TIMES, BEING HELD UP ONLY BY THE MEN GRIPPING THE ROPE.

DON'T LET GO NOW, LADS!

COME, CAPTAIN, YOU ARE NEARLY THERE!

TURNING FACE TO FACE AT THE TOP, THE TWO MEN SUDDENLY RECOGNISED EACH OTHER NOW THAT THEY HAD BOTH CALMED DOWN AND THE DANGER WAS OVER.

ENRICO! IT'S GOOD TO SEE YOU AGAIN, OLD FRIEND!

IT SEEMS AS IF YOU'VE REPAID AN OLD FAVOUR BY SAVING MY LIFE.

LEYTON BUTTED INTO THE FRIENDLY REUNION, ANNOYING BOTH BILL AND ENRICO.

DO I HAVE TO REMIND YOU, CAPTAIN, THAT THIS MAN IS ONE OF THE MURDERING ENEMY? HE'S NOT OUR FRIEND!

WE ARE ENEMIES, YES. BUT I WAS TRYING TO SAVE THE LIVES OF THOSE BRITISH PRISONERS!

HEY! THE FIGHT'S OUT THERE, NOT HERE. EVERY SECOND WE WASTE HERE, MASTRONI GETS FURTHER AWAY!

BILL KNEW THAT HE HAD TO PUT HIS FOOT DOWN, SO HE PULLED RANK ON LEYTON, REMINDING HIM WHO WAS IN CHARGE.

I CAN HELP YOU. I KNOW EXACTLY WHERE MASTRONI'S AMBUSH SITES ARE.

I HAD TO TRUST THIS MAN WITH MY LIFE ONCE! ALL YOU'VE GOT TO DO IS FOLLOW ORDERS. OKAY, LEYTON?

BILL WAS DETERMINED TO HUNT MASTRONI, AND WAS SURE THAT, WITH ENRICO'S HELP, HE COULD BRING THE KILLER TO JUSTICE.

OKAY, MEN. WE'VE GOT MORE CLIMBING TO DO. I KNOW IT'S HARD GOING, BUT THIS TIME WE'RE GOING TO HAVE A SURPRISE FOR MASTRONI.

ONCE BILL HAD TOLD THE MEN WHAT HE PLANNED WHICH MEANT GOING HIGHER AND HIGHER, LEYTON PUT IN A SNEERING COMMENT.

ARE YOU SURE YOU ARE CAPABLE OF THIS, WARWICK? WHAT ABOUT YOUR FEARS? PERHAPS I SHOULD TAKE OVER.

RESCUING ENRICO FROM THAT CLIFF-FACE MADE ME CONFRONT MY FEAR, LEYTON. AND I'VE BEATEN IT. I'LL BE OKAY. NOW I'M GOING TO BEAT MASTRONI.

MEANWHILE, THE ITALIANS WERE ALREADY IN POSITION AT A NARROW DEFILE WAITING FOR THE BRITISH TO COME THROUGH. BUT THE CAPTAIN WAS BEGINNING TO HAVE DOUBTS.

HAVE THEY GIVEN UP? THEY SHOULD HAVE BEEN HERE BY NOW! WHERE ARE THEY?

MASTRONI'S WONDERING STOPPED WHEN SUDDENLY SHELLS CRASHED INTO THE VERY MIDST OF HIS MEN'S POSITIONS.

AAARGH!

WHAT? THE BRITISH? BUT HOW COULD THEY KNOW WE WERE HERE!

THE SURPRISE WAS COMPLETE. THANKS TO ENRICO, BILL KNEW EXACTLY WHERE MASTRONI WOULD BE. CLIMBING HIGHER, HE HAD FOUND A POSITION TO LAUNCH HIS ATTACK.

THAT'S IT, LADS. TAKE CAREFUL AIM, CHOOSE YOUR TARGETS. WE DON'T HAVE A LOT OF AMMO.

MASTRONI IMMEDIATELY BROUGHT HIS HEAVY MACHINE-GUNS TO BEAR. BILL AND THE MEN WERE FORCED TO TAKE COVER AS THE BULLETS CRASHED ABOUT THEM.

THESE BRITISH NEVER GIVE UP. BUT SOON THEY'LL ALL BE DEAD!

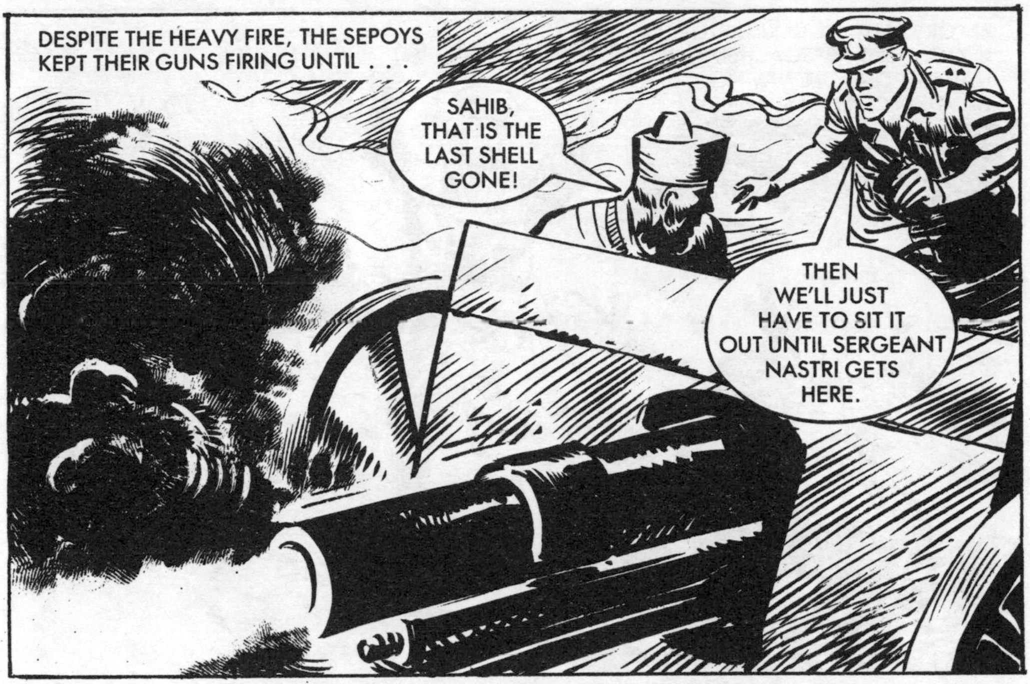
DESPITE THE HEAVY FIRE, THE SEPOYS KEPT THEIR GUNS FIRING UNTIL . . .
SAHIB, THAT IS THE LAST SHELL GONE!
THEN WE'LL JUST HAVE TO SIT IT OUT UNTIL SERGEANT NASTRI GETS HERE.

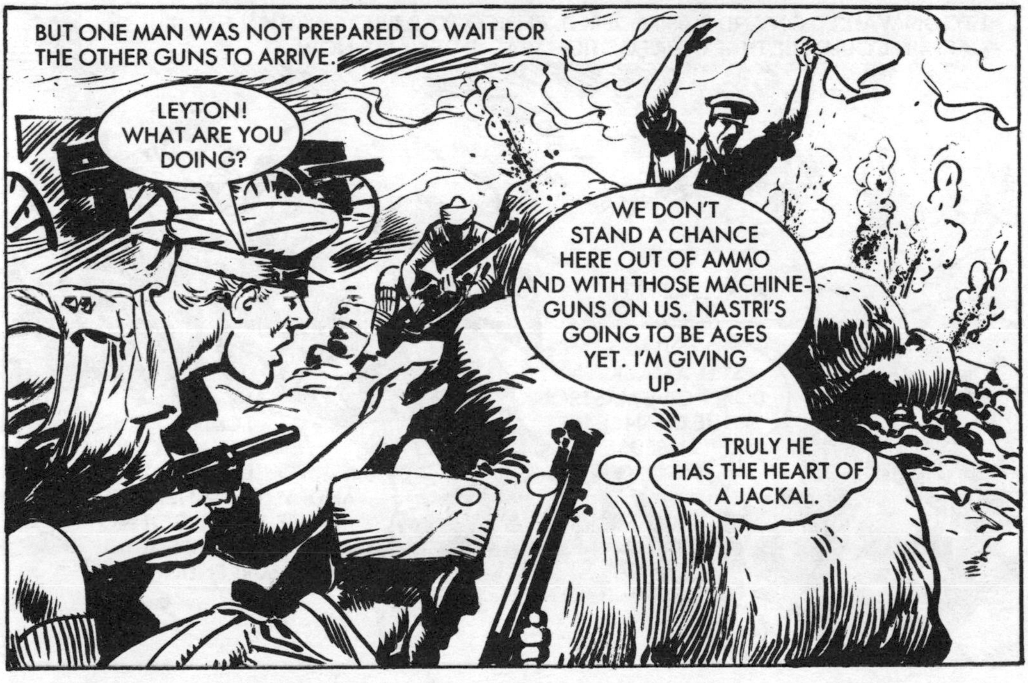
BUT ONE MAN WAS NOT PREPARED TO WAIT FOR THE OTHER GUNS TO ARRIVE.
LEYTON! WHAT ARE YOU DOING?
WE DON'T STAND A CHANCE HERE OUT OF AMMO AND WITH THOSE MACHINE-GUNS ON US. NASTRI'S GOING TO BE AGES YET. I'M GIVING UP.
TRULY HE HAS THE HEART OF A JACKAL.

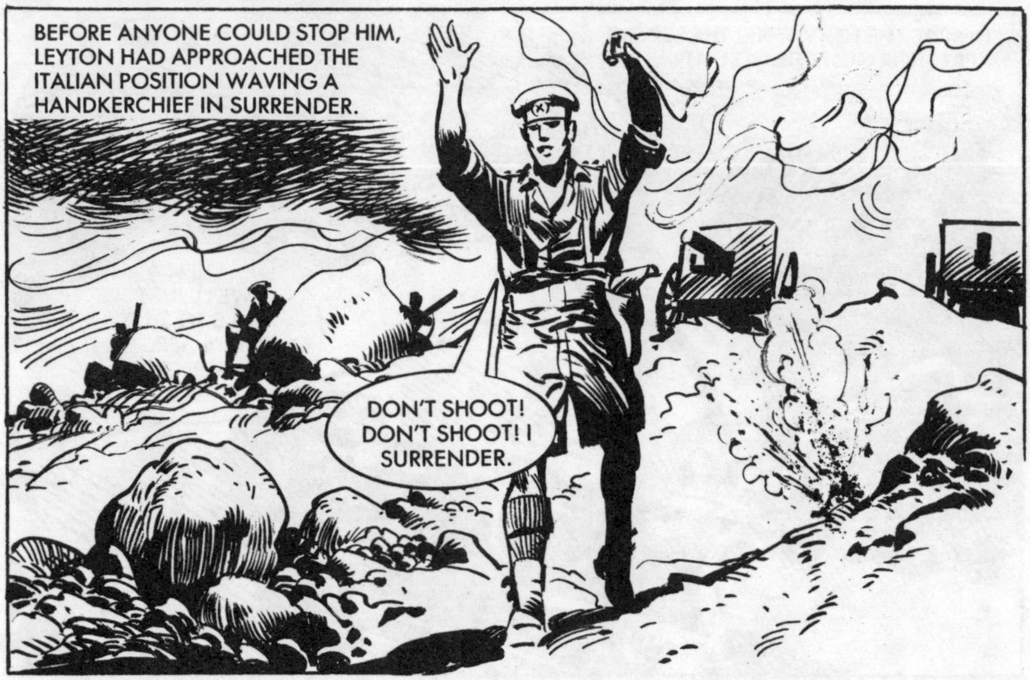
BEFORE ANYONE COULD STOP HIM, LEYTON HAD APPROACHED THE ITALIAN POSITION WAVING A HANDKERCHIEF IN SURRENDER.
DON'T SHOOT! DON'T SHOOT! I SURRENDER.

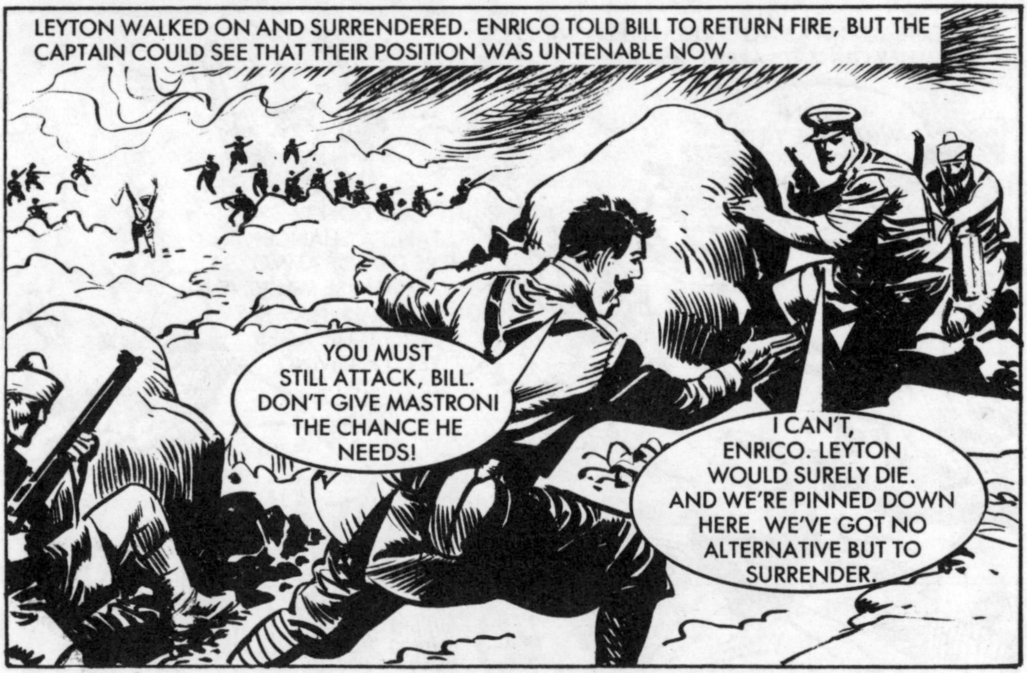
LEYTON WALKED ON AND SURRENDERED. ENRICO TOLD BILL TO RETURN FIRE, BUT THE CAPTAIN COULD SEE THAT THEIR POSITION WAS UNTENABLE NOW.
YOU MUST STILL ATTACK, BILL. DON'T GIVE MASTRONI THE CHANCE HE NEEDS!
I CAN'T, ENRICO. LEYTON WOULD SURELY DIE. AND WE'RE PINNED DOWN HERE. WE'VE GOT NO ALTERNATIVE BUT TO SURRENDER.

MASTRONI STOOD UP AND TRIUMPHANTLY GLOATED AS THEY WALKED DOWN TOWARDS HIS POSITION. HE WAS SURPRISED TO SEE ENRICO AND LAUGHED MOCKINGLY.

WELL, WELL, SERGEANT! SO NICE TO SEE YOU AGAIN. SO THAT'S HOW THEY FOUND US. I'LL MAKE SURE OF YOUR DEATH PERSONALLY THIS TIME.

ENRICO WARNED BILL THAT MASTRONI WOULD SHOOT THEM ALL — BUT THE CAPTAIN TOLD HIM NOT TO WORRY.

I'VE JUST SEEN SHAMI SIGNAL FROM BEHIND THE ITALIANS. HE'S UP ON THE SLOPES WITH THE OTHER GUNS. BE READY TO TAKE COVER WHEN HE FIRES . . .

THE BRITISH DIVED FOR COVER AS THE ITALIAN POSITIONS CAUGHT THE FULL BRUNT OF THE FIRE FROM SHAMI'S GUNS.

UUURGH!

MORE OF THEM! WE'RE TRAPPED — I'LL USE THE CONFUSION TO GET AWAY . . .

BUT BILL AND ENRICO SAW THE COWARDLY CAPTAIN RUN AWAY AND GAVE CHASE, ENRICO CLOSING IN ON HIM AS HE NEARED THE TOP OF THE SLOPE.

WAIT, MASTRONI! YOU DESERVE TO DIE FOR THE MURDER OF YOUR OWN MEN!

MASTRONI SPUN AROUND WITH SPEED AND SHOT ENRICO BEFORE HE COULD GRAB HIM.

FINE WORDS BUT BULLETS ARE BETTER, SERGEANT. DIE!

AAAR!

WITH THE LAST OF HIS STRENGTH ENRICO BARGED INTO MASTRONI, KNOCKING HIM OVER THE EDGE OF THE CLIFF.

AGH!

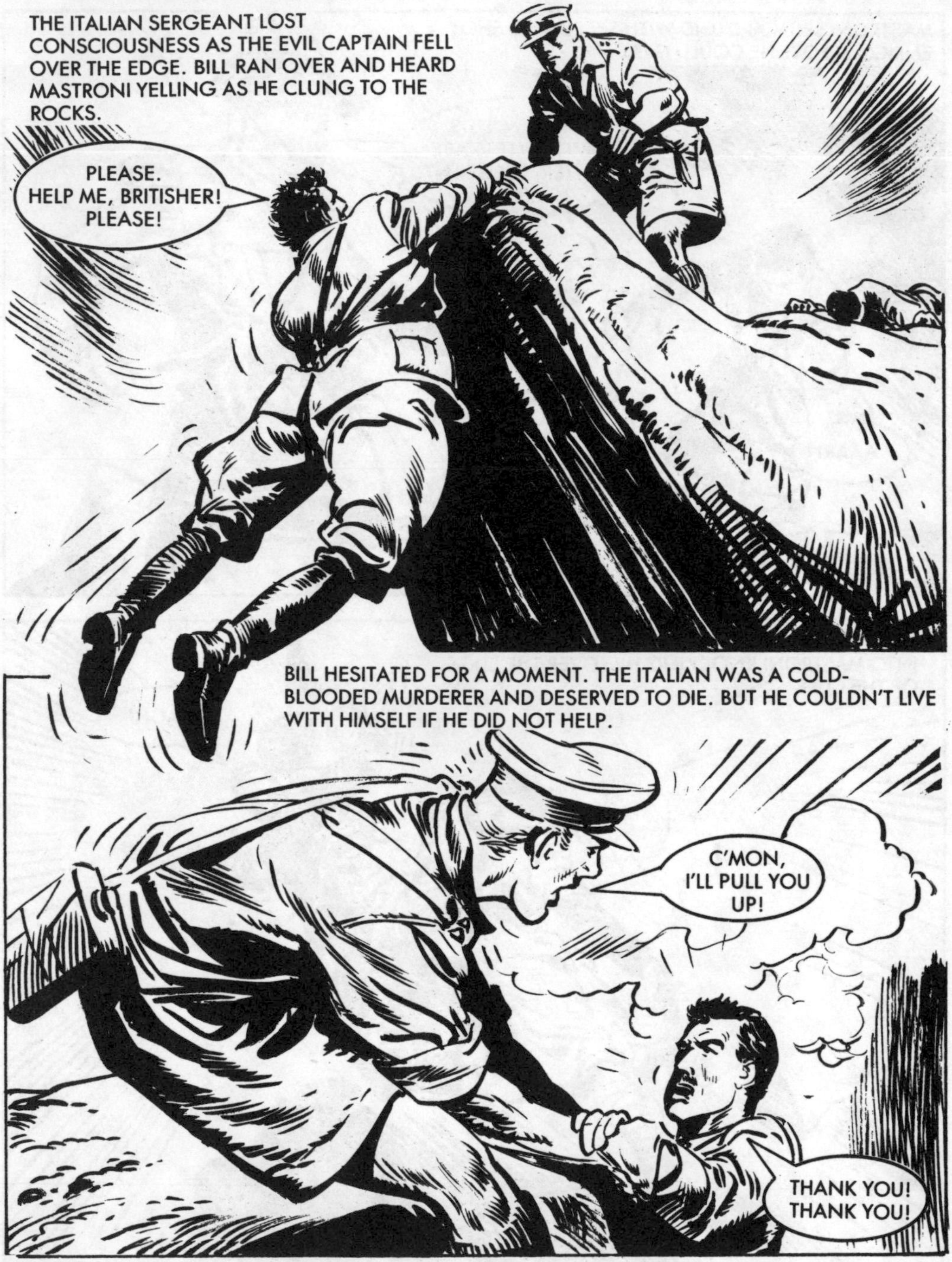
THE ITALIAN SERGEANT LOST CONSCIOUSNESS AS THE EVIL CAPTAIN FELL OVER THE EDGE. BILL RAN OVER AND HEARD MASTRONI YELLING AS HE CLUNG TO THE ROCKS.
PLEASE. HELP ME, BRITISHER! PLEASE!
BILL HESITATED FOR A MOMENT. THE ITALIAN WAS A COLD-BLOODED MURDERER AND DESERVED TO DIE. BUT HE COULDN'T LIVE WITH HIMSELF IF HE DID NOT HELP.
C'MON, I'LL PULL YOU UP!
THANK YOU! THANK YOU!

USING UP THE LAST OF HIS STRENGTH, THE CAPTAIN PULLED HIS ENEMY TO SAFETY.

THAT'S IT. YOU'LL BE OKAY NOW.

FOOL, ALL THESE ENGLISHMEN ARE WEAK. HE SHOULD HAVE LEFT ME TO DIE.

BILL SLUMPED TO THE GROUND BUT THE ITALIAN REACHED FOR HIS OWN FALLEN PISTOL.

MY MEN MAY BE DEAD BUT I'LL EXTRACT MY REVENGE.

EXHAUSTED, BILL STARED IN DISBELIEF AS MASTRONI AIMED THE PISTOL STRAIGHT AT HIM.

I TOLD YOU BEFORE WHO WAS THE MASTER RACE. IF YOU HAD LISTENED, THEN PERHAPS YOU WOULDN'T HAVE TO DIE NOW.

BUT BEFORE THE ITALIAN COULD SHOOT, ANOTHER SHOT SENT HIM SPRAWLING OVER THE EDGE OF THE CLIFF. BILL SPUN AROUND TO SEE WHAT HAD HAPPENED.

WHAT THE . . .? LEYTON! BUT HOW . . .?

LEYTON HAD SURVIVED THE BOMBARDMENT AND FOLLOWED MASTRONI UP. HE NOW REALISED WHAT A FOOL HE HAD BEEN IN HIS TREATMENT OF BILL.

THANKS FOR MY LIFE, LEYTON.

I SHOULD BE THANKING YOU FOR PUTTING UP WITH MY BEHAVIOUR FOR SO LONG! YOU WOULD HAVE BEEN WITHIN YOUR RIGHTS TO SEND ME BACK.

ALTHOUGH BADLY WOUNDED, ENRICO WOULD LIVE. AFTER HIS WOUND WAS BANDAGED, HE WAS TAKEN TO A FIELD HOSPITAL.

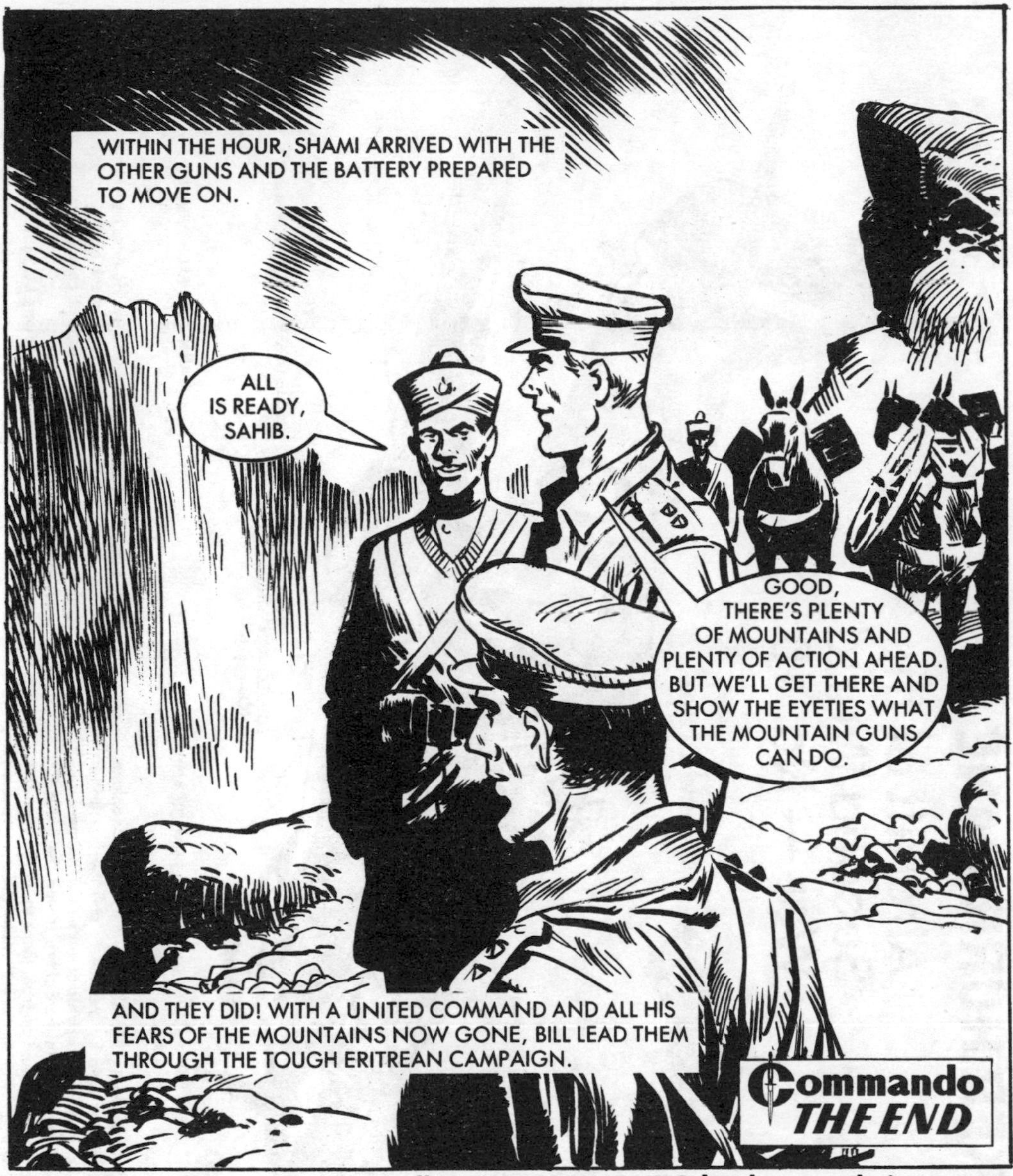
WITHIN THE HOUR, SHAMI ARRIVED WITH THE OTHER GUNS AND THE BATTERY PREPARED TO MOVE ON.
ALL IS READY, SAHIB.
GOOD, THERE'S PLENTY OF MOUNTAINS AND PLENTY OF ACTION AHEAD. BUT WE'LL GET THERE AND SHOW THE EYETIES WHAT THE MOUNTAIN GUNS CAN DO.
AND THEY DID! WITH A UNITED COMMAND AND ALL HIS FEARS OF THE MOUNTAINS NOW GONE, BILL LEAD THEM THROUGH THE TOUGH ERITREAN CAMPAIGN.
Commando THE END

HAWKER HURRICANE

Aircraft of the Second World War — No. 10

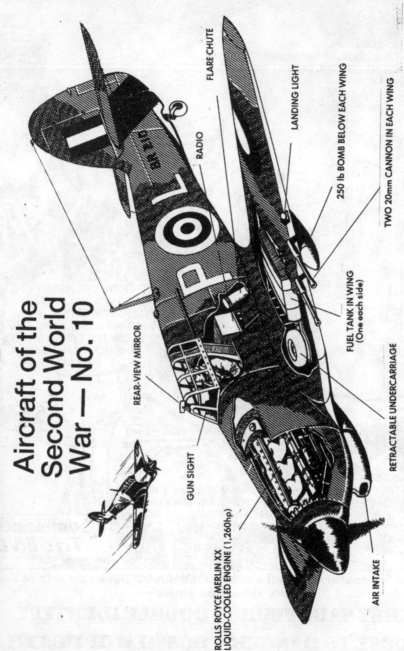

FLARE CHUTE

RADIO

LANDING LIGHT

250 lb BOMB BELOW EACH WING

TWO 20mm CANNON IN EACH WING

REAR-VIEW MIRROR

FUEL TANK IN WING
(One each side)

RETRACTABLE UNDERCARRIAGE

GUN SIGHT

ROLLS ROYCE MERLIN XX
LIQUID-COOLED ENGINE (1,260hp)

AIR INTAKE

THE famous "Hurri" was the first monoplane fighter used by the R.A.F. and the first British military aircraft capable of more than 300mph.

Together with the Spitfire it won the Battle Of Britain, then went on from there to serve in theatres of war all over the world. Many different versions were built. The Fleet Air Arm used it, one type had 40mm cannon below the wings for tank-busting, and it was also carried on a special catapult on merchant ships to protect convoys.

Total production of Hurricanes was 14,533.

THE FIGHTING FEW

NO ONE WILL DENY THAT THE BATTLE OF BRITAIN PRODUCED MORE HEROES THAN ANY OTHER ACTION OF THE SECOND WORLD WAR. THIS IS THE STORY OF THREE OF THOSE HEROES, THREE YOUNG R.A.F. PILOTS WHO OUTFLEW AND OUTFOUGHT THE MIGHTY LUFTWAFFE UNTIL THEY NEARLY DROPPED WITH EXHAUSTION.
YET, IN THIS SAVAGE AIR WAR, THEIR GREATEST FEAR WAS NOT OF THE NAZIS BUT OF A MAN WHO FLEW ALONGSIDE THEM IN A HURRICANE...

First published 1969

IN MID-SUMMER, 1940, WHEN THE 'BATTLE OF BRITAIN' OPENED WITH ATTACKS ON CHANNEL CONVOYS AND SOUTH COAST PORTS, R.A.F. FIGHTER COMMAND DEFENDED A FRONT THAT RAN FROM THE WASH TO LAND'S END.

WHEN THE PORTS WERE ATTACKED, THE SAVAGERY OF THE AIR BATTLES HAD TO BE SEEN TO BE BELIEVED.

FLYING OFFICER GAVIN ROBERTS, WHO HAD JUST JOINED A DEVON-BASED HURRICANE SQUADRON AFTER EIGHTEEN MONTHS OF TARGET-TOWING IN NORTHERN IRELAND, WAS FINDING THE GOING HARD ON HIS FIRST OPERATIONAL TRIP.

UP A BIT AND I'VE GOT HIM!

THEN AS GAVIN CLAIMED HIS FIRST VICTIM, A STRAY ANTI-AIRCRAFT SHELL FROM THE HARBOUR DEFENCES STRUCK HIS PLANE.

RIPPING BACK THE COCKPIT COVER, GAVIN PREPARED TO JUMP.

A SHARP JERK TOLD HIM HIS PARACHUTE HAD OPENED, AS THE HURRICANES CHASED OFF THE NAZI RAIDERS.

IN ACTUAL FACT HE WAS IN THE WATER FOR NO MORE THAN THREE MINUTES.

UP YOU COME!

HE'S ONE OF OURS. HOW ARE YOU, SIR?

WET!

LATE THAT AFTERNOON, DRESSED IN AN ASSORTMENT OF BORROWED CLOTHES, GAVIN WAS RETURNED TO HIS BASE, TO FACE THE JOKES FROM HIS TWO PALS, PILOT OFFICER 'JACKO' RAFT AND PILOT OFFICER JUAN RAMOS DE SILVA — 'LONG JOHN' TO HIS MATES.

ATTENTION! MAKE WAY FOR A NAVAL OFFICER!

GET A LOAD OF THAT. THE CRAZY COOT'S BEEN FOR A SWIM.

JACKO WAS A NEW ZEALANDER WHO'D COME TO BRITAIN AT THE START OF THE WAR AND LONG JOHN WAS THE NATURALISED BRITISH SON OF A PORTUGUESE BANKER.

BEFORE THE JOKING GOT OUT OF HAND, THE FLIGHT COMMANDER, FLIGHT LIEUTENANT DEMPSTER, BROKE IN —

WHAT HAPPENED TO YOU THEN?

I GOT CLOBBERED BY THE HARBOUR DEFENCES.

UNFRIENDLY OF THEM! STILL, THEY PICKED YOU OUT OF THE DRINK, SO I SUPPOSE YOU CAN'T COMPLAIN.

IGNORING FURTHER JIBES FROM JACKO AND LONG JOHN, GAVIN BEAT HIS RETREAT TO COLLECT NEW GEAR.

BUT THE C.O., SQUADRON LEADER CONNOR, DIDN'T FIND IT SO FUNNY. ACCORDING TO JACKO AND LONG JOHN HE COULN'T EVEN SMILE, LET ALONE LAUGH. AND NOT ONCE HAD ANYONE SEEN HIM NAIL A VICTIM.

DISPERSAL

LOST YOUR KITE ALREADY, ROBERTS? NOT A GREAT SHOW FOR YOUR FIRST OP.

SORRY, SIR. I'LL TRY TO DO BETTER...

EVEN BEFORE HE'D FINISHED, CONNOR HAD TURNED AND STRODE OFF WITHOUT ANOTHER WORD. HE WAS NOT WELL LIKED BY THE PILOTS.

THAT EVENING JACKO AND LONG JOHN BEGGED A LIFT TO THE NEAREST PUB IN GAVIN'S DECREPIT CAR.

NOTHING IN TODAY'S LITTLE PARTY EQUALS THE HORROR OF TRAVELLING IN THIS SOBBING RUIN.

YOU WEREN'T FISHED OUT OF THE DRINK WITH A BOAT-HOOK! BESIDES, THIS BEAUTY HAS A DIGNITY WHICH MODERN CARS LACK.

DIGNITY? I'D HAVE SWORN THE BRUTE HAD PALSY.

IN THE FRIENDLY ATMOSPHERE OF THE 'LOCAL', THE THREE YOUNG PILOTS FORMED AN UN-OFFICAL PARTNERSHIP.

I HEAR YOU'RE TAKING OVER THE SECOND SECTION SOON. WHAT ABOUT PICKING ME AND LONG JOHN FOR IT? WE CAN HOLD YOU UP WHEN YOU GET TIRED OF SWIMMING.

WHY NOT? IF YOU CAN STAND IT, I CAN. I'LL ASK THE FLIGHT COMMANDER.

NEXT MORNING THEY GOT THE IDEA APPROVED BY FLIGHT LIEUTENANT DEMPSTER. ANY SECTION THAT FORMS ITSELF VOLUNTARILY IS A GOOD TEAM.

IT SUITS ME OK. I'LL KEEP YOU TOGETHER AS MUCH AS I CAN. WHO COOKED THE IDEA UP ANYWAY?

I PROPOSED IT.

AND I SECONDED IT!

WELL, I SUPPOSE YOU'RE LUCKY, ROBERTS. ALTHOUGH YOU WOULDN'T THINK SO TO LOOK AT 'EM. YOU'D BETTER PRACTICE TOGETHER A BIT.

THANKS. I'LL MANAGE THESE CLOWNS.

AND SO FOR THE NEXT THREE DAYS THEY SPENT EVERY MINUTE THEY COULD IN THE AIR, UNTIL THEY FLEW PERFECTLY TOGETHER.

ON THE FOURTH MORNING, AS THEY PRACTICED CHANGES OF FORMATION, JACKO'S KEEN EYES SPOTTED A TARGET.

TALLYHO! BANDIT BELOW.

I SEE HIM. NUMBER ONE ATTACK. LINE ASTERN — GO!

IT WAS A DORNIER BOMBER ON A RECONNAISSANCE FLIGHT.

WHILE LONG JOHN AND JACKO HELD FORMATION ABOVE AND BEHIND THE GERMAN BOMBER, GAVIN OPENED HIS THROTTLE AND SWUNG DOWN TO THE ATTACK.

TURNING IN NOW!

TIMING IT PERFECTLY, GAVIN LET LOOSE AT THE NAZI PLANE.

FOLLOW ME IN, NUMBER TWO.

IT WAS A PERFECT ATTACK. AS GAVIN SWEPT DOWNWARDS AND AWAY, LONG JOHN OPENED UP.

REAR GUNNER STILL FIRING — WATCH HIM.

THIS WILL FIX HIM!

THEN LONG JOHN FINISHED HIS ATTACK. THE BIG DORNIER WAS BADLY DAMAGED AS JACKO OPENED FIRE.

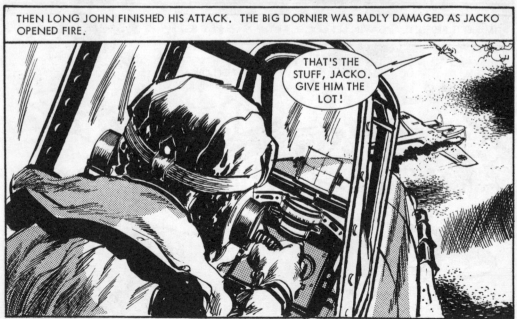

THAT'S THE STUFF, JACKO. GIVE HIM THE LOT!

THE END WAS SUDDEN AND SHOCKING.

LOOK AT THAT!

THEN THE COOL VOICE OF THE BASE CON-TROLLER RECALLED THEM TO REALITY.

ARE YOU PLAYING SOLDIERS OR HAVE YOU FOUND SOMETHING?

SORRY, ONE BANDIT DESTROYED HALF MILE OFF SHORE.

THEY LANDED BACK AT BASE AND WALKED INTO THE DISPERSAL HUT IN SOME EMBARRASSMENT.

SO YOU DOWNED A HUN? YOU MIGHT HAVE LET SOMEBODY KNOW YOU WERE STARTING A FIGHT!

SORRY. WE WERE RATHER BUSY AND I FORGOT ALL ABOUT IT.

THEN THE INTELLIGENCE OFFICER STEPPED FORWARD —

WELL, LET'S HAVE YOUR REPORTS ANYWAY. TO BEGIN WITH, WHO SHOT IT DOWN?

WE ALL DID!

YOU CAN'T ALL SHOOT DOWN A HUN. WHAT ACTUALLY HAPPENED?

GAVIN GAVE IT A SQUIRT AND SET ONE ENGINE ALIGHT. LONG JOHN THEN FIXED THE REAR GUNNER AND SET THE FUSELAGE ON FIRE. AND I GAVE IT A SQUIRT AND BLEW IT UP.

SO WE ALL SHOT IT DOWN. FAIR ENOUGH?

OK, SPLIT IT THREE WAYS. THEY'RE ALL MAD!

VICTORIES WERE OFTEN SPLIT TWO WAYS, BUT SELDOM THREE. SO GAVIN'S SECTION, NOW ALWAYS TOGETHER, CAME IN FOR A LOT OF GOOD-NATURED RIBBING.

I SUPPOSE YOU CHAPS SHARE EVERYTHING?

DISPERSAL

ALL BAR THE BATH. THERE'S NO ROOM IN THAT!

AND TIME AFTER TIME AGAIN THE MUCH-PRACTISED TEAMWORK CAME OFF.

BLAST 'EM, LADS!

IN FACT THEY ENJOYED THEIR WAR AND THIRSTED FOR THE HEAVIER ACTION ON THE BASES NEARER LONDON.

IN MID-AUGUST THEIR CHANCE CAME. EARLY ONE MORNING, WITH LESS THAN THREE HOURS NOTICE, THE WHOLE SQUADRON TOOK OFF FOR AN AERODROME IN SURREY, LED BY SQUADRON LEADER CONNOR.

AND ALL THEIR GUNS WERE EMPTY. FOR IN PLACE OF BELTS OF AMMUNITION, THE SQUADRON PILOTS WERE CARRYING THEIR PERSONAL LUGGAGE IN THE GUN BAYS.

THEN, AS THEY NEARED LONDON, A MESSAGE CAME IN FROM THEIR NEW OPERATIONS ROOM.

AERODROME UNDER ATTACK. ARE YOU FIT FOR ACTION?

NO. AIRCRAFT HAVE LUGGAGE IN GUN BAYS. WHAT ARE MY INSTRUCTIONS?

AND SO, WITH FUEL RUNNING LOW, THE HELPLESS SQUADRON CIRCLED ANXIOUSLY.

ORBIT WHERE YOU ARE. I'LL TRY TO SEND COVER.

AS THE MINUTES DRAGGED BY, THE SOUNDS OF BATTLE CAME NEARER.

KEEP YOUR EYES SKINNED.

BUT WHEN THE ATTACK CAME, IT WAS FROM A TOTALLY UNEXPECTED DIRECTION — FROM BELOW.
AGAIN, IT WAS JACKO WHO SPOTTED THE ENEMY.

IN A DISORDERLY SCRAMBLE THE SQUADRON SCATTERED, SIXTEEN FIRST-LINE FIGHTERS
INCAPABLE OF FIRING A SHOT. BUT HURRICANES FROM ANOTHER SQUADRON HAD APPEARED
AND WERE DIVING INTO ATTACK.

IT WAS A TIMELY INTERVENTION.

TAKEN COMPLETELY OFF-GUARD, THE MESSERSCHMITTS BROKE OFF THEIR ATTACK SWIFTLY AND STREAKED FOR HOME, LEAVING TWO OF THEIR NUMBER BLAZING.

AERODROME CLEAR. COME IN TO LAND NOW.

RATHER ASHAMED, THE SQUADRON LANDED AT THEIR NEW FRONT-LINE AERODROME TO BE GREETED BY THE LEADER OF THE FLIGHT THAT HAD DRIVEN OFF THEIR ATTACKERS. SQUADRON LEADER CONNOR THANKED HIM.

THANKS FOR CHIPPING IN THEN. WE'D HAVE BEEN IN A NASTY MESS IF YOU HADN'T.

THINK NOTHING OF IT, SIR. STILL I'D REMIND YOU THAT A FIGHTER HAS GUNS TO FIRE. YOU'LL NEED 'EM QUITE OFTEN UP HERE.

WHERE THE DEVIL DO YOU EXPECT US TO CARRY LUGGAGE THEN?

IN YOUR POCKETS, SIR, NOT IN YOUR GUN BAYS. BUT KEEP YOUR HAIR ON, LITTLE MAN. IT'S ONLY A BIT OF USEFUL ADVICE.

AND WITH THAT, THE COLOSSAL FIGURE WHO CARED NOTHING FOR RANK TURNED ON HIS HEEL AND STRODE AWAY.

INFURIATED BY THE BEHAVIOUR OF THE MASSIVE FLIGHT LIEUTENANT BUT NOT HAVING THE GUTS TO DO ANYTHING ABOUT IT, CONNOR PICKED ON LONG JOHN.

I WON'T BE TALKED TO LIKE THAT. DE SILVA SEEMS TO FIND IT FUNNY, HOWEVER.

SORRY, SIR. HE WAS TALKING ABOUT FIRING GUNS, AND ALL I HAD IN MY GUN BAYS WAS UNDERCLOTHES...

IF YOU FIND THAT FUNNY, WE HAVE DIFFERENT IDEAS OF HUMOUR. ARE YOU TRYING TO MAKE A FOOL OF ME?

NO, SIR. I JUST SAID...

GAVIN BROKE IN —

SIR, GO EASY...

NOW YOU'RE IN THIS TOO, ROBERTS. YOU THINK YOUR MINOR WEST COUNTRY SUCCESSES ENTITLE YOU TO RUN MY SQUADRON?

IT WAS FLIGHT LIEUTENANT DEMPSTER WHO BROKE IT UP.

I THINK WE'D BETTER CALL THIS OFF UNTIL WE'RE ALL CALMER. HADN'T YOU BETTER SEE THE STATION MASTER, SIR? YOU TWO BUZZ OFF AND GET SETTLED IN.

I SUPPOSE SO. WE'LL DISCUSS THIS LATER.

THE VOICE OF REASON HAD WON — THIS TIME.

AND SO IT WAS STILL ONLY TEN IN THE MORNING WHEN THE SQUADRON WAS AT READINESS ONCE MORE FOR THIS NEW AND VERY DIFFERENT SORT OF WAR.

CAN'T SAY I LIKED THE WAY THE C.O. BLEW UP.

I SHOULDN'T LET IT WORRY YOU. MOST ODD, THOUGH.

MAYBE IT WAS NERVES. MOST OF US HAVE SOME SOME- WHERE.

JUST BEFORE NOON THEY WERE SCRAMBLED TO COPE WITH A RAID ON A NEARBY FACTORY. BUT THE HEINKEL BOMBERS HAD A FIGHTER ESCORT.

BANDITS BEHIND! BREAK UPWARDS — QUICK!

IT WAS A PERFECT BOUNCE BY THE MESSERSCHMITTS.

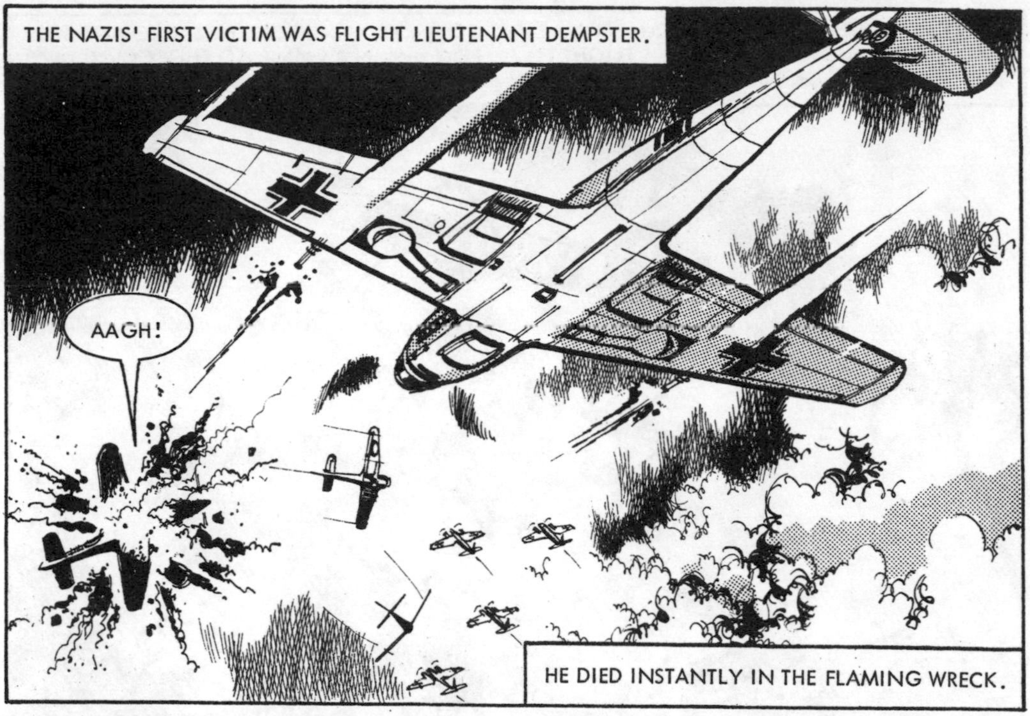
THE NAZIS' FIRST VICTIM WAS FLIGHT LIEUTENANT DEMPSTER.
AAGH!
HE DIED INSTANTLY IN THE FLAMING WRECK.

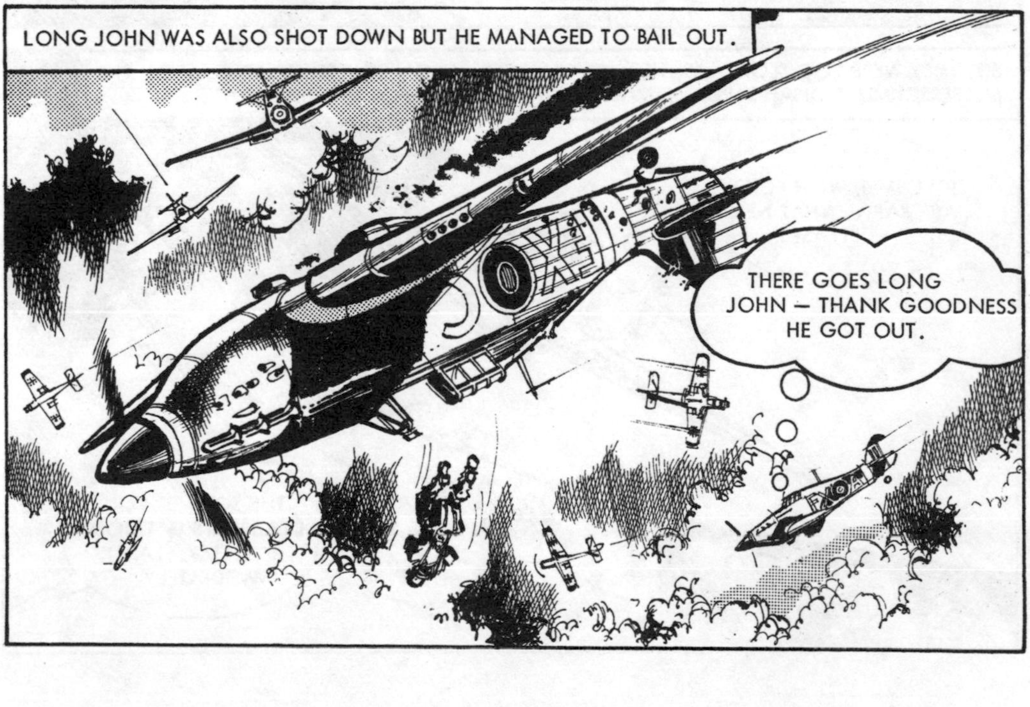
LONG JOHN WAS ALSO SHOT DOWN BUT HE MANAGED TO BAIL OUT.
THERE GOES LONG JOHN – THANK GOODNESS HE GOT OUT.

WHEN NO ORDERS CAME FROM SQUADRON LEADER CONNOR, GAVIN CALLED JACKO AND THE TWO HURRICANES FROM DEMPSTER'S FLIGHT TO FOLLOW HIM IN A CLIMB, SO THEY COULD DIVE BACK DOWN ON THE NAZI FIGHTERS.

BUT THEY WERE TOO SLOW. AS THE HURRICANE SQUADRON SCATTERED HOPELESSLY, THE MESSERSCHMITTS DISAPPEARED. GAVIN CONTACTED BASE FOR INSTRUCTIONS.

COLD WITH FURY, GAVIN RETURNED WITH THE SURVIVING AIRCRAFT, EACH WITHOUT HAVING FIRED A SHOT.

WE HAVE FULL AMMUNITION BELTS AND LOADS OF FUEL. HAVE YOU ANYTHING FOR US?

NO! GET OFF THE AIR AND SHUT UP.

AFTER THEY'D LANDED, THEY FOUND CONNOR IN A FOUL MOOD AND DEMANDING EXPLANATIONS.

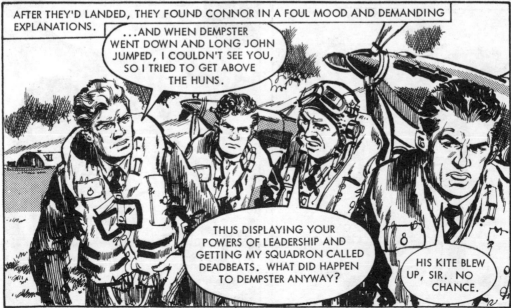

...AND WHEN DEMPSTER WENT DOWN AND LONG JOHN JUMPED, I COULDN'T SEE YOU, SO I TRIED TO GET ABOVE THE HUNS.

THUS DISPLAYING YOUR POWERS OF LEADERSHIP AND GETTING MY SQUADRON CALLED DEADBEATS. WHAT DID HAPPEN TO DEMPSTER ANYWAY?

HIS KITE BLEW UP, SIR. NO CHANCE.

THAT MEANS YOU'RE TEMPORARY FLIGHT COMMANDER, ROBERTS. I'D NEVER CONSIDER YOU PERMANENTLY, I'LL ADD. YOU'RE FAR TOO FULL OF YOURSELF...

WELL HE HASN'T GOT US INTO THE TIGHT SPOTS YOU'VE LED US INTO, SIR.

CHUCK IT, JACKO. WE'RE SUPPOSED TO BE FIGHTING GERMANS, NOT EACH OTHER.

BREATHING FIRE AND FURY ABOUT INSOLENCE, THE SQUADRON LEADER STRODE AWAY.

NOW JACKO REALLY BLEW UP.

WHAT A LOUSY RAT! HE'S THE ONLY ONE WHO BOOBS, BUT YOU GET THE BLAME!

LET IT REST. CONNOR JUST CAN'T ACCEPT RESPONSIBILITY OR MAKE DECISIONS.

YOU'RE THE BOSS. BUT THAT WALKING DUMMY'LL GET US ALL DEAD AND GONE YET.

ALTHOUGH THE TWO OTHER SQUADRONS SHARING THE
AERODROME TOOK OFF AGAIN IN THE EARLY AFTERNOON,
THE NEW ARRIVALS WERE NOT SCRAMBLED WITH THEM.
AND, LATER, LONG JOHN REAPPEARED.

THE WANDERER
RETURNS. HOW DID
YOU GET IN THAT
MESS?

GOT HIT IN THE ENGINE
AND SHOWERED WITH HOT OIL.
THEN I LANDED IN AN ORNAMENTAL
POND AND FRIGHTENED THE DUCKS
NO END. WHAT AIRCRAFT CAN
I HAVE NOW?

JUAN RAMOS DE SILVA WAS ALREADY BACK IN THE WAR.

TEN MINUTES LATER CAME THE ORDER TO
SCRAMBLE.

SCRAMBLE ALL
AIRCRAFT! FIFTY PLUS
BANDITS APPROACHING.
ORBIT BASE AT FIFTEEN
THOUSAND FEET.

THE USUAL WILD SPRINT BEGAN.

TO WAR
WE GO!

WITHIN TWO MINUTES THE HURRICANES WERE AIRBORNE.

I HOPE WE HAVE BETTER LUCK THIS TIME.

AT LESS THAN FIVE HUNDRED FEET WITH HIS FLIGHT ALREADY IN FORMATION, GAVIN LOOKED ROUND TO LOCATE THE SQUADRON COMMANDER AND THE LEADING FLIGHT.

WHAT THE DEVIL'S HE DOING SCRUBBING ABOUT DOWN THERE? BETTER FOLLOW HIM AND JOIN UP WHEN HE STARTS CLIMBING.

BUT FIVE MINUTES LATER THE LEADING FLIGHT WAS STILL AT GROUND LEVEL AND DEEP INTO RURAL SURREY. GAVIN CALLED ON HIS SECTION TO CLIMB AGAIN.

THE CONTROLLER SAID FIFTEEN THOUSAND FEET, SO FIFTEEN THOUSAND FEET IT IS. I HOPE I'M RIGHT!

CONNOR HAD NOT ONCE BROKEN RADIO SILENCE SINCE THEY'D TAKEN OFF AND MADE NO COMMENT AS GAVIN LED HIS SECTION OFF.

AND ALREADY A LARGE FORMATION OF HEINKEL BOMBERS WAS APPROACHING THE AIRFIELD TO BATTER IT OUT OF EXISTENCE.

KEEP IN TIGHT FORMATION.

BUT WHEN BASE PASSED ON THE NEWS TO CONNOR, THEY GOT A GRIM REPLY.

GAINING HEIGHT AND COMING IN FROM SOUTH. WILL BE TOO LATE.

BY GOOD LUCK GAVIN AND HIS SECTION HAD RETURNED AND WERE CIRCLING FAR ABOVE THE AERODROME AT THIS TIME.

IT APPEARED ALMOST AS IF CONNOR WAS TRYING TO KEEP AWAY FROM THE ACTION.

INTENT ON BREAKING UP THE ENEMY FORMATION BEFORE IT REACHED THE AERODROME, GAVIN DIVED DIRECTLY AT THE HEAD OF THE MASSIVE AIR ARMADA.

THE SIGHT OF THE KILLER HURRICANES CHILLED THE NAZIS' BLOOD.

FIRING BACK AT THE DIVING HURRIS, THE HEINKELS FLEW STEADILY ON.

AS GAVIN AND HIS FLIGHT SWUNG ROUND BEHIND THE ENEMY FORMATION, A SQUADRON OF SPITFIRES AND A FLIGHT OF HURRICANES FROM ANOTHER AERODROME FELL UPON THE NAZI HORDE.

AND IN THE NEXT FIVE MINUTES GAVIN DESTROYED HIS SECOND HEINKEL. JACKO AND LONG JOHN ALSO CLAIMED ANOTHER VICTIM EACH.

IT'S REALLY HOTTING UP NOW!

GAVIN THEN LED BACK TO BASE, TO FIND THE STATION COMMANDER, WING COMMANDER SUTTON, AND AN EXCITED RECEPTION COMMITTEE WAITING.

A SPLENDID SHOW, ROBERTS. NOT A BOMB ON THE AERODROME EITHER. BUT WHAT HAPPENED TO SQUADRON LEADER CONNOR AND THE OTHER FLIGHT?

HE DIDN'T CLIMB TO...ER, WE DIDN'T SEE HIM AFTER TAKE-OFF, SIR.

AND AT THAT VERY MOMENT THE OTHER FLIGHT LANDED — STILL IN PERFECT FORMATION.

AS THE TWO SENIOR OFFICERS WALKED AWAY, GAVIN HAD SOME TROUBLING THOUGHTS.

THAT'LL BE MY FIRST AND LAST OPERATION LEADING A FLIGHT. I KNOW AND THE OTHERS KNOW WHAT CONNOR IS LIKE, BUT DOES SUTTON?

GAVIN GOT HIS ANSWER LATER THAT AFTERNOON, WHEN HE WAS SUMMONED BY CONNOR.

WHO ORDERED YOU TO GO OFF ON YOUR OWN TODAY?

WITH A SINKING HEART GAVIN ADMITTED THAT HE'D GOT NO ORDER. HE REALISED NOW THAT CONNOR WAS OUT TO GET HIM AGAIN.

QUITE! YOU DIDN'T EVEN THINK I MIGHT HAVE A DIFFERENT PLAN OF ATTACK. I EXPECT TO BE OBEYED. I HAD NO ALTERNATIVE BUT TO ASK THE STATION COMMANDER TO POST YOU AWAY.

FRANKLY, I WAS OBEYING THE CONTROLLER'S INSTRUCTIONS AND NOTHING ELSE, SIR. WHEN DO I LEAVE?

YOU DON'T! SUTTON NOT ONLY PROMOTED YOU TO ACTING FLIGHT LIEUTENANT BUT INSISTED YOU LEAD A FLIGHT PERMANENTLY. HE EVEN HINTED I WAS AT FAULT THIS MORNING!

BUT PUT ONE FOOT WRONG, AND I'LL RUN YOU RIGHT OUT OF THE AIR FORCE, UNDERSTAND?

I DO, SIR.

ALMOST AS SOON AS HE GOT BACK TO DISPERSAL, THE SQUADRON WAS SCRAMBLED AGAIN AND JOINED THREE OTHER SQUADRONS IN ATTACKING A HORDE OF HEINKELS OVER KENT.

AS THE SQUADRON COMMANDER UNEXPECTEDLY LED THE FIRST SIX AIRCRAFT OUT THROUGH THE BOTTOM OF THE ENEMY FORMATION, GAVIN RECALLED HIS SECTION.

BREAK LEFT AND REFORM FOR ANOTHER POP AT 'EM.

GAVIN WAS ALREADY ATTACKING, WITH HIS SECTION, WHEN THE SQUADRON LEADER'S VOICE CAME THROUGH ON THE RADIO.

WHERE ARE YOU, ROBERTS? REFORM IMMEDIATELY FOR FRESH ATTACK.

AM ALREADY ATTACKING — SIR.

IT APPEARED THAT CONNOR WAS AGAIN KEEPING CLEAR OF THE FIGHT.

EVEN AS CONNOR BELLOWED AN ORDER TO GAVIN, Me109's DIVED DOWN ON THE HURRICANE.

REJOIN FORMATION IMMEDIATELY!

OH, SHUT UP! BANDITS SEVEN O'CLOCK HIGH. BREAK AND FIGHT.

WITH MOST OF THEIR AMMUNITION ALREADY EXPENDED, GAVIN'S SIX HURRICANES CHASED THE MESSERSCHMITTS.

WHEN YOU'RE OUT OF AMMO, GET ON THE DECK AND STREAK FOR HOME.

NEXT SECOND GAVIN'S OWN GUNS WERE EMPTY.

ONE AFTER THE OTHER THE PILOTS WERE FORCED TO OBEY HIS INSTRUCTIONS AS THE GERMANS MADE A BREAK FOR IT.

WHEN GAVIN LANDED BACK AT BASE THE OTHER FLIGHT WERE ALL DOWN INTACT. BUT ONLY JACKO HAD SO FAR LANDED OUT OF HIS OWN.

NO OTHER AIRCRAFT LANDED. CONNOR GRILLED LONG JOHN AND THE OTHER SURVIVING PILOT AS SOON AS THEY APPEARED.

WELL, WHAT HAPPENED?

I SAW GAVIN NAIL ONE JERRY. THEN I SAW DICK RIGBY AND SERGEANT CUTTER COLLIDE. THEY BOTH WENT STRAIGHT IN.

STILL GOING YOUR OWN SWEET WAY, ROBERTS! WHAT HAVE YOU GOT TO SHOW FOR IT? TWO GOOD PILOTS DEAD.

AND FIVE OR SIX HUNS PRANGED! WHAT DID YOU DO — SIR?

TENSION MOUNTED RAPIDLY.

I WARNED YOU, ROBERTS, AND NOW YOU'VE GOT RIGBY AND CUTTER KILLED. IF THE WING COMMANDER WON'T MOVE YOU, I'M GOING TO GROUP.

DO WHAT YOU LIKE, SIR. NO DOUBT I'M IN THE WRONG!

AT THAT THE SQUADRON LEADER STRODE AWAY.

BUT CONNOR HAD WORRIED GAVIN.

I SUPPOSE I DID KILL THOSE TWO.

NONSENSE! YOU CAN'T HELP IT IF PEOPLE COLLIDE. BESIDES, IF CONNOR HAD BEEN THERE, IT WOULD HAVE BEEN EASIER.

THANKS, CHAPS. I DO WORRY ABOUT THESE THINGS. NOW I'D BETTER PUT TWO RESERVE AIRCRAFT IN TO MAKE UP THAT SECTION.

AS A CURE FOR WORRY, NOTHING EQUALS RESPONSIBILITY.

THAT EVENING GAVIN WAS CALLED TO WING COMMANDER SUTTON'S OFFICE.

SQUADRON LEADER CONNOR HAS ASKED ME TO POST YOU AGAIN, BUT YOU MUST TRY TO HIT OFF WITH HIM. THE CONTROLLER ALSO TOLD ME YOU DID THE RIGHT THING THIS AFTERNOON.

I'LL TRY AS HARD AS I CAN, AND I'M AWFULLY GRATEFUL. I DO WANT TO STAY, SIR.

GOOD. HOW MANY DID YOU GET YOURSELF TODAY?

THREE CONFIRMED AND A POSSIBLE SIR.

EXCELLENT! KEEP AT IT.

GAVIN LEFT SUTTON, FEELING MUCH THE BETTER FOR THE INTERVIEW.

LATE THAT NIGHT, AS GAVIN WAS INSPECTING HIS HURRICANE, SQUADRON LEADER CONNOR APPEARED.

YOU'RE A FANTASTIC SALESMAN, ROBERTS. NOT ONLY DID SUTTON PERSUADE ME TO KEEP YOU ON, BUT THE CONTROLLER BACKED HIM UP. I DON'T GET IT!

THANKS FOR THE CHANGE OF MIND, SIR.

CONNOR STRODE OFF INTO THE NIGHT, COMPLETELY IGNORING GAVIN'S ATTEMPT TO BE REASONABLE AND KEEP THE PEACE.

EARLY NEXT MORNING THE SQUADRON WAS SCRAMBLED AGAIN AS GERMAN RAIDERS WERE SPOTTED.

BET YOU I GET THE FIRST KILL, LONG JOHN!

NOT A HOPE, YOU CROSS-EYED NEW ZEALAND NIT!

AGAIN, SQUADRON LEADER CONNOR LEFT THE AERODROME AT GROUND LEVEL.

STILL GRUBBING ALONG ON THE DECK! BUT, THIS TIME, I'LL STICK WITH HIM UNTIL HE DOES FINALLY DECIDE TO CLIMB.

THEN, WHEN THEY WERE FIFTEEN MILES FROM THE AERODROME, SQUADRON LEADER CONNOR SUDDENLY PULLED HIS STICK BACK AND BROUGHT THE SQUADRON UP IN A LONG CLIMBING TURN.

WONDERS WILL NEVER CEASE!

AS THE HURRICANES ARRIVED AT 16,000 FEET, READY TO CIRCLE THE AERODROME, THE HAWK-EYED JACKO SPOTTED THE RAIDERS FIRST.

TALLYHO! HERE'S THE BIGGEST SHOW EVER!

AS THE SQUADRON STREAKED TOWARDS THE ONCOMING BOMBERS, A RADIO CALL CAME FROM CONNOR.

MY ENGINE'S ACTING UP. YOU TAKE OVER, ROBERTS. AM RETURNING TO BASE.

UNDERSTOOD. REFORM FLIGHT AND PULL IN BEHIND ME.

BITTERLY GAVIN REALISED THAT CONNOR WAS PULLING OUT OF A FIGHT AGAIN.

AGAIN, DESPITE THE IMMENSITY OF THE ENEMY FORMATION, GAVIN USED THE DEVASTATING HEAD-ON ATTACK.

THE RESULT WAS UTTER CONFUSION AMONG THE NAZIS.

AS SOON AS HE WAS CLEAR OF THE MASS OF WEAVING AIRCRAFT, GAVIN PICKED A TURNING HEINKEL.

A MOMENT LATER HE WAS INVOLVED WITH A MESSERSCHMITT.

AT THE SAME TIME, FAR BELOW, SQUADRON LEADER BRIAN CONNOR WAS DIVING SWIFTLY HOMEWARDS WITH THREE NAZIS ON HIS TAIL.

THREE OF THEM — GOT TO TURN LEFT HARD!

CONNOR HAD LEFT THE FIGHT TO AVOID TROUBLE BUT NOW HE WAS REALLY IN A SPOT.

THE NAZI JUST REACHED THE SAFETY OF THE CLOUDS AS GAVIN RAN OUT OF AMMUNITION.

AND BECAUSE IT WAS THE ONLY CHANCE LEFT THE LONE SQUADRON LEADER TURNED AT BAY TO FIGHT.

GOT TO GET OUT OF THIS!

PANIC HAD GRIPPED CONNOR IN A FEARFUL HOLD.

THE BULLETS FOUND A TARGET IN ONE MESSERSCHMITT THEN CONNOR TURNED HIS GUNS ON ANOTHER NAZI.

AND THEN, WHEN VICTORY WAS IN HIS GRASP, CONNOR TURNED FOR CLOUD COVER, LEAVING THE THIRD GERMAN PLANE UNDAMAGED.

BUT THE GERMAN PILOT WAS NO NOVICE. HE QUICKLY GOT CONNOR IN HIS SIGHTS.

FAR ENOUGH, ENGLANDER!

SO DIED SQUADRON LEADER CONNOR, A MAN SCARED TO FIGHT.

HIS OWN COWARDICE HAD KILLED HIM.

BACK AT THE AERODROME, AS PILOTS LANDED AND REPORTS CAME IN, IT WAS OBVIOUS THAT THE SQUADRON HAD HAD A FIELD DAY.

WELL, HOW DID IT GO?

ONE HEINKEL NAILED AND ONE FIGHTER BADLY FRIGHTENED.

ONE HEINKEL — IN TINY LITTLE BITS. ITS BOMBS WENT UP.

THERE WAS STILL NO SIGN OF CONNOR OR JACKO WHEN WING COMMANDER SUTTON CAME TO SEE THEM.

WING COMMANDER SUTTON LEFT IT AT THAT. THEN THE TELEPHONE RANG HALF AN HOUR LATER...

IN THE LATE AFTERNOON GAVIN WAS CALLED TO WING COMMANDER SUTTON'S OFFICE.

THEY'VE LOCATED SQUADRON LEADER CONNOR TEN MILES AWAY — DEAD. THEY SAY HE TOOK ON THREE MESSERSCHMITTS AND GOT TWO OF THEM FIRST. JUST WHAT DID HAPPEN?

AS I SAID EARLIER, WE WERE ABOUT A MILE SHORT OF THE HEINKELS WHEN HE CALLED UP AND SAID HIS ENGINE WAS ACTING UP, SIR. HE TOLD ME TO TAKE OVER, SO WE PITCHED STRAIGHT IN.

DIDN'T SOMEBODY FROM 'B' FLIGHT GIVE HIM COVER?

NO, SIR. I CALLED THEM TO REFORM BEHIND 'A' FLIGHT. WE WERE ALMOST ON TOP OF THE HEINKELS.

WELL, HE SEEMS TO HAVE DIED WELL, BUT I THINK GROUP WILL WANT TO KNOW WHY AT LEAST ONE AIR-CRAFT DIDN'T STAY WITH HIM.

SUTTON NODDED IN AGREEMENT AND GAVIN LEFT THE OFFICE.

SO, FOR THE FIRST TIME IN WEEKS, THE FIGHTING THREE WERE SPLIT.

MINUTES LATER THEY REACHED THE LOCAL.

IT WOULDN'T SOUND TOO GOOD TO PEOPLE WHO DON'T KNOW THE WHOLE STORY. WHY NOT HAVE IT OUT WITH GROUP?

OH, I'LL WAIT AND SEE WHAT HAPPENS.

IT WASN'T UNTIL MUCH LATER IN THE EVENING THAT THEIR NATURAL EXUBERANCE TOOK OVER ONCE MORE.

SOON AFTER DAWN NEXT MORNING THE SQUADRON WAS SCRAMBLED TO HOLD OFF A BIG RAID'S FIGHTER ESCORT WHILE OTHER SQUADRONS ATTACKED THE BOMBERS.

EVERY MAN FOR HIMSELF ONCE WE DIVE IN.

GAVIN SCREAMED DOWN OUT OF THE SUN.

LOVELY! NOW PICK TARGETS AS NEAR THE FRONT AS YOU CAN.

JUST A MINUTE LATER GAVIN FOUND HIMSELF INVOLVED WITH THE GERMAN FORMATION LEADER WHO WAS OBVIOUSLY VERY EXPERIENCED.

I'M HALF BLACKED-OUT, BUT I CAN GET HIM IF I CAN HOLD ON.

REALISING THAT GAVIN WAS SLOWLY GAINING, THE HUN CHANGED HIS TACTICS IN A DESPERATE ATTEMPT TO GET ABOVE HIS ENEMY.

I'VE GOT TO SHOOT FAST — AND WELL!

AND HE DID.

POOR DEVIL! HE WAS REALLY GOOD.

GAVIN FLEW BACK TO BASE THOUGHTFULLY. NO NORMAL MAN KILLS FOR THE FUN OF IT.

BACK AT THE AERODROME —

YOU'RE THE LAST BACK. LONG JOHN'S LOST TWO AIRCRAFT AND ONE PILOT.

I'D BETTER GO OVER AND SEE HIM THEN.

LONG JOHN WAS A BIT DOWN IN THE MOUTH.

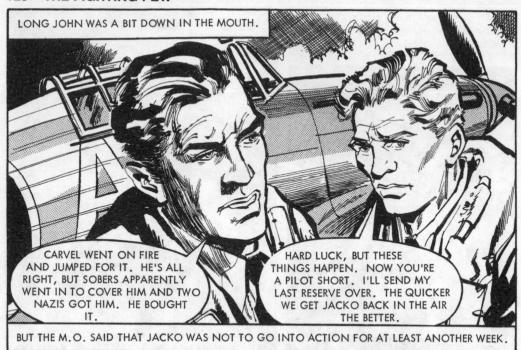

CARVEL WENT ON FIRE AND JUMPED FOR IT. HE'S ALL RIGHT, BUT SOBERS APPARENTLY WENT IN TO COVER HIM AND TWO NAZIS GOT HIM. HE BOUGHT IT.

HARD LUCK, BUT THESE THINGS HAPPEN. NOW YOU'RE A PILOT SHORT. I'LL SEND MY LAST RESERVE OVER. THE QUICKER WE GET JACKO BACK IN THE AIR THE BETTER.

BUT THE M.O. SAID THAT JACKO WAS NOT TO GO INTO ACTION FOR AT LEAST ANOTHER WEEK.

TWENTY MINUTES LATER THEY WERE OFF AGAIN TO INTERCEPT RAIDERS. AND THEY HAD AN EXTRA PLANE ALONG.

WHO THE DICKENS IS THAT TAGGING ON THE END?

PILOT JOINING SECTION TWO — IDENTIFY YOURSELF.

ADOLF HITLER HERE — AND RARING TO GO.

BEFORE GAVIN COULD SAY ANY MORE THEY CLASHED WITH SOME GERMAN FIGHTERS. THE MYSTERY PILOT SHOWED JUST HOW GOOD HE WAS.

ON THE WAY BACK TO BASE GAVIN DISCOVERED THE IDENTIFY OF THE MYSTERY PILOT.... JACKO.

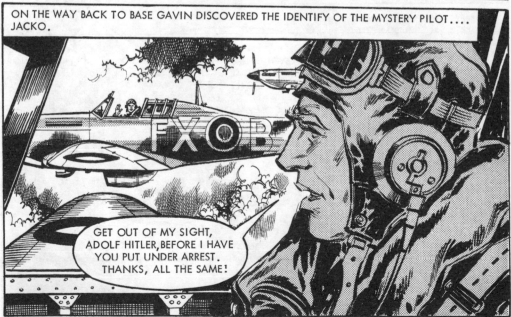

THE STATION COMMANDER, WING COMMANDER SUTTON, WAS WAITING WHEN GAVIN LANDED.

THE NEW SQUADRON LEADER HAS ARRIVED, WITH SOME RESERVE PILOTS. I SHOULDN'T SAY THIS BUT WATCH YOUR STEP WITH HIM. BRING ALL YOUR PILOTS DOWN TO 'B' FLIGHT NOW. HE WANTS TO TALK TO YOU.

RIGHT, SIR, AND THANKS VERY MUCH.

THE NEW C.O., SQUADRON LEADER, V.M. 'MICK' VERITY, WAS A VERY TOUGH CHARACTER INDEED.

YOU HAVEN'T DONE BADLY. BUT BY THE TIME I'VE FINISHED WITH YOU YOU'RE GOING TO HAVE THE MOST KILLS IN FIGHTER COMMAND! NOW I WANT TO SEE THE FLIGHT COMMANDERS ALONE.

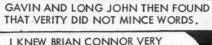

GAVIN AND LONG JOHN THEN FOUND THAT VERITY DID NOT MINCE WORDS.

I KNEW BRIAN CONNOR VERY WELL AND HE TOLD ME THIS UNIT LACKED TEAM SPIRIT AND LOYALTY. SO YOU TWO ARE VERY MUCH ON TRIAL. NOW, ROBERTS, A WORD WITH YOU ALONE...

AFTER LONG JOHN LEFT —

YOU'RE SENIOR FLIGHT COMMANDER, ROBERTS, UNTIL YOU PUT ONE FOOT WRONG. I HEARD ALL ABOUT YOU FROM CONNOR AND HE DIED BECAUSE YOU LET HIM DOWN. I'M STAYING ALIVE!

YES, SIR.

COMPARED WITH VERITY, CONNOR SEEMED A MILD AND PLEASANT MEMORY.

AND IN THE NEXT FEW DAYS THE FULL IMPACT OF VERITY'S AGGRESSIVENESS WAS FELT.

GIVE 'EM THE LOT. IF ONE GETS HOME, WE'VE BOOBED.

HIS POLICY OF 'ATTACK, ATTACK AND ATTACK AGAIN' MADE HIM AN INSPIRING LEADER — IN THE AIR.

ON THE GROUND, HOWEVER, HIS PRAISE WAS ALWAYS GRUDGING EVEN THOUGH THE SQUADRON'S SCORE AND GAVIN'S OWN SCORE MOUNTED STEADILY.

MY SCORE, SIR? ELEVEN CONFIRMED AND JACKO'S GOT SIX.

PRETTY FAIR, I SUPPOSE. WHAT MATTERS IS THAT YOU'RE EITHER REFORMED OR BEING CAUTIOUS.

IT SEEMED ALMOST AS IF THE GHOST OF CONNOR WAS STILL CHARGING AT GAVIN.

BUT WHILE GAVIN KEPT UP AN AIR OF APPARENT INDIFFERENCE, HIS TWO FRIENDS STILL VOICED THEIR WORRIES.

BUT WHY DON'T YOU SEE THE WINGCO, ASK HIM TO GET ONTO GROUP AND HAVE THE WHOLE THING PROPERLY THRASHED OUT.

VERITY MAY BE AN AWKWARD SORT OF TOUGH, BUT I THINK HE'D BE A FAIR GUY IF HE KNEW THE FACTS.

LOOK, POOR CONNOR IS DEAD AND I'M NOT GOING TO SLANDER HIS NAME.

THE NEWS THAT GAVIN HAD BEEN AWARDED THE D.F.C. CHEERED THEM UP SLIGHTLY. BUT THEN THEY WERE IN THE AIR AGAIN, INTERESTED ONLY IN STAYING ALIVE.

TWENTY-FIVE PLUS BANDITS APPROACHING BASE WITH MASSIVE ESCORT.

MESSAGE RECEIVED AND UNDERSTOOD.

A RAIDING FORCE OF THIS SIZE WASN'T HARD TO SPOT.

WE'LL HIT 'EM IN ONE SOLID LUMP AND THEN TAKE INDIVIDUAL TARGETS.

OUTNUMBERED FOUR TO ONE, THE HURRICANES HAD A REAL FIGHT ON THEIR HANDS.

THUMP THEM, LADS!

GAVIN, AS USUAL, WAS IN THE THICK OF IT.

WHERE DO THEY ALL COME FROM?

HE PULLED CLEAR OF THE BEDLAM.

THE WHOLE SKY IS LOUSY WITH THEM!

THEN HE PEERED ROUND TO FIND THE NEXT TARGET.

FAR BELOW, VERITY, WITH ONE OTHER HURRICANE, WAS FIGHTING GRIMLY AGAINST IMPOSSIBLE ODDS. GAVIN DECIDED TO HELP OUT.

AND CONVERTING HIS DIVE INTO A WILD TURN, GAVIN BROKE UP THE NAZI FORMATION.

AS THE SHATTERED GERMAN FORMATION BROKE AND RAN, GAVIN HAULED HIS AIRCRAFT ROUND INTO FORMATION ON HIS SQUADRON LEADER.

PRAISE FROM VERITY — THINGS WERE IMPROVING FOR GAVIN.

BACK AT BASE, VERITY PROVED JUST HOW MUCH A MAN HE WAS.

AND WHEN VERITY WAS PROMOTED TO WING COMMANDER, GAVIN TOOK OVER AS SQUADRON LEADER. BY NOW, THE LUFTWAFFE WAS REALLY ON THE RUN.

ANOTHER FOR THE SKIPPER!

WHAT A GUY!

Commando
THE END

WARSHIPS OF WORLD WAR 2

AFRIDI Class destroyers

(Britain, Canada, Australia)

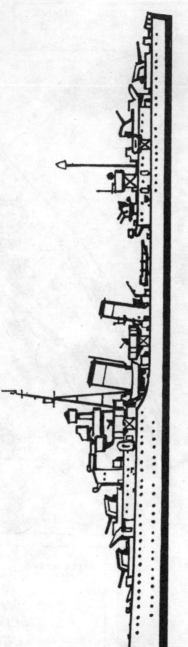

(Usually called "Tribal" class, with names like Cossack, Zulu, Sikh etc.)

Displacement 1960 tons
Length 115m (377 feet)
Speed 36 knots
Crew 190.

Armament — 8 120mm (4.7-inch)
4 40mm AA pom-poms
8 12.7mm (0.5-inch)
4 torpedo tubes.

BRIGHT BLADE of COURAGE

THIS IS A STORY OF PROUD SHIPS AND PROUD MEN, CHARGED TO SWEEP BRITAIN'S ENEMIES FROM THE SEAS. ABOVE ALL IT IS THE STORY OF THE MEN OF A CERTAIN FAMILY, NAVAL OFFICERS ALL, WHOSE SWORN DUTY WAS TO KEEP SAFE A VERY SPECIAL SWORD. BUT LET US START AT THE BEGINNING. THE YEAR IS 1798...

First published 1971

ABOUKIR BAY, IN EGYPT. THE BATTLE OF THE NILE WAS BEING HOTLY FOUGHT BETWEEN THE FLEETS OF BRITAIN AND FRANCE. ON BOARD A TRIM BRITISH FRIGATE, H.M.S. CUTLASS, STOOD CAPTAIN ROLAND WARDEN, ALREADY A VETERAN OF MANY A BATTLE.

THE FROGS ARE BREAKING OUR VAN! LAY HER ALONGSIDE THEIR FLAGSHIP, MISTER TEBBIT, AND WE'LL SEE HOW THEY LIKE THE TASTE OF BRITISH STEEL!

H.M.S. CUTLASS CAUGHT THE WIND SKILFULLY, AND LAID ALONGSIDE THE FRENCH FLAG-SHIP WITH A GRINDING CRASH. WARDEN WAS IN THE FOREFRONT OF THE RUSH.

AT 'EM, MY LADS!

DEATH TO THE FROGS!

STEEL SPARKED ON STEEL AS WARDEN AND HIS MEN HACKED THEIR WAY TOWARDS THE ENEMY COLOURS.

THAT ACTION CHANGED THE BATTLE. AS THE FRENCH FLEET SAW THEIR FLAGSHIP'S COLOURS STRUCK, ALL HEART FLED FROM THEM, AND THEY WERE EASY MEAT FOR THE BRITISH TARS. BUT WARDEN WAS DYING, FELLED BY A MUSKET BALL. WITH HIS LAST BREATH HE GASPED OUT A FINAL REQUEST.

H.M.S. CUTLASS SAILED FROM ABOUKIR BAY RICH IN GLORY, BUT SADDENED BY THE LOSS OF HER CAPTAIN. HIS SWORD WAS FASTENED TO THE MAINMAST FOR ALL EYES TO SEE. IT WAS THERE AT THE BATTLE OF COPENHAGEN IN 1801, AND AT TRAFALGAR FOUR YEARS LATER.

THERE HANGS OUR SWORD, JEM. A BRAVE SWORD FOR A BRAVE SHIP.

AND IN 1914, WHEN BRITAIN AGAIN FACED AN ENEMY ACROSS THE CHANNEL, THE SWORD WAS CARRIED INTO WAR BY A NEW H.M.S. CUTLASS — A FAST DESTROYER.

ANOTHER BROADSIDE, MEN! LET'S GIVE THE KAISER SOMETHING TO REMIND HIM OF KING GEORGE'S NAVY.

WHEN H.M.S. CUTLASS WAS SUNK IN 1916, THE SWORD WAS TAKEN OFF IN THE ONLY BOAT TO BE LAUNCHED.

THERE SHE GOES!

GOODBYE, OLD GIRL!

NOT UNTIL 1936 WAS A NEW H.M.S. CUTLASS BUILT. THE SWORD WAS WELCOMED ABOARD WITH A SPECIAL CEREMONY IN THE WARDROOM.

GENTLEMEN. I GIVE YOU THE BATTLE OF ABOUKIR BAY!

EVERY YEAR ON THE ANNIVERSARY OF THE BATTLE OF THE NILE THAT TOAST WAS DRUNK. NOW IT WAS 1940, AND AGAIN BRITAIN WAS FIGHTING FURIOUSLY FOR HER LIFE. H.M.S. CUTLASS WAS ON CONVOY DUTY, WATCHING OVER THE MERCHANT SHIPS THAT RISKED ALL TO KEEP BRITAIN FIGHTING.

THERE GOES ANOTHER ONE! MUST BE A U-BOAT PACK RIGHT UNDER OUR KEELS.

BESIDE THE CAPTAIN STOOD LIEUTENANT JOHN WARDEN, A DESCENDANT OF THE FIRST CAPTAIN WARDEN. JOHN HELD THE TRADITIONAL POST OF KEEPER OF THE SWORD. BUT NOW HE WAS CONCERNED WITH MORE MODERN WEAPONS.

DEPTH CHARGES, SIR?

YES, IF YOU CAN SORT ONE ECHO OUT FROM ANOTHER. THERE MUST BE HALF A DOZEN OF THEM AROUND.

BUT PROWLING U-BOATS WEREN'T THE ONLY PROBLEM. A PRIORITY SIGNAL ARRIVED...

PHEW! JERRY'S GOT THE GROSSADLER OUT IN THIS AREA. SHE WILL SLAUGHTER US!

FAST AND HEAVILY ARMED, THE BATTLE-CRUISER GROSSADLER WAS THE PRIDE OF THE NAZI FLEET. AND ALREADY SHE WAS HUNTING HER NEXT VICTIMS.

BRITISH CONVOY FIFTY KILOMETRES DUE EAST, SIR.

GUT! ALTER COURSE TO ENGAGE.

AND ABOARD H.M.S. CUTLASS THEY WERE PREPARING FOR THE COMING BATTLE TOO.

I HOPE THE TUBES ARE OK. LOOKS LIKE IT'S GOING TO BE A HOT DAY, CHIEF.

I WISH YOU MEANT WE'RE GOING TO SEE SOME SUN, SIR! NEVER DID LIKE SWIMMING IN COLD WATER.

CHIEF PETTY OFFICER BERT WOODLEY TOOK A SPECIAL INTEREST IN THE SWORD TOO, FOR HE ALWAYS REPRESENTED THE LOWER DECK AT THE CEREMONIES. BUT HE WAS MORE CONCERNED WITH HIS TORPEDO TUBES JUST NOW.

WE'VE GOT THE PRIDE OF THE GERMAN FLEET STEAMING OUR WAY. YOU'D BETTER MAKE SURE THESE TIN-FISH COME OUT FIGHTING, PARKER.

FIVE HOURS LATER THE GROSSADLER CLOSED WITH THE CONVOY. FOUR FIFTEEN-INCH GUN TURRETS SWUNG ROUND TO FACE THE MERCHANT SHIPS.

HER MIGHTY GUNS THUNDERED AND A TANKER EXPLODED IN A SHOCKING BLAST OF FIRE. GRIMLY H.M.S. CUTLASS TURNED TO FACE THE ENEMY.

THEN THE NEXT SALVO STRUCK — RIGHT ON THE DESTROYER'S BRIDGE.

SHE'LL BLAST US ALL OUT OF THE WATER!

WITH THE CAPTAIN WOUNDED, IT WAS UP TO JOHN TO TAKE OVER.

NELSON ALWAYS SAID TO GET CLOSE TO YOUR ENEMY. LET'S PROVE HIM RIGHT...

CUTLASS TURNED SHARPLY, POINTING HER GREYHOUND LENGTH AT THE BULKY GROSSADLER.

...OR WRONG.

IT WAS A DESPERATE MEASURE, BUT BY TAKING THE BRUNT OF THE NAZI FIRE JOHN HOPED TO LET SOME OF THE MERCHANTMEN SLIP AWAY UNDER COVER OF THE SMOKE. HE RAPPED OUT AN ORDER TO BERT WOODLEY.

STAND BY, TUBES. WE'LL GET IN A QUICK SHOT.

YOU'LL BE LUCKY, MISTER WARDEN, SIR.

BERT'S GLOOMY WORDS WERE PROVED RIGHT. MINUTES LATER H.M.S. CUTLASS WAS A BLAZING RUIN. ON BOARD THE GERMAN BATTLE-CRUISER, KAPITAN ERICH VON LIPPNER SPOKE IN AWE.

STOP FIRING! I'D LIKE TO SHAKE THAT CAPTAIN'S HAND IF HE'S STILL ALIVE. SEND OVER A BOAT.

THE ONCE-PROUD H.M.S. CUTLASS LAY BROKEN, A SHATTERED WRECK. THE BOARDING PARTY FROM THE GROSSADLER APPROACHED CAUTIOUSLY.

WHEN THE YOUNG GERMAN OFFICER REACHED THE LISTING DECK, A SCENE OF DEVASTATION MET HIM. ONLY BERT STILL LIVED.

IT WAS THE SAME ON THE WRECKED BRIDGE. THEN JOHN MADE A SLIGHT MOVEMENT.

HIMMEL, HOW COULD THEY HAVE STOOD THIS? ACH...ANOTHER ONE ALIVE. WE'LL TAKE THEM BOTH TO THE BOAT.

AS JOHN AND BERT WERE CARRIED INTO THE MOTOR BOAT THE GERMAN OFFICER SAW THE SWORD.

A FINE SOUVENIR OF A FINE SHIP.

THROUGH EYES MISTED WITH PAIN, JOHN SAW THE SWORD COME ABOARD THE GERMAN BATTLE-CRUISER.

THEN JOHN PLUMMETTED INTO A GREAT ABYSS OF BLACKNESS.

HE NEVER SAW THE END OF H.M.S. CUTLASS, FOR THE GROSSADLER SPED AWAY TO CHASE THE SCATTERED CONVOY.

NOR WAS HE AWARE OF BEING TRANSFERRED TO A SMALL GERMAN CARGO SHIP THAT WAS TO TAKE HIM TO FRANCE...AND A PRISON CAMP. BERT WAS THERE TOO.

JUST THE TWO OF US, EH? ALL THAT'S LEFT! AND THE SWORD GONE...RESTING A HUNDRED FATHOMS UNDER! WHAT A MESS!

A COUPLE OF DAYS LATER, JOHN RECOVERED ENOUGH TO TALK DURING THEIR EXERCISE PERIOD.

THE SWORD DIDN'T GO DOWN...A GERMAN OFFICER SWIPED IT. OUR SWORD IS NOW SAILING IN THE GROSSADLER.

WITH THE ENEMY, EH? STONE ME!

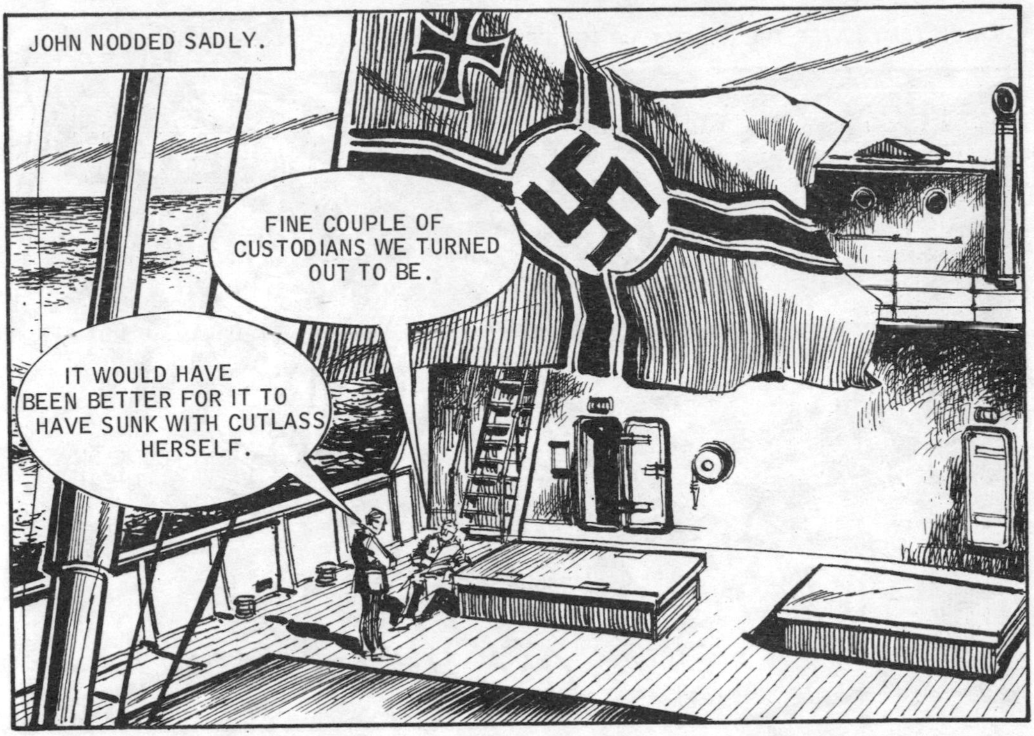
JOHN NODDED SADLY.
FINE COUPLE OF CUSTODIANS WE TURNED OUT TO BE.
IT WOULD HAVE BEEN BETTER FOR IT TO HAVE SUNK WITH CUTLASS HERSELF.

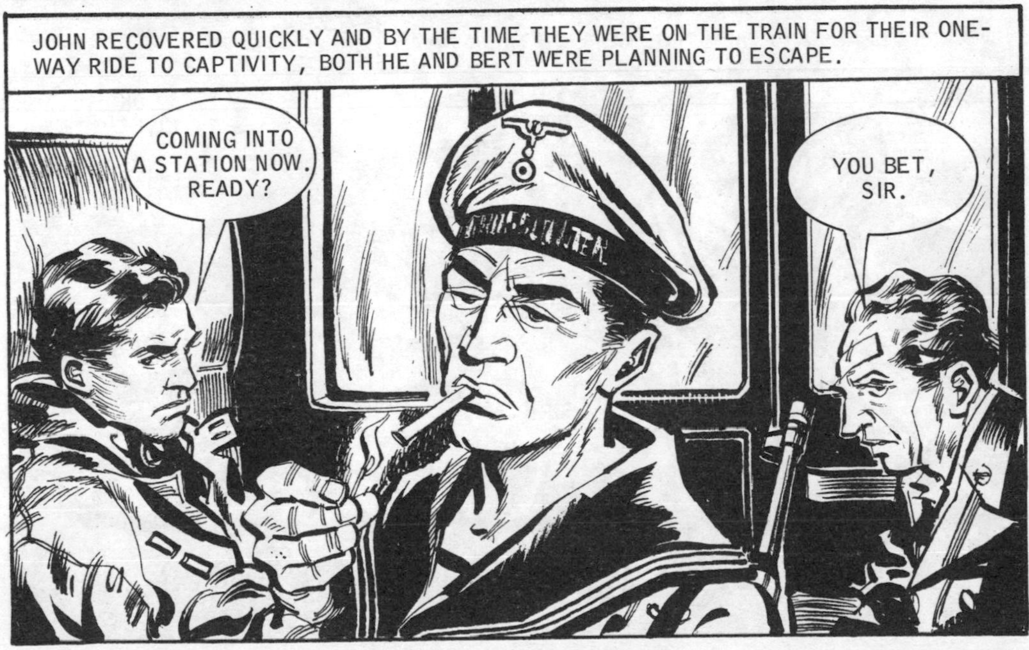
JOHN RECOVERED QUICKLY AND BY THE TIME THEY WERE ON THE TRAIN FOR THEIR ONE-WAY RIDE TO CAPTIVITY, BOTH HE AND BERT WERE PLANNING TO ESCAPE.
COMING INTO A STATION NOW. READY?
YOU BET, SIR.

AN INSTANT LATER THE GUARD PAID THE PRICE OF NEGLIGENCE.

COME ON, THEN!

A DARING LEAP, AND THEN THEY WERE ON THEIR WAY.

LOOK LIVELY!

AYE, AYE, SIR!

IT TOOK THEM SIX DESPERATE WEEKS TO GET BACK TO ENGLAND VIA THE FRENCH RESISTANCE.

VOILA, MESSIEURS. YOUR WHITE CLIFFS.

LOVELY SIGHT, EH, SIR?

JOHN WAS GIVEN A FEW WEEKS' HOME LEAVE, AND WENT TO STAY WITH HIS FATHER.

SO THE SWORD'S ON BOARD THE GROSSADLER?

AFRAID SO, DAD!

JOHN'S FATHER, REAR-ADMIRAL PHILIP WARDEN (RETIRED), NODDED GLUMLY.

WELL, I SUPPOSE THERE'S SOME CHANCE OF GETTING IT BACK. YOU REMEMBER WHAT THEY SAID ABOUT THE SWORD.

IN A DEEP, THROATY VOICE THE FORMER SEA-DOG SPOKE THE PROPHECY MADE YEARS BEFORE.

"UNLESS THE SWORD IS MOUNTED FIRMLY ON A SHIP CALLED CUTLASS, THINGS WILL NOT GO WELL FOR BRITAIN." THAT'S WHAT THEY SAY.

REAR-ADMIRAL WARDEN LED JOHN TO HIS STUDY.

AND IT'S COMING TRUE! WE'RE LOSING THOUSANDS OF TONS OF SHIPPING A WEEK! OUR ARMY'S BEING DRIVEN BACK, EVEN OUR TOWNS ARE BEING BOMBED. I TELL YOU, JOHN, UNTIL THAT SWORD IS RECOVERED, ENGLAND'S BACK IS TO THE WALL, AND NO MISTAKE!

THAT EVENING ADMIRAL SIR HERBERT MARTEN CAME TO VISIT JOHN'S FATHER. AFTER DINNER THE CONVERSATION TURNED TO THE SELF-SAME SUBJECT.

AND NOW THERE'S NOT A SHIP IN THE NAVY THAT BEARS THE NAME OF CUTLASS. SCANDALOUS, I CALL IT.

BUT, PHILIP, LET'S KEEP TO REALITIES.

SIR HERBERT WENT ON FIRMLY.

I LIKE NAVAL TRADITIONS TOO, BUT WE DON'T HAVE THE TIME FOR THEM JUST NOW. WE'LL USE THE NAME WHEN WE CAN.

IGNORING HIS HOST'S SNORT OF ANGER, HE TURNED TO JOHN.

AND ONCE YOU'RE ON A SHIP AGAIN, I DON'T WANT TO HEAR OF YOU CHASING AFTER THE GROSSADLER TO GET THAT SWORD BACK. YOUR FATHER WOULD, I KNOW, BUT I HOPE YOU'VE GOT MORE SENSE.

NAVY'S A LOT OF MILK-SOPS THESE DAYS. NO SPIRIT. NO FIRE!

JOHN RETURNED TO ACTIVE SERVICE, GAINING FAST PROMOTION TO COMMANDER AND EVENTUALLY GETTING HIS OWN SHIP, THE BRAND-NEW DESTROYER, H.M.S. VIPER. AND BERT WOODLEY WAS THERE TOO.

THANK HEAVEN I'VE GOT YOU TO BACK ME UP, CHIEF.

WE'LL BE GOING TO LOOK FOR THE GROSSADLER, SIR, I HOPE?

MURMANSK — THE ARCTIC RUN, THE MOST DREADED CONVOY ROUTE OF THEM ALL WITH PACKS OF KILLER U-BOATS LURKING EVERY MILE OF THE WAY.

DAYS AND NIGHTS WERE ONE CONTINUOUS BLUR OF BATTLE. JOHN STAYED ON HIS BRIDGE ALMOST ALL THE TIME, HIS EYES RED AND SORE WITH WATCHING OVER THE MERCHANTMEN FERRYING VITAL ARMS TO RUSSIA.

ANY ACTION ON THE RADAR, NUMBER ONE?

SCREEN'S CONFUSED, SIR. TOO MUCH ICE ABOUT.

THAT'S AN AMMO SHIP. TORPEDO. GET AFTER THE U-BOAT.

THE SHIP SPED THROUGH THE WATER, SEARCHING DESPERATELY FOR ANY TRACE OF THE LURKING SUBMARINE. THEN THE ASDIC OPERATOR REPORTED...

AN ARROW OF VENGEANCE SHE TORE THROUGH THE WATER, LAYING A PATTERN OF DEPTH CHARGES.

BLUNT CANISTERS OF DEATH THAT ROLLED AND TWIRLED THEIR WAY DOWN THROUGH THE ICY SEAS.

THEN ALL AT ONCE A LOOK-OUT GAVE AN EXCITED YELL.

THIS TIME ALL THEIR WEARY WORK HAD PAID OFF.

AND SO IT WENT ON. THE RETURN TRIP WAS EVEN WORSE, AND IT WAS A BATTERED H.M.S. VIPER WHICH LIMPED INTO A REPAIR YARD ON THE TYNE.

BEATS ME HOW THESE SHIPS EVER MAKE IT HOME!

YEAH. LOT OF WORK FOR US ON THAT ONE, SID.

JOHN GRABBED A FEW DAYS' LEAVE.

ROUGH TIME, BOY?

PRETTY ROUGH. IT JUST NEVER SEEMS TO END.

YES, I REMEMBER THAT FROM THE FIRST WAR. BUT IT PASSES, LAD. ANY NEWS OF THE GROSSADLER?

SHE'S STILL RAIDING OUR SHIPPING IN THE ATLANTIC.

JOHN'S FATHER WENT ON EARNESTLY.

DESTINY WILL TAKE YOU TO THAT SHIP, JOHN. JUST AS DESTINY WILL WRAP YOUR FINGERS ROUND THE HILT OF THE SWORD...AND ENGLAND WILL SEE THINGS COME RIGHT AGAIN.

WHEN H.M.S. VIPER WAS FIT FOR SEA AGAIN, SHE WAS RETURNED TO CONVOY DUTY, THIS TIME IN THE ATLANTIC, ESCORTING MERCHANTMEN AS FAR SOUTH AS GIBRALTAR. GETTING THE SHIPS THROUGH WAS VITAL TO BRITAIN...JUST AS SINKING THEM WAS VITAL TO THE GERMAN NAVAL HIGH COMMAND.

YOUR TASK IS VITAL TO THE REICH, GENTLEMEN. THE FUHRER DEPENDS ON YOU AND YOUR BOATS TO BRING THE ENGLISH TO THEIR KNEES.

AS THE EAGER YOUNG NAZIS TOOK THEIR U-BOATS TO SEA, JOHN AND BERT WERE IN THE ENGLISH CHANNEL, HEADING FOR GIBRALTAR.

GOOD TO SEE THE SUN AGAIN, SIR — AND I HEAR THE GROSSADLER'S OPERATING AROUND HERE.

I HOPE WE DON'T SEE HER THIS TRIP. THE CONVOY'S PRETTY VALUABLE AND THERE'S NOT MUCH OF AN ESCORT.

JOHN WENT ON SOLEMNLY.

I HEAR WE'LL HAVE JUST ABOUT EVERY U-BOAT IN THE GERMAN NAVY AFTER US THIS TRIP. AND THEIR RECCE PLANES WILL BE LOOKING FOR US TOO.

WELL, IT'S STILL BETTER THAN THAT PERISHING MURMANSK RUN!

ALL WAS PEACEFUL UNTIL THE EARLY EVENING. THEN, AS THEY ENTERED THE ATLANTIC ITSELF...

THERE WAS NO TIME TO CHANGE COURSE. THE SHIP LURCHED AS THE TORPEDO RAMMED DEEP INTO HER VITALS.

BUT THE DAMAGE WAS SUCH THAT JOHN WAS SOON FORCED TO THE INEVITABLE ORDER.

ABANDON SHIP! ABANDON SHIP!

ONCE ALL THE SURVIVORS WERE AWAY, JOHN JUMPED FOR IT HIMSELF. AND AGAIN BERT WAS THERE.

WELCOME ABOARD, SIR!

IT SEEMED IMPOSSIBLE THAT A SHIP OF VIPER'S POWER COULD BE SO QUICKLY OVERWHELMED. BUT WITHIN TEN MINUTES SHE SLIPPED DOWN, NOSE FIRST.

ALL THE SURVIVORS GOT AWAY, SIR. WE ONLY GOT ONE BOAT OFF, THOUGH.

LET'S MAKE FOR IT, THEN. PADDLE WITH YOUR HANDS.

THEN JOHN TURNED TO THE THIRD MAN.

AND WHO ARE YOU, LAD?

BARCLAY, E.J., SIR. STOKER MECHANIC, AFTER BOILER ROOM.

JOHN GRINNED.

STOKER, EH? WELL, WE'VE NO ENGINES ON BOARD HERE, SO PADDLE WITH YOUR HANDS AND HEAD FOR THE BOAT.

OK, SIR. BUT IT LOOKS LIKE DIRTY WEATHER COMING UP.

BARCLAY WAS ONLY TOO RIGHT. LONG BEFORE THEY REACHED THE BOAT, THE RISING WIND AND SEA SEPARATED THEM FROM THE OTHER SURVIVORS.

WHERE DO YOU RECKON WE'LL END UP, SIR?

FRENCH COAST SOMEWHERE...IF WE STAY AFLOAT THAT LONG!

STAY AFLOAT THEY DID...AND SEVEN HOURS LATER THEY DRAGGED THEMSELVES WEARILY UP A SANDY BEACH ON TO THE SHORE OF FRANCE.

BETTER HIDE THE FLOAT IN CASE IT LEADS JERRY TO US.

THEY SCRAPED A SHALLOW HOLE IN THE SAND AND CONCEALED THE FLOAT AS BEST THEY COULD. TWENTY MINUTES LATER THE JOB WAS COMPLETE.

WHAT NOW, SIR?

SOME FOOD IF WE CAN FIND IT, AND A BIT OF REST. THEN WE CAN MAKE PLANS.

THEY FOUND SOME CHEESES HANGING IN A FARM SHED AND ATE THEM HUNGRILY. THEN THEY MOVED CAREFULLY ALONG THE COAST.

IF WE KEEP GOING TILL WE SEE A TOWN, WE CAN FIND OUT WHERE WE ARE. MAYBE WE COULD PINCH A BOAT.

NOT ROW TO ENGLAND, SIR, SURELY?

IT WOULD GET YOUR WAISTLINE TRIMMED DOWN A BIT, CHIEF. YOU'VE HAD IT ALL TOO GOOD.

THEN I'D HATE TO SEE WHAT YOU CALL BAD!

IT WAS DUSK WHEN THEY CAME TO THE HILLS ENCIRCLING REAUVILLE, THE BIGGEST PORT IN THE AREA. AS THEY BREASTED A SLOPE AND SAW THE PORT...

NO! IT COULDN'T BE...

BUT IT IS!

BUT THERE COULD BE NO DOUBT...

IT'S THE GROSSADLER!

SIR...YOU DON'T PLAN TO PINCH THAT, DO YOU?

BERT WAS QUICK TO REPLY.

WE MIGHT. THERE'S SOMETHING THAT SHIP PINCHED FROM US ON BOARD.

TELL HIM ABOUT IT, CHIEF, WHILE I GO DOWN FOR A LOOK.

IT WAS WELL PAST MIDNIGHT WHEN JOHN RETURNED.

THEY'RE TAKING ON SUPPLIES. LOOKS LIKE THEY'RE LEAVING SOON.

JOHN GOT TO HIS FEET AND STARTED DOWN THE HILL.

COME ON, LET'S GET CLOSER, THEN WE'LL SEE IF ANYTHING CROPS UP.

JOHN KEPT HEARING HIS FATHER'S WORDS — "DESTINY WILL TAKE YOU TO THAT SHIP. JUST AS DESTINY WILL WRAP YOUR FINGERS ROUND THE HILT OF THAT SWORD."

ON THE WAY THEY FOUND SOME OLD CLOTHES IN A HUT AND QUICKLY PUT THEM ON. THEN THEY STROLLED THROUGH THE WINDING STREETS OF REAUVILLE.

BLIMEY! THESE JERRY MATELOTS ARE A TOUGH — LOOKING LOT.

ANOTHER HALF HOUR TOOK THEM TO THE DOCKS.

WHERE DO YOU RECKON THE SWORD WOULD BE, CHIEF?

TEN TO ONE IT'S IN THE CAPTAIN'S CABIN. HE'S AN OLD SEA DOG... RESPECTS THE TRADITIONS, HE DOES.

BUT JOHN WAS MORE INTERESTED IN THE TRAFFIC THAN IN TRADITION. HE NODDED TOWARDS ONE OF THE SUPPLY LIGHTERS.

WE COULD GET ABOARD THAT LIGHTER AND OUT TO THE SHIP, THEN CARRY A FEW BOXES TO THE CAPTAIN'S CABIN...

JUST WHAT I WAS THINKING, SIR.

IT WAS THE WORK OF A MOMENT TO PICK UP A FEW WOODEN BOXES.

COME ON, THEN.

BLIMEY!

AGAIN LUCK WAS WITH THEM. IN THAT JOSTLING, SWEATING CROWD OF WORKMEN, NOBODY NOTICED THREE EXTRA "LABOURERS".

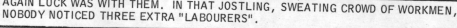

ONCE ABOARD THE GERMAN SHIP THEY CARRIED THEIR CASES AFT.

MONSIEUR LE CAPITAINE?

FOLLOWING THE SAILOR'S DIRECTION, THEY FOUND THE CAPTAIN'S CABIN.

THEY KNOCKED AND ENTERED. VON LIPPNER LOOKED UP, ANNOYED AT THE INTERRUPTION.

YES? WHAT IS IT?

VOTRE VIN, M'SIEUR.

BUT THE CAPTAIN DIDN'T SEEM VERY KEEN ON THE IDEA.

NEIN! RAUS, RAUS!

THERE WAS A HARD EDGE TO JOHN'S VOICE AS HE REPLIED.

WE'RE BRITISH SAILORS, CAPTAIN. YOU SPEAK ENGLISH?

MEIN GOTT! JA, I TALK ENGLISH.

JOHN WENT ON GRIMLY.

TWO YEARS AGO YOU SANK A DESTROYER AND TOOK A SWORD FROM HER BEFORE SHE SANK. WE WANT IT BACK.

THAT ONE?

YES, THAT ONE.

VON LIPPNER LOOKED AT THE SWORD, THEN STARED CLOSELY AT JOHN.

YOUR NAME?

COMMANDER JOHN WARDEN, ROYAL NAVY.

THE GERMAN CAPTAIN GASPED FOR A SPLIT SECOND. THEN...

A FAMOUS NAME. I KNEW YOUR FATHER BETWEEN THE WARS. WELL, I CAN'T STOP YOU TAKING THE SWORD, BUT I ASSURE YOU I SHALL RAISE THE ALARM IMMEDIATELY.

I KNOW. RIGHT, CHIEF...

IN SECONDS BERT WAS TYING THE GERMAN IN HIS CHAIR.

SEE HE'S SECURE, CHIEF. AND GAG HIM!

AYE, AYE, SIR. IT'S GREAT TO SEE THE OLD SWORD AGAIN!

BEFORE YOU GAG ME, COMMANDER...

THERE WAS A HINT OF A SMILE ON THE CAPTAIN'S FACE AS HE WENT ON.

LET ME CONGRATULATE YOU ON YOUR COURAGE. AND IF YOU REACH ENGLAND, GIVE MY REGARDS TO YOUR FATHER.

I WILL, SIR.

WRAPPING THE SWORD IN A LENGTH OF CLOTH, THEY HURRIED AWAY FROM THE CABIN AND MADE FOR THE RAIL. BUT THERE A SHOCK AWAITED THEM.

NO LIGHTERS! ALL THE PERISHIN' FROGS HAVE GONE ASHORE ALREADY!

ACT LIKE FRENCHMEN. GET EXCITED AND JUMP IN THE SEA. THEN LET THE CURRENT TAKE US ROUND TO THE OTHER SIDE OF THE QUAY.

WATCHED BY THE AMUSED GERMAN SAILORS, THEY RAN EXCITEDLY ALONG THE DECK, SHOUTING EVERY FRENCH WORD THEY KNEW...THEN JUMPED OVERBOARD.

JUST LIKE THE STUPID FRENCH. PROBABLY THEY WERE DRINKING BELOW DECKS.

BUT IN THE CAPTAIN'S CABIN...

THREE BRITISH SAILORS DRESSED AS FRENCH WORKMEN DID THIS. GET AFTER THEM. THEY MUST BE CAUGHT!

JA...JA, HERR KAPITAN. AT ONCE.

IN THE WATER, JOHN HEARD A KLAXON SOUND THE ALARM ABOARD THE GROSS-ADLER.

THEY'RE ON TO US! GET MOVING!

HELPED BY THE CURRENT THEY SWAM ROUND THE QUAY AND FOUND REFUGE AMONG A CLUTTER OF FISHING BOATS.

WE'LL STAY HERE FOR A WHILE.

BLIMEY, SIR, LOOK!

AN AMAZING SIGHT MET THEIR EYES.

TWO OF OUR M.T.B.s! WHAT ARE THEY DOING HERE?

CAPTURED BY THE GERMANS AND HAULED HERE TO ROT, I IMAGINE. LET'S PADDLE OVER AND TAKE A LOOK.

IT WAS TOO CLOSE TO SAILING TIME TO HAVE GERMAN SAILORS SCOURING THE PORT FOR THE FUGITIVES, SO THE CAPTAIN TOLD THE VILLAGE GENDARME TO WATCH OUT FOR THEM.

I SUPPOSE HE'LL RETURN TO THE WINE SHOP WHEN HE LEAVES HERE...AND THE ENGLANDERS WILL GET CLEAN AWAY. WELL, A CONVOY IS MORE IMPORTANT THAN THREE BRITISH SAILORS – EVEN THREE BRITISH SAILORS LIKE THAT!

MEANWHILE JOHN AND HIS TWO MEN HAD INSPECTED THE TWO M.T.B.s. TED BARCLAY HAD SERVED ON THESE CRAFT AND KNEW HIS WAY ABOUT THEM.

THIS IS THE BEST ONE, SIR. ENGINES IN PRETTY GOOD NICK, AND THERE'S EVEN A TORPEDO UP ONE OF THE TUBES.

A TORPEDO! WONDER WHY THEY DIDN'T REMOVE IT? HOW LONG HAS IT BEEN THERE, I WONDER?

BERT LOOKED DUBIOUS.

PROBABLY RUSTED IN THE TUBE BY NOW, SIR.

AND MAYBE NOT...

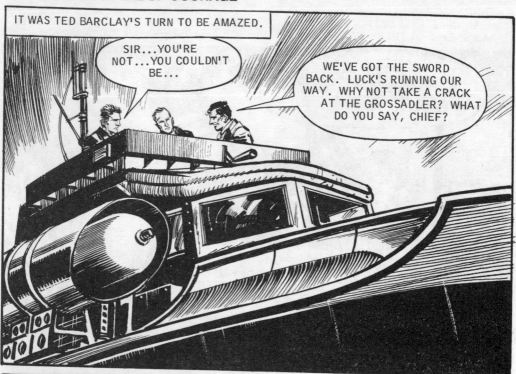

IT WAS TED BARCLAY'S TURN TO BE AMAZED.

SIR...YOU'RE NOT...YOU COULDN'T BE...

WE'VE GOT THE SWORD BACK. LUCK'S RUNNING OUR WAY. WHY NOT TAKE A CRACK AT THE GROSSADLER? WHAT DO YOU SAY, CHIEF?

WELL...ONE TORPEDO, EVEN IF IT WORKS, CAN'T DO MUCH HARM TO A SHIP THAT SIZE.

IT MIGHT HAVE HER BACK IN HERE FOR REPAIRS LONG ENOUGH TO LET ONE CONVOY THROUGH!

RIGHT, SIR, LET'S DO IT!

GOOD. NOW, YOUNG BARCLAY, YOU KNOW YOUR WAY ABOUT THESE BOATS. SHOW ME ROUND.

AYE, AYE, SIR!

ONCE ROUND THE SHIP, THEY GOT BUSY. BERT DISCOVERED GUN AMMUNITION STILL ON BOARD, AND JOHN FAMILIARISED HIMSELF WITH THE CONTROLS. FUEL WAS THEIR ONLY PROBLEM, AS THE PETROL TANKS WERE NEARLY EMPTY.

CAST OFF, CHIEF... AND WE'LL FILL HER UP. I THOUGHT I SAW SOME PETROL CANS ON THE JETTY OVER THERE.

A NERVE-RACKING JOURNEY WITH THE MIGHTY ENGINES RUNNING AS QUIETLY AS POSSIBLE TOOK THEM TO THE DARK AND SILENT JETTY WHICH JOHN HAD SEEN. AND SURE ENOUGH, THERE WAS A SIZEABLE STACK OF JERRICANS. WORKING AT TOP SPEED THEY POURED THE PRECIOUS PETROL INTO THE THIRSTY TANKS.

THAT'LL DO IT, CHIEF.

RIGHT, SIR. WAIT, THERE'S SOMETHING WE'VE FORGOTTEN, SIR.

THESE LITTLE MACKEREL BOATS DON'T HAVE NAMES, ONLY NUMBERS. WELL, SIR, WITH THE SWORD ABOARD, I THOUGHT...

OK. THERE'S BLACK PAINT AFT. BUT HURRY, CHIEF!

SOON BERT WAS ADMIRING HIS HANDIWORK.

NOW WE CAN'T GO WRONG, CAN WE?

ONLY THING TO WORRY ABOUT NOW IS THAT TORPEDO.

DURING THE NIGHT BERT CREPT BACK INTO THE HILLS AND RETURNED WITH THEIR UNIFORMS. HE WAS DETERMINED TO GO TO WAR IN STYLE. AS DAWN BROKE, THE NEW H.M.S. CUTLASS SLIPPED FURTIVELY AWAY FROM HER BERTH, PROUDLY FLYING A WHITE ENSIGN WHICH TED HAD FOUND IN A LOCKER.

GOOD LAD, THAT BARCLAY. HE'S HANDLING THOSE ENGINES LIKE A REAL GLASGOW ENGINEER.

ABOARD THE GROSSADLER THEY WERE TOO BUSY TO NOTICE THE LITTLE M.T.B. SNEAKING OUT INTO THE BAY.

READY FOR SEA AT LAST. TWO HOURS LATE, TOO. THESE CONFOUNDED FRENCH PORTS! TELL THEM TO STAND BY ON MAIN ENGINES, HERR SCHMIDT.

JA, HERR KAPITAN!

SOON THE HUGE SHIP WAS SLIPPING AWAY FROM REAUVILLE.

SIGNAL, HERR KAPITAN! BRITISH CONVOY, ONE HUNDRED KILOMETRES DUE WEST.

FROM THE LITTLE M.T.B. THREE PAIRS OF EYES WATCHED THE BATTLE-CRUISER STEAM THEIR WAY.

TALK ABOUT DAVID AND GOLIATH!

YEAH, BUT REMEMBER WHO WON THAT LITTLE SCRAP!

OTHER EYES WERE WATCHING THE GROSSADLER FROM A BRITISH SUNDERLAND ON RECONNAISSANCE.

THERE SHE IS, BOYS – THE BIG FAT BEAST COMING OUT TO FEED OFF THE CONVOYS.

ISN'T THAT AN M.T.B. DOWN THERE?

DOWN CAME THE SUNDERLAND.

YOU'RE RIGHT! SURELY IT'S NOT WAITING FOR THE GROSSADLER?

IT'S GOT A DIRTY GREAT NAME PAINTED ON THE SIDE. CUTLASS, IT SAYS. WHAT'S THIS – A JOKE?

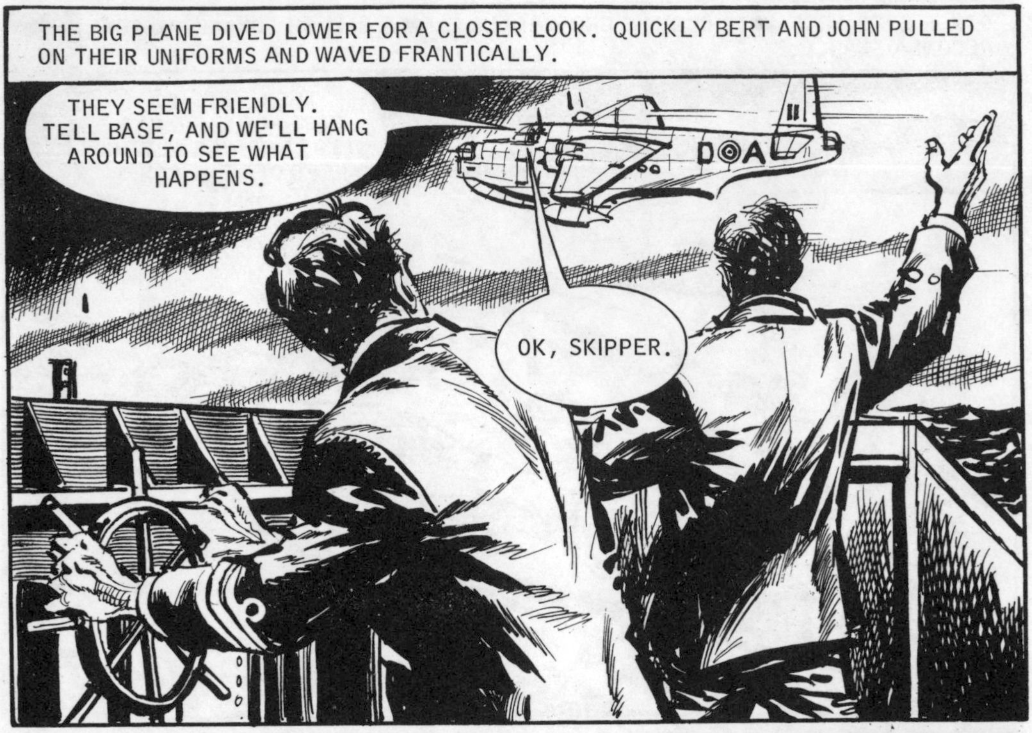
THE BIG PLANE DIVED LOWER FOR A CLOSER LOOK. QUICKLY BERT AND JOHN PULLED ON THEIR UNIFORMS AND WAVED FRANTICALLY.
THEY SEEM FRIENDLY. TELL BASE, AND WE'LL HANG AROUND TO SEE WHAT HAPPENS.
D◎A
OK, SKIPPER.

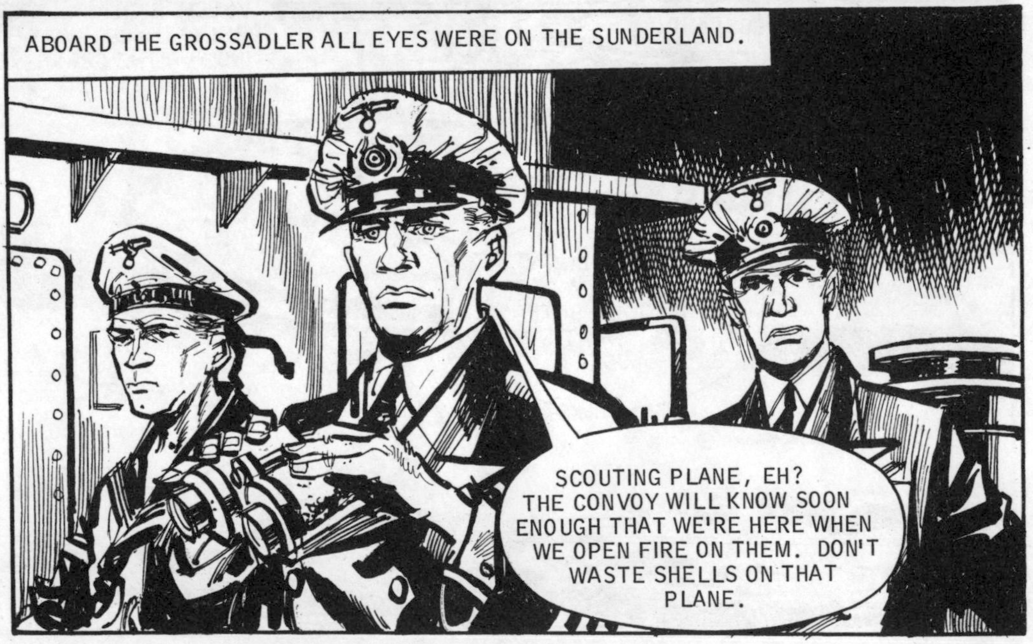
ABOARD THE GROSSADLER ALL EYES WERE ON THE SUNDERLAND.
SCOUTING PLANE, EH? THE CONVOY WILL KNOW SOON ENOUGH THAT WE'RE HERE WHEN WE OPEN FIRE ON THEM. DON'T WASTE SHELLS ON THAT PLANE.

AND JOHN KNEW IT WAS ONLY A MATTER OF TIME BEFORE THEY WERE SPOTTED. HE TURNED TO HIS TWO MEN.

LET'S ATTACK. BARCLAY, SET THE ENGINES ON FULL POWER, THEN COME BACK UP AND GIVE THE CHIEF A HAND ON THE GUN.

AYE, AYE, SIR!

THE SUNDERLAND'S STRANGE MESSAGE WAS RECEIVED IN THE ADMIRALTY, LONDON. JOHN'S FATHER HAPPENED TO BE THERE, CALLING ON ADMIRAL MARTEN.

"OLD M.T.B. WITH THE NAME CUTLASS ON SIDE STANDING BY TO ATTACK THE GROSSADLER". WHAT GIBBERISH IS THIS?

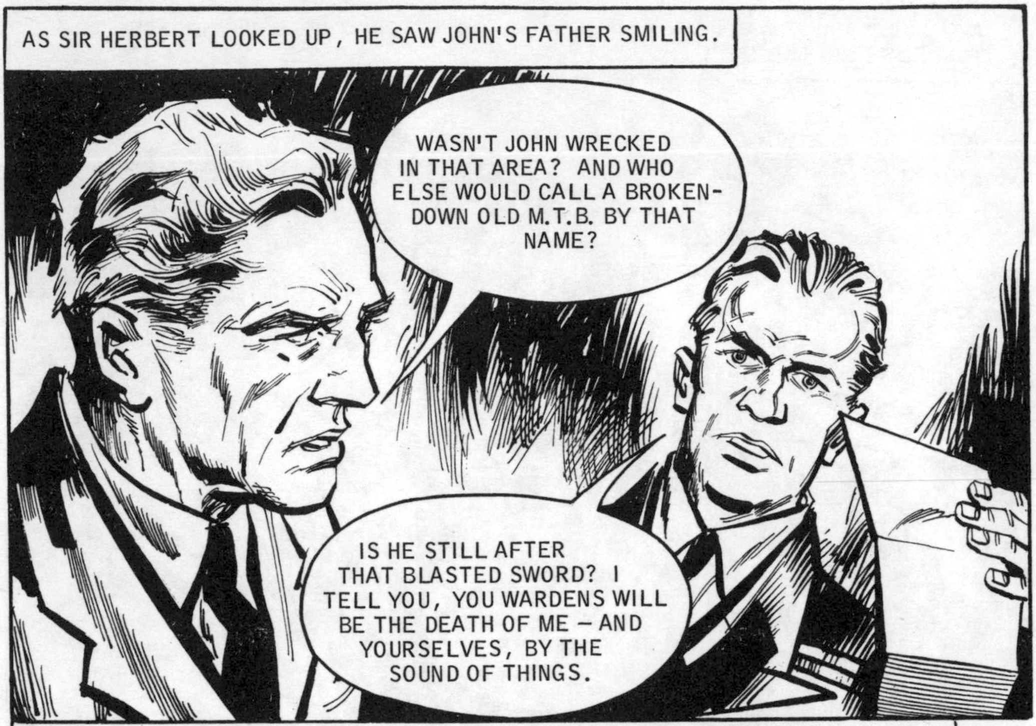
AS SIR HERBERT LOOKED UP, HE SAW JOHN'S FATHER SMILING.
WASN'T JOHN WRECKED IN THAT AREA? AND WHO ELSE WOULD CALL A BROKEN-DOWN OLD M.T.B. BY THAT NAME?
IS HE STILL AFTER THAT BLASTED SWORD? I TELL YOU, YOU WARDENS WILL BE THE DEATH OF ME – AND YOURSELVES, BY THE SOUND OF THINGS.

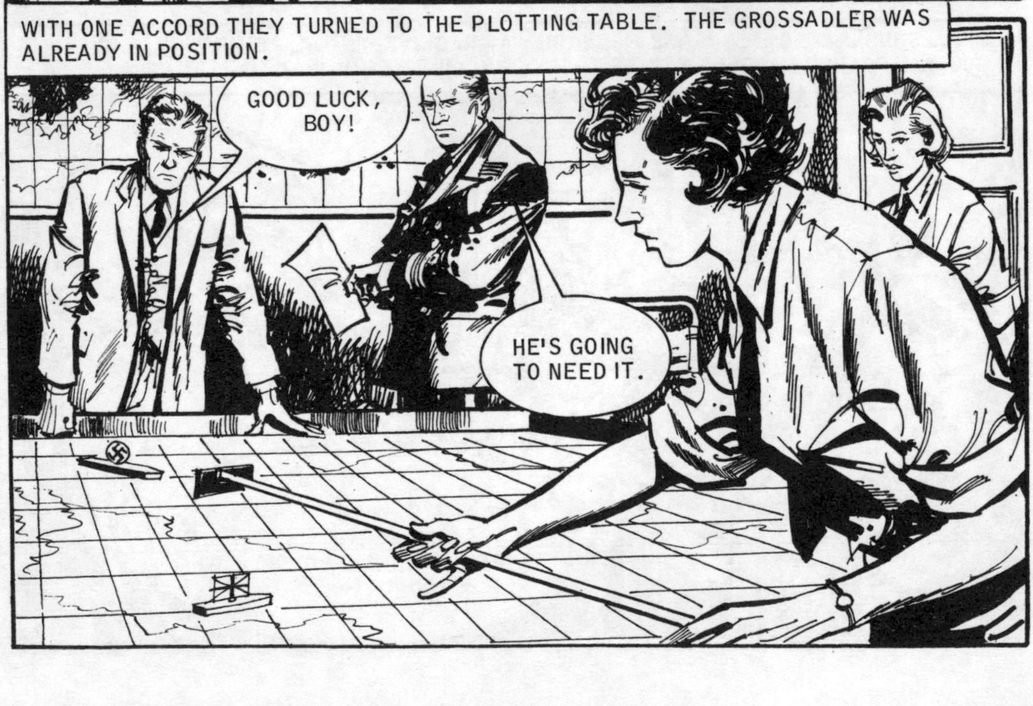
WITH ONE ACCORD THEY TURNED TO THE PLOTTING TABLE. THE GROSSADLER WAS ALREADY IN POSITION.
GOOD LUCK, BOY!
HE'S GOING TO NEED IT.

THE ACTION WAS ON. JOHN SENT HIS NEW MOUNT THUNDERING TOWARDS THE BATTLE-CRUISER.

UP AND AT 'EM, LADS!

MOMENTS LATER THEY WERE SPOTTED.

GOTT IN HIMMEL, A BRITISH TORPEDO BOAT! ACHTUNG, ACHTUNG!

QUICKLY THE AWESOME GUNS LOWERED UNTIL THEIR GAPING MUZZLES POINTED AT THE APPROACHING CRAFT. SEEING THEM, JOHN STEERED A WEAVING COURSE. ONE HIT FROM THOSE MONSTERS AND HIS BOAT WOULD VANISH COMPLETELY.

BIG, ISN'T IT?

MAKES IT A FATTER TARGET.

ABOVE THEM, THE CIRCLING SUNDERLAND CREW WATCHED WITH ROUNDED EYES, THE EXCITED RADIO OPERATOR COMMENTATING TO THE LISTENING BASE WHO RE-TRANSMITTED TO THE ADMIRALTY.

THEY'RE GOING IN!

THE FIRST SALVO MISSED, TEARING THE SEA TO SHREDS ON EITHER SIDE OF THE LEAPING, DUCKING TORPEDO BOAT.

THAT'S THE WAY, LADS. WE CAN STILL PULL THIS OFF...

BERT AND BARCLAY CONCENTRATED THEIR FIRE ON THE GUN CREWS.

BUT THE GUN PACKED UP AFTER A FEW HECTIC MINUTES. TED BARCLAY STUMBLED TO THE BRIDGE.

STAND BY TO FIRE THE TORPEDO IF I'M HIT!

RIGHT, SIR!

ABOARD THE GROSSADLER, CAPTAIN VON LIPPNER GREW MORE AGITATED AS HE SAW THE BRITISH CRAFT THRUSTING UNHARMED TOWARDS THEM.

IF THEY'VE GOT A TORPEDO ABOARD, THEY COULD HARM US. BRING EVERY GUN TO BEAR!

THE BATTLE-CRUISER OPENED UP WITH EVERYTHING. BERT WAS THE FIRST TO BE HIT.

AAGH!

JOHN AND BARCLAY WERE STRUCK MOMENTS LATER IN THAT OVERWHELMING BURST OF FIRE.

FIRE THE FISH, SIR...WHILE WE STILL CAN!

HOLDING THE BOAT STEADY, JOHN SENT THE TORPEDO FLASHING FROM ITS TUBE.

SHE'S GOING!

JUST PRAY THE WARHEAD IS STILL OK!

IT WAS. CAPTAIN VON LIPPNER CLOSED HIS EYES AS THE TORPEDO STREAKED THROUGH THE WATER AND STRUCK HOME DEEP IN A FUEL TANK. THE JOLT EVEN SHOOK THE BRIDGE.

WE'RE HIT, HERR KAPITAN!

JA, WE ARE HIT. CURSE THESE MAD, COURAGEOUS ENGLANDERS!

EVEN AS JOHN FIRED THE TORPEDO, AN AVALANCHE OF FIRE ENGULFED THE CRAFT. JOHN, BERT AND TED BARCLAY WERE FLUNG INTO THE WATER AS THE M.T.B. BEGAN TO SINK.

SHE'S GOING!

BERT WAS THE MOST SERIOUSLY WOUNDED OF THE THREE. JOHN AND BARCLAY HELD HIM UP AS THEY KICKED THEIR WAY FREE OF THE GREAT STAIN OF OIL THAT POURED FROM THE SHIP'S RUPTURED FUEL TANKS.

WE GOT HER, SIR!

YES, BUT WHAT HAPPENS TO US NOW?

THE GROSSADLER HAD STOPPED FIRING. ON THE BRIDGE CAPTAIN VON LIPPNER SALUTED A GALLANT ENEMY.

SHALL WE PICK THEM UP, HERR KAPITAN?

LET'S LEAVE THEM TO THEIR FRIENDS UP ABOVE. SUCH COURAGE SHOULD NOT BE ALLOWED TO WITHER IN A PRISON CAMP. AT MOMENTS LIKE THIS I AM PROUD TO BE A SAILOR. STEER BACK TO REAUVILLE.

AS THE GIANT SHIP LIMPED AWAY, THE SUNDERLAND LANDED AND WILLING HANDS REACHED OUT TO THE THREE EXHAUSTED MEN.

COME ON, LADS, THERE'S HOT GROG ABOARD!

THAT'LL GO DOWN WELL.

BERT WAS GRAVELY WOUNDED, BUT MANAGED A PALLID GRIN AS THE AIRCRAFT RAISED THEM OFF THE SEA.

THIS WILL BE SOME STORY TO TELL THE BOYS BACK HOME!

IT CERTAINLY HAD ITS MOMENTS, EH, TED?

YOU'VE SAID IT, SIR.

AT THE ADMIRALTY THEY WAITED IN AGONISED SUSPENSE, UNTIL...

THEY'RE SAFE...ALL THREE OF THEM. PICKED UP BY THE SUNDERLAND. AND THE GROSSADLER IS LIMPING BACK TO PORT.

I WOULD NEVER HAVE BELIEVED IT POSSIBLE. NEVER.

AFTER A SPELL IN HOSPITAL, THE THREE HEROES WERE FLOWN BACK TO LONDON FOR A VERY SPECIAL OCCASION.

COMMANDER JOHN WARDEN...THE VICTORIA CROSS.

AND FOR BERT AND BARCLAY THERE WAS THE DISTINGUISHED SERVICE MEDAL.

TODAY THERE'S A NEW H.M.S. CUTLASS IN THE ROYAL NAVY, A FINE MODERN SUPER-DESTROYER WHICH BEARS LITTLE RESEMBLANCE TO THE SHIPS OF WORLD WAR TWO. BUT IN THE WARDROOM THE SWORD STILL HANGS IN THE PLACE OF HONOUR, AND A NEW TOAST IS DRUNK ON THE ANNIVERSARY OF THE BATTLE OF THE NILE. THAT TOAST IS — "THE STORMING OF THE GROSSADLER".

AND THERE ARE SOME OF THE OFFICERS WHO WILL TELL YOU THERE'S ALWAYS AN EXTRA GUEST ON THESE NIGHTS, A NOBLE, DIMLY-SEEN FIGURE FROM THE PAST WHO STILL WATCHES OVER HIS FAMILY'S SWORD — CAPTAIN ROLAND WARDEN, R.N., VICTOR OF ABOUKIR BAY.

**Commando
THE END**

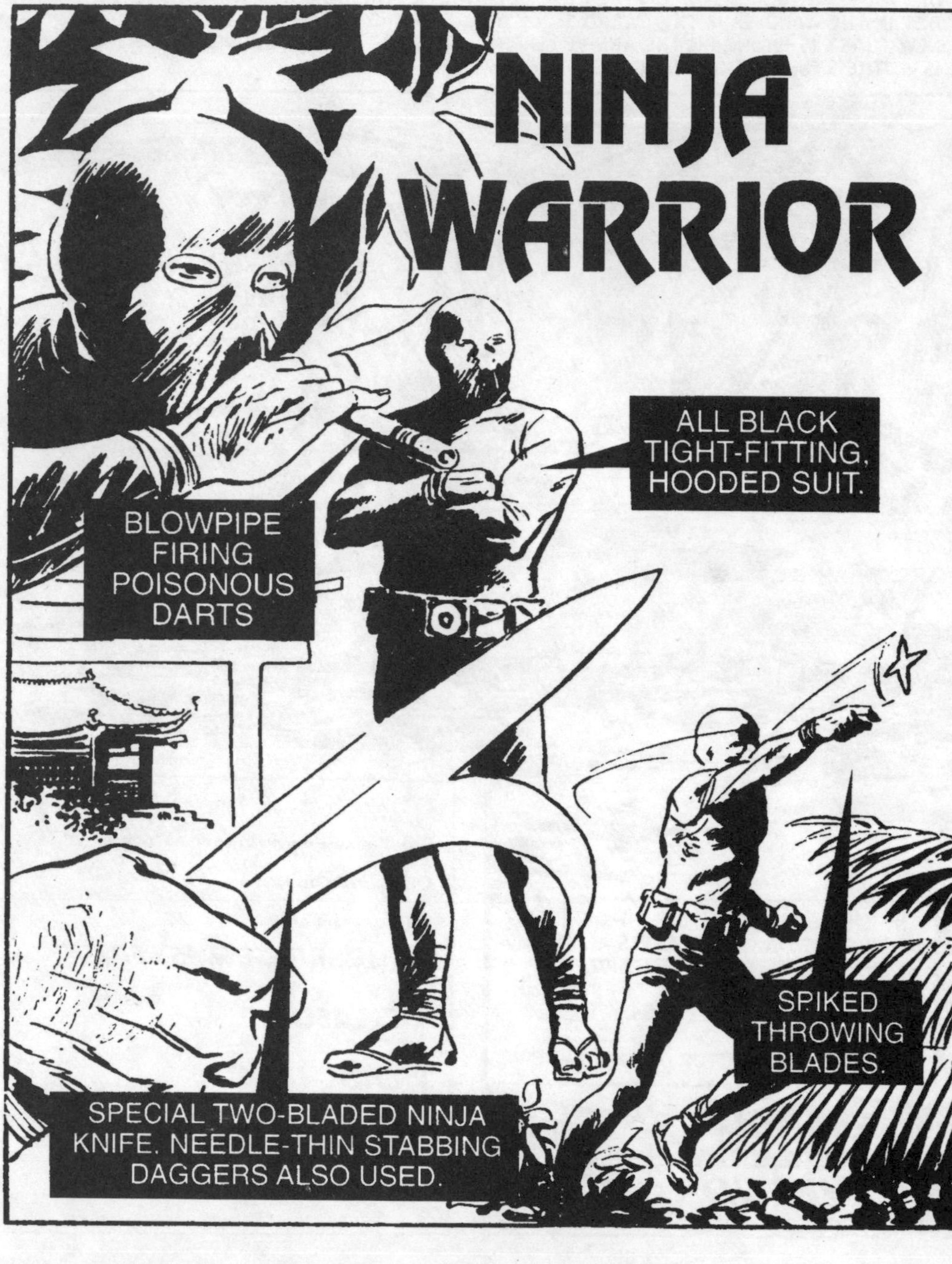
NINJA WARRIOR
ALL BLACK TIGHT-FITTING, HOODED SUIT.
BLOWPIPE FIRING POISONOUS DARTS
SPIKED THROWING BLADES.
SPECIAL TWO-BLADED NINJA KNIFE. NEEDLE-THIN STABBING DAGGERS ALSO USED.

THE HAUNTED JUNGLE

HIS NAME WAS TARO TARUKI, AND HE WAS THE MOST DANGEROUS MAN IN THE JAPANESE ARMY. A KARATE EXPERT WITH THE SPEED OF A TIGER AND THE CUNNING OF A COBRA, HE NOW LED A SPECIALLY TRAINED SQUAD OF PHANTOM KILLERS. IT WOULD NEED A SPECIAL BREED OF HERO TO TAKE HIM ON. SOMEONE LIKE SERGEANT DAVE THOMAS, COMMANDO EXTRAORDINARY...

First published 1972

IT ALL BEGAN IN A MARTIAL ARTS CLUB IN ENGLAND. DAVE THOMAS A KEEN YOUNG JUDO EXPERT, CALLED IN FOR HIS USUAL PRACTICE.

HI, SEEN THE NEWS? WE'RE TO BE HONOURED BY A VISIT FROM THE GREAT TARUKI HIMSELF.

TARUKI! THE KARATE EXPERT? HERE, LET ME SEE THAT.

NEWS OF THE IMPENDING KARATE DEMONSTRATION SOON SPREAD.

GOSH, I WON'T MISS THAT. THEY SAY HE CAN SMASH A TWO-INCH PLANK WITH HIS BARE FIST.

BALONEY! IT'S ALL RIGGED. I'M NOT WASTING MY TIME BY GOING TO SEE IT.

NOT MANY PEOPLE HAD HEARD OF KARATE IN THE DAYS BEFORE THE WAR, BUT DAVE AND HIS PALS, WITH THEIR KNOWLEDGE OF JUDO AND ALL THINGS JAPANESE, HAD.

TARO TARUKI

IT'S GOING TO BE A BIT OF A RUSH TO GET HERE AFTER WORK, BUT IT'LL BE WORTH IT.

TARO TARUKI WAS RECKONED THE FINEST KARATE EXPERT LIVING.

WHEN THE BIG DAY CAME, DAVE WAS INDEED LATE. HE STILL WASN'T THERE WHEN THE GREAT TARO TARUKI WAS ABOUT TO DEMONSTRATE THE BLOW THAT HAD MADE HIM FAMOUS.

YOU HAVE ALL INSPECTED THE PLANK WHICH IS TWO INCHES THICK. IF I CAN NOW HAVE COMPLETE SILENCE TO ENABLE ME TO CONCENTRATE, I WILL SHATTER THE PLANK WITH ONE BLOW.

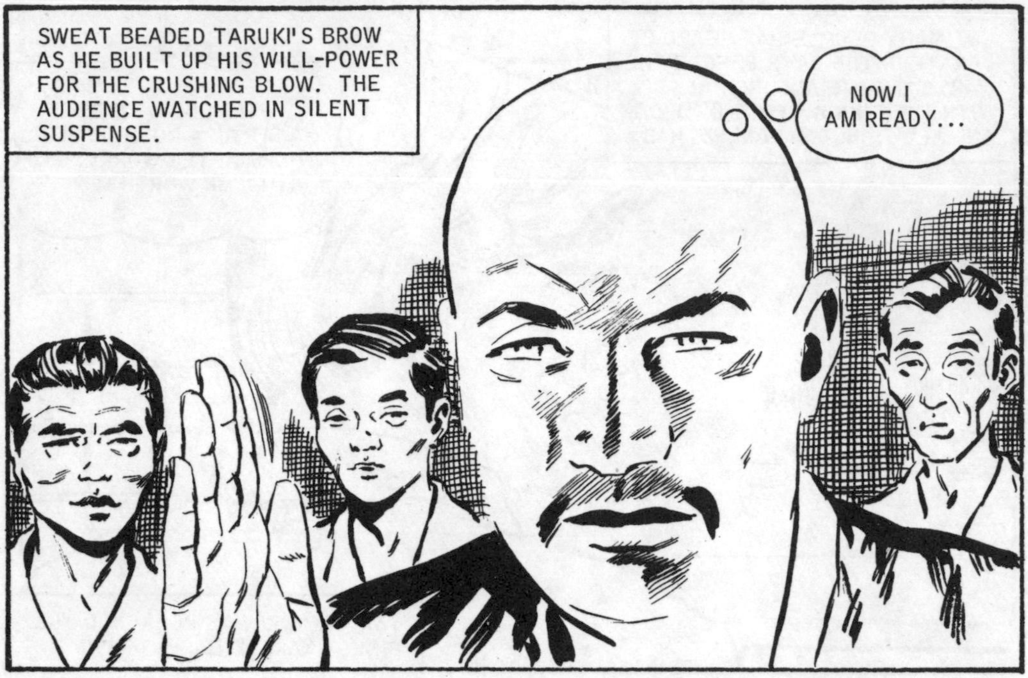
SWEAT BEADED TARUKI'S BROW AS HE BUILT UP HIS WILL-POWER FOR THE CRUSHING BLOW. THE AUDIENCE WATCHED IN SILENT SUSPENSE.
NOW I AM READY...

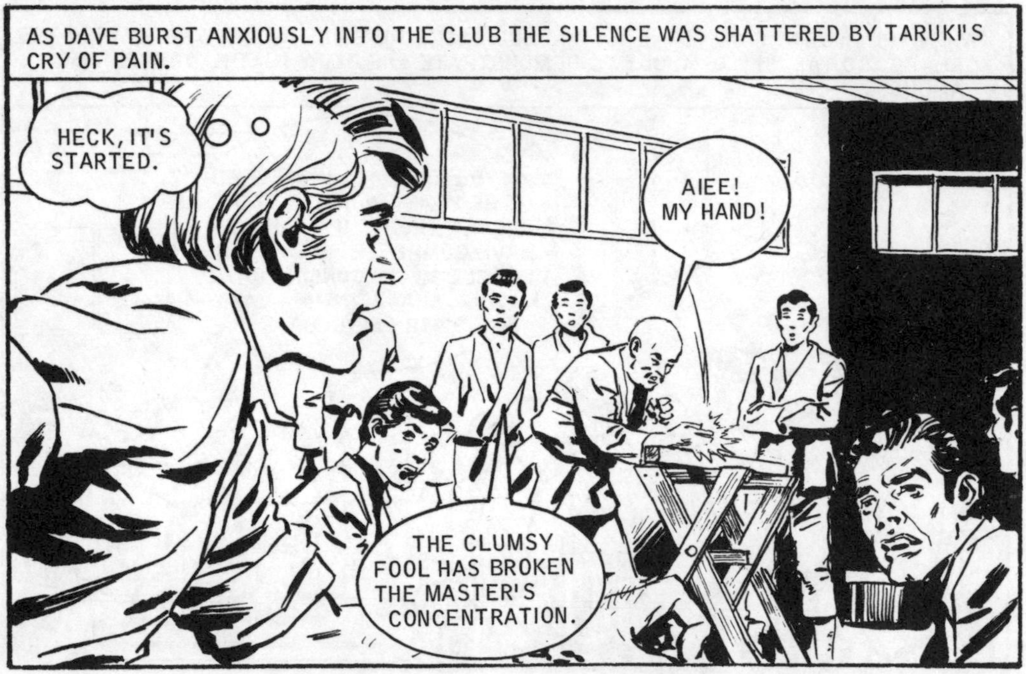
AS DAVE BURST ANXIOUSLY INTO THE CLUB THE SILENCE WAS SHATTERED BY TARUKI'S CRY OF PAIN.
HECK, IT'S STARTED.
AIEE! MY HAND!
THE CLUMSY FOOL HAS BROKEN THE MASTER'S CONCENTRATION.

THE EMBARRASSED DAVE APOLOGISED TO THE ORGANISER.

I'M SORRY, SIR, I WAS LATE...

BURSTING IN LIKE THAT! YOU'VE RUINED EVERYTHING.

THE DEMONSTRATION WENT ON — WITHOUT TARUKI WHO ANGRILY GLARED AT DAVE.

I HAVE LOST MUCH FACE THROUGH THAT CLUMSY PIG. I WILL MAKE HIM SUFFER IF WE MEET AGAIN.

AFTER THE DEMONSTRATION DAVE WAITED OUTSIDE TO APOLOGISE. BUT TARUKI GAVE HIM LITTLE CHANCE.

SO, THE FATES ARE KIND TO ME. WE HAVE A SCORE TO SETTLE, NO?

NOW HOLD ON A MINUTE...

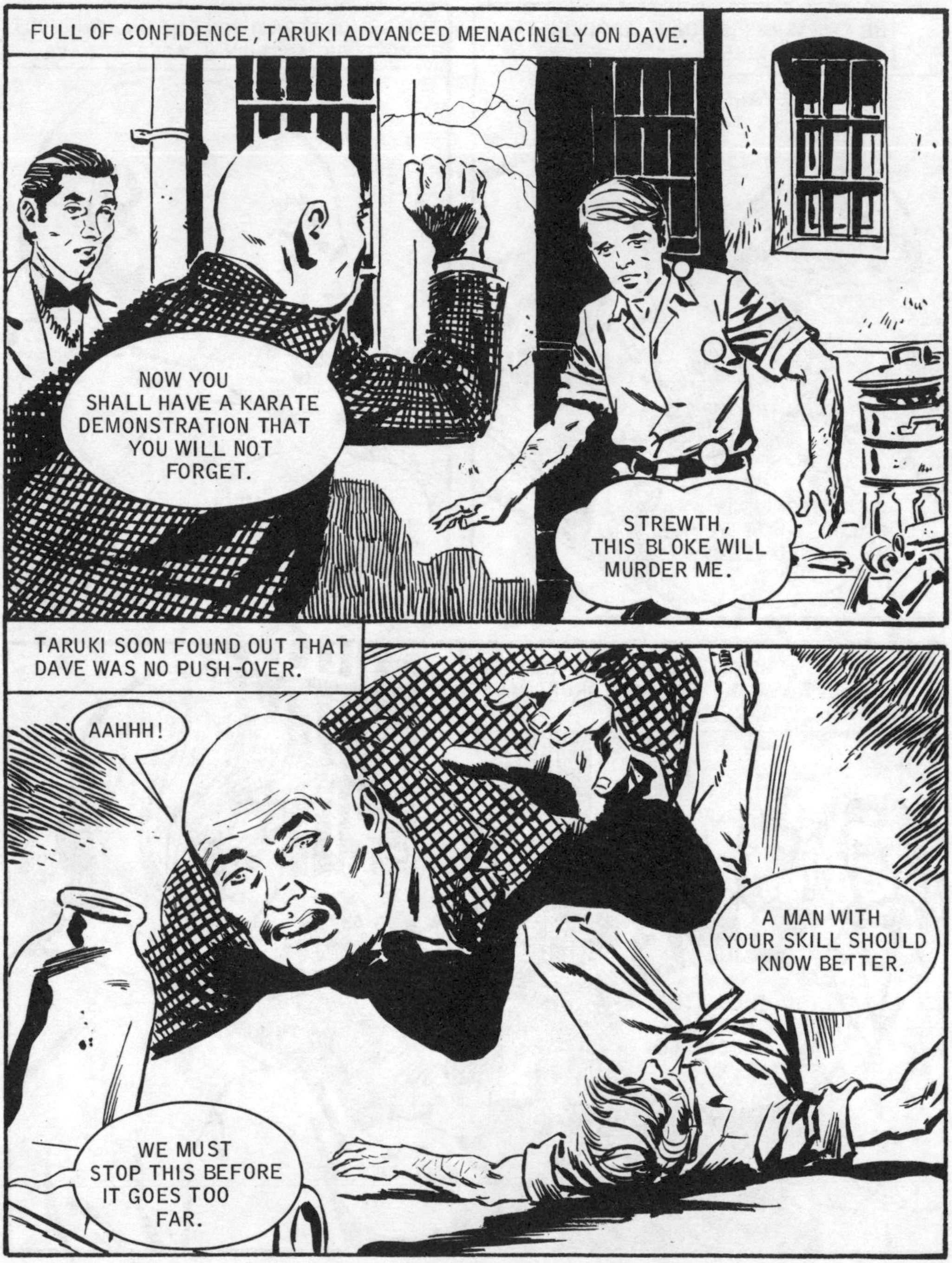
FULL OF CONFIDENCE, TARUKI ADVANCED MENACINGLY ON DAVE.
NOW YOU SHALL HAVE A KARATE DEMONSTRATION THAT YOU WILL NOT FORGET.
STREWTH, THIS BLOKE WILL MURDER ME.
TARUKI SOON FOUND OUT THAT DAVE WAS NO PUSH-OVER.
AAHHH!
A MAN WITH YOUR SKILL SHOULD KNOW BETTER.
WE MUST STOP THIS BEFORE IT GOES TOO FAR.

TARUKI LANDED AMIDST A GROUP OF MILK BOTTLES, CUTTING HIS FACE BADLY. THE SIGHT OF BLOOD SEEMED TO DRIVE HIM BERSERK.

I KILL! I KILL!

LOOK, I'M SORRY. I DIDN'T MEAN...

BUT FOR THE INTERVENTION OF TARUKI'S FRIENDS, DAVE WOULD ALMOST CERTAINLY HAVE BEEN KILLED.

YOUR KNOWLEDGE OF JUDO SERVED YOU WELL. BUT BE WARNED, TARO TARUKI WILL NOT REST UNTIL HIS HONOUR HAS BEEN REGAINED. I ADVISE YOU TO STAY WELL AWAY FROM HIM AND THIS CLUB.

YOU'RE RIGHT, THE MAN'S A FANATIC. A KARATE EXPERT WOULD BE TOO MUCH FOR THE LIKES OF ME TO HANDLE.

BUT SHORTLY AFTER, EUROPE ERUPTED INTO WAR AND DAVE FORGOT ALL ABOUT TARUKI.

WELL, IT'S HAPPENED. LOOKS LIKE I'LL BE WEARING UNIFORM BEFORE LONG.

DAVE WAS RIGHT. SOON HE WAS IN THE THICK OF IT, FIGHTING IN FRANCE AS THE NAZIS ADVANCED.

BLIMEY, IT'S HOT!

OFTEN THE FIGHTING WAS OF THE FIERCEST KIND – HAND TO HAND.

BLAST! THERE GOES MY RIFLE.

NOW THEN, ENGLANDER...

DAVE WAS THANKFUL THAT HE HAD NOT ALLOWED HIS JUDO TRAINING TO GO RUSTY.

UP AND OVER.

HIMMEL!

HE FOUGHT INSTINCTIVELY, FINDING HE PREFERRED USING HIS BARE HANDS RATHER THAN A RIFLE.

TIME FOR BED, JERRY!

I RECKON DAVE SCARED THESE CLOWNS HALF TO DEATH.

BUT THERE WERE NOT ENOUGH MEN LIKE DAVE TO STEM THE NAZI ASSAULT AND THE BRITISH ARMY RETREATED TO DUNKIRK TO BE SHIPPED HOME. BUT DAVE HAD NOT GONE UNNOTICED —

I'VE BEEN HEARING QUITE A LOT ABOUT YOUNG THOMAS LATELY. HE'S JUST THE KIND OF MAN WANTED BY THESE NEW COMMANDO UNITS. PERHAPS YOU'LL MENTION IT TO HIM, FORSYTHE.

YES, SIR. I'LL BET HE JUMPS AT THE CHANCE.

DAVE DID JUMP AT THE CHANCE, AND THE FOLLOWING WEEK FOUND HIM AT THE COMMANDO TRAINING CAMP.

ONE OF THE FIRST THINGS YOU LADS HAVE GOT TO MASTER IS UNARMED COMBAT. YOU'LL DO FOR A VOLUNTEER, THOMAS. STEP OUT HERE.

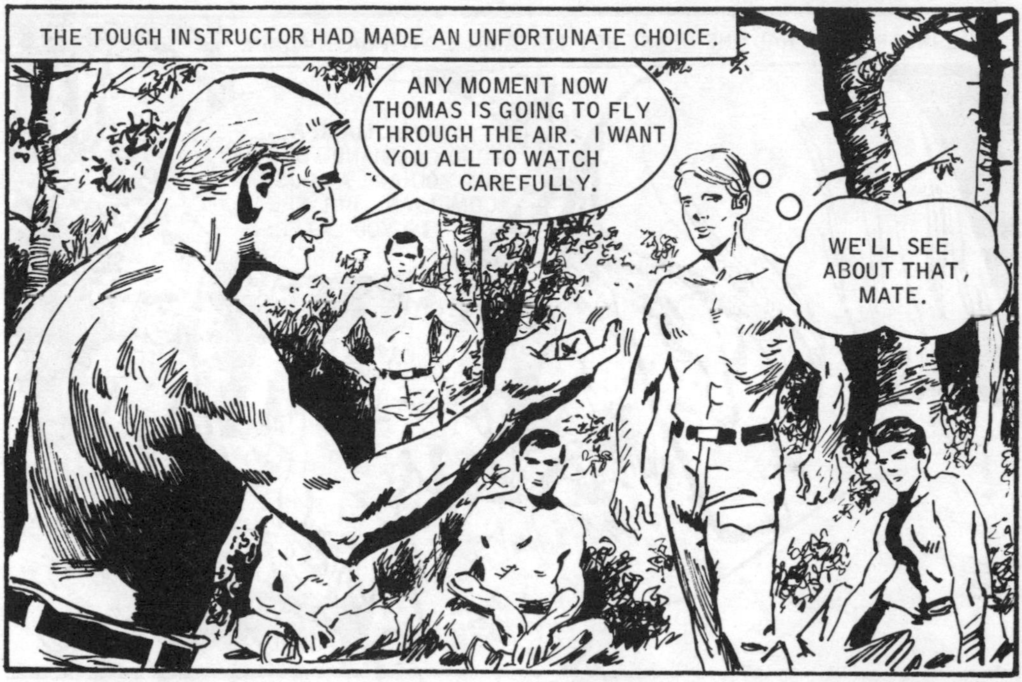
THE TOUGH INSTRUCTOR HAD MADE AN UNFORTUNATE CHOICE.
ANY MOMENT NOW THOMAS IS GOING TO FLY THROUGH THE AIR. I WANT YOU ALL TO WATCH CAREFULLY.
WE'LL SEE ABOUT THAT, MATE.

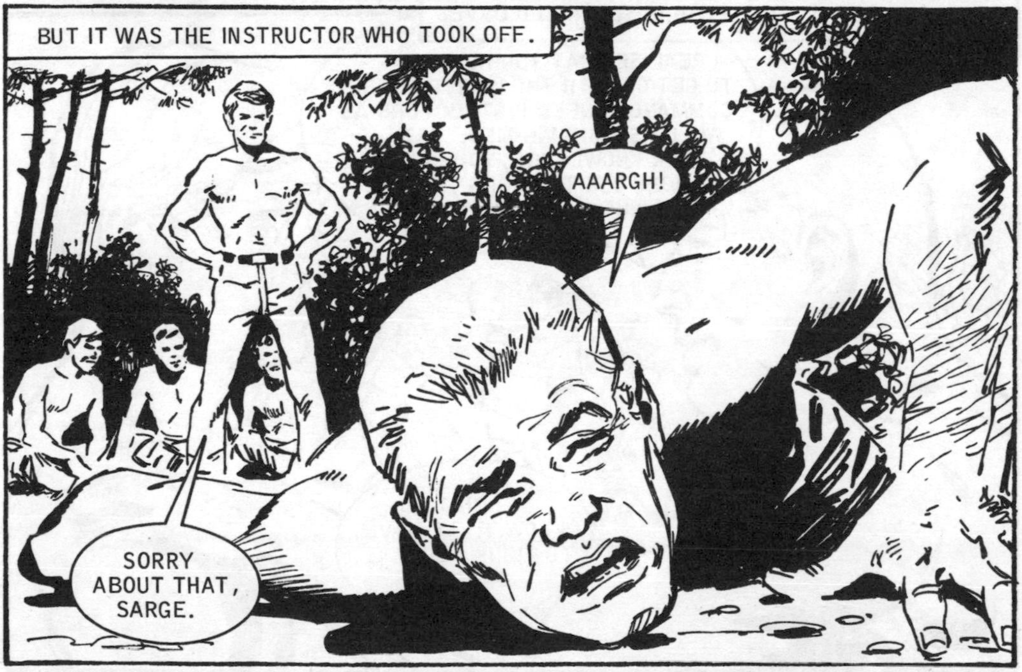
BUT IT WAS THE INSTRUCTOR WHO TOOK OFF.
AAARGH!
SORRY ABOUT THAT, SARGE.

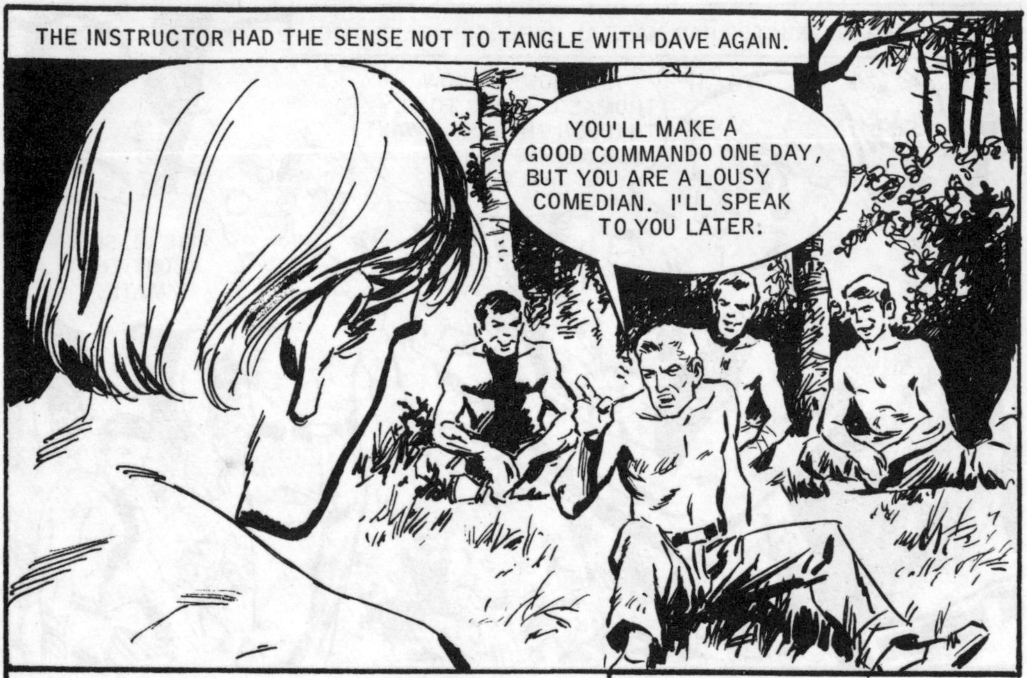
THE INSTRUCTOR HAD THE SENSE NOT TO TANGLE WITH DAVE AGAIN.
YOU'LL MAKE A GOOD COMMANDO ONE DAY, BUT YOU ARE A LOUSY COMEDIAN. I'LL SPEAK TO YOU LATER.

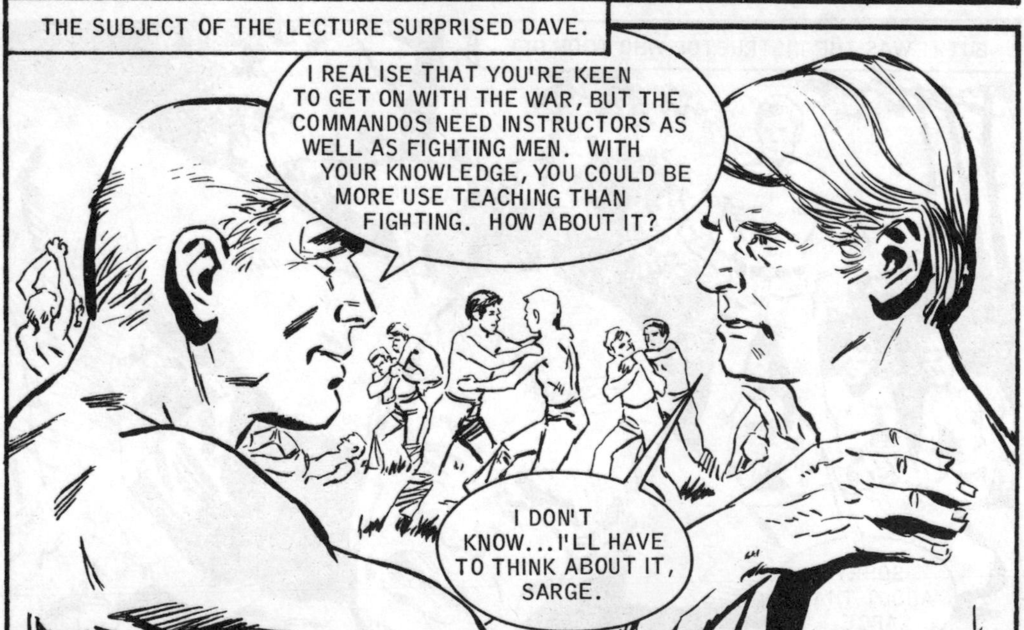
THE SUBJECT OF THE LECTURE SURPRISED DAVE.
I REALISE THAT YOU'RE KEEN TO GET ON WITH THE WAR, BUT THE COMMANDOS NEED INSTRUCTORS AS WELL AS FIGHTING MEN. WITH YOUR KNOWLEDGE, YOU COULD BE MORE USE TEACHING THAN FIGHTING. HOW ABOUT IT?
I DON'T KNOW...I'LL HAVE TO THINK ABOUT IT, SARGE.

EVENTUALLY DAVE AGREED AND BECAME A SERGEANT INSTRUCTOR.

BUT THE URGE FOR ACTION DEFEATED HIS INTEREST IN JUDO, AND HE APPLIED FOR ACTIVE SERVICE AGAIN.

DAVE'S REQUEST FOR ACTIVE SERVICE WAS RELUCTANTLY GRANTED, AND HE TASTED BATTLE AGAIN.

KEEP GOING! LOOK, THEY'RE PANICKING.

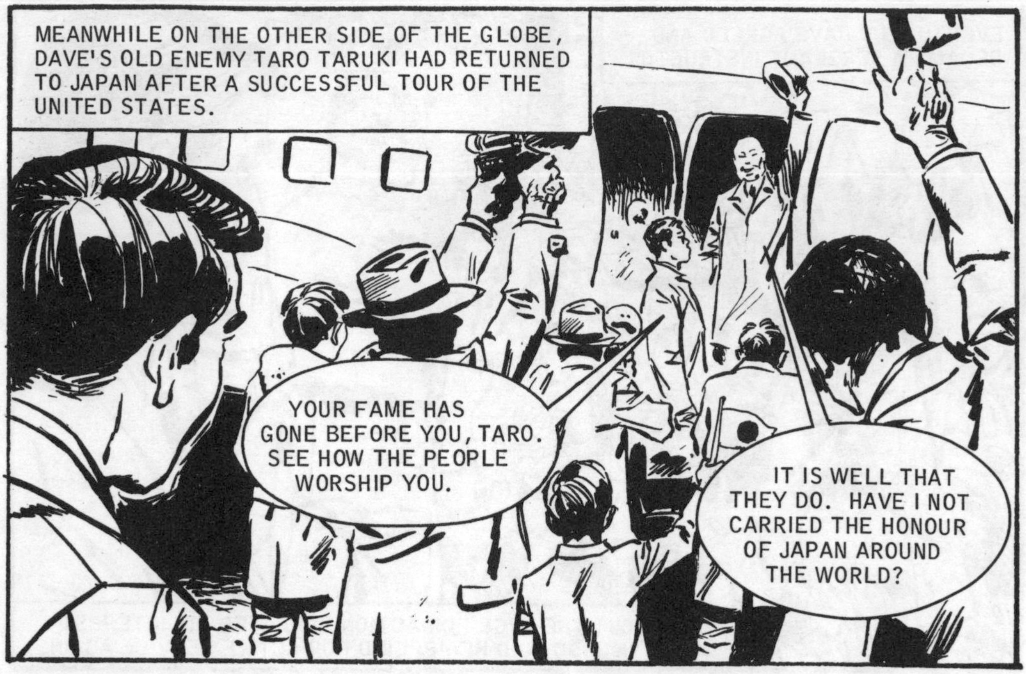
MEANWHILE ON THE OTHER SIDE OF THE GLOBE, DAVE'S OLD ENEMY TARO TARUKI HAD RETURNED TO JAPAN AFTER A SUCCESSFUL TOUR OF THE UNITED STATES.
YOUR FAME HAS GONE BEFORE YOU, TARO. SEE HOW THE PEOPLE WORSHIP YOU.
IT IS WELL THAT THEY DO. HAVE I NOT CARRIED THE HONOUR OF JAPAN AROUND THE WORLD?

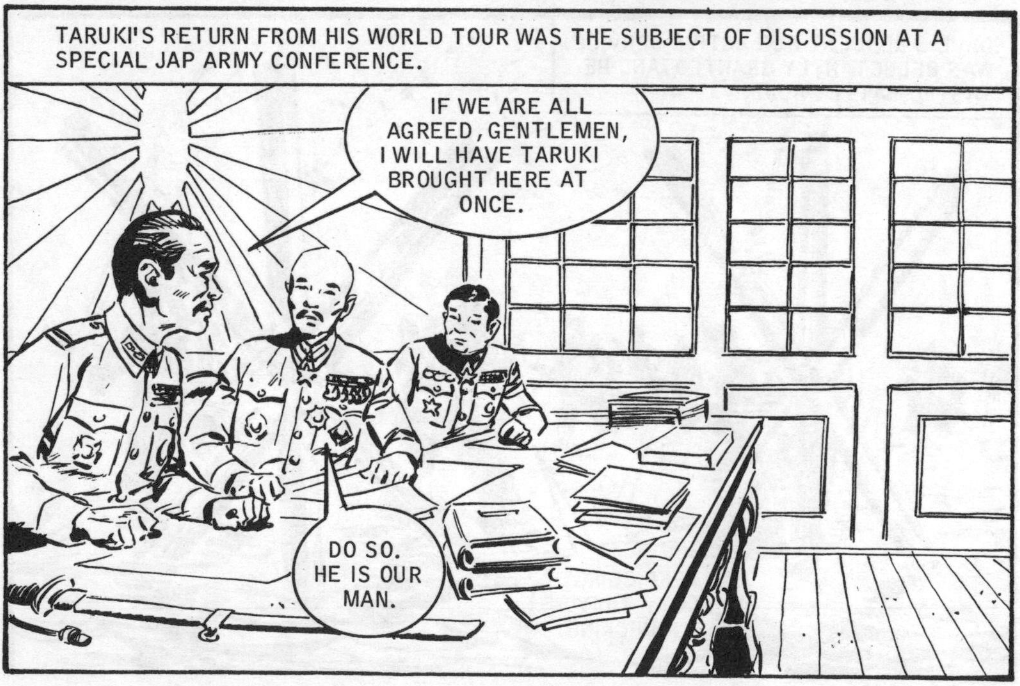
TARUKI'S RETURN FROM HIS WORLD TOUR WAS THE SUBJECT OF DISCUSSION AT A SPECIAL JAP ARMY CONFERENCE.
IF WE ARE ALL AGREED, GENTLEMEN, I WILL HAVE TARUKI BROUGHT HERE AT ONCE.
DO SO. HE IS OUR MAN.

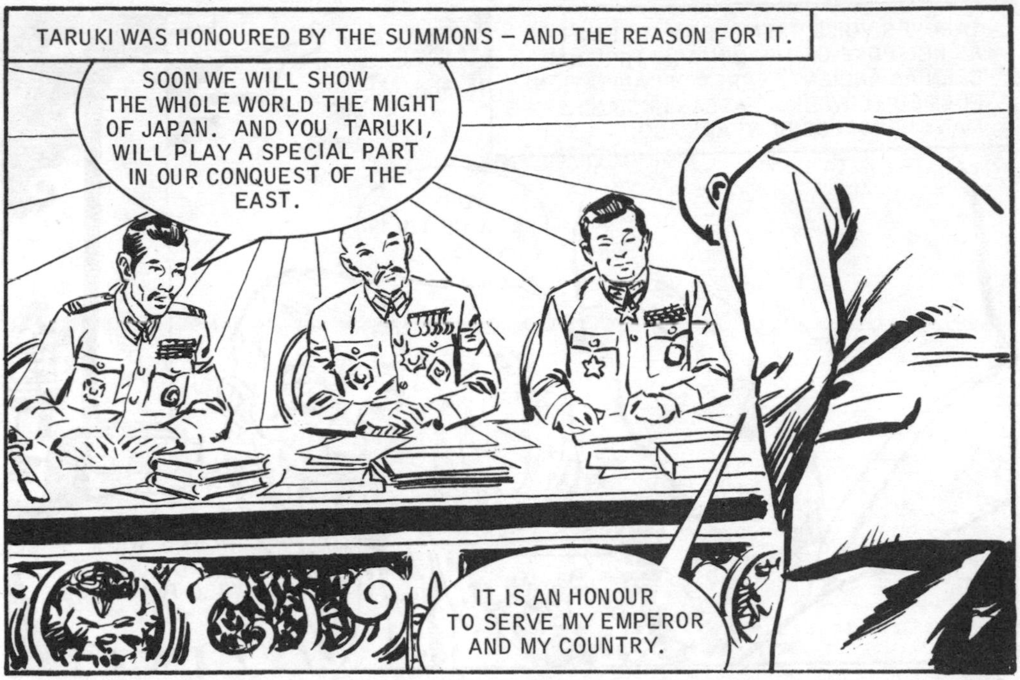
TARUKI WAS HONOURED BY THE SUMMONS – AND THE REASON FOR IT.
SOON WE WILL SHOW THE WHOLE WORLD THE MIGHT OF JAPAN. AND YOU, TARUKI, WILL PLAY A SPECIAL PART IN OUR CONQUEST OF THE EAST.
IT IS AN HONOUR TO SERVE MY EMPEROR AND MY COUNTRY.

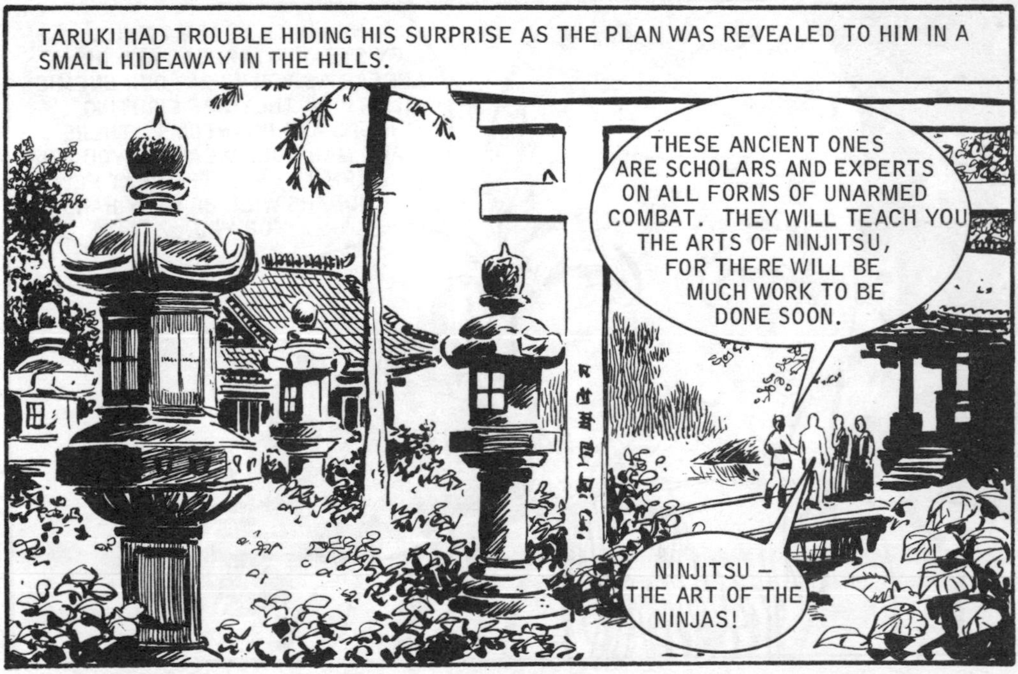
TARUKI HAD TROUBLE HIDING HIS SURPRISE AS THE PLAN WAS REVEALED TO HIM IN A SMALL HIDEAWAY IN THE HILLS.
THESE ANCIENT ONES ARE SCHOLARS AND EXPERTS ON ALL FORMS OF UNARMED COMBAT. THEY WILL TEACH YOU THE ARTS OF NINJITSU, FOR THERE WILL BE MUCH WORK TO BE DONE SOON.
NINJITSU – THE ART OF THE NINJAS!

TARUKI'S VOICE TREMBLED WITH EMOTION AS HE SPOKE OF THE NINJAS. THEY HAD BEEN AN ANCIENT SECRET ORGANISATION FORMED TO WORK AS ASSASSINS AND SPIES MANY HUNDREDS OF YEARS AGO.

YOU KNOW OF THEIR WAYS?

YES, WE KNOW. AND WE WILL TEACH YOU ALL.

YOU WILL LEARN TO KILL BY STEALTH, APPEAR AND DISAPPEAR AS YOU WISH. OUR ENEMIES WILL THINK THEY ARE FIGHTING GHOSTS AND PHANTOMS. THERE ARE MANY OLD WEAPONS YOU WILL LEARN TO USE. THE NEXT FEW MONTHS WILL BE VERY HARD FOR YOU...

AND THOSE MONTHS WERE HARD. FITTED OUT IN AN ALL-BLACK TIGHT-FITTING SUIT WITH HOOD HE TRAINED AS NEVER BEFORE TO BECOME A NINJA...

...TO FIRE DEADLY POISON DARTS...

...TO MASTER THE USE OF KNIVES, ESPECIALLY THE SPECIAL TWO-BLADED NINJA KNIFE AND THE NEEDLE-THIN STABBING DAGGERS.

...TO HURL WITH DEADLY ACCURACY THE SPIKED THROWING QUOITS.

ONCE HE WAS FULLY TRAINED AND PROMOTED TO COLONEL, TARUKI TOOK COMMAND OF SPECIALLY-CHOSEN MEN.

THERE THEY ARE — THE CREAM OF THE JAPANESE ARMY. YOU WILL TRAIN THESE MEN UNTIL THEY ARE FULLY-FLEDGED NINJAS. THEN THEY WILL FIGHT IN ADVANCE OF OUR ARMY AND STRIKE TERROR INTO OUR ENEMIES.

AN EXCELLENT SCHEME. DESTROYING THE ENEMY'S MORALE WILL MAKE OUR ADVANCE MUCH EASIER.

A SHORT TIME LATER THE JAPS LEAPT EXPLOSIVELY INTO THE WAR WHEN THEY ATTACKED PEARL HARBOUR.

AND TARUKI'S MEN DROPPED SILENTLY INTO BURMA.

AT LAST WE WILL DRAW BLOOD.

SWIFT AND DEADLY WERE THE NINJAS AS THEY CARRIED OUT THEIR TERRIBLE WORK, STRIKING SILENTLY AND NEVER LEAVING ANY SIGN.

AS THE DAYS WENT BY, MORE VICTIMS WERE ADDED TO THE NINJAS' LIST AND MORALE BEGAN TO CRUMBLE.

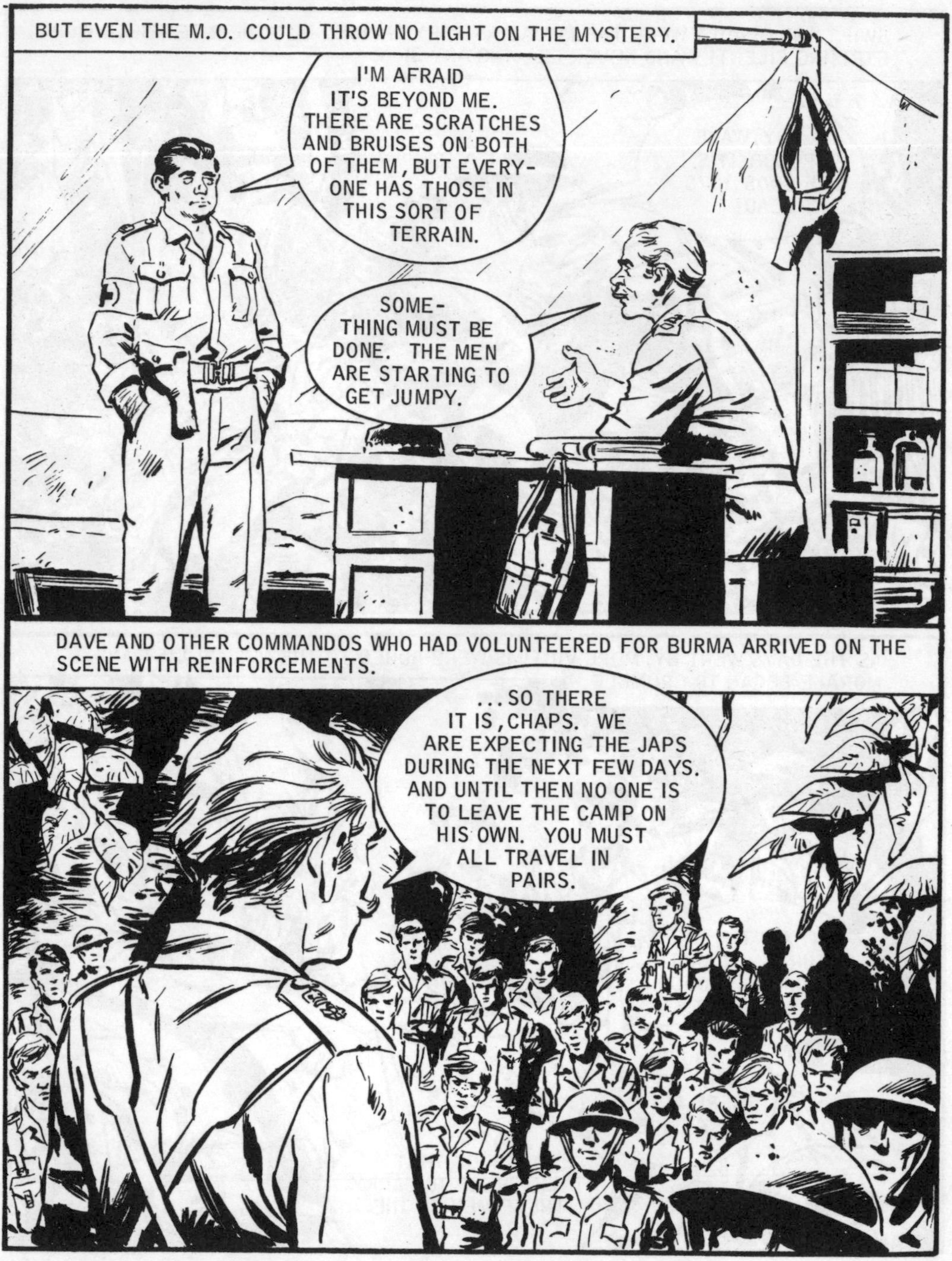
BUT EVEN THE M. O. COULD THROW NO LIGHT ON THE MYSTERY.
I'M AFRAID IT'S BEYOND ME. THERE ARE SCRATCHES AND BRUISES ON BOTH OF THEM, BUT EVERY-ONE HAS THOSE IN THIS SORT OF TERRAIN.
SOME-THING MUST BE DONE. THE MEN ARE STARTING TO GET JUMPY.
DAVE AND OTHER COMMANDOS WHO HAD VOLUNTEERED FOR BURMA ARRIVED ON THE SCENE WITH REINFORCEMENTS.
... SO THERE IT IS, CHAPS. WE ARE EXPECTING THE JAPS DURING THE NEXT FEW DAYS. AND UNTIL THEN NO ONE IS TO LEAVE THE CAMP ON HIS OWN. YOU MUST ALL TRAVEL IN PAIRS.

DAVE FOUND HIMSELF TALKING WITH ANOTHER SERGEANT CALLED NICK WEST.

I RECKON THE JAPS ARE ALREADY HERE. WE'VE LOST EIGHT MEN IN THE LAST THREE DAYS.

EIGHT MEN! BUT HOW?

DAVE'S NEW FRIEND AGREED TO SHOW HIM AROUND THE NEARBY NATIVE VILLAGE AND EXPLAINED ABOUT THE MYSTERY DEATHS.

...I RECKON THE JAPS ARE BEHIND IT ALL. IF THEY AIN'T, WHO IS?

NOT A MARK ON THEM, EH?

I'VE A FEELING I'VE HEARD THIS SOME- WHERE BEFORE.

DAVE WAS INTRIGUED BY THE NATIVE VILLAGE, BUT WEST WAS BEGINNING TO WORRY.

THIS NECKLACE IS JUST RIGHT FOR MY NIECE IN ENGLAND.

BUY THE BLINKING THING THEN, AND LET'S GET BACK BEFORE DARK.

AS DUSK APPROACHED, THE TWO MEN DOUBLED BACK TO BASE.

STEP ON IT. I DON'T WANT TO BE THE NINTH MYSTERY CORPSE.

BUT THEN THE NECKLACE BROKE.

HANG ON WHILE I GATHER THESE BEADS.

I'M OFF — SEE YOU BACK AT CAMP!

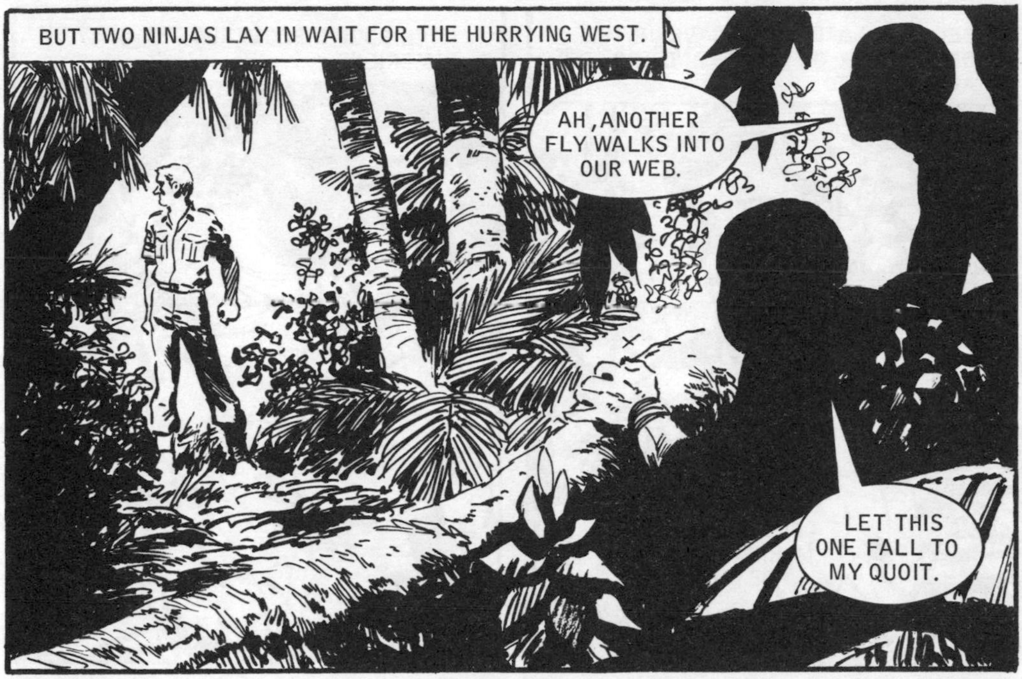
BUT TWO NINJAS LAY IN WAIT FOR THE HURRYING WEST.
AH, ANOTHER FLY WALKS INTO OUR WEB.
LET THIS ONE FALL TO MY QUOIT.

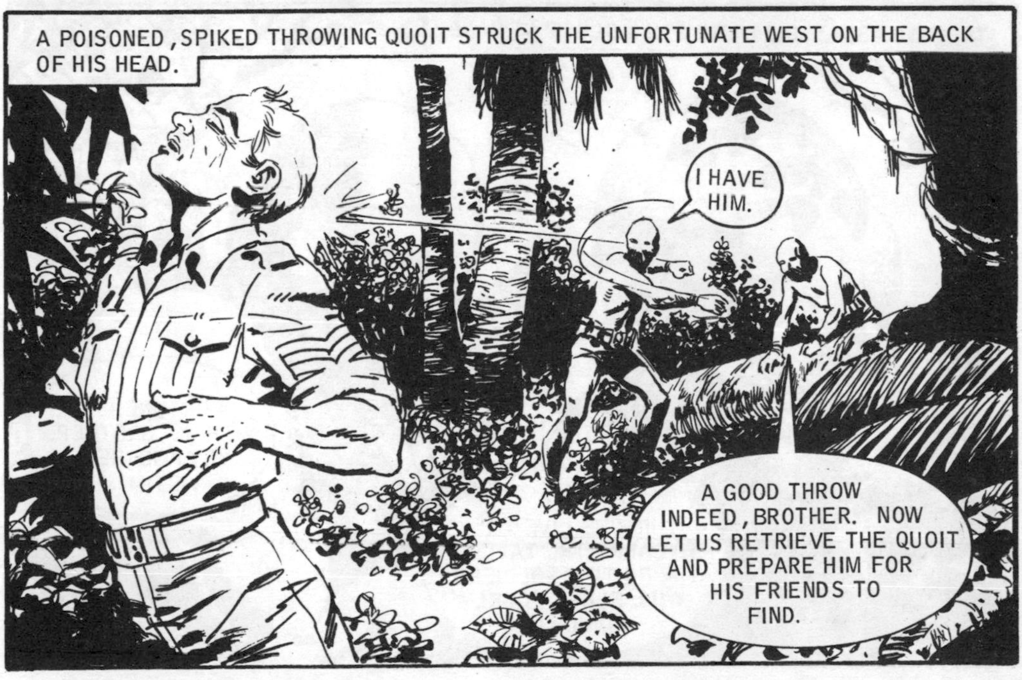
A POISONED, SPIKED THROWING QUOIT STRUCK THE UNFORTUNATE WEST ON THE BACK OF HIS HEAD.
I HAVE HIM.
A GOOD THROW INDEED, BROTHER. NOW LET US RETRIEVE THE QUOIT AND PREPARE HIM FOR HIS FRIENDS TO FIND.

SECONDS LATER DAVE GAVE UP THE SEARCH FOR THE BEADS AND TROTTED AFTER WEST.

BLASTED BEADS! I'LL COME BACK IN THE MORNING AND HAVE A BETTER LOOK.

DAVE SOON DISCOVERED THE BODY OF HIS FRIEND.

OH, NO, HE'S DEAD!

THE TWO ASSASSINS WERE STILL CLOSE AT HAND.

NAY, LET THIS ONE LIVE TO CARRY THE TALE. THE BRITISH SOLDIERS WILL SLEEP POORLY TONIGHT.

FORTUNE IS WITH US, BROTHER. YET ANOTHER VICTIM...

DAVE HEADED BACK FOR CAMP AND DISCOVERED THE SENTRIES WERE ALREADY JUMPY.

PACK IT IN, YOU TWERP! DO I LOOK LIKE A JAP?

I SHOOT FIRST AND LOOK AFTER. NO ONE'S CREEPING UP ON ME TONIGHT!

DAVE TOLD HIS STORY AND THE C.O. DISCUSSED IT WITH THE M.O.

I'M SORRY. IT'S JUST THE SAME AS ALL THE OTHERS — NO MARKS, NO SIGNS, NO SICKNESS.

THIS IS THE NINTH VICTIM IN FOUR DAYS. I'LL SEND OUT A SPECIAL PATROL AT DAWN.

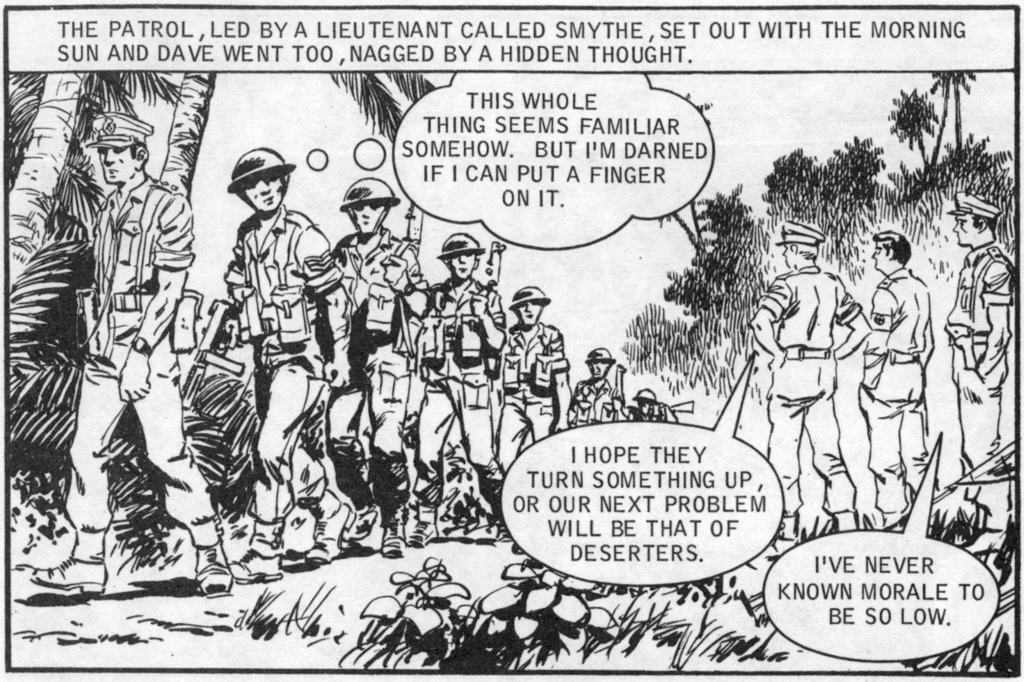
THE PATROL, LED BY A LIEUTENANT CALLED SMYTHE, SET OUT WITH THE MORNING SUN AND DAVE WENT TOO, NAGGED BY A HIDDEN THOUGHT.
THIS WHOLE THING SEEMS FAMILIAR SOMEHOW. BUT I'M DARNED IF I CAN PUT A FINGER ON IT.
I HOPE THEY TURN SOMETHING UP, OR OUR NEXT PROBLEM WILL BE THAT OF DESERTERS.
I'VE NEVER KNOWN MORALE TO BE SO LOW.

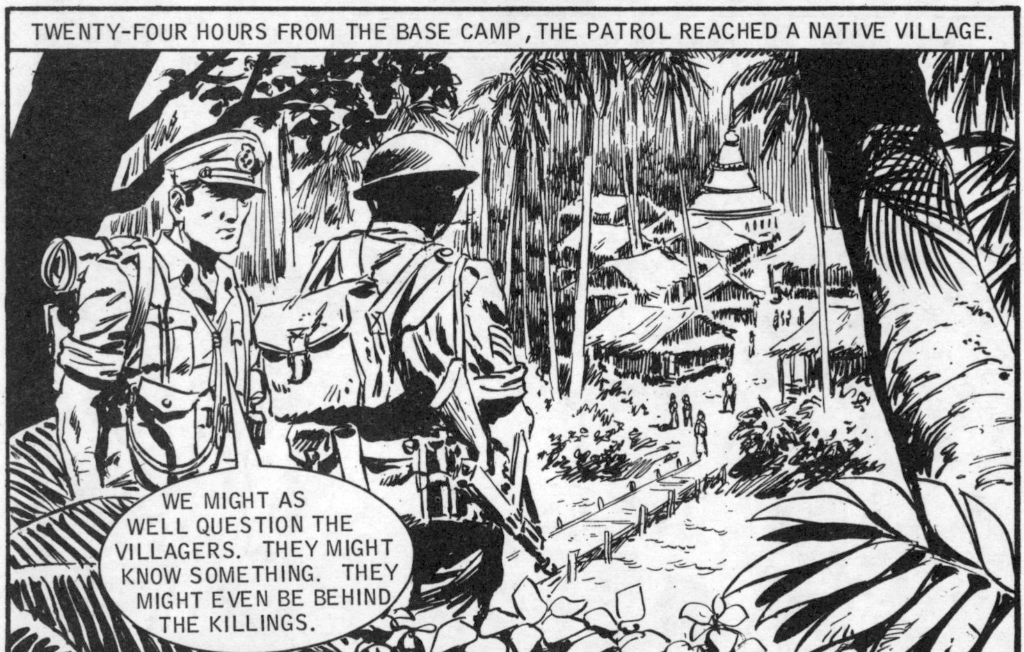
TWENTY-FOUR HOURS FROM THE BASE CAMP, THE PATROL REACHED A NATIVE VILLAGE.
WE MIGHT AS WELL QUESTION THE VILLAGERS. THEY MIGHT KNOW SOMETHING. THEY MIGHT EVEN BE BEHIND THE KILLINGS.

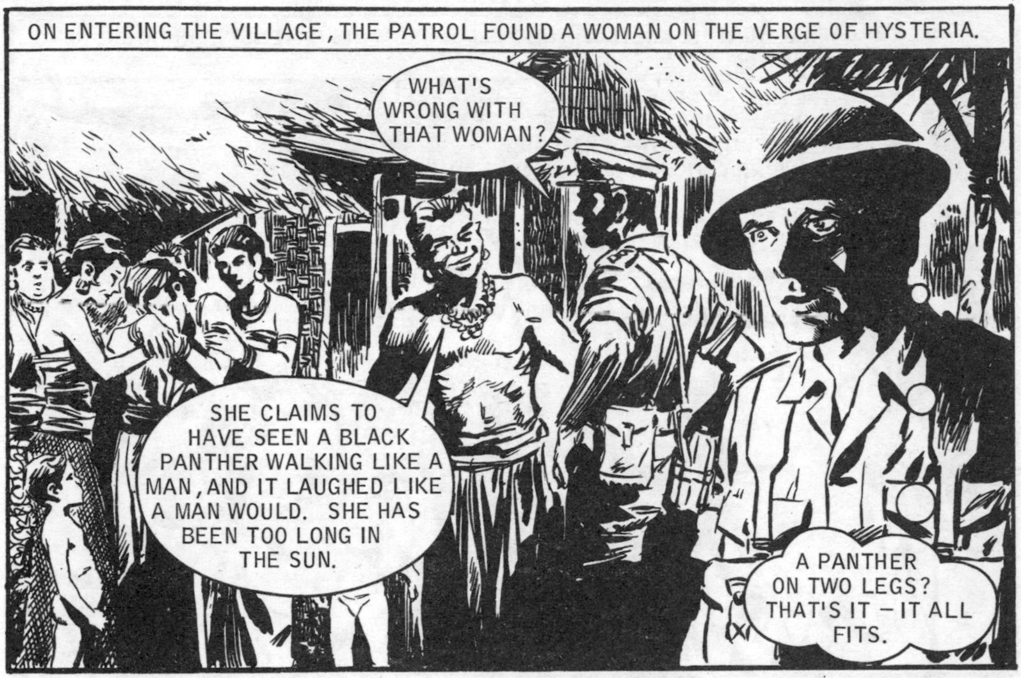
ON ENTERING THE VILLAGE, THE PATROL FOUND A WOMAN ON THE VERGE OF HYSTERIA.
WHAT'S WRONG WITH THAT WOMAN?
SHE CLAIMS TO HAVE SEEN A BLACK PANTHER WALKING LIKE A MAN, AND IT LAUGHED LIKE A MAN WOULD. SHE HAS BEEN TOO LONG IN THE SUN.
A PANTHER ON TWO LEGS? THAT'S IT – IT ALL FITS.

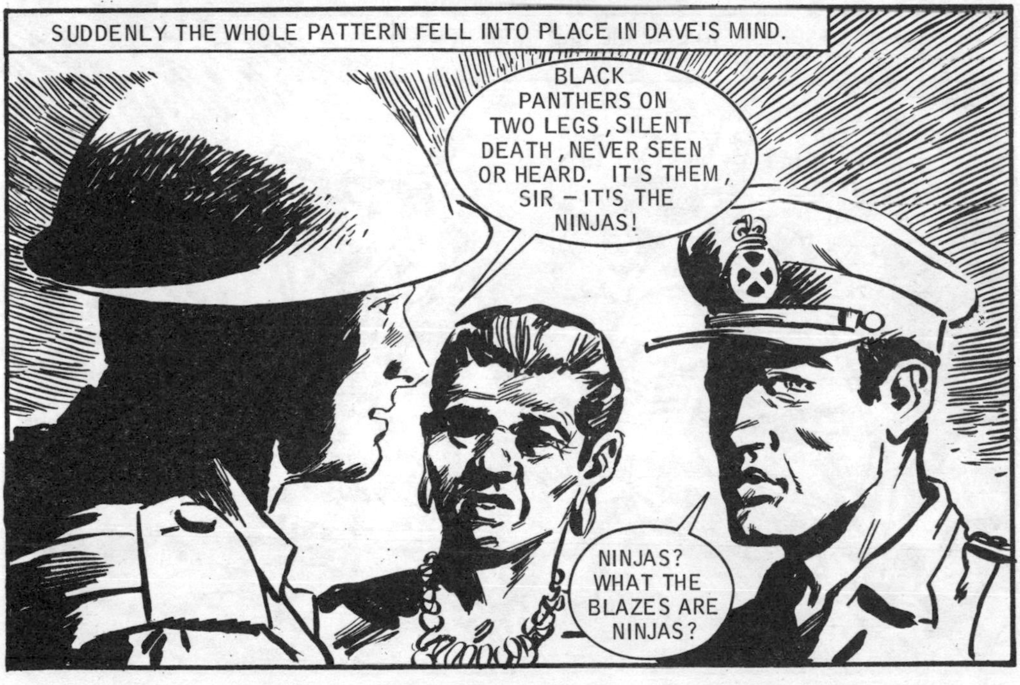
SUDDENLY THE WHOLE PATTERN FELL INTO PLACE IN DAVE'S MIND.
BLACK PANTHERS ON TWO LEGS, SILENT DEATH, NEVER SEEN OR HEARD. IT'S THEM, SIR – IT'S THE NINJAS!
NINJAS? WHAT THE BLAZES ARE NINJAS?

DAVE EXPLAINED WHAT HE KNEW OF THE NINJAS FROM HIS EXTENSIVE KNOWLEDGE OF JAPANESE HISTORY.

THEY'RE AN ANCIENT CULT, SIR, DATING BACK HUNDREDS OF YEARS. I THOUGHT THEY HAD DIED OUT, AND THE PRACTICE IS BANNED IN JAPAN. THEY MUST HAVE BEEN RAISED AGAIN AND PLANTED HERE TO SOFTEN US UP.

SOUNDS CRAZY TO ME, BUT WE'LL FOLLOW IT UP. ANY LEAD IS BETTER THAN NONE.

THE WOMAN DESCRIBED WHERE SHE HAD SEEN HER "PANTHER" AND THE AREA WAS SEARCHED.

THERE YOU ARE, SIR, A CLEAR PRINT OF A JAP CLEFT SOLE SANDAL.

YOU'RE RIGHT. NOW AT LEAST WE KNOW WHAT WE'RE UP AGAINST. ALTHOUGH, HOW MUCH GOOD WILL IT DO US?

DAVE SUDDENLY FOUND HIMSELF ACTING AS ADVISER TO THE PATROL.

IF YOU WERE A NINJA, WHERE WOULD YOU CHOOSE TO HIDE?

I'D STAY WITHIN A DAY'S MARCH OF THE ENEMY, BUT WELL AWAY FROM PATHS AND VILLAGES. I THINK THEY'RE NOT FAR FROM HERE, POSSIBLY IN THE MOUNTAINS.

THE MEN WERE NOW MORE CONFIDENT AND BIG BILL BATES SPOKE UP.

THEY KILLED MY BEST MATE. LET'S GET THEM. I'VE A SCORE TO SETTLE!

SMYTHE SPOKE SHARPLY —

CALM DOWN, BATES. WE'LL HEAD FOR THE HIGH GROUND AND MAKE CAMP. WE CAN MAKE A THOROUGH SEARCH AT DAWN.

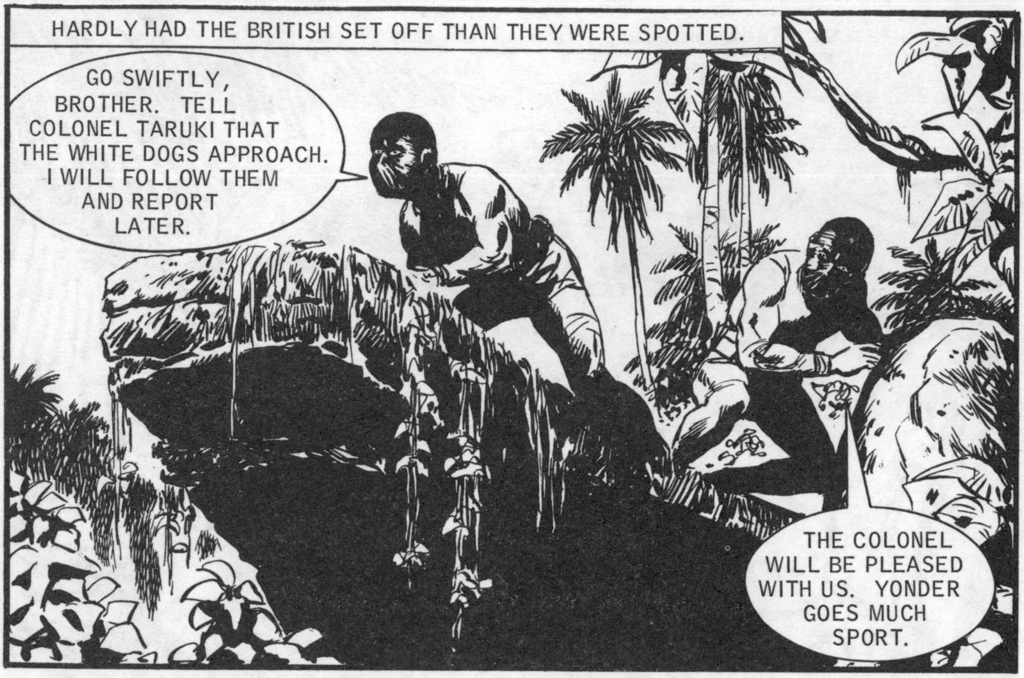
HARDLY HAD THE BRITISH SET OFF THAN THEY WERE SPOTTED.
GO SWIFTLY, BROTHER. TELL COLONEL TARUKI THAT THE WHITE DOGS APPROACH. I WILL FOLLOW THEM AND REPORT LATER.
THE COLONEL WILL BE PLEASED WITH US. YONDER GOES MUCH SPORT.

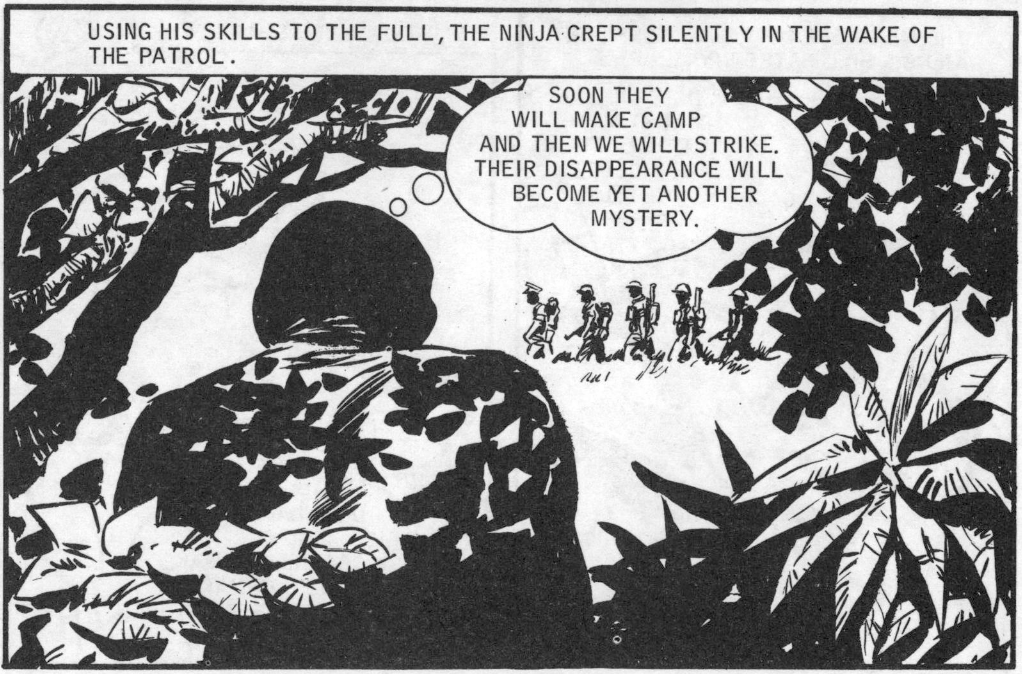
USING HIS SKILLS TO THE FULL, THE NINJA CREPT SILENTLY IN THE WAKE OF THE PATROL.
SOON THEY WILL MAKE CAMP AND THEN WE WILL STRIKE. THEIR DISAPPEARANCE WILL BECOME YET ANOTHER MYSTERY.

LATER THE PATROL STOPPED TO CAMP FOR THE NIGHT.

OK, LADS, TWO SENTRIES AND THREE-HOUR SHIFTS. KEEP YOUR EYES PEELED AND NO SMOKING.

TO THE SENTRIES, THREE HOURS FELT LIKE THREE WEEKS.   AND TO DICK PATTON IT WAS A REAL BIND.

TO HECK WITH THE ORDERS! I'M HAVIN' A SMOKE.

PATTON WAS A GOOD SOLDIER, BUT HE HAD LITTLE RESPECT FOR AUTHORITY.   AND HE WAS VERY NERVOUS.

AS PATTON CAUTIOUSLY LIT HIS CIGARETTE, THE NINJAS STRUCK AT THE OTHER SENTRY, USING A NEEDLE-THIN DAGGER.

IT TAKES PRACTICE TO LIGHT UP ON THE SLY.

AND THE KILLERS VANISHED AS SILENTLY AS THEY'D COME.

ONLY WHEN THE RELIEF SENTRIES APPEARED AND THE DEAD GUARD WAS FOUND DID PATTON LEARN OF HIS NARROW ESCAPE.

I NEVER HEARD A THING, SIR.

THERE WILL BE NO SLEEP FOR ANY OF US NOW.

AND DAVE HAD FOUND MORE TROUBLE.

SIR, PHILLIPS AND JOHNSON ARE DEAD TOO. AND THE RADIO'S GONE.

SMYTHE STARTED TO RAP OUT ORDERS, BUT A POISON DART FINISHED HIM.

WE'LL... AGH!

SIR!

EVERY MAN WAS IN COVER IN SECONDS AND THERE WAS NOTHING THAT DAVE COULD DO FOR THE OFFICER.

IT'S NO USE. THE POISON MUST ACT ALMOST INSTANTLY.

YOU KNOW MORE ABOUT THIS THAN ANY OF US, SARGE. IT'S A GOOD JOB YOU'RE TAKING COMMAND.

YET, DESPITE DAVE AND THE MEN BEING VERY ALERT, TWO MORE VICTIMS FELL THAT NIGHT.

SOON THERE WILL BE NONE...

WHEN DAWN FINALLY BROKE THE NINJAS HAD GONE — FOR THE MOMENT.

THE FOUR OF US WOULD STAND NO CHANCE IF WE TRIED TO MAKE IT BACK. I'M GOING AFTER THEM AND TAKING A FEW WITH ME.

THAT GOES FOR ME TOO!

AND ME!

PATTON COULD NOT BELIEVE HIS EARS.

THAT'S SUICIDE — COUNT ME OUT!

THEN YOU'D BETTER SHOVE OFF NOW! 'COS IF THE NINJAS DON'T GET YOU, I WILL!

BATES MEANT EVERY WORD HE SAID AND PATTON RELUCTANTLY BACKED DOWN.

MOMENTS LATER THE REMNANTS OF THE PATROL SET OUT FOR REVENGE, BUT ALREADY THEY WERE BEING WATCHED BY THREE NINJAS WHO WERE HIDDEN SO WELL THAT THE JUNGLE BIRDS HAD NOT EVEN SEEN THEM.

SO THERE ARE ONLY FOUR WHITE DOGS LEFT. SOON THERE WILL ONLY BE THREE...

STEALTH AND CUNNING BROUGHT ONE OF THE NINJAS UP BEHIND THE LAST MAN. THE JAP USED THE LEATHER THROTTLING ROPE ATTACHED TO BAMBOO HANDLES.

AAAGH!

HE SHOUTS...
I WAS NOT QUICK
ENOUGH.

BURLY BATES HEARD THE ATTACK AND WHIRLED QUICKLY. BUT IT WAS ALREADY TOO LATE TO SAVE HIS COMRADE.

MURDERING
LITTLE CREEP —
HOLD THAT!

THE NINJA DIED WITH HIS VICTIM.

THE OTHER TWO NINJAS RUSHED IN — BUT FOUND DAVE AND PATTON READY AND WAITING.

FAR ENOUGH, TOJO!

BOTH JAPS WERE DEAD BEFORE THEY HIT THE GROUND.

THEY BURIED THEIR DEAD COMRADE, THEN THEY SET ABOUT EXAMINING SOME OF THE NINJAS' WEAPONS.

A PROPER HORROR ARSENAL. NICE CHAPS THESE.

I'D LIKE TO WRING A FEW OF THEIR NECKS!

YOU'RE BOTH MAD — LET'S GET BACK TO BASE!

IRRITATED BY PATTON'S WHINING, DAVE SPUN ROUND AND FACED HIM.

OK, PATTON, IT'S TIME WE HAD THIS MADE CLEAR. WE SET OUT TO DO A JOB, AND WE'RE GOING TO DO IT. IF YOU WANT TO TAKE OFF INTO THE JUNGLE WITH THE NINJAS CREEPING ABOUT, YOU GO RIGHT AHEAD!

ALL RIGHT, I'LL STICK WITH YOU, BUT IT'S STILL SUICIDE.

THEN DAVE TOLD THEM OF HIS PLAN.

WE HAVEN'T MUCH CHANCE OF FINDING THEM, SO WE'LL WAIT FOR THEM TO FIND US. EACH OF YOU PUT ON A NINJA SUIT, AND THEN I'LL SHOW YOU WHAT WE'LL DO WITH OUR UNIFORMS...

THE OTHER TWO WERE PUZZLED BUT THEY PULLED ON THE NINJA SUITS AND THEN SAW WHAT DAVE HAD IN MIND WHEN HE FILLED THEIR BRITISH CLOTHING WITH DRIED GRASS TO MAKE QUITE REALISTIC DUMMIES.

THESE DUMMIES CAN ACT AS BAIT. WE'LL LIE LOW AND SEE IF ANY NINJAS COME CALLING.

BUT BATES HAD A FEW IDEAS OF HIS OWN TO ADD TO THE PLAN.

THIS GRENADE SHOULD GIVE A FEW OF 'EM A HEADACHE WHEN I PULL THE STRING...

GOOD THINKING!

MEANWHILE, A FEW MILES AWAY, TARUKI ADDRESSED HIS NINJA WARRIORS IN THEIR CAVE HIDE-OUT.

MANY OF OUR BROTHERS REST WITH THEIR ANCESTORS AND WE HAVE A SCORE TO SETTLE. WE HAVE TRIUMPHED OVER THE WHITE DOGS AND THEIR MODERN WEAPONS. TONIGHT WE WILL FINISH THE THREE WHO DEFY US!

AT DUSK SHADOWY FIGURES FLITTED TOWARDS THE CAMP.

SEE, MY BROTHER, THE WHITE FOOLS ARE EXHAUSTED. THIS WILL BE TOO EASY.

BUT BE WATCHFUL. NONE MUST ESCAPE.

BUT BIG BILL BATES WAS ON THE ALERT.

ONE MORE STEP, TOJO, AND THEN...

BATES' GRENADE BLASTED THREE NINJAS TO THEIR ANCESTORS.

AAARGH!

THERE WAS NO HIDING PLACE FROM THE HAIL OF LEAD THAT SWEPT THE AREA WHEN DAVE AND PATTON OPENED UP.

GIVE IT TO 'EM!

RETREAT — AT ONCE!

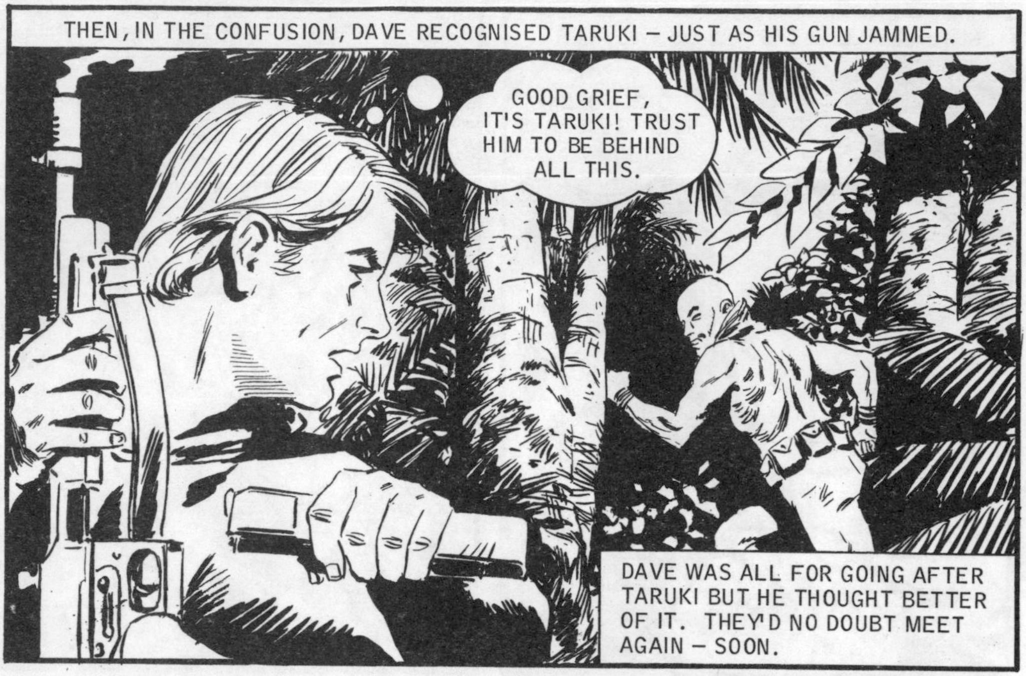
THEN, IN THE CONFUSION, DAVE RECOGNISED TARUKI – JUST AS HIS GUN JAMMED.
GOOD GRIEF, IT'S TARUKI! TRUST HIM TO BE BEHIND ALL THIS.
DAVE WAS ALL FOR GOING AFTER TARUKI BUT HE THOUGHT BETTER OF IT. THEY'D NO DOUBT MEET AGAIN – SOON.

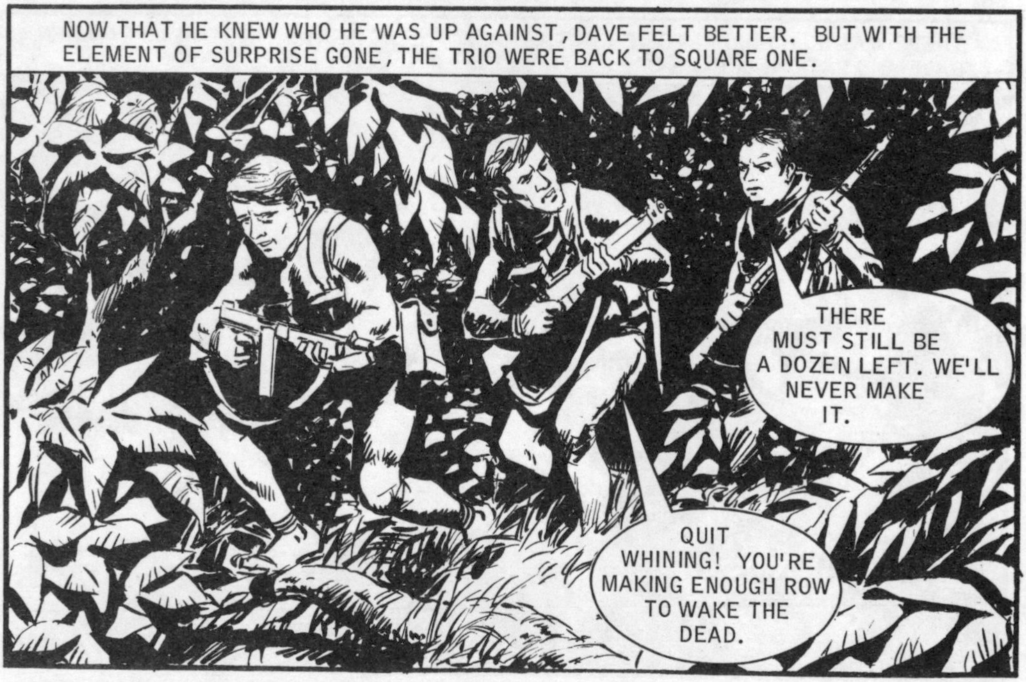
NOW THAT HE KNEW WHO HE WAS UP AGAINST, DAVE FELT BETTER. BUT WITH THE ELEMENT OF SURPRISE GONE, THE TRIO WERE BACK TO SQUARE ONE.
THERE MUST STILL BE A DOZEN LEFT. WE'LL NEVER MAKE IT.
QUIT WHINING! YOU'RE MAKING ENOUGH ROW TO WAKE THE DEAD.

PATTON'S HIGH-PITCHED VOICE HAD ALREADY CARRIED TO HOSTILE EARS.

LISTEN! THAT COULD BE THE WHITE ONES.

THEY WALK THIS PATH. WE WILL WAIT.

BUT DAVE DECIDED TO AVOID THE PATHS.

THEY'LL HAVE THE PATHS COVERED, SO WE'LL TAKE TO THE JUNGLE. AND PULL DOWN YOUR MASKS TO HIDE YOUR FACE.

ONCE AGAIN LUCK WAS WITH THE TRIO. THEIR SUITS HID THEIR REAL IDENTITY WHEN THEY UNWITTINGLY APPROACHED THE WAITING NINJAS.

SEE! THERE ARE SOME OF OUR BROTHERS.

QUICKLY — WARN THEM TO KEEP DOWN.

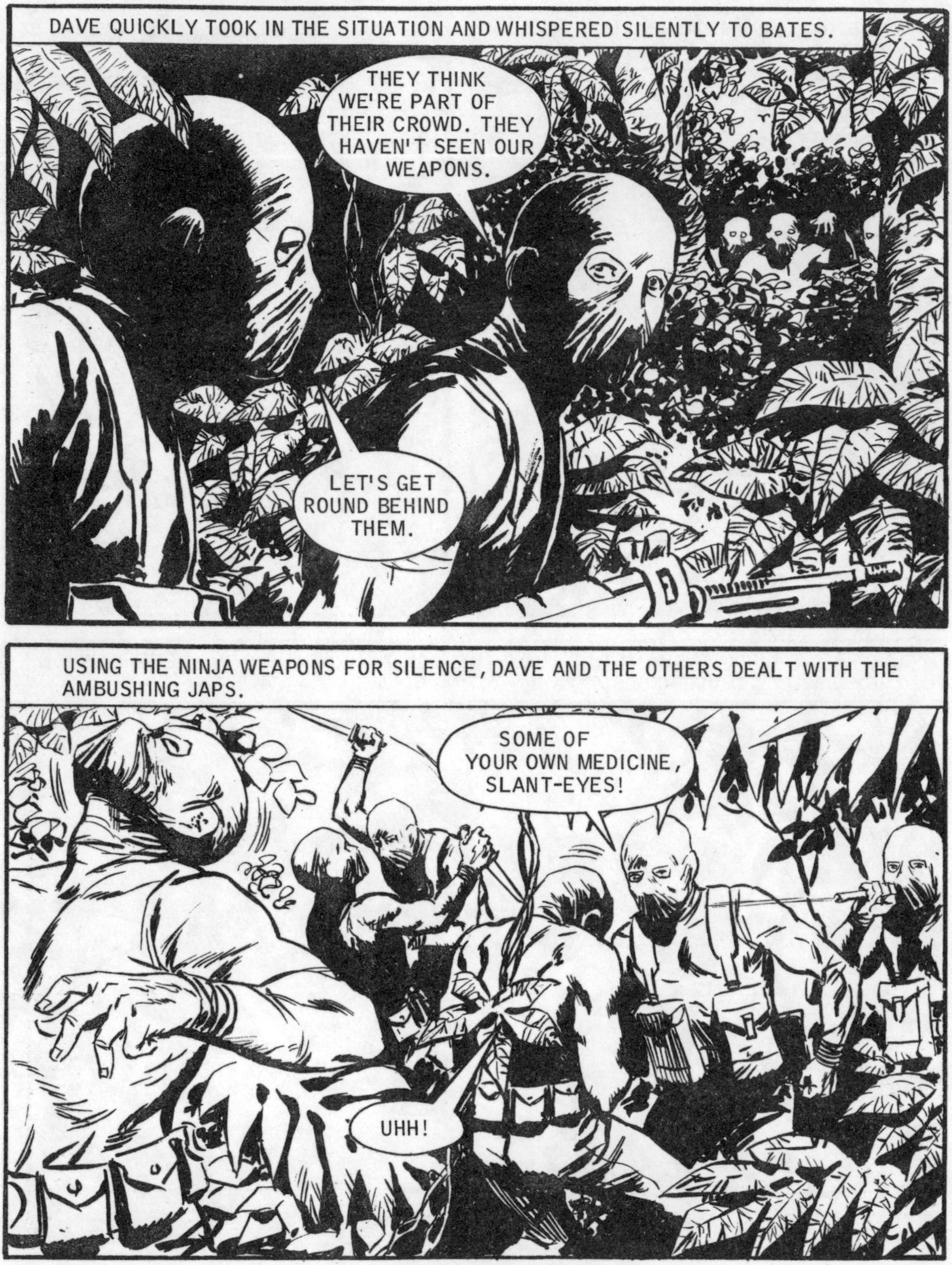
DAVE QUICKLY TOOK IN THE SITUATION AND WHISPERED SILENTLY TO BATES.
THEY THINK WE'RE PART OF THEIR CROWD. THEY HAVEN'T SEEN OUR WEAPONS.
LET'S GET ROUND BEHIND THEM.
USING THE NINJA WEAPONS FOR SILENCE, DAVE AND THE OTHERS DEALT WITH THE AMBUSHING JAPS.
SOME OF YOUR OWN MEDICINE, SLANT-EYES!
UHH!

HAVING REDUCED THE OPPOSITION BY THREE, DAVE'S PARTY MADE THEIR ESCAPE.

WE'LL HEAD UPHILL UNTIL WE'RE CLEAR OF THESE TREES AND CAN SEE ALL AROUND.

WHEN TARUKI DISCOVERED THE THREE BODIES, HE WAS LIVID.

NOW THEY USE OUR OWN WEAPONS AGAINST US. WE WILL FOLLOW AND BE AVENGED!

MEANWHILE THE THREE BRITISH SOLDIERS HAD FOUND REFUGE IN A MOUNTAIN CAVE.

IF WE PILE A FEW OF THESE BOULDERS AROUND THE ENTRANCE, THIS WILL MAKE A GOOD PLACE FOR A STAND.

OR A BLINKING TOMB!

BUT SOON SLANT EYES WERE WATCHING THE DESPERATE TRIO BUILDING THEIR DEFENCES.

CURSE THE DOGS! THEY MUST KNOW THAT WE HAVE NO MODERN WEAPONS. WE CANNOT ATTACK IN THE OPEN IN THIS MOONLIGHT.

DAVE DECIDED IT WAS TIME THEY GRABBED SOME WELL-EARNED REST, UNAWARE SO FAR OF THE DANGER WITHOUT.

TIME WE GRABBED SOME SHUT-EYE. YOU TAKE THE FIRST WATCH, PATTON.

HOW CAN THEY SLEEP WITH THAT LOT OUT THERE SOMEWHERE?

BUT DAVE AND BATES SOON SLEPT. PATTON'S FEAR INCREASED WITH EVERY MINUTE.

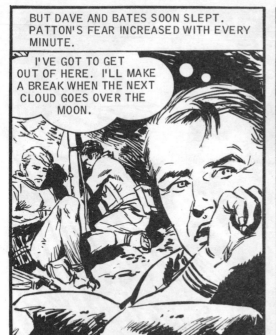

I'VE GOT TO GET OUT OF HERE. I'LL MAKE A BREAK WHEN THE NEXT CLOUD GOES OVER THE MOON.

ABANDONING BATES AND DAVE, PATTON SLIPPED AWAY.

SERVES 'EM RIGHT. I'D BE SAFE IN BASE BY NOW IF IT WEREN'T FOR 'EM.

BUT PATTON'S STEALTHY MOVEMENTS DID NOT GO UNSEEN BY THE SHARP EYES OF TARUKI.

AH! ONE RAT LEAVES ITS BURROW. HE SHALL HAVE THE DEATH THAT A RAT DESERVES.

PATTON'S NERVE BROKE AS HE BEGAN A PANIC-STRICKEN RUN THROUGH THE TREES.

THEY'RE ALL AROUND ME. MUST RUN... RUN...

BLIND WITH FEAR, PATTON RAN RIGHT INTO A TREACHEROUS SWAMP.

OH, NO — HELP, HELP!

PATTON'S CRIES REACHED DAVE'S EARS.

BATES, WAKE UP! SOUNDS LIKE PATTON'S IN TROUBLE.

HUH, WHAT...

NEITHER MAN COULD RISK GOING TO THE AID OF THE FOOLISH PATTON.

EVERY JAP FOR MILES WILL BE HEADING FOR HIM.

AND WE'LL GET JUMPED TOO IF WE GO.

MEANWHILE THE NINJAS HAD HOMED ON THEIR PREY. MAD WITH TERROR, PATTON TRIED TO BARGAIN FOR HIS LIFE.

I'M SINKING... I'LL DO ANYTHING, ONLY PULL ME OUT OF HERE. HELP ME!

WHAT HAVE YOU TO TRADE FOR YOUR MISERABLE LIFE? I WOULD LIKE TO WATCH YOU DROWN BUT YOUR WHINING ANNOYS ME.

THEN MY KNIFE WILL SILENCE HIM.

A THROWN KNIFE CUT SHORT PATTON'S PLEAS AND TARUKI AND HIS NINJAS HEADED BACK TO THE CAVE.

TARUKI'S IDEA WAS SOON PUT INTO ACTION. HE BELLOWED FROM THE JUNGLE.

A GREAT RAGE GRIPPED TARUKI AS HE REALISED WHO WAS IN THE CAVE.

SO THAT MEDDLING FOOL IS AT MY MERCY...

THE WHITE MAN CLAIMS VICTORY OVER OUR COLONEL.

THEN HE IS A WORTHY OPPONENT INDEED.

AND IN THE CAVE, DAVE TOLD BATES ABOUT HIS ENCOUNTER WITH TARUKI.

...SO IF I'M ANY JUDGE, PATTON WILL BE DEAD BY NOW.

I RECKON YOU'RE RIGHT. WE'LL JUST HAVE TO SIT IT OUT.

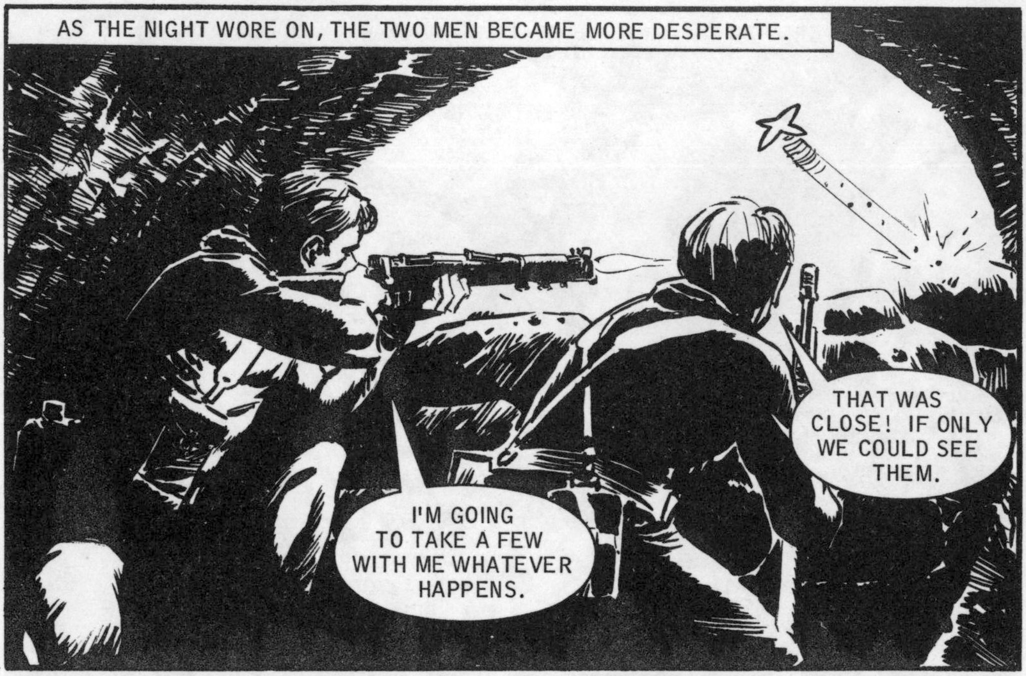
AS THE NIGHT WORE ON, THE TWO MEN BECAME MORE DESPERATE.
THAT WAS CLOSE! IF ONLY WE COULD SEE THEM.
I'M GOING TO TAKE A FEW WITH ME WHATEVER HAPPENS.

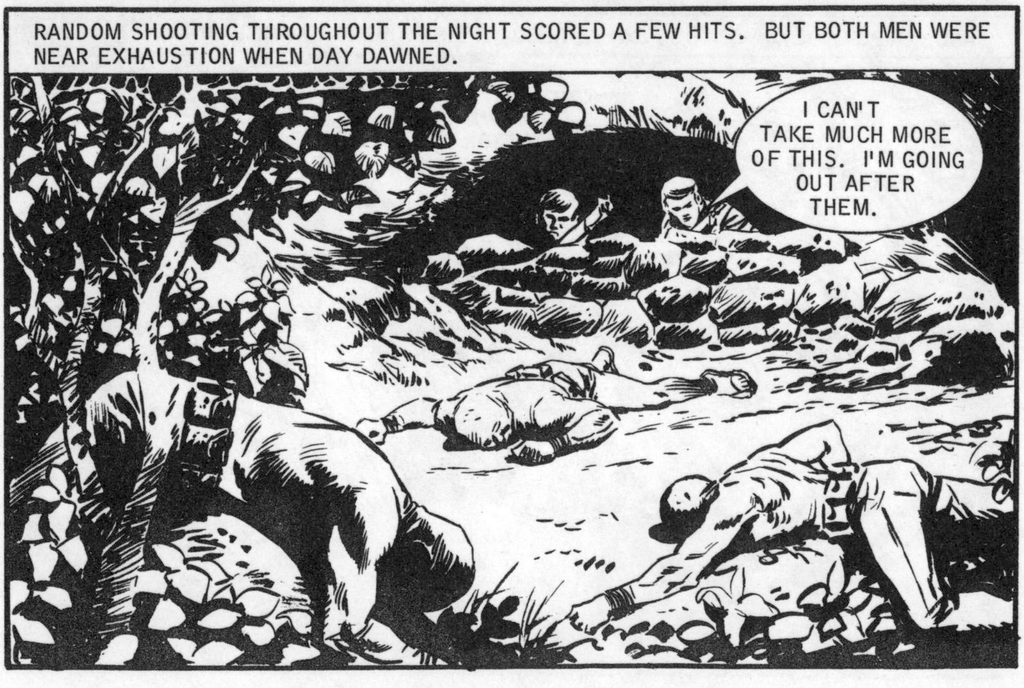
RANDOM SHOOTING THROUGHOUT THE NIGHT SCORED A FEW HITS. BUT BOTH MEN WERE NEAR EXHAUSTION WHEN DAY DAWNED.
I CAN'T TAKE MUCH MORE OF THIS. I'M GOING OUT AFTER THEM.

BEFORE DAVE COULD STOP HIM, BATES RAN INTO THE JAWS OF SURE DEATH, DETERMINED THAT HE WOULD NOT DIE ALONE.

THE BIG, BURLY HERO WAS CERTAINLY PUTTING ON A STIRRING LAST PERFORMANCE.

BY THE TIME TARUKI NAILED BATES, THERE WERE ONLY THREE NINJAS LEFT.

DIE, WHITE FOOL!

AAGH!

NOW ALL ALONE, DAVE WEIGHED UP HIS RESOURCES.

ONLY ONE AMMO CLIP LEFT, AND THE NINJA'S GEAR. I'VE GOT TO THINK OF SOMETHING...

AN IDEA FORMED IN DAVE'S MIND AS HE LOOKED AT THE TWO-BLADED NINJA KNIFE.

IT'S A SMALL CHANCE, BUT IT MIGHT WORK.

CAREFULLY DAVE PLAITED DRY GRASS AROUND THE METAL RING ON THE OTHER END OF THE ROPE FROM THE KNIFE.

THAT SHOULD JUST ABOUT DO IT.

THE METAL RING WAS THERE SO THAT THE NINJA COULD THROW THE KNIFE BUT HOLD ONTO THE RING AND THEN PULL BACK AND RETRIEVE THE KNIFE.

SETTING FIRE TO THE BUNDLE OF GRASS, DAVE LEAPT OUTSIDE AND HURLED THE KNIFE AS FAR AS HE COULD INTO THE JUNGLE.

JUST A FEW SECONDS IS ALL I NEED.

MORE BY GOOD LUCK THAN GOOD MANAGEMENT, DAVE GOT BACK TO SAFETY.

SO FAR, SO GOOD.

HE TURNED TO LOOK AT HIS HANDIWORK. THE FLYING KNIFE HAD PULLED THE ROPE AND THE BURNING GRASS AFTER IT, IN AMONGST THE DRY GRASS OF THE JUNGLE.

COP THAT LOT, TARUKI!

WITHIN SECONDS THE WHOLE JUNGLE WAS ABLAZE, AND UNDER COVER OF THE SMOKE HE GOT OUT OF THE CAVE.

THE LAST OF DAVE'S AMMO WAS PUT TO GOOD USE WHEN A NINJA LEAPT FROM THE FLAMES.

THAT'S ONE LESS! NOW I'LL HAVE TO RUN FOR IT.

DESPITE THE SMOKE DAVE WAS SPOTTED BY THE ONLY OTHER NINJA, APART FROM TARUKI HIMSELF, WHO WAS LEFT ALIVE.

YOU WILL NOT ESCAPE, WHITE PIG.

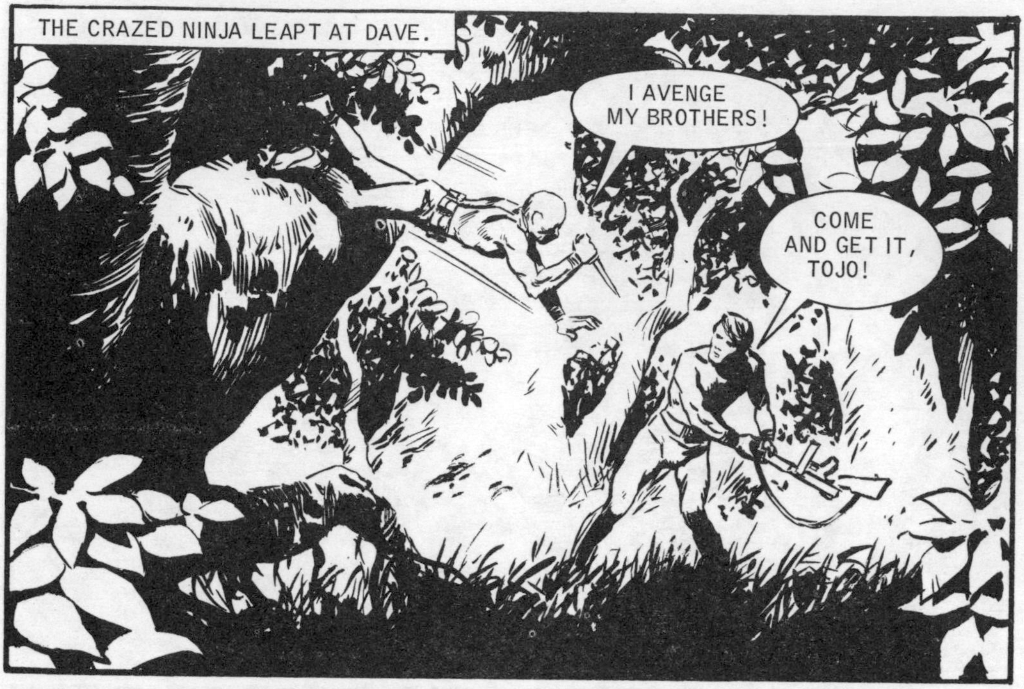
THE CRAZED NINJA LEAPT AT DAVE.
I AVENGE MY BROTHERS!
COME AND GET IT, TOJO!

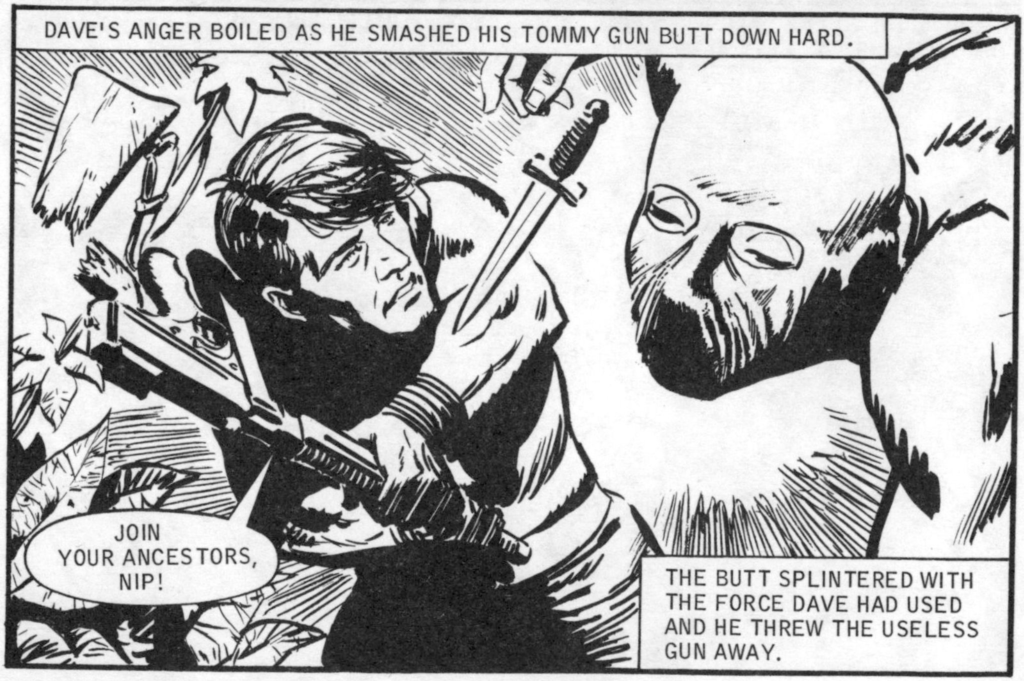
DAVE'S ANGER BOILED AS HE SMASHED HIS TOMMY GUN BUTT DOWN HARD.
JOIN YOUR ANCESTORS, NIP!
THE BUTT SPLINTERED WITH THE FORCE DAVE HAD USED AND HE THREW THE USELESS GUN AWAY.

TARUKI'S EYES GREW COLD AS HE WATCHED DAVE RUN OFF. HE ALONE WAS LEFT OF HIS ASSASSINS.

IT IS BETWEEN US NOW. AND I, TARUKI, WILL TRIUMPH.

DAVE'S HASTE PROVED TO BE HIS DOWNFALL. A TREE ROOT GOT IN HIS WAY...

BLAST!

THE STATE OF DAVE'S ANKLE PUT PAID TO ALL THOUGHTS OF FLIGHT.

I WON'T GET FAR WITH A TWISTED ANKLE. I'M FINISHED IF THE NINJAS CATCH UP WITH ME.

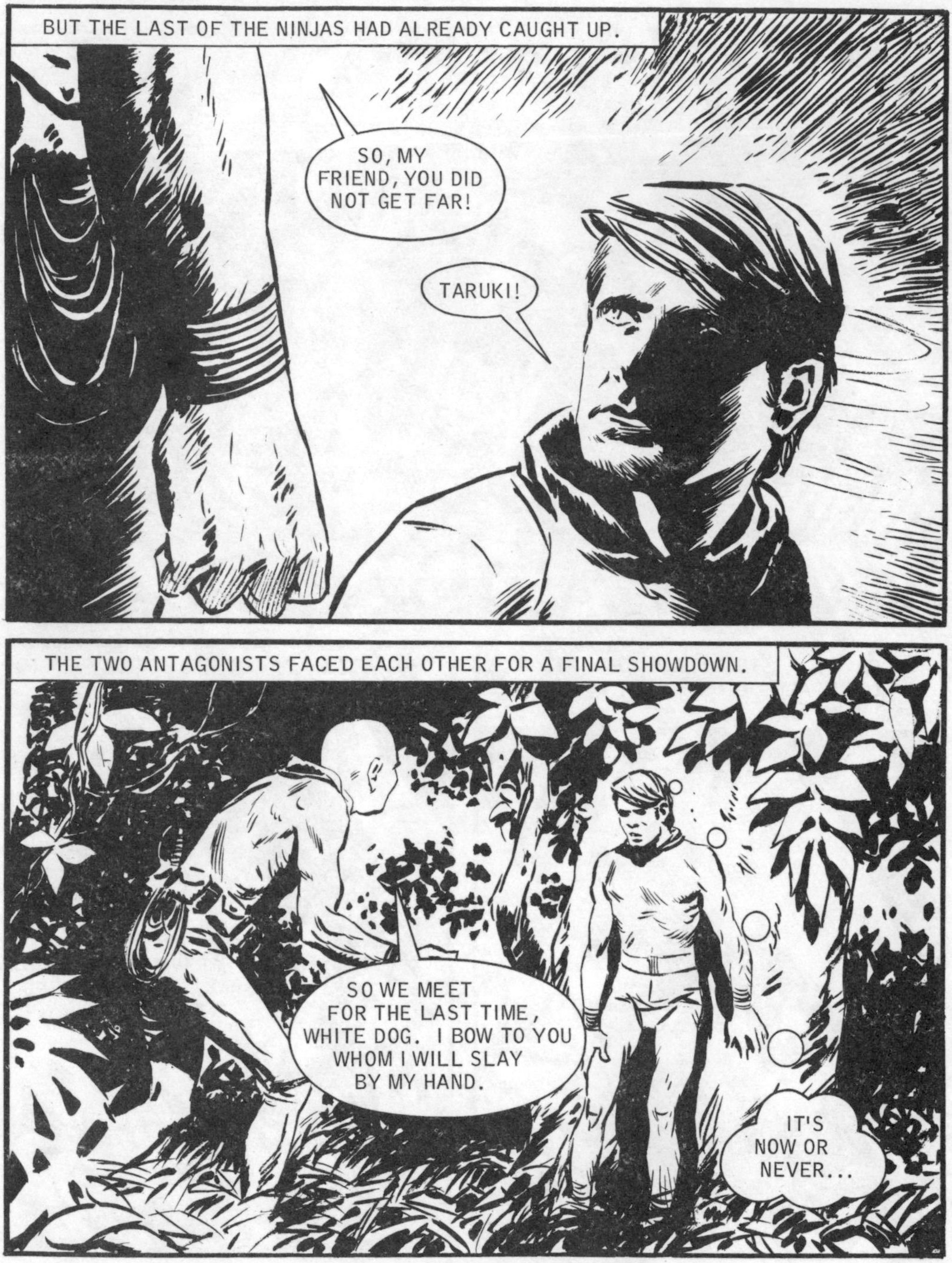
BUT THE LAST OF THE NINJAS HAD ALREADY CAUGHT UP.
SO, MY FRIEND, YOU DID NOT GET FAR!
TARUKI!
THE TWO ANTAGONISTS FACED EACH OTHER FOR A FINAL SHOWDOWN.
SO WE MEET FOR THE LAST TIME, WHITE DOG. I BOW TO YOU WHOM I WILL SLAY BY MY HAND.
IT'S NOW OR NEVER...

DAVE'S INJURED ANKLE SLOWED HIM DOWN ENOUGH FOR TARUKI TO GRAB THE ADVANTAGE.

ARE YOU PREPARED FOR A SLOW AND PAIN-FUL DEATH?

FOR WHAT SEEMED HOURS, TARUKI TAUNTED DAVE, ALWAYS JUST HITTING HIM HARD ENOUGH NOT TO DO GREAT DAMAGE.

HE'S JUST PLAYING WITH ME.

BUT AFTER ANOTHER ATTACK, DAVE LANDED CLOSE TO A SNAKE COILED ROUND A STICK.

I'M NOT FINISHED YET...

DAVE ACTED LIKE LIGHTNING. HE GRABBED THE STICK AND FLICKED IT FORWARD —

THE POISONOUS SNAKE ARCED THROUGH THE AIR TO LAND RIGHT IN THE HOOD OF TARUKI'S NINJA SUIT.

BY MY ANCESTORS!

YOU'RE WELCOME TO IT, MATE!

TARUKI DIED FROM THE BITE OF A KILLER FAR MORE DEADLY AND SILENT THAN ANY NINJA.

ONCE HE'D MADE SURE TARUKI WAS DEAD, DAVE CUT HIMSELF A CRUTCH FROM A TREE AND SET OFF BACK TO HIS BASE. IT WOULD BE A LONG, PAINFUL TREK BUT HE KNEW HE'D MAKE IT.

WELL, THAT'S THE NINJAS DONE FOR. I DOUBT IF THE JAPS WILL TRY THAT TRICK AGAIN. BUT IF THEY DO, WE'LL BE READY!

Commando
THE END

AVRO LANCASTER HEAVY BOMBER

Aircraft of the Second World War — No. 16

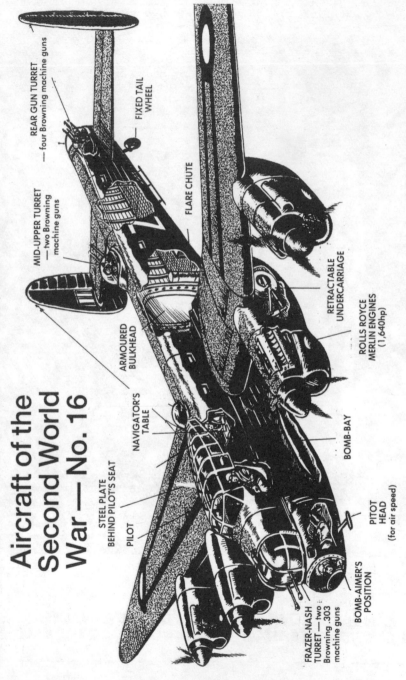

REAR GUN TURRET
— four Browning machine guns

FIXED TAIL WHEEL

MID-UPPER TURRET
— two Browning machine guns

FLARE CHUTE

ARMOURED BULKHEAD

NAVIGATOR'S TABLE

RETRACTABLE UNDERCARRIAGE

ROLLS ROYCE MERLIN ENGINES (1,640hp)

BOMB-BAY

STEEL PLATE BEHIND PILOT'S SEAT

PILOT

PITOT HEAD (for air speed)

BOMB-AIMER'S POSITION

FRAZER-NASH TURRET — two Browning .303 machine guns

DESCRIBED as the finest bomber of the war, the Lanc's main feature was its ability to take ever-increasing bomb loads. Designed originally to carry 4000 lb its pay-load was doubled and then trebled to 12,000 lb! Special modifications later enabled Lancasters to carry the fantastic Grand Slam bomb weighing 22,000 lb! Probably their most famous exploit was the Dam Busters raid, a strike which made these planes and their crews a living legend.

Tiger in the Tail

BRITISH BOMBERS LIKE THE FAIREY BATTLES, HAMPDENS AND LANCASTERS WERE FREQUENT TARGETS FOR MARAUDING ENEMY FIGHTERS, BUT THESE PARTICULAR THREE CARRIED A SECRET WEAPON— REAR-GUNNER CHARLIE STEVENS.

AS HE WAS FIRST IN THE FIRING LINE, CHARLIE WAS DETERMINED TO HAVE THE ODDS ON HIS SIDE. AFTER ALL, HE WAS GAMBLING WITH HIS LIFE.

First published 1972

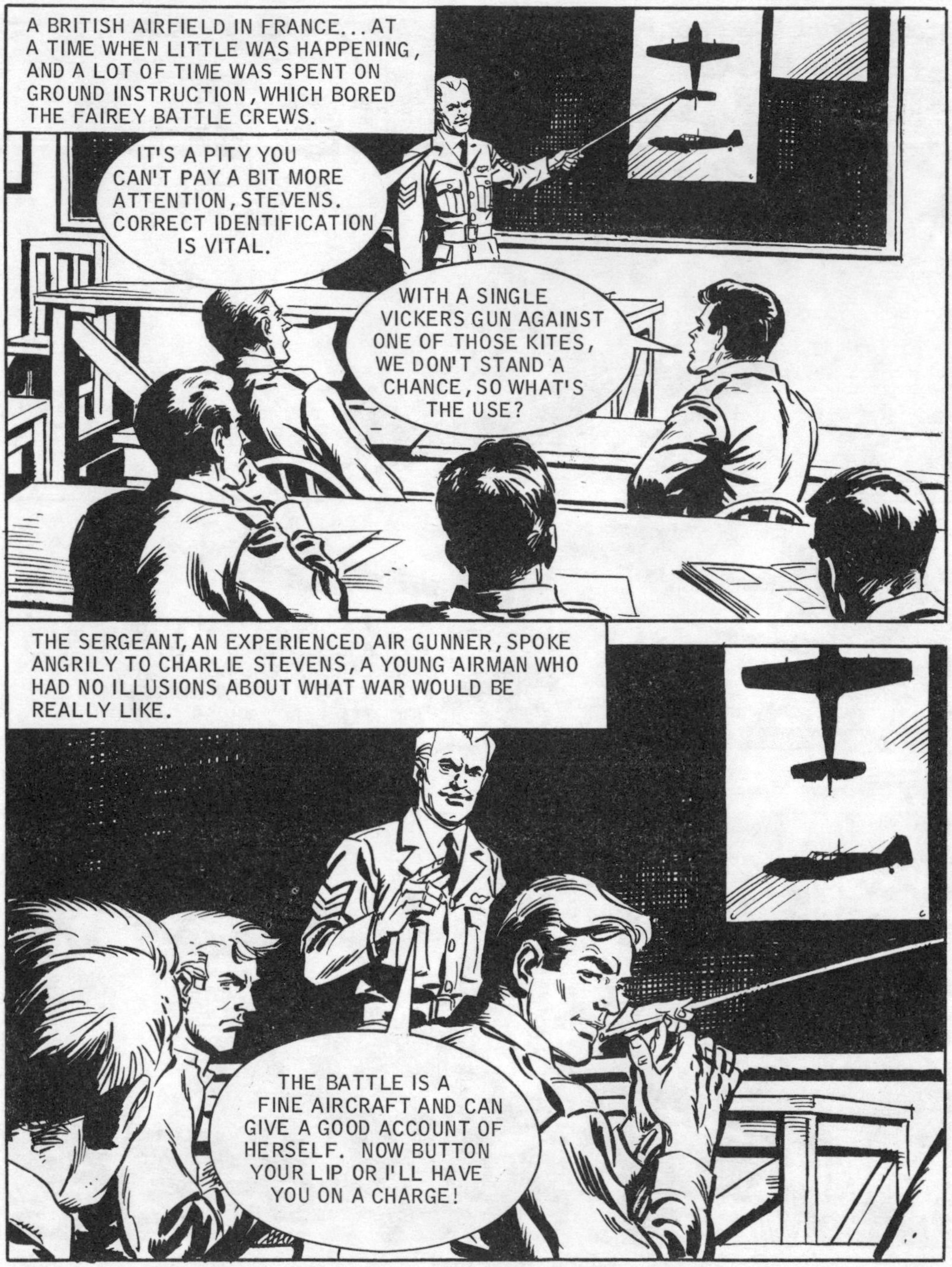
A BRITISH AIRFIELD IN FRANCE... AT A TIME WHEN LITTLE WAS HAPPENING, AND A LOT OF TIME WAS SPENT ON GROUND INSTRUCTION, WHICH BORED THE FAIREY BATTLE CREWS.
IT'S A PITY YOU CAN'T PAY A BIT MORE ATTENTION, STEVENS. CORRECT IDENTIFICATION IS VITAL.
WITH A SINGLE VICKERS GUN AGAINST ONE OF THOSE KITES, WE DON'T STAND A CHANCE, SO WHAT'S THE USE?
THE SERGEANT, AN EXPERIENCED AIR GUNNER, SPOKE ANGRILY TO CHARLIE STEVENS, A YOUNG AIRMAN WHO HAD NO ILLUSIONS ABOUT WHAT WAR WOULD BE REALLY LIKE.
THE BATTLE IS A FINE AIRCRAFT AND CAN GIVE A GOOD ACCOUNT OF HERSELF. NOW BUTTON YOUR LIP OR I'LL HAVE YOU ON A CHARGE!

BUT AT FIRST LIGHT ON THE 10TH MAY, 1940 THE GERMAN BLITZKRIEG BEGAN. GERMAN TANKS AND DIVE BOMBERS RUTHLESSLY BLASTED THEIR WAY THROUGH DUTCH AND BELGIAN NEUTRALITY TOWARDS THE BRITISH AND FRENCH ARMIES.

FORWARD — NO STOPPING UNTIL WE REACH THE SEA!

THE BATTLES WENT INTO ACTION IMMEDIATELY, THEIR CREWS ANXIOUS TO GET TO GRIPS WITH THE ENEMY.

ALL THESE ENEMY COLUMNS ARE CONVERGING ON THIS BRIDGE. OUR JOB'S TO DESTROY IT, AND LEAVE THE COLUMNS FOR LOW-FLYING HURRICANES TO ATTACK.

THEY WERE STILL TEN MILES FROM THEIR OBJECTIVE WHEN SEVEN MESSERSCHMITT FIGHTERS RACED IN TO THE ATTACK. CHARLIE, FLYING AS GUNNER FOR A PILOT CALLED BRABHAM, SPOTTED THEM FIRST.

BANDITS RIGHT BEHIND US, SKIPPER — COMING FAST!

OK, GUNNER. WE HOLD FORMATION AND CATCH 'EM IN OUR CROSSFIRE.

SINGLY, THE BATTLES WERE SITTING DUCKS, BUT IN FORMATION THEY COULD PRODUCE A DEVASTATING CURTAIN OF DEFENSIVE FIRE.

THAT SHOOK 'EM. WE'RE NOT AS USELESS AS I THOUGHT!

THE GERMANS WERE LEARNING A FEW LESSONS IN TACTICS THE HARD WAY.

KEEP OUT OF RANGE OF THOSE GUNNERS. STAND OFF AND USE YOUR CANNONS — SCHNELL!

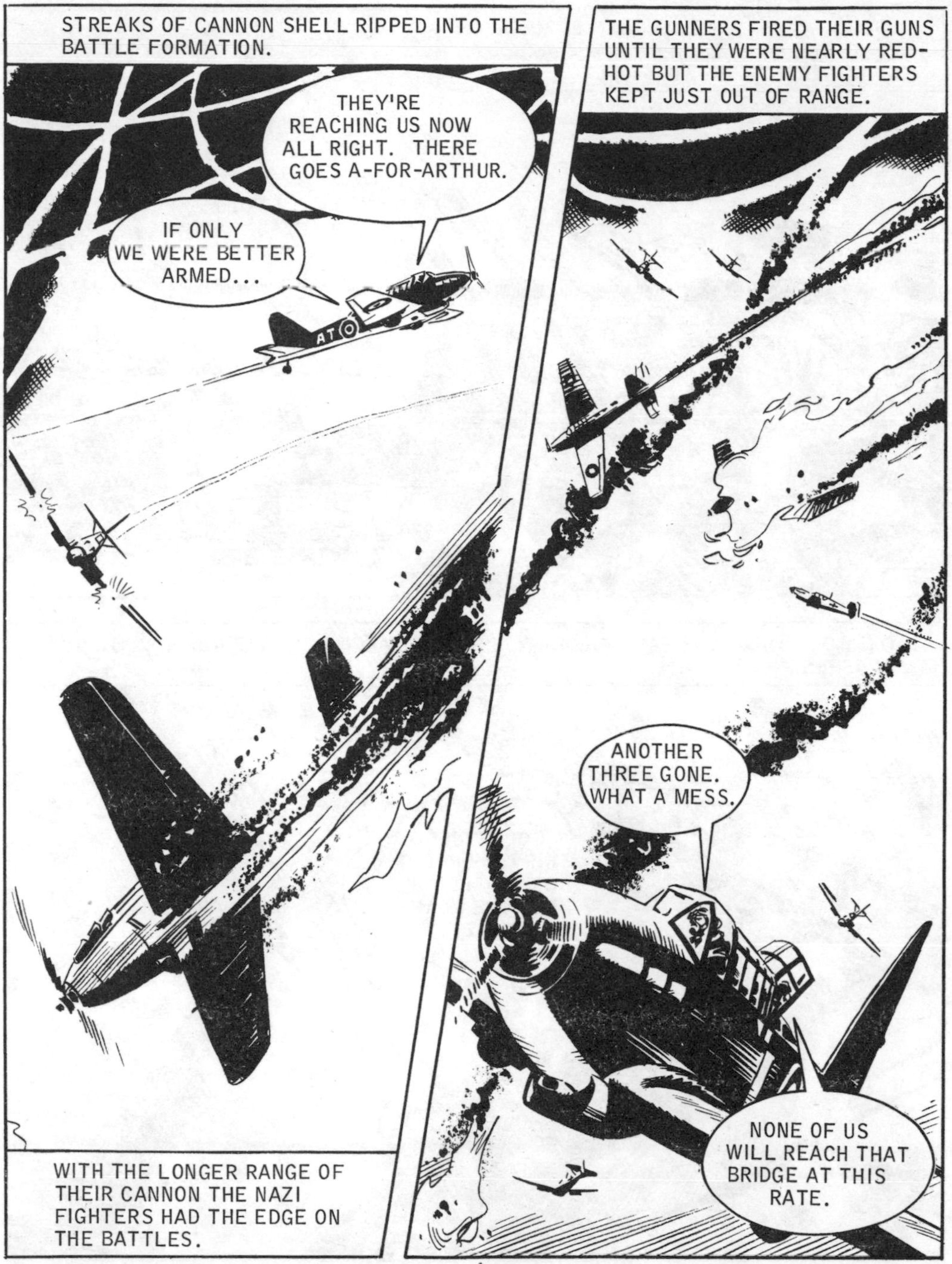
STREAKS OF CANNON SHELL RIPPED INTO THE BATTLE FORMATION.
THEY'RE REACHING US NOW ALL RIGHT. THERE GOES A-FOR-ARTHUR.
IF ONLY WE WERE BETTER ARMED...
AT
WITH THE LONGER RANGE OF THEIR CANNON THE NAZI FIGHTERS HAD THE EDGE ON THE BATTLES.
THE GUNNERS FIRED THEIR GUNS UNTIL THEY WERE NEARLY RED-HOT BUT THE ENEMY FIGHTERS KEPT JUST OUT OF RANGE.
ANOTHER THREE GONE. WHAT A MESS.
NONE OF US WILL REACH THAT BRIDGE AT THIS RATE.

SUDDENLY THE MESSERSCHMITTS SHEERED OFF AS THE BATTLES FLEW INTO RANGE OF ANTI-AIRCRAFT GUNS.

TARGET AHEAD. ATTACK AT WILL.

FEUER!

ONLY ONE THING WAS EASY...LOCATION OF THE TARGET. IT WAS RINGED WITH GUN FLASHES.

GOOD GRIEF, THIS IS MURDER! I CAN HARDLY SEE FOR THE FLAK SMOKE...

IT WAS LIKE AN EXECUTION.

COME ON, KEEP MOVING. SCHNELL! SCHNELL!

DON'T PANIC, KAMERAD. THOSE POOR DEVILS UP THERE WILL NEVER MAKE IT. YOUR PRECIOUS BRIDGE IS QUITE SAFE.

A SALVO OF CANNON SHELLS TORE INTO L-FOR-LEATHER, SMASHING THE ENGINE RADIATOR.

BAIL OUT, CHARLIE! WE'RE HIT BAD.

WE'RE STILL FLYING. I'LL STAY WITH YOU.

I SAID GET OUT — NOW! THAT ENGINE WILL SEIZE UP AT ANY MOMENT. THAT'S AN ORDER!

CHARLIE COULD DO NOTHING MORE THAN OBEY.

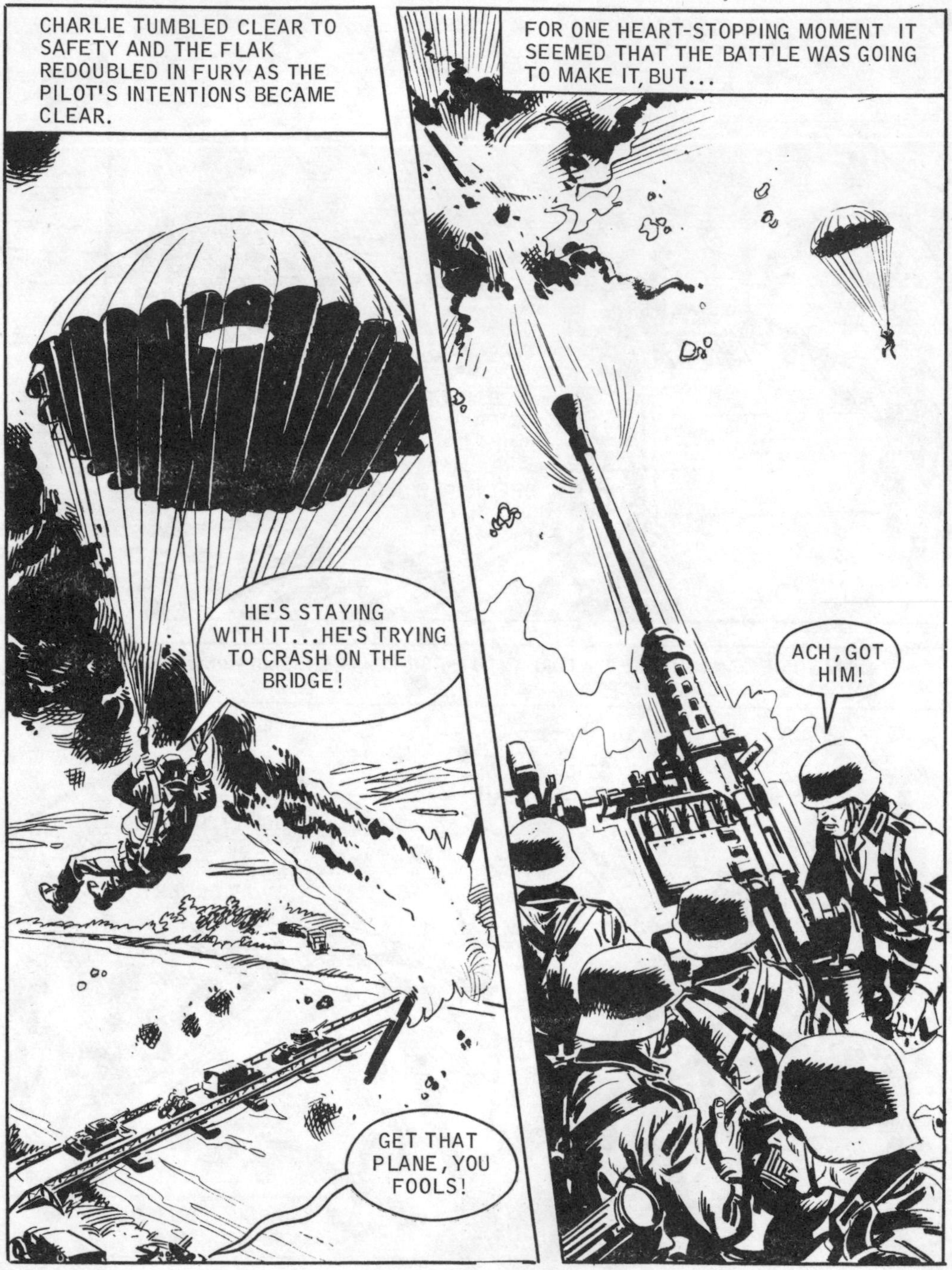
CHARLIE TUMBLED CLEAR TO SAFETY AND THE FLAK REDOUBLED IN FURY AS THE PILOT'S INTENTIONS BECAME CLEAR.
HE'S STAYING WITH IT...HE'S TRYING TO CRASH ON THE BRIDGE!
GET THAT PLANE, YOU FOOLS!
FOR ONE HEART-STOPPING MOMENT IT SEEMED THAT THE BATTLE WAS GOING TO MAKE IT, BUT...
ACH, GOT HIM!

FIERCE RAGE WELLED UP INSIDE CHARLIE WHEN HE LANDED AND SAW THAT NO BATTLES HAD SURVIVED THE MURDEROUS BARRAGE. HE GRABBED FOR HIS REVOLVER AS NAZIS CLOSED IN ON HIM.

ALL HE COULD THINK OF WAS REVENGE, BUT SUDDENLY HIS GUN ARM DROPPED LIFELESSLY TO HIS SIDE. IT WOULD ACHIEVE NOTHING TO DIE USELESSLY.

HE WAS ROUGHLY URGED TOWARDS A LARGE AIRCRAFT TRANSPORTER PARKED AT THE ROADSIDE.

YOU WILL GO BACK TO GERMANY WITH US, AS THE GUEST OF THE LUFTWAFFE.

WELL, TELL THIS GORILLA TO GET HIS POP-GUN OUT OF MY BACK. I'M NOT GOING TO PINCH YOUR BLASTED PLANE.

THE SERGEANT COULD SPEAK QUITE PASSABLE ENGLISH WHICH SEEMED TO INFURIATE CHARLIE EVEN MORE.

YOU WILL TRY NO FUNNY BUSINESS. HANS HERE WOULD LIKE YOU TO MAKE EXCUSE FOR HIM TO SHOOT. MEANWHILE WE WAIT UNTIL THOSE TRUCKS PASS. JA?

THE SERGEANT WAS COCKY, CONFIDENT THAT HIS AIR FORCE WAS SUPERIOR TO THE R.A.F.

YOU FOOLS, TO IMAGINE YOU COULD STOP US WITH SUCH ANTIQUATED PLANES.

SOME DAY YOU'LL GET ALL THIS BACK WITH INTEREST!

HAH! OUR MESSERSCHMITTS WILL MASSACRE YOUR AIR FORCE!

HUH, WE'LL SEE.

WHEN THE CONVOY WAS ABLE TO PROCEED AGAIN, CHARLIE WAS PUT IN THE TRAILER UNDER THE WATCHFUL EYE OF THE TRIGGER-HAPPY HANS. BUT —

ACHTUNG! HURRICANES ATTACKING.

EVERYBODY IN THE DITCH — SCHNELL!

IN THE ENSUING SCRAMBLE, CHARLIE SAW HIS CHANCE. HE LEAPT THE DITCH AND GOT CLEAN AWAY ACROSS THE FIELDS. HE DIDN'T STOP TO LOOK BACK AT THE CHAOS BEHIND HIM.

I'LL HEAD BACK FOR OUR LINES.

IT WAS A WEEK LATER BEFORE HE MANAGED TO REACH A FRENCH AIRFIELD OCCUPIED BY A HURRICANE SQUADRON.

AS YOU SEE, WE DON'T NEED ANY AIR GUNNERS HERE, BUT WE NEED EVERYBODY WE CAN GET OUR HANDS ON FOR GROUND DUTIES. YOU CAN MUCK IN WITH THE ARMOURERS.

YES, SIR.

THERE WAS A TENSENESS IN THE AIR. THE THUNDER OF GUNS COULD BE HEARD NOT VERY FAR AWAY.

THE FOLLOWING DAWN AN URGENT MESSAGE WAS RECEIVED. ENEMY TANKS WERE ATTEMPTING TO ENCIRCLE THE AREA.

AS THE LAST HURRICANE LEFT, BLACK SMOKE POURED ACROSS THE AIRFIELD AS ALL EQUIPMENT WAS DESTROYED.

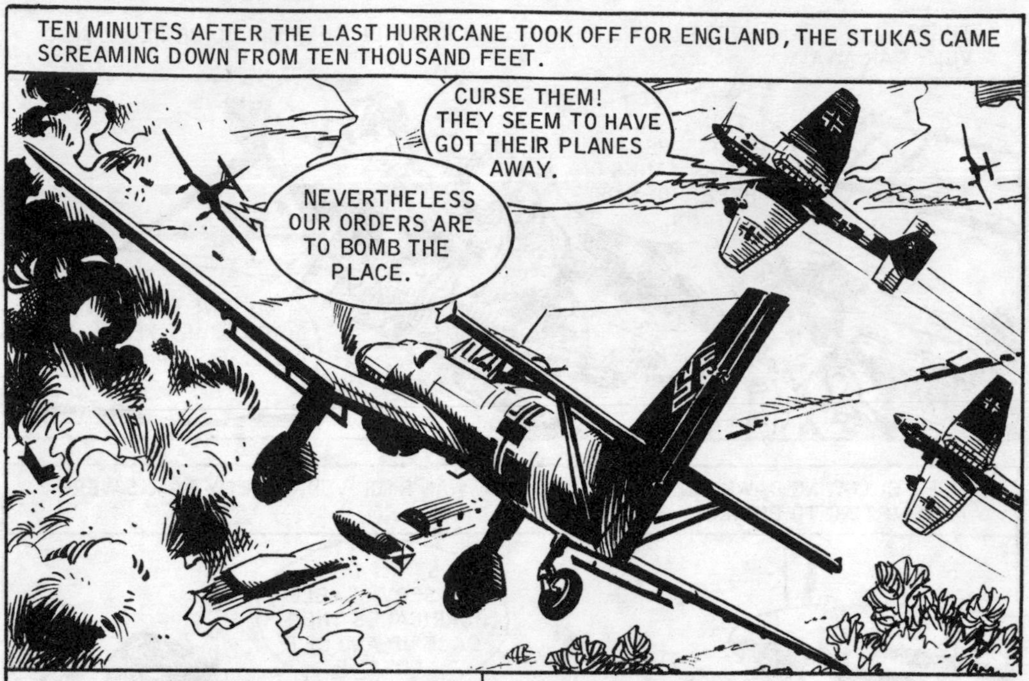
TEN MINUTES AFTER THE LAST HURRICANE TOOK OFF FOR ENGLAND, THE STUKAS CAME SCREAMING DOWN FROM TEN THOUSAND FEET.
CURSE THEM! THEY SEEM TO HAVE GOT THEIR PLANES AWAY.
NEVERTHELESS OUR ORDERS ARE TO BOMB THE PLACE.

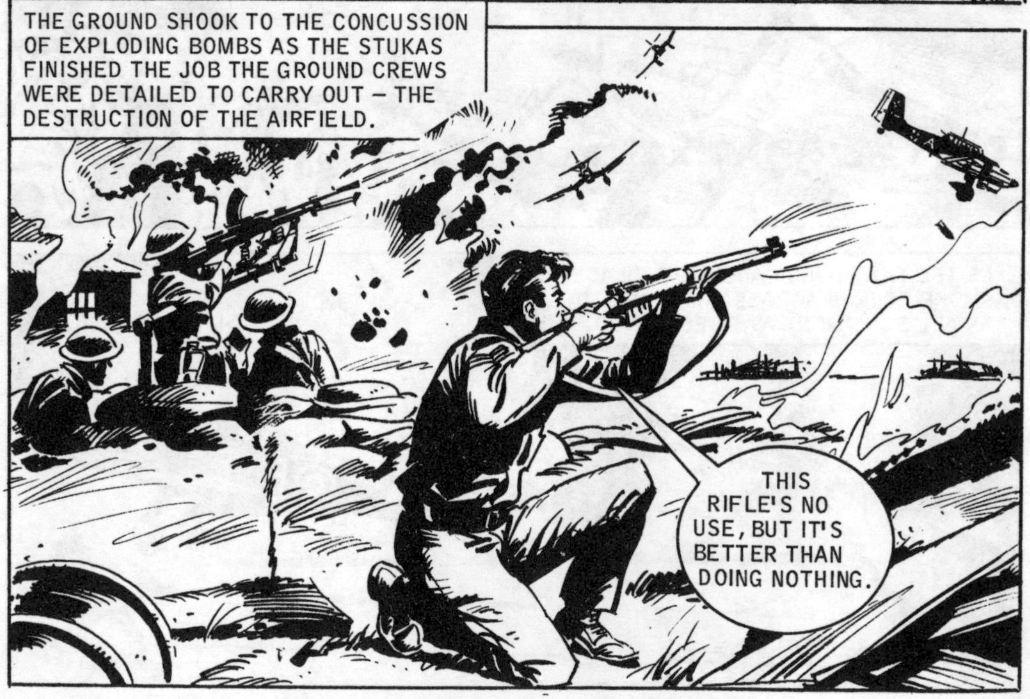
THE GROUND SHOOK TO THE CONCUSSION OF EXPLODING BOMBS AS THE STUKAS FINISHED THE JOB THE GROUND CREWS WERE DETAILED TO CARRY OUT – THE DESTRUCTION OF THE AIRFIELD.
THIS RIFLE'S NO USE, BUT IT'S BETTER THAN DOING NOTHING.

THE SWIFT GERMAN ADVANCE HAD PUT THE ALLIED ARMIES IN MORTAL DANGER. THE DECISION WAS MADE TO EVACUATE.

COME ON, SERGEANT, GET ABOARD. IT'S NO USE HANGING AROUND HERE ANY LONGER. WE'RE TO HEAD FOR DUNKIRK AS FAST AS WE CAN.

THEY RACED THROUGH THE BATTLE-TORN COUNTRYSIDE AND ON TO THE BLOOD-STAINED BEACHES AT DUNKIRK.

COME ON, THIS WAY FOR THE SKYLARK! WITH A BIT OF LUCK WE MIGHT GET AWAY TOMORROW.

YEAH, IF THESE STUKAS DON'T GET US FIRST.

THEY WERE AMONG THE LAST TO GET AWAY. IT WAS AN EXPERIENCE CHARLIE AND THOUSANDS OF OTHERS WOULD REMEMBER FOR THE REST OF THEIR LIVES.

SO THAT'S THE END OF IT. WHAT A CARVE-UP!

DON'T FEEL TOO BAD, MATE. WE'LL BE BACK... SOME DAY.

BY THE TIME THE GREAT AIR BATTLES OVER THE SOUTH OF ENGLAND BEGAN, CHARLIE HAD BEEN POSTED TO A BOMBING AND GUNNERY SCHOOL IN SCOTLAND.

WELL, SARGE, WE'RE WELL AWAY FROM IT ALL HERE.

I SUPPOSE THAT'S HOW IT SHOULD BE IF MEN HAVE GOT TO BE TRAINED, BUT I'D RATHER BE ON A SQUADRON.

AS A FLIGHT SERGEANT GUNNERY INSTRUCTOR, CHARLIE'S JOB WAS TO TRAIN THE GUNNER RECRUITS IN THE USE AND MAINTENANCE OF MACHINE GUNS.

YOU WILL NOTE THAT THE OBJECT IS TO SHOOT AT THE DROGUE TARGET, NOT THE PLANE TOWING IT. THE CREW WOULDN'T LIKE IT.

WITH THE DAILY REPORTS OF THE BATTLE OF BRITAIN COMING IN, CHARLIE AT TIMES FOUND THE ROUTINE AND THE REMARKS IRKSOME.

THIS IS THE VICKERS 'K' GUN...GAS OPERATED. WE USED THESE IN THE BATTLE OF FRANCE.

PRETTY LOUSY SHOW THOSE BATTLES PUT UP, DIDN'T THEY? LET'S HOPE WE'LL BE TRAINED TO SHOOT BETTER THAN THEIR GUNNERS.

THE INTERRUPTER'S MOCKING GRIN RUBBED CHARLIE ON A RAW SPOT. HE IMMEDIATELY ROSE IN DEFENCE OF HIS FELLOW GUNNERS.

WE DID OUR BEST WITH WHAT WE HAD. NO MAN CAN DO BETTER THAN THAT. IF WE'D HAD HEAVIER GUNS...

AH, COME OFF IT, SARGE. IT'S A POOR GUNNER THAT BLAMES HIS GUNS.

SHUT UP, BENNET, YOU FOOL.

CHARLIE'S ANGER SWELLED AND SUDDENLY ALL RESTRAINT WAS GONE.

LISTEN, YOU. WHEN YOU'VE FACED UP TO EXPLOSIVE CANNON SHELLS WITH ONLY ONE OF THESE GLORIFIED RIFLES TO DEFEND YOURSELF WITH, YOU'LL GRIN ON THE OTHER SIDE OF YOUR FAT FACE.

AT THAT MOMENT FLIGHT LIEUTENANT RICHARDS, THE CHIEF GUNNERY INSTRUCTOR, WALKED IN.

WHAT'S THE MEANING OF THIS, STEVENS? LEAVE THAT MAN ALONE!

RICHARDS TOOK CHARLIE OUTSIDE...

WE ALL KNOW YOU CHAPS HAD A ROUGH TIME, BUT THERE'S NO NEED TO BRAWL WITH THE PUPILS.

I'M SORRY, SIR. IT WON'T HAPPEN AGAIN.

THOROUGHLY FED UP, CHARLIE WENT OVER TO THE GUN MUSEUM. THERE WAS A NEW EXHIBIT — A U.S. AIR FORCE HALF-INCH BROWNING MACHINE GUN.

BY THUNDER, THAT'S THE ANSWER! WITH THESE IN THE BOMBERS' TURRETS, THE CREWS WOULD REALLY BE ABLE TO HIT BACK.

BROWNING 50

THAT NIGHT RICHARDS WAS ON HIS EVENING ROUNDS WHEN –

HELLO, THERE'S A LIGHT IN THE TURRET SHED. SOMEBODY'S BREAKING THE BLACK-OUT. THIS NEEDS INVESTIGATION.

RICHARD ENTERED THE SHED WHERE VARIOUS TYPES OF TURRETS WERE KEPT. HE WAS PUZZLED TO SEE CHARLIE STRUGGLING WITH A HEAVY MACHINE GUN.

WHAT THE DEVIL ARE YOU UP TO?

IT'S THIS HALF-INCH BROWNING FROM THE MUSEUM, SIR. I WONDERED IF IT COULD BE FITTED INTO ONE OF THESE BLENHEIM TURRETS.

CHARLIE EXPLAINED THAT IF THESE GUNS COULD BE FITTED INTO THE EXISTING TURRETS, MANY MORE PLANES WOULD GET HOME AFTER A RAID.

BELIEVE ME, SIR, YOU FEEL REALLY HELPLESS WHEN A JERRY LETS RIP WITH HIS CANNONS AND YOU JUST CAN'T GET NEAR IT WITH YOUR OWN GUNS.

RICHARDS REALISED THAT CHARLIE HAD THE EXPERIENCE TO KNOW WHAT HE WAS TALKING ABOUT.

I MUST SAY I'M IMPRESSED, BUT DON'T FORGET THE OFFICIAL POINT OF VIEW. IT STATES THAT OUR THREE-OH-THREE GUNS ARE SUFFICIENT. I ADVISE YOU TO FORGET THE WHOLE THING.

IT SEEMED THAT THE LESSONS WOULD HAVE TO BE LEARNED THE HARD WAY.

BUT THAT'S CRAZY. SOME DAY THE PEOPLE WHO MAKE THE DECISIONS WILL SEE I'M RIGHT.

BUT UNTIL THAT DAY COMES, THERE IS NOTHING MUCH YOU CAN DO ABOUT IT, SO COME ON — OUT OF HERE!

AFTER ALMOST A YEAR AS AN INSTRUCTOR, CHARLIE WAS POSTED TO A BOMBER SQUADRON, FLYING HAMPDENS. HE WAS MET BY THE OTHER TWO FLIGHT SERGEANTS IN THE CREW — BAINES AND NEAVE.

WELL, THIS IS OUR KITE. IF YOU'VE NEVER BEEN ON A HAMPDEN BEFORE, THEY CALL 'EM "FLYING TADPOLES". OUR MAIN JOB AT PRESENT IS MINE-LAYING.

BAINES WAS THE RADIO OPERATOR AND NEAVE WAS NAVIGATOR/BOMB AIMER.

THAT EVENING CHARLIE MET HIS SKIPPER — FLYING OFFICER NED RAMSAY.

THIS IS FLIGHT SERGEANT STEVENS. JUST ARRIVED FROM A BOMBING AND GUNNERY SCHOOL.

FOR CRYING OUT LOUD, ANOTHER ROOKIE! I'M GOING TO HAVE A GOOD MOAN ABOUT THIS.

JUST A MINUTE. I WAS AN INSTRUCTOR AT GUNNERY SCHOOL. I HAVE HAD SOME EXPERIENCE.

IRRITABLY RAMSAY TURNED ON HIS RADIO OPERATOR.

YOU'RE A ROOKIE UNTIL YOU PROVE YOURSELF OTHERWISE.

AW, GO EASY. CHARLIE HERE WAS IN THE BATTLE OF FRANCE.

KEEP OUT OF IT, BAINES. IF I SAY HE'S A ROOKIE, HE'S A ROOKIE.

BAINES TRIED TO APOLOGISE FOR HIS PILOT'S PEEVISH OUTBURST.

SORRY ABOUT THAT. RAMSAY'S NOT MUCH COP AS A PILOT, BUT WE'RE STUCK WITH HIM. HE'S OK IF YOU KEEP YOUR NOSE CLEAN.

IF HE TALKS TO ME LIKE THAT AGAIN, I WON'T BE KEEPING MY NOSE CLEAN.

SO CHARLIE JOINED A WORLD WHERE THE HAMPDENS WENT OUT NIGHT AFTER NIGHT IN ALL WEATHERS, DROPPING THEIR DEADLY CARGOES IN THE PORTS AND ESTUARIES OF OCCUPIED EUROPE.

ANOTHER ONE GONE.

ONE DARK NIGHT CHARLIE'S PLANE WAS DETAILED ALONG WITH FOUR OTHER HAMPDENS, TO LAY MAGNETIC MINES IN A GERMAN ESTUARY.

I WOULDN'T FANCY THEIR JOB ON A DIRTY NIGHT LIKE TONIGHT.

THEY'LL HAVE TO WORRY ABOUT THE FLAK MORE THAN THE WEATHER, FROM WHAT I HEAR.

IT WAS GOING TO BE A TOUGH OPERATION AND RAMSAY WAS IN A FOUL TEMPER.

COURSE IS ZERO-THREE-SEVEN DEGREES, SKIPPER. REMEMBER TO ALTER COURSE TO ZERO-FIVE-ONE DEGREES AT THE ESTUARY ENTRANCE AND KEEP CLOSE TO THE NORTH SHORE.

ALL RIGHT, ALL RIGHT. I WAS AT THE BRIEFING TOO, YOU KNOW.

THE FIVE HAMPDENS REACHED THE RIVER MOUTH WITHOUT INCIDENT, THEN EACH WENT ITS OWN WAY TOWARDS ITS DROPPING POINT.

NAVIGATOR HERE. YOU'RE TOO FAR SOUTH, SKIPPER. THERE'S A FLAK-SHIP MOORED ON THIS SIDE. WE'LL GET CLOBBERED.

YOU'RE THE ONE THAT'S WRONG. I'VE BEEN HERE BEFORE AND I KNOW MY WAY IN. NOW SHUT UP!

CHARLIE STEVENS, LISTENING TO THE ROW WITH GROWING ANGER, KNEW THAT RAMSAY COULD NEVER INSPIRE RESPECT NOR CONFIDENCE.

AS A NAVIGATOR, YOU'RE A DEAD LOSS.

ALL RIGHT, BUT JUST WATCH FOR THAT FLAK-SHIP. DON'T SAY I DIDN'T WARN YOU.

THE GERMAN COMMANDER WAITED PATIENTLY. THEN, WHEN THE HAMPDEN WAS OVERHEAD...

THE VICKERS GUNS IN THE TOP AND BOTTOM FIRING POSITIONS BLAZED OUT AS THE HAMPDEN BANKED AWAY SHARPLY.

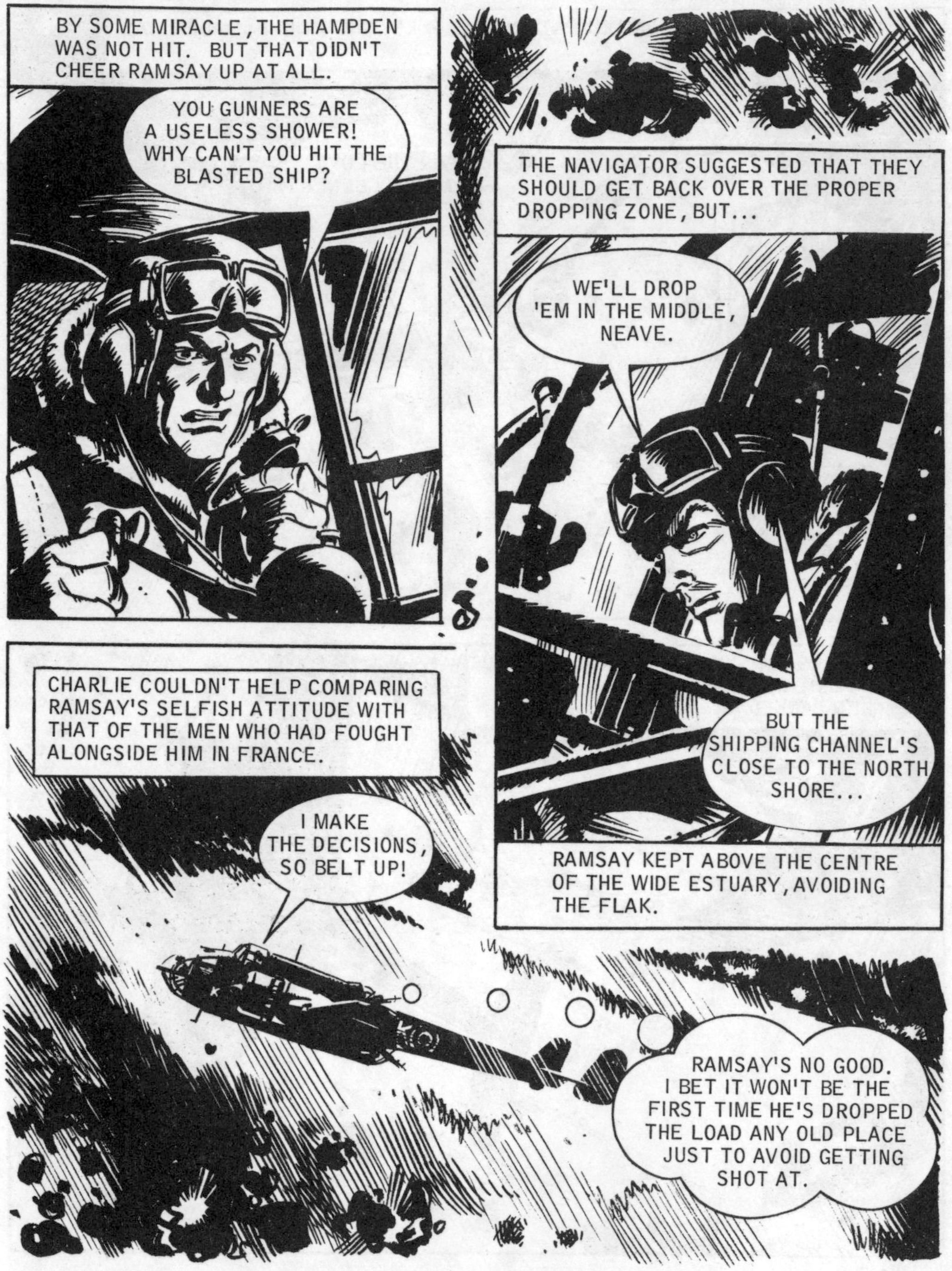
BY SOME MIRACLE, THE HAMPDEN WAS NOT HIT. BUT THAT DIDN'T CHEER RAMSAY UP AT ALL.
YOU GUNNERS ARE A USELESS SHOWER! WHY CAN'T YOU HIT THE BLASTED SHIP?
THE NAVIGATOR SUGGESTED THAT THEY SHOULD GET BACK OVER THE PROPER DROPPING ZONE, BUT...
WE'LL DROP 'EM IN THE MIDDLE, NEAVE.
BUT THE SHIPPING CHANNEL'S CLOSE TO THE NORTH SHORE...
RAMSAY KEPT ABOVE THE CENTRE OF THE WIDE ESTUARY, AVOIDING THE FLAK.
CHARLIE COULDN'T HELP COMPARING RAMSAY'S SELFISH ATTITUDE WITH THAT OF THE MEN WHO HAD FOUGHT ALONGSIDE HIM IN FRANCE.
I MAKE THE DECISIONS, SO BELT UP!
RAMSAY'S NO GOOD. I BET IT WON'T BE THE FIRST TIME HE'S DROPPED THE LOAD ANY OLD PLACE JUST TO AVOID GETTING SHOT AT.

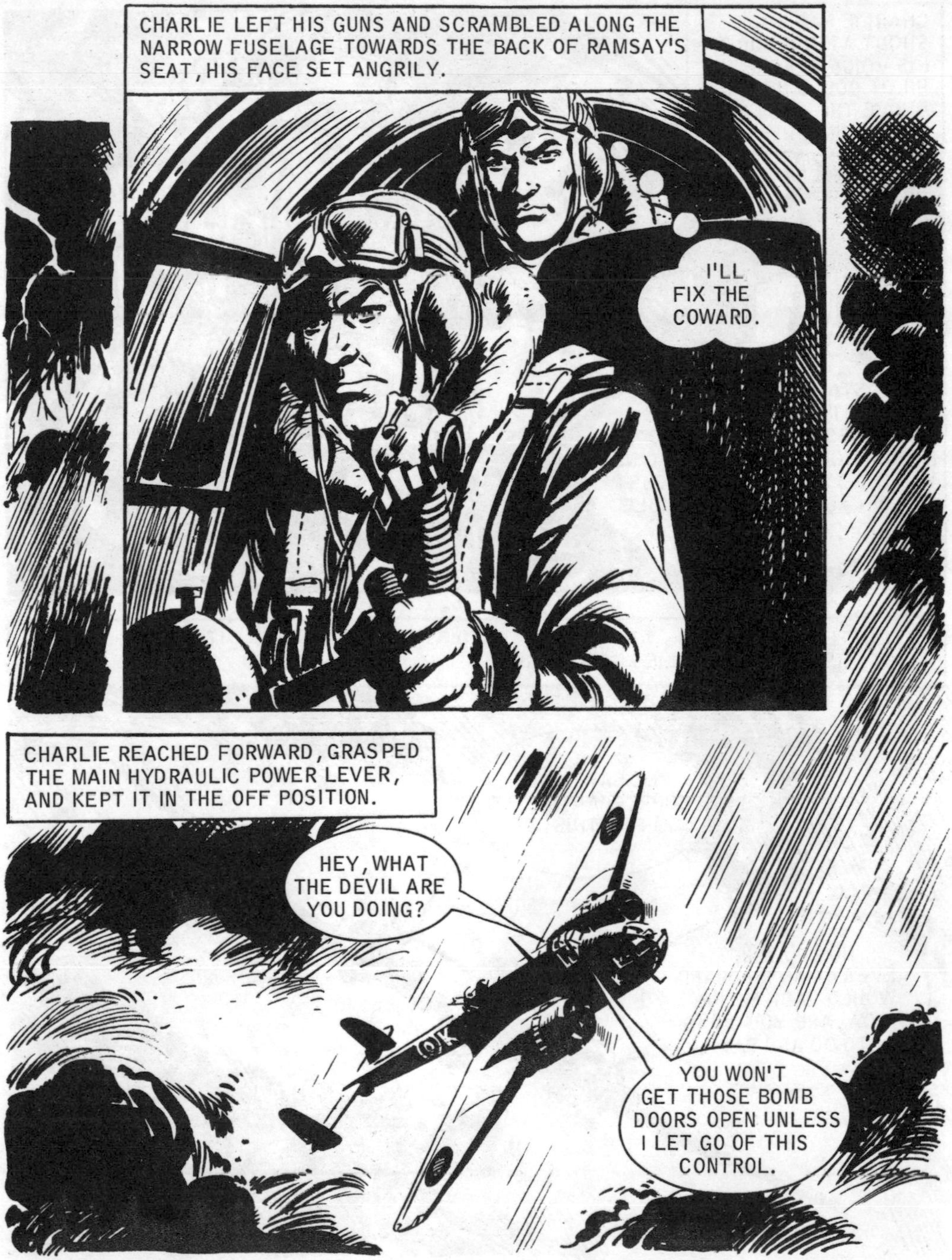
CHARLIE LEFT HIS GUNS AND SCRAMBLED ALONG THE NARROW FUSELAGE TOWARDS THE BACK OF RAMSAY'S SEAT, HIS FACE SET ANGRILY.
I'LL FIX THE COWARD.
CHARLIE REACHED FORWARD, GRASPED THE MAIN HYDRAULIC POWER LEVER, AND KEPT IT IN THE OFF POSITION.
HEY, WHAT THE DEVIL ARE YOU DOING?
YOU WON'T GET THOSE BOMB DOORS OPEN UNLESS I LET GO OF THIS CONTROL.

CHARLIE HAD TO SHOUT AT THE TOP OF HIS VOICE BEFORE THE PILOT COULD HEAR ABOVE THE ROAR OF THE ENGINES.

MY HAND STAYS WHERE IT IS UNTIL YOU DROP THESE MINES IN THEIR CORRECT POSITION. YOU'RE NOT GOING TO JETTISON OUR LOAD JUST BECAUSE YOU'RE TOO IDLE TO DO THE JOB PROPERLY.

SPLUTTERING WITH RAGE, RAMSAY BATTERED AT CHARLIE'S HAND WITH HIS CLENCHED FIST, BUT GRIMLY CHARLIE KEPT HIS GRIP.

I'LL HAVE YOU COURT-MARTIALLED FOR THIS!

NO YOU WON'T. EVERY MAN ON BOARD WOULD BACK ME UP. NOW, ARE YOU GOING TO DO AS I SAY?

RAMSAY SLAMMED THE BOMBER INTO A VICIOUS, TIGHT TURN, HOPING TO KNOCK CHARLIE OFF BALANCE, BUT CHARLIE HELD ON TIGHTLY.

HEY, TAKE IT EASY. WHAT'S GOING ON BACK THERE?

MORE BY MISTAKE THAN INTENTION, THE HAMPDEN FLEW OVER THE MAIN SHIPPING CHANNEL. CHARLIE LET GO THE POWER CONTROL AND THE BOMB DOORS WERE OPENED.

MINES GONE... BANG ON TARGET!

THE NAVIGATOR HAD PRESSED THE RELEASE BUTTON AND TWO MORE LOADS OF DEATH AND DESTRUCTION WENT UNSEEN INTO THE RIVER.

WHEN THEY GOT BACK, RAMSAY SAID NOTHING OF CHARLIE'S ACTION.

GOOD SHOW, RAMSAY. ALL AIRCRAFT RETURNED SAFELY AND CREWS REPORT GOOD RESULTS. A GOOD NIGHT'S WORK.

LATER, IN THE CREW ROOM...

DON'T THINK I'LL FORGET...

AH, BELT UP. SOMEBODY HAD TO PULL YOU UP.

SHORTLY AFTERWARDS THE SQUADRON WAS ONE OF THE FIRST TO BE RE-EQUIPPED WITH THE NEW BOMBER, THE LANCASTER.

BOMBS AWAY!

RAMSAY HAD BEEN GIVEN THREE SERGEANTS — CONWAY, REID AND BLAKE — TO MAKE UP HIS CREW TO SEVEN.

AFTER A FEW OPERATIONS, CAPTAINS OF AIRCRAFT WERE ASKED TO GIVE THEIR OPINIONS OF THE NEW BOMBERS.

I'M PUTTING IN A FAVOURABLE REPORT ON OUR LANCASTER. ANYBODY GOT ANYTHING TO ADD?

I'M NOT HAPPY ABOUT THAT REAR TURRET.

CHARLIE WAS THE ONLY MAN WITH A COMPLAINT. ALL THE OTHERS AGREED THAT IT WAS A GREAT PLANE.

CHARLIE STUCK OUT HIS CHIN GRIMLY. HE TOO THOUGHT THE LANC WAS A WINNER, BUT FOR THIS ONE WEAKNESS.

I MIGHT HAVE KNOWN YOU'D FIND SOMETHING WRONG. WHAT'S YOUR BEEF?

FOUR RIFLE-CALIBRE MACHINE GUNS IN THE TAIL ARE NO GOOD, EVEN WITH THE POWER TURRET.

RAMSAY WAS STILL NURSING HIS RESENTMENT AGAINST HIS TAIL GUNNER AND REPLIED SARCASTICALLY.

WELL, CLEVER DICK. WHAT SHOULD YOU HAVE — A SIXTEEN-INCH NAVAL GUN?

JUST TWO MACHINE GUNS, POINT FIVE CALIBRE. THAT WOULD MAKE IT JUST RIGHT.

STUNG BY CHARLIE'S ANSWER, RAMSAY CONTINUED TO NIGGLE AT HIS GUNNER.

THERE IS NO POINT IN SHIFTING YOUR FAILURE AS A GUNNER ONTO YOUR GUNS. IT DOESN'T WASH WITH ME.

DON'T TALK TO ME ABOUT FAILURES, RAMSAY.

WHAT'S HOLDING RAMSAY UP?

RAMSAY GLOWERED AT CHARLIE BUT SAID NO MORE AS HE HURRIED TO CATCH UP WITH THE OTHER AIRCRAFT.

I'LL GET RID OF THAT FOOL GUNNER YET.

THEIR TARGET WAS A LARGE GERMAN INDUSTRIAL TOWN AND THEY COULD EXPECT A HARD TIME AS THEY'D BE THE LAST SQUADRON TO ATTACK.

SUDDENLY, WHEN THEY WERE HALF WAY ACROSS THE NORTH SEA, CHARLIE OPENED FIRE.

WHAT THE BLAZES – WHO'S FIRING?

AT THE SUDDEN ROAR OF THE GUNS, RAMSAY HAD JUMPED WITH FEAR.

IT'S OK, I WAS JUST TESTING.

FOR CRYING OUT LOUD, CAN'T YOU WARN US FIRST?

RAMSAY'S TENSENESS COMMUNICATED ITSELF TO THE OTHERS.

SKIPPER'S A BIT JITTERY TO-NIGHT.

AREN'T WE ALL? LAST OVER THE TARGET'S A LOUSY DEAL.

IT WAS A VERY DARK NIGHT. THE GUNNERS' EYES ACHED AS THEY TRIED TO PENETRATE THE BLACKNESS.

THEN AHEAD LAY THE BURNING CITY, THE FIRES CLEARLY VISIBLE.

NAVIGATOR TO PILOT. TARGET IN TWO MINUTES.

OK, NAVIGATOR, I CAN SEE THE GLOW.

HOWEVER, UNKNOWN TO RAMSAY AND HIS CREW, A Ju88 WAS TAILING THEIR LANC.

THOR THREE TO BASE CONTROL. I AM IN THE BOMBER STREAM. ALREADY I HAVE VISUAL CONTACT.

KNOWING THAT HE WAS VIRTUALLY INVISIBLE TO THE LANC GUNNERS, THE NIGHT FIGHTER PILOT WAS IN NO HURRY TO ATTACK.

POOR FOOLS. LITTLE DO THEY KNOW WHAT AWAITS THEM.

THE FIRST THE LANCASTER'S CREW KNEW OF HIS PRESENCE WAS THE TEARING CRACK OF CANNON SHELLS AS THEY RAKED ALONG THE FUSELAGE.

YE GODS!

AAAAGH!

WITH ONE ENGINE OUT OF ACTION, THE BIG BOMBER BEGAN TO LOSE HEIGHT.

PILOT TO CREW, WHY DON'T YOU ANSWER? HECK! THE INTERCOM'S DEAD.

THE RADIO OPERATOR REPORTED TO RAMSAY.

THE FLIGHT ENGINEER AND MID-UPPER GUNNER HAVE HAD IT. THE NAVIGATOR'S WOUNDED BUT THE REAR GUNNER'S OK.

RIGHT. TELL THAT USELESS STEVENS TO KEEP HIS MIND ON THE JOB.

IMMEDIATELY RAMSAY HAD JUMPED TO THE WRONG CONCLUSION AND WAS BLAMING CHARLIE FOR NOT SPOTTING THE JUNKERS IN TIME.

FORTUNATELY THE LANCASTERS WERE BUILT TO TAKE AN INCREDIBLE AMOUNT OF PUNISHMENT. SOMEHOW RAMSAY NURSED THE RIDDLED WRECK ALL THE WAY.

RAMSAY REFUSED TO RELEASE THE UNINJURED MEMBERS OF HIS CREW UNTIL GROUP CAPTAIN BREWSTER, THE COMMANDING OFFICER, HAD LANDED.

I PUT THE RESPONSIBILITY FOR WHAT HAPPENED ON STEVENS, SIR. IF HE HAD BEEN ALERT HE WOULD HAVE SEEN THAT FIGHTER AND THIS WOULD NOT HAVE HAPPENED.

THAT'S NOT TRUE, SIR. I WAS ALERT, BUT IT WAS A DARK NIGHT AND THE FIGHTER APPEARED VERY QUICKLY.

THE GROUP CAPTAIN KNEW THAT RAMSAY AND HIS GUNNER DIDN'T HIT IT OFF, BUT...

I CAN'T ACCEPT THAT, STEVENS. YOU WILL BE GROUNDED UNTIL FURTHER NOTICE.

UNFORTUNATELY FOR CHARLIE, BREWSTER'S REAR GUNNER HAD HIMSELF SHOT DOWN A NIGHT FIGHTER AND THIS SEEMED TO ENDORSE RAMSAY'S COMPLAINT.

CHARLIE ONCE AGAIN FOUND HIMSELF IN THE ARMOURY.

COME ON, YOU LADS, KEEP YOUR MIND ON THE JOB.

THEN ONE AFTERNOON CHARLIE FOUND SOMETHING OF INTEREST.

HEY, TWO LOVELY BROWNINGS!

YEAH. A FORTRESS. CRASH-LANDED NEAR HERE SOME TIME AGO AND BURNED OUT. THE YANKS LEFT IT, SO WE BROUGHT IN THESE GUNS.

HEY, THIS IS GREAT. GUNS, AMMO — THE LOT. WOULD ANYBODY OBJECT IF I DID SOME WORK ON THIS?

IT'S OK BY ME, CHARLIE. THE YANKS DON'T WANT IT BACK.

THE ARMOURY STAFF WORKED HARD BUT IN ALL HIS SPARE MOMENTS, CHARLIE WAS AT WORK ON HIS OWN PLAN.

NOT MUCH TO DO NOW.

WITHIN A WEEK THE JOB WAS FINISHED.

THAT'S IT THEN — A COMPLETE HALF-INCH CALIBRE GUN INSTALLATION THAT WILL FIT INTO A LANC'S TAIL TURRET.

NOW ALL YOU'VE GOT TO DO IS PERSUADE RAMSAY TO LET YOU PUT IT IN YOUR LANCASTER, RIGHT?

THEN RAMSAY APPEARED —

YOU CAN STOP WASTING YOUR TIME HERE. YOUR GROUNDING'S OVER AND YOU'LL BE ON OPERATIONS TONIGHT.

JUST TAKE A LOOK IN HERE AND YOU'LL SEE I HAVEN'T BEEN WASTING MY TIME.

KNOWING RAMSAY'S ATTITUDE, CHARLIE HAD LITTLE HOPE OF APPROVAL FROM HIM AS HE LET HIM SEE THE TWIN BROWNINGS ON HIS IMPROVISED MOUNTING.

GIVE ME YOUR PERMISSION TO HAVE THIS INSTALLED, AND THEN ANY GERMAN NIGHT-FIGHTER PILOT WHO THINKS HE'S GOT US COLD IS IN FOR A SHOCK.

AND RAMSAY FORCIBLY CONFIRMED HIS FEARS.

YOU DON'T SERIOUSLY THINK I'D ALLOW THAT CONTRAPTION IN MY AIRCRAFT? IT'S NOT MY GUNS I WANT CHANGED — IT'S YOU!

AW, WHAT'S THE USE! YOU JUST WON'T SEE IT. I MIGHT HAVE KNOWN.

HE APPROACHED SOME OTHER PILOTS, BUT WITHOUT SUCCESS, AND FINALLY...

IT'S LIKE BEATING MY HEAD AGAINST A BRICK WALL. YOU JUST CAN'T GET ANY-WHERE. I'M GOING TO ABANDON THE WHOLE IDEA.

SO THE GUN MOUNTING WAS JUST LEFT TO GATHER DUST IN THE ARMOURY.

IT WAS ALMOST FOUR WEEKS LATER BEFORE THE ARMAMENT OFFICER APPROACHED GROUP CAPTAIN BREWSTER.

I FOUND SOMETHING RATHER UNUSUAL IN MY ARMOURY STORE TODAY, SIR. I WONDER IF YOU'D CARE TO LOOK AT IT SOMETIME.

NO TIME LIKE THE PRESENT. WHY DON'T WE GO OVER THERE NOW?

BREWSTER WAS SO IMPRESSED HE SENT FOR CHARLIE NEXT DAY AND HAD HIM DEMONSTRATE HIS INVENTION ON THE SHOOTING RANGE.

REMARKABLE! THE LAD'S GOT SOME-THING HERE ALL RIGHT.

AT LAST IT SEEMED HIS IDEAS WERE PAYING OFF.

HOW WOULD YOU LIKE TO BE MY TAIL GUNNER, STEVENS? THAT IS, WITH THIS GUN MOUNTING INSTALLED IN PLACE OF THE EXISTING ONE.

GREAT, SIR – JUST GREAT!

BUT ANOTHER DISAPPOINTMENT AWAITED HIM. THAT SAME AFTERNOON ALL CREWS WERE SUMMONED TO THE BRIEFING ROOM.

THE SQUADRON WILL BE TAKEN OFF THE OPERATIONS AND AN INTENSIVE TRAINING PROGRAMME WILL BEGIN. NO FURTHER DETAILS HAVE BEEN GIVEN.

BLAST! WHEN WILL I EVER GET THE CHANCE TO USE THOSE GUNS?

FOR THE NEXT FEW WEEKS THE LANCASTERS FLEW COMPLICATED COURSES AT LOW LEVEL, ALL OVER SCOTLAND AND NORTHERN ENGLAND.

IN TWENTY SECONDS CHANGE HEADING TO ONE-SIX-SEVEN DEGREES.

OK, NAVIGATOR. SOON BE FINISHED THIS LARK – I HOPE!

SOME MEMBERS OF THE PUBLIC DIDN'T TAKE TOO KINDLY TO THIS SORT OF FLYING.

OLD MACDONALD'S DOING HIS NUT!

I'LL HAVE THE LAW ON YE FOR THIS!

IT WAS INEVITABLE THAT THIS DANGEROUS LOW FLYING SHOULD RESULT IN ACCIDENTS AND SOME LANCASTERS WERE LOST.

CHARLIE, WITH HIS TWO BIG GUNS STILL UNFIRED, BEGAN TO GET SOMEWHAT RESTIVE.

JUST TWO DAYS AFTERWARDS, ALL THE CREWS WERE SUMMONED TO THE CLOSELY GUARDED BRIEFING ROOM WHERE A SCALE MODEL OF A CASTLE HAD BEEN MADE.

THIS IS IT, GENTLEMEN. ALTENHELM SCHLOSS IN AUSTRIA. WHAT GOES ON IN THERE, FEW PEOPLE KNOW, BUT IT IS IMPORTANT.

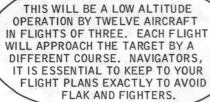

BREWSTER WENT ON TO EXPLAIN. THE ENEMY WERE USING THE CASTLE AS AN EXPERIMENTAL ATOMIC LABORATORY. IT HAD TO BE DESTROYED.

THIS WILL BE A LOW ALTITUDE OPERATION BY TWELVE AIRCRAFT IN FLIGHTS OF THREE. EACH FLIGHT WILL APPROACH THE TARGET BY A DIFFERENT COURSE. NAVIGATORS, IT IS ESSENTIAL TO KEEP TO YOUR FLIGHT PLANS EXACTLY TO AVOID FLAK AND FIGHTERS.

EVERY AIR GUNNER ON THE SQUADRON CHECKED AND DOUBLE-CHECKED HIS GUNS. THEIR LIVES MIGHT DEPEND ON THEM.

WELL, CHARLIE. YOUR THEORIES WILL SOON BE PUT TO THE TEST.

FOR ALL OUR SAKES, MATE, I HOPE THEY'RE RIGHT.

WITH THE LONGEST COURSE TO FLY, BREWSTER'S FLIGHT, WHICH INCLUDED RAMSAY, TOOK OFF FIRST.

WELL, HERE GOES...

THE FORMATION, AFTER CIRCLING, BEGAN THE FIRST LEG OF THE LONG TRIP.

NAVIGATOR TO PILOT. TURN ON TO COURSE NOW.

RIGHT, CHAPS, LET'S GET WEAVING.

THE LANCASTERS SWEPT ON, OVER THE SEA...THEN SUDDENLY CHARLIE SAW THE GREEN FIELDS OF NORTHERN GERMANY BELOW.

FLAK TO STARBOARD, SKIPPER.

OK REAR GUNNER, I SEE IT. IT'S WELL OUT OF RANGE.

SKIRTING TOWNS AND RIVERS THE FORMATION TWISTED AND TURNED, MAKING IT VIRTUALLY IMPOSSIBLE FOR FIGHTERS TO INTERCEPT.

THESE IMPUDENT BRITISHERS. WHERE IS THE LUFTWAFFE?

THEY WERE ALMOST AT THE TARGET, AND STILL THEY HAD NOT BEEN SEEN BY A SINGLE FIGHTER. THEN...

THE ENEMY ATTACKED VICIOUSLY AND QUICKLY CLAIMED A VICTIM.

THE DAMAGED LANC DISSOLVED IN A BOILING CLOUD OF EXPLODING FUEL AND BOMBS, AND TWO ATTACKING Me109s WERE SWALLOWED IN THE BLAST.

AT LEAST THEY TOOK TWO JERRIES WITH THEM.

THE REMAINING FOUR NAZI PILOTS CHANGED THEIR TACTICS, AND CONCENTRATED THEIR ATTACK ON RAMSAY'S PLANE.

SKIPPER, THEY'RE PICKING ON RAMSAY.

OK, STEVENS, HERE'S YOUR CHANCE TO SEE WHAT YOUR GUNS CAN DO. LET 'EM RIP.

WITH A BLASTING ROAR, CHARLIE'S GUNS LASHED OUT AND HEAVY SLUGS BATTERED THE LEADING MESSERSCHMITT INTO SCRAP.

AAGH!

SURPRISE, SURPRISE, TAIL-END CHARLIE'S BUMPER PARCEL!

BREWSTER THROTTLED BACK SLIGHTLY TO ALLOW RAMSAY TO CATCH UP.

NICE WORK, GUNNER. YOU'RE A REGULAR TIGER IN THAT TURRET.

THERE'S ANOTHER JUST COMING INTO MY SIGHTS...

ANOTHER GERMAN FIGHTER WILTED UNDER CHARLIE'S GUNS.

GOT YOU!

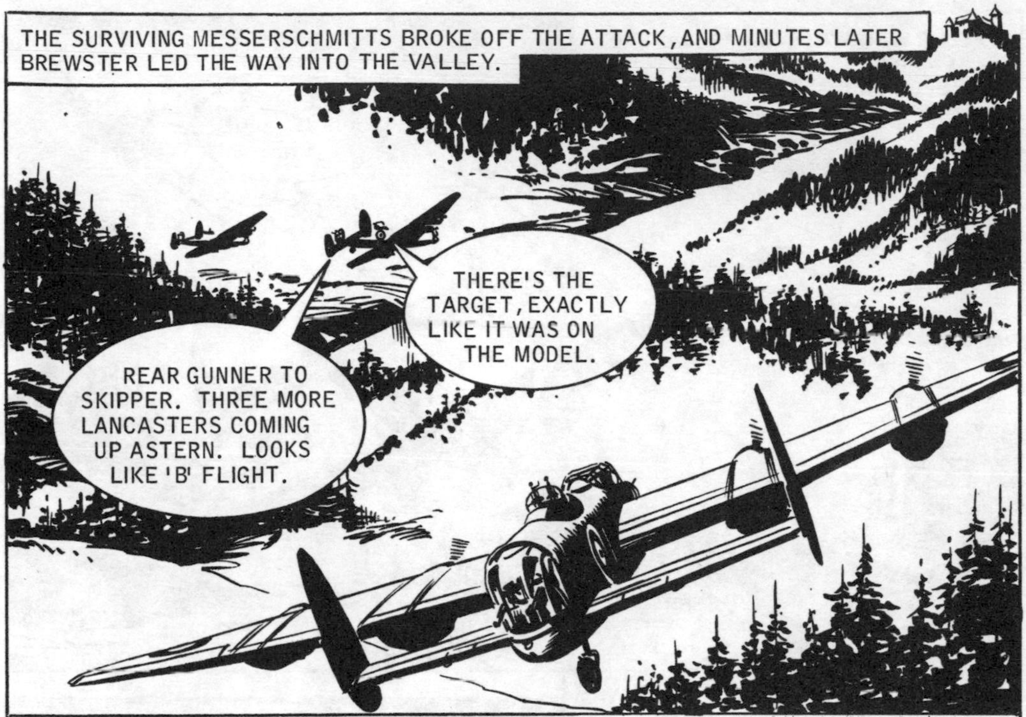
THE SURVIVING MESSERSCHMITTS BROKE OFF THE ATTACK, AND MINUTES LATER BREWSTER LED THE WAY INTO THE VALLEY.
THERE'S THE TARGET, EXACTLY LIKE IT WAS ON THE MODEL.
REAR GUNNER TO SKIPPER. THREE MORE LANCASTERS COMING UP ASTERN. LOOKS LIKE 'B' FLIGHT.

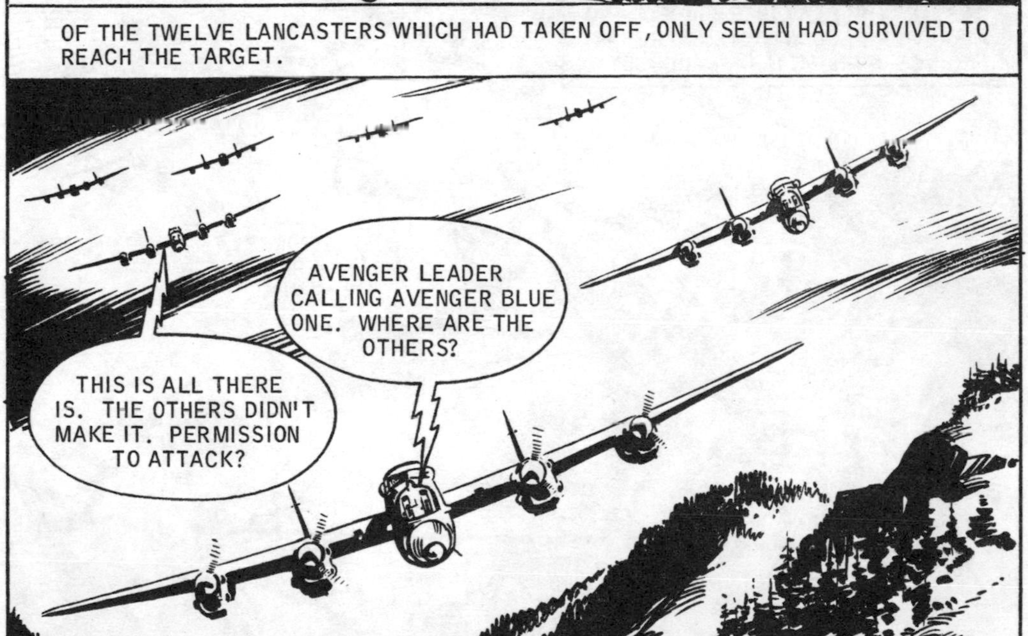
OF THE TWELVE LANCASTERS WHICH HAD TAKEN OFF, ONLY SEVEN HAD SURVIVED TO REACH THE TARGET.
AVENGER LEADER CALLING AVENGER BLUE ONE. WHERE ARE THE OTHERS?
THIS IS ALL THERE IS. THE OTHERS DIDN'T MAKE IT. PERMISSION TO ATTACK?

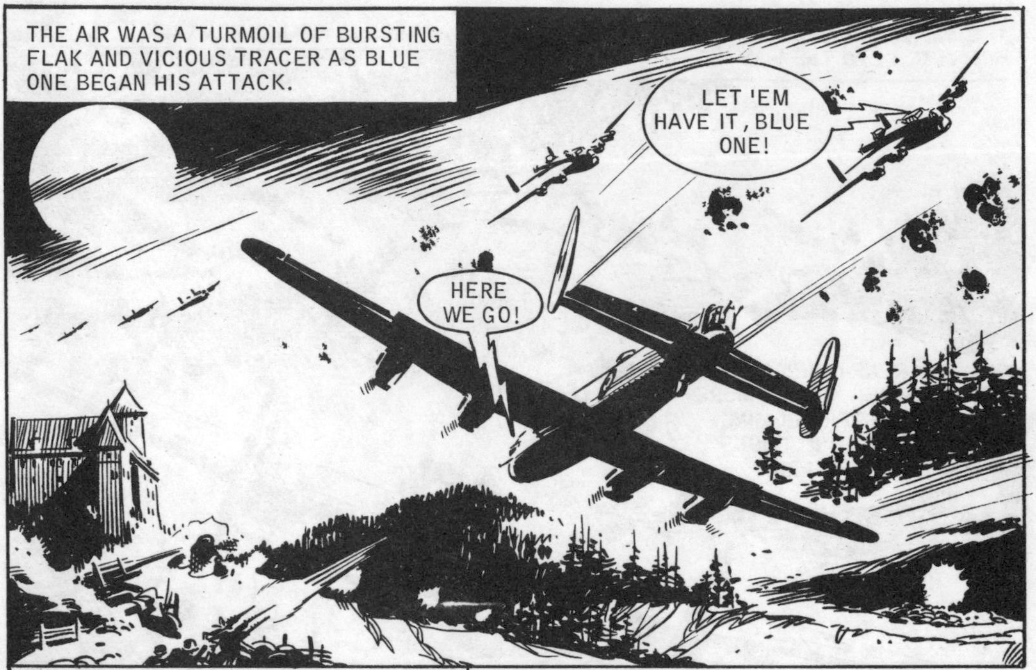
THE AIR WAS A TURMOIL OF BURSTING FLAK AND VICIOUS TRACER AS BLUE ONE BEGAN HIS ATTACK.
LET 'EM HAVE IT, BLUE ONE!
HERE WE GO!

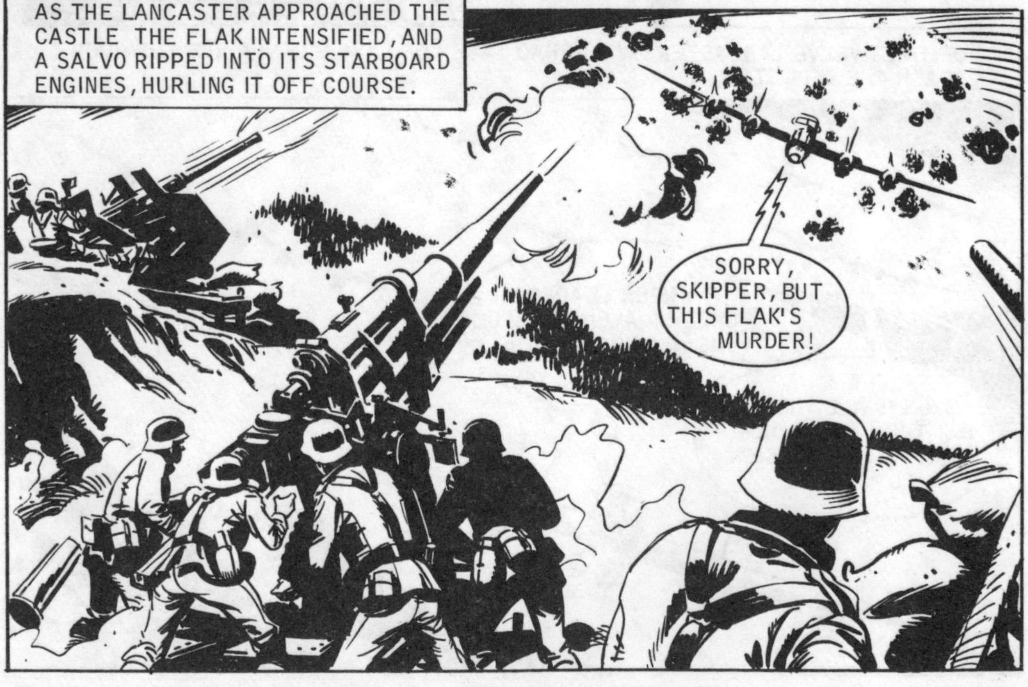
AS THE LANCASTER APPROACHED THE CASTLE THE FLAK INTENSIFIED, AND A SALVO RIPPED INTO ITS STARBOARD ENGINES, HURLING IT OFF COURSE.
SORRY, SKIPPER, BUT THIS FLAK'S MURDER!

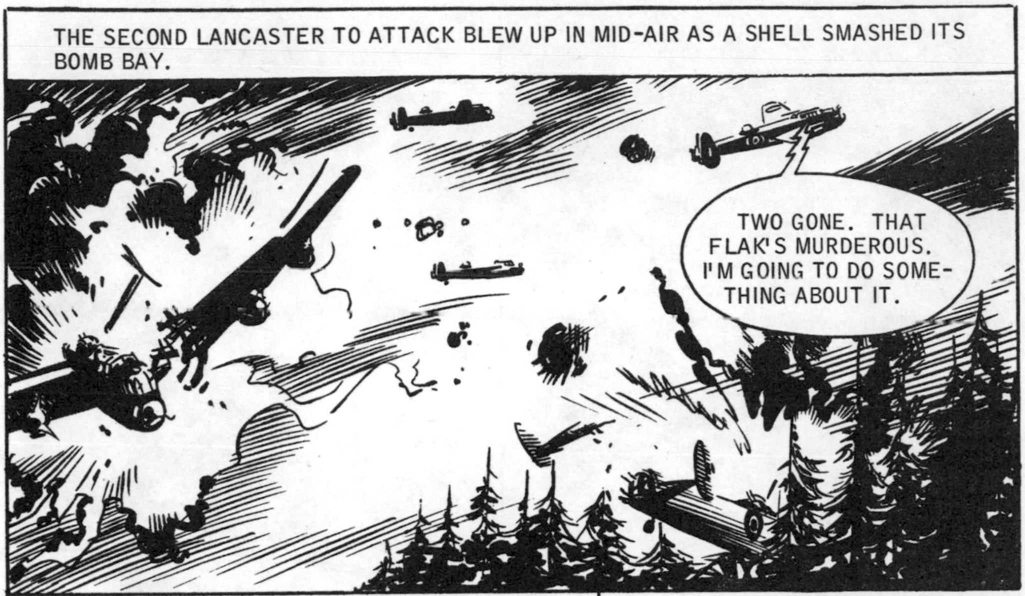
THE SECOND LANCASTER TO ATTACK BLEW UP IN MID-AIR AS A SHELL SMASHED ITS BOMB BAY.
TWO GONE. THAT FLAK'S MURDEROUS. I'M GOING TO DO SOMETHING ABOUT IT.

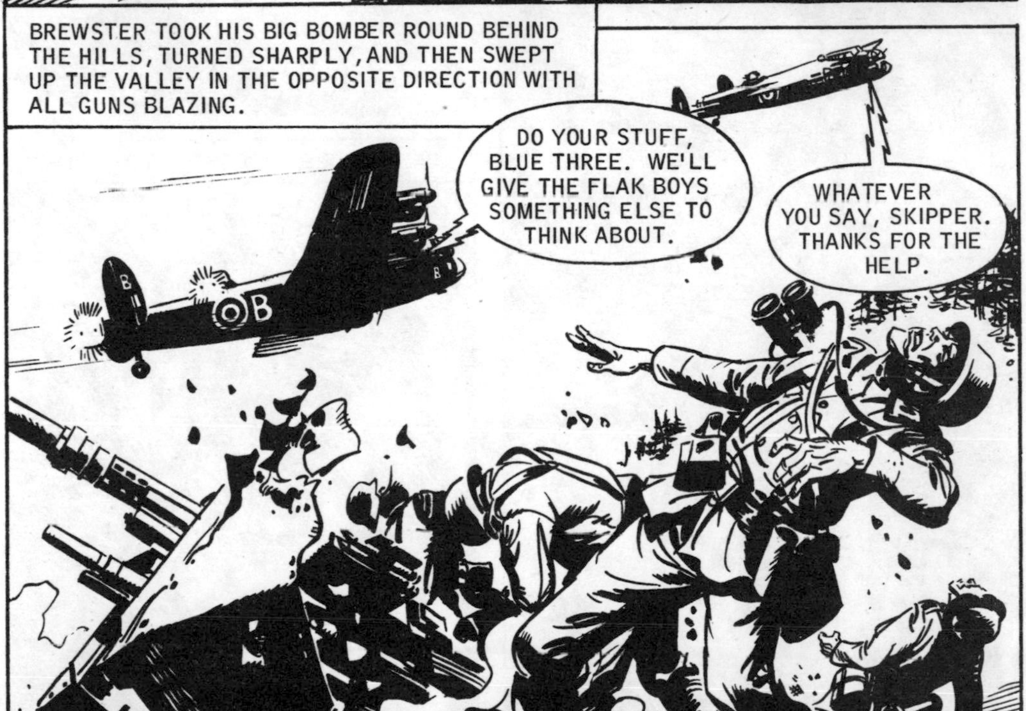
BREWSTER TOOK HIS BIG BOMBER ROUND BEHIND THE HILLS, TURNED SHARPLY, AND THEN SWEPT UP THE VALLEY IN THE OPPOSITE DIRECTION WITH ALL GUNS BLAZING.
DO YOUR STUFF, BLUE THREE. WE'LL GIVE THE FLAK BOYS SOMETHING ELSE TO THINK ABOUT.
WHATEVER YOU SAY, SKIPPER. THANKS FOR THE HELP.

BLUE THREE'S CARGO OF DESTRUCTION WAS DEAD ON THE TARGET.

WE DID IT, SKIPPER. IT'S SLAP ON TARGET!

NICE WORK, BLUE THREE.

AGAIN THE TACTIC WAS REPEATED, BUT THIS CREW WEREN'T SO LUCKY.

AAGH!

BREWSTER'S THOUGHTS WERE GRIM.

ONLY RAMSAY AND MYSELF LEFT NOW. IT'S UP TO US.

CHARLIE'S BIG GUNS SMOTHERED THE DEFENCES IN BULLETS AS RAMSAY WENT IN.

P-FOR-PETER GOT ONE ON TARGET. IT LOOKS GOOD.

KEEP YOUR GUNS GOING, TIGER!

BREWSTER'S HANDS WERE CLAMPED ROCK HARD ON THE CONTROLS AS HE STEERED THE HURTLING LANCASTER TOWARDS THE CASTLE.

IT'S UP TO US, LADS. HANG ON TIGHT.

AT THE PRECISE INSTANT THE BOMBS WERE RELEASED, THE LANCASTER STAGGERED UNDER A MORTAL BLOW.

AS BREWSTER FOUGHT TO KEEP CONTROL, THE GREAT CASTLE ERUPTED INTO A FLYING MASS OF RUBBLE AND DUST.

IN A TREMENDOUS CLOUD OF FLYING SPRAY, THE LANCASTER PLOUGHED INTO THE SHALLOWS OF THE RIVER.

ONLY CHARLIE, BREWSTER AND TWO OTHERS OF THE CREW WERE FIT TO ESCAPE WHEN THE NAZIS CAME HUNTING.

AS CHARLIE AND THE OTHERS HEADED FOR NEUTRAL SWITZERLAND, TWO LANCASTERS GOT BACK TO BASE. RAMSAY WAS ONE OF THE LUCKY ONES AND HE REPORTED THE MISSION AS A COMPLETE SUCCESS. HE HAD HAD PLENTY TIME TO THINK ABOUT HIS NASTINESS TO CHARLIE.

IF IT HADN'T BEEN FOR SERGEANT STEVENS' GUN TURRET, WE COULD NEVER HAVE DONE IT.

I'LL VOUCH FOR THAT. I RECKON ALL THE LANCS SHOULD BE EQUIPPED WITH THESE GUNS.

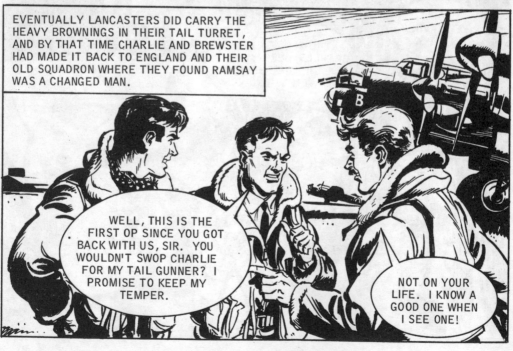

EVENTUALLY LANCASTERS DID CARRY THE HEAVY BROWNINGS IN THEIR TAIL TURRET, AND BY THAT TIME CHARLIE AND BREWSTER HAD MADE IT BACK TO ENGLAND AND THEIR OLD SQUADRON WHERE THEY FOUND RAMSAY WAS A CHANGED MAN.

WELL, THIS IS THE FIRST OP SINCE YOU GOT BACK WITH US, SIR. YOU WOULDN'T SWOP CHARLIE FOR MY TAIL GUNNER? I PROMISE TO KEEP MY TEMPER.

NOT ON YOUR LIFE. I KNOW A GOOD ONE WHEN I SEE ONE!

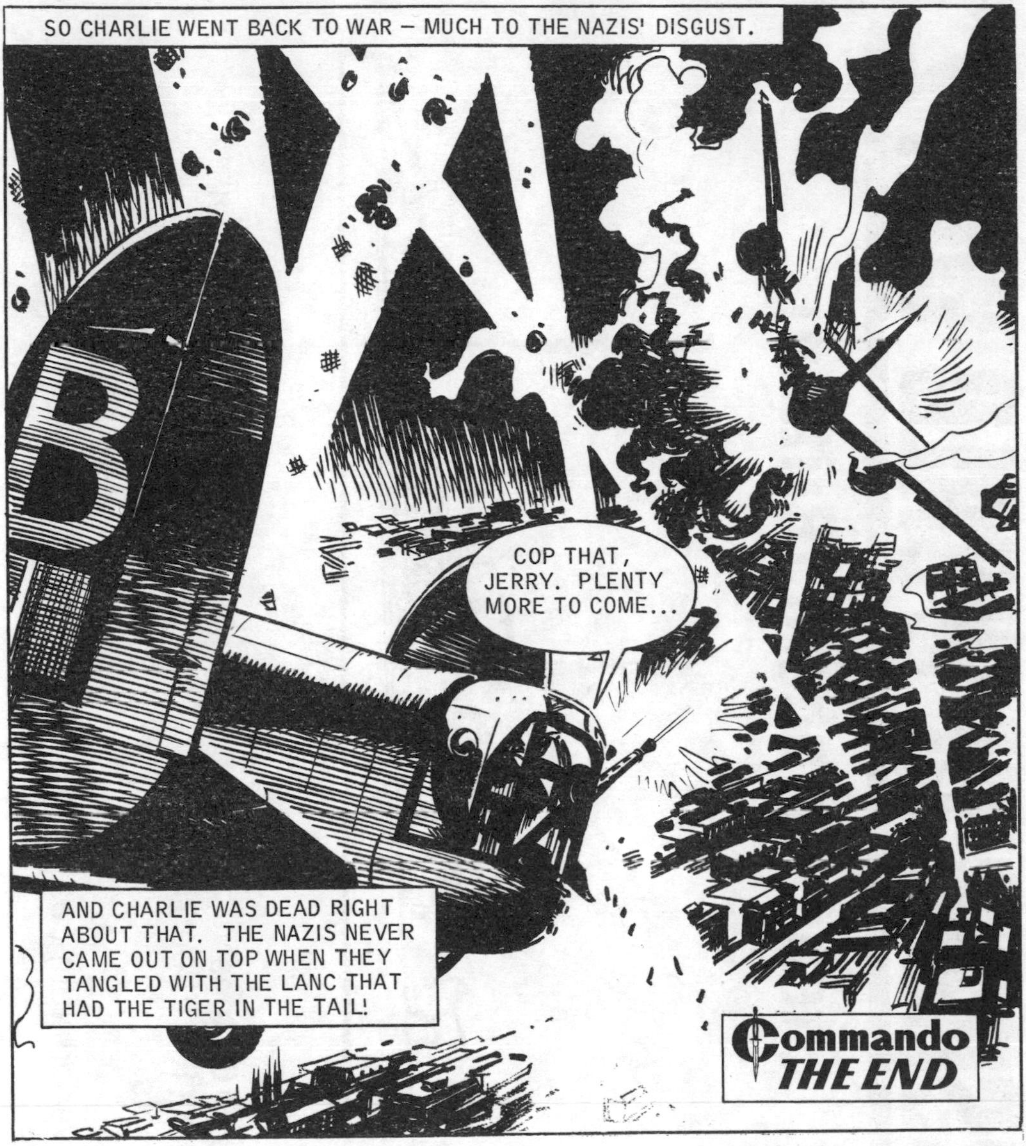
SO CHARLIE WENT BACK TO WAR – MUCH TO THE NAZIS' DISGUST.
COP THAT, JERRY. PLENTY MORE TO COME...
AND CHARLIE WAS DEAD RIGHT ABOUT THAT. THE NAZIS NEVER CAME OUT ON TOP WHEN THEY TANGLED WITH THE LANC THAT HAD THE TIGER IN THE TAIL!
Commando THE END

WARSHIPS OF WORLD WAR 2

Steam Gunboat (Britain)

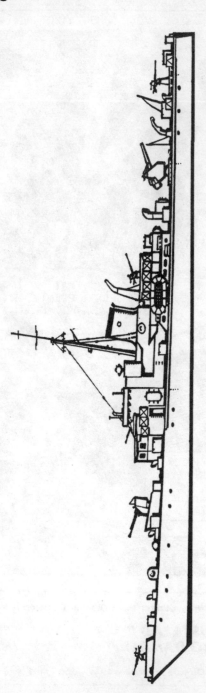

Displacement 165 tons
Length 44.3m (145.5 feet)
Speed 35 knots.
Crew 27
Armament (varied from boat
to boat) —

1 76mm (3-inch) high-angle:
1 2pdr (40mm) pom-pom:
3 20mm (0.79-inch):
2 twin 7.6mm (.303-inch):
2 torpedo tubes.

THE SPECIALISTS

A BRITISH MOTOR GUN BOAT ON PATROL ALONG THE COAST OF ENEMY-HELD YUGOSLAVIA HAD JUST BEEN BLOWN TO BITS AS TWO LURKING GERMAN S-BOATS STRUCK. ONLY ONE MAN WAS TO SURVIVE TO BE WASHED ASHORE . . .

First published 1986.

. . . WHERE AN ALERTED ENEMY PATROL PLUCKED HIM SEMI-CONSCIOUS FROM THE WATER. FOR SUB-LIEUTENANT ERIC GRANGE THE FUTURE WAS A PRISON CAMP.

HE'S STILL BREATHING.

HE'LL BE ALL RIGHT. BUT NONE OF THE OTHERS HAVE SURVIVED.

AFTER BEING INTERROGATED FIRMLY BUT FAIRLY BY THE LOCAL NAVAL COMMAND, HE WAS DESPATCHED TO A FORTRESS HIGH IN THE HILLS WHERE ALLIED OFFICERS CAPTURED IN AND AROUND THIS AREA WERE HELD.

NOT EXACTLY THE RITZ, BUT MAYBE IT WON'T BE TOO BAD.

THE ITALIANS WHO GUARDED THIS ESTABLISHMENT SEEMED A REASONABLE BUNCH. ERIC TOOK IN ALL THE DETAILS HE COULD AS HE WAS MARCHED TO HIS QUARTERS.

BEHAVE HERE AND THERE WILL BE NO TROUBLE.

WELL, WE'LL HAVE TO WAIT AND SEE.

HE FOUND HIMSELF IN A SMALL CELL WITH A CHEERFUL R.A.F. PILOT OFFICER BY THE NAME OF JOHN NEWTON.

WELCOME TO "CASTLE DOOM". IT'S NOT TOO BAD, BUT IT GETS A BIT BORING.

WE'LL HAVE TO DO SOMETHING ABOUT THAT THEN.

THE TWO LADS GOT ON WELL RIGHT AWAY. JOHN, WHO HAD BEEN SHOT DOWN NEAR-BY SOME MONTHS BEFORE, EXPLAINED ABOUT THE OTHER CAPTIVES.

THEY'RE MOSTLY R.A.F. TYPES LIKE MYSELF WITH ONE OR TWO OF YOU NAVY BODS AND A FEW ARMY BLOKES WHO HAD BEEN WORKING WITH THE PARTISANS.

WITH THE PLACE ONLY BEEN IN USE THE LAST FEW MONTHS, I CAN SEE WHY NODODY'S ESCAPED YET.

ANY BREAK-OUT WOULD BE BEYOND ONE OF JOHN'S OTHER FRIENDS, LIEUTENANT GUY RANSOME OF THE ARMY. HE HAD BEEN SHOT IN BOTH LEGS, CRIPPLED IN A BATTLE IN THE MOUNTAINS.

A NEW BLOKE, I SEE. DON'T GO TELLING HIM TOO MANY TALL STORIES, JOHN.

WOULD I EVER. SEE YOU AROUND . . .

ERIC MARVELLED AT THE WOUNDED MAN'S CHEERFULNESS AS HE HOBBLED ABOUT ON CRUTCHES.

HE'S AMAZING CONSIDERING ALL HE HAS TO PUT UP WITH.

HE'S TOUGH, ALL RIGHT. KEEPS HIMSELF TO HIMSELF AT TIMES, BUT HE'S A SHREWD BLOKE.

IN THE WEEKS WHICH FOLLOWED, ESCAPE BECAME THE FIRST PRIORITY OF THE TWO PALS. THEY TOOK EVERY CHANCE TO GET OUT OF CAMP ON LIGHT WORK DETAILS TO MAP AND SPY OUT THE LAND.

THEY'LL BE GETTING SUSPICIOUS THAT WE VOLUNTEER FOR THIS BREAD RUN SO OFTEN.

IF THEY HAVEN'T ALREADY. THEY WATCH US LIKE HAWKS.

ALL TOO SOON THEY WERE ON THEIR WAY BACK TO THE FORTRESS.

ANOTHER DAY WITH NO CHANCE OF ANY BREAK.

ACTUALLY ERIC HAD SPOKEN TOO SOON. A MOSQUITO FIGHTER CREW ON A SEARCH-AND-DESTROY MISSION . . .

. . . HAD SPOTTED THE VEHICLE.

THE SLEEK MOSSIE CAME IN WITH MACHINE GUNS HAMMERING. THE ITALIANS WERE TAKEN COMPLETELY BY SURPRISE.

THAT MADE THEM JUMP!

DIO MIO!

WHEN THE TRUCK TOPPLED OVER, THE AIRCRAFT CLIMBED AWAY, THE CREW PLEASED WITH A JOB WELL DONE.

AAGH!

RIGHT, LET'S GET HOME THEN.

MIRACULOUSLY NOBODY HAD BEEN KILLED, ALTHOUGH ALL THE ITALIANS HAD LOST INTEREST IN THEIR PRISONERS FOR THE MOMENT. THE TWO MATES GRABBED THE OPPORTUNITY TO SLIP AWAY.

ARE YOU OKAY?

YES, JUST A BIT BRUISED. I'LL BE FINE.

THEY HEADED FOR THE COAST. IT OFFERED THEIR BEST CHANCE.

IF WE CAN LAY OUR HANDS ON A BOAT, WE'RE HALF-WAY THERE.

THEIR TASK WAS STILL DAUNTING, THOUGH, ESPECIALLY WHEN THE ALARM WAS RAISED, THE LOCAL GARRISONS ALERTED.

NO SIGN HERE . . .

THE PAIR ON THE RUN WERE SOON AWARE OF THE PROBLEM AS THEY FOUND ROUTE AFTER ROUTE BLOCKED BY ENEMY SQUADS.

THEY'RE PULLING OUT ALL THE STOPS.

THEY'VE CERTAINLY SHORTENED THE ODDS FOR US.

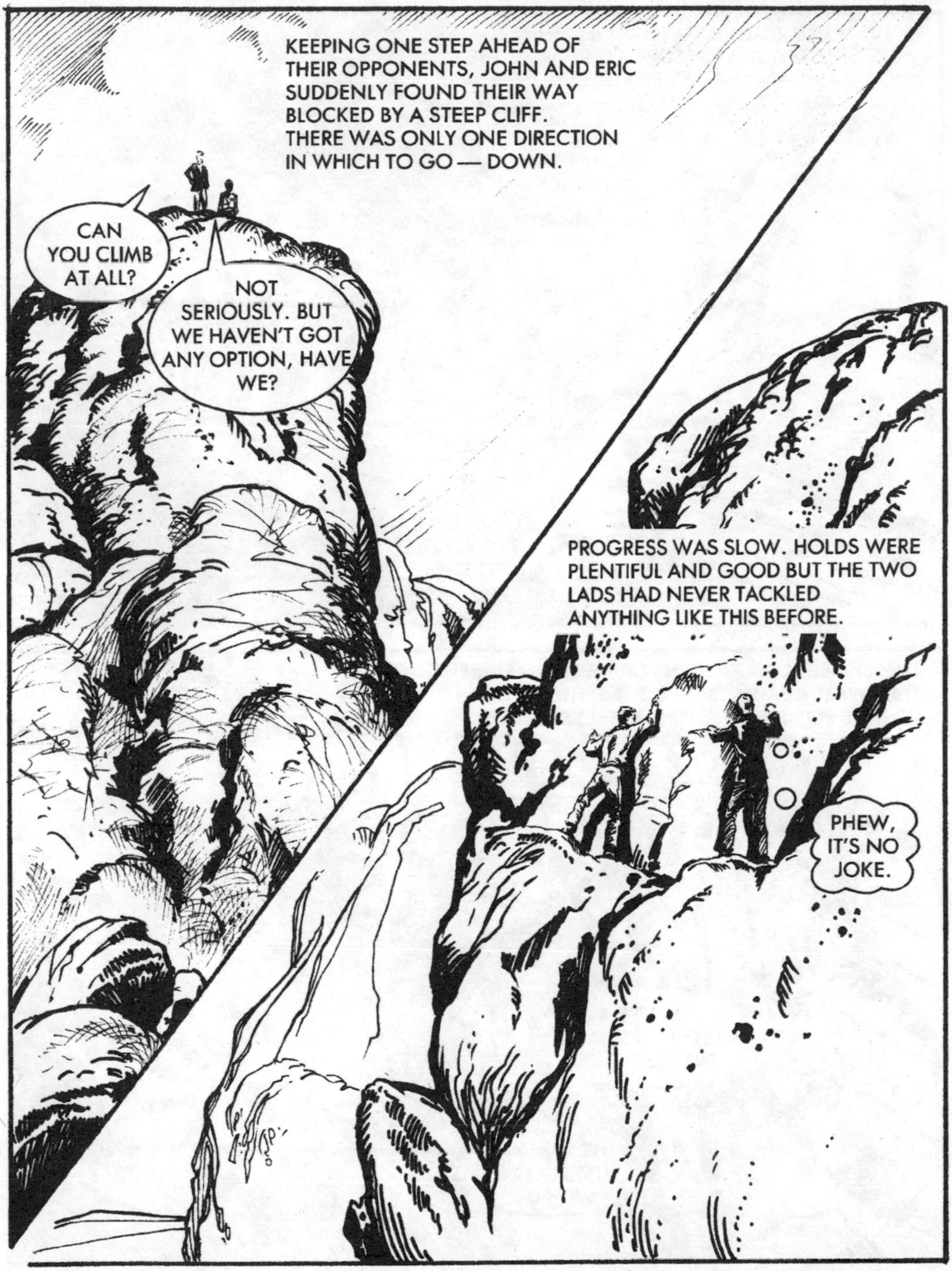
KEEPING ONE STEP AHEAD OF THEIR OPPONENTS, JOHN AND ERIC SUDDENLY FOUND THEIR WAY BLOCKED BY A STEEP CLIFF. THERE WAS ONLY ONE DIRECTION IN WHICH TO GO — DOWN.
CAN YOU CLIMB AT ALL?
NOT SERIOUSLY. BUT WE HAVEN'T GOT ANY OPTION, HAVE WE?
PROGRESS WAS SLOW. HOLDS WERE PLENTIFUL AND GOOD BUT THE TWO LADS HAD NEVER TACKLED ANYTHING LIKE THIS BEFORE.
PHEW, IT'S NO JOKE.

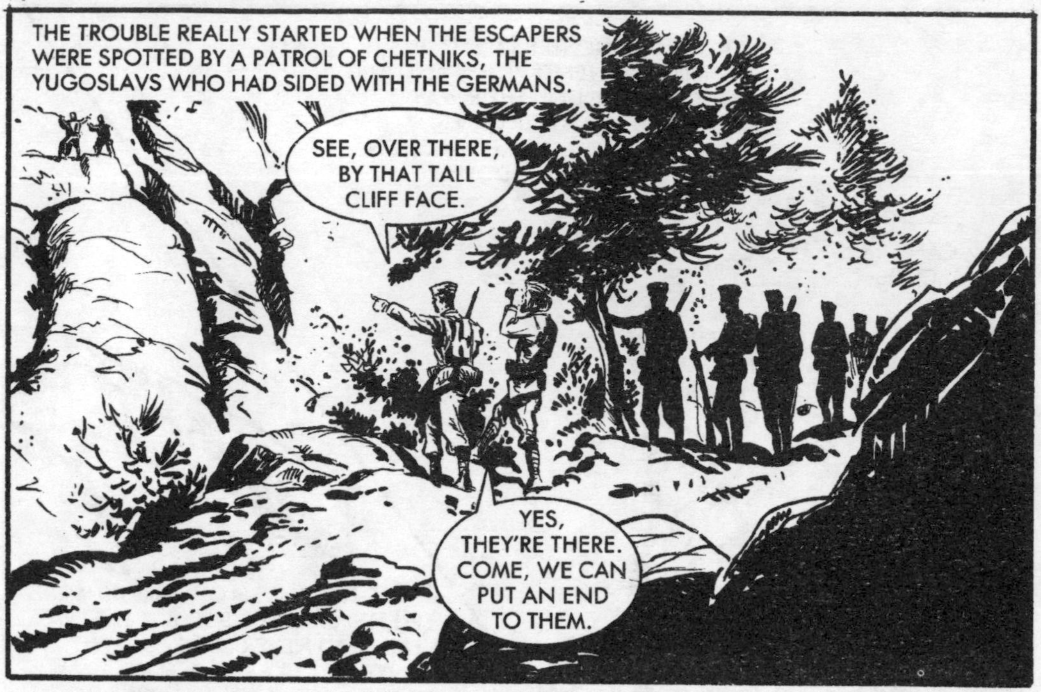
THE TROUBLE REALLY STARTED WHEN THE ESCAPERS WERE SPOTTED BY A PATROL OF CHETNIKS, THE YUGOSLAVS WHO HAD SIDED WITH THE GERMANS.
SEE, OVER THERE, BY THAT TALL CLIFF FACE.
YES, THEY'RE THERE. COME, WE CAN PUT AN END TO THEM.

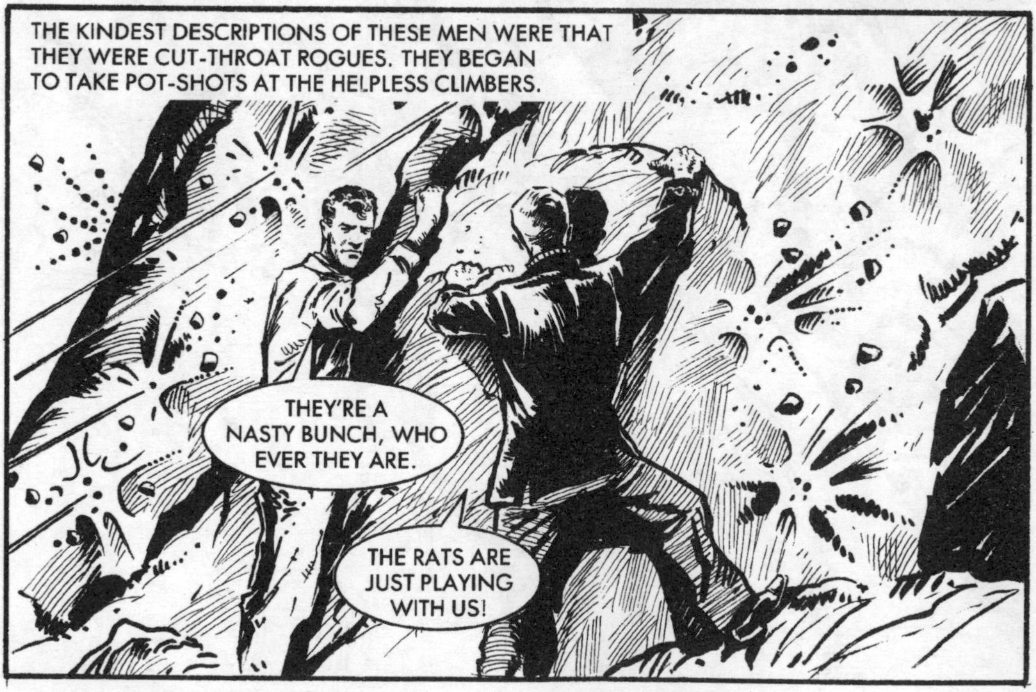
THE KINDEST DESCRIPTIONS OF THESE MEN WERE THAT THEY WERE CUT-THROAT ROGUES. THEY BEGAN TO TAKE POT-SHOTS AT THE HELPLESS CLIMBERS.
THEY'RE A NASTY BUNCH, WHO EVER THEY ARE.
THE RATS ARE JUST PLAYING WITH US!

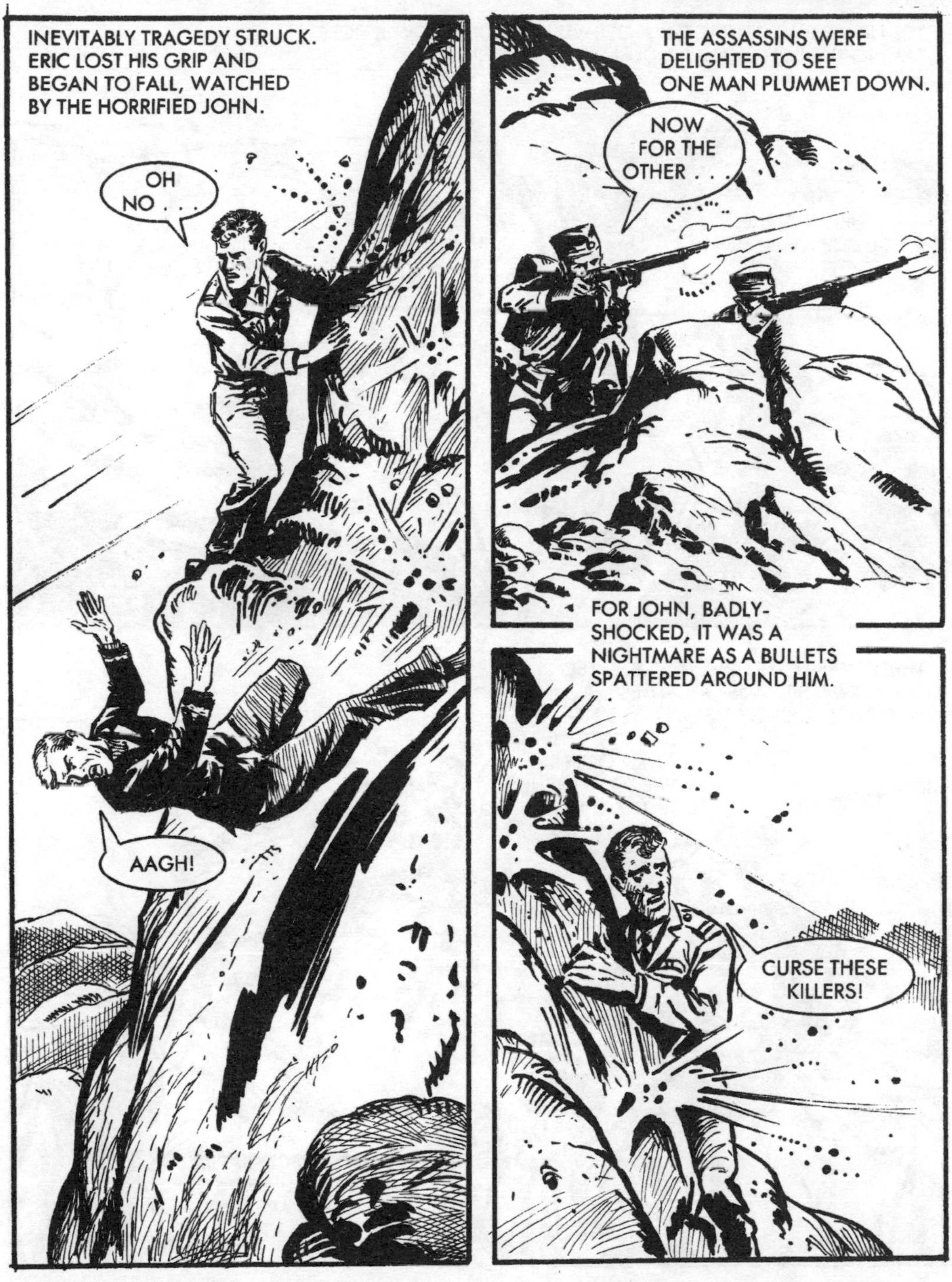
INEVITABLY TRAGEDY STRUCK. ERIC LOST HIS GRIP AND BEGAN TO FALL, WATCHED BY THE HORRIFIED JOHN.
OH NO . . .
AAGH!
THE ASSASSINS WERE DELIGHTED TO SEE ONE MAN PLUMMET DOWN.
NOW FOR THE OTHER . . .
FOR JOHN, BADLY-SHOCKED, IT WAS A NIGHTMARE AS A BULLETS SPATTERED AROUND HIM.
CURSE THESE KILLERS!

THE FIRING HAD ATTRACTED A GERMAN PATROL. THEIR OFFICER,
TAKING THE SCENE IN AT A GLANCE, WAS FURIOUS.

THERE WAS LITTLE LOVE LOST BETWEEN
THESE TWO SQUADS OF "ALLIES". A
BITTER QUARREL WAS SOON RAGING.

THE ENFORCED CEASE-FIRE HAD GIVEN JOHN A CHANCE TO CONTINUE THE DESCENT WHICH HAD IRONICALLY BECOME A LOT EASIER.

WE HAD ALMOST MADE IT WHEN ERIC FELL. BLAST THEM!

HE SEARCHED AS LONG AS HE DARED FOR ANY SIGN OF HIS FRIEND. IT WAS A FRUITLESS TASK, THOUGH, SO HE PRESSED ON ALONE.

HE WOULD NEVER HAVE SURVIVED ANYWAY . . . I'D JUST LIKE TO GET MY HANDS ON THE SCUM RESPONSIBLE.

FOR DAYS HE LIVED LIKE AN ANIMAL, EATING BERRIES, STEALING FOOD WHEN HE DARED ENTER ANY HOUSE ON THE EDGE OF A VILLAGE.

QUIET AS THE GRAVE. I DON'T LIKE LOOTING LIKE THIS, BUT I NEED THE GRUB.

TURNING TO LEAVE, HE FOUND HIS WAY BLOCKED BY TWO BURLY YUGOSLAVS.

AND WE WOULD BELIEVE YOU. WE HAVE NO LOVE FOR THE GERMANS.

OH, BLAST. LOOK, I CAN EXPLAIN . . .

HE HAD STRUCK LUCKY. THE VILLAGERS WERE ALL FIERCELY ANTI-NAZI AND HAD CONTACTS WITH THE PARTISANS.

DRASKO, THE SON OF THIS HOUSE, HAD BEEN A STUDENT UNTIL THE WAR HAD DISRUPTED HIS STUDIES. HE SPOKE GOOD ENGLISH.

YOU DON'T KNOW HOW MUCH I APPRECIATE THIS.

THINK NOTHING OF IT. SOON YOU WILL BE SAFE IN ITALY.

UNTIL ALL THE DETAILS WERE WORKED OUT, THE VILLAGERS HID HIM. DRASKO TALKED LONG AND OFTEN WITH HIM, THE TWO BECOMING GOOD FRIENDS.

THE RESISTANCE ARRANGED FOR JOHN TO BE PICKED UP BY A BRITISH MOTOR GUN BOAT WHICH HAD BROUGHT IN SUPPLIES.

YOU'RE SAFE NOW, RELAX.

HIS THOUGHTS CENTRED ON ERIC. HE COULD NOT FORGET THE GRIM FATE OF HIS MATE.

THE SOONER I'M FLYING AGAIN, THE SOONER I CAN PAY 'EM BACK FOR ERIC'S MURDER.

IT DIDN'T WORK OUT LIKE THAT. HE WAS DE-BRIEFED THOROUGHLY THEN FOUND HIMSELF ORDERED TO REPORT TO AN H.Q. IN THE ITALIAN PORT WHERE HE HAD BEEN LANDED.

IT'S STRANGE, ALL ORDERS AND NO EXPLANATIONS. THERE'S SOMETHING ODD GOING ON.

THE COLONEL HE WAS TO MEET DID NOT GIVE ANY NAME. HE WAS VERY WELCOMING YET THERE WAS A GLINT OF STEEL IN HIS EYES.

COME IN, WE DON'T STAND ON CEREMONY HERE. I'D LIKE TO HEAR ALL ABOUT YOUR ADVENTURES.

YES, SIR.

THE SENIOR OFFICER ASKED QUITE A
FEW BACKGROUND QUESTIONS THEN BEGAN
ON THE REALLY PROBING ONES.

DID YOU
BY ANY CHANCE
COME ACROSS A BLOKE
CALLED RANSOME IN
THAT PRISON?

YES, HE
WAS ON CRUTCHES
WHEN I LEFT.

THE ARMY MAN PRODUCED A
PHOTOGRAPH WHICH JOHN
CONFIRMED WAS THAT OF
THE PRISONER HE HAD SEEN.

WELL, THAT'S NOT
HIS REAL NAME OR RANK.
WHAT I HAVE TO TELL YOU
NOW IS TOP SECRET
— ABSOLUTELY SO.

"GUY", IT TRANSPIRED,
WAS A LEADING BRITISH
AGENT, A KEY LINK IN
THE ALLIED LIAISON
WITH THE PARTISANS.

TIME AFTER TIME HE
HAD BEEN PARACHUTED
BEHIND THE LINES.

GRIMLY THE COLONEL EXPLAINED THAT ON THE LAST OPERATION, THE OPERATIVE'S LUCK HAD RUN OUT. HE HAD BEEN WOUNDED AND CAPTURED.

SO FAR THEY THINK HE'S JUST ANOTHER OFFICER, BUT SOONER OR LATER THEY'RE GOING TO BLOW HIS COVER. AND HE'S IN NO FIT STATE TO ESCAPE UNDER HIS OWN STEAM.

YES, SIR, I'D AGREE WITH THAT.

SO IT HAD BEEN DECIDED THAT A SQUAD OF SPECIALLY-TRAINED COMMANDOS WOULD BE SENT IN TO SOMEHOW SNATCH GUY FROM ENEMY HANDS, THEN RETURN WITH HIM TO ALLIED TERRITORY.

WHEW, THAT'S SOME UNDERTAKING, SIR. AND WHY TELL ME ALL THIS?

I HAD HOPED YOU COULD HELP. YOUR KNOWLEDGE OF THE AREA WOULD PROVE INVALUABLE.

THE PILOT WAS ASTONISHED. HE WAS NOT TRAINED AS A FOOT SOLDIER, NEVER MIND A COMMANDO.

IT'S MADNESS, SIR — WITH RESPECT . . . I'D JUST BE A LIABILITY TO SPECIALISTS LIKE THESE GUYS.

WHAT ABOUT YOUR FRIEND ERIC? DON'T YOU WANT A CHANCE TO HIT BACK AT THE ENEMY IN THE VERY AREA WHERE HE WAS KILLED?

THAT SWUNG IT. JOHN AGREED, SEEING THE SENSE IN THE STATEMENT, EVEN ALTHOUGH HE KNEW IT HAD BEEN PLANNED TO BRING SUCH A REACTION.

GOOD MAN. YOUR RECORD MADE US THINK YOU'D PLAY ALONG. WE'LL SEE YOU GET SOME BASIC TRAINING FIRST.

THANKS, SIR, I THINK I'M GOING TO NEED IT.

THE TWO OFFICERS IN CHARGE OF THE SNATCH SQUAD — CAPTAIN BRUCE WALKER AND LIEUTENANT ED DRIVER — WERE OLD HANDS AT TOUGH ASSIGNMENTS. THEIR WELCOME FOR JOHN, NOW KITTED OUT, WAS SLIGHTLY COOL.

LOOK, I KNOW I'LL NEVER BE ANYTHING LIKE AS GOOD AS YOU BLOKES, BUT JUST GIVE ME A CHANCE.

FAIR ENOUGH, YOU'RE HONEST. WE'LL SEE HOW THINGS GO.

A WEEK WAS ALL THE TIME ALLOTTED TO TRAIN HIM TO A REASONABLE DEGREE OF PROFICIENCY. HIS PROGRESS WAS MONITORED CLOSELY.

HOW'S HE COMING ALONG?

NOT BAD, CONSIDERING. HE'S KEEN, BUT HE'S NOT REALLY OUR TYPE OF MATERIAL.

READY OR NOT, JOHN WAS ONE OF THE TWELVE SPECIALISTS WHO WENT ASHORE ONE DARK NIGHT ON THE COAST OF YUGOSLAVIA FROM A GUN BOAT WHICH HAD FERRIED THEM THERE.

THERE'S NO TURNING BACK NOW.

THE R.A.F. PILOT STROVE TO APPEAR CALM BEFORE THESE TOUGH VETERANS.

HOW'S IT GOING?

FINE. MY LAST TREK ACROSS THESE MOUNTAINS REALLY GOT ME IN TRAINING FOR THIS.

THE ROUTE ON WHICH THE INTRUDERS WERE TRAVELLING WAS AN OLD SMUGGLERS' PATH. UNFORTUNATELY THE GERMANS HAD BEEN KEEPING WATCH ON IT IN AN ATTEMPT TO CAPTURE SOME BLACK-MARKETEERS WHO HAD BEEN MAKING USE OF IT.

SIR, I SAW SOME MEN TO THE WEST. THEY WERE MOVING FAST BUT I COULDN'T MAKE THEM OUT CLEARLY.

PROBABLY FROM ONE OF OUR MOUNTAIN REGIMENTS, ALTHOUGH H.Q. HAD NO WORD OF THIS.

THE ENEMY OFFICER LOST HIS CALM HOWEVER WHEN HE ZEROED IN ON THE MEN WITH HIS FIELD-GLASSES.

MEIN GOTT, ENGLANDERS! RADIO H.Q. THEN PREPARE AN AMBUSH.

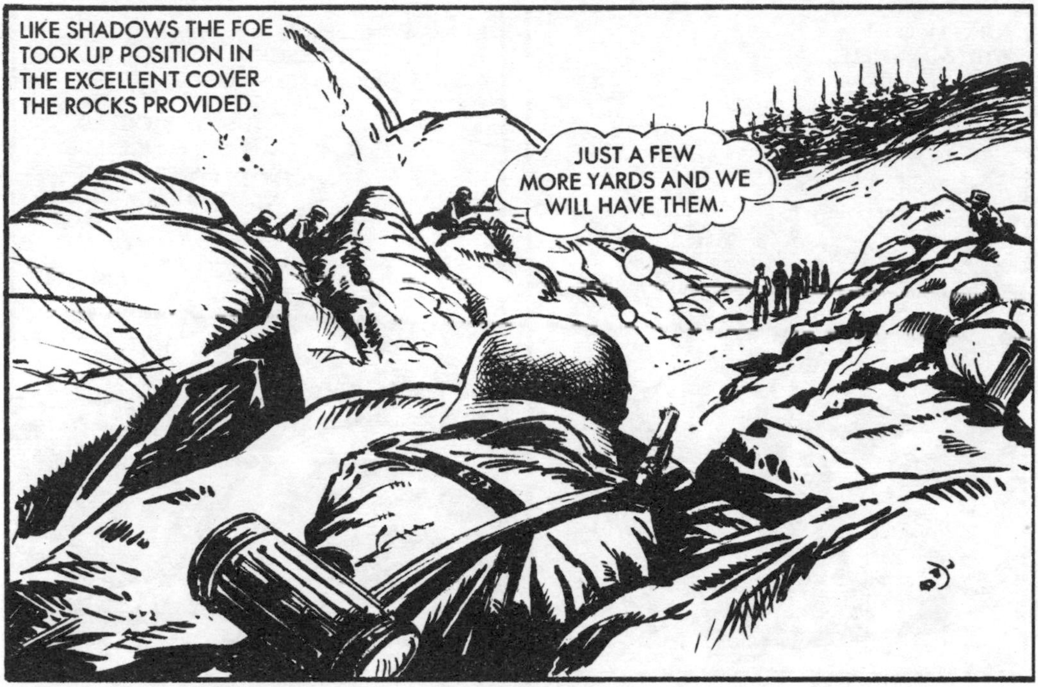
LIKE SHADOWS THE FOE TOOK UP POSITION IN THE EXCELLENT COVER THE ROCKS PROVIDED.
JUST A FEW MORE YARDS AND WE WILL HAVE THEM.

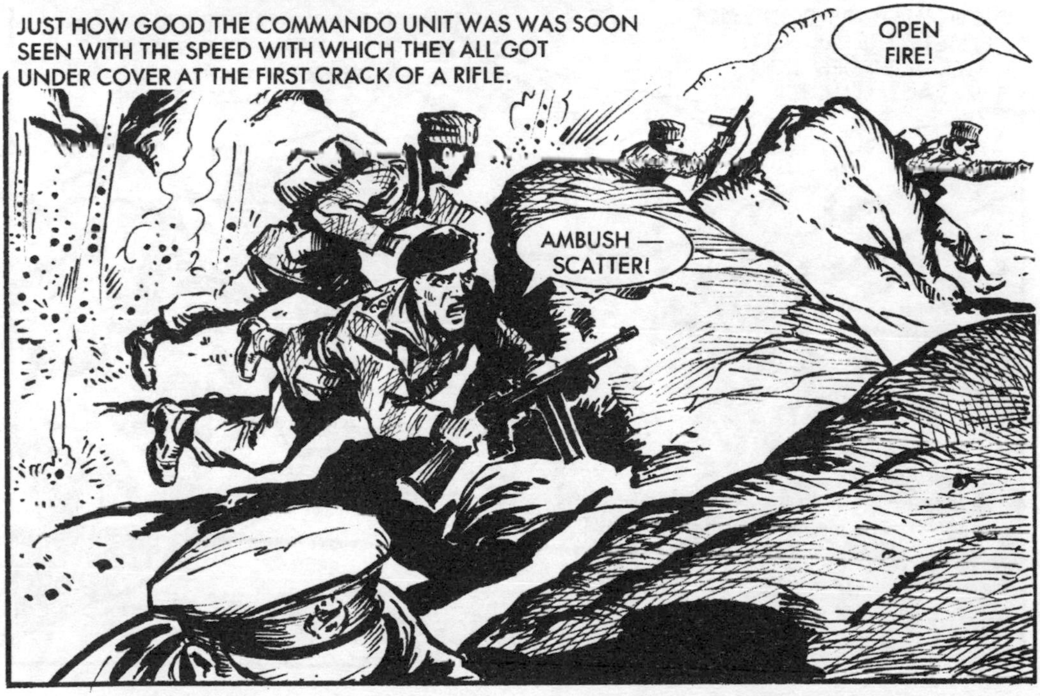
JUST HOW GOOD THE COMMANDO UNIT WAS WAS SOON SEEN WITH THE SPEED WITH WHICH THEY ALL GOT UNDER COVER AT THE FIRST CRACK OF A RIFLE.
OPEN FIRE!
AMBUSH — SCATTER!

JOHN MADE IT WITH SOME HELP FROM BRUCE.

YOU'VE GOT TO MOVE FAST IN A SPOT LIKE THIS.

BY NOW THE SPECIALISTS WERE FIGHTING BACK. CALMLY BRUCE ASSESSED THE SET-UP.

THEY'VE BLOCKED ANY ADVANCE, BUT WE CAN ALWAYS GO BACK.

THE ENEMY HAD THE SUPERIOR NUMBERS, THE RAIDERS THE BETTER MARKSMEN. SOON IT WAS A STALEMATE.

AAGH!

I THINK WE'D BEST RETREAT THEN MAKE A DETOUR. THEY'RE BOUND TO HAVE RADIOED THEIR BASE.

THAT, IT SEEMED, WOULD NOT BE NECESSARY AS THE AMBUSHERS WERE STRUCK FROM BEHIND BY A NEW FORCE JOINING IN THE SKIRMISH.

AAGH!

TEUFEL, WHAT'S GOING ON?

TO THE BRITISH IT WAS AN INCREDIBLE SIGHT TO SEE THEIR OPPONENTS CUT DOWN SO COMPLETELY.

WHO'S DOING IT? I CAN'T SEE A SIGN OF A SOUL.

WHOEVER IT IS, THEY'RE NOT PULLING THEIR PUNCHES.

THE RESCUERS SOON ROSE FROM COVER AS THE LAST GERMANS BEGAN TO FALL. THEY WERE A RAGGED BUNCH OF YUGOSLAVS WHO LIKED TO BE TERMED PARTISANS BUT WERE MORE LIKE BANDITS.

BRUCE WAS SMART ENOUGH TO WARN HIS MEN TO BE READY FOR TROUBLE AS THE CUT-THROAT BAND MOVED DOWN TOWARDS THEM.

THE LEADING MAN CALLED OUT TO THE WAITING COMMANDO UNIT IN BROKEN ENGLISH.

I NO SPEAK GOOD BUT OUR LEADER CAN. HE COME SOON.

WE'RE GLAD TO SEE YOU, FRIENDS.

A FIGURE CAME DOWN PAST THE OTHERS THEN. HIS ARRIVAL BROUGHT A STARTLED CRY FROM JOHN.

LOOK, IT'S HIM — I DON'T BELIEVE IT!

WHAT ARE YOU ON ABOUT?

AT FIRST JOHN HAD THOUGHT IT WAS A GHOST.
BUT NO, HERE WAS ERIC, SOLID AND ALIVE,
ALTHOUGH A LOT SCRUFFIER THAN BEFORE.

AGAIN WE WIN. YOU BRING US LUCK!

A HEALTH TO OUR LEADER!

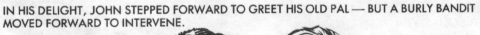

IN HIS DELIGHT, JOHN STEPPED FORWARD TO GREET HIS OLD PAL — BUT A BURLY BANDIT
MOVED FORWARD TO INTERVENE.

ERIC! IT'S GREAT TO SEE YOU . . .

BACK, GET BACK!

WHO ARE YOU?

THE COLD, EMPTY STARE IN ERIC'S EYES TOLD ITS OWN STORY.

HE SURVIVED THE FALL SOMEHOW, BUT HE'S LOST HIS MEMORY. AND HE'S CHANGED . . .

HIS SUSPICIONS WERE SOON CONFIRMED WHEN ERIC SPOKE.

I DON'T KNOW YOU AND WE HAVE NO TIME TO WASTE. ALREADY THE NAZIS COULD BE COMING.

WHEN AN OFFER OF SHELTER WAS ACCEPTED, ERIC LED THE WAY. BRIEFLY JOHN EXPLAINED ALL WHICH HAD JUST OCCURRED TO THE PUZZLED COMMANDO OFFICERS.

. . . BUT AS YOU SAW, HE DIDN'T KNOW ME FROM ADAM THERE.

ALL VERY STRANGE. ED, TRY TO FIND OUT MORE ABOUT THIS.

BY THE TIME THE CAMP WAS REACHED, ED, A FLUENT SPEAKER OF THE LANGUAGE, HAD SOON LEARNED THAT THESE MEN HAD FOUND ERIC TRAPPED IN SOME BUSHES HALF-WAY DOWN THE CLIFF, MORE DEAD THAN ALIVE.

THEY HAD TAKEN CARE OF HIM UNTIL HE HAD BEEN STRONG AGAIN. HIS NAME AND BACKGROUND HAD BEEN GLEANED FROM HIS IDENTITY DISCS, YET HE COULD REMEMBER NOTHING ELSE.

THE NEW RECRUIT HAD GONE ALONG ON RAIDS WITH THE SLAVS, IMPRESSING ALL WITH HIS COURAGE AND SKILL. SO MUCH SO THAT HE HAD BECOME THEIR LEADER BY COMMON CONSENT.

HE KNOWS NO FEAR!

AS HE LEARNED ALL THIS, BRUCE TURNED TO JOHN.

THIS IS TOO FISHY. I SAY WE TELL YOUR FRIEND NOTHING ABOUT OUR MISSION.

YES, I'VE GOT TO AGREE.

ERIC HIMSELF INTERRUPTED THEM.

WE WILL EAT NOW. FOLLOW ME . . .

AS THEY ATE, JOHN STUDIED HIS OLD MATE MORE CLOSELY. NEVER ONCE DID HIS EXPRESSION OR TONE OF VOICE CHANGE, NOR WAS THERE ANY FLICKER OF RECOGNITION.

HE'S LIKE A ROBOT. HE MUST HAVE DAMAGED HIS BRAIN IN THE FALL.

THAT'S MY BET TOO. HE CERTAINLY ISN'T NORMAL.

ALL TALK CEASED AS TWO
MORE YUGOSLAVS APPEARED
WITH A PRISONER. BRUCE
SPOTTED THEM FIRST.

HELLO,
IT'S ONE OF
THEIR OWN. I WONDER
WHAT HE'S
DONE?

WAIT A
MINUTE, I KNOW
HIM. IT'S DRASKO, THE
GUY WHO HELPED
ME ESCAPE.

BEFORE JOHN COULD RISE TO HIS FEET TO INTERVENE,
ERIC GLARED FURIOUSLY AT THE PRISONER AFTER ONE
OF HIS AIDES HAD WHISPERED IN HIS EAR.

TRAITOR!
YOU TRIED TO
BETRAY US — YOU'LL
PAY THE PENALTY!
SHOOT HIM!

IMMEDIATELY JOHN CONFRONTED ERIC BEFORE HE COULD BE STOPPED.

LOOK, I DON'T KNOW WHAT THIS IS ALL ABOUT, BUT HE'S NO TRAITOR. HE HELPED ME ESCAPE.

HOW MUCH DID YOU PAY HIM? HIS KIND CAN ALWAYS BE BOUGHT. BUT TODAY HE'LL DIE.

REALISING WHATEVER HE SAID WOULD MAKE NO DIFFERENCE, JOHN ACTED, SENDING ONE OF THE MEN HOLDING DRASKO SPINNING.

QUICK, RUN FOR IT!

AAGH!

THE CONDEMNED MAN NEEDED NO SECOND BIDDING. HE SPRINTED OFF LIKE A HARE.

SHOOT HIM, BRING HIM DOWN!

A BRAWL WAS CLOSE TO DEVELOPING AS ERIC BEGAN TO YELL FURIOUSLY AT JOHN WHILE ALL THE OTHERS MILLED AROUND.

YOU DEFIED ME, LET HIM ESCAPE! WHY, YOU FOOL . . .

AW, BELT UP. YOU WERE READY TO KILL A FRIEND OF MINE.

THE PEACE WAS RESTORED, ODDLY ENOUGH, BY SOME OF ERIC'S HENCHMEN WHO MADE LIGHT OF THE SITUATION, JOKING THAT WHAT WAS NEEDED BY ALL WAS A SOUND SLEEP.

WE WILL TALK IN THE MORNING. IT WILL MAKE MORE SENSE THEN.

I DOUBT IT. THERE'S A LOT MORE TO THIS THAN MEETS THE EYE.

IN THE HUT ALLOCATED TO THEM, THE THREE BRITISH OFFICERS POOLED TOGETHER ALL THE BITS OF INFORMATION THEY HAD GLEAMED FROM THE SITUATION.

IT LOOKS TO ME AS IF SOME OF THESE CUT-THROATS ARE CONTROLLING YOUR FRIEND, JOHN, MAKING USE OF HIM SOMEHOW.

HE CERTAINLY ISN'T THE SAME BLOKE I KNEW, SO IT'S VERY POSSIBLE. BUT WHAT'S IT ALL ABOUT?

THE TASK TO FIND OUT MORE FELL TO ED. HE SLIPPED OUT INTO THE NIGHT TO EAVESDROP ON ANYTHING AT ALL, BUT SOON HOMED IN ON TWO OF THE GROUP'S SPOKESMEN.

WE MUST BE CAREFUL WITH THESE BRITISH. THEY ARE TOUGH.

THEY'LL DIE ALL THE SAME ONCE WE KNOW WHERE THEIR GOLD IS. ALL WE NEED IS PATIENCE.

WITH THIS CRYPTIC KNOWLEDGE TO ADD TO WHAT THEY ALREADY KNEW, ED GOT BACK TO THE OTHERS UNSEEN.

GOLD? BUT WE HAVEN'T GOT ANY, HAVE WE?

NO, NOT THIS TIME. WE HAVE HAD IN THE PAST, THOUGH, FOR PARTISANS TO USE AS BRIBES, THINGS LIKE THAT.

AND I BET THESE CUT-THROATS HAVE HEARD OF THAT, SO THEY THINK WE'LL HAVE SOME ALONG THIS TIME AS WELL.

GRIMLY THE BRITISH TRIO REALISED WHAT THIS MEANT.

THEY'RE LIABLE TO TURN NASTY, SO THE QUICKER WE GET OUT OF HERE THE BETTER.

THE MEN WERE BRIEFED, THE COMMANDO SQUAD MADE TO LEAVE. ANY SENTRIES WERE SILENTLY RENDERED UNCONSCIOUS.

YOU'LL HAVE A SORE HEAD TOMORROW, MATE.

THEY WERE ALMOST OUT OF SIGHT WHEN THEY WERE SPOTTED BY A LONE GUARD PATROLLING AT IRREGULAR INTERVALS.

THE BRITISH ARE TRYING TO LEAVE! QUICK, WAKE UP!

CURSE HIM!

MORE TO DISCOURAGE PURSUIT THAN ANYTHING ELSE, THE RETREATING MEN OPENED FIRE.

THIS WILL SLOW THEM DOWN.

IT HAD BETTER.

THE TACTIC WORKED WELL.
ERIC SAW NO GREAT
ADVANTAGE IN RUNNING
THESE MEN TO THE GROUND.

LET THEM
GO. OTHERS LIKE
THEM WILL SOON
APPEAR FOR US
TO TACKLE.

THE NOISE HAD ATTRACTED TROUBLE, HOWEVER,
IN THE FORM OF A SQUAD OF CRACK ENEMY
MOUNTAIN TROOPS WHO HAD JUST STRUCK CAMP.

IT CAME
FROM OVER THERE.
NOT MORE THAN TWO
MILES AWAY I
WOULD SAY.

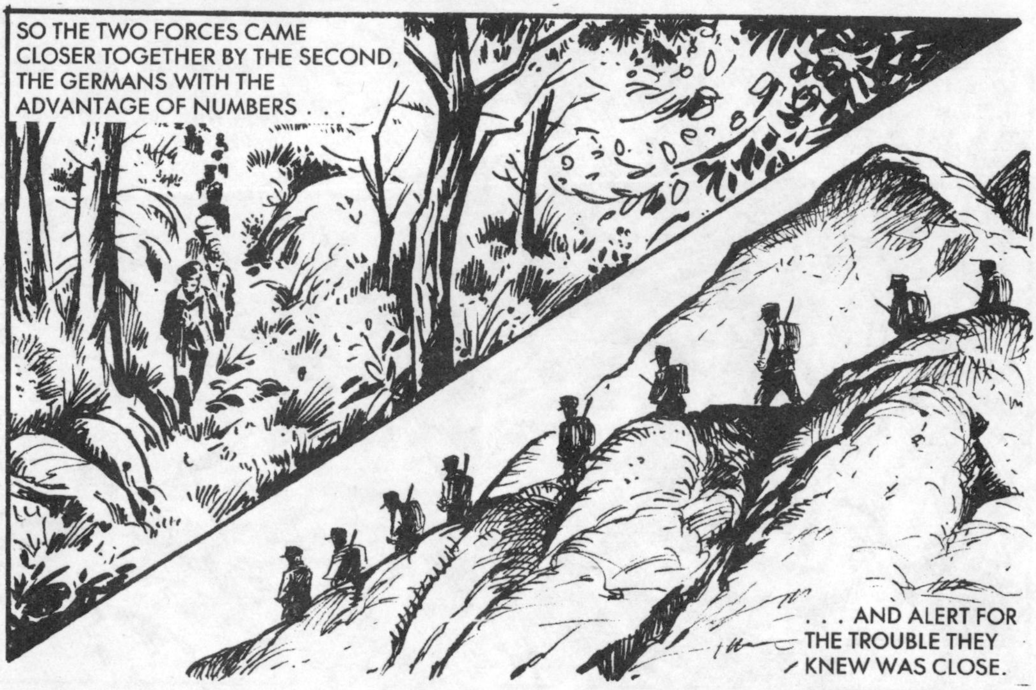
SO THE TWO FORCES CAME CLOSER TOGETHER BY THE SECOND, THE GERMANS WITH THE ADVANTAGE OF NUMBERS . . .
. . . AND ALERT FOR THE TROUBLE THEY KNEW WAS CLOSE.

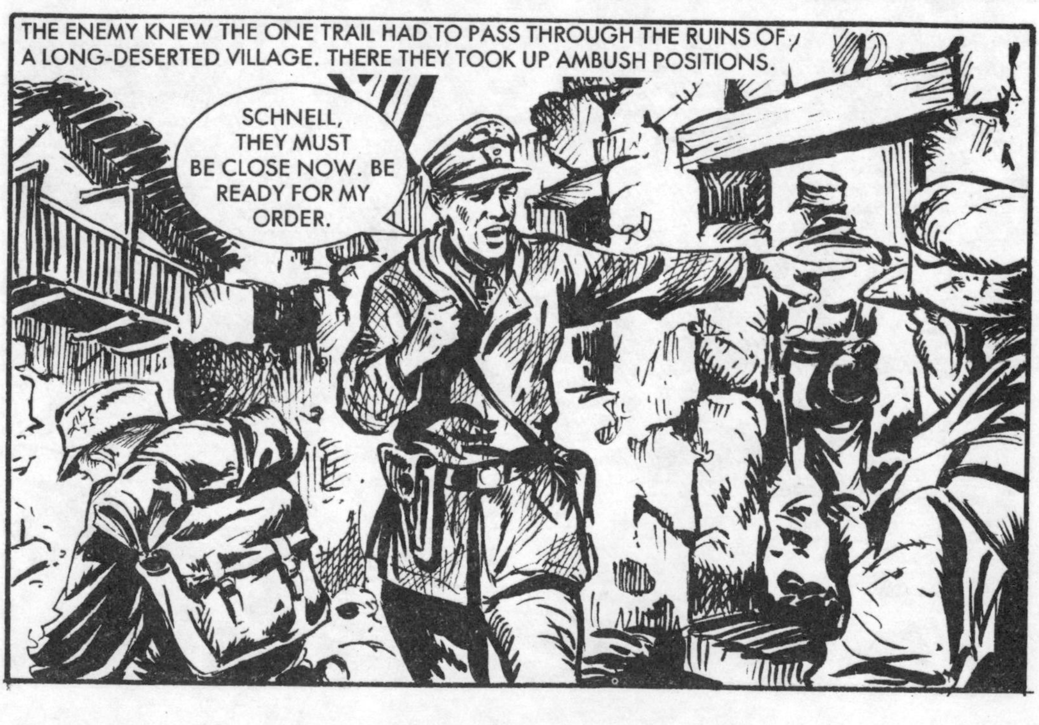
THE ENEMY KNEW THE ONE TRAIL HAD TO PASS THROUGH THE RUINS OF A LONG-DESERTED VILLAGE. THERE THEY TOOK UP AMBUSH POSITIONS.
SCHNELL, THEY MUST BE CLOSE NOW. BE READY FOR MY ORDER.

MEANWHILE THE SPECIALISTS TREKKED NEARER TO THIS HIDDEN DANGER.

KEEP MOVING —WAIT A MINUTE, WHAT WAS THAT?

SLOWLY DRASKO, THE MAN JOHN HAD SAVED, CAME OUT OF COVER, HIS HANDS RAISED.

DO NOT SHOOT. I COME TO HELP.

THE YUGOSLAV'S GRATITUDE AND HONESTY WAS OBVIOUS. ALL OTHER QUESTIONS WERE PUT ASIDE FOR THE MOMENT AS HE WARNED OF THE AMBUSH UP AHEAD.

IF I LEAD YOU, YOU CAN COME ROUND BEHIND THEM, ATTACK FROM THE RIVER.

GOOD FOR YOU, DRASKO. YOU'RE A FRIEND IN NEED ALL RIGHT.

THE GOING WAS ALMOST IMPOSSIBLE. EVEN GOATS WOULD HAVE TRIED TO AVOID THIS ROUTE.

IT IS NOT MUCH FURTHER.

YOU SAID THAT HALF-AN-HOUR AGO.

MEANWHILE THE GERMAN TROOPS HAD BEEN WAITING FOR WHAT SEEMED LIKE AN ETERNITY.

WHERE ARE THEY? THERE'S NO OTHER TRACK TO FOLLOW, BUT THEY SHOULD HAVE BEEN HERE BY NOW.

PERHAPS THEY'RE RESTING OR SOMETHING.

A GRENADE LOBBED INTO ONE OF THE HOUSES ENDED ALL SPECULATION.

HIMMEL!

THAT EXPLOSION WAS FOLLOWED BY A BLAST OF GUNFIRE.

WINKLE 'EM OUT, LADS!

THE TRAPPED ENEMY WRE FINISHED ALMOST AT ONCE. BRAVELY THEY FOUGHT ON.

WATCH THEM, LADS, THEY'RE TOUGH!

AAGH!

THE ENEMY HELD OUT TO THE LAST MAN, THE LAST BULLET. BRUCE HIMSELF CLAIMED THE FINAL PAIR.

THEY'RE BRAVE MEN, THAT'S FOR SURE.

THE GRIM BATTLE HAD BEEN WATCHED FROM ABOVE BY JOHN AND DRASKO WHO WERE GLAD THEY HAD NOT BEEN MORE CLOSELY INVOLVED.

IT IS FINISHED.

YES, THANKS TO YOU. BUT WHAT WAS ALL THAT ABOUT LAST NIGHT ABOUT YOU BEING A TRAITOR?

DRASKO EXPLAINED HIS SIDE OF THINGS AS BRUCE CAME OVER TO JOIN THEM WITH A SCHMEISSER FOR THE SLAV. HIS CLAIM THAT THE BAND LED BY ERIC WERE ONLY BANDITS RANG TRUE.

ME THEY WANT DEAD BECAUSE I TALKED OUR VILLAGERS OUT OF GIVING THEM FOOD AND DRINK AS A BRIBE TO LEAVE US ALONE.

THE OLD PROTECTION RACKET. BUT WHERE DOES JOHN'S FRIEND FIT INTO ALL THIS?

APPARENTLY IT WAS SOME VILLAGERS WHO HAD ACTUALLY FOUND AND NURSED ERIC BEFORE THE BRIGANDS HAD TAKEN HIM AWAY.

THEY SAY HE IS NOT WELL IN THE HEAD, KNOWS NO FEAR, DOES NOT REALISE THE DANGER HE IS IN.

SOUNDS LIKE HE'S JUST A PUPPET AND THEY PULL THE STRINGS.

THE YUGOSLAV CONFIRMED THIS, ADDING THAT HE HAD HEARD SOME OF THE CUT-THROATS BOAST THAT ERIC WAS THEIR PASSPORT TO FORTUNE.

GRIMLY BRUCE TURNED TO JOHN.

I HATE TO DO IT, BUT I SAY WE JUST LEAVE ERIC AND GET ON WITH OUR JOB.

IT'S HARD, BUT THERE'S NO OTHER WAY.

BY THAT THEY MEAN THE MONEY YOUR AGENTS OFTEN CARRY. THEY WOULD KILL FOR THIS.

WITH THAT DECIDED, JOHN THEN SUGGESTED AND BRUCE APPROVED THAT DRASKO BE INFORMED OF THE BARE OUTLINE OF THEIR REAL MISSION.

I'M SUPPOSED TO GUIDE THEM TO THIS PLACE, BUT I BET YOU COULD DO IT EVEN BETTER.

MORE THAN THAT. I KNOW HOW TO GET INTO THE JAIL UNSEEN.

"BEFORE THE WAR, ITALIAN ARCHAEOLOGISTS CAME TO THE FORTRESS TO DIG IN AND AROUND THE BUILDINGS FOR ANY TRACE OF OLD ROMAN REMAINS."

"MY FATHER WORKED WITH THEM AS THE BOSS OF THE LOCAL LABOURERS THEY USED, WITH ME AS A MESSENGER BOY."

"THEY FOUND VERY LITTLE BUT ONE ITALIAN, WHO SPOILED ME ROTTEN, SHOWED ME A DRAINAGE TUNNEL THEY HAD FOUND."

"AFTER THAT THEY FILLED EVERYTHING IN, WENT BACK TO ITALY. BUT EVEN TODAY I KNOW HOW TO GET INTO THAT TUNNEL."

THE INTRUDERS COULD HARDLY BELIEVE THEIR LUCK. BRUCE QUESTIONED DRASKO FIRMLY—

YOU'RE SURE OF THIS? YOU'RE NOT MISTAKEN?

NEVER. I CAN GET YOU IN AND OUT WITH NO TROUBLE IF WE ARE LUCKY.

SPURRED ON BY THIS NEWS THE BRITISH, GUIDED BY THE SLAV, MADE GOOD TIME UNTIL AT LAST THE PRISON CAME IN VIEW AS EVENING FELL.

LOOK, THERE IT IS. I WILL SHOW YOU WHERE WE GO WHEN NIGHT COMES.

GREAT WORK. LET'S GET TO IT.

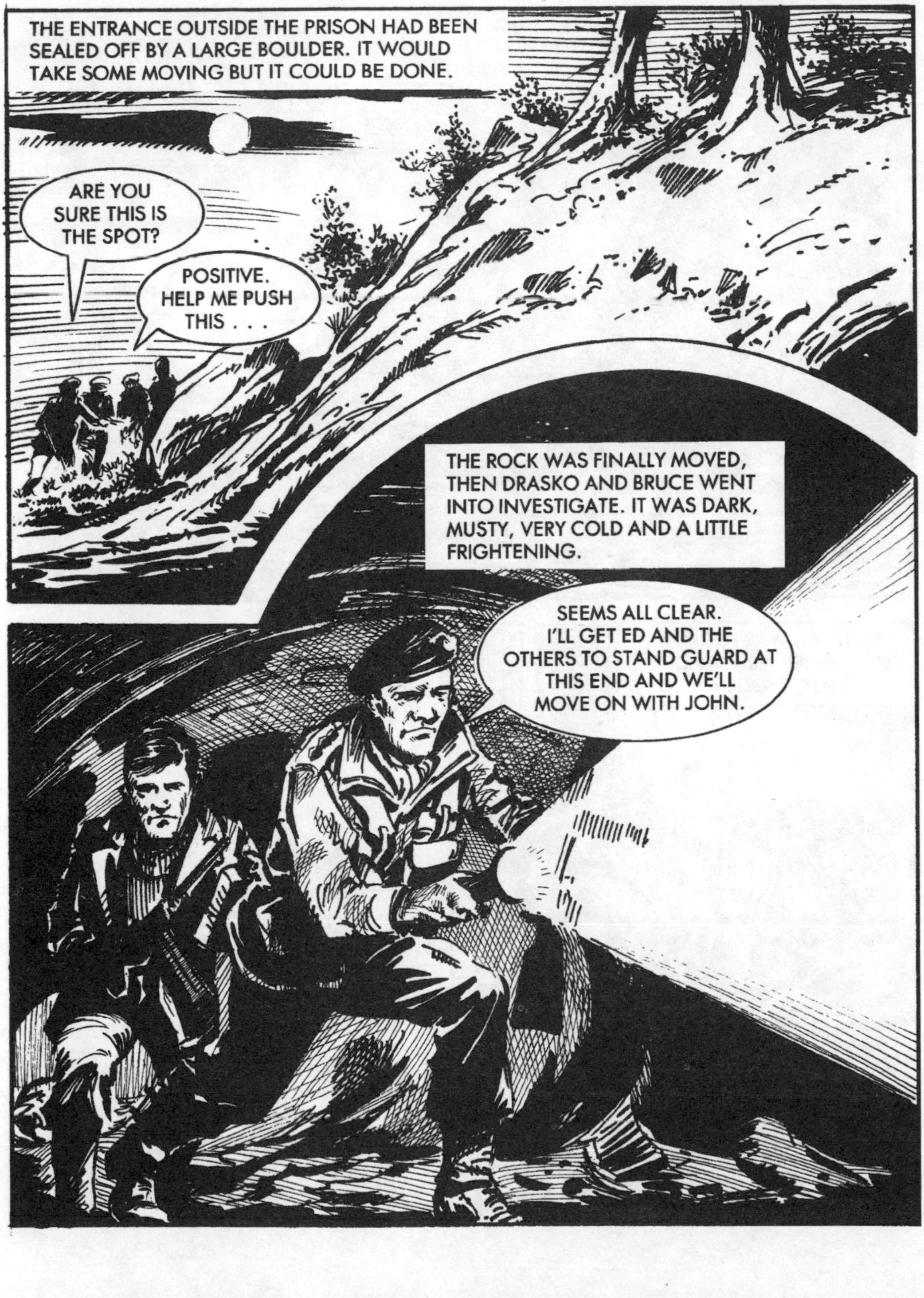
THE ENTRANCE OUTSIDE THE PRISON HAD BEEN SEALED OFF BY A LARGE BOULDER. IT WOULD TAKE SOME MOVING BUT IT COULD BE DONE.
ARE YOU SURE THIS IS THE SPOT?
POSITIVE. HELP ME PUSH THIS . . .
THE ROCK WAS FINALLY MOVED, THEN DRASKO AND BRUCE WENT INTO INVESTIGATE. IT WAS DARK, MUSTY, VERY COLD AND A LITTLE FRIGHTENING.
SEEMS ALL CLEAR. I'LL GET ED AND THE OTHERS TO STAND GUARD AT THIS END AND WE'LL MOVE ON WITH JOHN.

THE TUNNEL CAME OUT IN A DUSTY CELLAR PILED HIGH WITH OLD BOXES AND BARRELS. THE THREE RAIDERS SLIPPED IN THERE WITH THE MINIMUM OF SOUND.

GOOD, LET'S SEE HOW WE CAN GET OUT OF HERE NOW.

THE DOOR WAS LOCKED OF COURSE. BRUCE SOON PICKED IT, THOUGH.

OKAY, HERE WE GO.

THEY FOUND THEMSELVES IN A CORRIDOR WHICH BOTH DRASKO AND JOHN KNEW LED UP INTO THE MAIN YARD.

YOU LEAD, JOHN, SINCE YOU WERE HERE MOST RECENTLY.

THE GUARDS WERE FEW AND FAR BEWEEN. EXPERTLY BRUCE RENDERED ANY THEY MET UNCONSCIOUS.

I WOULDN'T LIKE TO HAVE HIM AS AN ENEMY.

THE FIRST CELL THEY REACHED WAS OPENED, MUCH TO THE AMAZEMENT OF THE AWAKENED OCCUPANTS, TO HELP DISCOVER GUY'S EXACT WHEREABOUTS.

SSH, DON'T MAKE A SOUND.

WHAT THE . . .

WHAT THE INTRUDERS HEARD WAS VERY DISTURBING. BATCH BY BATCH THE PRISONERS HAD BEEN MOVED BACK NORTH TO GERMANY. ONLY ONE GROUP OF ABOUT TWELVE REMAINED.

WHAT ABOUT GUY RANSOME? HAVE THEY MOVED HIM?

NO, HE'S STILL WITH US. THE POOR BLOKE CAN HARDLY GET ABOUT, EVEN WITH CRUTCHES.

SOON THEY HUNTED HIM DOWN. HE AWAKENED AT THE CODE-WORD HE HAD USED WHICH BRUCE NOW SPOKE QUIETLY.

"KNIGHT TEMPLAR" —WE'VE BEEN SENT TO GET YOU.

EH, WHAT? BY GLORY . . . AND IT'S JOHN TOO!

WITH ONLY A FEW LEFT OF THE OTHER CAPTIVES, BRUCE DECIDED TO TAKE THEM ALONG TOO. THE WITHDRAWAL BEGAN, JOHN AND DRASKO SUPPORTING GUY.

JUST KEEP QUIET, DO WHAT YOU'RE TOLD AND WE'LL ALL GET BACK TO ITALY.

AMEN TO THAT.

THE ESCAPE ROUTE WAS A REVELATION TO THE PRISONERS WHO ONLY WISHED THEY HAD KNOWN ABOUT IT BEFORE.

YES, BUT THEN WE DIDN'T KNOW ABOUT IT EITHER. THE EYETIES STILL OBVIOUSLY DON'T.

THEY'LL HAVE A FIT WHEN THEY DISCOVER IT!

OUT IN THE OPEN COUNTRY, ED WAS ASTONISHED TO SEE SO MANY COME BACK FROM THE FORAY INTO THE FORTRESS.

IT'S LIKE A PRIVATE ARMY.

THE MORE THE MERRIER. TELL THE LADS TO GET READY TO MOVE OUT.

A SPECIAL LIGHT-WEIGHT STRETCHER HAD BEEN BROUGHT ALONG TO TRANSPORT GUY. AS SOON AS HE HAD BEEN STRAPPED ONTO IT, THE TREK TO SAFETY BEGAN.

WE'LL REST REGULARLY TO GIVE THE PRISONERS A CHANCE TO KEEP UP. OTHERWISE, JUST STAY ALERT.

THANKS TO THE EXTRA GUIDANCE FROM DRASKO, DAWN FOUND THEM HIGH IN THE HILLS WITH NO SIGN OF PURSUIT. BRUCE WAS NOT READY TO RELAX YET, THOUGH.

KEEP YOUR EYES PEELED, WE'RE NOT CLEAR.

THEIR PROGRESS HAD BEEN TOO GOOD TO BE TRUE. THE ROGUES THEY HAD CLASHED WITH BEFORE UNFORTUNATELY WERE ALSO ON THE MOVE THAT MORNING. THEY SPRUNG AN AMBUSH—

BANDITS, NOT GERMANS! THEY'RE IN THE ROCKS TO THE LEFT.

AAGH!

THE BRITISH LAY LOW UNDER THE RAGGED FIRE.

YOUR MATE ERIC IS WITH THEM. I SAW HIM.

CONFOUND IT!

INDEED HE WAS, FIGHTING LIKE SOME ROBOT.

WE HAVE THEM TRAPPED!

NOT THIS TIME THEY DIDN'T. ED AND ANOTHER COMMANDO HAD WORKED THEIR WAY UNSEEN UP THE HILLSIDE TO OUT-FLANK THE RENEGADES.

LET 'EM HAVE IT!

AAGH!

THAT TWO-MAN SPEARHEAD GAVE THE OTHER SPECIALISTS TIME TO MOVE UP FROM COVER.

THEY'RE BREAKING NOW!

AAGH!

BY NOW BRUCE AND JOHN WERE UP THERE WITH THE BEST OF THEM, DOING GREAT DAMAGE.

THAT'S THE WAY, FLY-BOY!

AAGH!

IN THE BEDLAM WHICH FOLLOWED, JOHN SUDDENLY FOUND HIMSELF ALONE — UNTIL ERIC OF ALL PEOPLE ROSE INTO VIEW.

YE GODS!

I'LL KILL YOU AND ALL LIKE YOU!

AS JOHN FROZE, THE OTHER MAN DIDN'T. HE BLAZED AWAY—

BLAST, THAT JUST MISSED!

OUT OF SELF-PRESERVATION, JOHN RETURNED THE FIRE.

ERIC, YOU FOOL, CAN'T YOU SEE IT'S ME?

THE MOMENT OF ANGER TURNED TO CONCERN AS
JOHN SAW HIS OPPONENT FALL AS HE WAS HIT.

LUCKILY THE VICTIM HAD ONLY BEEN HIT BY ROCK SPLINTERS AND
KNOCKED COLD. HE CAME ROUND WITH JOHN CROUCHING OVER HIM.

SLOWLY, PIECE BY PIECE, ERIC FITTED HIS MEMORY TOGETHER AGAIN. HE WAS HORRIFIED TO HEAR OF SOME OF HIS ANTICS.

WHAT? MY NAME WILL BE MUD NOW . . .

DON'T WORRY ABOUT IT, MATE. I THINK I CAN ALMOST UNDERSTAND.

BRUCE APPEARED THEN JUST AS THE TWO PALS CLEARED UP THE MISUNDERSTANDING.

IT'S OKAY, HE'S ON OUR SIDE NOW.

WELL, THAT'S A RELIEF. TELL ME ALL ABOUT IT WHILE WE GET OUT OF HERE.

AT LEAST THEY WOULD NOT BE HINDERED BY THE RENEGADE PARTISANS — NONE OF THEM HAD SURVIVED.

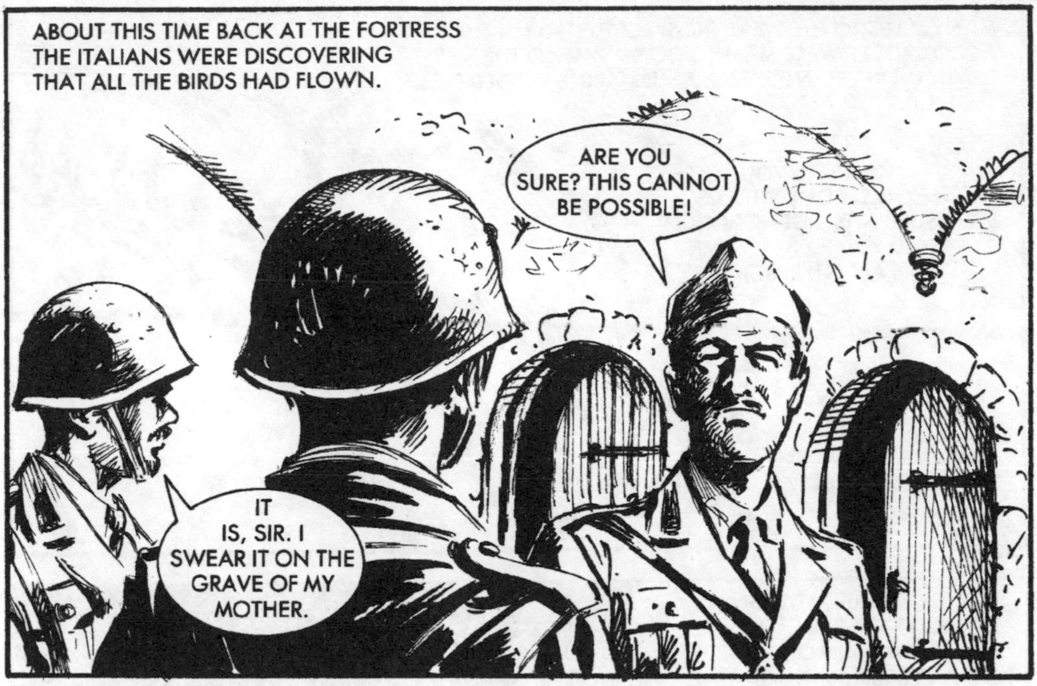
ABOUT THIS TIME BACK AT THE FORTRESS THE ITALIANS WERE DISCOVERING THAT ALL THE BIRDS HAD FLOWN.
ARE YOU SURE? THIS CANNOT BE POSSIBLE!
IT IS, SIR. I SWEAR IT ON THE GRAVE OF MY MOTHER.

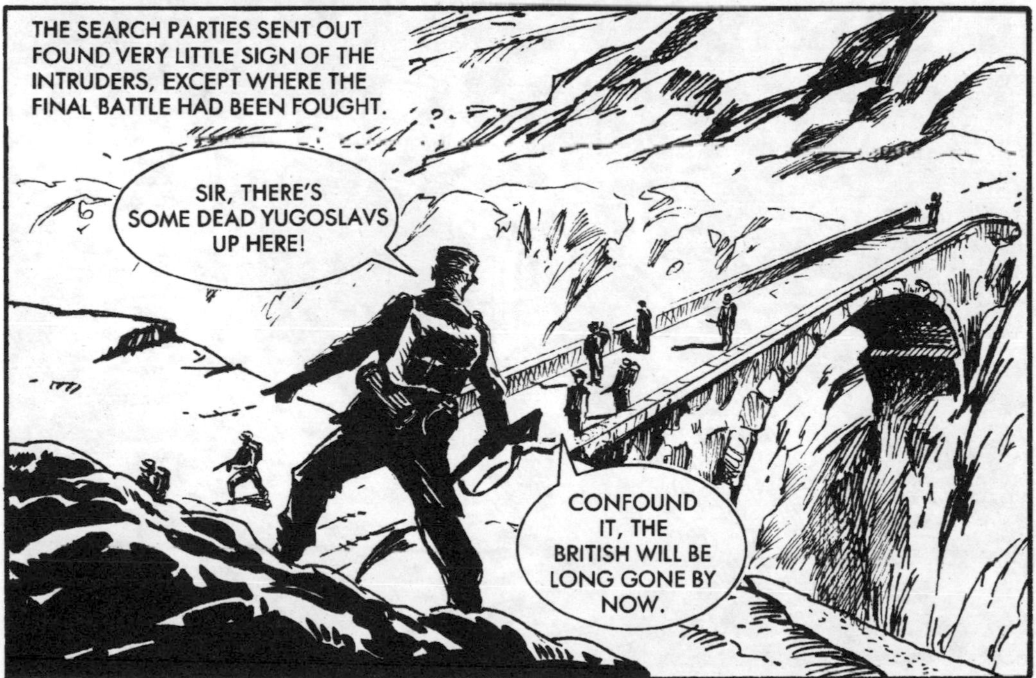
THE SEARCH PARTIES SENT OUT FOUND VERY LITTLE SIGN OF THE INTRUDERS, EXCEPT WHERE THE FINAL BATTLE HAD BEEN FOUGHT.
SIR, THERE'S SOME DEAD YUGOSLAVS UP HERE!
CONFOUND IT, THE BRITISH WILL BE LONG GONE BY NOW.

MANY MILES TO THE WEST THE SPECIALISTS AND THEIR ACCOMPLICES WERE MAKING GOOD TIME TO THE RENDEZVOUS POINT WHERE A SUBMARINE WOULD PICK THEM UP.

DRASKO, YOU SHOULD COME WITH US. I'M SURE INTELLIGENCE COULD FIND YOU PLENTY WORK AS AN INTERPRETER.

IS THAT SO? THEN I AGREE.

THE PRE-ARRANGED SIGNAL BROUGHT THE SUB CLOSE IN SHORE. THE MEN ON LAND WERE SAFELY FERRIED ABOARD . . .

. . . BEFORE THE SLEEK CRAFT SLIPPED BELOW THE WAVES ON THE FIRST STAGE OF THE RUN TO SAFETY.

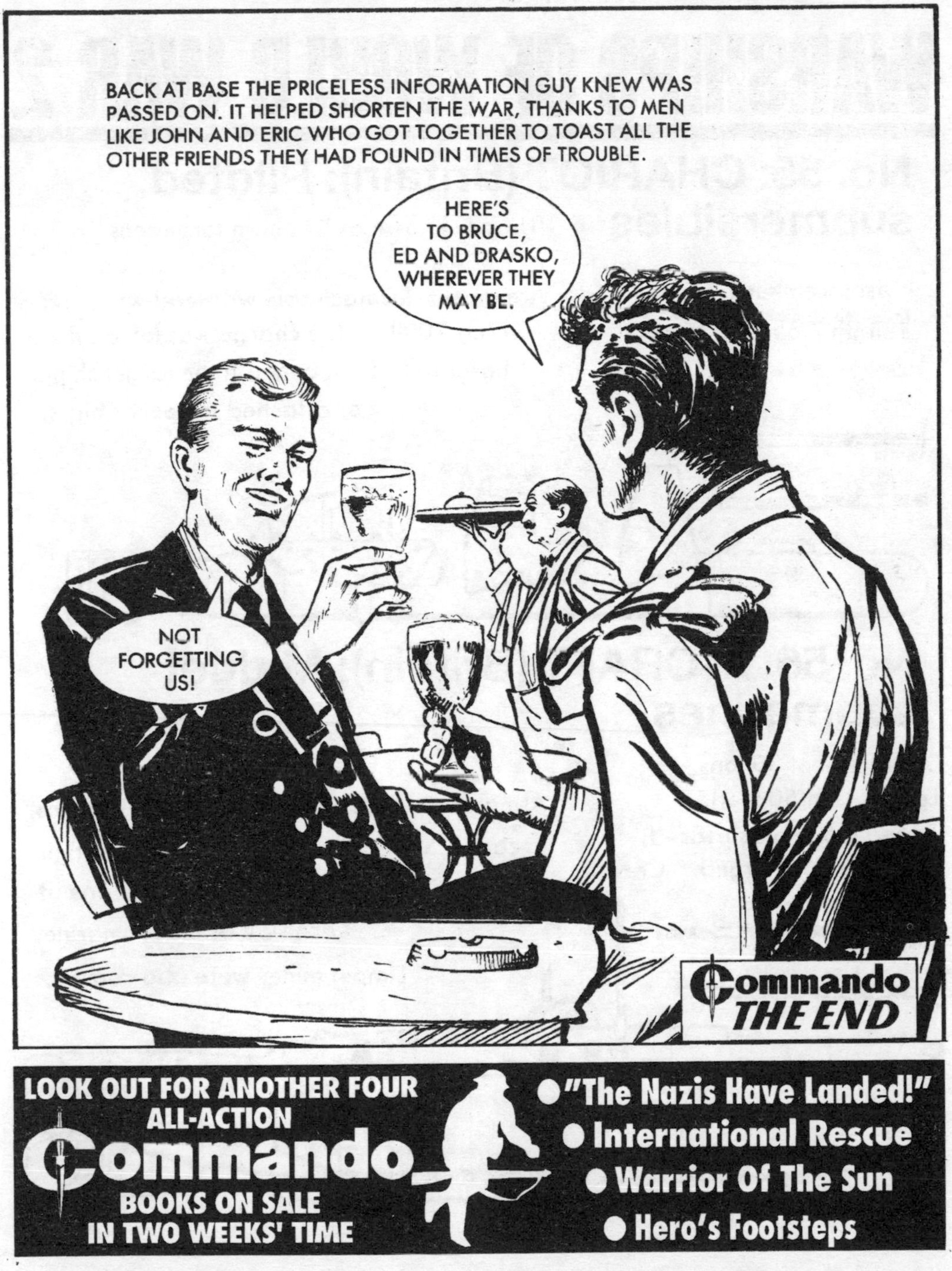
BACK AT BASE THE PRICELESS INFORMATION GUY KNEW WAS PASSED ON. IT HELPED SHORTEN THE WAR, THANKS TO MEN LIKE JOHN AND ERIC WHO GOT TOGETHER TO TOAST ALL THE OTHER FRIENDS THEY HAD FOUND IN TIMES OF TROUBLE.
HERE'S TO BRUCE, ED AND DRASKO, WHEREVER THEY MAY BE.
NOT FORGETTING US!
Commando THE END

WARSHIPS OF WORLD WAR 2

No. 55: CHARIOT (Britain): Piloted submersibles (Usually known as " human torpedoes ")

Displacement 1.5 tons.
Length 7.65m(25 feet).
Speed 3.5 knots.   Crew 2.

Armament—Detachable warhead weighing 317kg(700lbs). The charge was left on the harbour bottom beneath the target ship, or attached to keel or bilge.

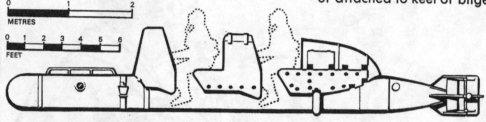

No. 56: X-CRAFT (Britain): Midget submarines

Displacement 30 tons.
Length 15m(50 feet).
Speed 6.5 knots surfaced,
4.5 knots submerged.   Crew 4.

Armament—2 detachable explosive charges, each 5.5 tons. These were 9.1m(30 feet) in length, streamlined, and carried one at each side of the submarine.

Limpet mines were also carried.

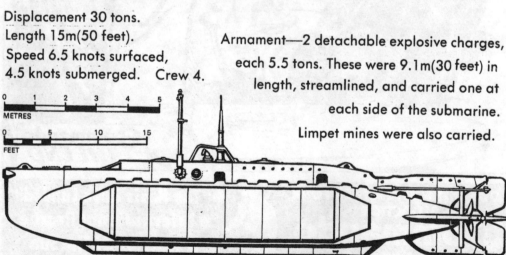

MIGHTY MIDGET

THE MEDITERRANEAN, NINETEEN-FORTY-TWO. A BRITISH SUBMARINE MOVED ACROSS THE SURFACE, CHARGING HER BATTERIES AT NIGHT FOR YET ANOTHER DAY'S OPERATIONS AGAINST THE GERMAN SUPPLY LINES.

ON THE BRIDGE, THE LATEST RECRUIT TO THE CREW, LIEUTENANT DICK ROLLAND, ALLOWED HIMSELF A SMILE OF SATISFACTION. IT WAS A LONG WAY FROM THE QUIET LIFE AS SERVICE MANAGER IN HIS FATHER'S GARAGE — AND HE WAS RELISHING EVERY SECOND OF IT!

DICK'S THOUGHTS WERE INTERRUPTED BY THE ARRIVAL OF THE SUB'S CAPTAIN — COMMANDER JENKINS, AN ABLE AND WELL-LIKED SKIPPER.

I'LL TAKE OVER, DICK. DOWN YOU GO AND GET YOURSELF A MUG OF COCOA.

THANKS, SIR. I COULD DO WITH ONE.

KEEN AND WILLING, AN OFFICER FROM THE ROYAL NAVAL VOLUNTEER RESERVE, DICK HAD SOON WON THE RESPECT OF JENKINS, A REGULAR NAVY MAN.

BUT EN ROUTE TO THE GALLEY, DICK WAS INTERCEPTED BY LIEUTENANT REX PRENDLE, THE SECOND-IN-COMMAND, WHO SHARPLY DEMANDED TO KNOW WHERE HE WAS GOING.

COCOA? YOU'RE NOT WORKING IN A GARAGE NOW. IF YOU'VE NOTHING BETTER TO DO, GO UP-DATE THE MANUALS.

ALSO REGULAR NAVY, PRENDLE WAS ONE OF THE FEW WHO FOOLISHLY LOOKED DOWN UPON THE MEN OF THE R.N.V.R. IT WASN'T THE FIRST TIME DICK HAD FALLEN FOUL OF HIS ARROGANCE.

HE THINKS ALL RESERVISTS ARE JUST USELESS AMATEURS, BUT I'LL SHOW HIM.

IN FACT PRENDLE DID NOT SEEM TO LIKE ANYBODY. FROM A FAMILY WHICH HAD SERVED AFLOAT FOR GENERATIONS, HE WAS HARD ON ALL THOSE UNDER HIS RANK, THEN A SMILING YES-MAN WHEN DEALING WITH HIS SUPERIORS.

MORE SIGNIFICANT EVENTS WERE OCCURRING ON THE SURFACE HOWEVER WHERE THE LOOKOUT HAD JUST RAISED THE ALARM.

AN ITALIAN DESTROYER, SIR — OFF THE PORT BOW! IT LOOKS LIKE SHE'S SEEN US . . .

DIVE! DIVE! DIVE!

JENKINS, WITH ALL HIS EXPERIENCE, WAS IN NO DOUBT AS TO THE SERIOUSNESS OF THEIR SITUATION. HE WAS BELOW DECKS IN SECONDS, RAPPING OUT ORDERS.

RIG FOR SILENT RUNNING. STAND BY FOR DEPTH-CHARGING.

AYE, AYE, SIR.

WITHIN MINUTES, THE SUBMARINERS KNEW THEY HAD INDEED BEEN SPOTTED. THE ITALIAN DESTROYER RELEASED HER DEADLY CHARGES, THE FIRST EXPLOSIONS SENDING UP SPOUTS OF WATER.

THE ATMOSPHERE IN THE CRAMPED SUB WAS TENSE AS SHE SHOOK TO THE EXPLOSIONS. DICK COULD NOT FAIL TO NOTICE THOUGH THAT PRENDLE WAS A LOT JUMPIER THAN ANY OF THE OTHERS.

PRENDLE DOESN'T LOOK SO CONFIDENT NOW THAT THE CHIPS ARE DOWN.

THAT GAVE HIM SOME GRIM SATISFACTION. ALL ELSE WAS FORGOTTEN AS SUDDENLY THE BRITISH CRAFT LISTED OVER AS A CHARGE EXPLODED VERY CLOSE.

THEY WERE LUCKY TO SURVIVE THAT ENCOUNTER. AS THE SUBMARINE RIGHTED HERSELF, THE ONLY REAL CASUALTY WAS JENKINS WITH A BAD GASH ON HIS HEAD.

THE SKIPPER'S HURT, SIR.

GET HIM TO HIS BUNK. COXSWAIN — CHECK THE BOAT FOR DAMAGE.

DICK GAVE THAT ORDER. NO SOUND CAME FROM THE ASHEN-FACED PRENDLE WHO SLIPPED AWAY QUIETLY AS IF TO BUSY HIMSELF ELSEWHERE. AS SECOND-IN-COMMAND, HE SHOULD HAVE ASSUMED CONTROL.

FINALLY THE DETONATIONS CEASED. THE CREW WERE STILL LOOKING TO DICK FOR THEIR ORDERS —

HYDROPHONES REPORT THE EYETIE WITHDRAWING, SIR. IT LOOKS LIKE WE'VE MADE IT.

THANK GOODNESS FOR THAT. I CAN'T BELIEVE PRENDLE — JUST FOLDING UP . . .

GRIMLY HE WENT TO CHECK ON THE SKIPPER'S CONDITION.

IT WASN'T GOOD, AS HE REPORTED TO PRENDLE WHEN HE EVENTUALLY FOUND HIM SKULKING IN THE WARDROOM.

HE'S BADLY CONCUSSED. HE NEEDS A HOSPITAL.

WELL . . . RIGHT. SET COURSE FOR MALTA.

AS DICK PREPARED TO LEAVE, PRENDLE MUSTERED ALL HIS NORMAL ARROGANCE TO GIVE HIM A WARNING —

WHAT HAPPENED JUST NOW COULD RUIN MY CAREER. KEEP YOUR MOUTH SHUT IF YOU KNOW WHAT'S GOOD FOR YOU.

THAT'S BETWEEN YOU AND YOUR CONSCIENCE . . . SIR.

WITH NO FURTHER ENEMY ACTION, PRENDLE GRADUALLY RECOVERED HIS NERVE. BY THE TIME THEY REACHED THE SAFETY OF MALTA HE WAS BACK TO HIS OVER-BEARING, UNPLEASANT SELF.

GET THAT CASING PARTY SMARTENED UP, ROLLAND. I WANT EVERYTHING LOOKING GOOD AS WE COME ALONGSIDE.

AS SOON AS WE'RE IN SIGHT OF PORT HE STARTS ACTING LIKE HE RULES THE WAVES.

NONE OF THE CREW WERE AT ALL FOOLED. YET, LIKE DICK, THEY KNEW IT WAS USELESS TO CREATE ANY SORT OF FUSS WITHOUT COMPLETE PROOF. PRENDLE WAS TOO WELL CONNECTED FOR THAT.

AT THE SUBMARINE DEPOT, THE CAPTAIN IN COMMAND GREETED THEM AS THEY CAME ALONGSIDE. DICK COULD HARDLY BELIEVE PRENDLE'S CONCEIT AS HE TOOK THE CREDIT FOR THEIR RETURN.

YOU DID A GOOD JOB BRINGING THIS BOAT HOME, PRENDLE.

THANK YOU, SIR. IT WASN'T EASY WITH SUCH AN INEXPERIENCED CREW.

THE SHIRKER HAD COVERED HIS FAULTS WELL. HE WAS ACTING MORE UNPLEASANTLY THAN EVER BEFORE THE DAY WAS OUT.

SMARTING AT ALL THIS, NEXT MORNING AT H.Q., DICK READ A BULLETIN CALLING FOR VOLUNTEERS FOR " SPECIAL AND HAZARDOUS DUTIES ".

ANYTHING TO GET AWAY FROM PRENDLE. I'LL PUT MY NAME DOWN.

WITH PRENDLE IN COMMAND UNTIL JENKINS RECOVERED, HE HOPED HE WOULD BE ACCEPTED.

A SELECTION BOARD SOON SPELLED OUT THE DETAILS. THE WORK INVOLVED WAS TO DO WITH MIDGET SUBMARINES, A WEAPON DICK HAD ONLY HEARD VAGUELY ABOUT.

WE'RE TRAINING CREWS FOR THESE CRAFT. IF YOU'RE STILL INTERESTED, WE'LL RECOMMEND YOU.

THANK YOU, SIR.

AFTER TWO WEEKS LEAVE, DICK REPORTED FOR TRAINING AT A DEPOT-SHIP, WHICH LAY AT ANCHOR IN A LOCH IN SCOTLAND. HIS FIRST VIEW WAS OF A BLEAK, COLD ANCHORAGE, THE SCENE PARTLY OBSCURED BY DRIVING RAIN.

I MUST HAVE BEEN MAD TO LEAVE THE MED FOR THIS.

CAPTAIN CALSHOT, THE C.O. OF THE TRAINING SCHOOL, GREETED HIS NEW STUDENT WARMLY. HERE WAS AN OFFICER WHO MUCKED IN WITH HIS MEN IN THEIR DANGEROUS WORK.

GLAD TO HAVE YOU WITH US. YOUR MECHANICAL BACKGROUND WILL COME IN HANDY. I'LL SHOW YOU ROUND.

CALSHOT HAD ONE PIECE OF UNWELCOME NEWS, HOWEVER.

I THINK YOU KNOW ONE OF OUR OTHER NEW TRAINEES — LIEUTENANT PRENDLE.

OH . . . YES, SIR. THAT'S RIGHT . . .

PRENDLE WAS THE LAST PERSON DICK HAD EXPECTED OR WANTED TO SEE ON THE COURSE. THE INFORMATION REALLY SHOOK HIM.

THAT EVENING IN THE MESS, DICK MET HIS FELLOW TRAINEES. SOME OF THEM KNEW PRENDLE OF OLD AND HE WAS INTERESTED TO HEAR THEIR VIEWS AS TO WHY HE HAD VOLUNTEERED FOR THE COURSE.

ALL TALK ON THE SUBJECT CEASED WHEN THE MAN IN QUESTION APPEARED. HE WAS FAR FROM FRIENDLY WHEN DICK GREETED HIM.

I DON'T WANT YOU FOULING UP MY CHANCES, ROLLAND. KEEP OUT OF MY WAY AND DON'T CAUSE ME TROUBLE.

GOOD FOR HIS CAREER, OLD BOY. HE'S BEEN PROMISED COMMAND OF A FLEET SUB IF HE DOES WELL HERE.

CLEARLY HE WAS WORRIED ANY TALK ABOUT HIS BEHAVIOUR UNDER STRESS WOULD GET OUT. DICK REALISED HIS LIFE WAS GOING TO BE VERY DIFFICULT.

WHEN THE COURSE STARTED, FOR SOME IT WAS A PAINFUL SHOCK. CALSHOT BELIEVED IN HAVING HIS MEN AT THE PEAK OF PHYSICAL FITNESS.

THIS IS RIDICULOUS. ANYONE WOULD THINK WE WERE RAW RECRUITS . . .

SAVE YOUR BREATH, MR PRENDLE, SIR. YOU'VE ANOTHER THREE MILES.

AS TRAINING PROGRESSED, THE VOLUNTEERS WERE INTRODUCED TO NEW SKILLS. FOR DICK, IT WAS A CHALLENGING EXPERIENCE.

THEY'RE CERTAINLY MAKING SURE WE'RE READY FOR ANYTHING. AND PRENDLE THOUGHT HE WAS GOING TO HAVE AN EASY TIME OF IT!

FINALLY, AFTER WEEKS OF PREPARATION, DICK, PRENDLE AND THE OTHER " SURVIVING " VOLUNTEERS WERE INTRODUCED TO THEIR NEW WEAPON — THE MIDGET SUBMARINE.

. . . OR X-CRAFT AS WE CALL THEM. FORTY-EIGHT FEET LONG, FIVE AND A HALF FEET IN DIAMETER. TOTAL WEIGHT, FULLY LOADED, THIRTY-NINE TONS. A CREW OF FOUR.

IT SHOULD BE A PIECE OF CAKE WITH ALL MY BIG BOAT EXPERIENCE.

ONLY A MAN LIKE PRENDLE WOULD HAVE SPOKEN SO ARROGANTLY.

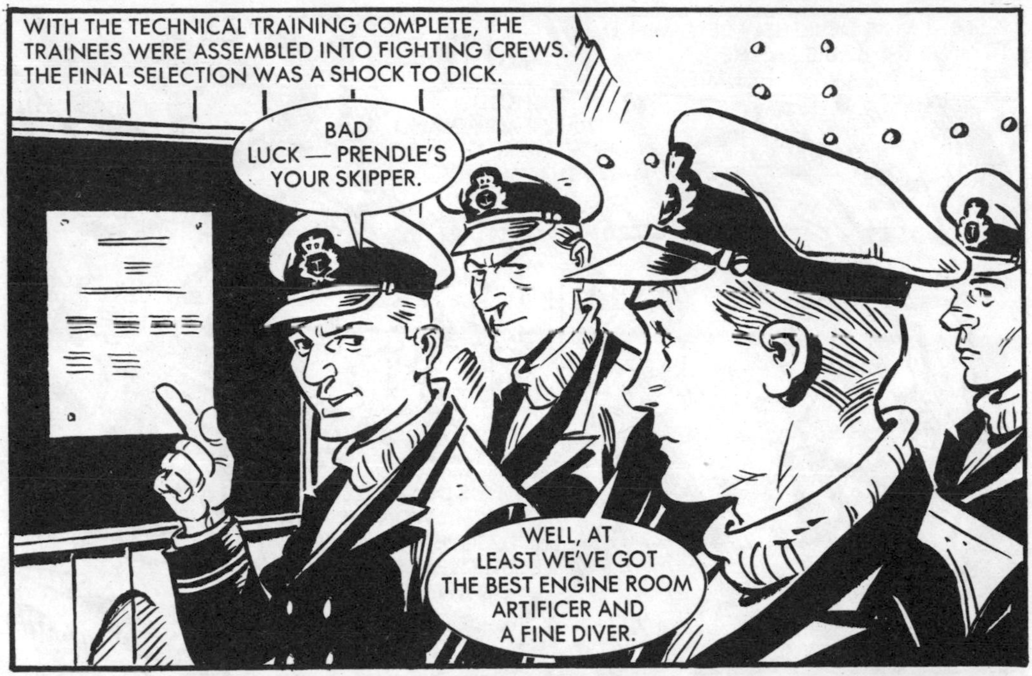
WITH THE TECHNICAL TRAINING COMPLETE, THE TRAINEES WERE ASSEMBLED INTO FIGHTING CREWS. THE FINAL SELECTION WAS A SHOCK TO DICK.
BAD LUCK — PRENDLE'S YOUR SKIPPER.
WELL, AT LEAST WE'VE GOT THE BEST ENGINE ROOM ARTIFICER AND A FINE DIVER.

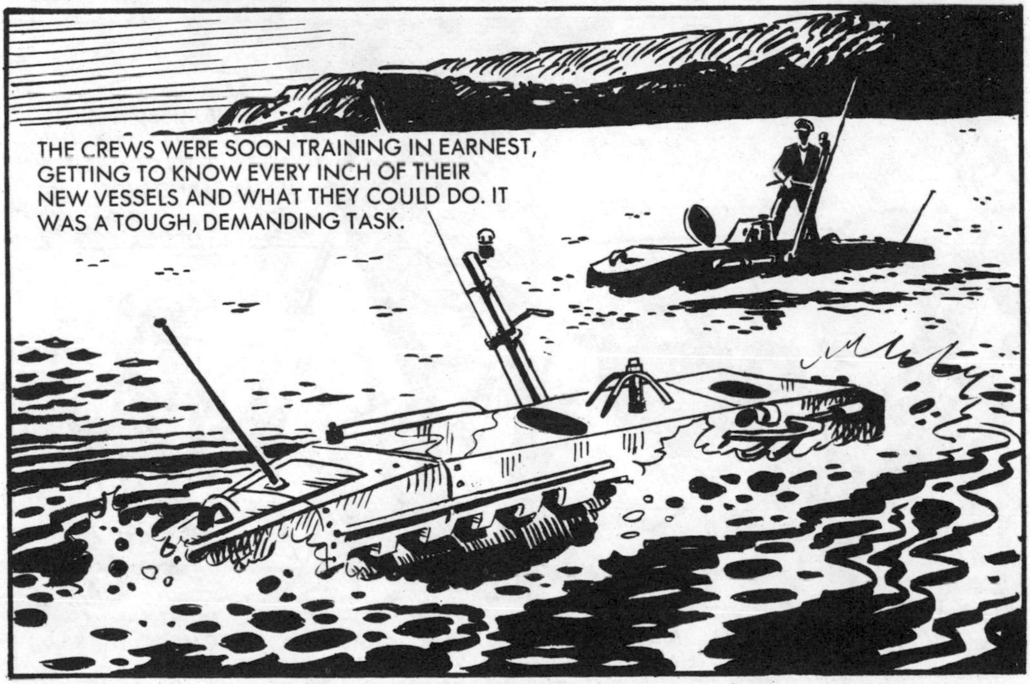
THE CREWS WERE SOON TRAINING IN EARNEST, GETTING TO KNOW EVERY INCH OF THEIR NEW VESSELS AND WHAT THEY COULD DO. IT WAS A TOUGH, DEMANDING TASK.

PRENDLE WAS OBVIOUSLY DETERMINED TO HAVE THE BEST BOAT. HE PUSHED HIS TEAM TO THE LIMIT.

HOLD THAT HEADING AND DEPTH. WE'RE GOING TO TRY THAT MANOEUVRE AGAIN.

HE'S DEAD KEEN NOW. BUT I WONDER HOW HE'LL COPE WITH A JERRY DESTROYER BREATHING DOWN HIS NECK.

UNFORTUNATELY, IN HIS SEARCH FOR PERFECTION, HE HAD LOST NONE OF HIS BITING ARROGANCE.

AS A TEAM YOU'RE RUBBISH. YOU'RE GOING TO HAVE TO BUCK UP TO COME UP TO MY STANDARDS.

THE OTHER TWO MEMBERS OF THE CREW — ENGINE ROOM ARTIFICER LARRY TANNER AND LEADING SEAMAN SAM RAMAGE, THEIR DIVER — HAD QUICKLY COME TO THE SAME CONCLUSION AS DICK THAT THEIR SKIPPER WAS A PAIN IN THE NECK.

IT HAD BEEN A PARTICULARLY GRUELLING DAY FOR SAM. LARRY SOON HEARD ALL ABOUT IT.

SIX TIMES HE HAD ME IN AND OUT OF THAT DIVING CHAMBER!

CHEER UP, MATE. I'VE HEARD THAT MR ROLLAND IS BEING CONSIDERED FOR A COMMAND. PRENDLE MIGHT GET MOVED.

AS USUAL, RUMOUR WAS CLOSE TO TRUTH. CALSHOT SOUGHT OUT PRENDLE THAT EVENING.

YOUNG DICK ROLLAND SEEMS TO BE SQUARING UP WELL. WE NEED SOME MORE SKIPPERS, SO LET HIM COMMAND ON TOMORROW'S EXERCISE.

DICK COULDN'T BELIEVE HIS LUCK WHEN HE HEARD THE ORDERS. HE WAS SURPRISED TO FIND PRENDLE ALSO UNUSUALLY HELPFUL . . . ALTHOUGH HIS TONGUE WAS AS BITING AS EVER.

I'LL TAKE THE WHEEL MYSELF. WE DON'T WANT THAT FOOL TANNER MESSING UP YOUR CHANCES.

THE EXERCISE WAS TO MAKE A MOCK ATTACK ON A CRUISER ANCHORED IN THE LOCH. WITH SO MUCH AT STAKE, DICK PLANNED HIS APPROACH CAREFULLY.

IT'S WORKING OUT JUST RIGHT.

RUDDER — TEN DEGREES STARBOARD.

IT WAS A SIMPLE ORDER. PRENDLE SWUNG THE WHEEL IN RESPONSE . . . BUT THE WRONG WAY. DICK WAS QUICK TO DETECT THE ERROR —

WE'RE TURNING TO PORT — CANCEL THAT WHEEL!

ALREADY IT WAS TOO LATE. WITH A JOLT, THE SMALL SUBMARINE STRUCK ONE OF THE MANY ROCKY OUTCROPS IN THE LOCH.

IN THOSE FEW SECONDS, DICK REALISED THAT PRENDLE HAD LOST HIM HIS CHANCE OF A COMMAND.

YOU'VE PUT US AGROUND!

SORRY, OLD BOY, BUT YOU'RE THE SKIPPER. YOU SHOULD HAVE MADE THE ORDER CLEARER.

GRITTING HIS TEETH, DICK GAVE THE ORDER TO SURFACE. THE DAMAGE WAS SLIGHT BUT CAPTAIN CALSHOT'S DISPLEASURE WAS OBVIOUS.

ROLLAND! RETURN TO THE DEPOT-SHIP AND REPORT TO MY OFFICE.

AS DICK PREPARED TO FACE THE MUSIC, LARRY OFFERED HIM SOME WORDS OF SUPPORT. HE AND SAM HAD BOTH HAD THEIR FILL OF PRENDLE.

IF IT'S ANY CONSOLATION, SIR, WE HEARD THAT ORDER CLEAR ENOUGH.

THANKS, LARRY, BUT I DON'T THINK THAT'S GOING TO HELP ME WITH THE C.O.

HE WAS RIGHT. BLAMING PRENDLE WOULD ONLY SEEM LIKE AN EXCUSE AND WORSEN HIS CASE. CALSHOT PULLED NO PUNCHES.

I'M VERY DISAPPOINTED IN YOU. IF WE WEREN'T SO SHORT OF CREWS, I'D HAVE YOU THROWN OFF THE COURSE.

INSTEAD, DICK LEARNED HE HAD TO CONTINUE SERVING UNDER PRENDLE.

AS HE LEFT THE C.O.'s OFFICE, HE FOUND IT DIFFICULT TO CONTROL HIS BITTERNESS. THERE WAS NO DOUBT HE WAS REALLY UP AGAINST IT.

IT SEEMS PRENDLE WILL TRY ANYTHING TO GET RID OF ME AND SAVE HIS PRECIOUS CAREER.

A FEW DAYS LATER, HOWEVER, ALL ELSE WAS FORGOTTEN WHEN THE TWO TRAINED CREWS WERE CALLED TO A BRIEFING.

WELL, NOW YOU'VE GOT A TARGET — A GERMAN BATTLE-CRUISER LYING HERE ON THE BRITTANY COAST.

THE WARSHIP HAD BEEN CAUGHT BY BRITISH SURFACE UNITS WHILE COMMERCE RAIDING IN THE NORTH ATLANTIC. ALTHOUGH DAMAGED, SHE HAD MANAGED TO ESCAPE. NOW A FRENCH RESISTANCE GROUP HAD REPORTED HER AT A NAVAL ANCHORAGE IN FRANCE WHERE BOMBERS COULD NOT GET IN CLOSE BECAUSE OF THE TERRAIN.

THE OPERATION WAS TO BE LAUNCHED FROM A CHANNEL PORT. THAT SAME NIGHT, THE
TWO TEAMS SPED SOUTH TO JOIN THE X-CRAFT ALREADY WAITING THERE. IT GAVE DICK
PLENTY OF TIME FOR THOUGHT.

I MUST BE A FOOL FOR NOT TELLING THE C.O. HOW PRENDLE LOST HIS NERVE IN THE MED., BUT IT'S TOO LATE NOW. THEY'D ONLY THINK IT WAS SOUR GRAPES . . .

THE NEXT FORTY-EIGHT HOURS WERE ONES OF FEVERISH PREPARATION.
SLOWLY THE JIGSAW CAME TOGETHER WITH THE ARRIVAL OF TWO
CONVENTIONAL SUBMARINES WHICH WOULD TOW THE X-CRAFT AS
CLOSE AS POSSIBLE TO THE FRENCH COAST.

THEY'RE GOING TO PUT MEN ABOARD OUR CRAFT WHILE WE TRAVEL IN THE SUBS.

SOUNDS GOOD. AT LEAST WE'LL GET SOME KIP BEFORE THE ACTION STARTS.

THAT SAME NIGHT, THE SMALL FLOTILLA SET OFF. GRIMLY DICK WATCHED FROM THE CONNING TOWER OF ONE OF THE LARGE SUBMARINES.

WELL, HERE WE GO. IT'S TOO LATE FOR PRENDLE TO BACK OUT NOW.

THE X-CRAFT WERE TOWED SUBMERGED BY DAY, THEN ON THE SURFACE AT NIGHT. ON THE SECOND NIGHT, AS THEY ENTERED THE NOTORIOUS BAY OF BISCAY, THE WEATHER WORSENED.

A TYPICAL BISCAY GALE. WE COULD HAVE DONE WITHOUT THIS.

AS THE STORM ROARED OVERHEAD, DICK DETECTED SIGNS OF AGITATION IN PRENDLE. WAS HIS NERVE SLIPPING ALREADY? THE SUDDEN ARRIVAL OF A BRIDGE MESSENGER ENDED FURTHER SPECULATION.

THE SKIPPER WANTS YOU ON THE BRIDGE IMMEDIATELY, GENTLEMEN. THE OTHER MIDGET'S IN TROUBLE.

SHE WAS INDEED. ALREADY THE CREW WERE ABANDONING HER.

SHE TOOK A WAVE DOWN THE HATCH WHILE SHE WAS VENTILATING. I'M AFRAID SHE'S HAD IT.

THE LOSS OF HALF THE FORCE WAS A BAD SET-BACK. IT GAVE PRENDLE . . .

. . . THE VERY EXCUSE DICK SUSPECTED HE WAS LOOKING FOR.

WE CAN'T GO ON WITH JUST ONE UNIT. WE'LL HAVE TO CALL IT OFF.

HE'S GIVING UP . . .

IT WAS A TIME FOR BRUTAL MEASURES. DICK KNEW FULL WELL ONE X-CRAFT COULD STILL DO THE JOB.

WE'RE GOING ON — OR I'LL MAKE SURE EVEN THE FIRST SEA LORD KNOWS HOW YOU LOST YOUR NERVE!

CURSE YOU! OKAY, YOU WIN THIS TIME, BUT ONE DAY I'LL RID MYSELF OF YOU FOR GOOD!

WITH THAT THREAT RINGING IN HIS EARS, DICK STAYED ON DECK WHILE THE FURIOUS PRENDLE STAMPED BELOW.

I HATED DOING THAT, BUT IT WAS THE ONLY WAY.

LUCKILY NOBODY ELSE HAD HEARD THE EXCHANGE ABOVE THE ROAR OF THE BUFFETING WIND.

ONLY ONE SUBMARINE NOW SAILED ON. JUST AFTER MIDNIGHT, THEY REACHED THE POSITION OFF THE FRENCH COAST WHERE THEY WERE TO SLIP THEIR TOW.

WE'LL BE WAITING HERE FOR YOU TOMORROW. GOOD LUCK.

THE X-CRAFT COMMANDED BY PRENDLE CAST OFF. SOON THE MOTHER SUB HAD DISAPPEARED INTO THE DARKNESS BEHIND THEM.

FOUR HOURS CRUISING BROUGHT THE MOUTH OF THE RIVER IN SIGHT WHICH LED TO THE ANCHORAGE. IT WAS TIME FOR THE X-CRAFT TO PLAY HER TRUE ROLE.

THERE'S THE LIGHTHOUSE . . . PREPARE TO DIVE!

LARRY, SAM AND DICK WENT ABOUT THEIR DUTIES LIKE A TEAM. PRENDLE ALONE DID NOT FIT IN WITH THE OTHERS.

AS THE X-CRAFT CAUTIOUSLY ENTERED THE RIVER, PRENDLE WAS FAR FROM HAPPY AS HE SURVEYED THE DANGERS THROUGH HIS PERISCOPE.

PATROL BOATS AND SHORE BATTERIES — I DON'T LIKE THIS AT ALL.

IN SPITE OF HIS FEAR AND THE ELABORATE DEFENCES, THE MIDGET SUBMARINE PASSED THROUGH UNDETECTED.

I JUST HOPE IT'S AS EASY TO GET OUT.

SLOWLY THEY CREPT BENEATH THE ASSORTED SHIPS IN THE NAVAL ANCHORAGE. LARRY SUMMED UP THE FEELINGS OF THEM ALL.

I'VE NEVER SEEN A SUB MOVE ON TIPTOE, BUT THIS ONE FEELS LIKE IT'S DOING IT.

A GRAVE PROBLEM STILL HAD TO BE TACKLED. NOW THEY HAD TO NEGOTIATE A SHARP CURVE IN THE RIVER.

ACCORDING TO THE RESISTANCE CHAPS, OUR TARGET IS LYING FURTHER UP-RIVER, ROUND THE NEXT BEND.

AS THE MIDGET ROUNDED THE OBSTACLE SUCCESSFULLY, THERE LAY THE GLITTERING PRIZE. IT PRESENTED A DAUNTING PICTURE TO PRENDLE WHO WAS BECOMING MORE AGITATED BY THE SECOND.

TORPEDO NETS, MORE PATROL BOATS — THIS IS MADNESS! WE'LL NEVER PENETRATE THOSE DEFENCES.

DICK KNEW HE HAD TO KEEP PUSHING OR THE MISSION WOULD BE A FAILURE.

SAM WILL SOON CUT US THROUGH THOSE NETS. LET'S GET RIGHT UP TO THEM.

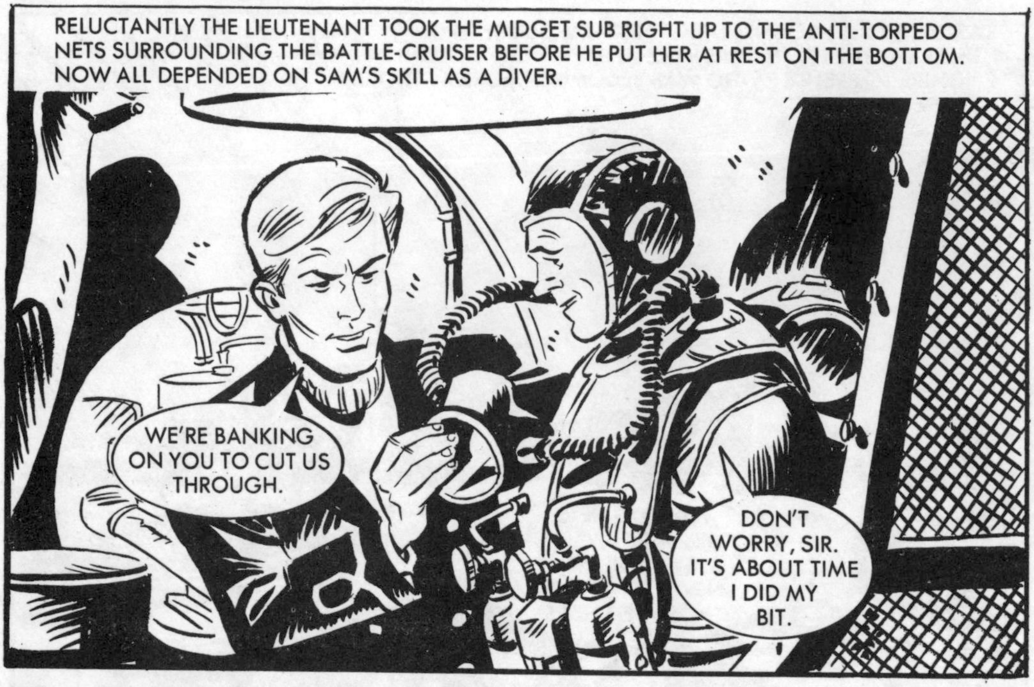
RELUCTANTLY THE LIEUTENANT TOOK THE MIDGET SUB RIGHT UP TO THE ANTI-TORPEDO NETS SURROUNDING THE BATTLE-CRUISER BEFORE HE PUT HER AT REST ON THE BOTTOM. NOW ALL DEPENDED ON SAM'S SKILL AS A DIVER.
WE'RE BANKING ON YOU TO CUT US THROUGH.
DON'T WORRY, SIR. IT'S ABOUT TIME I DID MY BIT.

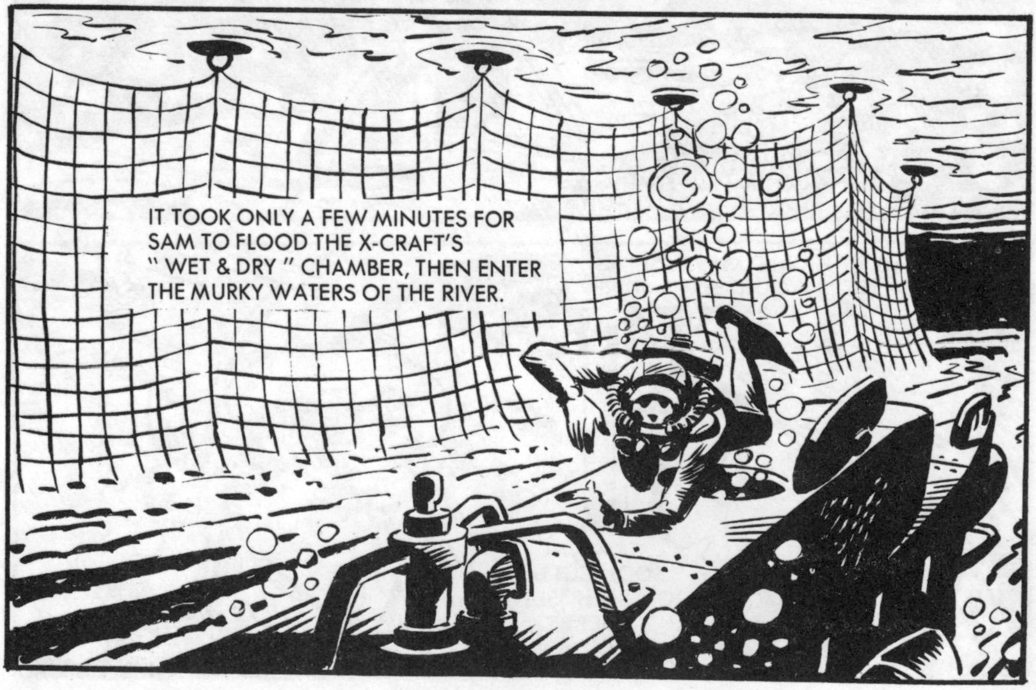
IT TOOK ONLY A FEW MINUTES FOR SAM TO FLOOD THE X-CRAFT'S " WET & DRY " CHAMBER, THEN ENTER THE MURKY WATERS OF THE RIVER.

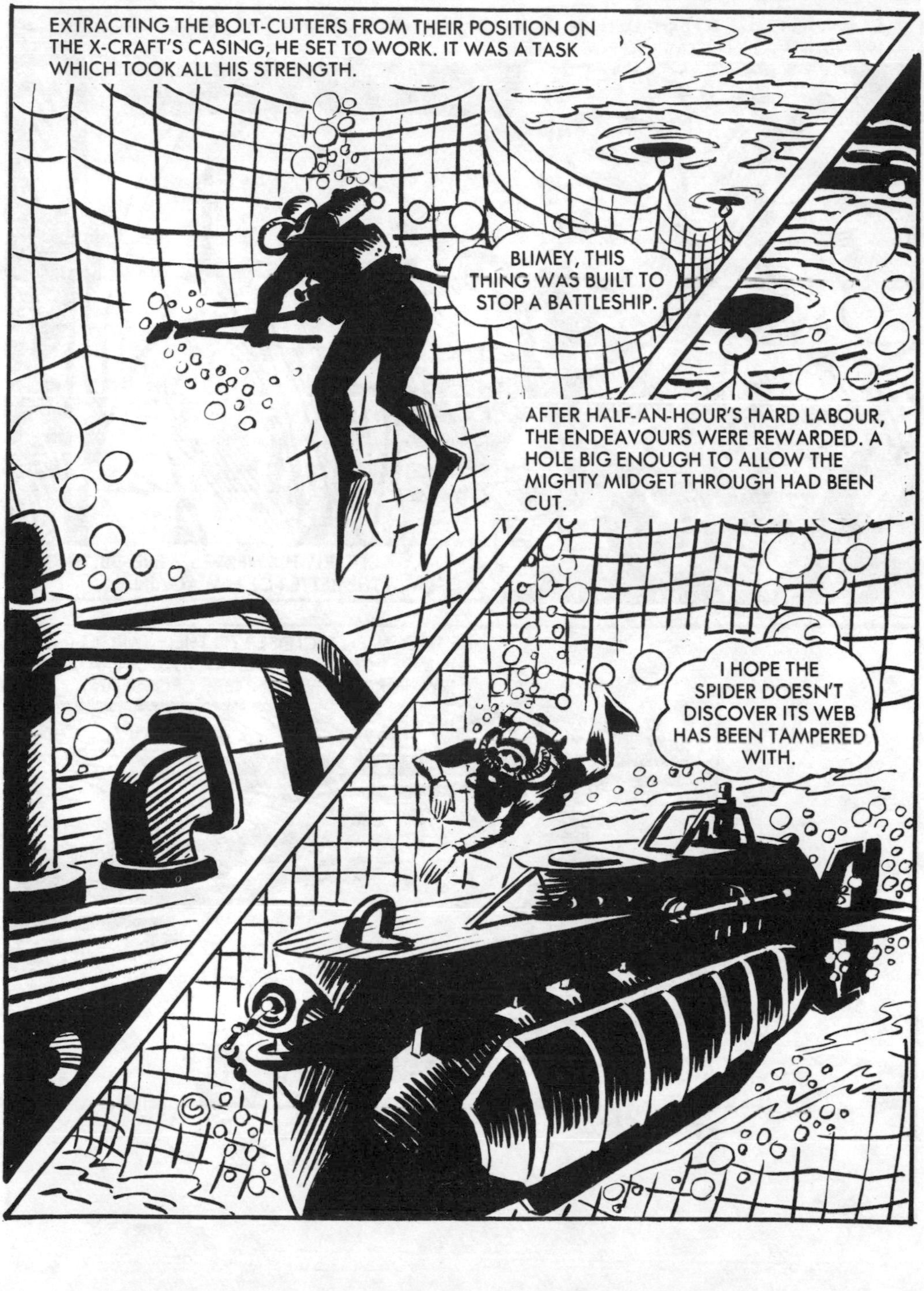
EXTRACTING THE BOLT-CUTTERS FROM THEIR POSITION ON THE X-CRAFT'S CASING, HE SET TO WORK. IT WAS A TASK WHICH TOOK ALL HIS STRENGTH.
BLIMEY, THIS THING WAS BUILT TO STOP A BATTLESHIP.
AFTER HALF-AN-HOUR'S HARD LABOUR, THE ENDEAVOURS WERE REWARDED. A HOLE BIG ENOUGH TO ALLOW THE MIGHTY MIDGET THROUGH HAD BEEN CUT.
I HOPE THE SPIDER DOESN'T DISCOVER ITS WEB HAS BEEN TAMPERED WITH.

SAM WAS CLOSE TO EXHAUSTION. DICK GOT HIM A HOT DRINK RIGHT AWAY BUT PRENDLE WAS IN NO MOOD FOR GRATITUDE.

YOU CERTAINLY TOOK YOUR TIME, RAMAGE. NOW LET'S GET THIS JOB OVER WITH.

CLEARLY HIS NERVES WERE GETTING THE BETTER OF HIM AGAIN.

AS THEY SLIPPED CLOSER TO THEIR TARGET IN THE MOST CRITICAL PHASE OF THE OPERATION, THEY ALL KEPT THEIR FINGERS CROSSED.

SO FAR, SO GOOD. NOW TO DROP THE CHARGES.

AS DICK TURNED THE RELEASING WHEEL IN THE X-CRAFT'S CONTROL-ROOM, THE FIRST TWO-TON CHARGE DROPPED AWAY TO LAND BENEATH THE SHIP'S VULNERABLE STERN.

THE SECOND CHARGE WAS PLACED AMIDSHIPS. THE THOUGHT OF FOUR TONS OF AMATOL, TIMED TO EXPLODE IN NINETY MINUTES, HAD ROBBED PRENDLE OF ALL CAUTION.

NOW LET'S GET OUT OF HERE, QUICK. ENGINE FULL ASTERN.

DICK KNEW THIS WAS TOO MUCH POWER IN SUCH A CONFINED AREA.

STEADY! THE NORTHERN SECTION OF THE NET MUST BE CLOSE BY HERE.

DON'T TELL ME MY JOB!

BUT IT WAS TOO LATE TO ARGUE. ENGINE RACING, THE VESSEL HURTLED BACKWARD TO HIT THE NET.

IMMEDIATELY THE PROPELLERS AND HYDROPLANES WERE TANGLED IN IT.

THE CREW REALISED AT ONCE THEY WERE IN A BAD SITUATION. PRENDLE WAS THE FIRST TO PANIC.

THAT'S TORN IT! WE'RE SNAGGED.

WE'VE GOT TO DO SOMETHING. THOSE CHARGES GO OFF IN EIGHTY MINUTES. ENGINE FULL AHEAD.

FOR A FEW FRANTIC MINUTES THE SHAKING LIEUTENANT TRIED TO WORK THEM FREE, ALTHOUGH IT WAS USELESS. THE MIDGET SUB WAS HELD FAST.

SAM KNEW THERE WAS ONLY ONE THING THEY COULD DO NOW.

I'LL GO OUT AND CUT THE NET AWAY, SIR.

YOU'RE RIGHT, IT'S OUR ONLY HOPE. BUT NOT YOU, SAM. IT'S MY TURN.

DICK COULD SEE SAM WAS STILL EXHAUSTED FROM HIS PREVIOUS LABOURS. LUCKILY THEIR RIGOROUS TRAINING HAD MADE ALL THE OTHERS COMPETENT IN THIS ROLE AS WELL AS THEIR OWN.

WITH THE TIME FUSES TICKING ONLY FIFTY YARDS AWAY, DICK LOST LITTLE TIME CHANGING INTO SOME DIVING GEAR THEN LEAVING THE X-CRAFT.

WHAT A MESS. PRENDLE ISN'T FIT TO COMMAND A RUBBER DUCK!

THE JOB WASN'T QUITE AS FORMIDABLE AS IT HAD APPEARED. TWENTY MINUTES LATER . . .

ALMOST THROUGH! THANK GOODNESS THE PROP CUT SOME OF THE NET TO BEGIN WITH.

AFTER SEVERING THE FINAL STRANDS, DICK TAPPED THREE TIMES ON THE HULL, THE SIGNAL FOR " SLOW ASTERN ".

SLOWLY THE MIDGET SUB EASED HERSELF AWAY FROM THE ENSNARING WEB.

EASY DOES IT, WE'LL SOON BE FREE.

CLEAR OF THE NET, THE VESSEL TURNED AROUND. TO DICK'S SHOCK, IT THEN BEGAN TO MOVE AWAY WITH INCREASING SPEED.

I CAN'T BELIEVE IT . . . THEY'RE NOT STOPPING. THEY'RE GOING WITHOUT ME!

INSIDE THE CRAFT, LARRY AND SAM COULDN'T BELIEVE IT EITHER. OBVIOUSLY PRENDLE HAD NO INTENTION OF STOPPING FOR THE VERY MAN WHO HELD SUCH A THREAT TO HIS CAREER.

SIR, WE'VE GOT TO WAIT FOR MR ROLLAND.

I'M NOT RISKING THIS BOAT ANOTHER MINUTE. NOW, OBEY ORDERS AND STEER YOUR COURSE!

THEY HAD NO ALTERNATIVE. WHAT WAS WORSE, PRENDLE WOULD PROBABLY BE ABLE TO JUSTIFY THIS ACTION IF THEY ESCAPED.

MEANWHILE DICK HAD FORCED HIMSELF TO PUT ASIDE HIS BITTERNESS TO APPLY HIS MIND TO SURVIVAL.

FIRST THINGS FIRST. THE SOONER I CLEAR THIS AREA AND GET ASHORE, THE BETTER.

THE CURRENTS WERE TRICKY — VISIBILITY WAS NO MORE THAN A FEW YARDS.

I MUST BE CLOSE TO THE RIVER-BANK NOW, I HOPE SO . . . I'M JUST ABOUT ALL IN.

CAUTIOUSLY HE SURFACED TO FIND HIMSELF CLOSE TO SOME STEEP AND WOODED TERRAIN.

GOOD, DESERTED. THOSE TREES WILL GIVE ME SOME COVER.

HAULING HIMSELF ASHORE, HE HID ALL THE DIVING GEAR EXCEPT FOR HIS SUIT.

I'LL GET RID OF THIS THEN HAVE A DEKKO FROM HIGHER UP . . .

ALONE, ON THE RUN IN ENEMY TERRITORY, HIS FUTURE DIDN'T LOOK TOO BRIGHT AS HE TOOK STOCK.

I DON'T KNOW HOW I'LL GET OUT OF THIS MESS, BUT I'M NOT CAUGHT YET.

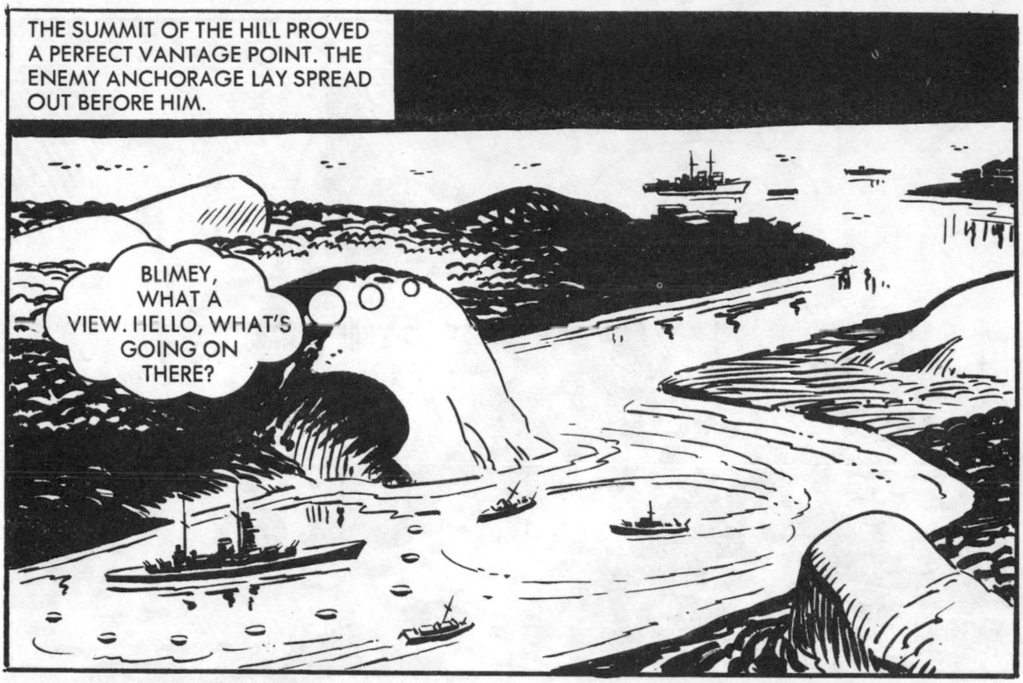
THE SUMMIT OF THE HILL PROVED A PERFECT VANTAGE POINT. THE ENEMY ANCHORAGE LAY SPREAD OUT BEFORE HIM.
BLIMEY, WHAT A VIEW. HELLO, WHAT'S GOING ON THERE?

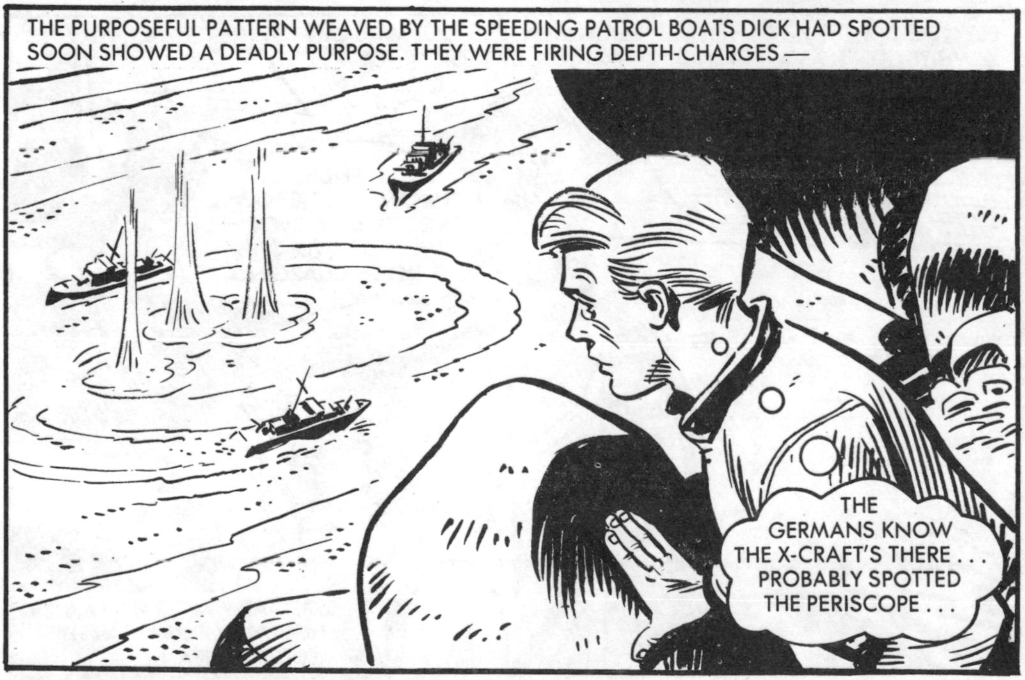
THE PURPOSEFUL PATTERN WEAVED BY THE SPEEDING PATROL BOATS DICK HAD SPOTTED SOON SHOWED A DEADLY PURPOSE. THEY WERE FIRING DEPTH-CHARGES —
THE GERMANS KNOW THE X-CRAFT'S THERE . . . PROBABLY SPOTTED THE PERISCOPE . . .

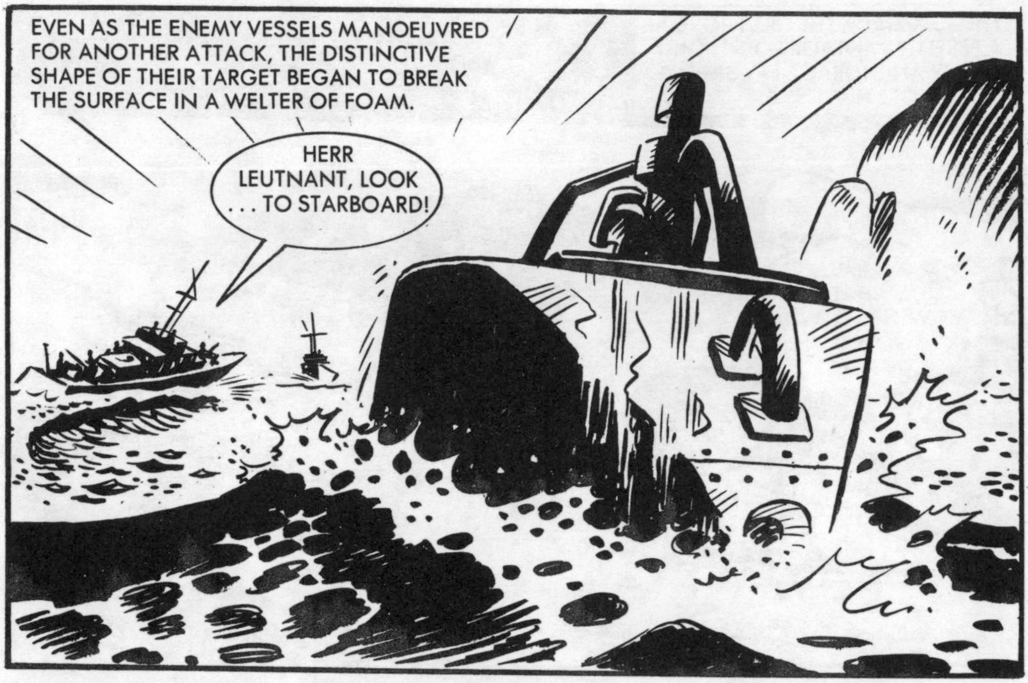
EVEN AS THE ENEMY VESSELS MANOEUVRED FOR ANOTHER ATTACK, THE DISTINCTIVE SHAPE OF THEIR TARGET BEGAN TO BREAK THE SURFACE IN A WELTER OF FOAM.
HERR LEUTNANT, LOOK . . . TO STARBOARD!

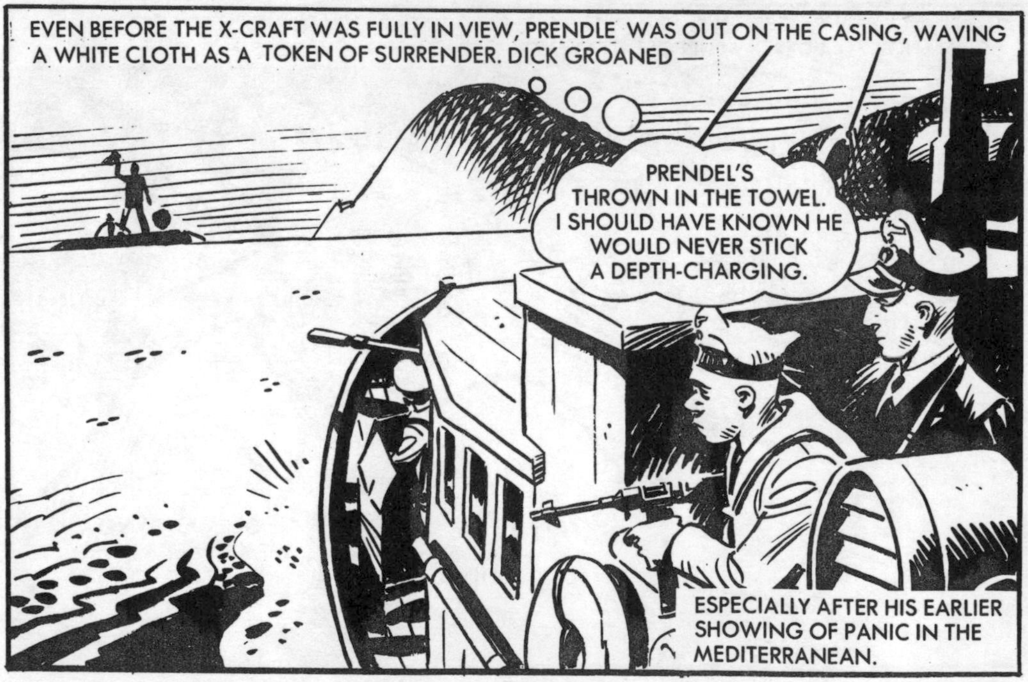
EVEN BEFORE THE X-CRAFT WAS FULLY IN VIEW, PRENDLE WAS OUT ON THE CASING, WAVING A WHITE CLOTH AS A TOKEN OF SURRENDER. DICK GROANED —
PRENDEL'S THROWN IN THE TOWEL. I SHOULD HAVE KNOWN HE WOULD NEVER STICK A DEPTH-CHARGING.
ESPECIALLY AFTER HIS EARLIER SHOWING OF PANIC IN THE MEDITERRANEAN.

IT WAS A MADDENING SIGHT FOR DICK TO SEE THE THREE MEN BEING TRANSFERRED TO A PATROL BOAT BEFORE THE MIDGET SUB WAS TAKEN IN TOW.

SO NOW THE ENEMY HAVE AN X-CRAFT TO EXAMINE. PRENDLE JUST HANDED IT TO THEM ON A PLATE!

HE KNEW THAT GERMAN EXPERTS WOULD SOON UNRAVEL AND COPY THE MIDGET'S SECRETS.

AS HE TURNED AWAY IN DISGUST, HE DISCOVERED HE HAD EVEN MORE TO WORRY ABOUT — A GERMAN SCHMEISSER WAS INCHES FROM HIM . . .

WHAT THE . . .

LUCKILY THE SUB-MACHINE GUN WAS HELD BY A FRENCHMAN ACCOMPANIED BY TWO OTHER HARD-FACED CHARACTERS. WITH GREAT EFFORT, DICK SUMMONED UP HIS SCHOOL FRENCH, HOPING THEY WERE RESISTANCE FIGHTERS.

WHO.. WHO ARE YOU?

PARDON ME, MONSIEUR, BUT THAT IS MY QUESTION. WHAT ARE YOU . DOING HERE?

LUCKILY THE REPLY HAD COME IN ENGLISH WHICH WAS BETTER THAN DICK'S STAB AT THE LOCAL LINGO.

A VIOLENT DOUBLE EXPLOSION TOOK ALL THEIR ATTENTION THEN, SHAKING THE VERY GROUND ON WHICH THEY STOOD.

SACRE BLEU! WHAT WAS THAT?

THE CHARGES! I'D FORGOTTEN ALL ABOUT THEM.

AT LEAST THE WELL-PLACED CHARGES FROM THE MIGHTY MIDGET HAD GONE OFF AS PLANNED.

THE DESTRUCTION OF THE ENEMY BATTLE-CRUISER SEEMED TO GIVE THE FRENCHMEN AS MUCH SATISFACTION AS IT DID DICK.

BRAVO! SHE IS SUNK.

NOT QUITE — SHE'S RESTING ON THE BOTTOM. IT'LL BE A LONG TIME THOUGH BEFORE SHE BOTHERS ANY MORE ATLANTIC CONVOYS.

NOW THAT IT WAS CLEAR HIS COMPANIONS WERE ANTI-GERMAN, IT SEEMED A GOOD TIME FOR INTRODUCTIONS.

I'M DICK ROLLAND FROM THE SUB THAT PLANTED THOSE CHARGES.

CONGRATULATIONS. IT IS I, EMILE TOUSSAINT, WHO INFORMED YOUR NAVY OF HER PRESENCE. NOW, LET US LEAVE THIS PLACE.

AS EMILE LED HIM TO A WAITING LORRY, DICK FELT GREATLY RELIEVED. THE CRUISER HAD BEEN CRIPPLED AND NOW, AT LEAST, HE HAD HELP.

AS DAWN BROKE, THE LORRY TOOK THEM TO THE RESISTANCE H.Q., A SECLUDED FARMHOUSE CLOSE TO THE ANCHORAGE. WHILE DICK WAS GIVEN FOOD AND CLOTHING, EMILE RADIOED LONDON.

YOUR NAVY ASK THAT YOU MAKE FOR A COASTAL INLET TWENTY KILOMETRES FROM HERE. A SUBMARINE WILL WAIT THERE UNTIL DAWN TOMORROW.

THAT'S MARVELLOUS, EMILE. WILL YOU BE COMING WITH ME?

THE RESISTANCE LEADER'S EXPRESSION HARDENED.

I'M AFRAID NOT, MY FRIEND. YOUR NAVY HAS ASKED THAT I DESTROY YOUR LITTLE SUBMARINE. WE MUST PREPARE FOR THAT ATTACK TONIGHT.

DICK OCCUPIED HIS AFTERNOON HELPING THE RESISTANCE PREPARE FOR THE EVENING OPERATION. HIS THOUGHTS WERE TROUBLED —

EMILE AND HIS LADS SEEM FIRST-CLASS TYPES. IT'S A PITY THEY HAVE TO RISK THEIR LIVES CORRECTING PRENDLE'S MISTAKE.

THEN HIS ATTENTION WAS DIVERTED BY A FRENCHMAN WHO HAD JUST ARRIVED IN THE FARMYARD.

AFTER A DEEP DISCUSSION WITH THE STRANGER, EMILE TOLD DICK WHAT NEWS HE HAD BROUGHT.

THAT MAN WORKS AS A CLEANER AT THE NAVAL DEPOT ON THE RIVER — YOUR SUBMARINE IS THERE.

THEY HAD ALSO LEARNED THAT THAT NIGHT, SENIOR NAVAL OFFICERS WERE TO ARRIVE FROM PARIS TO INSPECT THE MIDGET AND INTERROGATE THE PRISONERS.

THIS LAST PIECE OF INFORMATION MADE UP DICK'S MIND TO BEG TO BE ALLOWED TO GO ON THE RAID.

I KNOW WHERE BEST TO PUT THE CHARGES ON THE MIDGET, AND THERE'S A CHANCE I CAN RESCUE MY OLD CREW.

ALL RIGHT, IF THAT'S WHAT YOU WANT. COME, I WILL EXPLAIN.

THE PLAN WAS BOLD YET SIMPLE. EVERY MAN WAS WELL BRIEFED.

IN THE EVENING TWILIGHT THEY SET OFF, WELL HIDDEN IN THE BACK OF THE OLD TRUCK BEHIND SACKS OF FARM PRODUCE. DICK COULDN'T RESIST A PRIVATE CHUCKLE.

" JOIN THE NAVY AND SEE THE WORLD " . . . THEY DIDN'T MEAN THIS!

ONCE IN POSITION AT A CHOSEN SPOT ON A CERTAIN ROAD, DICK FOUND THE WAITING MORE NERVE-RACKING THAN ANY DEPTH-CHARGING.

ARE YOU SURE THIS WILL WORK?

PATIENCE, MON AMI . . . RELAX.

THIS ROUTE WAS THE ONLY WAY TO THE NAVY DEPOT FOR THE SENIOR OFFICERS COMING FROM PARIS. ALREADY THE SMALL CONVOY WAS SPEEDING THROUGH THE NIGHT, TOWARDS THE WAITING RESISTANCE MEN.

IT WAS A BAD BLOW TO LOSE THE CRUISER, BUT THIS CAPTURED MIDGET SUBMARINE WILL GIVE US MANY SECRETS.

JA, KARL. AND I UNDERSTAND THE BRITISH CAPTAIN SEEMS READY TO GIVE US ANY INFORMATION WE NEED.

AS THE VEHICLES ROUNDED THE NEXT BEND, THEY FOUND THEIR ROUTE BARRED BY AN OLD TRUCK WHICH HAD " BROKEN DOWN " ON THE ROAD — EMILE'S TRUCK.

SOME FRENCH FOOLS IGNORING THE CURFEW. GO AND INVESTIGATE, BUT BE CAREFUL.

THE YOUNG AIDE WHO STRODE FORWARD WAS IN AN IMPATIENT MOOD.

IDIOTS! GET THIS HEAP OF SCRAP-METAL OFF THE ROAD!

HE GOT AN UNEXPECTED ANSWER FROM DICK —

SORRY, MATE, BUT YOUR MOTHER REALLY SHOULD HAVE TAUGHT YOU BETTER MANNERS.

THEN IT WAS THE TURN OF EMILE AND HIS MEN TO SUBDUE THE OTHER GERMANS WHICH THEY DID WITH RUTHLESS EFFICIENCY. NOT ONE SHOT WAS FIRED.

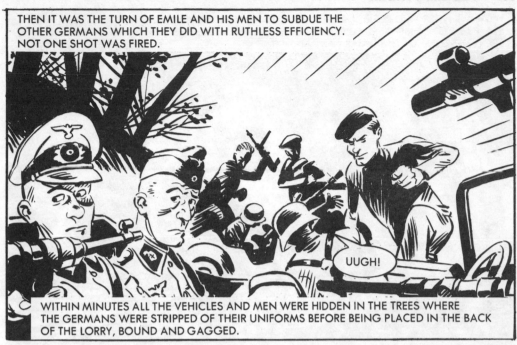

WITHIN MINUTES ALL THE VEHICLES AND MEN WERE HIDDEN IN THE TREES WHERE THE GERMANS WERE STRIPPED OF THEIR UNIFORMS BEFORE BEING PLACED IN THE BACK OF THE LORRY, BOUND AND GAGGED.

THE UNIFORMS WERE THEN BORROWED, EMILE ASSUMING THE ROLE OF THE SENIOR OFFICER WITH DICK AND MARCEL — THE GROUP'S SECOND-IN-COMMAND AND A FLUENT GERMAN SPEAKER — AS HIS AIDES.

WITH ANOTHER TWO RESISTANCE FIGHTERS HIDDEN IN THE BOOT OF THE STAFF CAR, THE DISGUISED GROUP SET OFF. JUST A FEW KILOMETRES BROUGHT THEM TO THE GATES OF THE DEPOT.

WELL, HERE WE GO. I HOPE MARCEL IS AS GOOD AT SPEAKING GERMAN AS HE SAYS.

TRUST US, MY FRIEND. TEN YEARS WITH THE FOREIGN LEGION TEACHES A MAN MUCH.

THE GUARD DETAIL WERE EXPECTING THEM. EMILE'S TRUST IN MARCEL'S SKILL WAS SOON JUSTIFIED.

FIRST WE GO TO THE SMALL SUBMARINE. THEN WE WILL COLLECT THE BRITISH PRISONERS.

AT ONCE, SIR. WE HAVE THEM IN THE GUARD-ROOM. THEY WILL BE READY.

DICK BREATHED AGAIN AS THE BOGUS CONVOY MOVED OFF ONCE MORE.

SO FAR SO GOOD. HEAD FOR THE MAIN JETTY. THEY'RE SURE TO HAVE THE X-CRAFT TIED UP THERE.

THERE INDEED, SHE WAS, MOORED AT THE JETTY, GUARDED BY TWO GERMAN SAILORS WHO SNAPPED TO ATTENTION AT THE APPROACH OF THE VEHICLES.

SHE LOOKS IN GOOD SHAPE. PRENDLE GAVE IN WITHOUT GETTING A SCRATCH.

WITH A MERE NOD TO EACH OTHER AS A SIGNAL, MARCEL AND DICK THRUST THEIR SCHMEISSERS MENACINGLY INTO THE FACES OF THE GERMAN SENTRIES.

HANDE HOCHE!

THE AMAZED ENEMY DETAIL WAS QUICKLY DISARMED, THEN TIED UP AND GAGGED.

WHILE THE OTHERS HID THE GUARDS, EMILE AND DICK SET ABOUT RIGGING THE X-CRAFT WITH EXPLOSIVES.

WE'VE GOT TO HURRY. THE GATE-HOUSE OFFICER IS SURE TO HAVE CALLED THE DEPOT H.Q. TO TELL THEM WE'RE HERE.

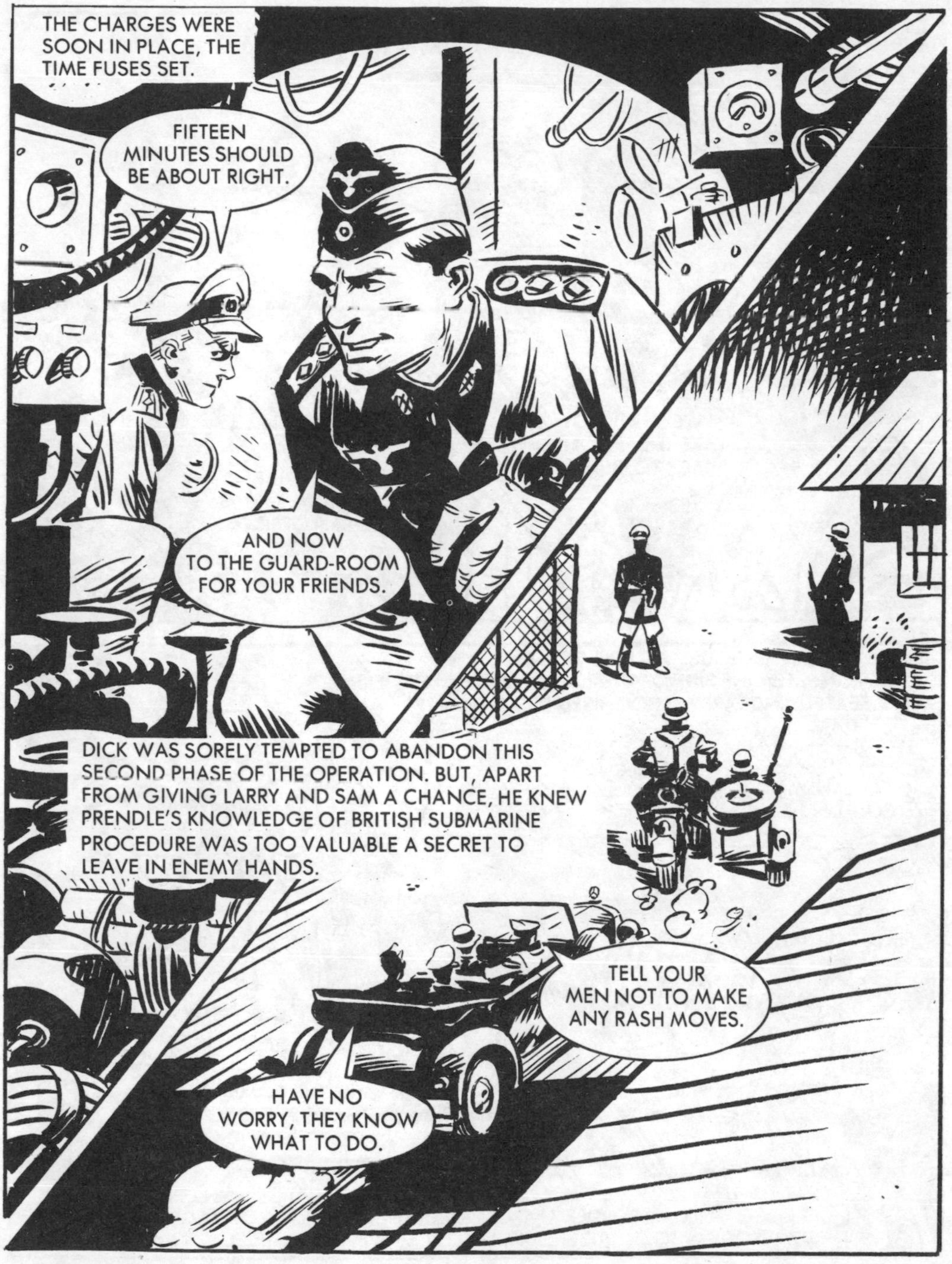
THE CHARGES WERE SOON IN PLACE, THE TIME FUSES SET.
FIFTEEN MINUTES SHOULD BE ABOUT RIGHT.
AND NOW TO THE GUARD-ROOM FOR YOUR FRIENDS.
DICK WAS SORELY TEMPTED TO ABANDON THIS SECOND PHASE OF THE OPERATION. BUT, APART FROM GIVING LARRY AND SAM A CHANCE, HE KNEW PRENDLE'S KNOWLEDGE OF BRITISH SUBMARINE PROCEDURE WAS TOO VALUABLE A SECRET TO LEAVE IN ENEMY HANDS.
TELL YOUR MEN NOT TO MAKE ANY RASH MOVES.
HAVE NO WORRY, THEY KNOW WHAT TO DO.

ONCE AGAIN MARCEL'S GERMAN WAS PUT TO THE TEST AS THEY CONFRONTED THE OFFICER IN CHARGE OF THE GUARD-ROOM.

WE SHALL NOW TAKE THE PRISONERS BACK TO OUR H.Q.

I CAN'T BELIEVE IT'S THIS EASY . . . THIS GERMAN OFFICER'S NO FOOL.

INSIDE THE GUARD-HOUSE, MARCEL DEALT WITH THE FORMALITIES. TO ONE SIDE OF THE ROOM THE X-CRAFT'S CREW WERE SEATED AND LARRY RECOGNISED DICK AT ONCE.

MR ROLLAND? IT COULDN'T BE.

I HOPE LARRY DOESN'T GIVE THE GAME AWAY. THAT OFFICER LOOKS PRETTY SUSPICIOUS.

IN FACT HE WAS MORE THAN JUST SUSPICIOUS. HE HAD GROWN UP ON THE FRANCO-GERMAN BORDER AND COULD DETECT THE TRACE OF ACCENT EVEN FROM SOMEBODY WHO COULD SPEAK GERMAN AS WELL AS MARCEL.

OUT CAME A LUGER, FOLLOWED BY THE COMMAND TO STAY STILL.

I DID NOT KNOW OUR NAVY RECRUITED FRENCHMEN!

BLAST! HE'S TUMBLED US.

EVEN AS THE GERMAN SPOKE, THE TIME FUSE ABOARD THE X-CRAFT TICKED ITS FINAL SECOND.

WITH A THUNDEROUS EXPLOSION THE MIDGET SUB BLEW APART, DEMOLISHING HALF THE JETTY AND LIGHTING UP THE EVENING SKY.

AS THE GUARD-ROOM SHOOK WITH THE CONCUSSION, EMILE TOOK ADVANTAGE OF THE GERMANS' SURPRISE AND ORDERED DICK AND THE OTHERS TO THE GROUND.

MEIN GOTT! WHAT WAS THAT?

ON THE FLOOR — EVERYBODY!

EMILE'S ACTION WAS FOLLOWED UP BY HIS MEN WAITING OUTSIDE. THEY BURST IN THE DOOR WITH WEAPONS BLAZING.

USHERING ALONG THE DELIGHTED LARRY AND SAM WITH THE ASHEN-FACED PRENDLE, THE RESCUE PARTY DECIDED IT WAS TIME FOR A SPEEDY WITHDRAWAL.

THEY NEEDED EVERY BIT OF THE TWO VEHICLES'
ACCELERATION AS THE STILL-REELING GERMANS DID
EVERYTHING IN THEIR POWER TO STOP THEM LEAVING.

I DON'T THINK
THEY WANT TO SEE
US GO, MES AMIS!

FINALLY THEY WERE CLEAR, DRIVING FAST FOR THE HILLS,
LEAVING THE GERMANS WITH THEIR HANDS FULL FIGHTING
THE BLAZE.

ONE AND A
HALF HOURS TO
DAWN. WE'RE GOING TO
HAVE TO HURRY TO
CATCH THAT SUB.

AFTER A FEW MORE KILOMETRES, EMILE ORDERED THE CAR STOPPED. IT WAS TIME FOR THE FRENCH LEADER AND HIS MEN TO BID FAREWELL TO THE ENGLISHMEN.

AU REVOIR, MY FRIEND. WE SHOULD LIKE TO COME WITH YOU, BUT OUR FIGHT IS HERE.

GOODBYE, EMILE. WE SHAN'T FORGET THE DEBT WE OWE YOU.

AFTER EMILE HAD GIVEN DICK PRECISE DIRECTIONS FOR THE RENDEZVOUS WITH THE SUBMARINE, THEY SPED ALONG THE COAST ROAD, LARRY AT THE WHEEL. PRENDLE SPOKE FOR THE FIRST TIME SINCE THE BREAKOUT.

THANKS, ROLLAND . . . AFTER WHAT HAPPENED, I DIDN'T DESERVE IT.

FORGET IT, PRENDLE. YOU'RE NOT SAFE YET. JERRY IS SURE TO HAVE PUT UP ROAD-BLOCKS.

THESE FEARS WERE CONFIRMED ALL TOO SOON. A MAKE-SHIFT CONTROL POINT LAY ONLY A SHORT DISTANCE AHEAD.

PUT YOUR FOOT DOWN, LARRY. IT'S OUR ONLY CHANCE.

AYE, AYE, SIR! FULL AHEAD.

THERE WAS ONLY ONE WAY ROUND AND LARRY TOOK IT. A GERMANY MOTOR-CYCLE COMBINATION SUFFERED BADLY.

SORRY WE CAN'T STOP FOR A CHAT.

THE ENEMY OFFICER QUICKLY RALLIED HIS MEN, ORDERING THEM INTO THEIR TRUCK. THE CHASE WAS ON.

QUICKLY — THE BRITISH PIRATES MUST NOT ESCAPE!

ALTHOUGH THE CAR HAD THE EDGE IN SPEED, THE CREW KNEW THAT TO CONTINUE WOULD LEAD THE ENEMY TO THE SUBMARINE ONLY TWO KILOMETRES AWAY. NOW THEY ALSO HAD SOMETHING ELSE TO CONSIDER.

SIR! IT'S MR PRENDLE — HE'S BEEN HIT!

IT'S NOTHING, JUST A SCRATCH. STOP THE CAR ACROSS THE ROAD AROUND THAT BLIND CORNER.

DICK'S FIRST THOUGHT WAS THAT, ONCE AGAIN, PRENDLE WAS GIVING IN.

ARE YOU MAD, PRENDLE? THAT TRUCK WILL BE HERE IN MINUTES.

EXACTLY, AND THE SUB IS ONLY A MILE OVER THAT HILL. YOU THREE HEAD OFF ACROSS COUNTRY. LEAVE ME TO HOLD UP JERRY.

THERE WAS NO TIME TO ARGUE. AS DICK HANDED OVER A SCHMEISSER, HE GUESSED PRENDLE'S WOUND WAS MORE SERIOUS THAN HE WOULD ADMIT.

YOU NEVER STOP SURPRISING ME, PRENDLE.

WELL, THERE'S BEEN A PRENDLE IN THE ROYAL NAVY FOR CENTURIES. I DON'T INTEND BEING REMEMBERED AS THE COWARD OF THE FAMILY.

EVEN AS DICK AND PRENDLE SHOOK HANDS, THE GERMAN PLATOON NEARED THE VITAL CORNER.

FASTER, SCHMIDT! WE CANNOT BE FAR BEHIND . . .

PRENDLE'S REARGUARD TOOK THE GERMANS COMPLETELY BY SURPRISE. HE PEPPERED THE TRUCK'S CABIN, KILLING THE OFFICER, BADLY WOUNDING THE DRIVER.

AAAAGH!

CAREERING OUT OF CONTROL, THE TRUCK CONTINUED ON A COLLISION COURSE WITH THE STAFF CAR BEHIND WHICH PRENDLE WAS HUNCHED.

COME ON, NAZIS! I WANT TO GO OUT IN STYLE AND I NEED YOU FOR THAT.

HE DID NOT EVEN TRY TO ESCAPE. HE PLANNED TO DIE FIGHTING.

BEFORE HE COULD SPEAK AGAIN, THE TRUCK RAMMED THE CAR AND EXPLODED. HIS LAST BULLETS HAD FOUND THE GERMAN PETROL TANK.

THE AWESOME FUNERAL PYRE STOPPED THE ESCAPING TRIO IN THEIR TRACKS.

THEY WERE ALL STUNNED BY THEIR OFFICER'S SACRIFICE, BUT THEY KNEW HE HAD DIED TO HELP THEM ESCAPE. THE BEST WAY TO HONOUR HIS COURAGE WAS TO KEEP MOVING.

WHEN THE THREE SAILORS HAD MADE THEIR WAY DOWN TO THE DESIGNATED BEACH, DESPAIR OVERTOOK THEM — THE HORIZON WAS EMPTY. THEN, ONLY MINUTES LATER, THE WATER BOILED AS A BRITISH SUBMARINE'S BOWS BROKE THE SURFACE.

THEY HAD ME WORRIED FOR A MOMENT THERE, SIR.

YOU SHOULDN'T HAVE BEEN, SAM. THE SUBMARINE SERVICE NEVER FORGETS HER OWN . . .

SOON A DINGHY WAS PUT ASHORE FOR THEM. EAGERLY THEY CLAMBERED ABOARD.

GLAD YOU COULD MAKE IT, DICK — WHERE'S PRENDLE?

HE WASN'T SO LUCKY . . .

There's non-stop action in your next four exciting Commando books!
Out in two weeks:—

" *THE SQUADRON THAT WOULDN'T DIE* " " *WHO NEEDS LUCK?* "
" *COWBOY IN KHAKI* "   " *FIND THEM, SINK THEM!* "

THE BRITISH COMMANDO

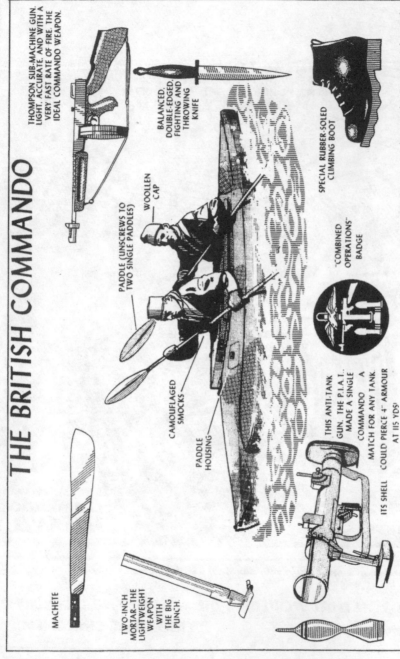

THOMPSON SUB-MACHINE GUN. LIGHT, ACCURATE, AND WITH A VERY FAST RATE OF FIRE, THE IDEAL COMMANDO WEAPON.

BALANCED, DOUBLE-EDGED, FIGHTING AND THROWING KNIFE

SPECIAL RUBBER-SOLED CLIMBING BOOT

WOOLLEN CAP

PADDLE (UNSCREWS TO TWO SINGLE PADDLES)

"COMBINED OPERATIONS" BADGE

CAMOUFLAGED SMOCKS

PADDLE HOUSING

THIS ANTI-TANK GUN, THE P.I.A.T., MADE A SINGLE COMMANDO A MATCH FOR ANY TANK. ITS SHELL COULD PIERCE 4" ARMOUR AT 115 YDS!

MACHETE

TWO-INCH MORTAR—THE LIGHTWEIGHT WEAPON WITH THE BIG PUNCH.

BEFORE a man could don the distinctive green beret, he had to live through the toughest four months of his life.

He learned to live off the land, handle all kinds of weapons and stick to a rock-face like a fly.

From early morning to lights-out he did everything at the double, including the toughest assault courses ever invented!

All the stunts were carried on, under live fire, and to crown it all there was no such thing as sick parade. Report sick—and you were returned to your unit the same day!

But when a man finally put on the green beret and became a Commando, he could be justly proud. He knew he was among the finest fighters in the world.

Not a German in Europe, no matter where, didn't finger his throat and peer around nervously at the news that a band of these super-soldiers was on the loose.

VLR
VERY LONG RANGE

DURING THE SECOND WORLD WAR AN AMAZING VARIETY OF GUNS WERE DEVELOPED FOR SPECIAL PURPOSES . . . HOUSE-TO-HOUSE FIGHTING, SNIPING, RESISTANCE OPERATIONS AND SUCH.

BUT FEW WERE AS REMARKABLE AS THE ONE INVENTED BY THE BRITISH . . . THE MASSIVELY POWERFUL VLR — THE VERY LONG RANGE AUTOMATIC RIFLE — WHICH WAS TO TRIGGER A DEADLY MANHUNT ACROSS THE WILDS OF OCCUPIED NORWAY.

First published 1988.

ONE DAY IN THE THIRD YEAR OF THE WAR, MAJOR SHAWCROSS, THE GRUFF C.O. OF A FIRING RANGE IN NORTHUMBERLAND, LEARNED THAT HIS ESTABLISHMENT WAS TO BE TAKEN OVER FOR A WEEK BY SCIENTISTS IN ORDER TO TEST A NEW RIFLE.

DON'T YOU FELLOWS HAVE ANYTHING BETTER TO DO THAN MESS UP MY SCHEDULES WITH YOUR CRACKPOT INVENTIONS?

THIS ONE'S DIFFERENT, MAJOR. WE CALL IT THE VLR — FOR VERY LONG RANGE.

AS FAR AS SHAWCROSS WAS CONCERNED, A LEE-ENFIELD IN THE HANDS OF A TRAINED MAN WAS AS GOOD AS ANY INFANTRY WEAPON. NO AMOUNT OF ENTHUSIASTIC EXPLANATION WAS GOING TO CHANGE HIS MIND.

IT'S THE BULLETS WHICH ARE REALLY REVOLUTIONARY. THEY'RE FITTED WITH COMPRESSED GAS CARTRIDGES WHICH BOOST THEIR VELOCITY TEN-FOLD.

REALLY? I SUSPECT YOU'LL BE TELLING ME NEXT THAT THEY CAN EVEN FIND THEIR OWN WAY TO THE TARGET!

RELUCTANTLY THE BOFFINS WERE FORCED TO ADMIT THAT THEIR BRAND NEW CONCEPT DIDN'T GO QUITE AS FAR AS THAT. WITH A SMALL GROWL OF TRIUMPH, THE MAJOR SUMMONED A PRIVATE SOLDIER.

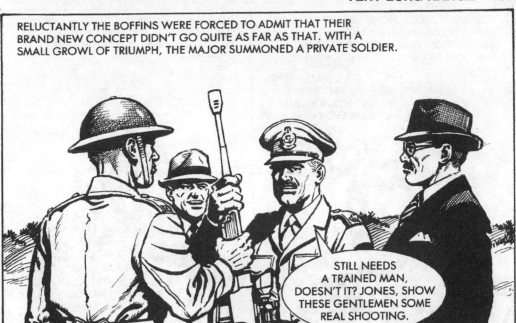

STILL NEEDS A TRAINED MAN, DOESN'T IT? JONES, SHOW THESE GENTLEMEN SOME REAL SHOOTING.

PRIVATE JONES WAS A NOTED CRACKSHOT. IT DIDN'T TAKE HIM LONG TO FAMILIARISE HIMSELF WITH THE VLR, TO SET THE TELESCOPIC SIGHTS TO HIS LIKING.

RED FLAG'S UP, JONES. FIRE WHEN READY.

IF YOU DON'T MIND ME SAYING SO, MAJOR, I THINK THE TARGET'S STILL A BIT TOO CLOSE. THIS GUN DOES HAVE EXCEPTIONAL POWER.

FOR SHAWCROSS, MORE ACCUSTOMED TO LEE-ENFIELDS AND THEIR LIKE, THE SUGGESTION THAT HIS LONGEST RANGE WAS NOT FAR ENOUGH WAS AN INSULT.

IT'S A FULL MILE! I'LL RECONSIDER IF ANY OF YOUR WONDER BULLETS EVEN REACH THE TARGET.

THE PRIVATE FIRED FIVE TIMES IN RAPID SUCCESSION. WHATEVER HIS C.O. THOUGHT, JONES KNEW THIS WAS SOMETHING SPECIAL.

VIRTUALLY NO KICK-BACK, YET I CAN FEEL THE POWER. IT HANDLES BETTER THAN ANYTHING I'VE EVER TRIED.

AS SOON AS THE ALL CLEAR WAS SOUNDED, A CORPORAL AT THE TARGET EMERGED FROM THE PROTECTION OF THE CONCRETE BUNKER NEARBY TO INSPECT THE RESULTS. HE WHISTLED APPRECIATIVELY WHEN HE SAW WHAT JONES HAD DONE.

FIVE HITS RIGHT IN THE BULL FROM A MILE AWAY! THAT'S WHAT I CALL REAL SHOOTING.

THE STARTLING NEWS WAS RELAYED BY TELEPHONE TO SHAWCROSS WHO RECEIVED IT WITH A SHEEPISH EXPRESSION.

YOU'RE QUITE SURE? GOOD LORD, IT SEEMS I SPOKE TOO SOON, GENTLEMEN. MY APOLOGIES.

THINK NOTHING OF IT. BUT PLEASE ASK YOUR MEN TO RETRIEVE THE SPENT BULLETS. WE NEED THEM FOR EXAMINATION.

THE REQUEST WAS PASSED ON, BUT WHEN THE CORPORAL WENT TO INSPECT THE HEAVY BACK-STOP BEHIND THE TARGET HE GOT A NASTY SHOCK.

BLIMEY, THEY ALL WENT THROUGH LIKE A KNIFE THROUGH BUTTER. I'VE NEVER KNOWN THAT HAPPEN BEFORE!

AS ANOTHER SOLDIER JOINED HIM, THE N.C.O. STARED OUT AT THE FLAT MOORLAND BEYOND.

HOW FAR DO YOU THINK THEY WENT, CORP?

SEARCH ME. I ONLY HOPE THERE'S NOBODY OUT THERE.

AS IT HAPPENED, A FEW MINUTES EARLIER AND TWO MILES BEYOND THE TARGET, A COMMANDO OFFICER, CAPTAIN ROBERT TERRY, WAS LEADING HIS MEN ON A BACK-BREAKING TREK ACROSS THE ROUGH, MIST-COVERED TERRAIN.

NO SLACKING, CHAPS. ANOTHER TEN MILES TO COVER YET.

WHO NEEDS TO WORRY ABOUT JERRIES? ONE OF THE SKIPPER'S NORMAL ROUTE MARCHES IS ENOUGH TO KILL A MAN.

AT LEAST HE DOESN'T ASK US TO DO ANYTHING HE CAN'T DO HIMSELF.

COMMANDO TRAINING WAS, BY ITS VERY NATURE, TOUGH AND ARDUOUS. ACCIDENTS WERE COMMON — BUT NOT OF THE SORT WHICH SUDDENLY BEFELL TWO OF THE MEN.

AAARGH, MY ARM!

MY LEG, UUUGH!

WHAT THE BLAZES? ARE YOU TWO TRYING TO BE FUNNY?

IT WAS INSTANTLY APPARENT THAT BOTH MEN WERE IN GREAT PAIN. THE CAUSE OF THEIR AGONY ASTOUNDED ROBERT.

GOOD GRIEF, THEY'VE BOTH BEEN SHOT. BUT BY WHOM, AND WHERE FROM? DID ANYBODY HEAR ANYTHING?

NO, SIR, NOT A PEEP.

AS SOON AS ROBERT HAD WORKED OUT THE APPROXIMATE DIRECTION OF THE MYSTERIOUS ROUNDS, HE SET OFF IN GRIMLY-DETERMINED MANNER TO TRACK DOWN THE CULPRIT, LEAVING A MAN TO TEND TO THE VICTIMS.

THEY MUST HAVE COME FROM THIS GENERAL BEARING. WHOEVER FIRED THEM HAD BETTER LOOK OUT!

SHAWCROSS, MEANWHILE, HAD ORDERED THE RANGE CORPORAL
AND HIS MEN TO LOOK FOR THE SPENT BULLETS, A SEEMINGLY-
HOPELESS TASK IN THE ENDLESS HEATHER. THE MENACING EMERGENCE
OF ROBERT AND HIS MEN FROM THE MIST PUT AN END TO THAT.

YOU THERE, DON'T MOVE — WE'VE GOT YOU COVERED!

WHA...AT?

AS THE N.C.O. TRIED TO EXPLAIN, THE FURIOUS
ROBERT HEARD ONLY WHAT HE WANTED TO.

THEY WERE TEST-FIRING A NEW GUN, SIR, BUT THE BULLETS SORT OF . . .

I KNOW WHAT THEY DID — HIT TWO OF MY MEN! I'LL SORT THIS OUT WITH WHOEVER'S IN CHARGE!

THE MAJOR WAS UNDERSTANDABLY PUT OUT WHEN ROBERT CAME STORMING UP ACCUSING HIM OF EVERY CRIME UNDER THE SUN.

WHAT SORT OF SHOW DO YOU RUN HERE? NO WARNINGS, NO SIGNALS, NO NOTHING! I'LL BE REPORTING THIS!

DO CALM DOWN. WHAT ARE YOU BABBLING ABOUT? EVERYTHING'S QUITE IN ORDER.

THE REPLY ENRAGED ROBERT EVEN FURTHER. THE TWO OFFICERS WERE VERY SOON SHOUTING ANGRILY AT EACH OTHER.

I'VE GOT TWO WOUNDED MEN BECAUSE YOU IGNORED ALL SAFETY REGULATIONS!

NOW YOU LOOK HERE, I DO EVERYTHING BY THE BOOK. IF YOU PERSIST, I'LL THROW IT AT YOU!

TACTFULLY JONES INTERVENED WITH A REQUEST FOR ROBERT TO SHOW THEM ON THE MAP WHERE THE CASUALTIES HAD OCCURRED.

ROBERT, AN EXCELLENT MAP READER, HARDLY HESITATED BEFORE JABBING HIS FINGER FIERCELY AT A LOCATION WHICH MADE THE MARKSMAN STARE IN AMAZEMENT.

EVEN AS ROBERT OPENED HIS MOUTH TO CARRY ON WITH THE ARGUMENT, THE REMARKS FROM JONES AND THE SCIENTIST SANK IN.

ALMOST REVERENTLY, ROBERT TOOK THE VLR IN HIS HANDS, NO LONGER INTERESTED IN THE BICKERING GOING ON AROUND HIM BETWEEN THE MAJOR AND THE CIVILIANS.

YOU SHOULD HAVE TOLD ME IT HAD A RANGE OF THREE MILES!

YOU NEVER ASKED!

THREE MILES! AND NOT JUST PLUNGING FIRE, BUT FLAT TRAJECTORY. THIS COULD BE THE ANSWER TO THE NORWEGIAN PROBLEM.

THE NEXT MORNING HE WENT TO SEE COLONEL BEVAN, HIS COMMANDING OFFICER, TO WHOM HE PUT FORWARD AN IMAGINATIVE BUT VERY DANGEROUS SUGGESTION.

WITH THIS NEW RIFLE YOUR PREVIOUS OBJECTION TO THE PROPOSED MISSION NO LONGER APPLIES. I'M SURE WE COULD PULL IT OFF.

I MUST SAY I'D HOPED THE AIR FORCE COULD HAVE TAKEN IT ON, BUT THE ANTI-AIRCRAFT DEFENCES AROUND THE TARGET ARE TOO HEAVY.

THE C.O. DID RECKON, HOWEVER, THAT IT WOULD BE IMPOSSIBLE TO OBTAIN ANY EXPERIMENTAL WEAPONS BEFORE THEY WERE PROPERLY TESTED. ROBERT ALREADY HAD AN ANSWER FOR THAT.

WHAT BETTER WAY TO ASSESS THEM THAN IN ACTION, SIR? A FEW HOURS' COMBAT WOULD PROVE THEM MORE THOROUGHLY THAN SIX MONTHS IN A LAB.

VERY WELL, I'LL SEE WHAT I CAN DO.

BEVAN PULLED THE NECESSARY STRINGS. HE MANAGED TO OBTAIN TWO OPERATIONAL PROTOTYPES OF THE VLR ALONG WITH A QUANTITY OF THE SPECIAL AMMUNITION.

A WEEK LATER ROBERT AND HIS TEAM PARACHUTED DOWN TO A BLEAK MOORLAND HIGH IN THE NORWEGIAN MOUNTAINS.

EACH MAN KNEW JUST HOW VITAL THIS RAID WAS.

ROBERT HAD ONE VLR, HIS SECOND-IN-COMMAND, LIEUTENANT ROLF KARLSVILK OF THE FREE NORWEGIAN FORCES, THE OTHER. A VETERAN COMMANDO IN HIS OWN RIGHT, BECAUSE HE KNEW THE AREA, ROLF WAS ALSO THE GUIDE.

WE MUST HEAD EAST TO LOWER COUNTRY. I'M AFRAID IT'S GOING TO BE A LONG HIKE.

THAT'S WHAT WE'VE BEEN TRAINING FOR. WE'LL SET OFF AS SOON AS THE CHUTES ARE BURIED.

THE FOLLOWING MORNING, CLOSE TO THE SAME SPOT, A MAGNIFICENTLY-ANTLERED ELK WAS BROWSING PEACEFULLY, UNAWARE OF THE TELESCOPIC SIGHTS TRAINED ON IT UNTIL A SINGLE SHOT RANG OUT.

GOT HIM!

THE MARKSMAN WAS COLONEL OSKAR VON WECHMAR, AN ARISTOCRATIC PRUSSIAN STAFF OFFICER INDULGING IN HIS PASSION FOR HUNTING. WITH HIM WAS A SMALL SQUAD OF MOUNTAIN TROOPS COMMANDED BY THE KEEN LEUTNANT RUDI RUGGERHEIM.

THE HUNTING PARTY TRUDGED OVER TO THE KILL WHICH VON WECHMAR EXAMINED WITH PROFESSIONAL SKILL.

BY SHEER BAD LUCK THE ELK, BEFORE ITS DEATH, HAD DISTURBED THE SPOT WHERE THE COMMANDOS HAD BURIED THEIR PARACHUTES THE PREVIOUS NIGHT. THE COLONEL RAN HIS PRACTISED EYE OVER THE FIND.

DEFINITELY BRITISH, AND THEY'VE NOT BEEN HERE LONG, JUDGING BY THEIR CONDITION.

IT WAS A CHALLENGE THE STAFF OFFICER WAS UNABLE TO RESIST. HE EXPLAINED A PLAN OF ACTION, BASED ON THE FACT THAT THE INTRUDERS COULD NOT HAVE GONE FAR YET.

SO WE BEGIN A NEW HUNT, IN PURSUIT OF THE MOST CHALLENGING PREY OF ALL . . . HUMAN BEINGS!

WITH RESPECT, WE SHOULD SEND SOMEBODY TO THE NEAREST ARMY POST TO SOUND THE ALARM.

VON WECHMAR OVER-
RULED RUGGERHEIM'S
SENSIBLE SUGGESTION FOR
PRACTICAL REASONS OF HIS OWN.

THE RAIDERS, MEANWHILE,
HAD ALREADY DESCENDED
TO A LESS WILD REGION.

THE SIGNS SHOW THEY
WENT THIS WAY, THE SHORTEST
ROUTE DOWN TO CIVILISATION.
BESIDES, WE MIGHT NEED
EVERY GUN. FOLLOW ME!

THE
ROAD AHEAD IS
PATROLLED BY GERMANS,
BUT WE MUST
CROSS IT.

LEAD
THE WAY.

UNFORTUNATELY FOR THE BRITISH THE
CROSSING POINT WAS CLOSE TO A THUNDERING
WATERFALL, WHICH BLOTTED OUT THE SOUND OF
APPROACHING TRUCKS UNTIL IT WAS TOO LATE.

ACHTUNG!

JERRIES!

THE LAST THING THE GERMAN PATROL HAD EXPECTED TO ENCOUNTER IN THIS LONELY WILDERNESS WAS A GROUP OF BRITISH COMMANDOS. THE ENEMY WERE TOTALLY UNPREPARED FOR THE FEROCITY OF THE RAIDERS' REACTION.

THE FIRST LORRY WAS WRECKED YET THE SECOND SEEMED TO HAVE A CHARMED LIFE AS IT TURNED AND FLED BACK DOWN THE MOUNTAIN ROAD, UNSCATHED BY THE FIERCE GUNFIRE.

THE ROUTE, HOWEVER, HUGGED THE VALLEY SIDE, OUT OF LINE OF FIRE UNTIL IT CROSSED A BRIDGE NEARLY TWO MILES DOWNSTREAM.

WE'LL NEVER HAVE A BETTER CHANCE TO TRY OUT THESE NEW GUNS THAN WHEN THE TRUCK REACHES THERE, ROLF.

I HOPE YOU'RE RIGHT. IT MUST BE ALL OF THREE KILOMETRES AWAY.

NOT UNREASONABLY THE YOUNG N.C.O. IN COMMAND OF THE SURVIVING VEHICLE FELT IT WAS SAFE ENOUGH TO PAUSE ON THE STRUCTURE IN ORDER TO SURVEY THE SCENE THROUGH BINOCULARS.

WHAT CAN YOU SEE, FELDWEBEL?

THE ENGLANDERS ARE STILL THERE . . . PREPARING TO FIRE AT US. BAH, LET THEM WASTE THEIR AMMUNITION.

A MOCKING SMILE PLAYED ACROSS HIS FACE.

BOTH MARKSMEN HAD COMPLETELY FAMILIARISED THEMSELVES WITH THE VLRs BY NOW. AFTER A NECESSARY DELAY TO FOCUS THEIR POWERFUL TELESCOPIC SIGHTS, THEY FIRED SIMULTANEOUSLY.

REMEMBER, NONE OF THEM CAN BE PERMITTED TO ESCAPE.

FAR BELOW THE CORPORAL'S CONTEMPT TURNED ABRUPTLY TO HORROR AS THE ULTRA-HIGH VELOCITY BULLETS SMASHED INTO THE TARGET.

AAARGH!

MEIN GOTT! HOW CAN THEY REACH US FROM THAT DISTANCE?

ANOTHER FACTOR OF THE NEW DESIGN ADDED TO THE CONFUSION. THE ENEMY WAS SO FAR AWAY FROM THE GUNS THAT NO SHOOTING COULD BE HEARD, JUST SHARP, PINGING SOUNDS AS METAL DRILLED THROUGH METAL. THEN ONE ROUND IGNITED A FUEL PIPE —

OFF THE BRIDGE, SCHNELL — TAKE COVER!

ONLY THE N.C.O., ALTHOUGH WOUNDED IN THE SHOULDER, ESCAPED DEATH.

AAAGH!

UUUGH!

THE NEW GUNS, FIRED IN ANGER FOR THE FIRST TIME, HAD AMPLY DEMONSTRATED THEIR FEARSOME POWER.

IF THEY PERFORM AS WELL LATER, IT'LL BE A PIECE OF CAKE. TIME WE STARTED MOVING AGAIN.

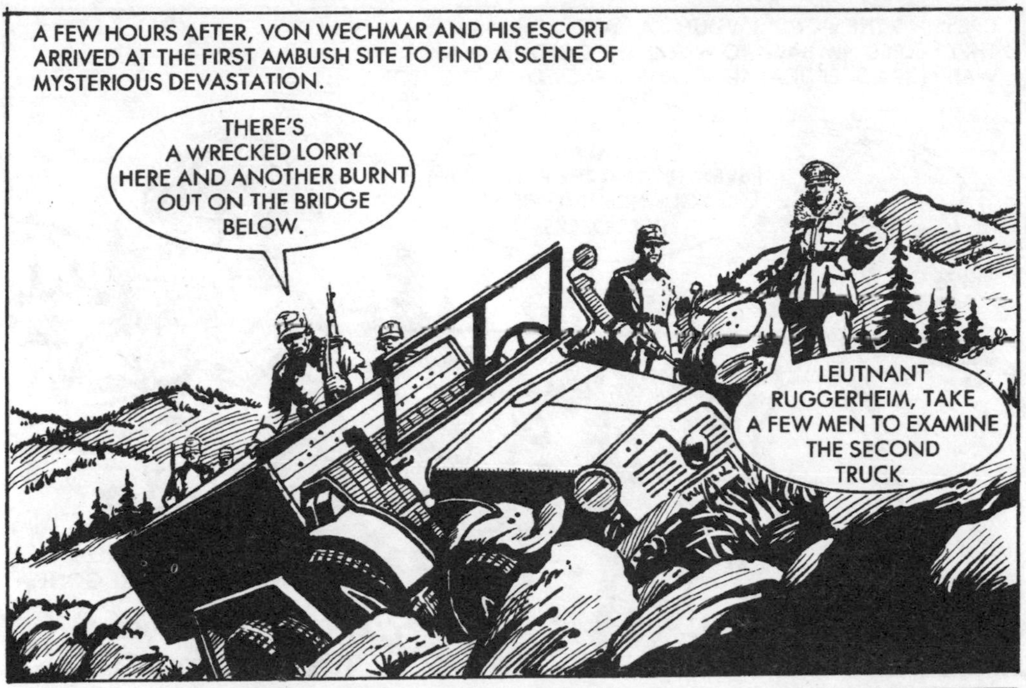
A FEW HOURS AFTER, VON WECHMAR AND HIS ESCORT ARRIVED AT THE FIRST AMBUSH SITE TO FIND A SCENE OF MYSTERIOUS DEVASTATION.
THERE'S A WRECKED LORRY HERE AND ANOTHER BURNT OUT ON THE BRIDGE BELOW.
LEUTNANT RUGGERHEIM, TAKE A FEW MEN TO EXAMINE THE SECOND TRUCK.

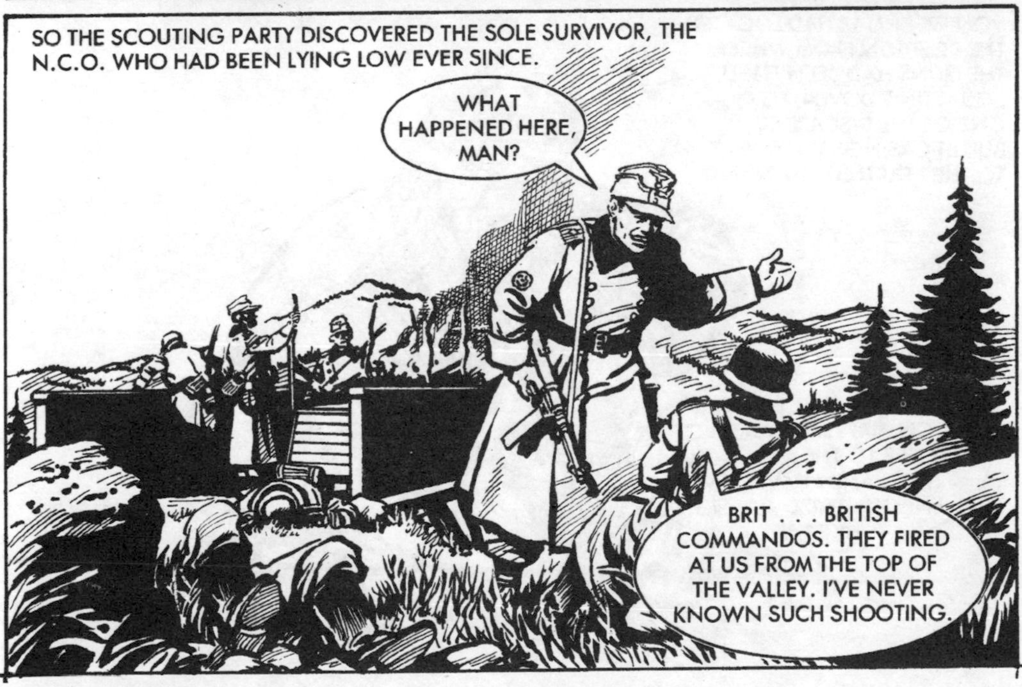
SO THE SCOUTING PARTY DISCOVERED THE SOLE SURVIVOR, THE N.C.O. WHO HAD BEEN LYING LOW EVER SINCE.
WHAT HAPPENED HERE, MAN?
BRIT . . . BRITISH COMMANDOS. THEY FIRED AT US FROM THE TOP OF THE VALLEY. I'VE NEVER KNOWN SUCH SHOOTING.

DRESSING THE VICTIM'S WOUND AS WELL AS POSSIBLE, THEY HELPED HIM BACK TO WHERE THE COLONEL WAS WAITING. A SCEPTICAL RUGGERHEIM PASSED ON THE STORY.

HE MUST BE MISTAKEN. IT'S EVEN BEYOND THE RANGE OF YOUR HUNTING RIFLE, HERR OBERST.

IT SEEMS INCREDIBLE, I AGREE, BUT WHILE YOU WERE GONE I TOOK A GOOD LOOK AROUND.

VON WECHMAR HAD LOCATED THE POSITION FROM WHERE THE GUNS HAD BEEN FIRED. SQUATTING DOWN, HE PICKED UP ONE OF THE DISCARDED BULLET CASINGS TO DISPLAY TO THE STARTLED LEUTNANT.

UNLESS THEY FLOATED ON AIR, THEY CAME NO CLOSER TO THE BRIDGE THAN HERE. AND I HAVE NEVER ENCOUNTERED A DESIGN LIKE THIS.

THE CASUALTY WAS UNABLE TO GIVE AN ACCURATE DESCRIPTION OF THE FIRE-ARMS. HE SAID ENOUGH TO SEND A SURGE OF EXCITEMENT THROUGH THE PRUSSIAN HUNTER, THOUGH.

THEY LOOKED ORDINARY FROM THAT DISTANCE, HERR OBERST. THERE CERTAINLY DIDN'T SEEM TO BE ANYTHING UNUSUAL ABOUT THEM.

EXCEPT THAT THEY FIRED HIGH VELOCITY BULLETS OVER A KILLING RANGE OF AT LEAST THREE KILOMETRES, JA?

HOT ON THE SCENT, VON WECHMAR COULD NOT AFFORD TO BE SLOWED DOWN BY THE INJURED N.C.O., WHO WAS LEFT BEHIND IN THE CARE OF ONE OF RUGGERHEIM'S MEN.

OUR PRIORITY IS TO CATCH UP WITH THESE COMMANDOS. IT IS IMPERATIVE THAT WE LEARN MORE ABOUT THE REMARKABLE GUNS THEY APPEAR TO BE CARRYING.

MEANWHILE ROBERT'S FORCE HAD ARRIVED CLOSE TO A BIG ALUMINIUM SMELTING WORKS SUPPLYING LARGE QUANTITIES OF THE VITAL METAL TO THE GERMAN WAR MACHINE.

NO WONDER THE R.A.F. WERE SO CAGEY ABOUT RAIDING THIS PLACE. IT'S BETTER PROTECTED THAN HITLER'S CHANCELLORY. NOT THAT IT'S OUR ACTUAL TARGET, THOUGH.

HIS ATTENTION TURNED TO THEIR PRIME OBJECTIVE — THE HYDRO-ELECTRIC POWER STATION ALONGSIDE THE SMELTING WORKS. ITS TURBINES WERE FED BY WATER CHANNELLED DOWN BY HUGE PIPES FROM A MOUNTAIN RESERVOIR.

THE SMELTING PLANT'S WELL-PROTECTED. EVEN IF IT WERE TO BE DESTROYED, IT COULD BE REBUILT VERY QUICKLY.

ON THE OTHER HAND, WITHOUT ENORMOUS AMOUNTS OF ELECTRICITY, THE FACTORY WAS USELESS.

THE PLANNERS HAD KNOWN THAT A SKILLED TEAM COULD PROBABLY ENTER THE POWER STATION BY COMING DOWN THE OUTSIDE OF THE WATER PIPES, EXCEPT FOR THE THREAT POSED BY THE TWO GERMAN OBSERVATION POSTS ON EITHER SIDE.

THERE SEEMED NO WAY TO DEAL WITH THEM QUICKLY AND QUIETLY UNTIL THESE BEAUTIES SHOWED UP.

HOW VITAL A ROLE THE NEW GUNS WERE DESTINED TO PLAY WAS CLEAR.

A GOOD MARKSMAN CAN TAKE OUT THE OBSERVATION POST GUARDS FROM HERE, TWO MILES AWAY.

SO THAT'S WHY YOU CHOSE ME IN PARTICULAR?

ROLF HAD BEEN A NATURAL CHOICE, NOT ONLY BECAUSE HE KNEW THE AREA BUT BECAUSE HE HAD BEEN A PRE-WAR SHOOTING CHAMPION.

AND SOMEHOW I DON'T THINK YOU'D HAVE TOO MANY QUALMS ABOUT SHOOTING GERMANS.

NOT AFTER WHAT THEY'VE DONE TO MY COUNTRY.

ROBERT EXPLAINED THE FINAL DETAILS OF THE MISSION TO THE RAPTLY ATTENTIVE NORWEGIAN MARKSMAN WHO WAS TO REMAIN WHERE HE WAS WHILE THE OTHERS MOVED TO THE FAR SIDE OF THE VALLEY.

WHEN YOU SEE ME SIGNAL FROM THE TOP OF THE WATER PIPES, THAT'S WHEN YOU HIT THE OBSERVATION POSTS.

YOU CAN RELY ON ME.

LEAVING ROLF WITH ONE OF THE VLRs, TAKING THE OTHER ONE HIMSELF, ROBERT AND HIS MEN SET OFF ON THEIR ARDUOUS JOURNEY. CROSSING THE BOTTOM OF THE GREAT VALLEY WAS MERELY THE FIRST HAZARD.

THEY CROSSED A REMOTE RAILWAY LINE IN THE COVER OF AN ABANDONED WAGON.

LET'S GO — MOVE, MOVE!

THERE FOLLOWED A LONG TOUGH CLIMB UP THE FAR SIDE. IT WAS A DAUNTING TASK FOR WHICH THEY HAD TRAINED LONG AND HARD.

KEEP MOVING. IF A JERRY PLANE CAME BY NOW, WE'D STICK OUT LIKE SORE THUMBS.

IT TOOK THE COMMANDOS THREE GRUELLING HOURS TO REACH THE RESERVOIR HIGH ABOVE, WHERE THE OUTLET WAS UNDER CONSTANT SCRUTINY FROM A GUARD HUT.

TWO OUTSIDE, AND TWO INSIDE, SIR.

THIS IS A JOB FOR THE NEW GUN THEN.

THE DISTANCE, NORMALLY CONSIDERED A FAIR SNIPING RANGE, WAS NOW THE EQUIVALENT OF FIRING AT A BARN DOOR.

IT'S TOO EASY.

THE TWO OFF-DUTY SOLDIERS INSIDE SAW THEIR COMRADES COLLAPSE BENEATH THE IMPACT OF THE SPECIAL AMMO.

GOTT IN HIMMEL! WHAT'S HAPPENED TO THEM?

BEFORE THE SURVIVORS COULD REACT FURTHER, ROBERT TURNED HIS ATTENTION TO THE HUT. THE INCREDIBLY POWERFUL BULLETS SMASHED THROUGH THE WOODEN WALLS AS IF THEY DIDN'T EVEN EXIST, KILLING BOTH MEN.

AAARGH!

A FEW MINUTES LATER ROBERT STOOD BY THE PIPES, SIGNALLING TO ROLF WHO WAS INVISIBLE IN THE FORESTED SLOPES OVER TWO MILES AWAY.

I HOPE OUR NORWEGIAN FRIEND'S KEEPING HIS EYES PEELED.

HE HAD NO NEED TO WORRY. THE MARKSMAN, HIMSELF A SKILLED AND EXPERIENCED HUNTER, HAD NOT RELAXED HIS VIGILANCE FOR A SECOND.

THEY'VE MADE IT. NOW IT'S UP TO ME.

ROLF HAD SPENT HIS TIME SETTING AND REFINING HIS TELESCOPIC SIGHTS TO WHAT HE JUDGED TO BE NEAR PERFECTION.

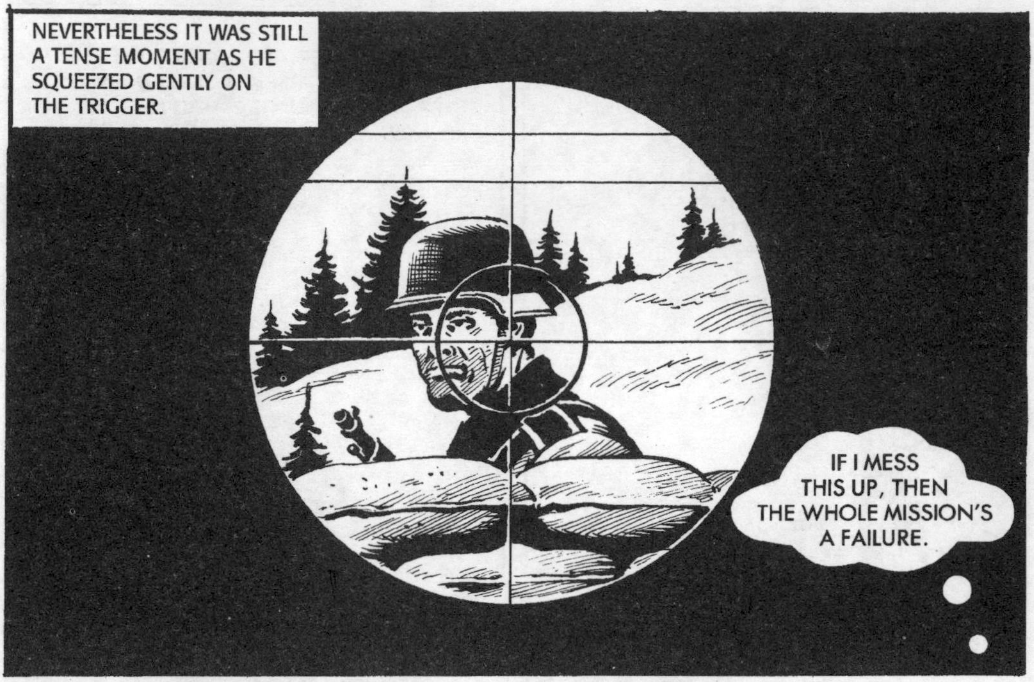
NEVERTHELESS IT WAS STILL A TENSE MOMENT AS HE SQUEEZED GENTLY ON THE TRIGGER.
IF I MESS THIS UP, THEN THE WHOLE MISSION'S A FAILURE.

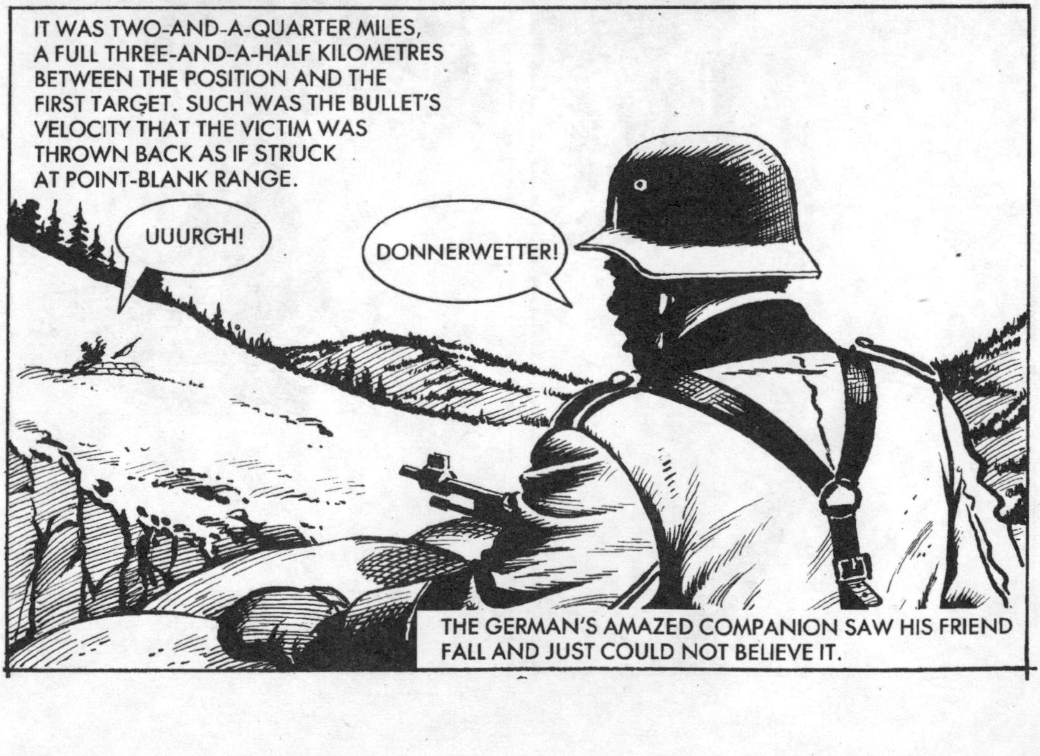
IT WAS TWO-AND-A-QUARTER MILES, A FULL THREE-AND-A-HALF KILOMETRES BETWEEN THE POSITION AND THE FIRST TARGET. SUCH WAS THE BULLET'S VELOCITY THAT THE VICTIM WAS THROWN BACK AS IF STRUCK AT POINT-BLANK RANGE.
UUURGH!
DONNERWETTER!
THE GERMAN'S AMAZED COMPANION SAW HIS FRIEND FALL AND JUST COULD NOT BELIEVE IT.

IT WAS ONLY A MATTER OF MOMENTS BEFORE THE NORWEGIAN CRACKSHOT FOUND AND STRUCK HIS SECOND TARGET. WATCHING FROM ABOVE, ROBERT WAS READY TO MOVE AN INSTANT LATER.

THE FINAL ABSEILING DESCENT HAD BEEN PRACTISED DOZENS OF TIMES BEFORE AT A SIMILAR HYDRO-ELECTRIC STATION IN THE SCOTTISH HIGHLANDS, ENSURING THAT THE REAL THING WAS ACCOMPLISHED SMOOTHLY AND RAPIDLY.

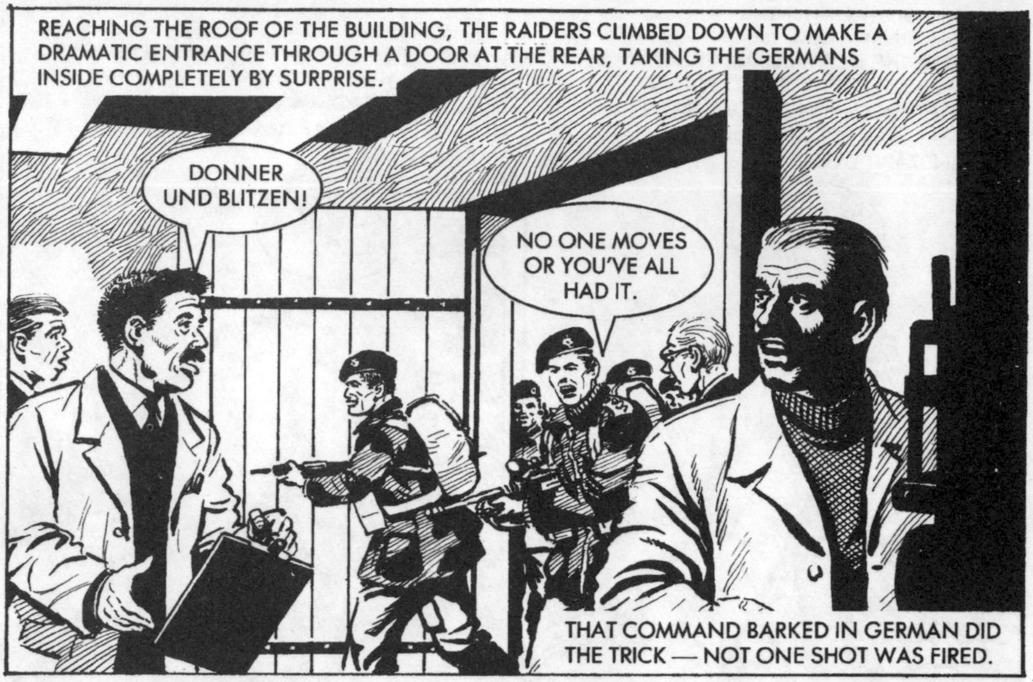
REACHING THE ROOF OF THE BUILDING, THE RAIDERS CLIMBED DOWN TO MAKE A DRAMATIC ENTRANCE THROUGH A DOOR AT THE REAR, TAKING THE GERMANS INSIDE COMPLETELY BY SURPRISE.
DONNER UND BLITZEN!
NO ONE MOVES OR YOU'VE ALL HAD IT.
THAT COMMAND BARKED IN GERMAN DID THE TRICK — NOT ONE SHOT WAS FIRED.

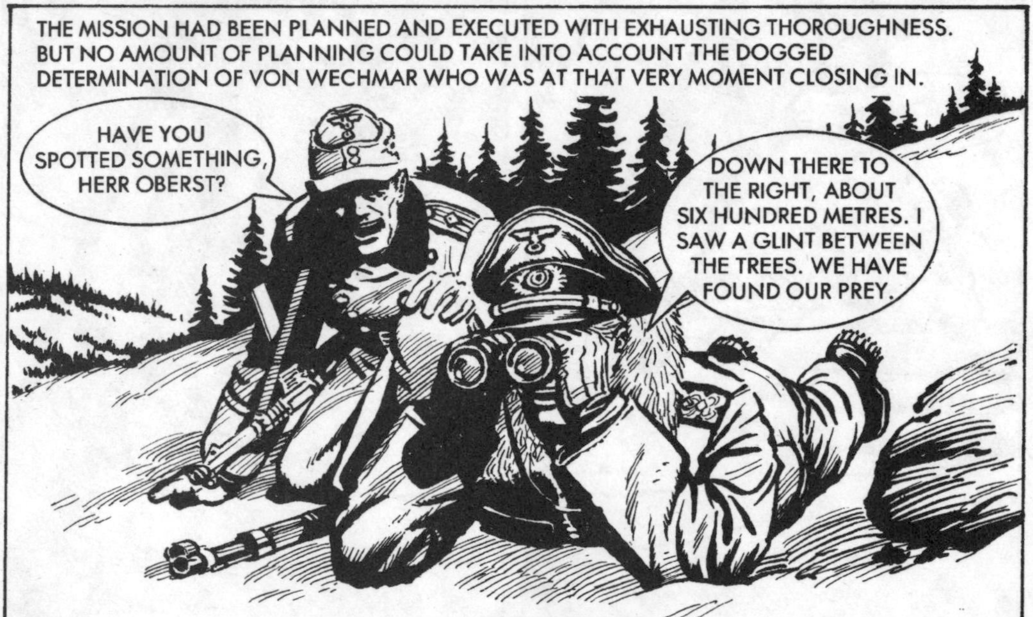
THE MISSION HAD BEEN PLANNED AND EXECUTED WITH EXHAUSTING THOROUGHNESS. BUT NO AMOUNT OF PLANNING COULD TAKE INTO ACCOUNT THE DOGGED DETERMINATION OF VON WECHMAR WHO WAS AT THAT VERY MOMENT CLOSING IN.
HAVE YOU SPOTTED SOMETHING, HERR OBERST?
DOWN THERE TO THE RIGHT, ABOUT SIX HUNDRED METRES. I SAW A GLINT BETWEEN THE TREES. WE HAVE FOUND OUR PREY.

BUT VON WECHMAR WASN'T THE ONLY EXPERIENCED HUNTER. BORN AND BRED IN THESE MOUNTAIN FORESTS, ROLF SENSED THE APPROACH OF DANGER LONG BEFORE HE SPOTTED IT.

SOMETHING DISTURBED THAT BIRD. THERE'S SOMEBODY UP THERE.

WHEN THE FIRST GERMAN TROOPER UNWISELY SHOWED HIMSELF AGAINST THE SKYLINE, ROLF WAS READY AND WAITING.

UUURH!

ANOTHER MAN WAS LOST BEFORE THE COLONEL FULLY APPRECIATED THE DEADLY SKILLS OF HIS ADVERSARY. FOR HIM IT MERELY SERVED TO INCREASE THE CHALLENGE.

AAARGH!

RUGGERHEIM, TAKE THE MEN THAT WAY. GO DOWNHILL, MAKE LOTS OF NOISE.

IT WAS THE OLDEST PLOY IN THE BOOK, DISTRACTING A QUARRY. THAT WAS ALSO THE REASON IT WAS SO EFFECTIVE.

BEFORE THEY WERE QUIET AS MICE, NOW THEY SOUND LIKE A HERD OF STAMPEDING ELEPHANTS. WHAT ARE THEY PLAYING AT?

VON WECHMAR WAS ENACTING A VERY DEADLY GAME OF HIDE-AND-SEEK. EVEN AS ROLF SENSED MOVEMENT BEHIND HIM AND WHIRLED ROUND, HE KNEW HE WOULD PAY FOR THOSE FEW SECONDS OF DISTRACTION WITH HIS LIFE.

AAARGH!

A CLOSE RUN THING, MY FRIEND, BUT NOT QUITE CLOSE ENOUGH.

THE COLONEL SEIZED THE DEAD NORWEGIAN'S VLR IN TRIUMPH AS RUGGERHEIM AND HIS MEN RAN UP.

SO THIS IS THE MARVELLOUS GUN, EH? BUT WHY HAVE THE BRITISH BROUGHT IT HERE?

I DON'T KNOW, SIR, BUT MAYBE THERE ARE OTHER COMMANDOS NEARBY.

VON WECHMAR GAVE A GRUNT OF DISDAIN AS HE SURVEYED THE VALLEY BEYOND THROUGH HIS BINOCULARS. HE WAS POSITIVE HE WOULD HAVE DETECTED THEM.

I CAN ASSURE YOU OF THAT. HOWEVER, THIS MAN WAS CLEARLY HERE FOR A REASON AND . . . TEUFEL!

WHAT IS IT, HERR, OBERST?

IN A SINGLE REVEALING MOMENT, THE PURPOSE OF THE MISSION BECAME CRYSTAL CLEAR TO VON WECHMAR.

ROPES DOWN THE WATER PIPES FEEDING THE HYDRO STATION, AND DEAD SENTRIES IN THE OBSERVATION POSTS. SO THAT'S WHAT THEY NEEDED THE GUNS FOR!

THE IMPLICATIONS OF WHAT HE HAD SEEN WERE IMMEDIATELY OBVIOUS TO THE FAST-THINKING HUNTER. HE WASTED NO TIME BEFORE SNAPPING OUT A COMMAND.

TAKE YOUR MEN DOWN BELOW AND ALERT THE GARRISON. I SHALL REMAIN HERE.

ALREADY HE WAS HOPING HE MIGHT HAVE A CHANCE TO TURN THEIR OWN AMAZING WEAPON AGAINST THE RAIDERS.

LEFT ALONE, HE SETTLED DOWN TO EXAMINE THE GUN WITH METICULOUS THOROUGHNESS. THE CARTRIDGES HE TOOK FROM NEXT TO ROLF'S BODY ESPECIALLY INTRIGUED HIM. THE MORE HE STUDIED THEM THE MORE IMPRESSED HE BECAME.

THERE SEEMS TO BE SOME SORT OF COMPRESSED GAS CYLINDER FITTED TO THE BASE. IT MUST BE HOW THE VELOCITY IS BOOSTED SO MUCH. MOST INGENIOUS.

PEERING THROUGH THE POWERFUL TELESCOPIC SIGHTS, HE PRACTICALLY SMACKED HIS LIPS IN ANTICIPATION WHEN HE SAW A COMMANDO GUARDING THE REAR DOOR.

THAT MUST BE WHERE THE BRITISH ENTERED. PRESUMABLY IT WILL ALSO BE THEIR EXIT. I CAN HARDLY WAIT TO PICK OFF THE FIRST ONE WHO SHOWS HIMSELF.

IT WAS ALSO CLEAR TO THE GERMAN THAT THE RAIDERS HAD PICKED THEIR SPOT WELL. NO HEAVY VEHICLES COULD GET DOWN THE SIDE OR BEHIND THE COMPLEX BECAUSE IT WAS SET TIGHT INTO THE SIDE OF THE MOUNTAIN.

BY THIS TIME, THE RAIDERS HAD IMMOBILISED THE FEW GERMANS INSIDE AND WERE JUST FINISHING LAYING EXPLOSIVE CHARGES IN THE MAIN GENERATING HALL.

TIMERS ARE READY FOR SETTING, SKIPPER.

SET THEM FOR FIVE MINUTES. THAT'LL GIVE US PLENTY OF TIME TO GET CLEAR AND PUT THESE JERRIES OUT OF HARM'S WAY.

UNFORTUNATELY FOR ROBERT AND HIS MEN, RUGGERHEIM HAD JUST REACHED THE GARRISON WHERE HE WAS RAISING THE ALARM.

BRITISH COMMANDOS ARE IN THE POWER STATION!

RAUS, RAUS — TO THE AREA — SCHNELL!

THE RAIDERS' LOOK-OUT ABOVE THE HEAVY STEEL ENTRANCE DOORS SOON SPOTTED THE COMMOTION.

JERRIES COMING!

THE DOORS SHOULD DELAY THEM LONG ENOUGH FOR US TO GET OUT.

THIS WAS WHAT VON WECHMAR HAD BEEN WAITING FOR. AS THE FIRST RETREATING MAN EMERGED . . .

. . . THE COLONEL SQUEEZED THE TRIGGER, MARVELLING AT THE EFFECT OF THIS REVOLUTIONARY WEAPON.

IT WAS A TERRIBLE SHOCK FOR THE SABOTEURS TO FIND THAT THEIR ESCAPE ROUTE WAS CUT OFF. ROBERT REALISED IMMEDIATELY WHAT THE CAUSE OF IT HAD TO BE.

NOTHING OVERLOOKS US FROM THE VALLEY BOTTOM, WHICH MEANS THE SHOT MUST HAVE COME FROM ROLF'S POSITION.

HE MUST BE DEAD THEN . . . AND A JERRY'S GOT HIS VLR!

REACHING A SUITABLE WINDOW, ROBERT SEARCHED THE FAR SIDE OF THE VALLEY THROUGH HIS OWN TELESCOPIC SIGHTS UNTIL HE FOUND WHAT HE WAS LOOKING FOR.

IT'S A GERMAN OFFICER. I'M GOING TO TRY AND KEEP HIM PINNED DOWN. AS SOON AS I START SHOOTING, THE REST OF YOU GET GOING.

HIS OWN ATTENTION FIXED FIRMLY ON THE EXIT, VON WECHMAR WAS TAKEN BY SURPRISE AS A VOLLEY OF SHOTS SMASHED INTO THE TREES JUST ABOVE HIM, THE MASSIVE VELOCITY OF THE BULLETS SUFFICIENT TO BRING DOWN A SHOWER OF BRANCHES.

MEIN GOTT!

REALISING THAT HE WAS NOW ON THE RECEIVING END, HE DUCKED INTO BETTER COVER.

IF I SHOW MYSELF, I'LL NEVER HAVE TIME TO LOCATE WHOEVER'S SHOOTING BEFORE HE NAILS ME. I'LL HAVE TO WAIT FOR HIM TO CHANGE MAGAZINES.

AT ROBERT'S RATE OF FIRE, THIS WAS ONLY A MATTER OF MOMENTS, BY WHICH TIME HIS SERGEANT WAS SHOUTING URGENTLY.

COME ON, SKIPPER! THE CHARGES GO IN THIRTY SECONDS!

RIGHT. LET'S HOPE OUR SNIPER KEEPS HIS HEAD DOWN.

THE SHORT LULL GAVE THE GERMAN TIME TO WRIGGLE FORWARD AGAIN TO SET UP FOR MORE ACTION.

HE WAS GOOD ALL RIGHT, THAT MARKSMAN, BUT LET'S SEE WHERE HE IS NOW.

THE FIRST ROBERT KNEW THAT VON WECHMAR WAS BACK IN BUSINESS WAS WHEN THE MAN ABOVE HIM WAS ABRUPTLY SHOT OFF THE ROPE HE WAS USING TO HAUL HIMSELF BACK UP THE CLIFF.

AAAARGH!

THE SNIPER'S ON TO US! WE'RE SITTING DUCKS OUT HERE.

AS IT HAPPENED, TWO OTHER EVENTS WERE COMING TO A HEAD AT THE SAME TIME. OUTSIDE THE POWER STATION, RUGGERHEIM HAD CALLED UP A SELF-PROPELLED GUN TO BLAST DOWN THE HEAVY DOORS.

FEUER!

MEANWHILE, INSIDE THE BUILDING, THE CHARGES EXPLODED ON SCHEDULE . . .

. . . RIPPING APART THE MASSIVE TURBINES, RUPTURING THE HUGE WATER FEEDER PIPES ENTERING FROM ABOVE.

WHILE THIS WAS HAPPENING, VON WECHMAR WAS STRUGGLING TO CENTRE HIS SIGHTS ON ROBERT, A DIFFICULT TASK GIVEN THE DEGREE OF MAGNIFICATION NECESSARY OVER SUCH A LONG RANGE.

AT LAST I'VE GOT HIM!

THE SLIGHTEST MOVEMENT ON THE GERMAN'S PART COULD JERK HIS AIM OFF OUT OF ALL PROPORTION.

EVEN AS THE COLONEL SQUEEZED THE TRIGGER, A HUGE CLOUD OF SMOKE AND STEAM ERUPTED THROUGH THE ROOF OF THE POWER STATION, BLOTTING OUT HIS VIEW. THE BULLET JUST MISSED AND NO MORE.

THAT WAS TOO CLOSE FOR COMFORT. LET'S GET OUT OF HERE WHILE THE COVER LASTS!

AT THE SAME MOMENT, RUGGERHEIM WAS LEADING AN ASSAULT TOWARDS THE SHATTERED ENTRANCE, CERTAIN THAT THE BRITISH WERE STILL INSIDE.

FORWARD!

TO THEIR HORROR, THE GERMANS WERE MET INSTEAD BY A GIGANTIC WALL OF WATER FROM THE RUPTURED PIPES WHICH SWEPT AWAY EVERYTHING IN ITS PATH.

NEIN . . . EEEAAR!

THE LEUTNANT, LIKE MANY OF HIS MEN, DROWNED IN THE FLOOD.

IT WAS SEVERAL MINUTES BEFORE THE SMOKE AND STEAM CLEARED SUFFICIENTLY FOR VON WECHMAR TO INSPECT THE DAMAGE DONE. HE SAW THE ABANDONED ROPES.

SO THEY THINK THEY'VE GOT AWAY, DO THEY?

THE HUNTER WHO HAD BEEN CHEATED OF HIS PREY WAS IN NO MOOD TO ABANDON THE CHASE. CASTING ASIDE HIS OWN RIFLE IN FAVOUR OF THE VLR, HE SET OFF ALONE, DETERMINED TO EVEN THE SCORE.

WE'LL SEE WHO'S THE BEST WITH THESE GUNS, MY BRITISH FRIENDS.

BACK IN BRITAIN, THE REMAINING PROTOTYPE VLR HAD BEEN SUBJECTED TO A GRUELLING SERIES OF FIRING TESTS, THE EFFECTS OF WHICH WERE BEGINNING TO TROUBLE ONE OF THE SCIENTISTS INVOLVED.

STILL WORRIED ABOUT THE ENERGY GENERATED BY COMPRESSED GAS CHARGES?

WE'VE MADE THE BARREL OUT OF THE STRONGEST ALLOY AVAILABLE, BUT IT'S STILL WARPING SLIGHTLY WITH EACH SHOT FIRED.

WHAT MIGHT HAVE BEEN NOTHING MORE THAN AN ACADEMIC PROBLEM TOOK ON A NEW IMPORTANCE WITH TWO OF THE WEAPONS ALREADY OPERATING IN THE FIELD.

IT GRADUALLY BECOMES LESS ACCURATE WITH EACH USE.

BUT THAT ALSO MEANS THERE WILL INEVITABLY COME A POINT WHEN . . .

THE WORDS WERE LEFT UNSAID, FOR THERE COULD BE ONLY ONE RESULT. HURRIEDLY THE TWO MEN SET UP THE GUN AT AN INDOOR RANGE. THEY TOOK COVER WHILE THEY OPERATED A SERIES OF RODS TO PULL THE TRIGGER.

WE'RE USING LIVE AMMO, AREN'T WE?

NATURALLY. BLANKS JUST SEND HOT GASES DOWN THE BARREL. WE'VE GOT TO KNOW WHAT HAPPENS TO HIGH-VELOCITY METAL TAKING THE SAME ROUTE.

THEY WERE HALF WAY THROUGH THE THIRD MAGAZINE WHEN IT HAPPENED. THOUGH STILL UNDETECTABLE TO HUMAN EYES, THE BARREL FINALLY WARPED SUFFICIENTLY TO DEFLECT THE HIGH VELOCITY BULLET FROM A STRAIGHT LINE TRAJECTORY — WITH DEVASTATING CONSEQUENCES.

GOOD LORD! IT BLEW APART LIKE A BOMB!

WE'D BETTER HOPE THAT THE COMMANDO MARKSMEN HAVEN'T HAD A LOT OF SHOOTING TO DO . . . OR ELSE.

THERE WAS, OF COURSE, NO WAY OF WARNING ROBERT. HE AND HIS SURVIVING MEN WERE AT THAT MOMENT LOOKING DOWN ON A LAKE HIGH IN THE DESOLATE MOUNTAINS OF CENTRAL NORWAY FROM WHICH A FLYING BOAT WOULD EVACUATE THEM.

THIS IS THE PLACE. WE'VE GOT AN HOUR BEFORE THE PLANE'S DUE TO ARRIVE. WE'LL WAIT DOWN BY THE SHORE.

WHAT THE RAIDERS DID NOT KNOW WAS THAT VON WECHMAR, HAVING PICKED UP THEIR TRACKS, WAS FOLLOWING THEM RUTHLESSLY.

THEY MUST BE MAKING FOR A RENDEZVOUS. PERHAPS AN AIRCRAFT IS COMING TO PICK THEM UP.

LIKE A MAN POSSESSED HE STALKED ON, HIS SKILLED EYES TELLING HIM THAT HE WAS GAINING ALL THE TIME.

THEY CAN'T BE MORE THAN TEN MINUTES AHEAD OF ME NOW.

CRESTING A FINAL RISE, HE FOUND HIMSELF LOOKING DOWN AT THE LAKE WHERE, FAR BELOW, HIS QUARRY WAS IN PLAIN SIGHT.

TRACED THEM AT LAST. BUT WHAT ARE THEY DOING AMONG THOSE ROCKS?

A ROWING BOAT WAS IN FACT CAREFULLY CONCEALED THERE, LEFT A FEW DAYS EARLIER BY MEMBERS OF THE NORWEGIAN RESISTANCE AFTER A RADIOED REQUEST FROM LONDON, THOUGH FOR SECURITY PURPOSES THEY HAD NOT BEEN TOLD WHY.

YOU CAN ALWAYS RELY ON THE NORWEGIANS NOT TO LET YOU DOWN. IT'S A PITY ROLF DIDN'T MAKE IT.

IT WAS, IN MORE WAYS THAN ONE. THE NORWEGIAN'S OWN UNERRING HUNTING INSTINCTS MIGHT WELL HAVE DETECTED VON WECHMAR'S PRESENCE.

AS IT WAS, THE NAZI HAD ALREADY SELECTED HIS FIRST TARGET.

THEIR OFFICER WILL BE THE FIRST TO DIE.

ONCE AGAIN, THE DISTANCE FROM WHICH THE GUN WAS FIRED CONCEALED THE SOUND UNTIL THE BULLET STRUCK HOME, JUST MISSING ROBERTS.

GOOD GRIEF — ROLF'S KILLER MUST BE BACK AGAIN!

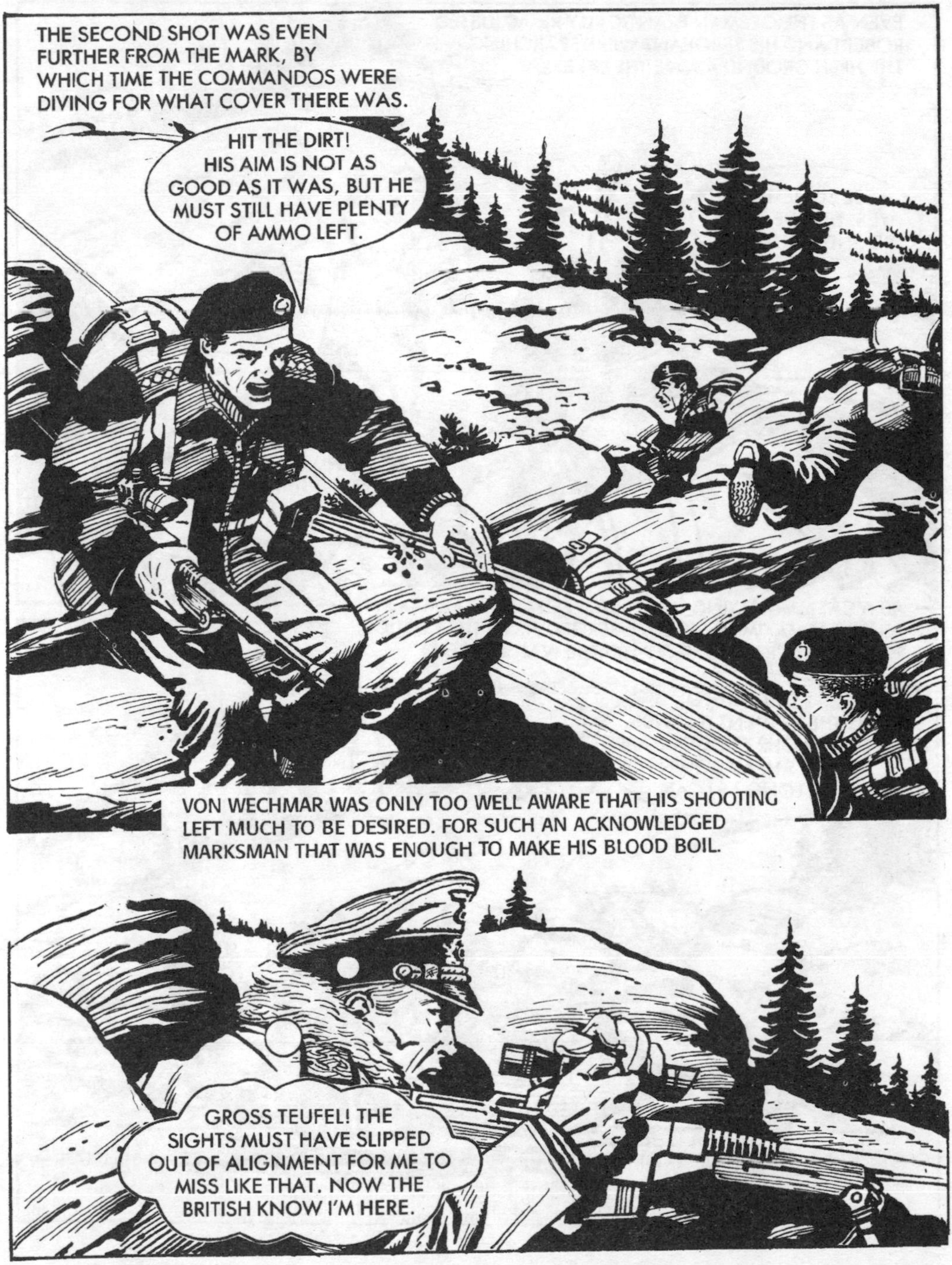
THE SECOND SHOT WAS EVEN FURTHER FROM THE MARK, BY WHICH TIME THE COMMANDOS WERE DIVING FOR WHAT COVER THERE WAS.
HIT THE DIRT! HIS AIM IS NOT AS GOOD AS IT WAS, BUT HE MUST STILL HAVE PLENTY OF AMMO LEFT.
VON WECHMAR WAS ONLY TOO WELL AWARE THAT HIS SHOOTING LEFT MUCH TO BE DESIRED. FOR SUCH AN ACKNOWLEDGED MARKSMAN THAT WAS ENOUGH TO MAKE HIS BLOOD BOIL.
GROSS TEUFEL! THE SIGHTS MUST HAVE SLIPPED OUT OF ALIGNMENT FOR ME TO MISS LIKE THAT. NOW THE BRITISH KNOW I'M HERE.

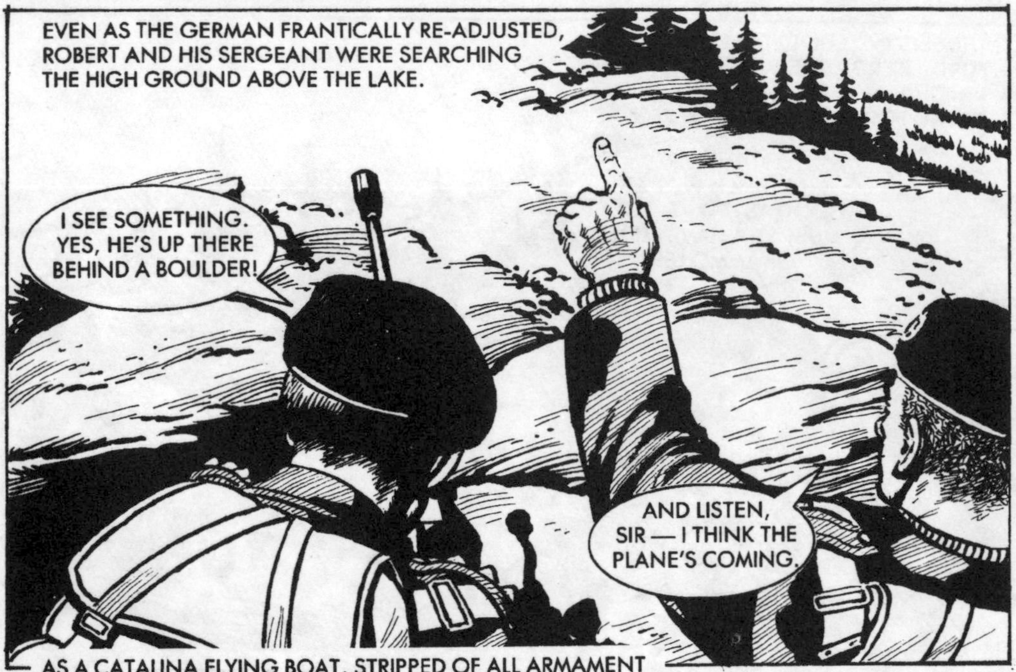
EVEN AS THE GERMAN FRANTICALLY RE-ADJUSTED, ROBERT AND HIS SERGEANT WERE SEARCHING THE HIGH GROUND ABOVE THE LAKE.
I SEE SOMETHING. YES, HE'S UP THERE BEHIND A BOULDER!
AND LISTEN, SIR — I THINK THE PLANE'S COMING.

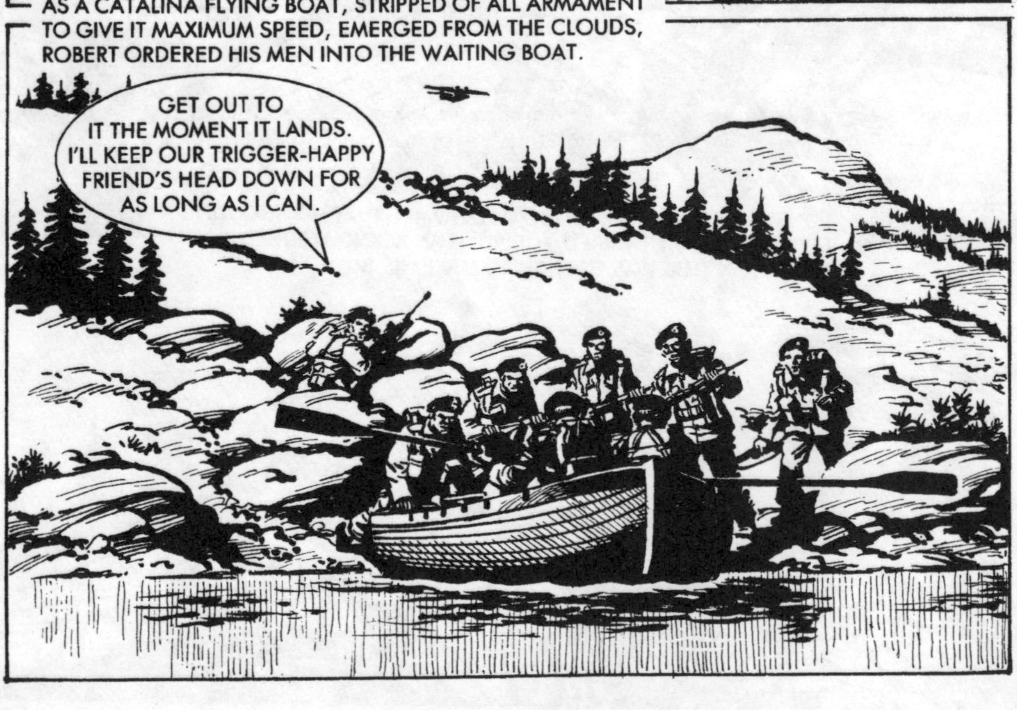
AS A CATALINA FLYING BOAT, STRIPPED OF ALL ARMAMENT TO GIVE IT MAXIMUM SPEED, EMERGED FROM THE CLOUDS, ROBERT ORDERED HIS MEN INTO THE WAITING BOAT.
GET OUT TO IT THE MOMENT IT LANDS. I'LL KEEP OUR TRIGGER-HAPPY FRIEND'S HEAD DOWN FOR AS LONG AS I CAN.

VON WECHMAR WAS READY TO OPEN FIRE AGAIN WHEN THE CATALINA FLEW IN ABOVE HIM.

SO THAT'S HOW THEY'RE GETTING AWAY, OR SO THEY THINK. WITH THE PROBLEM SORTED, THOUGH, THIS GUN IS QUITE CAPABLE OF SHOOTING THE PILOTS.

THE NAZI ROSE FOR A BETTER VIEW, SO CAUGHT UP IN THE EXCITEMENT OF THE HUNT THAT HE HAD COMPLETELY FORGOTTEN THERE WAS A WEAPON OF EQUAL POWER IN THE VICINITY, AND THAT ITS OWNER WAS AFTER HIS BLOOD.

I'VE GOT YOU NOW, FRITZ!

THIS TIME IT WAS ROBERT'S TURN TO GRIT HIS TEETH. IN SPITE OF HAVING THE TARGET IN THE CENTRE OF HIS SIGHTS, HIS SHOT STILL NARROWLY MISSED.

MEIN GOTT, I'D FORGOTTEN ABOUT THE OTHER GUN. LUCKY FOR ME THAT HE'S SHOOTING AS BADLY AS I WAS JUST NOW.

LIKE VON WECHMAR, ROBERT ALSO BLAMED HIS SIGHTS. BUT INSTEAD OF TRYING TO CORRECT THEM HE SETTLED INSTEAD FOR A POLICY OF SHOOTING STEADILY AT THE GERMAN'S POSITION TO GIVE HIS MEN TIME TO REACH WATER DEEP ENOUGH FOR THE CATALINA TO TAXI TO SAFETY.

WE CAN'T LEAVE YOU BEHIND, SKIPPER!

DON'T WORRY ABOUT ME. I'LL BE ALONG AS SOON AS THE CAT REACHES YOU.

JUDGING IT FINELY, HE EMPTIED A MAGAZINE
TO COINCIDE WITH THE AIRCRAFT'S BEST POSITION.

SARGE, GET READY TO CATCH THE GUN. WE CAN'T LEAVE IT BEHIND.

RUNNING UP TO THE EDGE OF THE LAKE, ROBERT
THREW THE VLR WITH ALL HIS MIGHT, HIS
SERGEANT MANAGING TO SNATCH IT OUT OF THE AIR.

GOOD FIELDING!

FOR PITY'S SAKE, SKIPPER, YOU'RE A SITTING DUCK!

THE WARNING CAME IN THE NICK OF TIME. JUST AS ROBERT LAUNCHED HIMSELF INTO THE WATER ANOTHER HIGH VELOCITY SHOT STRUCK HOME WHERE HE HAD BEEN STANDING AN INSTANT BEFORE.

HECK, THAT JERRY NEVER GIVES UP.

EVEN IN THE WATER, ROBERT WAS A CLEAR TARGET. BUT TO HIS HUGE RELIEF, THE TWO OR THREE BULLETS WHICH WERE ACTUALLY FIRED CAME NOWHERE NEAR TO HITTING HIM.

HIS AIM IS GETTING WILDER WITH EVERY SHOT. HE MUST BE GETTING THE JITTERS.

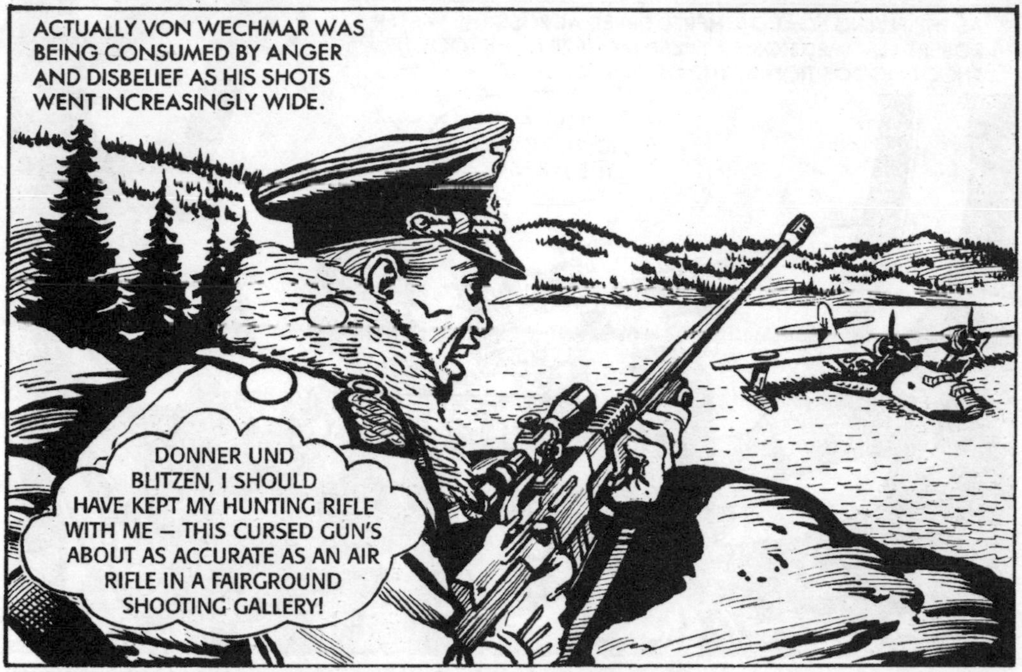
ACTUALLY VON WECHMAR WAS BEING CONSUMED BY ANGER AND DISBELIEF AS HIS SHOTS WENT INCREASINGLY WIDE.
DONNER UND BLITZEN, I SHOULD HAVE KEPT MY HUNTING RIFLE WITH ME – THIS CURSED GUN'S ABOUT AS ACCURATE AS AN AIR RIFLE IN A FAIRGROUND SHOOTING GALLERY!

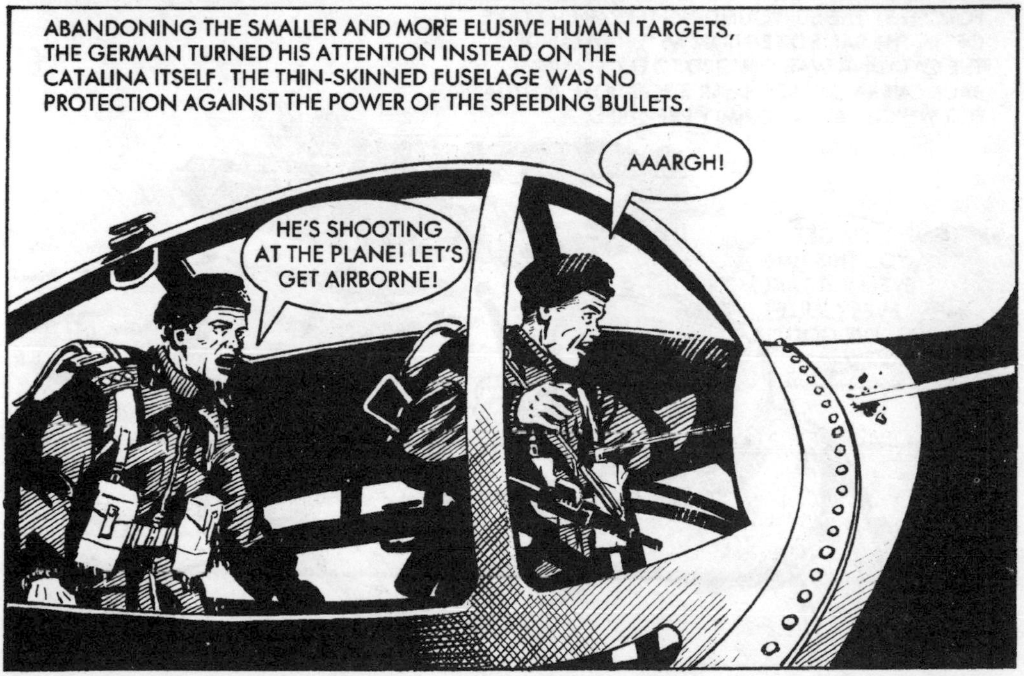
ABANDONING THE SMALLER AND MORE ELUSIVE HUMAN TARGETS, THE GERMAN TURNED HIS ATTENTION INSTEAD ON THE CATALINA ITSELF. THE THIN-SKINNED FUSELAGE WAS NO PROTECTION AGAINST THE POWER OF THE SPEEDING BULLETS.
HE'S SHOOTING AT THE PLANE! LET'S GET AIRBORNE!
AAARGH!

AS THE FLYING BOAT GATHERED SPEED ACROSS THE WATER, ROBERT SLAMMED HOME A FRESH MAGAZINE. HE TOOK UP A SHOOTING POSITION BY THE OPEN SIDE TURRET.

I'LL HAVE ANOTHER CRACK AT THE JERRY . . .

FORCED BY THE SURROUNDING TERRAIN TO TAKE OFF IN THE SAME DIRECTION AS IT HAD LANDED, THE CATALINA WAS OBLIGED TO FLY STRAIGHT BACK OVER VON WECHMAR'S POSITION, A SITUATION FOR WHICH HE WAS GRIMLY PREPARED.

I'LL GET YOU THIS TIME, EVEN IF IT TAKES EVERY BULLET I'VE GOT!

THE ROAR OF THE ENGINES MADE IT IMPOSSIBLE TO KNOW HOW MUCH SHOOTING WAS ACTUALLY GOING ON. THEN EVEN AS ROBERT WILDLY RETURNED FIRE HIS VLR WAS ABRUPTLY RIPPED FROM HIS GRASP BY A LUCKY HIT FROM WON WECHMAR.

AAARH . . . THE GUN — I'VE LOST IT!

THE WEAPON DROPPED LIKE A STONE TO STRIKE THE ROCKY SHORELINE — WHERE, TO ROBERT'S ASTONISHMENT, IT EXPLODED VIOLENTLY.

YE GODS! THAT MUST HAVE BEEN THE MAGAZINE GOING UP. THOSE GAS-BOOSTED BULLETS ARE AS POWERFUL AS A CRATE OF GRENADES.

VON WECHMAR DIDN'T EVEN NOTICE THE EXPLOSION. HE WAS COMMITTED BODY AND SOUL TO DESTROYING THE ENEMY, UNLEASHING SHOT AFTER SHOT WITH CRISP REGULARITY.

YOU WILL NOT GET AWAY!

FOR THE MEN ON BOARD, UNABLE TO STRIKE BACK, THERE WAS NOTHING TO DO EXCEPT PRESS THEMSELVES AGAINST THE SIDES OF THE FUSELAGE AND PRAY.

HE'S GOING TO HIT SOMETHING VITAL SOONER OR LATER!

ACCURACY NO LONGER A CONSIDERATION, THE NAZI WAS INDEED BANKING ON THE LAW OF AVERAGES TO COME TO HIS RESCUE. WHEN A THIN TRAIL OF SMOKE APPEARED FROM ONE ENGINE HE LET OUT A CRY OF TRIUMPH.

A HIT!

IT WAS THE LAST THING HE EVER SAID. AS HE SQUEEZED THE TRIGGER YET AGAIN HE WAS TOTALLY UNAWARE THAT THE REASON FOR THE GUN'S INCREASING INACCURACY HAD BEEN THE STEADY WARPING OF THE BARREL.

AAAAAARGH!

THE VLR BLEW UP SAVAGELY — THE OBSESSED GERMAN DIED IN HIS TRACKS.

MEANWHILE THE ENGINE FIRE HAD BEEN PUT OUT, THE PILOT SPOTTING THE EXPLOSION BELOW AS HE ASSESSED THE DAMAGE TO HIS KITE. WHEN HE INFORMED HIS PASSENGERS, ROBERT SNATCHED UP BINOCULARS TO STUDY THE SCENE.

IT MUST HAVE BLOWN LIKE MINE DID. IT COULD HAVE BEEN A FAULT WITH THE GUN, I SUPPOSE.

AT LEAST THE JERRIES DON'T HAVE ONE NOW.

THEIR WORRY WAS REPLACED WITH RELIEF WHEN TWO GUARDIAN MOSQUITOES DETAILED TO ESCORT THE CATALINA BUT HELD BACK EARLIER BY BAD WEATHER . . .

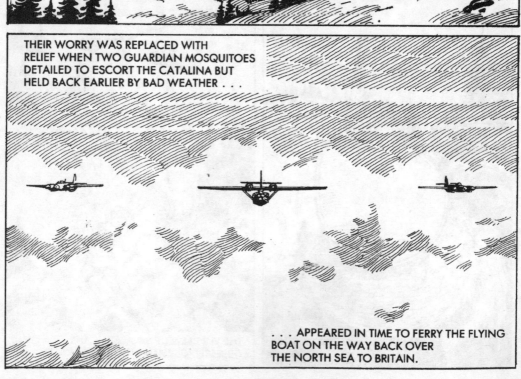

. . . APPEARED IN TIME TO FERRY THE FLYING BOAT ON THE WAY BACK OVER THE NORTH SEA TO BRITAIN.

THE RAIDERS REACHED THE SAFETY OF A SCOTTISH ANCHORAGE AFTER A FEW HOURS' FLIGHT. THERE, ROBERT'S RELIEVED C.O. MET HIM WITH NEWS FROM THE SCIENTISTS.
IT SEEMS THE VLRs PROVED TO BE AS LETHAL AS THE BULLETS THEY FIRED. THEY'RE FIT ONLY FOR THE SCRAPHEAP.
DON'T WORRY, SIR. . . . THEY'RE ALREADY ON IT!
Commando
THE END

DE HAVILLAND MOSQUITO MK. IV

NOSE OF MK. VI FIGHTER VERSION,
FOUR M/GUNS AND FOUR CANNON

SPECIFICATION

Power Plant—   Two Rolls - Royce "Merlin" twelve-cylinder, Vee, liquid-cooled engines powering D.H. three-bladed, constant speed, fully-feathering airscrews.

Dimensions—   Span —54 ft. 2 in.
Length—40 ft. 6 in.
Height—12 ft. 6 in.

Weight (empty)—   19,093 lb.

Bomb Load—   4000 lb.

Speed—   408 m.p.h.

A wonder-plane, beautiful to look at, successful in everything it did, and able to lick the fastest enemy fighters to a frazzle . . . . That was the amazing "Mossie", the fighter-bomber that left the Germans wondering what had hit them. Built of steel-strong plywood at a time when supplies of metal were running low, it used its amazing speed to penetrate deep into enemy territory and drop its 4000-lb. bomb-load from rooftop level with hair-splitting accuracy.

FLAK FEVER

THE AIRCREWS CALLED IT "FLAK FEVER" — THE SYMPTOMS
WERE A DRY MOUTH, A RACING PULSE AND HANDS THAT
REFUSED TO KEEP STEADY WHEN THE SKY FILLED WITH
SPARKLING ENEMY TRACER. BUT THE FEAR IT BROUGHT ON
WASN'T THE SORT OF THING A MAN REPORTED TO THE
MEDICAL OFFICER...UNLESS HE WANTED TO BE THOUGHT
A COWARD.

First published 1977

MOSQUITO PILOT TERRY FRANKLIN AND HIS NAVIGATOR JACK DILLON EVEN TRIED TO JOKE AWAY THEIR FEARS ABOUT IT.

HEY, SKIPPER, WHAT'S THE BEST CURE FOR FLAK FEVER?

A DIRECT HIT, MATE — ONE BIG BANG AND YOU FORGET ALL YOUR TROUBLES.

BUT IT WASN'T REALLY FUNNY, WHEN FOUR AIRCRAFT HAD BEEN LOST IN LESS THAN A WEEK.

ACH, WE'VE HIT ONE OF THE SCHWEIN!

SUDDENLY THE AIRCRAFT BESIDE TERRY FLICKED INTO A DIVE AS ONE WING BROKE AWAY.

MIKE AND DOUGIE HAVE HAD IT.

THE SQUADRON C.O. WAS THE NEXT TO GO, PLUNGING HEADLONG INTO THE TARGET HE WAS ATTACKING. IT SEEMED NO ONE COULD FLY THROUGH THE FLAK AND SURVIVE.

MAKING SURE TO HIT THEIR TARGETS ON THE FIRST PASS, THE TWO REMAINING AIRCRAFT CLIMBED STEEPLY AWAY.

IT HAD BEEN LIKE THE WORST NIGHTMARE — BUT THE HOLES IN TERRY'S AIRCRAFT WERE REAL ENOUGH.

THE C.O. AND THE FLIGHT COMMANDER HAVE HAD IT. ARE YOU OK, JACK?

I RECKON SO, SKIPPER, BUT THE MICE HAVE BEEN AT THE CANOPY AND IT'S A BIT DRAUGHTY.

EVEN NOW JACK TRIED TO MAKE A JOKE OF IT BUT TO TERRY'S EAR IT SOUNDED TERRIBLY FORCED.

THEY MADE IT BACK TO THEIR BASE IN ENGLAND, AND LANDED SMOOTHLY AFTER A STEADY APPROACH, BUT FOUND THEIR COMPANION AIRCRAFT HAD COLLAPSED ITS UNDERCARRIAGE ON TOUCHDOWN.

THE JERRIES MUST BE SLIPPING. THEY ONLY GOT THREE OUT OF FIVE.

MAYBE WE SHOULD GO BACK THIS AFTERNOON AND GIVE THEM SOME MORE PRACTICE.

BUT THERE WERE NO MORE JOKES, FORCED OR OTHERWISE, AS THE AIRMEN MADE THEIR WAY GLUMLY TO THE BRIEFING ROOM TO REPORT.

HOW DOES IT FEEL TO BE ACTING FLIGHT COMMANDER, TERRY? PROMOTION'S QUICK IN THIS OUTFIT.

I COULD LOSE THE JOB THE SAME WAY THAT I JUST GOT IT, MATE — WHICH ISN'T A VERY CHEERFUL THOUGHT.

THE MOOD IN THE MESS THAT NIGHT WAS SOMBRE, FOR SIX MOSQUITO CREWS HAD BEEN LOST IN A WEEK.

WE'RE LIVING ON BORROWED TIME.

MAYBE A NEW SQUADRON COMMANDER WILL CHANGE OUR LUCK. IT'S TIME WE WERE RESTED.

THE SUBJECT OF THE NEW SQUADRON COMMANDER STARTED ARGUMENTS AS TO HIS POSSIBLE IDENTITY.

HEY, TERRY, THE ADMIN OFFICER WANTS YOU. ASK HIM ABOUT THE NEW BOSS.

WHEN TERRY PUT DOWN THE RECEIVER, THE OTHERS CROWDED AROUND HIM EAGERLY.

THE NEW BLOKE ARRIVES TOMORROW, AND WE SHAN'T BE GOING ON REST. IT'S RON FISHER.

FISHER? HE'S THE BLOKE WHO ALMOST WON A V.C. FOR SINKING A JERRY CRUISER.

WING COMMANDER RON FISHER WAS A MOSQUITO ACE — AND HIS APPOINTMENT COULD MEAN ONLY MORE, NOT LESS, OPERATIONS.

FISHER ARRIVED NEXT MORNING, WITH A HOWL OF ENGINES AS HE BEAT UP THE AIRFIELD WITH HAIR-RAISING LOW-LEVEL AEROBATICS.

IF HE COMES ANY LOWER THERE'LL BE ANOTHER VACANCY FOR SQUADRON COMMANDER!

RON WAS SMALL AND DYNAMIC, THE TYPE TO GET THINGS DONE IN A HURRY AND JUST AS HE WANTED — BUT THE CREWS WERE NOT IMPRESSED.

WE'LL HAVE TO MAKE SOME CHANGES AROUND HERE. YOU LOOK LIKE A BUNCH OF MOURNERS AT A FUNERAL.

TOO TRUE — IT'S OUR OWN!

HOWEVER THE PROMISE OF THE LATEST MARK OF AIRCRAFT CHEERED THEM UP SLIGHTLY WHEN RON ANNOUNCED HIS PLANS.

MORE CREWS, TO GET THE SQUADRON UP TO STRENGTH. AND WE'RE TAKING A WEEK OFF OPERATIONS, AS YOU'VE HAD A BAD TIME LATELY.

GOOD SHOW, I CAN DO WITH SOME LEAVE.

BUT THE WEEK OFF OPERATIONS WAS NO HOLIDAY. INSTEAD, THE CREWS DID INTENSIVE TRAINING UNDER RON'S EVER—CRITICAL EYE.

TARGET AREA. KEEP OFF

THAT'S BETTER, THE STANDARD'S IMPROVING. THERE'S NO POINT IN FLYING TO A TARGET AND MISSING IT WHEN YOU GET THERE.

EVERY DAY, FROM DAWN TILL DUSK, THE SQUADRON PRACTISED ROCKET FIRING AND GUNNERY AND PERFECTED ITS FLYING.

OK, LET'S GO AND BEAT UP THE COUNTRY-SIDE.

AND BY THE END OF THE WEEK THE AIRCREWS WERE BEGINNING TO LAUGH AND JOKE ALMOST LIKE THEIR FORMER SELVES.

DID YOU SEE THOSE COWS SCATTER WHEN WE WENT OVER? THEY'LL BE GIVING BUTTER INSTEAD OF MILK TONIGHT.

EVEN A FEW DAYS HAS MADE A DIFFERENCE. THEY'VE GOT BACK THEIR CONFIDENCE. THEY'RE A TEAM AGAIN.

HOWEVER THERE WERE SOME TENSE EXPRESSIONS WHEN RON ANNOUNCED THAT OPERATIONS WOULD BEGIN AGAIN IMMEDIATELY.

TO SHOW THE JERRIES WE'RE BACK IN BUSINESS, TOMORROW MORNING WE'RE HITTING THEIR AIRFIELD AT AUGONNE.

THE LAST TIME WE ATTACKED AUGONNE WE LOST THREE KITES AND THEIR CREWS.

ONCE AGAIN FLAK FEVER WAS BEGINNING TO WORK ON THE MOSSIE CREWS.

EVEN TERRY, WHO HAD BEEN CONFIRMED IN HIS NEW JOB AS FLIGHT COMMANDER, BEGAN TO FEEL UNEASY ABOUT THE COMING JOB.

UNLESS WE CATCH THE JERRIES BY SURPRISE TOMORROW, JACK, THEY'RE GOING TO MASSACRE US!

THE OLD MAN DOESN'T THINK SO, SKIPPER. ANYWAY, I'M GOING TO THE FLICKS TO TRY AND FORGET ABOUT IT.

JACK WAS STILL THINKING ABOUT THE FORTHCOMING ATTACK AS HE CYCLED TO THE CAMP CINEMA, AND...

LOOK WHERE YER GOIN'!

AAAGHHH!

HE WAS NOT BADLY HURT, BUT THERE WAS NO CHANCE THAT HE WOULD BE ABLE TO FLY FOR A FEW DAYS.

I'LL PROBABLY END UP WITH SOME SPROG NAVIGATOR FOR TOMORROW'S SHINDIG.

SORRY, SKIPPER.

A LAST—MINUTE CREW CHANGE WAS REGARDED AS A BAD OMEN — AND RON HAD GUESSED HOW TERRY WOULD BE FEELING.

FLYING OFFICER WILF TYLER HAD FLOWN WITH RON ON MORE THAN FIFTY OPERATIONS AND TERRY HAD GOOD REASON TO BE PLEASED.

ONCE THE SQUADRON WAS AIRBORNE, RON KNEW FROM THE RAGGED FORMATION THAT HIS PILOTS WERE JUMPY.

THEY'VE GOT A BAD CASE OF FLAK FEVER. IF THIS TRIP'S A FAILURE, THEY'LL BE FINISHED AS A SQUADRON...

ONE PILOT WAS A LOT HAPPIER THOUGH. TERRY HAD FOUND THAT WILF'S CALM EFFICIENCY WAS JUST WHAT HE NEEDED.

COFFEE, SKIPPER? MIGHTN'T GET A CHANCE LATER.

HIS HAND'S AS STEADY AS A ROCK. NOT MUCH WRONG WITH HIS NERVES.

BUT THE BOREDOM ENDED OVER HOSTILE COUNTRYSIDE. AT LOW LEVEL THE MOSQUITOES MET LITTLE OPPOSITION.

MUST BE HITLER'S BIRTHDAY— THE FLAK'S ON HOLIDAY.

EVERY MAN KNEW IT WAS TOO GOOD TO LAST, AND AS THEY REACHED AUGONNE AIRFIELD THE FLAK ROSE AHEAD LIKE A DEADLY CURTAIN.

I RECKON THEIR HOLIDAY'S OVER.

THEY'RE JUST TRYING TO MAKE US FEEL AT HOME, SKIPPER.

LINING UP HIS SIGHTS ON A LARGE HANGAR, TERRY TRIED TO FORGET THE LETHAL DISPLAY OF FIREWORKS.

IT'S IMPOSSIBLE. THEY CAN'T MISS ME...

AS HE FLASHED OVER THE HANGAR HE REALISED TOO LATE...

...THAT HE HAD FAILED TO SWITCH HIS GUNS FROM SAFE AND NO DEADLY BROADSIDE LEAPT FROM THEM.

OF ALL THE STUPID MISTAKES!

NEVER MIND, SKIPPER. WE SCARED 'EM PROPER!

ANGER OVERCOMING HIS FEAR, TERRY BANKED AND RETURNED FOR A SECOND ATTACK.

LOOK AT THOSE KITES, SKIPPER.

THIS TIME THERE WAS NO MISTAKE, AND HIS CANNON SHELLS DEVASTATED THE PARKED JUNKERS.

ENCOURAGED BY TERRY'S EXAMPLE, THE OTHER PILOTS OF HIS FLIGHT ATTACKED WITH RECKLESS ABANDON.

THE RAID WAS SHORT AND SHARP, JUST LIKE THE BEATING THEY INFLICTED ON THE GERMANS.

NICE WORK, BLUE FLIGHT. LET'S GO HOME NOW.

NOT A SINGLE MOSQUITO HAD BEEN LOST, DESPITE THE MURDEROUS FLAK.

A HOLIDAY MOOD PREVAILED AS THE CREWS RETURNED TO THEIR BASE BUT TERRY WAS WORRIED.

IF WILF TELLS RON ABOUT MY STUPID MISTAKE, HE'LL THINK I'VE LOST MY NERVE.

SO WHEN RON CALLED HIM ASIDE AFTER THE DEBRIEFING, TERRY EXPECTED THE WORST — THEN FOUND HIMSELF BEING CONGRATULATED.

THAT SECOND ATTACK OF YOURS WAS A GREAT HELP, TERRY. YOU SHOWED THEM THAT FLAK ISN'T SUCH A BOGEY.

SO WILF DIDN'T MENTION WHAT HAPPENED. HE KEPT IT TO HIMSELF...

WHEN TERRY THANKED THE NAVIGATOR, HE JUST GRINNED AND SHRUGGED IT OFF.

WE ALL MAKE MISTAKES. ONCE I GOT THE WINGCO LOST IN THE MIDDLE OF GERMANY.

MAYBE, BUT I'VE LEARNED MY LESSON. I SHAN'T FORGET MY GUN SWITCHES AGAIN.

AND THAT NIGHT IN THE MESS JACK, STILL SUFFERING A LITTLE FROM HIS ACCIDENT, WAS QUICK TO SENSE THE NEW AIR OF CONFIDENCE.

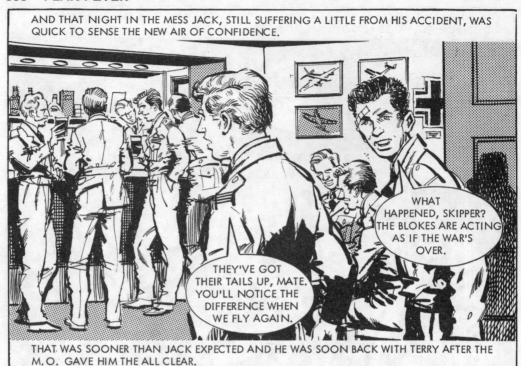

WHAT HAPPENED, SKIPPER? THE BLOKES ARE ACTING AS IF THE WAR'S OVER.

THEY'VE GOT THEIR TAILS UP, MATE. YOU'LL NOTICE THE DIFFERENCE WHEN WE FLY AGAIN.

THAT WAS SOONER THAN JACK EXPECTED AND HE WAS SOON BACK WITH TERRY AFTER THE M.O. GAVE HIM THE ALL CLEAR.

DURING THE NEXT FEW WEEKS THE MOSQUITOES HIT TARGETS ALL OVER FRANCE AND HOLLAND.

ACHTUNG, MOSKITOS!

AND WITH EACH NEW SUCCESS THE CREWS GAINED CONFIDENCE.

ROTTEN SHOTS HERE, SKIPPER.

WE'LL SHOW 'EM HOW IT SHOULD BE DONE!

WE'RE CERTAINLY PROVIDING WORK FOR THE BUILDERS.

IT SEEMED AS IF RON HAD SHARED HIS COURAGE AND DETERMINATION AMONG THE WHOLE SQUADRON AS WEEK FOLLOWED SUCCESSFUL WEEK.

BUT RON HAD ALREADY EXCEEDED HIS TOUR OF DUTY, AND DESPITE HIS PROTESTS HE WAS ORDERED ON LEAVE.

WE SHALL MISS YOU, SIR. YOU PULLED THIS OUTFIT INTO SHAPE AND MADE IT SOMETHING TO BE PROUD OF.

I'M GLAD YOU FEEL LIKE THAT, TERRY. BECAUSE YOU'RE GOING TO HAVE EVEN MORE REASON TO BE PROUD.

ALTHOUGH YOU HAVEN'T MUCH SENIORITY, I'VE RECOMMENDED THAT YOU TAKE OVER THE SQUADRON FROM ME.

I...I DON'T KNOW WHAT TO SAY, SIR.

THIS WAS THE LAST NEWS TERRY HAD EXPECTED AND HIS DELIGHT WAS EVIDENT.

ONE OF TERRY'S OLDEST FRIENDS, SAM BRADY, WAS TO TAKE OVER FROM HIM AS FLIGHT COMMANDER.

RON ISN'T LEAVING FOR A COUPLE OF DAYS, SO THAT'LL GIVE US TIME TO SORT THINGS OUT. I'VE GOT ALL THE RECORDS UP TO DATE.

THAT'S JUST AS WELL, TERRY. I WAS NEVER MUCH GOOD AT FLYING A DESK.

BUT RON WAS FATED TO MAKE ONE LAST TRIP WITH THE SQUADRON.

ALL AIRCREWS TO ASSEMBLE IMMEDIATELY FOR A BRIEFING. THERE'S AN EMERGENCY OP — SHIPPING TARGET!

ROGER, SIR!

THE CAUSE FOR THE FLAP WAS THE "VULKAN", A GERMAN CRUISER, LOOSE IN THE CHANNEL WITH ITS ATTENDANT DESTROYER ESCORT.

THE WEATHER'S GETTING WORSE, SO THERE ISN'T MUCH TIME. WE'VE GOT TO SINK THE VULKAN OR IMMOBILISE HER FOR THE BOMBERS WHO WILL FOLLOW UP.

SOUNDS LIKE A TOUGH ONE, SAM.

LOW CLOUDS AND RAIN WERE FORECAST FOR THE SEARCH AREA BUT THE CREWS WERE FULL OF CONFIDENCE.

THIS IS THE LAST TIME YOU'LL BE MY WING-MAN, SAM. YOU'LL BE LEADING THE FLIGHT IN FUTURE.

DON'T FORGET YOU'LL BE LEADING THE SQUADRON, MATE. SO I'LL BE RIGHT BEHIND YOU.

OVER THE CHANNEL THE VISIBILITY GREW WORSE, AND RON DIDN'T THINK MUCH OF THEIR CHANCES OF SUCCESS.

IF WE DON'T FIND THE JERRY SHIPS, SKIPPER, THE BOMBERS CERTAINLY WON'T.

BUT LUCK STAYED WITH THEM, FOR ON THE EDGE OF THE SEARCH AREA THE LOW CLOUDS PARTED TO REVEAL THEIR QUARRY.

HIMMEL, ENEMY AIRCRAFT! START MAKING SMOKE!

RON JUST HAD TIME TO FIRE HIS ROCKETS AS A DESTROYER LOOMED AHEAD THROUGH THE MURK.

THE DENSE SMOKE SCREEN ADDED TO THE CONFUSION AS THE REMAINING MOSQUITOES SOUGHT THEIR TARGET.

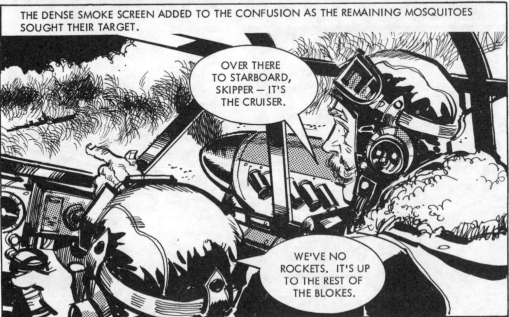

BUT FLYING IN THE SMOKE-SCREEN PRODUCED ITS OWN HAZARDS — AND TERRY FOUND HIMSELF ON A COLLISION COURSE.

IT'S SAM — HE HASN'T SEEN US!

THE CRASH WHICH FOLLOWED WAS INEVITABLE.   THERE JUST WASN'T TIME TO TAKE ANY AVOIDING ACTION.

WE'VE HAD IT!

TERRY WAS TOO BUSY TRYING TO KEEP CONTROL OF HIS OWN PLANE TO BE AWARE OF SAM'S MOSSIE PLUNGING INTO THE SEA.

BALE OUT, JACK! I CAN'T HOLD HER!

JACK OBEYED THE ORDER INSTANTLY, LEAVING TERRY TO BATTLE FOR CONTROL AS THE MOSSIE HEADED FOR THE WAVES.

I'M TOO LOW TO BALE OUT NOW. BUT SHE'S STARTING TO PULL OUT OF THE DIVE.

THE RECOVERY DIDN'T LAST LONG, FOR SECONDS LATER THE MOSSIE SMASHED INTO THE SURFACE OF THE CHOPPY SEA.

WHERE'S THE DINGHY? IT SHOULD HAVE FLOATED CLEAR BY NOW.

BY THIS TIME VULKAN HAD ESCAPED INTO THE SMOKE-SCREEN AND GERMAN LONG-RANGE FIGHTERS HAD ARRIVED.

THAT'S NO MOSSIE, SKIPPER — IT'S A JUNKERS EIGHTY-EIGHT!

I'LL JUST MAKE ANOTHER QUICK SWEEP TO SEE IF WE CAN SPOT THE VULKAN AGAIN.

RON DIDN'T FIND THE VULKAN — BUT HE DID SEE TERRY'S DINGHY BOBBING ON THE WAVES.

GET A POSITION REPORT OFF TO AIR–SEA RESCUE, WILF — IT'S ONE OF OURS.

A GERMAN FIGHTER ATTEMPTED TO INTERFERE, BUT RON TURNED SAVAGELY WITH HIS CANNONS FIRING.

AAAGHHH!

GOT HIM!

AFTER A REASSURING SWOOP OVER THE DINGHY, RON TURNED FOR HOME WITH HIS FUEL RUNNING LOW.

AT LEAST SOMEONE'S SEEN ME. I WONDER IF THEY'VE FOUND JACK?

BUT IT WAS MANY HOURS BEFORE TERRY, SUFFERING FROM A BROKEN ARM AND EXPOSURE, WAS PICKED UP BY A BRITISH RESCUE LAUNCH.

IT'LL BE DARK IN A FEW MINUTES AND WE'LL HAVE TO GIVE UP THE SEARCH FOR YOUR NAVIGATOR.

POOR OLD JACK... IF ONLY I HADN'T TOLD HIM TO BALE OUT.

EVEN IN HOSPITAL, DESPITE THE ENFORCED REST, TERRY COULD NOT STOP BLAMING HIMSELF FOR JACK'S DEATH.

WHAT'S UP, SIR? YOU WERE SHOUTIN' YOUR 'EAD OFF!

IT WAS A NIGHTMARE... FLAK AND FIGHTERS, AND I COULDN'T GET OUT OF MY COCKPIT.

AS THE WEEKS PASSED THE NIGHTMARES STOPPED, BUT THE MEMORIES REMAINED.

AFTER MY MEDICAL TOMORROW AND A BIT OF LEAVE, I'LL BE SENT BACK TO DUTY. BUT I DON'T KNOW IF I CAN FACE FLYING AGAIN.

AFTER LEAVE HE WAS GIVEN A TEMPORARY OFFICE JOB, REVERTING BACK TO FLIGHT-LIEUTENANT, AND GRADUALLY HE RETURNED TO NORMAL.

YOU'RE A LUCKY BLIGHTER, TERRY. I WOULDN'T MIND AN OFFICE JOB MYSELF. THE FLAK GETS WORSE ALL THE TIME!

I WONDER IF I COULD TAKE IT AGAIN? I'LL NEVER KNOW IF I DON'T GO BACK TO A SQUADRON AND TRY..

THEN HE HAD A SURPRISE VISITOR. IT WAS WILF, WHO TOLD HIM THAT HE AND RON FISHER WERE WORKING WITH AN EXPERIMENTAL UNIT.

THE SKIPPER'S BEEN TRYING TO TRACK YOU DOWN EVER SINCE YOU WENT ON LEAVE. HE'S GOT A JOB FOR YOU AS SOON AS YOU'RE FIT.

TELL HIM I'M FIT NOW. I'LL START PACKING RIGHT AWAY, IF YOU LIKE!

WILF WOULD SAY NOTHING ABOUT THE WORK, EXCEPT THAT IT WAS SECRET AND INVOLVED FLYING.

THEN I'M YOUR MAN. I'VE HAD ENOUGH OF DESKS TO LAST ME FOR LIFE!

RON MUST HAVE HAD INFLUENCE, FOR IN LESS THAN A WEEK TERRY WAS ON HIS WAY, POSTED TO AN EAST ANGLIAN AIRFIELD.

IF IT'S TEST FLYING THERE WON'T BE ANY FLAK, AND I CAN BREAK MYSELF IN AGAIN GENTLY.

TO HIS SURPRISE HE LEARNED THAT RON WAS EXPERIMENTING WITH RADIO–CONTROLLED BOMBERS.

WE GOT THE IDEA FROM THE YANKS. THEY STUFF THEIR WORN–OUT LIBERATORS WITH EXPLOSIVES, AND GUIDE THEM TO THE TARGET FROM A MUSTANG.

SO THE R.A.F.'S GOING ONE BETTER, AND USING HALIFAXES AND MOSSIES. AND A NEW SUPER–EXPLOSIVE!

THE UNIT HAD ONLY JUST BEEN FORMED, BUT RON HAD DEMANDED AND GOT THE BEST MEN HE COULD FIND.

I WANT A CRACK OUTFIT, ONE THAT CAN TACKLE THE REALLY TOUGH TARGETS NOBODY ELSE CAN HIT.

SO MUCH FOR MY HOPES OF TEST FLYING. IT LOOKS AS IF I'LL BE OPERATIONAL AGAIN.

PROUD OF HIS COMMAND, RON TOOK TERRY TO SEE THE RADIO REMOTE-CONTROL SYSTEM.

THE MOSSIE NAVIGATOR USES THAT CONTROL BOX TO GUIDE THE HALIFAX. AS YOU CAN SEE, IT ISN'T COMPLICATED.

NO. IT'S SIMPLE ENOUGH. BUT THE YANK MUSTANG PILOTS MUST KEEP PRETTY BUSY WORKING IT AND FLYING THE PLANE SINGLE-HANDED!

RON WASTED NO TIME AND THE FOLLOWING MORNING TERRY WAS DETAILED TO TRY THE SYSTEM FOR HIMSELF, WITH RON AS HIS PILOT.

TED AND BARRY WILL FLY THE HALIFAX AND WE'LL BE IN THE MOSSIE. YOU CAN HANDLE THE REMOTE-CONTROL.

FOR THIS TRIP WE'RE LOADED WITH SANDBAGS FOR BALLAST, AND NOT HIGH-EXPLOSIVES.

THE HALIFAX WOULD BE FLOWN NORMALLY ON TAKE-OFF AND LANDING, AS THE REMOTE CONTROL EQUIPMENT COULD NOT HANDLE COMPLICATED MANOEUVRES.

BUT ON A REAL OPERATION THE HALIFAX PILOTS WOULD BALE OUT BEFORE THE AIRCRAFT CROSSED THE BRITISH COAST...

...LEAVING THEIR AIRCRAFT TO BE FLOWN BY REMOTE CONTROL.

ONCE AIRBORNE, THE TWO AIRCRAFT CLIMBED TO A SAFE HEIGHT TO BEGIN THEIR EXERCISE.

BAKER ONE TO SUGAR, WE'RE READY TO TAKE CONTROL.

ROGER, BAKER ONE, SHE'S ALL YOURS!

TERRY FOUND THE CONTROL SYSTEM SURPRISINGLY EASY TO USE AND HE WAS SOON ENJOYING HIMSELF.

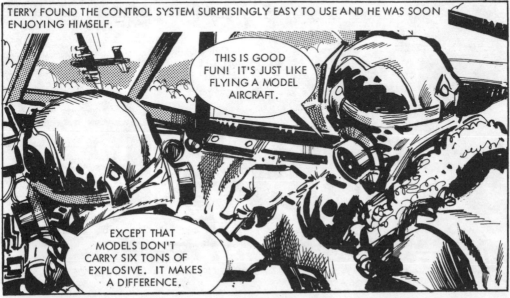

THIS IS GOOD FUN! IT'S JUST LIKE FLYING A MODEL AIRCRAFT.

EXCEPT THAT MODELS DON'T CARRY SIX TONS OF EXPLOSIVE. IT MAKES A DIFFERENCE.

ON THE RETURN JOURNEY RON SLID INTO CLOSE FORMATION WITH THE HALIFAX — AND TERRY GREW TENSE.

THERE'S NO DANGER. RON'S A SUPERB PILOT. I'VE JUST GOT TO GET USED TO HAVING OTHER KITES AROUND AND FORGET ABOUT COLLISIONS.

BUT THAT NIGHT, FOR THE FIRST TIME IN WEEKS, THE NIGHTMARES RETURNED.

LOOK OUT, SAM, WE'RE GOING TO COLLIDE! THE FLAK'S GETTING THICKER... LOOK OUT! AAAGH!

HE AWOKE WITH A START, SWEAT POURING OFF HIM. AND THE REST OF THE NIGHT PASSED VERY UNEASILY.

RON'S KEEN EYE DIDN'T FAIL TO NOTICE THE EXTRA WORRY AND FATIGUE LINES ON TERRY'S FACE NEXT MORNING.

YOU LOOK A BIT ROUGH, TERRY. BEEN CELEBRATING?

NO, THERE WAS A MOUSE IN MY ROOM. ITS GNAWING KEPT ME AWAKE ALL NIGHT. I'LL GET A TRAP SET TONIGHT.

TERRY'S NEW NAVIGATOR WAS JOE PRICE, A KEEN YOUNGSTER WHO HAD BEEN TRAINING IN THE USE OF THE CONTROL BOX.

WE GAVE JOE A FEW HOURS ON TIGER MOTHS, FOR EXPERIENCE, AND HE'S PICKING UP THE SYSTEM FAST.

I FIND IT EASIER THAN FLYING THE TIGER MOTH.

JOE WAS CAREFUL AND STEADY, AND SOON TERRY BEGAN TO FEEL MORE CONFIDENT IN HIS NEW ROLE.

DO YOU THINK THE HALIFAX BODS WOULD FANCY SOME AEROBATICS, SKIPPER?

THEY'D PROBABLY BALE OUT IF YOU TRIED — THEY STILL DON'T TRUST NAVIGATORS AS PILOTS.

BUT THERE WERE TECHNICAL TROUBLES WITH THE RADIO EQUIPMENT WHICH CAUSED CONSTANT WORRIES.

I'M SORRY, SQUADRON-LEADER, BUT ALL THE EQUIPMENT HAS SNAGS. WE'RE DOING OUR BEST TO SORT THEM OUT.

I KNOW, BUT I'VE GOT FOUR TEAMS TRAINED NOW, AND THERE ARE PEOPLE AT H. Q. WHO'D LIKE AN EXCUSE TO SCRUB THE WHOLE BUSINESS.

AND TO ADD MORE TROUBLE, TERRY'S NEW-FOUND CONFIDENCE RECEIVED A SEVERE JOLT ON HIS NEXT TRIP WITH JOE.

TURN TO STARBOARD. WE'LL GO HOME NOW. AND HAND ME THE MAP, I'LL NAVIGATE.

ROGER, SKIPPER.

JOE LOOKED DOWN AT HIS RADIO CONTROLS AFTER HANDING THE MAP TO TERRY...

HEY, WATCH IT!

TERRY GLANCED UP TO SEE THE HALIFAX BANKING TOWARDS HIM, AND PULLED THE MOSQUITO INTO A TIGHTER TURN.

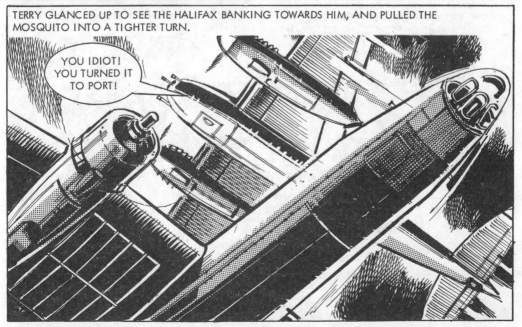

YOU IDIOT! YOU TURNED IT TO PORT!

THE HALIFAX CREW HURRIEDLY DISCONNECTED THE RADIO–CONTROL LINK — AND SWITCHED IT TO MANUAL CONTROL. IT HAD BEEN A NEAR THING.

THE RETURN FLIGHT WAS COMPLETED IN GRIM SILENCE WITH BOTH CREWS ONLY TOO WELL AWARE OF HOW CLOSE TO DEATH THEY HAD BEEN.

THE DAYS PASSED IN ENDLESS TRAINING UNTIL AT LAST RON DECIDED THEY WERE READY TO EXPERIMENT WITH AN EXPLOSIVE–LADEN HALIFAX.

YOU FLY THE MOSSIE AND I'LL WORK THE RADIO CONTROL, AS IT'S THE FIRST FULL TEST.

THE HALIFAX MAKES MY HAIR BRISTLE WHEN I THINK HOW MUCH EXPLOSIVE IS PACKED INTO IT!

TAKE–OFF TIME WAS TENSE AND NOT ONLY FOR THE TWO AIRCREW INVOLVED.

I'M GLAD I'M NOT SITTIN' IN THAT FLYIN' BOMB. IF THEY PRANGED, THEY'D WIPE OUT THE AIRFIELD.

WHEN THE TWO AIRCRAFT REACHED THE COAST, RON TOOK REMOTE CONTROL AND THE HALIFAX CREW BALED OUT.

THERE THEY GO — SHE'S ALL OURS NOW!

THEN, WITHOUT WARNING, CAME DISASTER. WITH A TREMENDOUS EXPLOSION THE HALIFAX DISAPPEARED.

IT'S BLOWN UP!

TERRY FOUGHT DESPERATELY WITH HIS CONTROLS AS THE BLAST THREW THE MOSQUITO INTO A VICIOUS SPIN.

SHE'S NOT ANSWERING — THE SPIN'S GETTING TIGHTER.

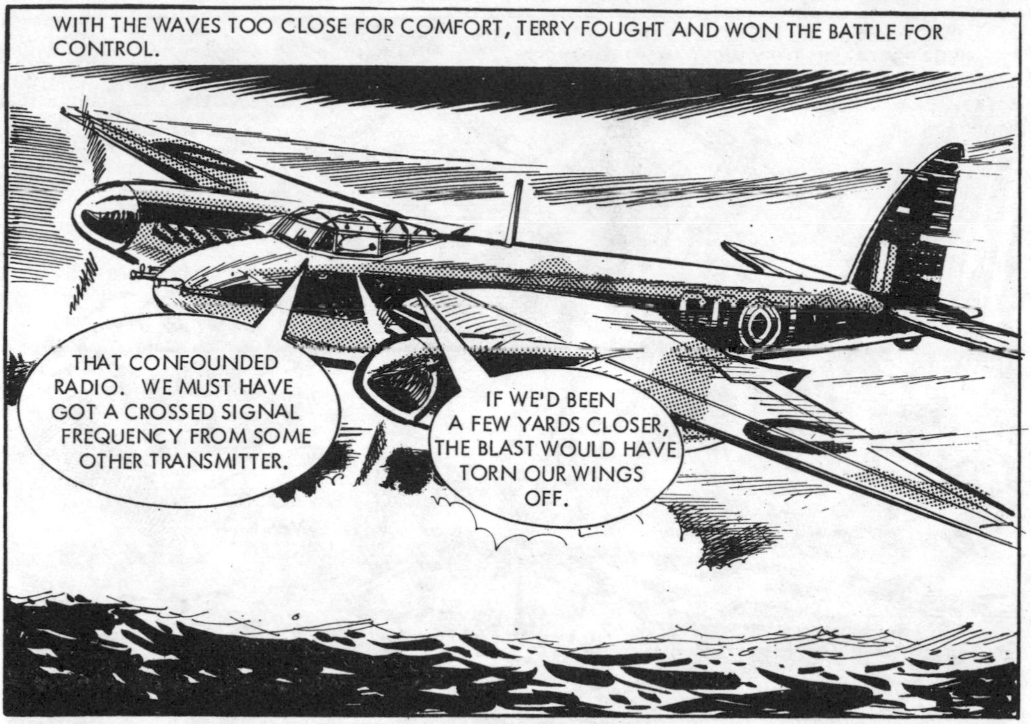
WITH THE WAVES TOO CLOSE FOR COMFORT, TERRY FOUGHT AND WON THE BATTLE FOR CONTROL.
THAT CONFOUNDED RADIO. WE MUST HAVE GOT A CROSSED SIGNAL FREQUENCY FROM SOME OTHER TRANSMITTER.
IF WE'D BEEN A FEW YARDS CLOSER, THE BLAST WOULD HAVE TORN OUR WINGS OFF.

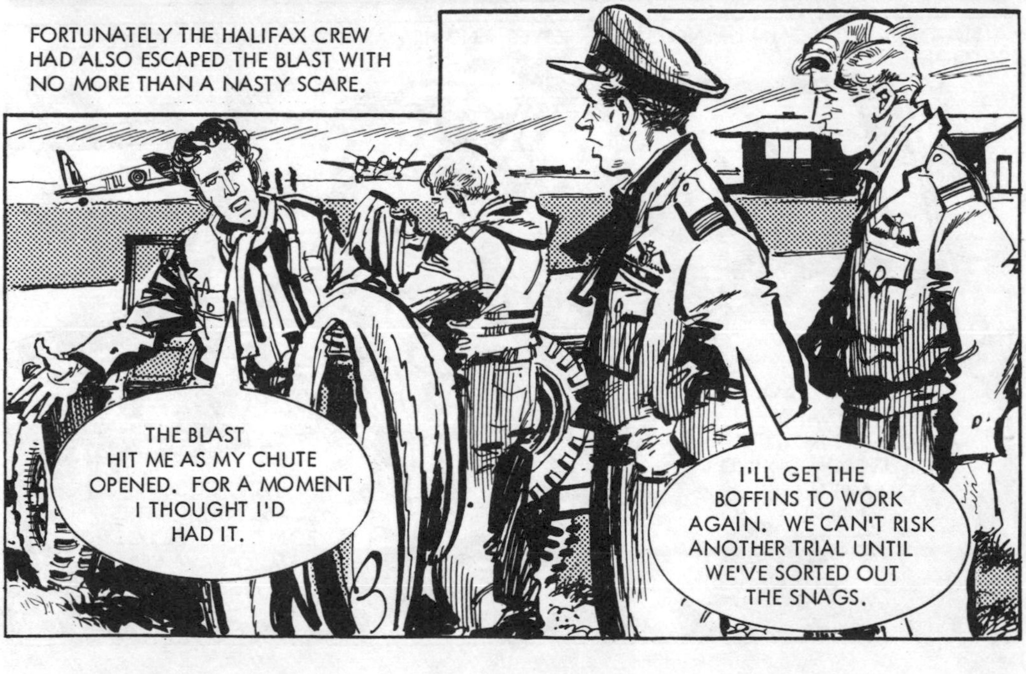
FORTUNATELY THE HALIFAX CREW HAD ALSO ESCAPED THE BLAST WITH NO MORE THAN A NASTY SCARE.
THE BLAST HIT ME AS MY CHUTE OPENED. FOR A MOMENT I THOUGHT I'D HAD IT.
I'LL GET THE BOFFINS TO WORK AGAIN. WE CAN'T RISK ANOTHER TRIAL UNTIL WE'VE SORTED OUT THE SNAGS.

THERE WERE MORE TESTS, THIS TIME WITHOUT ANY MISHAPS — AND THEY WERE MOST IMPRESSIVE.

EASY DOES IT...SMACK ON TARGET!

BUT TERRY WAS AGAIN LIVING ON HIS NERVES, AND HE WAS BEGINNING TO DREAD EACH FLIGHT.

ANOTHER DIRECT HIT. H.Q. WON'T HAVE ANY ARGUMENTS NOW TO STOP US FROM TAKING ON A REAL TARGET.

I WISH I COULD FEEL AS ENTHUSIASTIC AS RON DOES. HE DOESN'T SEEM TO HAVE ANY NERVES.

THEN HEADQUARTERS AGREED TO TRY THE NEW WEAPON — BUT ON A NORMAL DAYLIGHT BOMBING RAID.

WHY ARE WE FLYING WITH AN ORDINARY BOMBER FORMATION? DON'T THEY TRUST US ON OUR OWN?

I TOLD YOU SOMEONE AT H. Q. WANTS TO SEE OUR OUTFIT DISBANDED. BUT I'LL SHOW THEM!

RON DECIDED TO USE TWO HALIFAXES, WITH WILF AND JOE PRICE GUIDING THEM FROM MOSQUITOES.

WE'RE GOING WITH A BOMBER FORMATION THAT WILL ATTACK THIS FACTORY, AND OUR TARGET IS THE POWER STATION HERE, BY THE RAILWAY. THEY'LL BOMB FIRST, AND THEN IT'S OUR TURN.

ONCE THEY WERE AIRBORNE, WILF AND JOE TOOK OVER CONTROL OF THE TWO HALIFAXES FROM THE CREW ON BOARD THE BOMBERS.

EVERYTHING UNDER CONTROL, SKIPPER. SHE'S RESPONDING PERFECTLY.

THE PILOTLESS HALIFAXES AND THEIR MOSQUITO CONTROLLERS JOINED A SMALL BOMBER FORMATION HEADING FOR FRANCE...

...KEEPING WELL CLEAR OF THE FORCE.

THEY'RE A BIT JUMPY AT HAVING US AROUND.

I DON'T BLAME 'EM, SKIPPER.

DESPITE A HOT RECEPTION FROM THE GERMAN FLAK, THE BOMBERS HIT THE FACTORY THAT WAS THEIR TARGET.

OK, WILF, DO YOUR STUFF. THE BOMBERS HAVE FINISHED.

ROGER, SKIPPER. WATCH OUT FOR THE BANG.

GUIDED FROM THE MOSQUITOES, THE TWO HALIFAXES DIVED STEEPLY TOWARDS THE POWER STATION. AND THE GERMANS BELOW JUMPED TO THE WRONG CONCLUSION.

ACH, WE'VE HIT TWO OF THEM — THEY'RE CRASHING.

DESPITE THE FLAK, TERRY CIRCLED TO WATCH THE TREMENDOUS EXPLOSIONS AS THE HALIFAXES HOMED IN ON THEIR TARGETS.

NICE WORK, JOE — A DIRECT HIT.

IT CERTAINLY SHOOK THE JERRIES — LOOK AT THE FLAK.

AS THEY TURNED FOR HOME THE MOSQUITO WAS JARRED BRUTALLY BY SHELL SPLINTERS THAT PEPPERED THE COCKPIT.

WITH THE WOUNDED MAN FILLING HIS THOUGHTS TERRY HEADED STRAIGHT FOR BASE WHERE HE AND RON TOUCHED DOWN SAFELY.

TWO NEAR CRASHES AND THE LOSS OF TWO NAVIGATORS PROVED TOO MUCH FOR TERRY. AFTER A GREAT DEAL OF ANGUISHED THOUGHT HE WENT TO SEE RON IN HIS ROOM.

I'VE HAD IT, SIR. I CAN'T FACE FLYING AGAIN. I WANT TO BE GROUNDED.

HAVE YOU THOUGHT WHAT IT MEANS, TERRY? THEY CALL IT LACK OF MORAL FIBRE. CAN YOU FACE THAT?

I DON'T CARE WHAT THEY CALL IT! EVERYONE HAS HIS BREAKING POINT, AND I'VE REACHED MINE.

ALL RIGHT, TERRY, IF THAT'S WHAT YOU WANT. WE'LL TALK AGAIN IN THE MORNING.

THE FOLLOWING MORNING TERRY REPEATED HIS REQUEST, AND RON HAD TO AGREE TO REMOVE HIM FROM FLYING.

UNTIL YOUR POSTING COMES THROUGH YOU CAN WORK IN MY OFFICE. I NEED A HAND WITH THE PAPER-WORK.

EVERYONE APPEARED TO ACCEPT THE STORY THAT TERRY WAS JUST WAITING FOR A NEW NAVIGATOR.

BUT I'LL BET THEY ALL KNOW THE TRUTH. I WONDER WHO'LL BE THE FIRST TO TELL ME I'M YELLOW?

MEANWHILE, DUE TO THE SUCCESS OF THE FIRST ATTACK, RON HAD PERSUADED HEADQUARTERS TO LET HIM TRY ANOTHER.

WE'VE BEEN GIVEN A CRACK AT THE VULKAN. SHE'S BEEN SHELTERING IN A NORWEGIAN FIORD SINCE OUR WARSHIPS DAMAGED HER.

WHY HAVEN'T OUR HEAVY BOMBERS HIT HER? SHE'S A SITTING TARGET NOW!

RON EXPLAINED THAT OVERHANGING CLIFFS PROTECTED THE ENEMY SHIP FROM HIGH-LEVEL BOMBING.

AND THEY'VE GOT TERRIFIC FLAK DEFENCES. BUT ONE OF OUR HALIFAXES COULD DIVE THROUGH THE FLAK AND TAKE THE JERRIES BY SURPRISE.

THERE'S ONLY ONE HALIFAX AIRWORTHY UNTIL THE REPLACEMENTS ARRIVE. BUT ONE WOULD BE ENOUGH.

AFTER PLANNING THE DETAILS OF THE RAID, RON DECIDED TO TAKE HIS MOSQUITO FOR AN AIR TEST.

I HOPE THE BOFFINS HAVE CHECKED THE RADIO, SIR. WE DON'T WANT ANY SNAGS ON THE RAID.

WE CERTAINLY DON'T. I'VE A SCORE TO SETTLE WITH THE VULKAN.

FROM THE OFFICE WINDOW TERRY WATCHED RON'S MOSQUITO GATHER SPEED SMOOTHLY DOWN THE RUNWAY — THEN DISASTER STRUCK SWIFTLY.

THEY'RE SWINGING OFF THE RUNWAY! THEY'RE GOING TO PRANG.

A BURST TYRE HAD CAUSED THE ACCIDENT — AND A FUEL BOWSER WAS DIRECTLY IN THE PATH OF THE AIRCRAFT.

AAAGHH!

BLIMEY, RUN!

EVEN AS TERRY RAN DESPERATELY ACROSS THE AIRFIELD, HE KNEW THERE WAS NOTHING HE COULD DO.

THE C.O.'S HAD IT, SIR, BUT I THINK HIS NAVIGATOR'S OK. HE WAS THROWN CLEAR AS THEY HIT.

THE SKIPPER... YOU'VE GOT TO GET HIM OUT...

BUT IT WAS SOON CLEAR TO ALL THAT THERE WAS NO HOPE FOR RON — PERHAPS THE BRAVEST PILOT ANY OF THEM HAD KNOWN.

AND ALTHOUGH SHOCKED, BRUISED AND BURNED, WILF REFUSED TO GET INTO THE AMBULANCE.

I'M OK, TERRY. I'LL FLY WITH YOU, AND WE CAN STILL GET THE VULKAN.

HE MUST BE CRAZY. HAS HE FORGOTTEN THAT I'VE BEEN GROUNDED?

THEN IT DAWNED ON TERRY THAT RON HAD NOT TOLD ANYONE OF HIS REQUEST TO BE TAKEN OFF FLYING DUTIES.

YOU'RE IN TEMPORARY COMMAND NOW THE SKIPPER'S GONE, AND YOU HAVEN'T A NAVIGATOR. SO I'M VOLUNTEERING.

IT WAS AS IF RON HAD GIVEN HIM A LAST CHANCE TO PROVE THAT HE WAS NOT A COWARD AND TERRY ACCEPTED IT GRATEFULLY.

IF I LET HIM DOWN NOW, I SHALL NEVER BE ABLE TO LIVE WITH MY CONSCIENCE. AND IF WILF CAN FACE IT, SO CAN I.

FIGHTING BACK THE PANIC THAT ROSE WITHIN HIM AT THE THOUGHT OF THE FLAK TERRY KNEW THAT HE HAD NO CHOICE.

PERMISSION TO CARRY ON WITH THE RAID WAS OBTAINED, AND THE FOLLOWING MORNING THE OPERATION BEGAN.

ARE YOU SURE YOU FEEL OK, WILF? BY RIGHTS YOU SHOULD BE IN A HOSPITAL BED.

DON'T WORRY ABOUT ME, SKIPPER. SINKING THE VULKAN IS GOING TO BE THE BEST TONIC I COULD HAVE.

BUT AS THEY LINKED UP WITH THE HALIFAX AND MOSSIE ESCORT AND HEADED FOR THE COAST, WILF BEGAN TO HAVE TROUBLE.

WHAT'S WRONG? IT'S ALMOST TIME FOR THE HALIFAX PILOTS TO BALE OUT.

I CAN'T GET ANY RESPONSE TO MY SIGNALS. CAN YOU MOVE IN A BIT CLOSER?

TERRY SLID CLOSER TO THE HALIFAX UNTIL THE TWO AIRCRAFT WERE ALMOST SIDE BY SIDE.

THAT'S BETTER. SHE'S RESPONDING NOW.

BUT WE'RE FAR TOO NEAR HER!

A GRIM DECISION FACED TERRY, FOR THE TWO AIRCRAFT WERE DANGEROUSLY CLOSE TO EACH OTHER.

WE'LL HAVE TO STAY AT THIS DISTANCE, SKIPPER. ANY FURTHER AWAY AND WE LOSE RADIO CONTACT.

THAT MEANS WE'LL HAVE TO DIVE ALONGSIDE THE HALIFAX TO GUIDE IT ON TO THE TARGET! WE'VE EVERY EXCUSE TO TURN BACK. NOBODY WOULD BLAME ME...

TERRY HESITATED — BUT HE KNEW WHAT RON WOULD HAVE DONE UNDER SIMILAR CIRCUMSTANCES.

WE'LL GO AHEAD AS PLANNED. TELL THE HALIFAX PILOTS TO BALE OUT.

THE ESCORTING MOSQUITO PILOTS DREW AWAY HURRIEDLY WHEN THEY SAW THE HALIFAX CREW BALE OUT.

THE CONTROL BODS MUST BE CRAZY, FLYING SO CLOSE. THAT THING COULD GO UP ANY TIME.

AND EVEN WILF SEEMED TO LOSE SOME OF HIS CONFIDENCE AS THE LITTLE FORMATION HEADED OVER THE SEA FOR NORWAY.

BLIMEY, SKIPPER, THIS IS HARD WORK. I THOUGHT PILOTS HAD AN EASY TIME TILL I TRIED THIS CLOSE FORMATION STUFF.

YOU WON'T BE ABLE TO NAVIGATE AS WELL. ONE OF THE ESCORT HAD BETTER COPE WITH THAT.

WITH ONE OF THE ESCORTING MOSQUITOES LEADING THE WAY, THEY CONCENTRATED ON KEEPING THE HALIFAX STEADY.

HAVE YOU THOUGHT WHAT WOULD HAPPEN IF THE RADIO GOES ON THE BLINK — EVEN FOR A FEW SECONDS?

I'D RATHER NOT CONSIDER IT, CHUM. EVERY TIME WE HIT AN AIR POCKET IT TAKES YEARS OFF MY LIFE.

BY THE TIME THEY SIGHTED THE NORWEGIAN COAST BOTH MEN WERE DAZED WITH FATIGUE.

SORRY, BLUE LEADER, WE'RE A BIT OFF COURSE. WE'LL HAVE TO TURN.

THE TURN, WITH THE HALIFAX YAWING CLUMSILY ONLY A FEW FEET FROM THE MOSQUITO, SEEMED TO LAST FOR EVER.

CLOSER, SKIPPER, I'VE LOST CONTACT...AH, THAT'S BETTER.

BUSY KEEPING OUT OF THE WAY OF THE CLUMSY HALIFAX, TERRY WAS STILL AWARE OF THE FLAK RISING IN BLACK PUFFS ABOVE THE FIORD.

I CAN SEE THE CRUISER. WE'LL HAVE TO DIVE WITH THE HALIFAX UNTIL WE'RE SURE IT'LL SCORE A HIT.

DON'T LEAVE IT TOO LATE, SKIPPER. THERE'LL BE A LOT OF BLAST FROM THE EXPLOSION.

THE GERMANS WERE PUZZLED AND SUSPICIOUS AS THE ATTACKERS APPROACHED.

THEY CAN'T BOMB ACCURATELY FROM THAT HEIGHT. IS IT A TRICK?

MAYBE THEY'RE DECOYS. WATCH OUT FOR ANOTHER FORCE SNEAKING IN AT LOW LEVEL.

PROTECTED BY THE OVERHANGING CLIFF, THE CRUISER WAS TAKING NO CHANCES AND PUT UP A DAUNTING BARRAGE OF SHELLS.

ONE SHELL SPLINTER IN THAT HALIFAX AND WE'LL BE SPREAD ACROSS NORWAY.

MUST KEEP GOING. MUST IGNORE THE FLAK... MUST!

THE HALIFAX AND MOSQUITO BEGAN TO DIVE TOGETHER, STRAIGHT INTO THE HAIL OF METAL FROM THE DEFENDING GUNS.

HIMMEL, WE'VE HIT THE BIG BOMBER. AND ONE OF THE MOSQUITOES!

AS THEIR SPEED INCREASED THE HALIFAX BECAME MORE DIFFICULT TO CONTROL, AND TERRY HAD LITTLE TIME TO SPARE TO WORRY ABOUT THE FLAK DEFENCES.

LEFT A BIT, WILF! HOLD IT THERE!

THE CRUISER GREW SWIFTLY IN SIZE AS IT FILLED THE MOSSIE'S SCREEN SO THAT EVERY DETAIL ON THE DECK BECAME VISIBLE.

I CAN EVEN SEE THE GUNNERS' FACES! PULL OUT, SKIPPER.

JUST ANOTHER FEW SECONDS! WE CAN'T AFFORD TO MISS.

SUDDENLY TERRY KICKED HARD AT THE CONTROLS AS THE CLIFF ROSE AHEAD LIKE A WALL.

I'VE LEFT IT TOO LATE. WE'LL NEVER BE ABLE TO TURN IN TIME.

WHILE TERRY FOUGHT FOR CONTROL OF HIS MOSQUITO, THE HALIFAX WITH ITS DEADLY CARGO OF EXPLOSIVES HEADED UNCHECKED TOWARDS THE CRUISER.

A SUICIDE ATTACK... AAAGHHH!

AN EARTH-SHATTERING BLAST TORE THE CRUISER APART, FLAME LICKING INTO EVERY CORNER. AND THE MAMMOTH SHOCK WAVE BROUGHT ROCKS TUMBLING FROM THE CLIFF FACE, DOWN INTO THE SEETHING WATER.

AAAIIEE!

THE SAME EXPLOSION SOLVED TERRY'S PROBLEMS BY LIFTING THE MOSQUITO CLEAR OF THE CLIFF TOP.

THE MOSQUITO ESCORT REFORMED AROUND TERRY AS THE LAND DEFENCES CEASED FIRING, SHOCKED BY THE ENORMITY OF THE EXPLOSION.

AS THE MOSQUITOES RACED OUT TO SEA, THERE WAS LITTLE HOPE OF ENEMY FIGHTERS CATCHING THE SLEEK, DEADLY RAIDERS, BUT WILF CAST A SLIGHTLY ANXIOUS EYE AT THE NEAREST ESCORT KITE —

NOT TOO CLOSE, SKIPPER. MY NERVES ARE STILL JUMPING.

IT'S OK, YOU CAN RELAX NOW. YOU DON'T HAVE TO WORRY ABOUT FLYING THAT ONE.

TERRY KNEW THAT HE HAD OVERCOME HIS OWN FEARS ONCE AND FOR ALL.

I RECKON THE FEAR OF BEING THOUGHT A COWARD WAS WORSE THAN THE FEAR OF THE FLAK ITSELF.

UNFORTUNATELY THE EXPERIMENT WITH THE HALIFAXES WAS DISCONTINUED, AS THERE WERE NOT ENOUGH TARGETS SUITABLE FOR SUCH SPECIALIST ATTACKS. BUT TERRY SOON FOUND ANOTHER JOB — THE COMMAND OF A MOSQUITO SQUADRON WITH WILF AS HIS NAVIGATOR.

THESE NEW LADS ARE SHAPING UP WELL, SKIPPER.

YES, RON WOULD HAVE BEEN PROUD OF THEM.

Commando
THE END

The next four action-packed Commando books will be in the shops in two weeks' time. Look out for:

"FIGHTING REPORTER"   "DEATH ON THE WIND"

"FALSE HEROES"   "NAZI HIJACK"

JAPANESE SOLDIER

THIS heavily-laden figure is a Jap infantryman in full kit. He is armed with a Type 38 6.5 mm. rifle, used from the start of the war. Other interesting items include his half tent, which could be pitched alone or joined with others, and it also doubled as a rain cape. His mess tin holds sufficient cooked rice for several days' rations, a valuable time-saver when on the march. Also shown are the extraordinary "tabi" or jungle boots, in which the big toe is separated from the rest of the foot.

In the background is the "Senninbari," the embroidered belt of a thousand stitches, a form of good-luck charm which many soldiers wore round their waists in the belief that it made them safe from enemy bullets.

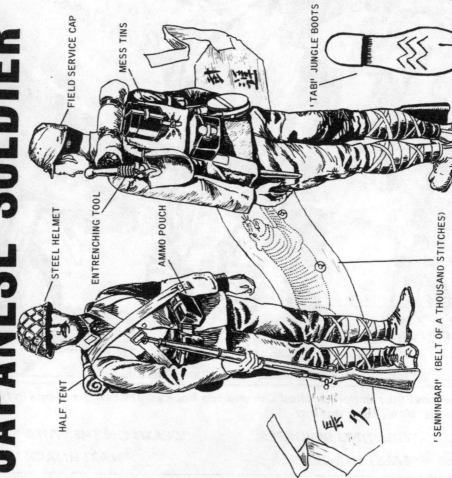

STEEL HELMET

FIELD SERVICE CAP

ENTRENCHING TOOL

MESS TINS

AMMO POUCH

'TABI' JUNGLE BOOTS

HALF TENT

'SENNINBARI' (BELT OF A THOUSAND STITCHES)

FIGHT OR DIE!

THEY WERE ALL VOLUNTEERS, ALL SEVEN OF THEM. BUT WHEN THEY HAD PUT THEIR NAMES FORWARD, NOT ONE OF THEM KNEW THAT THEIR TASK BEHIND THE ENEMY LINES IN BURMA WAS RECKONED TO BE A SUICIDE MISSION. THEIR CHANCES OF SURVIVAL WERE NIL . . . THEY WERE ON A ONE-WAY TRIP!

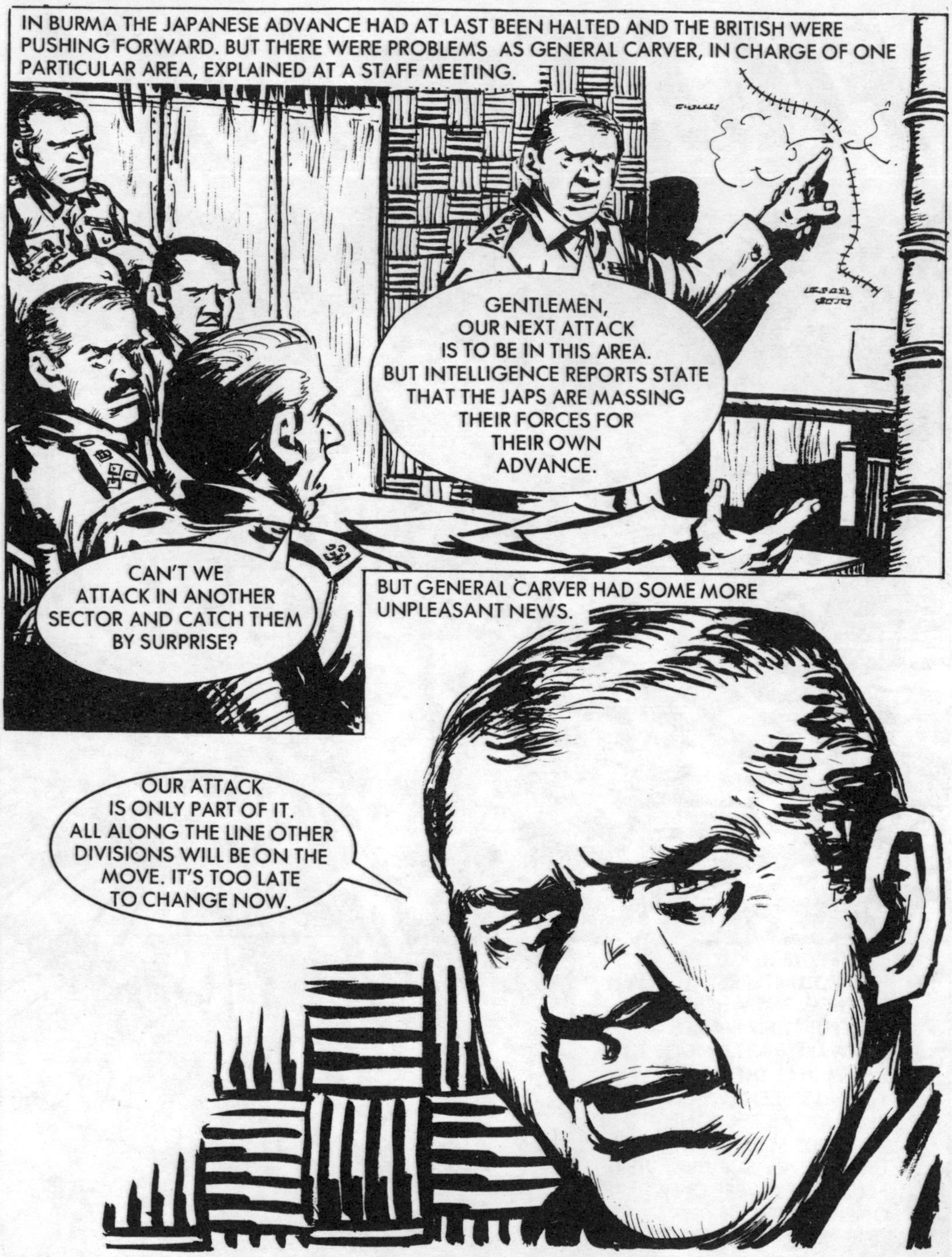
IN BURMA THE JAPANESE ADVANCE HAD AT LAST BEEN HALTED AND THE BRITISH WERE PUSHING FORWARD. BUT THERE WERE PROBLEMS AS GENERAL CARVER, IN CHARGE OF ONE PARTICULAR AREA, EXPLAINED AT A STAFF MEETING.
GENTLEMEN, OUR NEXT ATTACK IS TO BE IN THIS AREA. BUT INTELLIGENCE REPORTS STATE THAT THE JAPS ARE MASSING THEIR FORCES FOR THEIR OWN ADVANCE.
CAN'T WE ATTACK IN ANOTHER SECTOR AND CATCH THEM BY SURPRISE?
BUT GENERAL CARVER HAD SOME MORE UNPLEASANT NEWS.
OUR ATTACK IS ONLY PART OF IT. ALL ALONG THE LINE OTHER DIVISIONS WILL BE ON THE MOVE. IT'S TOO LATE TO CHANGE NOW.

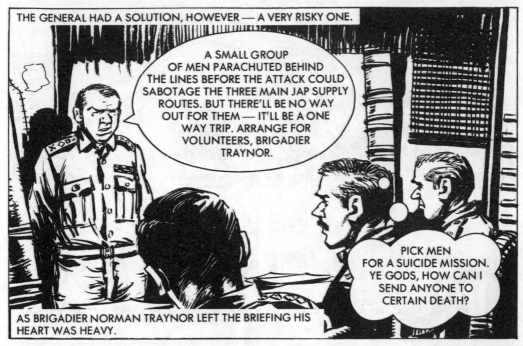

THE GENERAL HAD A SOLUTION, HOWEVER — A VERY RISKY ONE.

A SMALL GROUP OF MEN PARACHUTED BEHIND THE LINES BEFORE THE ATTACK COULD SABOTAGE THE THREE MAIN JAP SUPPLY ROUTES. BUT THERE'LL BE NO WAY OUT FOR THEM — IT'LL BE A ONE WAY TRIP. ARRANGE FOR VOLUNTEERS, BRIGADIER TRAYNOR.

PICK MEN FOR A SUICIDE MISSION. YE GODS, HOW CAN I SEND ANYONE TO CERTAIN DEATH?

AS BRIGADIER NORMAN TRAYNOR LEFT THE BRIEFING HIS HEART WAS HEAVY.

THE GENERAL WANTED SEVEN VOLUNTEERS FOR THE JOB, AND TRAYNOR HURRIEDLY ORGANISED FOR THEM TO BE SELECTED. WITHIN HOURS HE HAD THE LIST OF NAMES OF MEN FOR THIS ONE-WAY TRIP.

HERE THEY ARE, SIR. ONE OFFICER AND SIX MEN — THE PICK OF VOLUNTEERS FROM ALL UNITS.

DO THEY KNOW THEIR CHANCES OF SURVIVAL?

THOUGH THEY HADN'T BEEN TOLD OF THE MISSION, A HINT HAD BEEN GIVEN OF ITS DANGERS.

ALL WERE WARNED IT WOULD BE DICEY, SIR.

TRAYNOR TOOK THE PAPERS AND GLANCED OVER THE NAMES — AND THERE WAS ONE VOLUNTEER WHO SHOOK HIM RIGID.

LIEUTENANT R. HUNTER — MY GRANDSON!

ROGER HUNTER WAS HIS DAUGHTER'S SON — AND HE WAS SENDING HIM ON A MISSION FROM WHICH HE WOULDN'T RETURN.

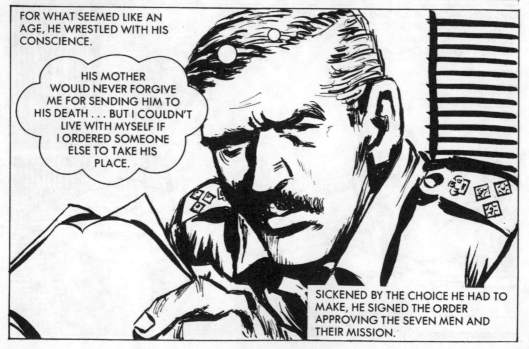

FOR WHAT SEEMED LIKE AN AGE, HE WRESTLED WITH HIS CONSCIENCE.

HIS MOTHER WOULD NEVER FORGIVE ME FOR SENDING HIM TO HIS DEATH . . . BUT I COULDN'T LIVE WITH MYSELF IF I ORDERED SOMEONE ELSE TO TAKE HIS PLACE.

SICKENED BY THE CHOICE HE HAD TO MAKE, HE SIGNED THE ORDER APPROVING THE SEVEN MEN AND THEIR MISSION.

MEANWHILE, UNAWARE OF THE BRIGADIER'S THOUGHTS, LIEUTENANT ROGER HUNTER WAS ON HIS WAY TO THE BRIEFING.

I WONDER WHAT THE MISSION IS? IF THERE'S ANY REAL DANGER I SUPPOSE GRANDFATHER WILL TRY AND STOP ME GOING.

THE OTHER SIX VOLUNTEERS HAD ALREADY ARRIVED AT THE CAMP WHERE THE BRIEFING WAS TO BE HELD. PRIVATE DAVE PRIOR, ONE OF THE DOOMED MEN, HAD SOME SURPRISING NEWS.

DID YOU KNOW THAT LIEUTENANT HUNTER IS THE BRIGADIER'S GRANDSON?

EH? THAT MEANS THIS JOB'LL BE A PIECE OF CAKE. OLD TRAYNOR WON'T RISK HIS GRANDSON'S LIFE.

CORPORAL JOHNNY RICHARDSON SNORTED AS HE SPOKE. HE HAD LITTLE TIME FOR THE STAFF OFFICERS WHO SAW NO COMBAT.

SECONDS LATER ROGER ARRIVED WITH THE MAJOR WHO WAS TO BRIEF THEM. THEY ALL LISTENED INTENTLY AS THE INTELLIGENCE OFFICER EXPLAINED THE MISSION.

YOU ARE TO CUT THE JAPS' MAIN SUPPLY LINES — TWO ROADS AND ONE RAILWAY. BOTH THE RAILWAY AND ONE OF THE ROADS CROSS LIGHTLY-GUARDED BRIDGES . . .

THE BRIEFING WAS LONG AND THOROUGH. AT ITS CONCLUSION THEY WERE TOLD THAT SINCE THEY ALL HAD PARACHUTE TRAINING THEY WOULD BE DROPPED THAT NIGHT. BUT NO MENTION OF THEIR WITHDRAWAL WAS MADE UNTIL ROGER ASKED DIRECTLY.

WHAT ARE THE ARRANGEMENTS FOR GETTING BACK, SIR?

ER . . . YOU'LL BE TOLD ALL THAT WHEN YOU RADIO H.Q. AND CONFIRM THE SUCCESS OF THE MISSION.

THE INTELLIGENCE OFFICER THEN SEEMED TO BE IN A TEARING HURRY AND MARCHED AWAY.

AS THE MAJOR DEPARTED, PRIVATE RON HART TURNED TO FELLOW PRIVATE BILL WATSON, THE RADIO EXPERT, AND GAVE HIM A FRIENDLY WARNING.

YOU'D BETTER TAKE GOOD CARE OF YOUR RADIO, BILL, OR WE'LL NEVER GET BACK.

DON'T WORRY, I WILL. SEEMS ODD THOUGH, HAVING TO WAIT TILL AFTER BEFORE WE'RE TOLD HOW WE'LL BE PICKED UP.

PRIVATE HARRY LOMAX HAD BEEN LISTENING TO THE TWO MEN, AND HE VOICED HIS OWN THOUGHTS.

MAYBE WE'RE NOT SUPPOSED TO COME BACK.

OH, COME OFF IT. REMEMBER WE'VE GOT THE BRIGADIER'S GRANDSON WITH US. H.Q. WON'T LEAVE HIM STUCK IN THE JUNGLE.

ROGER'S SECOND-IN-COMMAND, SERGEANT FRED TURNBULL, THE EXPLOSIVES EXPERT, HAD HEARD THE THREE MEN'S DISCUSSION AS THEY LEFT THE HUT AND WHEN HE CAUGHT UP WITH THEM HE HAD A FEW THINGS TO SAY.

OK, YOU THREE IDIOTS. THIS SORT OF TALK WON'T DO ANYONE ANY GOOD. WE'VE A JOB TO DO — ONCE THAT'S DONE WE'LL GET BACK AGAIN.

RIGHT, SARGE!

THOUGH TURNBULL HIMSELF HAD DOUBTS ABOUT THIS MISSION, HE KNEW HE HAD TO TRY TO KEEP UP MORALE.

AS DUSK FELL THEY WERE ALL EQUIPPED AND WERE ARRIVING AT A SMALL AIRSTRIP.

THERE'S OUR TRANSPORT.

WITHIN MINUTES THEY WERE ABOARD THE DAKOTA AND WERE HEADING FOR THEIR DROP ZONE.

BE CAREFUL.ON THE WAY DOWN—THE CLEARING ISN'T VERY BIG.

AFTER A SHORT AND UNEVENTFUL FLIGHT THEY WERE NEARLY THERE AND WERE READY TO PARACHUTE DOWN.

FIVE MINUTES TO DROP, SIR.

THANKS, SERGEANT.

THEN, JUST AS THEY WERE ABOUT TO JUMP, THE R.A.F. SERGEANT GAVE A SHOCK REPLY TO ROGER'S PARTING STATEMENT.

WELL, THIS IS IT. I WOULDN'T LIKE TO HAVE YOUR JOB OF LANDING TO PICK US UP AGAIN.

PICK YOU UP? WE WEREN'T TOLD ANYTHING ABOUT COMING BACK FOR YOU. ONCE WE DROP YOU WE START FERRYING SUPPLIES AGAIN.

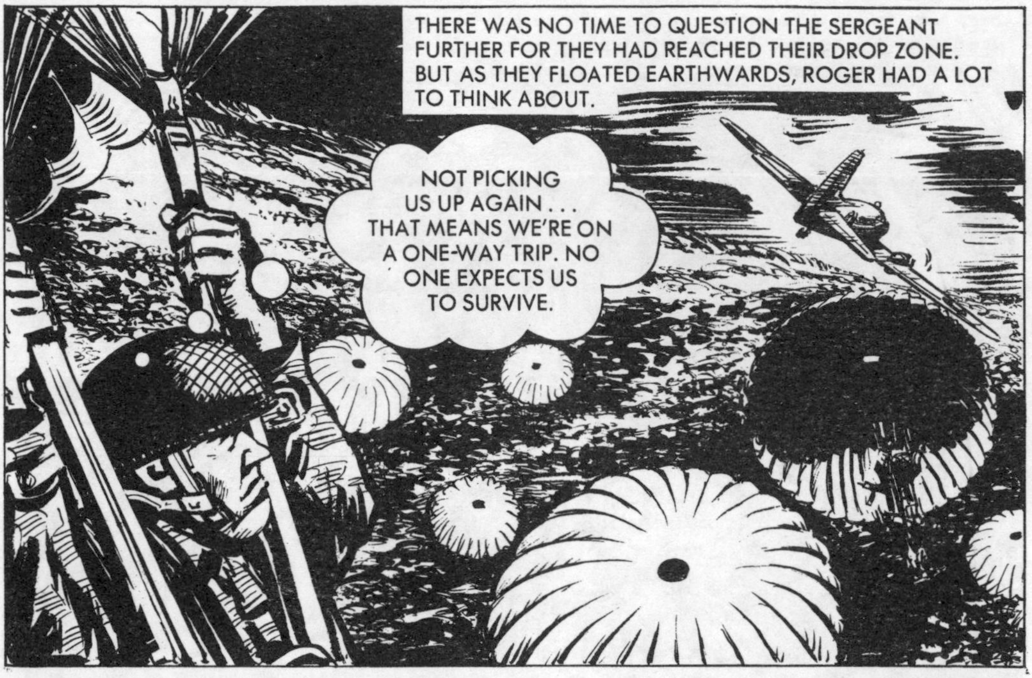
THERE WAS NO TIME TO QUESTION THE SERGEANT FURTHER FOR THEY HAD REACHED THEIR DROP ZONE. BUT AS THEY FLOATED EARTHWARDS, ROGER HAD A LOT TO THINK ABOUT.
NOT PICKING US UP AGAIN . . . THAT MEANS WE'RE ON A ONE-WAY TRIP. NO ONE EXPECTS US TO SURVIVE.

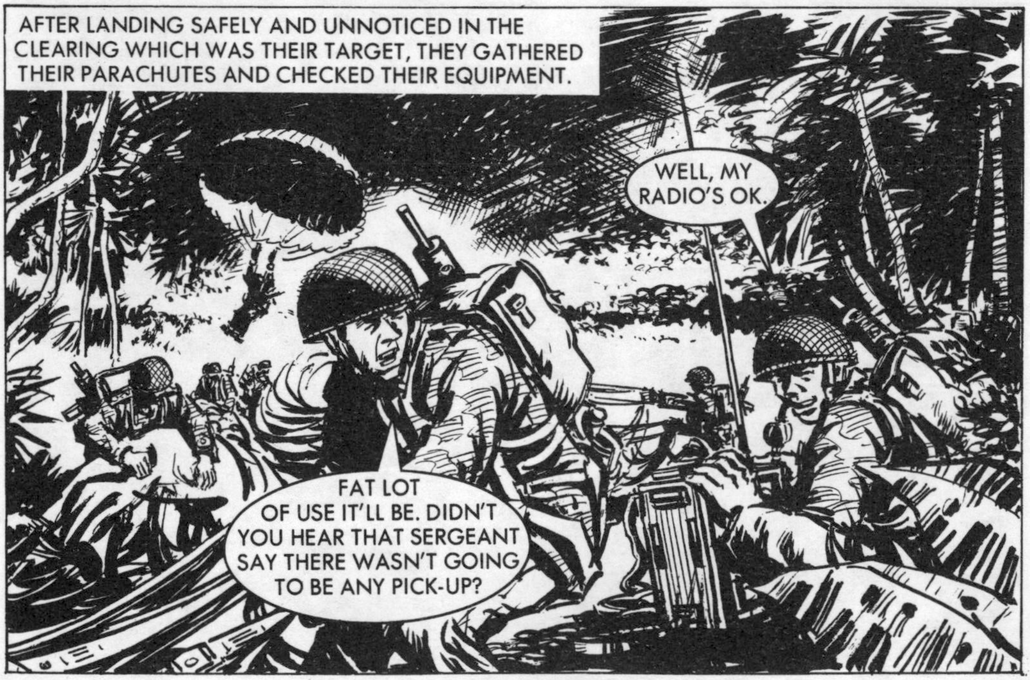
AFTER LANDING SAFELY AND UNNOTICED IN THE CLEARING WHICH WAS THEIR TARGET, THEY GATHERED THEIR PARACHUTES AND CHECKED THEIR EQUIPMENT.
WELL, MY RADIO'S OK.
FAT LOT OF USE IT'LL BE. DIDN'T YOU HEAR THAT SERGEANT SAY THERE WASN'T GOING TO BE ANY PICK-UP?

LOMAX HADN'T BEEN THE ONLY ONE TO GRUMBLE, AND ROGER KNEW THAT HE'D HAVE TO ACT FAST TO STOP THEM BECOMING DEMORALISED. WHEN THEY WERE READY TO MOVE OUT, HE CALLED THEM TOGETHER.

WE'VE GOT A JOB TO DO, A VITALLY IMPORTANT ONE. THE SOONER WE GET IT DONE THE SOONER WE'LL GET BACK.

AN' HOW ARE WE GOIN' TO GET BACK, SIR? THE R.A.F. AREN'T COMIN' BACK FOR US.

RICHARDSON, DISDAINFUL AS EVER OF H.Q. PLANS, HAD VOICED ALL THEIR THOUGHTS.

ROGER HAD NO ANSWER FOR THE MEN, HE COULD ONLY TELL THEM WHAT HE BELIEVED.

WE'LL GET BACK SOMEHOW. ONCE OUR JOB'S DONE WE RADIO H.Q. — THEY'RE BOUND TO HAVE SOMETHING WORKED OUT.

YEAH, THAT'S RIGHT. THE BRIGADIER'S GRANDSON WON'T BE LEFT IN THE LURCH.

FOR THE TIME BEING, ROGER'S WORDS HAD DONE THE TRICK AND THEY PREPARED TO MOVE OFF.

AS ROGER LED THEM TOWARDS THE ROAD BRIDGE WHICH WAS TO BE THEIR FIRST TARGET, EACH MAN WARILY SCANNED THE JUNGLE FOR ANY SIGN OF ENEMY ACTIVITY.

WE SHOULD REACH THE BRIDGE IN ABOUT-HALF AN-HOUR.

BUT IT SEEMED THE BRITISH FORCE WASN'T THE ONLY ONE OUT THAT NIGHT — A JAP PATROL WAS ON THE PROWL.

THIS IS A WASTE OF TIME. THE WHITE-EYES WILL NOT BE NEAR THIS AREA.

THE JAP OFFICER COULDN'T HAVE BEEN MORE WRONG, FOR AT THE NEXT CLEARING HE CAME FACE TO FACE WITH ROGER'S MEN.

WHITE-EYES!

JAPS!

ROGER AND HIS MEN WERE THE FIRST TO RECOVER FROM THE SURPRISE OF THIS ENCOUNTER. THEY DIVED FOR COVER AND THEIR STEN GUNS CHATTERED A FRACTION OF A SECOND BEFORE THE JAPS RESPONDED.

RIGHT, MEN. HIT 'EM HARD!

DON'T LET THE WHITE DOGS ESCAPE.

THOUGH THE RAIDERS HAD GOT SOME OF THE ENEMY PATROL, THE REST QUICKLY FOUND GOOD COVER. ROGER REALISED THEY WERE WASTING PRECIOUS TIME IN THIS FIGHT.

YOU THREE GIVE ME COVERING FIRE, I'M GOING TO TRY TO OUTFLANK THEM.

FOR AN OFFICER HE'S GOT GUTS!

RICHARDSON WAS BEGINNING TO REVISE HIS OPINION OF ROGER.

SO ROGER SET OFF ON HIS ONE-MAN MISSION.

IT LOOKED AS IF THERE WERE TWO GROUPS OF THEM. I HOPE I CAN GET THEM BOTH.

HE GOT NEAR ENOUGH WITHOUT BEING SEEN TO USE HIS FIRST GRENADE.

HERE GOES.

THE GRENADE EXPLODED, KILLING THE TWO JAPS. TWO OTHERS WERE UNWISE ENOUGH TO LOOK UP IN SURPRISE, BUT AS ROGER DEALT WITH THEM HE FAILED TO SEE THE JAP OFFICER RISE UP BEHIND HIM AND TAKE AIM WITH HIS PISTOL.

NOW YOU DIE!

GET THAT JAP OFFICER BEFORE HE SHOOTS MR HUNTER!

THE WORDS HAD SCARCELY LEFT SERGEANT TURNBULL'S LIPS WHEN RICHARDSON RUSHED FORWARD, HIS STEN GUN BLAZING.

OH NO, YOU DON'T, YOU SLANT-EYED NIP!

ARRGH!

WHAT THE . . .

AS THEY REGROUPED IN THE CLEARING, ROGER'S FIRST ACT WAS TO THANK THE TOUGH LITTLE CORPORAL FOR SAVING HIS LIFE.

THANKS, RICHARDSON. IF YOU HADN'T BEEN SO QUICK I'D HAVE HAD IT.

I WAS ONLY GIVING YOU COVERING FIRE LIKE YOU SAID, SIR.

ALL KNEW THAT THE FIRING COULD HAVE ALERTED ANY OTHER JAPS IN THE AREA SO THEY QUICKLY PREPARED TO MOVE OFF AGAIN.

THE SOONER WE'RE OUT OF HERE, THE BETTER. LET'S GET MOVING.

AND EVERYONE KEEP THEIR EYES PEELED.

THEY HAD BEEN LUCKY, HAVING HAD NO CASUALTIES IN THAT ENCOUNTER.

AS THEY HEADED TOWARDS THE BRIDGE, DAVE PRIOR QUIZZED RICHARDSON ABOUT HIS RECKLESS ACTION.

YOU COULD HAVE GOT YOURSELF KILLED, RUSHING OUT INTO THE OPEN LIKE THAT, CORP.

IF MR HUNTER HAD BOUGHT IT, WE'D ALL BE IN THE SOUP. AS LONG AS HE STAYS ALIVE, THE TOP BRASS ARE BOUND TO FETCH US BACK.

WITHOUT FURTHER INCIDENT THEY REACHED A HILL OVER-LOOKING THEIR FIRST OBJECTIVE — A LIGHTLY-GUARDED RAILWAY BRIDGE.

THERE IT IS — THINK YOU CAN DESTROY IT, TURNBULL?

NO PROBLEM, SIR. I'LL TURN IT TO MATCHWOOD — IF SOMEONE CAN DEAL WITH THE JAPS WHILE I PLACE THE EXPLOSIVES.

ROGER DETAILED PRIVATES LOMAX AND PRIOR TO DISPOSE OF THE TWO SENTRIES WHILE HE AND THE OTHERS COVERED THE AREA TO WATCH FOR ANY APPROACHING ENEMY TROOPS.

ONCE THE GUARDS ARE OUT OF THE WAY WE'LL MOVE IN AND COVER THE APPROACHES WHILE YOU HELP THE SERGEANT.

RIGHT, SIR.

AND BEFORE THEY MELTED INTO THE JUNGLE THEY WERE WARNED TO MAKE NO NOISE.

SOON ALL WERE IN POSITION AND PRIOR AND LOMAX WERE READY.

READY, HARRY — NOW!

AS IF ONE, THEY LEAPT AT THE STARTLED GUARDS.

AIEEE!

THE BIG, BURLY PRIOR HAD LITTLE DIFFICULTY IN DEALING WITH HIS OPPONENT, BUT LOMAX FOUND THE GOING A LOT HARDER.

HE'S STRONGER THAN HE LOOKS.

THAT TAKES CARE OF THAT.

TURNING, PRIOR SAW THAT LOMAX WAS STILL IN TROUBLE AND IMMEDIATELY WENT TO HELP, USING HIS STEN AS A CLUB.

TAKE THAT!

THANKS, DAVE, I THOUGHT I'D BITTEN OFF MORE THAN I COULD CHEW THERE.

LIKE A WELL-OILED MACHINE THEY ALL WENT INTO ACTION. EVEN AS THE LAST GUARD FELL, TURNBULL HOISTED HIMSELF ONTO THE BRIDGE AND BEGAN PLANTING THE EXPLOSIVES AND ROGER LED THE OTHERS FROM COVER TO GUARD THE APPROACH.

I'VE LAID THE EXPLOSIVES, I'VE ONLY GOT TO PUT THE FUSES IN NOW.

BLIMEY, THAT WAS QUICK WORK, SARGE.

THE EXPLOSIVES WERE SOON SET AND THEY REJOINED THE OTHERS.

THAT'S THAT DONE, SIR. THE BRIDGE'LL GO UP IN FIVE MINUTES.

WE'D BETTER GET CRACKING, THEN. MOVE OUT, MEN.

ONCE MORE THEY SET OFF, THIS TIME KNOWING THAT THEIR PRESENCE IN THE JUNGLE WOULD NOT BE A SECRET FOR LONG.

ONLY A FEW SECONDS NOW, SIR.

ONCE THAT BRIDGE GOES UP, WE'LL HAVE EVERY JAP IN THIS AREA AFTER US.

THE EXPLOSIVES WENT OFF ON TIME, COMPLETELY DESTROYING THE BRIDGE WITH AN EARTH-SHAKING ROAR.

COR, I WISH I'D HAD A BETTER VIEW OF THAT.

IF YOU DON'T GET A MOVE ON, HART, YOU WON'T BE SEEING ANYTHING AGAIN—THE JAPS'LL BE AFTER US NOW WITH A VENGEANCE.

ROGER WASN'T WRONG. THE NOISE OF THE EXPLOSION CARRIED FOR MILES ACROSS THE STILL NIGHT AIR AND THE JAPANESE H.Q. WERE SOON INFORMED ABOUT WHAT HAD HAPPENED.

RAIDERS HAVE DESTROYED THE MOULANG BRIDGE. FIND THEM—THEY MUST NOT LIVE TO BOAST OF THEIR SUCCESS OR DO MORE DAMAGE.

THE HUNT WAS NOW ON.

IT WASN'T LONG BEFORE ROGER SPOTTED THE FIRST OF THE PATROLS.

GET DOWN, MEN.

THEY DIVED FOR COVER.

LUCKILY THE PATROL PASSED BY WITHOUT NOTICING THEM.

THEY'RE STILL TOO CLOSE FOR US TO MOVE SAFELY, WE'LL HAVE TO STAY HIDDEN.

THE TENSION GREW AS THEY WAITED, AND CORPORAL RICHARDSON COULDN'T HELP BUT GIVE VENT TO HIS FEELINGS OF DISCONTENT.

NO WONDER THE BRASS HATS DIDN'T THINK UP A WAY TO GET US OUT — THEY DON'T EXPECT US TO BE STILL ALIVE.

YEAH, IT LOOKS AS IF YOU'RE RIGHT, CORP.

ROGER HAD OVERHEARD RICHARDSON'S COMMENT AND KNEW THAT IF HE DIDN'T DO SOMETHING THEN THE GROUP'S MORALE WOULD DISINTEGRATE.

I DON'T MIND IF I'VE GOT A CHANCE — BUT NONE OF US'LL GET BACK FROM THIS ONE-WAY TRIP.

YOU VOLUNTEERED FOR THIS, CORPORAL, LIKE WE ALL DID. IF YOU DON'T LIKE RISKING YOUR NECK YOU SHOULDN'T HAVE VOLUNTEERED.

ROGER'S VOICE TOOK ON A DETERMINED TONE AS HE SPOKE.

YOU'RE ALL GOOD MEN — AND DESPITE THE FACT THAT H.Q. DON'T SEEM TO WANT YOU BACK, I'M GOING TO MAKE SURE THAT WE RETURN IN ONE PIECE. BUT I CAN'T DO THAT UNLESS WE ALL WORK AS A TEAM.

HIS LITTLE SPEECH SANK HOME AND ALL FELL STRANGELY SILENT, EACH OCCUPIED WITH HIS OWN THOUGHTS.

IF THAT HASN'T PULLED THEM TOGETHER, NOTHING WILL.

I DON'T BELIEVE A WORD OF WHAT HE SAID — BUT I'LL FIGHT TO GET BACK ALIVE.

IT WAS YOUNG HARRY LOMAX WHOSE VOICE WAS HEARD NEXT AS HE SUMMED UP THE FEELINGS OF THEM ALL.

WE'VE ALL GOT TO DIE SOMETIME, BUT AS LONG AS I'M ALIVE I'M GOING TO FIGHT.

QUIET — THERE'S A JAP HEADING THIS WAY.

TURNBULL'S HARSH WHISPER MADE THEM TAKE COVER AS THE JAPANESE SOLDIER AMBLED PAST, SCANT FEET AWAY FROM THEM, BUT LUCKILY HE WAS UNAWARE OF THEIR PRESENCE.

IF YOU LOOK THIS WAY, WE'LL BE THE LAST THING YOU EVER SEE.

THE JAP TRUDGED ON BY AND BY THE TIME HE WAS FAR ENOUGH AWAY IT WAS DAWN AND ROGER LED HIS MEN TOWARDS THEIR NEXT OBJECTIVE — THE HEAVILY-USED ROAD.

NOW THAT HE'S GONE WE CAN MOVE ON. IT SHOULD TAKE US ABOUT AN HOUR TO REACH THE ROAD.

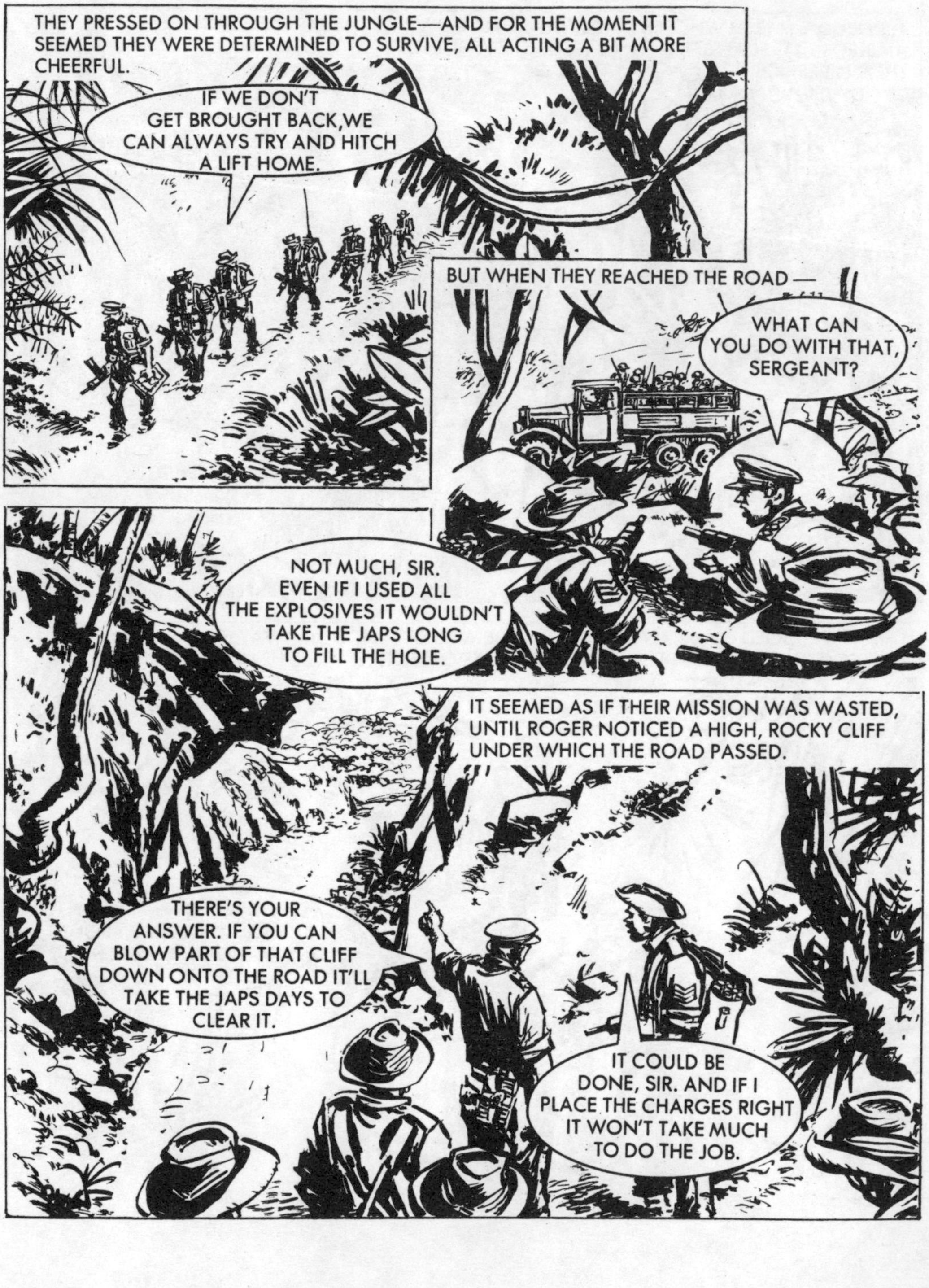
THEY PRESSED ON THROUGH THE JUNGLE—AND FOR THE MOMENT IT SEEMED THEY WERE DETERMINED TO SURVIVE, ALL ACTING A BIT MORE CHEERFUL.
IF WE DON'T GET BROUGHT BACK, WE CAN ALWAYS TRY AND HITCH A LIFT HOME.
BUT WHEN THEY REACHED THE ROAD —
WHAT CAN YOU DO WITH THAT, SERGEANT?
NOT MUCH, SIR. EVEN IF I USED ALL THE EXPLOSIVES IT WOULDN'T TAKE THE JAPS LONG TO FILL THE HOLE.
IT SEEMED AS IF THEIR MISSION WAS WASTED, UNTIL ROGER NOTICED A HIGH, ROCKY CLIFF UNDER WHICH THE ROAD PASSED.
THERE'S YOUR ANSWER. IF YOU CAN BLOW PART OF THAT CLIFF DOWN ONTO THE ROAD IT'LL TAKE THE JAPS DAYS TO CLEAR IT.
IT COULD BE DONE, SIR. AND IF I PLACE THE CHARGES RIGHT IT WON'T TAKE MUCH TO DO THE JOB.

BUT AS HE WAS LEADING HIS MEN ACROSS THE ROAD TOWARDS THE CLIFF, HE SPOTTED VEHICLES HEADING THEIR WAY — AND THE JAPS HAD SEEN THEM.

THE BRITISH HAD BEEN TOO QUICK FOR THE APPROACHING JAPS. THEY MELTED INTO COVER AND OPENED FIRE AT THE LEADING TRUCK BEFORE THE ENEMY COULD REACT.

HOT LEAD HAS SLAMMED INTO THE FIRST TRUCK, RENDERING IT USELESS.

BUT THESE JAPS WERE BATTLE-SEASONED TROOPS AND WERE NOT EASILY PANICKED.

THE RAIDERS ARE OVER THERE. OPEN FIRE.

LOOKS LIKE WE'RE GOING TO HAVE A REAL SCRAP ON OUR HANDS.

TWO JAPS WERE SENT TO ONE SIDE WITH A MACHINE GUN AND WHEN IT OPENED UP, IT PINNED DOWN THE DEFENDERS.

BLAST THAT MACHINE GUN. IF WE MOVE WE'LL BE CUT TO RIBBONS.

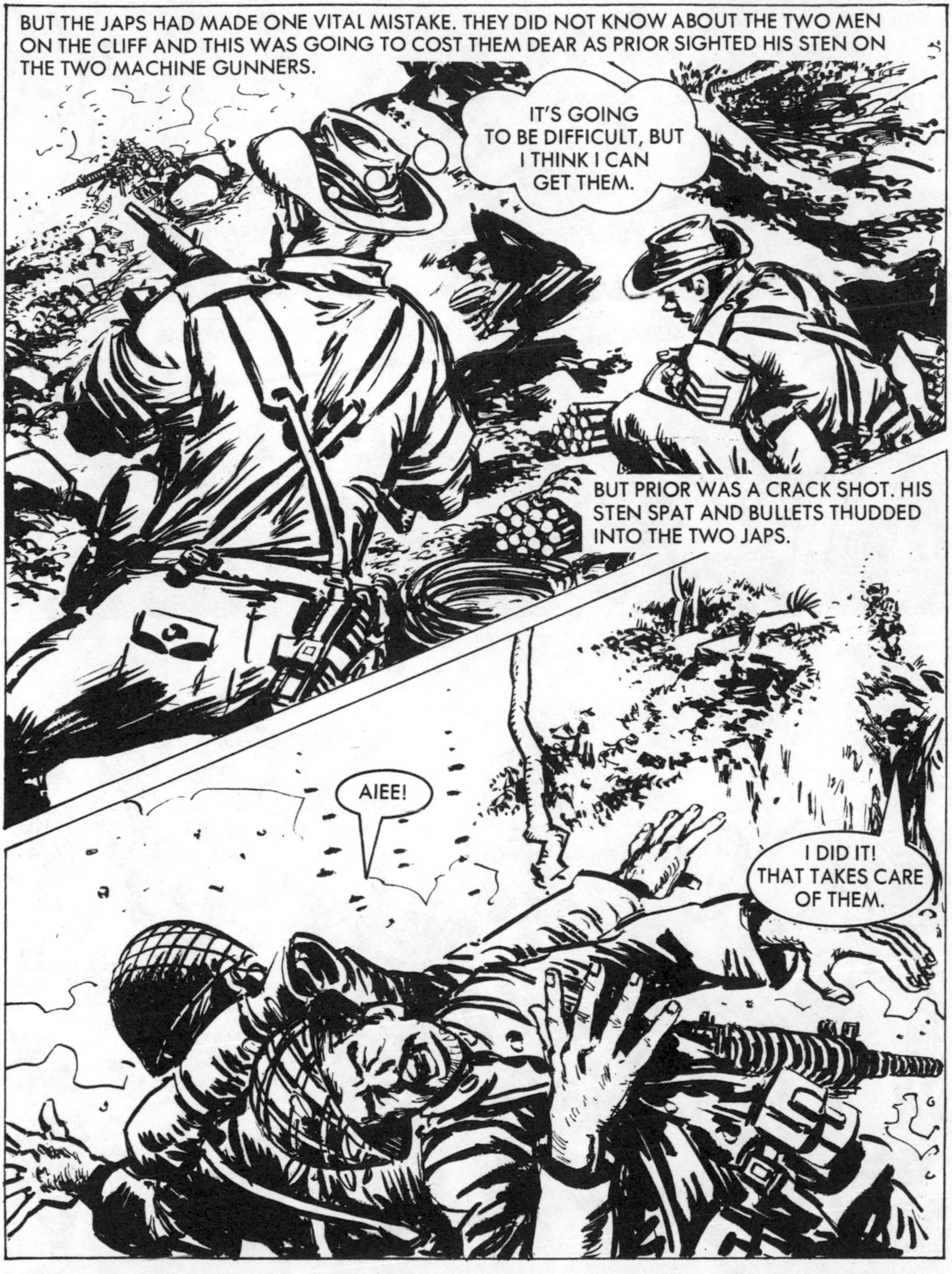
BUT THE JAPS HAD MADE ONE VITAL MISTAKE. THEY DID NOT KNOW ABOUT THE TWO MEN ON THE CLIFF AND THIS WAS GOING TO COST THEM DEAR AS PRIOR SIGHTED HIS STEN ON THE TWO MACHINE GUNNERS.
IT'S GOING TO BE DIFFICULT, BUT I THINK I CAN GET THEM.
BUT PRIOR WAS A CRACK SHOT. HIS STEN SPAT AND BULLETS THUDDED INTO THE TWO JAPS.
AIEE!
I DID IT! THAT TAKES CARE OF THEM.

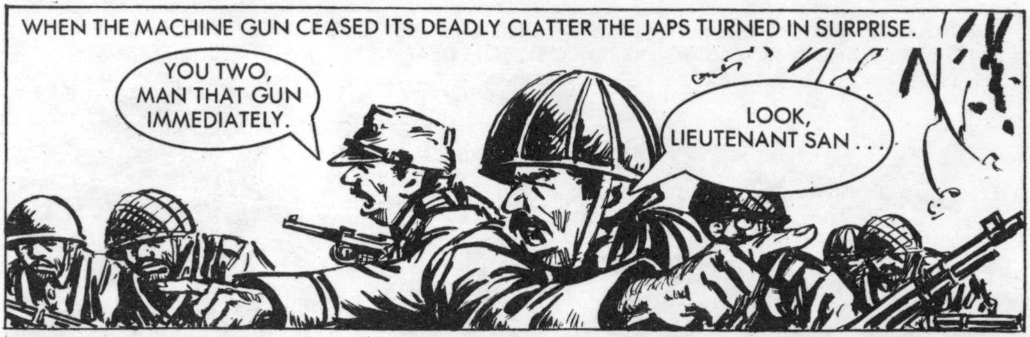
WHEN THE MACHINE GUN CEASED ITS DEADLY CLATTER THE JAPS TURNED IN SURPRISE.
YOU TWO, MAN THAT GUN IMMEDIATELY.
LOOK, LIEUTENANT SAN . . .

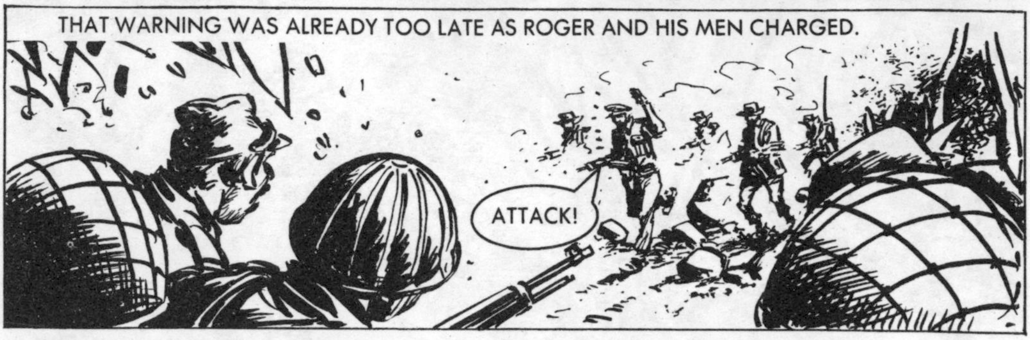
THAT WARNING WAS ALREADY TOO LATE AS ROGER AND HIS MEN CHARGED.
ATTACK!

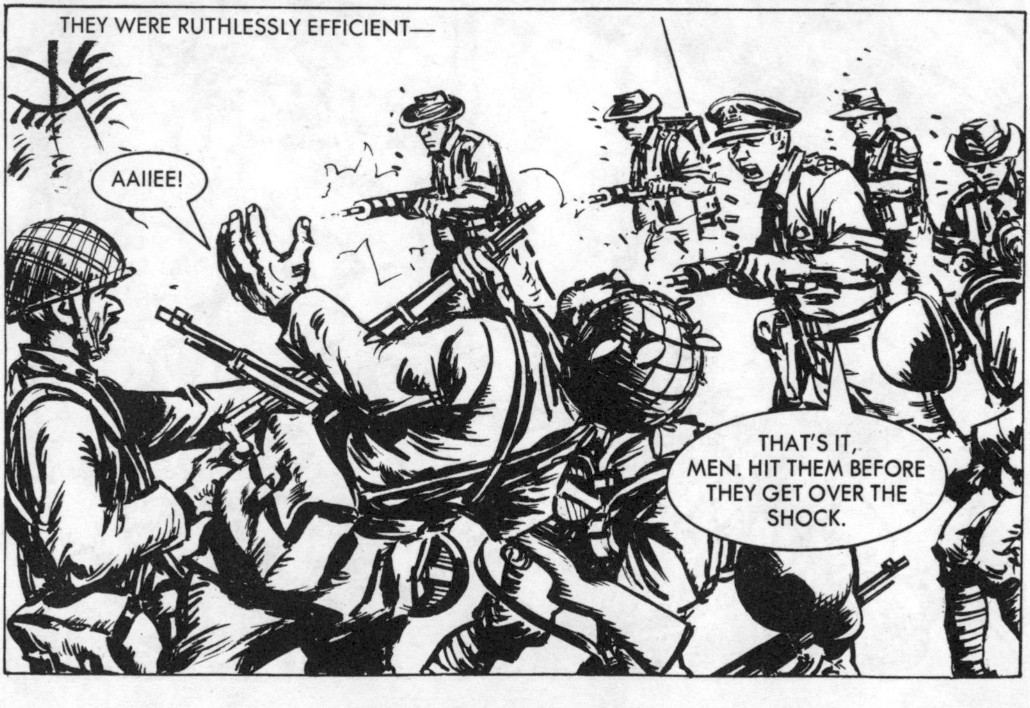
THEY WERE RUTHLESSLY EFFICIENT—
AAIIEE!
THAT'S IT, MEN. HIT THEM BEFORE THEY GET OVER THE SHOCK.

AND ON THE CLIFF, PRIOR WAS GETTING IMPATIENT. IT DIDN'T SEEM RIGHT TO HIM THAT HE SHOULD BE LEFT OUT OF THE BATTLE THAT RAGED BELOW.

HURRY UP, SARGE. OUR MOB'LL BE SLAUGHTERED DOWN THERE.

YOU CAN'T HURRY A JOB LIKE THIS, I'VE ANOTHER BUNDLE TO SET YET.

PRIOR GRIPPED HIS STEN TIGHTER AND WATCHED IN HELPLESS FURY AS THE BRITISH AND JAPS STRUGGLED.

THERE'S MEN BEING CUT TO RIBBONS. DOWN THERE — AND I CAN'T DO A THING TO HELP.

BECAUSE THE FIGHTING WAS SO CONFUSED, HE KNEW HE DAREN'T OPEN FIRE FROM HIS VANTAGE POINT FOR FEAR OF HITTING ONE OF HIS OWN MEN.

BUT MIRACULOUSLY NEITHER ROGER NOR HIS MEN HAD BEEN HURT. THE SPEED AND SURPRISE OF THEIR CHARGE HAD NUMBED THE JAPANESE TROOPS. NOW ROGER WAS PLANNING THEIR GETAWAY.

MAKE FOR THEIR TRUCK — THAT'S OUR TICKET OUT OF HERE.

BUT JUST AS THEY RAN FOR THE TRUCK AND SCRAMBLED ABOARD, HART GAVE A SCREAM OF PAIN.

ARGH!

THEY'VE GOT HART!

RICHARDSON HAD SEEN HART FALL, AND IT WAS HE WHO LEAPT OUT TO DRAG HIM TO SAFETY WHILE THE OTHERS GAVE COVERING FIRE.

COME ON, CORP. WE CAN'T HANG ABOUT ALL DAY.

JUST SHUT UP AND KEEP THOSE JAPS BUSY!

EVEN AS THE TWO MEN WERE HOISTED ABOARD, ROGER GUNNED THE ENGINE AND THE TRUCK ROARED OFF.

THANKS, CORP! I THOUGHT I WAS GOING TO BE LEFT BEHIND.

I DON'T WANT ANYONE LEFT BEHIND — I WANT TO PROVE THE TOP BRASS WRONG!

AS WATSON BANDAGED HART'S LEG, THE TRUCK SQUEALED TO A HALT UNDER THE OVERHANG TO PICK UP THE TWO SABOTEURS — TURNBULL AND PRIOR.

DON'T WORRY, HART, IT'S ONLY A FLESH WOUND.

WE'D BETTER GET WEAVING, SIR. THAT LOT WILL BLOW IN LESS THAN A MINUTE.

THE TRUCK ROARED OFF AND JUST AS IT SLOWED FOR A BEND THERE WAS THE SOUND OF AN EXPLOSION.

THE SARGE HAS DONE IT AGAIN!

BUT WHEN ROGER AND TURNBULL STOLE A QUICK GLANCE ROUND, THEY SAW THAT THE OVERHANG WAS INTACT.

IT HASN'T BLOWN!

I DON'T UNDERSTAND IT . . .

TURNBULL'S EFFICIENCY WASN'T AT FAULT, FOR ONE SET OF FUSES HAD A SLIGHTLY DIFFERENT TIMING. AND, SECONDS LATER, WHEN THEY WENT OFF, THEY SENT TONS OF ROCK CASCADING DOWNWARDS.

ON THE ROAD, THE JAPS PURSUING THE FLEEING RAIDERS, STOPPED IN STUNNED HORROR AS THE CLIFF FACE FELL TOWARDS THEM.

AIEE! WE ARE DOOMED.

THERE WAS NO ESCAPE FOR THE JAPANESE AS THE MANY TONS OF ROCK SWEPT DOWN ON THEM.

AIEEE!

WHEN THEY REACHED SOME HIGH GROUND, ROGER STOPPED THE TRUCK AND THEY ALL PILED OUT TO LOOK DOWN AND SURVEY THEIR HANDIWORK.

PHEW, WHAT A MESS!

YES, THE JAPS WON'T CLEAR THAT LOT IN A HURRY. IT'LL TAKE THEM DAYS.

WHILE THE OTHERS RESTED, ROGER GOT OUT HIS MAP AND PLANNED THE ROUTE TO THEIR FINAL OBJECTIVE — THE ROAD BRIDGE.

SINCE WE'VE GOT THE TRUCK WE MAY AS WELL USE IT. WE CAN FOLLOW THIS ROAD AND THEN CUT OFF AND HEAD FOR THE BRIDGE.

SO THEY SET OFF AGAIN. BUT THIS TIME THEY KNEW THAT THEIR THIRD AND FINAL TARGET WOULD BE THE TOUGHEST YET.

EVERY JAP FOR MILES WILL BE LOOKING FOR US, AND THEY'LL BE SURE TO HAVE THAT BRIDGE WELL GUARDED.

IF WE GET TO IT, I'LL FIND SOME WAY TO DESTROY IT, SIR!

WHEN THEY CAME TO THE END OF THE TRACK AND WERE ABOUT TO JOIN THE MAIN ROAD, THEY FOUND THAT IT WAS PARTICULARLY BUSY.

A JAP CONVOY ON OUR ROUTE — JUST OUR LUCK. WE'LL HAVE TO WAIT UNTIL IT'S CLEAR.

NO WE WON'T. LISTEN . . .

AFTER OUTLINING HIS PLAN TO THE ASTONISHED SERGEANT HE STOPPED THE TRUCK AND TOLD THE OTHERS.

KEEP OUT OF SIGHT BUT BE READY FOR TROUBLE — WE'RE JOINING A JAP CONVOY.

HE'S CRAZY — WE WON'T STAND A CHANCE.

THOUGH RICHARDSON KEPT HIS THOUGHTS TO HIMSELF, THE OTHERS SEEMED TO THINK THE SAME.

AFTER REMOVING THEIR BUSH HATS, THEY DROVE TOWARDS THE JUNCTION.

DO WE TAG ON TO THE END, SIR?

NO, THE LAST MAN SHOULD REALISE THERE SHOULDN'T BE ANYONE BEHIND HIM.

ROGER TOOK ADVANTAGE OF THE FIRST GAP IN THE TRAFFIC.

HERE WE GO!

IT WAS PERHAPS JUST AS WELL THAT ROGER HAD DECIDED ON THIS BOLD MOVE, FOR THERE WAS A CHECK-POINT FURTHER ALONG THE ROAD. ONLY THE LEADING TRUCK WAS STOPPED. THE REST WERE WAVED THROUGH.

THAT WAS A BIT OF LUCK, THEY'RE NOT BOTHERING ABOUT US.

AS THEY NEARED THE BRIDGE, ROGER TURNED OFF THE MAIN ROAD AGAIN ONTO ANOTHER NARROW TRACK.

WE DAREN'T STAY WITH THIS CONVOY FOR TOO LONG.

BY USING NARROW JUNGLE TRAILS, THEY DROVE AS CLOSE AS THEY COULD TO THEIR TARGET, BUT THERE CAME A TIME WHEN THEY HAD TO LEAVE THE TRUCK AND STRIKE OUT ACROSS COUNTRY AGAIN.

ONCE WE GET TO THE TOP OF THIS HILL WE SHOULD BE ABLE TO SEE THE BRIDGE. THINK YOU CAN MAKE IT, HART?

OF COURSE I CAN, SIR. MY WOUND'S NOT THAT BAD.

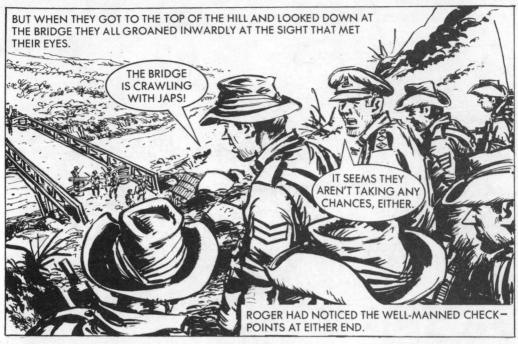

BUT WHEN THEY GOT TO THE TOP OF THE HILL AND LOOKED DOWN AT THE BRIDGE THEY ALL GROANED INWARDLY AT THE SIGHT THAT MET THEIR EYES.

THE BRIDGE IS CRAWLING WITH JAPS!

IT SEEMS THEY AREN'T TAKING ANY CHANCES, EITHER.

ROGER HAD NOTICED THE WELL-MANNED CHECK—POINTS AT EITHER END.

IT LOOKED AS IF THEY WOULDN'T BE ABLE TO GET NEAR ENOUGH TO GET ON THE BRIDGE, LET ALONE PLACE THEIR CHARGES.

SHALL I RADIO H.Q. AND TELL THEM WE'VE DONE ALL WE COULD?

WAIT A MINUTE, THERE MIGHT BE A WAY TO DESTROY THAT THING.

THE TOUGH EXPLOSIVES EXPERT WENT ON TO OUTLINE WHAT HE HAD IN MIND.

IF WE PACKED THE TRUCK WITH EXPLOSIVES I COULD DRIVE IT ONTO THE BRIDGE AND DETONATE IT IN THE MIDDLE. AT FULL SPEED THE JAPS WOULDN'T STOP ME.

IT'S A GOOD IDEA, BUT I'LL DO THE DRIVING — I TOLD YOU I'D MAKE SURE YOU ALL GOT BACK SAFELY.

AS THEY MARCHED BACK TO THE TRUCK THE PLAN WAS DISCUSSED THOROUGHLY — AND RICHARDSON SEEMED DEAD SET AGAINST IT.

YOU CAN'T DRIVE THE TRUCK, SIR — YOU WON'T STAND A CHANCE.

I'M NOT GOING TO LET ANYONE ELSE GO IN MY PLACE. REMEMBER, I GAVE YOU ALL MY WORD THAT WE'D SUCCEED AND THAT YOU'D ALL GET BACK SAFELY.

THEY REACHED THE TRUCK AND WHILE TURNBULL SAW TO THE EXPLOSIVES, THE REST OF THE MEN TRIED TO TALK ROGER OUT OF THIS RISKY VENTURE.

LOOK, SIR, IF YOU'RE GOING THEN WE'RE COMING WITH YOU.

HE'S RIGHT, SIR, YOU'RE NOT GOING TO LEAVE US BEHIND.

FOR ONCE THEY WERE ALL IN AGREEMENT. ROGER HAD LED THEM WELL SO FAR, AND THEY WEREN'T GOING TO LET HIM THROW HIS LIFE AWAY.

FACED WITH SO MUCH PRESSURE, ROGER HAD NO CHOICE BUT TO MODIFY HIS PLAN TO TAKE INTO ACCOUNT THIS SUDDEN RUSH OF VOLUNTEERS.

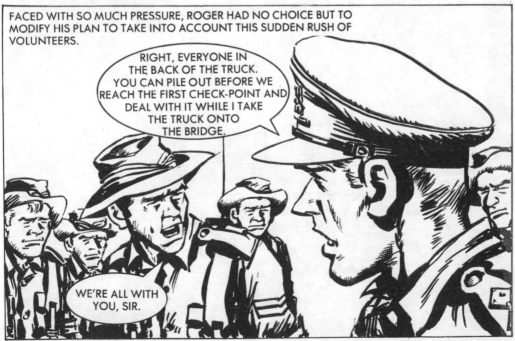

RIGHT, EVERYONE IN THE BACK OF THE TRUCK. YOU CAN PILE OUT BEFORE WE REACH THE FIRST CHECK-POINT AND DEAL WITH IT WHILE I TAKE THE TRUCK ONTO THE BRIDGE.

WE'RE ALL WITH YOU, SIR.

TURNBULL SOON HAD THE EXPLOSIVES RIGGED UP AND THEY SET OFF ONCE AGAIN.

IF THIS DOESN'T WORK, WE'VE ALL HAD IT.

TRAVELLING ALONG THE MAIN ROAD WITHOUT INCIDENT, THEY SOON CAME TO THE BRIDGE.

SO FAR SO GOOD!

ROGER SLOWED THE TRUCK AS HE NEARED THE CHECK-POINT AND HIS MEN DIVED FROM THE BACK AND ROLLED INTO COVER AT THE SIDE OF THE ROAD.

I'D BETTER BE CAREFUL, I DON'T WANT TO BUST THE RADIO.

ONCE HIS MEN WERE SAFELY OUT, ROGER GUNNED THE ENGINE AND AS THE TRUCK SMASHED THROUGH THE STARTLED JAP GUARDS AT THE CHECK-POINT, HIS MEN OPENED FIRE ON THEM.

AIEE! WHAT'S GOING ON?

KEEP FIRING, LADS. GIVE MR HUNTER A CHANCE.

HERE GOES!

WITH THE EXPLOSIVE-PACKED TRUCK ON COURSE, ROGER LEAPT FROM IT, HIS STEN GUN BLAZING.

TURNBULL'S SET SHORT FUSES — I'D BETTER GET CLEAR FAST!

BEFORE THE SERGEANT HAD ROLLED FROM THE BACK OF THE TRUCK, HE HAD LIT THE FUSES ON THE EXPLOSIVES, SO EVERY SECOND WAS VITAL.

THE SWIFT ATTACK HAD TAKEN THE JAPS BY SURPRISE AND AS ROGER MADE HIS WAY BACK TO HIS MEN THE FEW REMAINING ENEMY TROOPS ON THAT SIDE OF THE BRIDGE, WERE SWIFTLY DEALT WITH.

RIGHT, MEN, LET'S GET OUT OF HERE.

AIEE!

THEY DIDN'T NOTICE THEIR TRUCK, HALF-WAY ACROSS THE BRIDGE, COLLIDING WITH ANOTHER VEHICLE . . .

. . . BUT THEY ALL HEARD THE RESULTING EXPLOSION. FOR AS THE CHARGES DETONATED THE BRIDGE WAS BLOWN TO SMITHEREENS.

BLIMEY, SIR, I DIDN'T HAVE ENOUGH EXPLOSIVES LEFT TO DO THAT!

IT MUST HAVE HIT AN AMMO TRUCK.

THE RESULT WAS ONE BEYOND THEIR WILDEST DREAMS.

WITH THE JAPS ON THEIR SIDE OF THE BRIDGE WIPED OUT, AND THOSE ON THE OTHER SIDE CUT OFF, THEY MOVED OUT CHEERFULLY WITH NO IMMEDIATE PURSUIT.

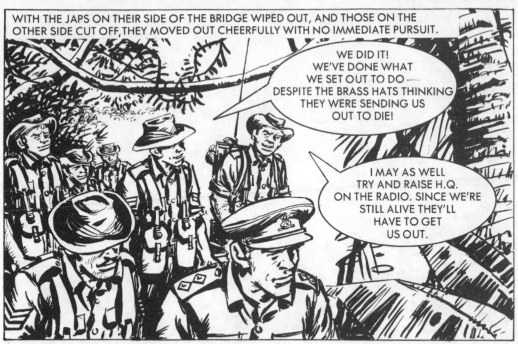

WE DID IT! WE'VE DONE WHAT WE SET OUT TO DO — DESPITE THE BRASS HATS THINKING THEY WERE SENDING US OUT TO DIE!

I MAY AS WELL TRY AND RAISE H.Q. ON THE RADIO. SINCE WE'RE STILL ALIVE THEY'LL HAVE TO GET US OUT.

BECAUSE OF THE DISTANCE TO H.Q. WATSON HAD TROUBLE IN RAISING THEM. BUT FINALLY —

I'M THROUGH TO H.Q.

RIGHT, FIND OUT HOW WE GET BACK.

THEIR REQUEST FOR TRANSPORT WAS RELAYED TO BRIGADIER TRAYNOR, BUT —

THEY'RE TOO FAR BEHIND ENEMY LINES TO BE REACHED. THERE'S NOTHING WE CAN DO TO HELP THEM.

AS TRAYNOR'S REPLY CAME THROUGH, ALL WERE CLUSTERED EAGERLY AROUND WATSON, DESPERATE TO HEAR THE NEWS.

WELL, WHAT DID HE SAY? WHEN DO WE GET PICKED UP?

WE DON'T! ALL HE SAID WAS " WELL DONE " AND " CARRY ON ".

THERE WAS A MOMENT'S INCREDULOUS SILENCE WHICH WAS BROKEN ONLY WHEN RICHARDSON MOUNTED A SCATHING ATTACK ON THE PLANNERS AT H.Q.

BLOOMIN' TOP BRASS! WE RISK OUR NECKS AND THAT'S ALL THE THANKS WE GET!

I THOUGHT YOU SAID THE BRIGADIER WOULDN'T RISK HIS OWN GRANDSON? YOU SAID WE'D BE SAFE IF WE STUCK CLOSE TO HIM, BUT IT LOOKS LIKE HE'S FOR THE CHOP THE SAME AS THE REST OF US!

BOTH ROGER AND TURNBULL HAD HEARD THESE BITTER RECRIMINATIONS AND WERE ABOUT TO PUT A STOP TO THEM WHEN ANOTHER SOUND ATTRACTED ATTENTION—THE DISTANT RUMBLE OF HEAVY ARTILLERY FIRE.

THAT SOUNDS LIKE OUR GUNS. THE BIG PUSH MUST HAVE STARTED.

THAT'S NOT ALL— LISTEN.

THEIR EARS STRAINING, THEY HEARD THE OMINOUS SOUND OF APPROACHING ENEMY TROOPS.

KNOWING THAT THEY'D BE FOLLOWED IF THEY RAN, ROGER LED HIS MEN IN A WILD CHARGE. THE JAPS WERE TAKEN COMPLETELY UNAWARES.

LET'S KNOCK 'EM FOR SIX.

YOU LOUSY JAPS!

AIEE— THE RAIDERS!

RICHARDSON, WELL TO THE FORE, VENTED HIS FURY ON THE UNSUSPECTING JAPS.

TAKEN BY SURPRISE, THE SMALL ENEMY PATROL WAS NO MATCH FOR THE HALF-CRAZED CHARGE AND THEY WERE SOON MOWN DOWN.

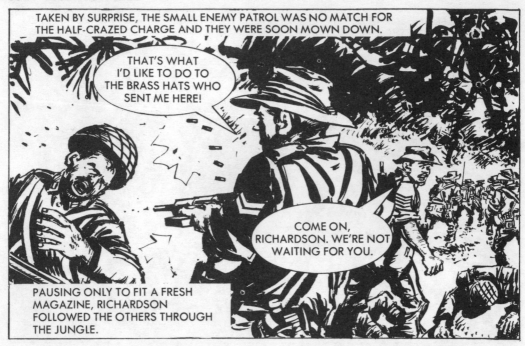

THAT'S WHAT I'D LIKE TO DO TO THE BRASS HATS WHO SENT ME HERE!

COME ON, RICHARDSON. WE'RE NOT WAITING FOR YOU.

PAUSING ONLY TO FIT A FRESH MAGAZINE, RICHARDSON FOLLOWED THE OTHERS THROUGH THE JUNGLE.

FOR WHAT SEEMED LIKE AN AGE THEY CUT THROUGH THE JUNGLE UNTIL THEY CAME OUT INTO A LARGE CLEARING.

LOOK AT THAT!

A DAKOTA COULD LAND HERE! WATSON, RADIO H.Q.

AND BACK AT HEADQUARTERS, TRAYNOR WAS QUICKLY INFORMED.

HUNTER HAS FOUND A CLEARING BIG ENOUGH FOR A DAKOTA TO LAND—AND WE'VE A PLANE SPARE JUST NOW!

BY HEAVENS! THAT'S MARVELLOUS NEWS!

TO TRAYNOR IT LOOKED AS IF HE COULD RESCUE HIS GRANDSON AND HIS MEN AFTER ALL, BUT AS HE LIFTED THE PHONE TO AUTHORISE THE PICK – UP THERE WAS AN INTERRUPTION AS ANOTHER OFFICER BURST IN.

SIGNAL FROM ' B ' COMPANY, SIR. THEY ARE LOW ON AMMO AND SURROUNDED. THEY REQUEST AN URGENT AIR DROP OF SUPPLIES OR THEY'LL BE WIPED OUT, LEAVING OUR LEFT FLANK EXPOSED.

AGHAST AT THE DECISION HE HAD TO MAKE, TRAYNOR PUT DOWN THE PHONE.

' B ' COMPANY SHOULD BE ABLE TO HOLD OUT FOR ANOTHER COUPLE OF HOURS. WE COULD PICK UP THE RAIDERS FIRST.

NO, WE CAN'T RISK THE JAPS BREAKING THROUGH ON OUR LEFT FLANK.

THOUGH THE TWO STAFF OFFICERS THOUGHT THAT THE MEN SHOULD BE PICKED UP, TRAYNOR KNEW THAT HE DAREN'T RISK LETTING THE JAPS BREAK THROUGH.

ARRANGE FOR THE SUPPLIES FOR 'B' COMPANY TO BE LOADED ON THE DAKOTA.

VERY WELL, SIR.

SO THE GRIM NEWS WAS RELAYED TO ROGER AND HIS MEN.

H.Q. SAYS THEY HAVE NO PLANES AVAILABLE, SIR. WE CAN EITHER WAIT HERE UNTIL THEY DO OR TRY TO LINK UP WITH THE ADVANCE.

SOME CHOICE —WE EITHER GET KILLED HERE OR ON THE WAY.

NOW THAT IT WAS DEFINITE THAT THEY WERE NOT TO BE RESCUED, THE MEN'S MORALE HAD DETERIORATED RAPIDLY—UNTIL ROGER ASSERTED COMMAND.

WE'VE GOT THIS FAR AND SURVIVED, SO LET'S GET MOVING AGAIN. REMEMBER, I GAVE YOU ALL MY WORD THAT I'D GET YOU BACK SAFELY—AND I INTEND TO KEEP IT.

GRUDGINGLY THE MEN FOLLOWED HIM ON THE LONG TREK TOWARDS THEIR LINES.

I'LL NEVER TRUST AN OFFICER AGAIN.

SHUT UP, RICHARDSON. YOU HEARD MR HUNTER—HE'LL GET US OUT.

THEY TRUDGED ON FOR MILE AFTER WEARY MILE, UNTIL—

A JAP CAMP!

LOOKS LIKE SOME SORT OF H.Q.

THEY STOPPED AND AS ROGER AND TURNBULL LOOKED DOWN AT THE CAMP, PRIOR GRINNED WICKEDLY AND SPOKE TO RICHARDSON.

YOU KNOW, CORP, BRASS HATS ARE BRASS HATS—AND THERE'S PLENTY OF 'EM DOWN THERE. THEY'D MAKE GOOD TARGET PRACTICE.

YEAH, AND WE'D HAVE THE WHOLE OF THE JAP ARMY AFTER US, NOT JUST HALF.

IF WE HIT THEIR COMMUNICATIONS, THEY WOULDN'T KNOW WHERE TO LOOK FOR US.

THE TOUGH LITTLE CORPORAL DIDN'T NEED MUCH CONVINCING AND PUT FORWARD THE IDEA TO ROGER.

ME AND THE LADS HAVE BEEN THINKIN', SIR. WHY DON'T WE KNOCK THAT H.Q. FOR SIX.

THERE'S NO NEED. WE CAN PASS IT BY AND GET BACK SAFELY TO OUR LINES.

ROGER TURNED AND FACED HIS MEN. HE THOUGHT FOR A MOMENT THEN SHRUGGED BRIEFLY AS HE MADE HIS DECISION.

AFTER CREEPING QUIETLY THROUGH THE JUNGLE TO GET AS CLOSE AS THEY COULD WITHOUT BEING SEEN, THEY BURST FROM COVER AND ATTACKED THE CAMP, THROWING GRENADES AND FIRING RAPIDLY.

RICHARDSON CERTAINLY GOT HIS REVENGE ON HIGH RANKING OFFICERS, FOR A GRENADE HE THREW INTO A HUT KILLED THREE OF THEM.

THAT'S WHAT I'D LIKE TO DO TO THE BRITISH TOP BRASS.

CONFUSION REIGNED AS THE RAIDERS BLITZED THE CAMP. TURNBULL DEALT WITH TWO JAPS WHO TRIED TO GET TO A MACHINE GUN.

OH NO YOU DON'T!

AIEEE!

ARGH!

ROGER AND HIS MEN WERE FULL OF FIGHTING SPIRIT AND SUCH WAS THE SUDDENNESS AND FEROCITY OF THE ATTACK THAT THE JAPS WERE TOO SURPRISED TO PUT UP MUCH OF A FIGHT.

THAT'S IT, MEN.

IN THE MIDDLE OF ALL THAT CHAOS ONE OFFICER KEPT HIS HEAD AND RUSHED TO THE RADIO ROOM WHERE HE URGENTLY DEMANDED ASSISTANCE TO DEAL WITH WHAT HE THOUGHT WAS A FULL-SCALE ATTACK.

WE ARE COMPLETELY OUTNUMBERED. REQUEST IMMEDIATE REINFORCEMENTS . . .

IT WAS THE LAST MESSAGE HE WOULD SEND FOR SCANT SECONDS LATER RICHARDSON AND PRIOR BURST IN, USING THEIR STENS AND GRENADES TO GOOD EFFECT.

UNKNOWN TO ROGER AND HIS MEN, THEIR ATTACK, AND THAT BRIEF RADIO MESSAGE, WERE TO HAVE FAR REACHING EFFECTS. A PUZZLED OFFICER REPORTED TO GENERAL CARVER WHO WAS IN COMMAND OF THE BRITISH OFFENSIVE.

INTELLIGENCE REPORT, SIR. ONE OF THE ENEMY BATTALIONS HAS PULLED OUT OF THE LINE FOR NO APPARENT REASON.

THEN WE'LL SWITCH OUR MAIN ASSAULT TO THAT SECTOR.

THOUGH THEY DIDN'T KNOW IT, THE JAPS HAD BEEN SENT TO STEM THE ATTACK BY ROGER AND HIS MEN.

THE GENERAL'S PLAN WORKED, AND THE NEWS WAS RELAYED TO TRAYNOR WHO WAS STILL PRE-OCCUPIED WITH THOUGHTS OF HIS OWN.

WE'VE BROKEN THROUGH, SIR. THE JAPS ARE SHORT ON SUPPLIES AND ARE BEING FORCED TO RETREAT.

SO ROGER'S MISSION WAS NOT IN VAIN. BUT IS HE DEAD OR ALIVE?

TRAYNOR WAS DETERMINED TO RESOLVE THIS QUESTION IF HE COULD AND WITHIN MINUTES HE WAS IN HIS STAFF CAR, HEADING FOR THE SHATTERED JAPANESE LINES.

IF ROGER KEPT GOING HE SHOULD BE SOMEWHERE IN THIS AREA — IF HE'S STILL ALIVE.

URGING HIS DRIVER TO GO FASTER, TRAYNOR RACED ALONG TOWARDS THE FRONT LINE. THEN A CAPTAIN WAVED FOR HIS CAR TO STOP.

THE ENEMY'S REPORTED TO BE JUST UP AHEAD, SIR.

WE'LL PROCEED.

I CAN'T SHRINK FROM THE SAME DANGER I PUT ROGER IN.

BUT FURTHER ALONG THE ROAD, GRENADE EXPLOSIONS ROCKED THE CAR.

AARGH!

EVEN AS THE VEHICLE HEELED OVER, SEVERAL JAPS APPEARED FROM THE JUNGLE AND LET LOOSE A FUSILLADE OF SHOTS.

BY SHINTO, THESE WHITE-EYES WILL NOT LIVE TO SEE THE DAWN OF A NEW DAY.

AS THE JAPS CLOSED IN ON THEM, TRAYNOR GROPED WILDLY FOR HIS REVOLVER.

THE BLASTED THING MUST HAVE FALLEN OUT OF THE HOLSTER WHEN WE WENT OVER.

WITH NO GUN AND HIS DRIVER UNCONSCIOUS IN THE FRONT, IT LOOKED AS IF TRAYNOR HAD HAD IT.

BUT BEFORE THE ADVANCING JAPS REACHED HIM, THERE WAS THE CRACKLE OF STEN GUN FIRE FROM THE JUNGLE AND THE JAPS WENT DOWN LIKE NINEPINS.

AIEE!

GOOD GRIEF! SOME OF OUR LADS HAVE CAUGHT UP WITH US.

THEN THE MEN RESPONSIBLE STEPPED OUT OF THE JUNGLE INTO VIEW — AND BRIGADIER TRAYNOR GAPED IN DISBELIEF.

KEEP ONE EYE OPEN FOR ANY MORE JAPS WHILE I SEE HOW THE OCCUPANTS ARE.

GREAT SCOTT! IT'S ROGER!

WHEN ROGER REACHED THE CAR AND SAW WHO HE HAD RESCUED, HE WAS JUST AS SURPRISED AS HIS GRANDFATHER HAD BEEN.

SIR! WHAT THE BLAZES ARE YOU DOING HERE?

ROGER, THANK HEAVENS YOU'RE OK.

AFTER HELPING TRAYNOR AWAY FROM THE WRECKED CAR, ROGER STEPPED BACK, SALUTED AND GAVE HIS REPORT IN TRUE MILITARY FASHION.

MISSION SUCCESSFULLY COMPLETED, SIR. SORRY WE COULDN'T GET BACK SOONER, BUT WE DIDN'T HAVE ANY TRANSPORT.

ROGER, IF I COULD HAVE DONE ANYTHING TO HELP IT WOULD HAVE BEEN DONE, BELIEVE ME.

AS TRAYNOR SPOKE TO THE GROUP OF MEN WHO HAD MIRACULOUSLY SURVIVED THE SUICIDE MISSION, EVEN RICHARDSON FELT A SURGE OF PRIDE.

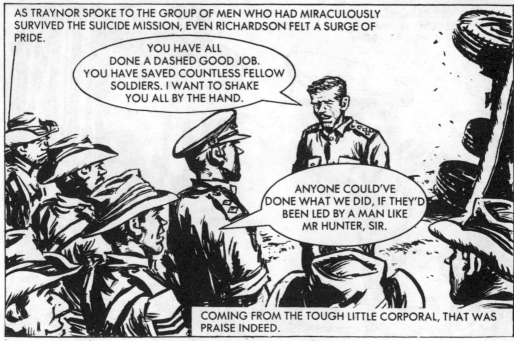

YOU HAVE ALL DONE A DASHED GOOD JOB. YOU HAVE SAVED COUNTLESS FELLOW SOLDIERS. I WANT TO SHAKE YOU ALL BY THE HAND.

ANYONE COULD'VE DONE WHAT WE DID, IF THEY'D BEEN LED BY A MAN LIKE MR HUNTER, SIR.

COMING FROM THE TOUGH LITTLE CORPORAL, THAT WAS PRAISE INDEED.

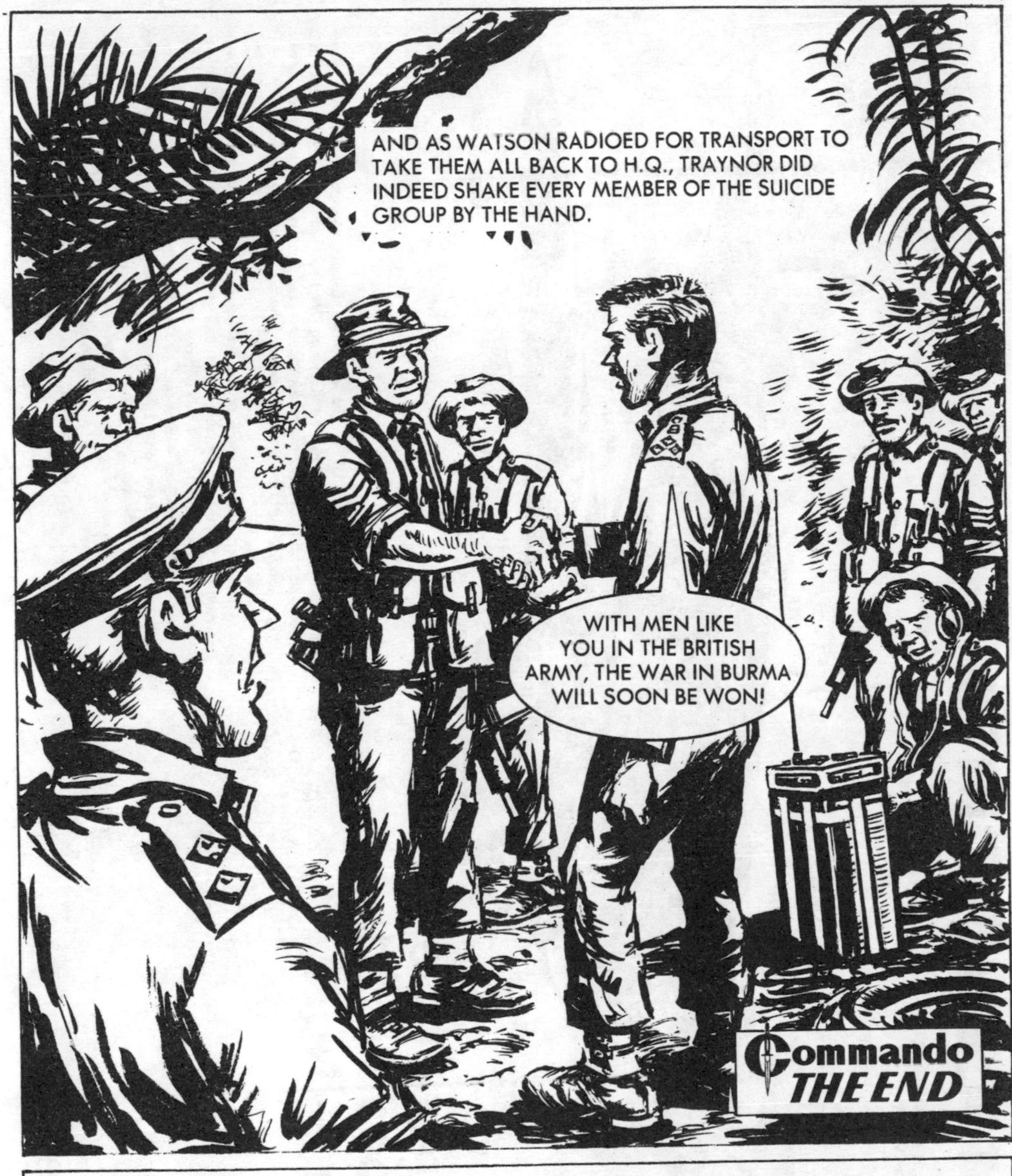
AND AS WATSON RADIOED FOR TRANSPORT TO TAKE THEM ALL BACK TO H.Q., TRAYNOR DID INDEED SHAKE EVERY MEMBER OF THE SUICIDE GROUP BY THE HAND.
WITH MEN LIKE YOU IN THE BRITISH ARMY, THE WAR IN BURMA WILL SOON BE WON!
Commando
THE END

Four action-packed Commando books hit the shops in three weeks! Don't miss:—

" AGAINST ALL ODDS "
" AIR GUNNER "
" BOYS' WAR "
" GHOST RIDER "

BRISTOL BEAUFIGHTER

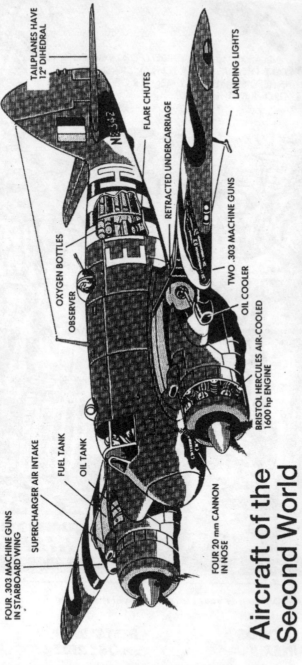

FOUR .303 MACHINE GUNS
IN STARBOARD WING

SUPERCHARGER AIR INTAKE

FUEL TANK

OIL TANK

FOUR 20 mm CANNON
IN NOSE

BRISTOL HERCULES AIR-COOLED
1600 hp ENGINE

OIL COOLER

TWO .303 MACHINE GUNS

OBSERVER

OXYGEN BOTTLES

RETRACTED UNDERCARRIAGE

FLARE CHUTES

LANDING LIGHTS

TAILPLANES HAVE
12° DIHEDRAL

Aircraft of the
Second World
War — No. 2

A T the outbreak of World War Two Britain found she had no plane
comparable with the German Me110 fighter. The Spitfire and
Hurricane did not have the endurance needed for flying long patrols, day or
night, and so, utilising many Beaufort bomber parts, the Bristol Beaufighter
was built.

It helped remove some of the weight put on the Boulton-Paul Defiant
during the German night blitz on Britain, and was the only plane capable of
carrying interception radar sets without sacrificing fire-power.

Used by Coastal Command from Norway to the Bay of Biscay,
torpedo-armed Beaufighters became the scourge of enemy shipping. These
were called Torbeaus.

Rommel's supply columns in the Western Desert also learned to fear the
day-fighter Beau, and it was nicknamed "Whispering Death" by the Japs
who fell foul of it in the Far East.

OF ALL THE ALLIED AIRCRAFT, FEW WERE AS FEARED BY THE GERMANS AS MUCH AS THE BRISTOL BEAUFIGHTERS WHICH COMBINED SPEED AND POWER WITH A DEVASTATING PUNCH. THIS IS THE STORY OF ONE OF THOSE BEAU SQUADRONS, AND THE EXTRAORDINARY MAN WHO LED IT.

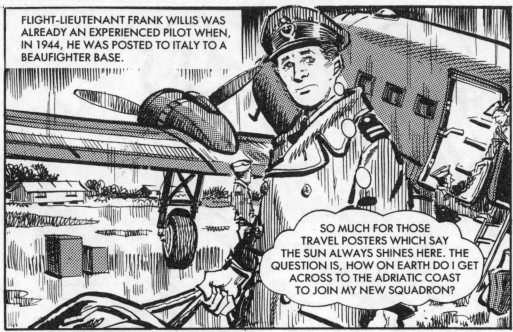

FLIGHT-LIEUTENANT FRANK WILLIS WAS ALREADY AN EXPERIENCED PILOT WHEN, IN 1944, HE WAS POSTED TO ITALY TO A BEAUFIGHTER BASE.

SO MUCH FOR THOSE TRAVEL POSTERS WHICH SAY THE SUN ALWAYS SHINES HERE. THE QUESTION IS, HOW ON EARTH DO I GET ACROSS TO THE ADRIATIC COAST TO JOIN MY NEW SQUADRON?

FRANK NEEDN'T HAVE WORRIED. A CHEERFUL FLIGHT SERGEANT EMERGED OUT OF THE POURING RAIN, AN UMBRELLA IN HIS HAND.

FLIGHT-SERGEANT DAWSON, SIR, BUT EVERYONE CALLS ME "GEORDIE", 'COS I COME FROM TYNESIDE. THE SQUADRON-LEADER SENT ME TO PICK YOU UP.

YOU'VE DRIVEN ACROSS ITALY JUST FOR ME? SINCE WHEN DO MERE FLIGHT-LIEUTENANTS QUALIFY FOR THE RED CARPET TREATMENT?

CONSIDERING THAT HIS NEW BASE WAS OVER A HUNDRED MILES AWAY, THE LAST THING FRANK EXPECTED WAS TO FIND TRANSPORT LAID ON. BUT AS GEORDIE EXPLAINED, THIS WAS NO NORMAL SQUADRON.

THE BOSS BELIEVES IN LOOKING AFTER HIS MEN, SIR. WHEN YOU'VE BEEN JAMMY ENOUGH TO GET A POSTING TO JOIN FEARLESS FREDDY, YOUR TROUBLES ARE OVER.

FEARLESS FREDDY?

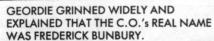
GEORDIE GRINNED WIDELY AND EXPLAINED THAT THE C.O.'s REAL NAME WAS FREDERICK BUNBURY.

EVERYONE CALLS HIM FEARLESS FREDDY — THE BEST DARNED LEADER EVER.

I THINK I'M GOING TO LIKE MY NEW POSTING.

AS THEY DROVE ON, THE SUN CAME OUT AND THE DEVASTATION CAUSED BY THE FIGHTING BECAME APPARENT. FRANK, WHO HAD FLOWN UP UNTIL NOW FROM BRITISH BASES, HAD NEVER SEEN ANYTHING LIKE IT.

I HAVEN'T SEEN A BUILDING INTACT FOR TEN MILES.

THAT'S WHAT IT'S LIKE HERE. THE JERRIES DEFEND EVERY MILE.

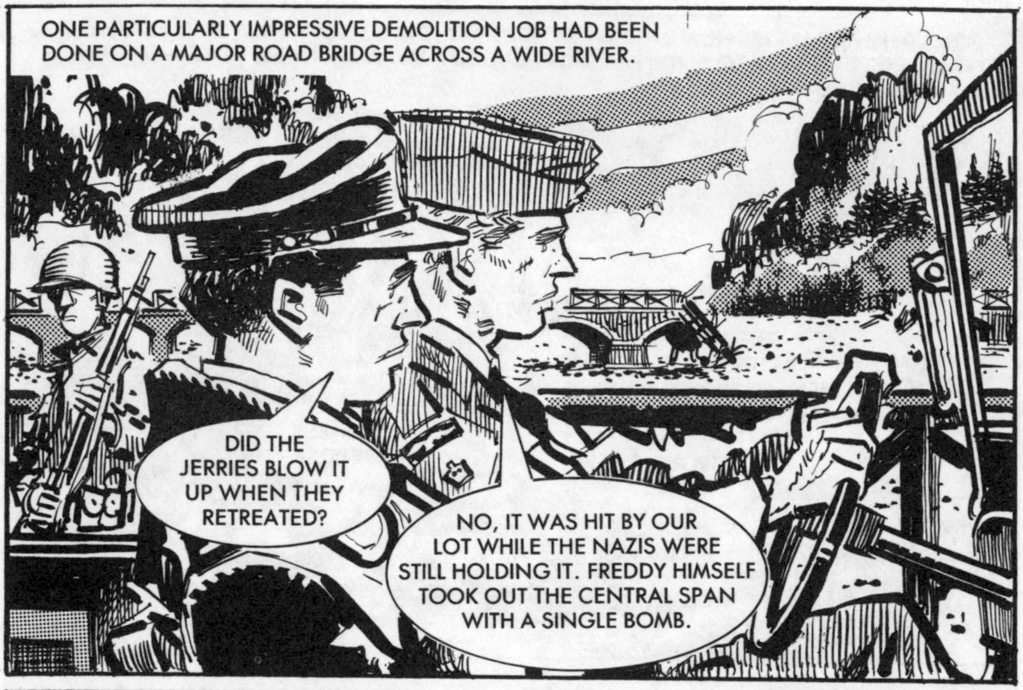
ONE PARTICULARLY IMPRESSIVE DEMOLITION JOB HAD BEEN DONE ON A MAJOR ROAD BRIDGE ACROSS A WIDE RIVER.
DID THE JERRIES BLOW IT UP WHEN THEY RETREATED?
NO, IT WAS HIT BY OUR LOT WHILE THE NAZIS WERE STILL HOLDING IT. FREDDY HIMSELF TOOK OUT THE CENTRAL SPAN WITH A SINGLE BOMB.

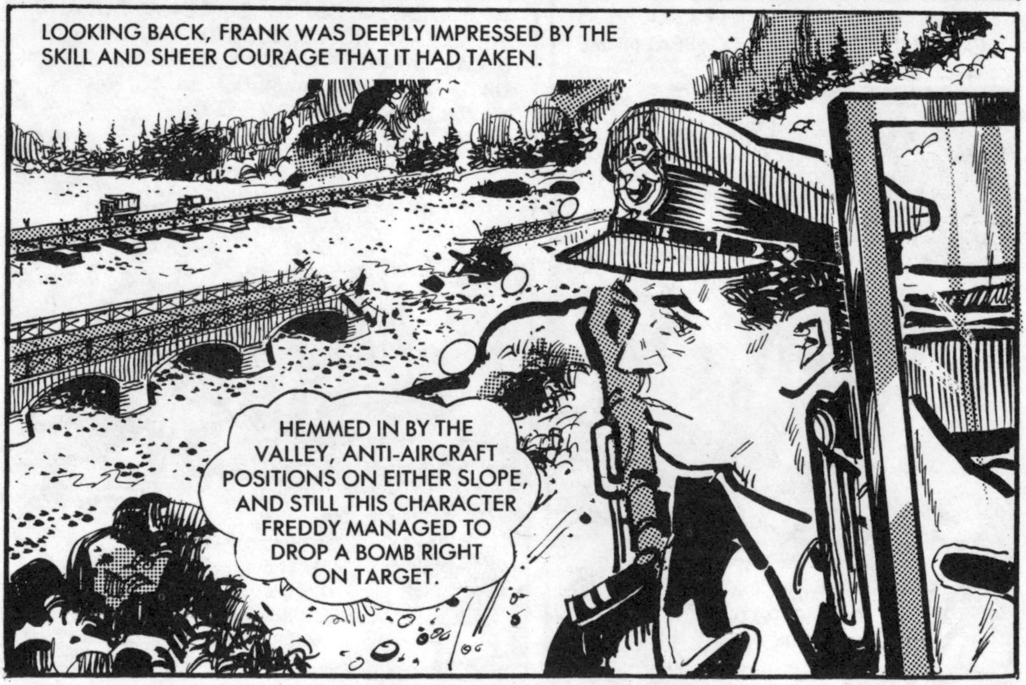
LOOKING BACK, FRANK WAS DEEPLY IMPRESSED BY THE SKILL AND SHEER COURAGE THAT IT HAD TAKEN.
HEMMED IN BY THE VALLEY, ANTI-AIRCRAFT POSITIONS ON EITHER SLOPE, AND STILL THIS CHARACTER FREDDY MANAGED TO DROP A BOMB RIGHT ON TARGET.

A FEW HOURS LATER THEY REACHED THE AIRFIELD AND FRANK WAS ABLE AT LAST TO MEET THE LEGENDARY FREDDY.

FRANK FOUND HIMSELF IN ACTION THE VERY NEXT DAY AS FREDDY LED HIS PLANES IN AN ATTACK AGAINST GERMAN POSITIONS FURTHER UP THE COAST.

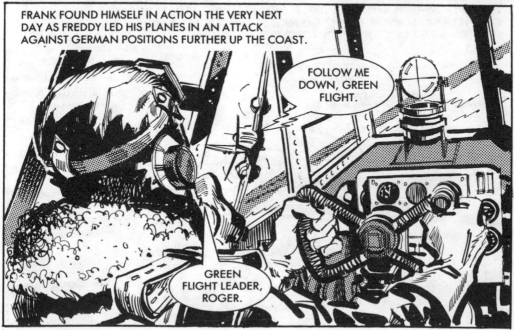

ALMOST IMMEDIATELY FRANK WAS TREATED TO AN AWESOME FLYING DISPLAY BY FREDDY, WHO NEITHER EXPECTED NOR WANTED HIS OTHER PILOTS TO TRY TO COPY HIM.

THE VERY LOW-LEVEL APPROACH SUCCEEDED IN TAKING THE MAIN DEFENCES COMPLETELY BY SURPRISE. LUCKILY THE NAVIGATOR, SERGEANT ANDY WHITTON, HAD A GOOD STOMACH FOR THIS SORT OF FLYING.

IN A SINGLE SWOOP FREDDY HAD TAKEN OUT MOST OF THE GERMAN HEAVY ANTI-AIRCRAFT GUNS AND HAD CLEARED A PATH FOR THE PLANES FOLLOWING.

THE SQUADRON-LEADER'S LAID THIS LOT OUT ON A PLATE FOR US. DOES HE ALWAYS TAKE ALL THE RISKS, GEORDIE?

THAT'S THE WAY HE IS. HE NEVER ASKS ANYONE TO DO ANYTHING HE CAN'T DO HIMSELF.

THE ATTACK WAS A COMPLETE SUCCESS. FRANK PULLED BACK THE STICK TO REJOIN THE REST.

JUST CROSSING ALLIED LINES, SKIPPER.

THANKS, GEORDIE. NOW WE CAN RELAX AND ENJOY THE VIEW.

FRANK HAD HARDLY SPOKEN WHEN HIS BEAU WAS BUFFETTED BY ANTI-AIRCRAFT FIRE.

WHAT THE BLAZES?

THE CULPRITS TURNED OUT TO BE SOME TRIGGER-HAPPY AMERICAN GUNNERS WHO HAD MISTAKEN THE BEAUFIGHTERS FOR JUNKERS EIGHTY-EIGHTS. EVEN AS FRANK STRUGGLED TO REGAIN CONTROL, THE YOUNG AMERICAN OFFICER IN COMMAND, CAPTAIN FORD NIXON, FRANTICALLY CALLED A HALT.

CEASE FIRE, YOU NUMBSKULLS! THOSE ARE LIMEY PLANES!

IT WAS JUST ANOTHER ACCIDENT OF WAR, BUT AS FRANK GRADUALLY REGAINED HEIGHT, HE WAS STARTLED TO SEE FREDDY'S PLANE HURTLE DOWN.

WHERE THE DEVIL'S HE GOING?

TO FRANK'S AMAZEMENT, THE C.O. SWEPT LOW AND UNLEASHED A BURST OF CANNON FIRE WHICH SENT THE ERRANT GUNNERS DIVING FOR COVER.

THOUGH FREDDY HAD DELIBERATELY SHOT WIDE TO AVOID CAUSING ANY CASUALTIES, HE LEFT ONE VERY ANGRY AMERICAN OFFICER TO PICK HIMSELF UP FROM THE MUD.

BACK AT BASE, FRANK AND GEORDIE EXAMINED THE DAMAGE DONE BY THE AMERICANS AND REALISED HOW LUCKY THEY HAD BOTH BEEN.

A COUPLE OF FEET TO THE LEFT OR RIGHT AND WE'D BE A NEW HOLE IN THE LANDSCAPE RIGHT NOW.

EVEN SO, I NEVER EXPECTED FREDDY TO REACT SO FEROCIOUSLY.

HOWEVER, WHEN FRANK SUGGESTED TO FREDDY THAT HIS REACTION MIGHT HAVE BEEN A BIT EXTREME, HE RECEIVED A SHARP RETORT.

WHEN YOU'VE BEEN HERE AS LONG AS I HAVE, YOU GET SICK TO DEATH OF THE WAY THE YANKS TRY AND BLAST EVERYTHING OUT OF THE SKY. AND WHEN IT'S ONE OF MY BEAUS ON THE RECEIVING END, I DON'T LIKE IT ONE LITTLE BIT!

NEXT DAY AN ANGRY VISITOR ARRIVED IN THE SHAPE OF CAPTAIN FORD NIXON FROM THE GUN SITE. FRANK DIDN'T NEED THREE GUESSES TO REALISE WHO HE WAS.

HEY, YOU, WHERE'S THE GUY IN CHARGE? I'VE GOT A FEW THINGS TO SAY TO HIM!

OH-OH, LOOKS LIKE TROUBLE'S ARRIVED.

SOON ALMOST EVERYBODY WAS AWARE OF THE AMERICAN'S ARRIVAL, BUT FREDDY, LOUNGING OUTSIDE HIS OFFICE, SEEMED TO TAKE ABSOLUTELY NO NOTICE.

SQUADRON-LEADER, MIND TELLING ME WHICH OF YOUR MEN FLIES A BEAUFIGHTER WITH THE LETTERS B.T.?

AS A MATTER OF FACT, OLD CHAP, IT HAPPENS TO BE ME.

SUDDENLY FREDDY WAS ON HIS FEET, JABBING THE STARTLED YOUNG OFFICER IN THE CHEST IN A VERY MENACING FASHION.

AND BEFORE YOU ASK, I'M ALSO THE ONE WHO SHOT YOU UP YESTERDAY. AND NEXT TIME I'LL NOT MISS — YOU COULD HAVE KILLED ONE OF MY CREWS!

I . . . I . . . I GUESS WE NEARLY DID. OKAY, I CAN SEE WHY YOU GOT SO MAD AT US.

IN THE FACE OF THIS ACCUSATION, FORD NIXON'S BRAVADO COLLAPSED. HE WAS, AFTER ALL, VERY YOUNG AND INEXPERIENCED, AS WERE THE MEN HE COMMANDED.

A MISTAKE ON OUR PART COULD EASILY MEAN DISASTER. I'M REALLY SORRY. IT WON'T HAPPEN AGAIN.

IN THAT CASE I WON'T BE FIRING ANY ROCKETS AT YOU. BY THE WAY, CALL ME FREDDY.

BY THE TIME THE AMERICAN LEFT, IT WAS AS IF HE AND
FREDDY WERE OLD FRIENDS. AGAIN, FRANK WAS IMPRESSED BY
THE SQUADRON-LEADER'S TALENT FOR WINNING PEOPLE OVER.

I'LL KEEP IN TOUCH — AND I'LL SEE ABOUT GETTING YOU AND YOUR BOYS SOME EXTRA RATIONS.

VERY GENEROUS OF YOU. WE'LL LOOK FORWARD TO IT.

FREDDY COULD EVEN TALK A STARVING LION OUT OF EATING HIM.

A FEW DAYS LATER THE SQUADRON WAS MOVED NORTH
TO A RECENTLY CAPTURED AIRFIELD. FREDDY LED THE
PLANES IN OVER A LARGE VILLA ON THE PERIMETER.

LOOK AT THAT PILE DOWN THERE, LADS. WHAT SAY WE BAG IT FOR OUR BILLETS?

SOUNDS GREAT.

ON THE GROUND, HOWEVER, THE R.A.F. BILLETING OFFICER HAD SOME BAD NEWS.

I'M AFRAID THE ARMY'S ALREADY REQUISITIONED THE VILLA AS A BRIGADE H.Q., SIR. WE'VE BEEN ALLOCATED THIS EX-PRISON CAMP.

LET'S TAKE A LOOK INSIDE, SHALL WE?

IF ANYTHING, THE INTERIORS OF THE HUTS WERE EVEN WORSE THAN THE OUTSIDE.

HECK, IT'S CRAWLING WITH FLEAS!

ER — WE'VE BEEN PROMISED DISINFECTANTS AND NEW MATTRESSES . . .

IGNORING THE FEEBLE PROTESTS OF THE BILLETING OFFICER, FREDDY ROARED UP TO THE VILLA WHERE A FEW SOLDIERS WERE ALREADY UNPACKING CRATES.

YES, THIS WILL DO NICELY. TELL THE PONGOES TO PACK UP AGAIN AND GET LOST!

BUT . . . BUT, SIR . . .

THE SOLDIERS WERE SENSIBLE ENOUGH TO TAKE THE HINT AND RETIRE GRACEFULLY, BUT WITHIN THE HOUR AN IRATE ARMY STAFF COLONEL APPEARED.

HOW DARE YOU THROW MY MEN OUT? I WANT YOU TO MOVE RIGHT NOW — YOU'VE ALREADY BEEN ALLOCATED SUITABLE ACCOMMODATION.

OH, REALLY. IS THAT WHAT YOU CALL IT?

COLONEL REGINALD ROE, AS POMPOUS AS HE WAS ANNOYING, TURNED PALE AS FREDDY, WITH A SNARL, POINTED DOWN TO THE CAMP.

IF YOU THINK A BUNCH OF DESK-JOCKEYS ARE GOING TO LORD IT UP HERE WHILE MY MEN LIVE IN THOSE SQUALID SLUMS, YOU CAN THINK AGAIN.

SO YOU REFUSE TO MOVE? WE'LL SEE ABOUT THAT, MISTER BUNBURY!

LATER, A BAD-TEMPERED R.A.F. STAFF OFFICER ARRIVED. ROE HAD FRIENDS IN HIGH PLACES, AND THE NEW ORDERS BROUGHT BY GROUP-CAPTAIN IAIN CLITHERS WERE FIRM.

THE BRASS HAS COME DOWN LIKE A TON OF BRICKS. YOU'RE TO MOVE POST-HASTE.

I'M SORRY, SIR, BUT SUCH CONDITIONS WILL EFFECT MY MEN'S FLYING. I SHALL BE FORCED TO DECLARE MY ENTIRE SQUADRON NON-OPERATIONAL!

IT WAS THE RIGHT OF ANY SQUADRON COMMANDER TO MAKE SUCH A DECLARATION, PROVIDED HE WAS PREPARED TO BACK UP HIS DECISION. FREDDY AND CLITHERS HAD NEVER GOT ON — AND IT SHOWED.

I SHALL, OF COURSE, DEFEND ALL THIS BEFORE A COURT OF ENQUIRY IF NEED BE. IN THE MEANTIME, HOWEVER, MY SQUADRON REMAINS GROUNDED!

YOU'LL PUSH YOUR LUCK TOO FAR ONE OF THESE DAYS! VERY WELL, I SHALL RELAY YOUR DECISION TO H.Q.

IN THE END, ANOTHER RECENTLY CAPTURED AIRFIELD, THIS TIME WITH ACCEPTABLE ACCOMMODATION, WAS FOUND. NEXT MORNING, HOWEVER, AS THEY WAITED TO FLY OUT, FREDDY DISAPPEARED FOR A FEW HOURS.

HERE HE COMES AT LAST.

AYE, BUT WHAT'S HE BRINGING WITH HIM IN THOSE TRUCKS?

FREDDY TOLD FRANK TO JOIN HIM, AND THE MYSTERIOUS CONVOY HEADED UP TO THE VILLA, WHICH WAS EMPTY, WAITING THE ARMY'S RETURN.

I DON'T UNDERSTAND, SIR. WHAT'S GOING ON?

JUST A LITTLE SURPRISE I'VE FIXED UP FOR THE PONGOES. YOU'LL SEE.

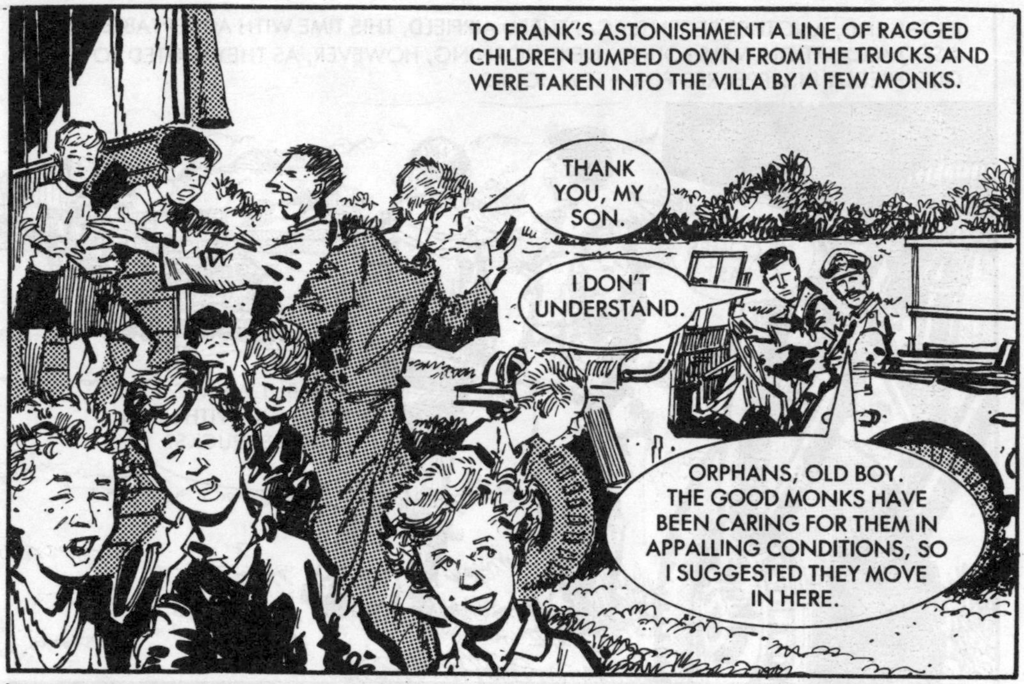
TO FRANK'S ASTONISHMENT A LINE OF RAGGED CHILDREN JUMPED DOWN FROM THE TRUCKS AND WERE TAKEN INTO THE VILLA BY A FEW MONKS.
THANK YOU, MY SON.
I DON'T UNDERSTAND.
ORPHANS, OLD BOY. THE GOOD MONKS HAVE BEEN CARING FOR THEM IN APPALLING CONDITIONS, SO I SUGGESTED THEY MOVE IN HERE.

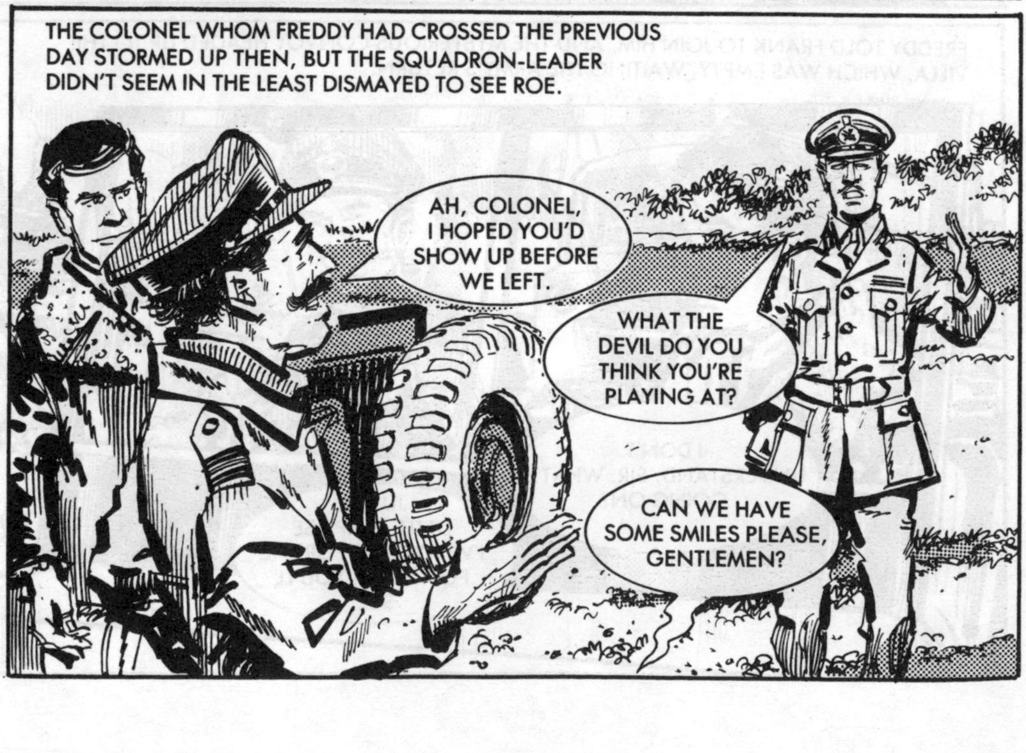
THE COLONEL WHOM FREDDY HAD CROSSED THE PREVIOUS DAY STORMED UP THEN, BUT THE SQUADRON-LEADER DIDN'T SEEM IN THE LEAST DISMAYED TO SEE ROE.
AH, COLONEL, I HOPED YOU'D SHOW UP BEFORE WE LEFT.
WHAT THE DEVIL DO YOU THINK YOU'RE PLAYING AT?
CAN WE HAVE SOME SMILES PLEASE, GENTLEMEN?

FRANK SUDDENLY REALISED THAT FREDDY HAD BROUGHT MORE THAN JUST THE ORPHANS AND THEIR GUARDIANS ALONG.

PRESS? WHAT THE BLAZES ARE THEY DOING HERE?

OH, THEY'VE COME TO RECORD THE ARMY'S GENEROUS ACT — GIVING UP A LUXURY VILLA FOR POOR ORPHANS.

GOOD LORD, FREDDY'S STUMPED 'EM GOOD AND PROPER!

WITH THE STORY ALREADY CLEARED FOR PUBLICATION, IT WAS IMPOSSIBLE FOR THE ARMY TO BE SEEN TO GO BACK ON ITS OFFER, EVEN IF IT HAD BEEN MADE FOR THEM BY FREDDY.

BUT . . . BUT WHAT ARE WE GOING TO DO FOR A STAFF H.Q.?

SOME NICE EMPTY BARRACKS DOWN THERE. A GOOD FUMIGATING AND THEY'LL BE LIKE HOME FROM HOME. BYE.

FREDDY SHOT OFF, ALL BUT RUNNING OVER THE FEET OF THE FURIOUS ROE.

DURING THE FLIGHT TO THE NEW AIRFIELD, FRANK TOLD GEORDIE ALL ABOUT IT, BUT HIS NAVIGATOR SOUNDED A NOTE OF CAUTION.

HIS NAVIGATOR ANDY WAS SAYING THAT HE'S MADE A LOT OF POWERFUL ENEMIES AT H.Q. — IF HE DOESN'T WATCH HIS STEP, HE COULD BE IN REAL TROUBLE.

GEORDIE'S RIGHT. I HADN'T THOUGHT OF THAT.

NOT THAT THERE WAS MUCH TIME TO WORRY. THE NEXT DAY SAW THE START OF A SERIES OF HARD-HITTING MISSIONS AGAINST GERMAN COASTAL SHIPPING AMONG THE ISLANDS OFF THE COAST OF YUGOSLAVIA.

LET'S HIT 'EM!

GERMAN GUNNERS ON A NEARBY ISLAND OPENED UP WITH EVERYTHING THEY HAD AND CAUGHT ONE OF THE ATTACKING BEAUS IN A HAIL OF FLAK.

THAT'S SCOTTIE MACLEOD'S CRATE!

AS FRANK WATCHED ANXIOUSLY, TWO FIGURES BALED OUT.

THEY'VE BOTH GOT CLEAR, BUT THIS CLOSE TO OCCUPIED TERRITORY MEANS THEY'RE BOUND TO END UP IN A P.O.W. CAGE.

COMMANDER TO GREEN FLIGHT LEADER, TAKE THE REST OF 'EM HOME. ANDY WILL CALL UP AIR-SEA RESCUE AND WE'LL KEEP THOSE LADS COVERED UNTIL THEY GET HERE.

FRANK PROTESTED VIGOROUSLY AS HE REALISED WHAT FREDDY INTENDED TO DO.

IT'LL TAKE AIR-SEA RESCUE AN HOUR TO GET HERE. YOU WON'T HAVE THE FUEL FOR THAT.

I'LL STRETCH IT OUT. NOW GET LOST— THAT'S AN ORDER.

RELUCTANTLY FRANK OBEYED, BUT THE MOMENT HE TOUCHED DOWN, HE ORDERED AN EMERGENCY REFUELLING.

GET A MOVE ON, I HAVEN'T GOT ALL DAY!

A FEW MINUTES LATER FRANK'S PLANE WAS STREAKING BACK ACROSS THE ADRIATIC WHERE THEY AT LAST CAUGHT SIGHT OF A FAST LAUNCH.

THERE'S THE RESCUE LAUNCH, GEORDIE. IT SHOULD BE ON THE SCENE IN A FEW MINUTES.

AYE, BUT WHAT'S FEARLESS FREDDY FLYING ON RIGHT NOW? AIR?

AMAZINGLY FREDDY WAS STILL AIRBORNE. NOT ONLY THAT, HE WAS DEALING WITH A GERMAN E-BOAT TO ENSURE THAT HIS TWO DOWNED MEN STAYED FREE LONG ENOUGH TO BE RESCUED.

PUSH OFF, FRITZ!

EVEN AS FREDDY BROKE OFF HIS ATTACK ON THE CRAFT, A DIVING FOCKE-WULF 190 SENT DEBRIS FLYING FROM HIS PLANE.

WE'RE GETTING PASTED, ANDY — HOLD ON TIGHT!

A NEW COMPETITOR ENTERED THE RING THEN, IN THE AVENGING SHAPE OF FRANK'S BEAUFIGHTER, ITS NOSE CANNONS BLASTING THE ONE-NINETY TO OBLIVION.

FREDDY WAS UNSTINTING IN HIS PRAISE FOR FRANK'S ACTION, BUT THIS TIME IT WAS THE SQUADRON-LEADER WHO GOT HIS MARCHING ORDERS.

AS SOON AS THE DITCHED MEN HAD BEEN PICKED UP, FRANK TURNED FOR HOME, AND SOON CAUGHT UP WITH FREDDY.

HE'S TRYING FOR MAXIMUM FUEL ECONOMY, GEORDIE.

I'M AMAZED HE'S GOT ANY LEFT.

SUDDENLY THE OTHER BEAU STARTED TO GAIN HEIGHT. PUZZLED, FRANK MOVED CLEAR, THEN HE REALISED WHAT FREDDY WAS DOING.

HE'S ABOUT TO RUN OUT OF FUEL AND HE'S GOING FOR ALL THE HEIGHT HE CAN GET IN ORDER TO GLIDE!

MOMENTS LATER A FEW LAST PUFFS OF EXHAUST FROM FREDDY'S ENGINES PROVED FRANK'S POINT.

HE'S OUT OF JUICE AND IT'S STILL A COUPLE OF MILES TO LAND. SURELY HE AND ANDY SHOULD BALE OUT NOW, WHILE THEY'VE STILL GOT THE HEIGHT.

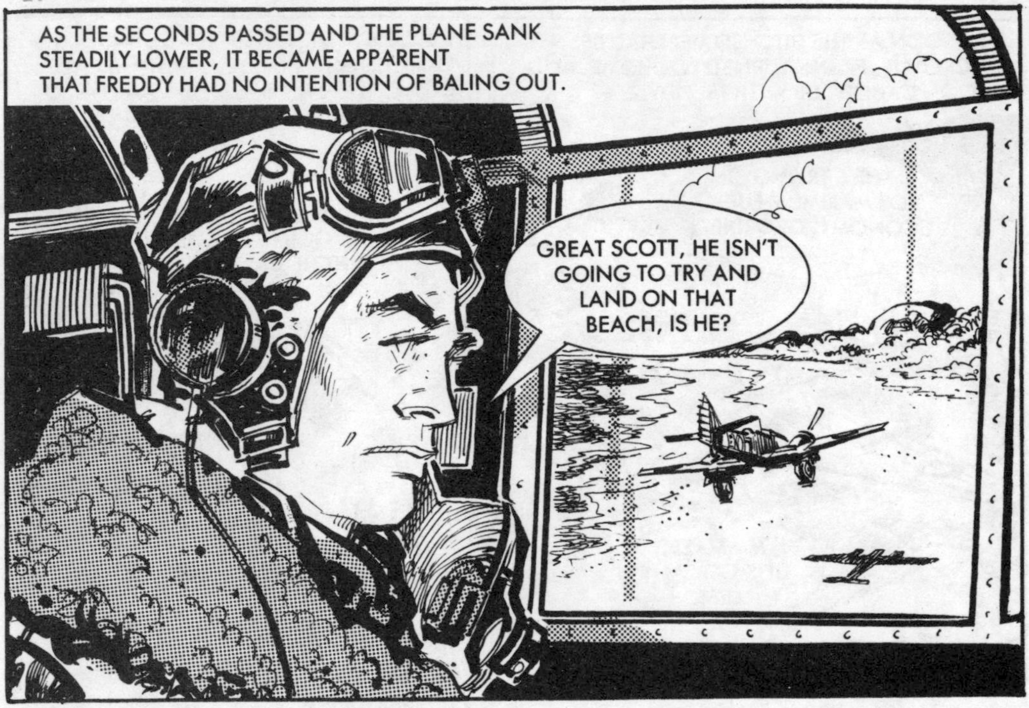
AS THE SECONDS PASSED AND THE PLANE SANK STEADILY LOWER, IT BECAME APPARENT THAT FREDDY HAD NO INTENTION OF BALING OUT.
GREAT SCOTT, HE ISN'T GOING TO TRY AND LAND ON THAT BEACH, IS HE?

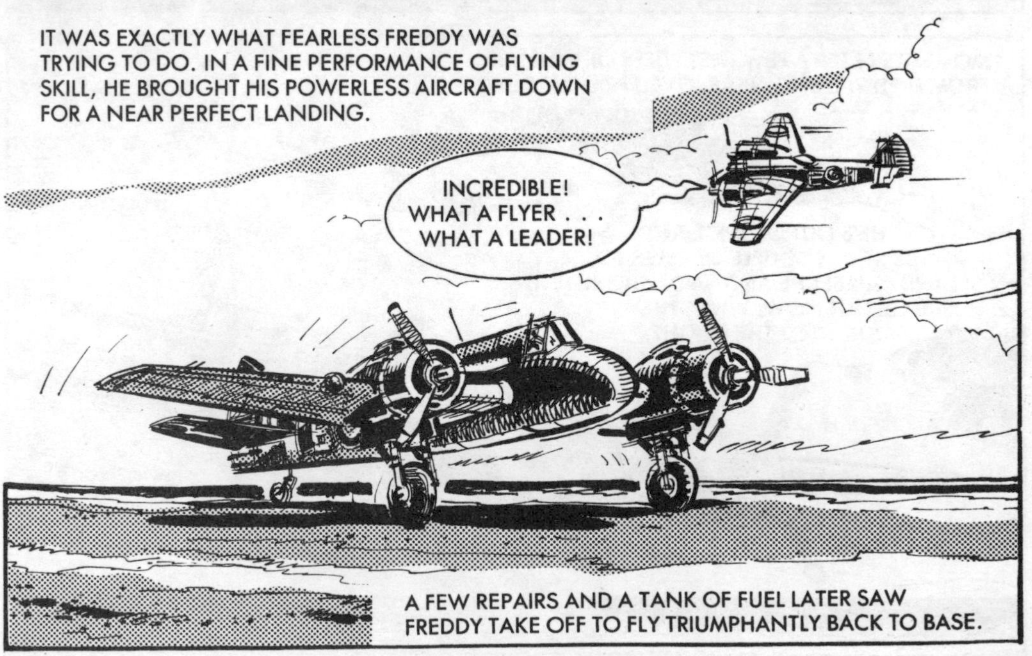
IT WAS EXACTLY WHAT FEARLESS FREDDY WAS TRYING TO DO. IN A FINE PERFORMANCE OF FLYING SKILL, HE BROUGHT HIS POWERLESS AIRCRAFT DOWN FOR A NEAR PERFECT LANDING.
INCREDIBLE! WHAT A FLYER . . . WHAT A LEADER!
A FEW REPAIRS AND A TANK OF FUEL LATER SAW FREDDY TAKE OFF TO FLY TRIUMPHANTLY BACK TO BASE.

AS THE WEATHER WORSENED, FREDDY INDULGED IN ANOTHER HABIT THAT WAS OFFICIALLY FROWNED UPON — FLYING SOLO MISSIONS IN BAD WEATHER, LOOKING FOR TARGETS OF OPPORTUNITY. FRANK WANTED TO GO, BUT FREDDY SAID NO.

HE SAYS HE ISN'T PREPARED TO RISK ANOTHER CREW, BUT IT MIGHT BE BETTER IF HE DIDN'T GO AT ALL. H.Q. DON'T LIKE SOLO MISSIONS.

AYE, BUT THEY DON'T COMPLAIN EITHER WHEN HE COMES BACK AFTER BAGGING A JERRY CONVOY OR TWO.

IT WASN'T ONLY CONVOYS WHICH WERE ON THE RECEIVING END. THE LUFTWAFFE ALSO FELL VICTIM TO HIS SURPRISE ATTACKS IN WEATHER WHICH WOULD HAVE GROUNDED LESSER PILOTS.

DONNER UND BLITZEN!

BEFORE LONG, FREDDY'S REGULAR ONSLAUGHTS HAD MADE HIM A MARKED MAN IN THE ENEMY CAMP.

A LONE BEAUFIGHTER, HERR OBERST. ITS IDENTIFICATION LETTERS WERE B.T. — THE SAME AS THE AIRCRAFT WHICH ATTACKED US A FEW DAYS AGO.

SO, THIS SQUADRON-LEADER BUNBURY IS BECOMING A THORN IN OUR SIDE.

TO COLONEL HERTZOG, THE GERMAN AIR COMMANDER IN THIS SECTOR, FREDDY'S RAMPAGES WERE BECOMING MORE THAN A NUISANCE. THE IDENTITY OF THE PILOT HAD BEEN GLEANED BY LUFTWAFFE INTELLIGENCE.

IT WOULD BE PLEASANT TO SEE HIM SHOT DOWN, BUT HE IS TOO GOOD A FLYER FOR ME TO BANK ON THAT. HOWEVER, ONE WAY OR ANOTHER, I WANT THIS MAN GROUNDED . . . PERMANENTLY!

MEANWHILE, ON THE GROUND, THE SLOGGING MATCH BETWEEN THE ALLIED AND GERMAN ARMIES CONTINUED FIERCELY. FOR THE COLONEL IN CHARGE OF ONE EMBATTLED GERMAN UNIT, THE FUTURE LOOKED BLEAK.

OUR LINE OF RETREAT IS CUT OFF, HERR GENERAL. YOU MUST ALLOW ME TO SURRENDER. TO HOLD OUT ANY LONGER IS A FUTILE WASTE OF LIVES.

THE FUHRER HAS ORDERED NO SURRENDER! HOLD OUT UNTIL A RELIEF FORCE BREAKS THROUGH — THAT IS AN ORDER!

WEARILY THE COLONEL LOOKED OUT OF HIS BUNKER, PAST WHICH THE DEAD AND WOUNDED WERE BEING CONSTANTLY CARRIED.

I WILL NOT TOLERATE THIS USELESS CARNAGE ANY LONGER. I MUST CONTACT THE ENEMY COMMANDER.

THE GERMAN COMMANDER DID JUST THIS UNDER A FLAG OF TRUCE. THE DETAILS OF A SURRENDER WERE THRASHED OUT WITH HIS BRITISH OPPOSITE NUMBER.

THEY'VE A LOT OF WOUNDED, SIR. THEIR C.O. WANTS THEM PROPERLY CARED FOR.

ARRANGE FOR AMBULANCES AND MEDICS TO BE BROUGHT FORWARD IMMEDIATELY. THERE'S NO WORRY ABOUT AIR ATTACKS IN THIS WEATHER.

AT THE SAME TIME HERTZOG WAS VISITING GERMAN ARMY H.Q. ON A LIAISON MISSION AND FOUND THE PLACE BUZZING WITH ACTIVITY.

ONE OF OUR FRONT-LINE UNITS HAS SURRENDERED WITHOUT PERMISSION, HERR OBERST. THE GENERAL'S HOPPING MAD.

IS HE NOW? PERHAPS I SHOULD HAVE A WORD WITH HIM.

HERTZOG HAD BEEN TOYING WITH A VERY SPECIAL IDEA FOR SOME TIME. THE GENERAL, FURIOUS AT THE UNAUTHORISED SURRENDER, WAS OPEN TO SUGGESTIONS.

IF WE CAN PULL IT OFF, IT WILL BENEFIT BOTH THE WEHRMACHT AND THE LUFTWAFFE. EVEN THE WEATHER IS PERFECT.

IT'S A GOOD IDEA, HERTZOG. WHATEVER HAPPENS, WE CAN'T LOSE. I'LL CONTACT YOUR H.Q. TO CLEAR YOUR WAY.

THE SAME FOUL WEATHER HAD ALSO BLANKETED THE BEAUFIGHTER BASE, BUT IT WASN'T GOING TO STOP FREDDY EMBARKING ON ANOTHER SOLO MISSION, IN SPITE OF FRANK'S PLEAS.

YOU CAN'T GO UP IN THIS SOUP, SIR. YOU WON'T SEE PAST YOUR NOSE.

JUST THE SORT OF WEATHER JERRY THINKS IT'S SAFE TO MOVE IN, FRANK. DON'T WORRY, I KNOW WHAT I'M DOING.

IT WASN'T FEARLESS FREDDY'S FLYING THAT FRANK WAS WORRIED ABOUT. IT WAS JUST A STRANGE FEELING THAT HIS SQUADRON-LEADER WAS ABOUT TO RUN OUT OF LUCK.

JUST COME BACK SAFELY, THAT'S ALL I ASK. THE SQUADRON NEEDS YOU.

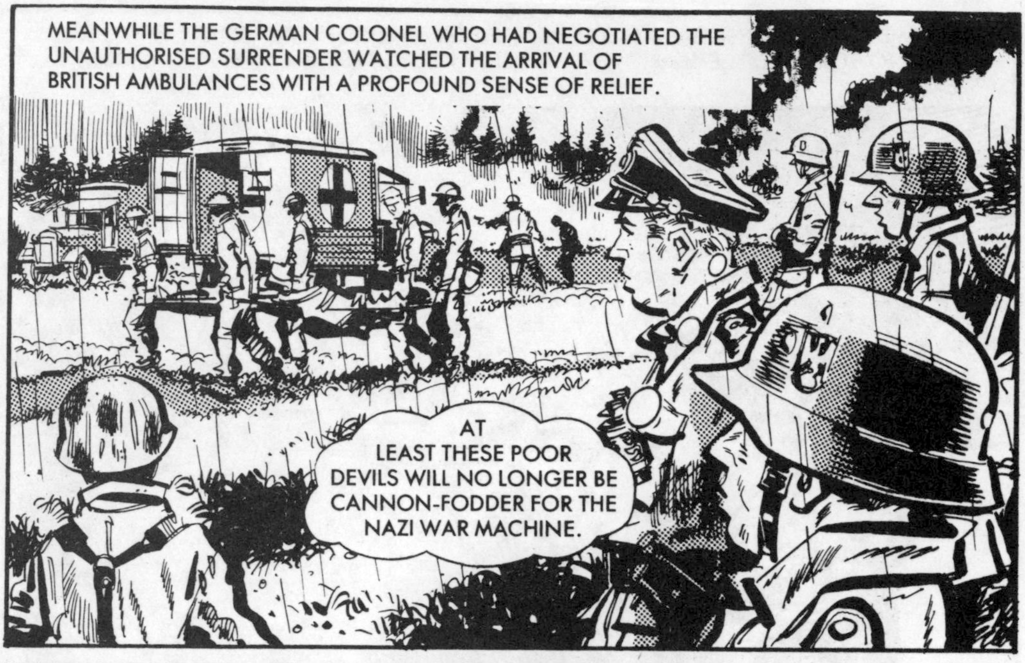
MEANWHILE THE GERMAN COLONEL WHO HAD NEGOTIATED THE UNAUTHORISED SURRENDER WATCHED THE ARRIVAL OF BRITISH AMBULANCES WITH A PROFOUND SENSE OF RELIEF.
AT LEAST THESE POOR DEVILS WILL NO LONGER BE CANNON-FODDER FOR THE NAZI WAR MACHINE.

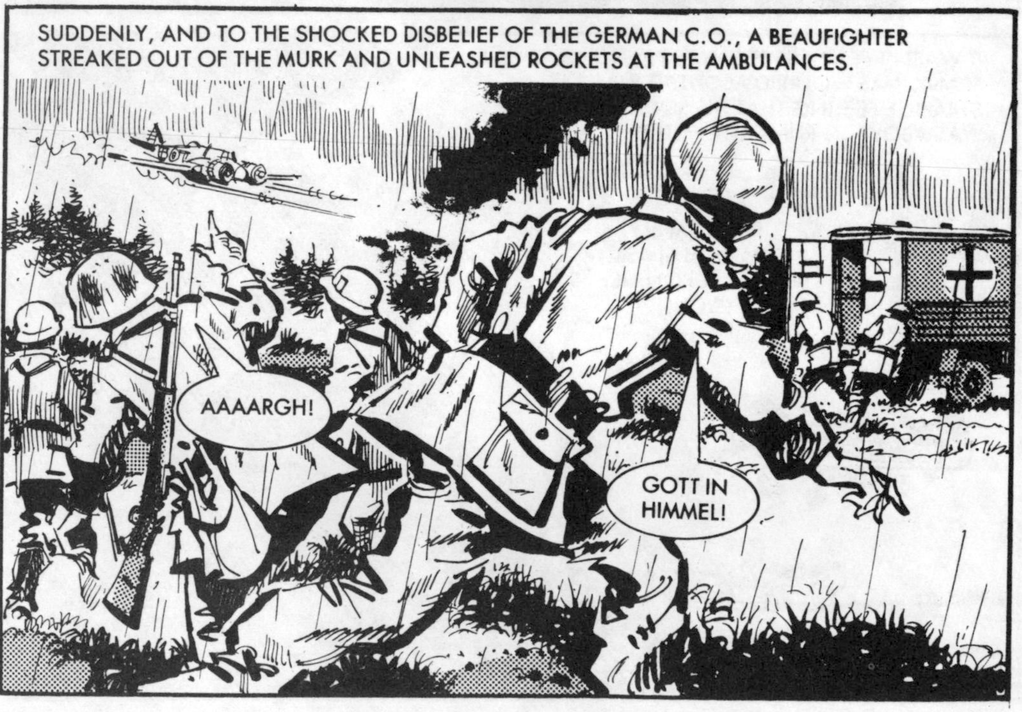
SUDDENLY, AND TO THE SHOCKED DISBELIEF OF THE GERMAN C.O., A BEAUFIGHTER STREAKED OUT OF THE MURK AND UNLEASHED ROCKETS AT THE AMBULANCES.
AAAARGH!
GOTT IN HIMMEL!

THE BRITISH COMMANDER WAS EQUALLY HORRIFIED.

BRING ALL GUNS TO BEAR ON THAT LUNATIC! BLOW HIM OUT OF THE SKY!

EVERY BRITISH GUN THAT COULD BE USED IN AN ANTI-AIRCRAFT ROLE . . .

. . . WAS BROUGHT TO BEAR ON THE ROGUE BEAU.

ALMOST MIRACULOUSLY THE AIRCRAFT ESCAPED DESTRUCTION, THOUGH NOT WITHOUT SUSTAINING SOME DAMAGE.

IT'S FLYING OFF, SIR — BUT WE GOT A LOOK AT THE IDENTIFICATION LETTERS. THEY WERE B.T.

SOMEBODY'S GOING TO ANSWER FOR THIS.

A LITTLE LATER, FREDDY RETURNED TO BASE, CALLING AHEAD BY RADIO TO REPORT THAT ANDY HAD BEEN INJURED. ANXIOUSLY, FRANK AND GEORDIE DROVE OUT TO MEET HIM.

HE'S CERTAINLY BEEN SHOT UP, BUT HE CAN STILL BRING HER DOWN LIKE A FEATHER.

LOOKS LIKE MY PREMONITION WAS HALF RIGHT. I HOPE ANDY ISN'T TOO BADLY HURT.

ANDY WAS CARRIED AWAY UNCONSCIOUS AS FREDDY TOLD FRANK HE HAD SPOTTED A FEW JERRY TRUCKS MOVING SOUTH THROUGH THE RAIN — BUT NOT A CAMOUFLAGED FLAK POSITION.

I NEVER KNEW IT WAS THERE UNTIL IT BLASTED US. I SHOULD'VE TAKEN YOUR ADVICE, AND STAYED ON THE GROUND.

YOU DID WHAT YOU THOUGHT BEST, SIR. THESE THINGS HAPPEN.

WHAT MIGHT HAVE BEEN WRITTEN OFF AS A BAD DAY TURNED ABRUPTLY INTO A DISASTROUS ONE WITH THE ARRIVAL OF GROUP-CAPTAIN CLITHERS AND SOME R.A.F. POLICE.

FRANK WAS APPALLED TO LEARN THAT FREDDY WAS BEING ACCUSED OF MOUNTING A MURDEROUS ATTACK ON AMBULANCES COLLECTING WOUNDED. ALL PROTESTATIONS OF INNOCENCE WERE IN VAIN.

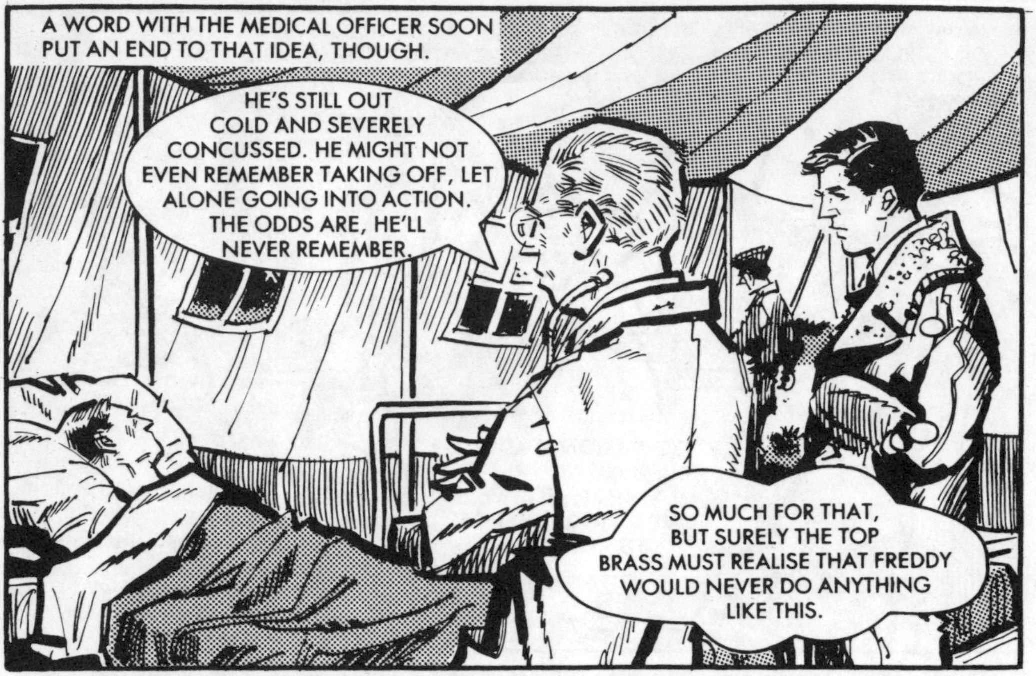
A WORD WITH THE MEDICAL OFFICER SOON PUT AN END TO THAT IDEA, THOUGH.
HE'S STILL OUT COLD AND SEVERELY CONCUSSED. HE MIGHT NOT EVEN REMEMBER TAKING OFF, LET ALONE GOING INTO ACTION. THE ODDS ARE, HE'LL NEVER REMEMBER.
SO MUCH FOR THAT, BUT SURELY THE TOP BRASS MUST REALISE THAT FREDDY WOULD NEVER DO ANYTHING LIKE THIS.

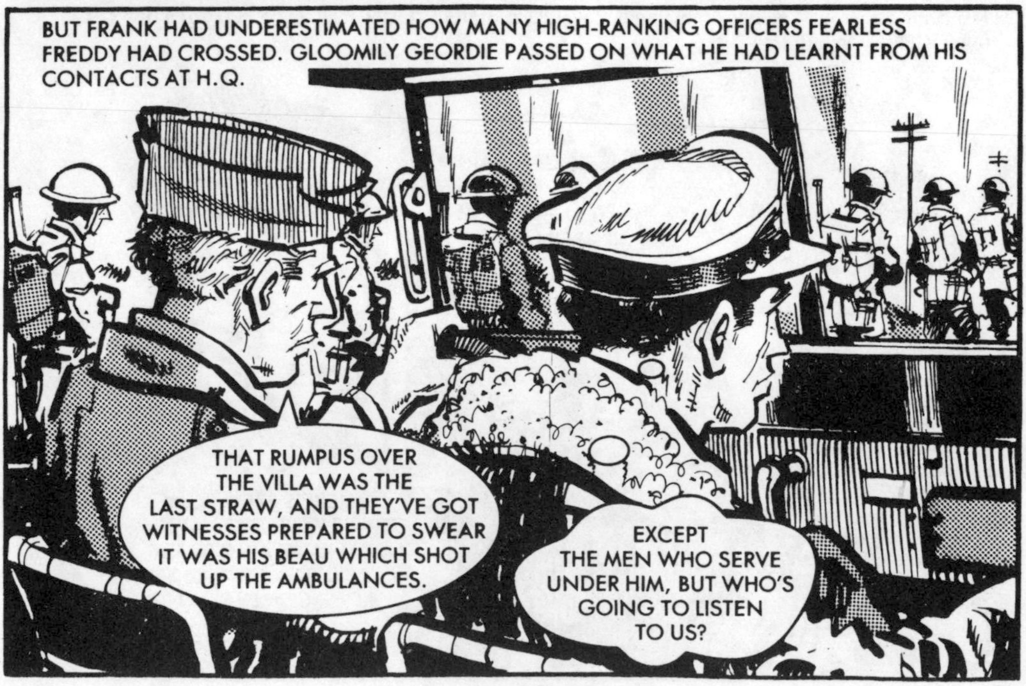
BUT FRANK HAD UNDERESTIMATED HOW MANY HIGH-RANKING OFFICERS FEARLESS FREDDY HAD CROSSED. GLOOMILY GEORDIE PASSED ON WHAT HE HAD LEARNT FROM HIS CONTACTS AT H.Q.
THAT RUMPUS OVER THE VILLA WAS THE LAST STRAW, AND THEY'VE GOT WITNESSES PREPARED TO SWEAR IT WAS HIS BEAU WHICH SHOT UP THE AMBULANCES.
EXCEPT THE MEN WHO SERVE UNDER HIM, BUT WHO'S GOING TO LISTEN TO US?

IT WAS INTO THIS DOOM-LADEN ATMOSPHERE THAT FORD NIXON, THE AMERICAN GUNNERY OFFICER, ARRIVED WITH THE GOODS HE HAD PROMISED.

HEY, FELLAS, BRIGHTEN UP. I'VE BROUGHT YOU THE EXTRA RATIONS I PROMISED TO YOUR SQUADRON-LEADER.

WITH A SIGH FRANK TRIED TO EXPLAIN, BUT BEFORE HE COULD SAY ANYTHING THE CAPTAIN PRATTLED ON MERRILY.

YOUR BOSS FLEW OVER US SO LOW YESTERDAY HE ALMOST TOOK OUR HELMETS OFF, BUT AT LEAST HE DIDN'T OPEN FIRE!

HE FLEW OVER YOU YESTERDAY? EXACTLY WHEN?

THE AMERICAN REPLIED UNHESITATINGLY, THE INCIDENT STILL FRESH IN HIS MIND.

HEY, CAP'N, IT'S THAT NUTTY LIMEY AGAIN.

PROBABLY REMINDING ME TO DELIVER THOSE RATIONS. IT'S JUST COMING UP TO FOUR O'CLOCK. SWITCH ON FORCES RADIO, ROSCOE, FOR THE BASEBALL RESULTS.

TO FORD'S ASTONISHMENT, FRANK PRACTICALLY DRAGGED HIM INTO THE BRIEFING ROOM AND SHOWED HIM SOME LARGE-SCALE MAPS.

YEAH, THIS IS WHERE WE ARE, ON THIS RIDGE. WHAT'S THIS ABOUT?

IT'S ABOUT SAVING THE BEST SQUADRON-LEADER EVER. AND IF YOU'RE RIGHT, WE'VE JUST TAKEN A BIG LEAP IN THE RIGHT DIRECTION.

AFTER THE AMERICAN HAD LEFT, FRANK EXPLAINED TO GEORDIE THAT FREDDY HAD LANDED AT THE BASE AT EXACTLY FOUR O'CLOCK — WHEN THE YANKS HAD CLAIMED HE HAD FLOWN OVER THEM.

. . . WHICH MEANS THE PLANE THEY SAW COULDN'T HAVE BEEN HIS!

FINE, SKIPPER, BUT WHAT ABOUT THE FACT THAT THE ONLY BEAU WITH THE LETTERS B.T. IS FREDDY'S?

FRANK ALREADY HAD A THEORY OF HIS OWN, THOUGH.

THERE MUST BE TWO BEAUS WITH THE LETTERS B.T.!

BUT THAT'S IMPOSSIBLE . . . HEY, WHERE ARE YOU GOING?

GEORDIE FOUND FRANK MAKING A PHONE CALL. APPARENTLY FIXING UP SOME SORT OF MEETING.

I'LL BE THERE IN AN HOUR WITH A FEW OF THE OTHER LADS AS WELL.

NOW WHAT?

"NOW WHAT" TURNED OUT TO BE A TRIP TO THE PHOTO-RECONNAISSANCE CENTRE, WHERE FRANK, GEORDIE, AND A FEW MATES WERE SHOWN INTO THE ARCHIVES SECTION BY A TUBBY FLYING OFFICER.

AUTHORISED PERSONNEL ONLY

THANKS FOR THIS, BILL.

ONLY TOO GLAD TO HELP, OLD BOY. RIGHT, THE COAST'S CLEAR, IN YOU GO.

BILL PERTWEE HAD SERVED UNDER FREDDY UNTIL HE HAD BEEN GROUNDED FOR MEDICAL REASONS. NOW HE WORKED IN PHOTO-RECONNAISSANCE EVALUATION, AND WAS QUITE PREPARED TO BREAK THE RULES FOR FREDDY'S SAKE.

THESE WERE ALL TAKEN IN THE LAST FEW MONTHS. WHAT EXACTLY ARE WE LOOKING FOR?

AN INTACT, OR RELATIVELY UNDAMAGED, BEAUFIGHTER IN GERMAN HANDS. IT'S THE ONLY LOGICAL EXPLANATION FOR THIS MYSTERY.

AIRCRAFT OF ALL TYPES WENT MISSING IN WAR. IT WAS NOT IMPOSSIBLE THAT AN INTACT BEAUFIGHTER MIGHT HAVE FALLEN INTO GERMAN HANDS. GEORDIE, HOWEVER, RAISED A STRONG POINT.

OF COURSE, IF IT WAS A JERRY-OPERATED PLANE, DOES THAT MEAN THEY SET OUT DELIBERATELY TO IMPERSONATE THE BOSS?

THEY'D HAVE GOOD REASON, GEORDIE. HE'S BEEN A THORN IN THEIR SIDE FOR A LONG TIME.

HOURS LATER FRANK'S OPTIMISM HAD EVAPORATED. THEY'D STUDIED HUNDREDS OF PICTURES WITHOUT ANY SIGN. WITH A SIGH, FRANK TRIED ANOTHER CUPBOARD.

WHAT'S THIS LOT, BILL?

PHOTOS OF LUFTWAFFE AIRFIELDS TAKEN FROM THE GROUND BY ITALIAN PARTISANS. THE QUALITY'S USUALLY SO BAD THEY'RE NEXT TO USELESS.

THE QUALITY WAS INDEED BAD AND IT SEEMED HOPELESS . . . UNTIL THE LAST FEW PICS WERE SCRUTINISED UNDER THE MAGNIFYING GLASS.

SKIPPER, TAKE A GANDER AT THIS.

IT'S A BEAU ALL RIGHT. BILL, WHERE WAS THIS TAKEN, AND WHEN?

BILL CHECKED THE CODED INFORMATION ON THE BACK OF THE PHOTOGRAPH AND TURNED TO A MAP.

IT'S A RESERVE AIRFIELD HERE. HARDLY USED AT ALL, WHICH IS WHY WE HAVEN'T BOTHERED WITH IT MUCH. THE PICTURE WAS TAKEN THREE WEEKS AGO.

SURELY WE'VE GOT ENOUGH EVIDENCE NOW TO SECURE FREDDY'S RELEASE.

ALREADY APPOINTED TEMPORARY SQUADRON-LEADER UNTIL MATTERS WERE SETTLED, FRANK HAD EVERY RIGHT TO VISIT FREDDY, WHO WAS BEING HELD IN SECURE QUARTERS AT THE LOCAL R.A.F. H.Q.

. . . AS SOON AS THIS IS PRESENTED IN EVIDENCE, THEY'LL HAVE TO LET YOU GO.

I AGREE IT COULD BE A BEAU, BUT SO WHAT? THIS WAS TAKEN WEEKS AGO, AND IT DOESN'T SHOW ANY IDENTIFICATION LETTERS.

FRANK TRIED TO PROTEST, BUT FREDDY CUT HIM SHORT. HE HAD DISCOVERED HE HAD MADE TOO MANY ENEMIES AMONG THE BRASS FOR THEM TO LET HIM GO EASILY.

BY ALL MEANS, SEE WHAT YOU CAN DO, BUT WHEN YOU'VE FAILED, COME BACK AND SEE ME AGAIN.

ACTUALLY, FRANK DIDN'T BELIEVE THINGS WERE THAT BAD, BUT HE QUICKLY LEARNT OTHERWISE WHEN HE WENT TO SEE CLITHERS.

A FUZZY PICTURE TAKEN WEEKS AGO AT A VIRTUALLY DISUSED AIRFIELD A HUNDRED MILES FROM THE FRONT? THAT WON'T DO AT ALL!

FREDDY'S RIGHT. THEY'RE NOT EVEN PREPARED TO GIVE HIM THE BENEFIT OF THE DOUBT.

THE GROUP CAPTAIN EVEN ADDED A FURTHER CUTTING REMARK TO THE EFFECT THAT FRANK WAS NOT AUTHORISED TO BE IN POSSESSION OF THE PICTURE.

THERE'S CLEARLY BEEN A BREACH OF SECURITY WHICH I WILL HAVE INVESTIGATED. YOUR SQUADRON-LEADER MIGHT NOT BE THE ONLY ONE IN TROUBLE!

NO WONDER FREDDY TROD ON SO MANY TOES. WHEN THEY BELONG TO CLOTS LIKE THIS, THEY DESERVE TO BE TRODDEN ON.

DEFEATED, FRANK WENT BACK TO REPORT TO FREDDY WHO DIDN'T SEEM IN THE LEAST DISMAYED BY IT.

I DON'T KNOW WHAT TO DO NOW.

THE ONLY THING THAT'S GOING TO GET ME OFF THE HOOK IS TO PRODUCE THE SECOND BEAU. TO DO THAT, YOU MUST HELP ME ESCAPE!

FRANK GASPED, BUT EVEN AS HE TRIED TO OBJECT, FEARLESS FREDDY WAS MOVING SMOOTHLY INTO ACTION, NO LONGER EVEN LISTENING.

HELP YOU ESCAPE, BUT . . .

OH, CORPORAL, THE FLIGHT-LIEUTENANT'S READY TO LEAVE NOW.

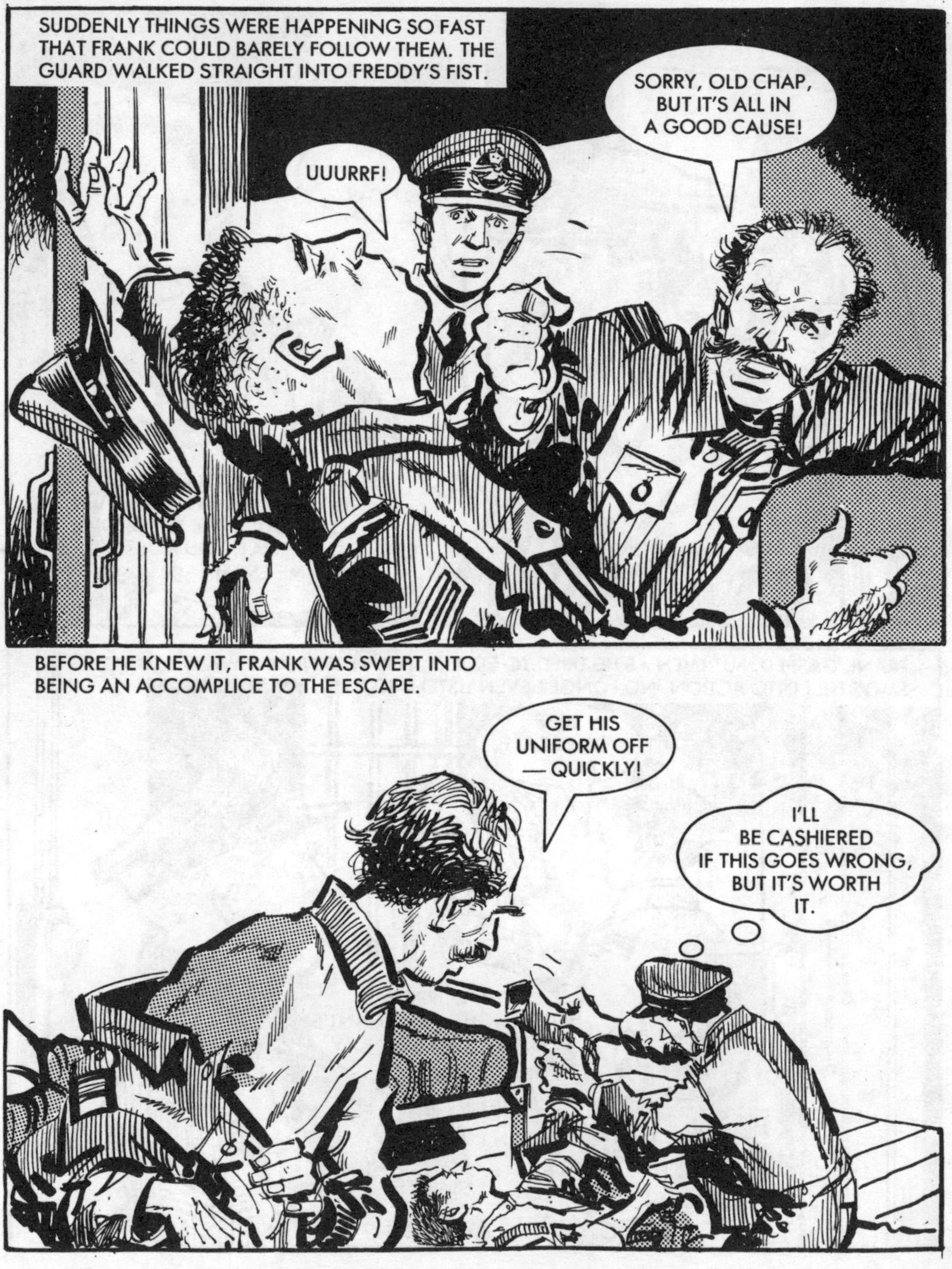
SUDDENLY THINGS WERE HAPPENING SO FAST THAT FRANK COULD BARELY FOLLOW THEM. THE GUARD WALKED STRAIGHT INTO FREDDY'S FIST.
UUURRF!
SORRY, OLD CHAP, BUT IT'S ALL IN A GOOD CAUSE!
BEFORE HE KNEW IT, FRANK WAS SWEPT INTO BEING AN ACCOMPLICE TO THE ESCAPE.
GET HIS UNIFORM OFF — QUICKLY!
I'LL BE CASHIERED IF THIS GOES WRONG, BUT IT'S WORTH IT.

A FEW MINUTES LATER THE TWO MEN CALMLY WALKED OUT, FREDDY IN THE SERVICE POLICEMAN'S UNIFORM. HOWEVER, THEIR LUCK RAN OUT.

HECK, ISN'T THAT . . . ?

THE PONGO WHO DIDN'T WANT TO LEAVE THE VILLA? AFRAID SO!

GOOD LORD, IT'S . . .

THERE WAS NO TIME TO WASTE. AS ONE, FREDDY AND FRANK ACTED, GENTLY BUT FIRMLY DUMPING ROE AND HIS DRIVER.

SORRY, SIR, BUT WE NEED YOUR CAR!

EH . . . WHAT?

BUT NOT THE DRIVER — OUT YOU COME, OLD CHAP!

A FRANTIC TEN-MINUTE DRIVE WHICH PROVED THAT FREDDY DROVE AS FEARLESSLY AS HE FLEW BROUGHT THEM TO THEIR AIRFIELD.

ROUND UP A COUPLE OF CREWS, FRANK. I'LL GET THE GROUND CREWS TO READY SOME KITES FOR TAKE-OFF.

THERE WAS NO SHORTAGE OF VOLUNTEERS WILLING TO TAKE CHANCES FOR THEIR BOSS. IN RECORD TIME FOUR PLANES WERE MADE READY, FRANK AT THE CONTROLS OF FREDDY'S USUAL PLANE, FREDDY ACTING AS NAVIGATOR.

FIRST — MAKE SURE THAT THE CAPTURED BEAU IS STILL AT THAT AIRFIELD. IF IT IS, WE'LL TAKE IT FROM THERE.

AND IF IT ISN'T, WE'LL ALL BE BREAKING ROCKS FOR THE REST OF THE WAR.

IN THE END THE BEAUFIGHTERS TOOK OFF JUST A FEW MOMENTS AHEAD OF THE ARRIVAL OF A FORMIDABLE FORCE OF R.A.F. POLICE.

STOP THOSE PLANES!

SHOUT LOUDER, THEY CAN'T HEAR YOU.

A HUNDRED MILES TO THE NORTH, AT THE RESERVE AIRFIELD, COLONEL HERTZOG WAS WELCOMING A VISITOR — THE RUTHLESS GENERAL WITH WHOM HE HAD PLOTTED.

GOOD OF YOU TO COME, HERR GENERAL.

I THOUGHT I'D LIKE TO TAKE A LOOK FOR MYSELF AT THIS PLANE OF YOURS WHICH DID SUCH STERLING WORK.

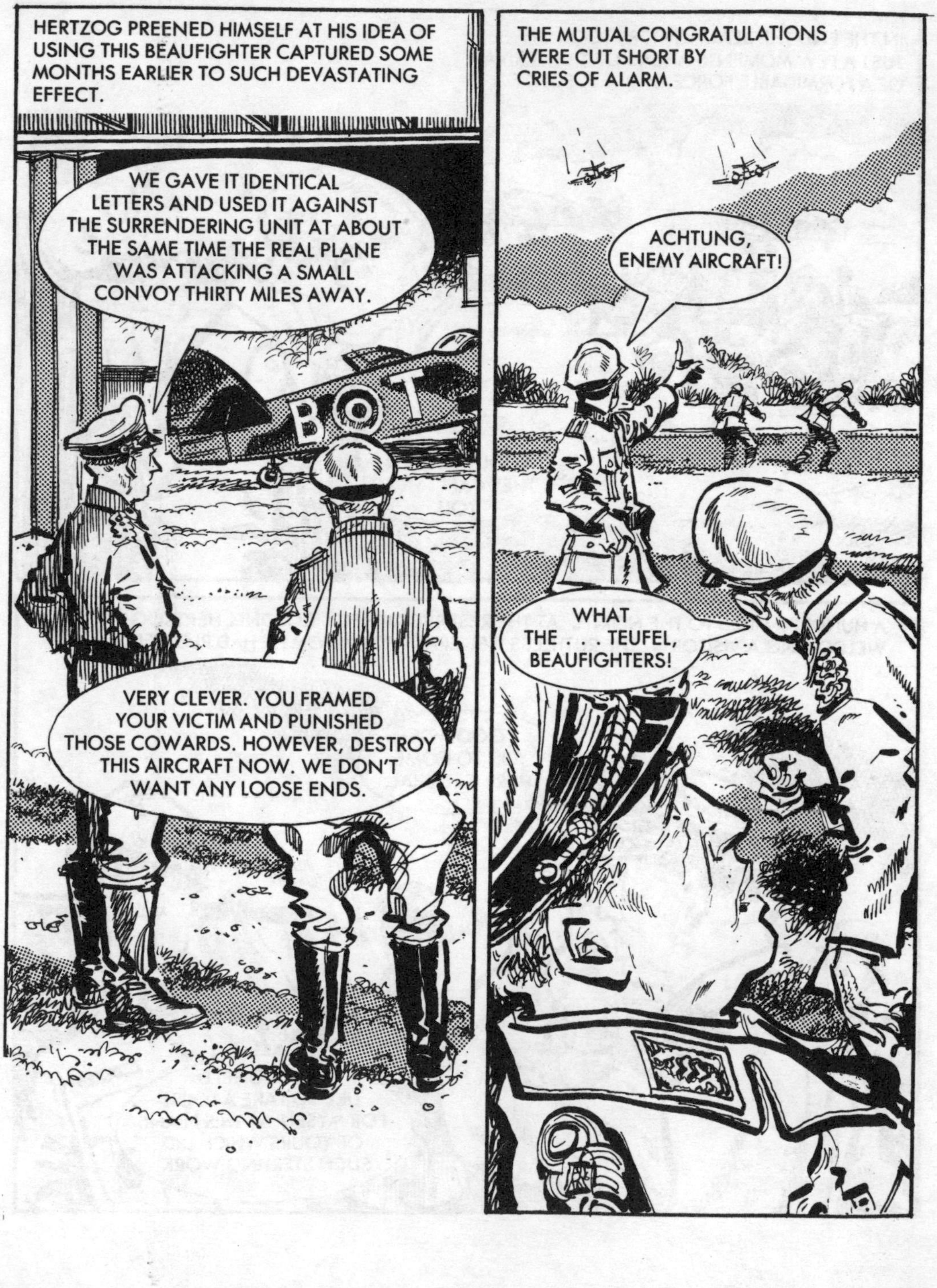
HERTZOG PREENED HIMSELF AT HIS IDEA OF USING THIS BEAUFIGHTER CAPTURED SOME MONTHS EARLIER TO SUCH DEVASTATING EFFECT.
WE GAVE IT IDENTICAL LETTERS AND USED IT AGAINST THE SURRENDERING UNIT AT ABOUT THE SAME TIME THE REAL PLANE WAS ATTACKING A SMALL CONVOY THIRTY MILES AWAY.
VERY CLEVER. YOU FRAMED YOUR VICTIM AND PUNISHED THOSE COWARDS. HOWEVER, DESTROY THIS AIRCRAFT NOW. WE DON'T WANT ANY LOOSE ENDS.
THE MUTUAL CONGRATULATIONS WERE CUT SHORT BY CRIES OF ALARM.
ACHTUNG, ENEMY AIRCRAFT!
WHAT THE . . . TEUFEL, BEAUFIGHTERS!

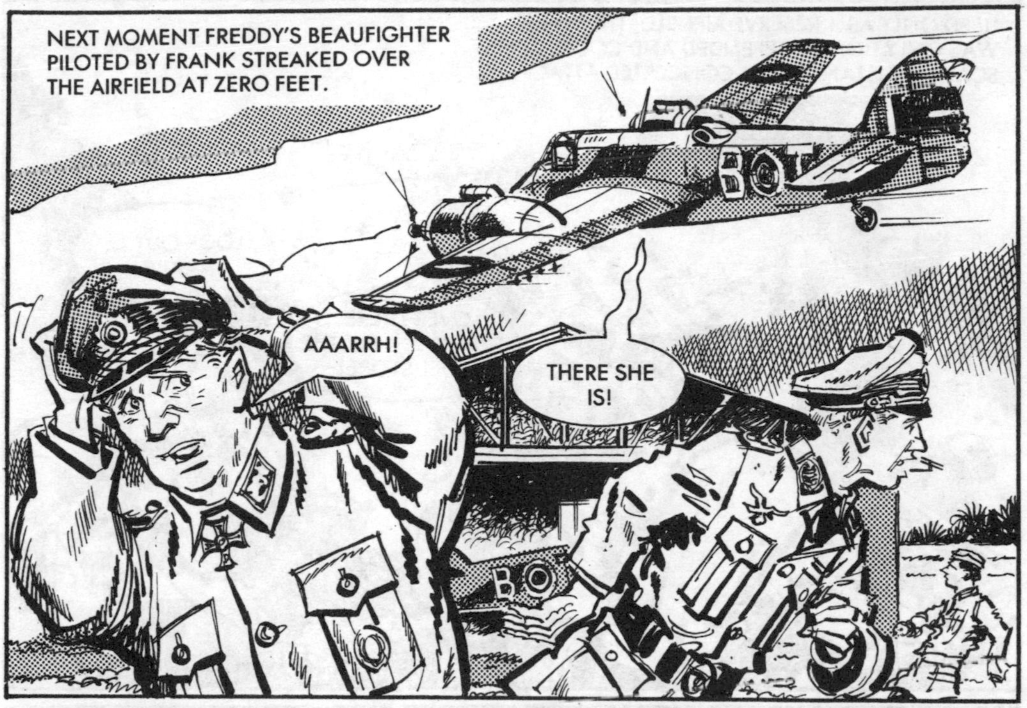
NEXT MOMENT FREDDY'S BEAUFIGHTER PILOTED BY FRANK STREAKED OVER THE AIRFIELD AT ZERO FEET.
AAARRH!
THERE SHE IS!

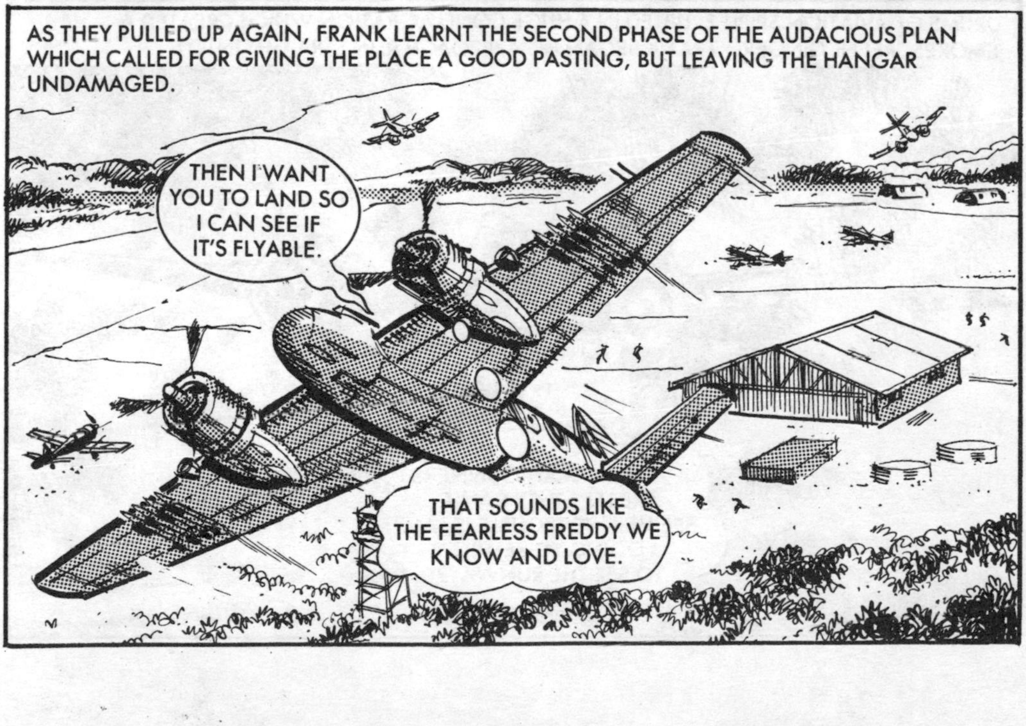
AS THEY PULLED UP AGAIN, FRANK LEARNT THE SECOND PHASE OF THE AUDACIOUS PLAN WHICH CALLED FOR GIVING THE PLACE A GOOD PASTING, BUT LEAVING THE HANGAR UNDAMAGED.
THEN I WANT YOU TO LAND SO I CAN SEE IF IT'S FLYABLE.
THAT SOUNDS LIKE THE FEARLESS FREDDY WE KNOW AND LOVE.

USED ONLY AS A RESERVE AIRFIELD, THE PLACE WAS ONLY LIGHTLY DEFENDED AND COULD OFFER SCANT RESISTANCE TO A CONCERTED ATTACK.

DRUMS OF AVIATION SPIRIT ERUPTED IN A HUGE CONFLAGRATION WHICH CREATED A SMOKESCREEN. GINGERLY FRANK BEGAN HIS APPROACH RUN STRAIGHT INTO IT.

IN THE EVENT FRANK GOT IT RIGHT, BUT ONLY JUST.

HECK, A FEW MORE INCHES AND WE'D HAVE BEEN IN THE MUD.

GOOD WORK, FRANK. TAXI OVER TO THE HANGAR.

HERTZOG MEANWHILE WAS HELPING THE DAZED GENERAL TO HIS FEET.

WH . . . WHAT'S HAPPENING?

I'M NOT SURE. QUICKLY, WE MUST SEEK SHELTER.

BEFORE EITHER OF THEM COULD MOVE, THERE WAS THE SUDDEN ROAR OF AERO ENGINES AS A BEAUFIGHTER LOOMED ABRUPTLY OUT OF THE SMOKE, SENDING THEM SPINNING TOWARDS A DITCH.

GOTT IN HIMMEL . . . AAAARGH!

WE'RE HERE . . . I THINK!

AS FRANK ROLLED TO A STOP, FREDDY CLAMBERED OUT AND RACED ACROSS TO THE CAPTURED BEAUFIGHTER.

AN HOUR AGO HE WAS LOCKED UP FACING TRIAL, NOW LOOK AT HIM.

FREDDY REACHED THE AIRCRAFT AND MADE A RAPID CHECK OF ALL THE INSTRUMENTS.

FUEL, HALF FULL. OIL PRESSURE NORMAL. NOT EXACTLY A TEXTBOOK PRE-FLIGHT CHECK, BUT IT'LL DO FOR NOW . . .

THEN FRANK WINCED AS A SHOT RANG OUT AND A BULLET RICOCHETED PAST FREDDY.

YE GODS!

DIE, YOU SCUM!

GOOD GRIEF, THIS COULD FOUL THINGS UP.

FRANK RELEASED THE BRAKES AND REVVED UP A SINGLE ENGINE, CAUSING HIS PLANE TO PIVOT SLOWLY ROUND. IT TOOK A FEW MOMENTS FOR HERTZOG TO REALISE THE DANGER.

COME ON, TURN, BLAST YOU . . . TURN.

WAS IS DAS?

THE LUFTWAFFE COLONEL DODGED TOO LATE.

CLOSE BY, THE GENERAL HAD FINALLY STAGGERED OUT OF THE DITCH. DAZED AND BEWILDERED, HE CALLED OUT PLAINTIVELY.

HERTZOG! HERTZOG, WHERE ARE YOU?

THERE WAS NO REPLY, OF COURSE, FROM HERTZOG, BUT THE GENERAL DID RECEIVE AN ANSWER OF SORTS AS TWO BEAUFIGHTERS LOOMED OUT OF THE SMOKE.

MEIN GOTT . . . AAARGH!

I DON'T KNOW WHY THIS BLOKE KEEPS GETTING IN THE WAY.

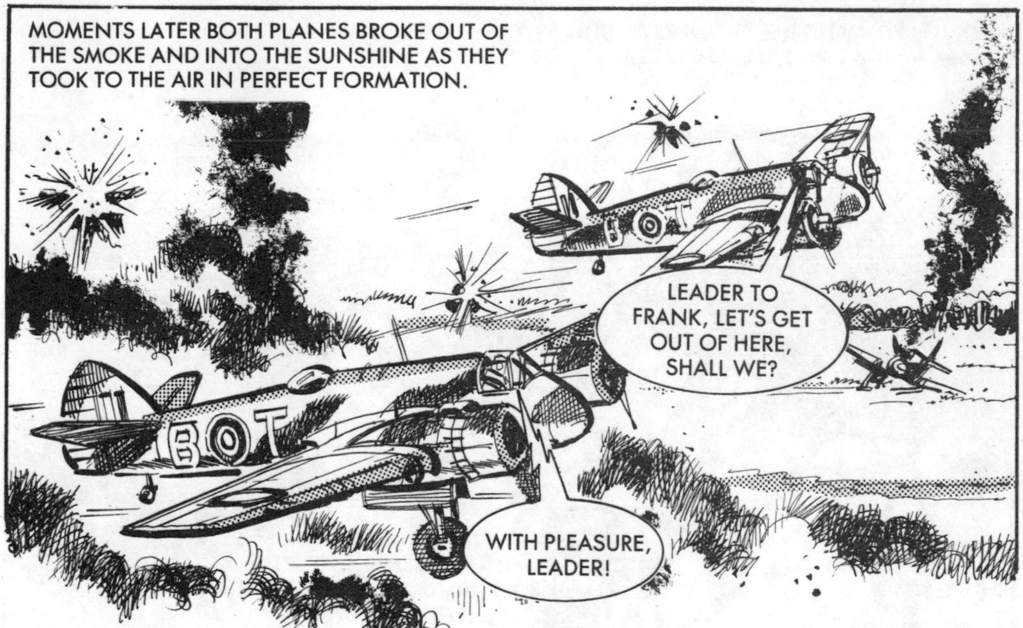
MOMENTS LATER BOTH PLANES BROKE OUT OF THE SMOKE AND INTO THE SUNSHINE AS THEY TOOK TO THE AIR IN PERFECT FORMATION.
LEADER TO FRANK, LET'S GET OUT OF HERE, SHALL WE?
WITH PLEASURE, LEADER!

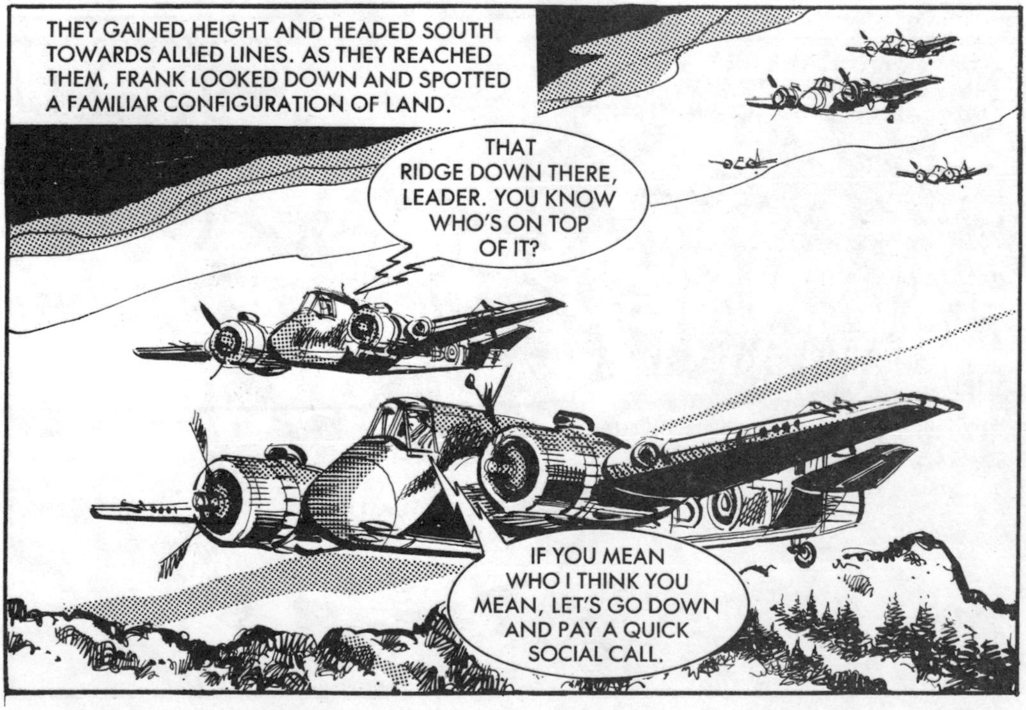
THEY GAINED HEIGHT AND HEADED SOUTH TOWARDS ALLIED LINES. AS THEY REACHED THEM, FRANK LOOKED DOWN AND SPOTTED A FAMILIAR CONFIGURATION OF LAND.
THAT RIDGE DOWN THERE, LEADER. YOU KNOW WHO'S ON TOP OF IT?
IF YOU MEAN WHO I THINK YOU MEAN, LET'S GO DOWN AND PAY A QUICK SOCIAL CALL.

FORD NIXON AND HIS GUNNERS COULD ONLY GAPE AS THE TWO BEAUFIGHTERS HURTLED OVER.

HOLY TOLEDO — THEY'RE BOTH LETTERED B.T.! THE CRAZY LIMEYS HAVE PULLED IT OFF!

A FEW MINUTES LATER THE PLANES LANDED BACK HOME, TO BE MET BY A FULL SCALE RECEPTION COMMITTEE.

THEY'RE GOING TO HAVE TO BELIEVE US NOW.

OH, THEY WILL EVENTUALLY, BUT THEY WON'T MAKE IT EASY FOR US . . . YOU CAN BET ON THAT.

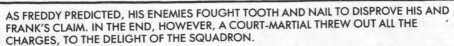

AS FREDDY PREDICTED, HIS ENEMIES FOUGHT TOOTH AND NAIL TO DISPROVE HIS AND FRANK'S CLAIM. IN THE END, HOWEVER, A COURT-MARTIAL THREW OUT ALL THE CHARGES, TO THE DELIGHT OF THE SQUADRON.

THREE CHEERS FOR FEARLESS FREDDY AND FRANK . . . HIP, HIP . . .

WITH FRIENDS LIKE THESE, FRANK, IT DOESN'T MATTER WHO YOU'VE GOT FOR ENEMIES.

MORE GOOD NEWS CAME WITH THE RECOVERY OF ANDY THE NAVIGATOR — ALTHOUGH HE COULD NOT REMEMBER A BLIND THING ABOUT THAT FATEFUL DAY.

THERE WAS STILL THE PROBLEM OF THE RECAPTURED BEAUFIGHTER. AS FREDDY STOOD ON THE AIRFIELD LOOKING AT IT PARKED ALONGSIDE HIS OWN PLANE, A WICKED GLEAM CAME INTO HIS EYES.

I'VE BEEN TOLD WE CAN HAVE THIS KITE OFFICIALLY. OF COURSE, SHE'LL HAVE TO BE RE-LETTERED, BUT BEFORE WE DO THAT . . .

I DAREN'T ASK.

BACK AT H.Q., ROE AND CLITHERS, FREDDY'S ARCH ENEMIES, PREPARED TO DRIVE TO A CONFERENCE, NEITHER MAN HAPPY WITH THE OUTCOME OF THE COURT-MARTIAL.

I MEAN, I DON'T DOUBT HE WASN'T RESPONSIBLE FOR SHOOTING UP THE AMBULANCES, BUT THE FELLOW'S SUCH A BOUNDER.

I QUITE AGREE. HE GOT OFF FAR TOO LIGHTLY.

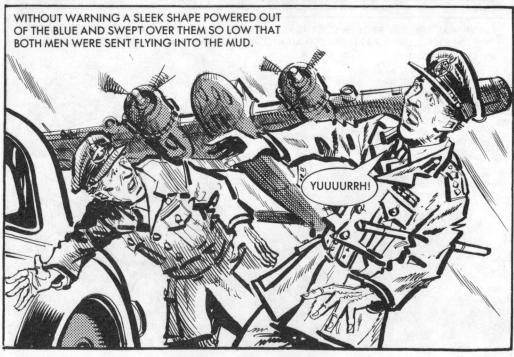

WITHOUT WARNING A SLEEK SHAPE POWERED OUT OF THE BLUE AND SWEPT OVER THEM SO LOW THAT BOTH MEN WERE SENT FLYING INTO THE MUD.

YUUUURRH!

AS IF TO GIVE THEM EVERY CHANCE TO IDENTIFY IT, THE BEAUFIGHTER BANKED SLOWLY ROUND BEFORE FLYING OFF.

B.T.! IT'S HIM. IT'S BUNBURY!

WE'VE GOT HIM THIS TIME!

ROE AND CLITHERS HAD BARELY STOOD UP BEFORE A SECOND BEAUFIGHTER THUNDERED OVER THEM.

YEAAARH!

FINALLY IT DAWNED ON THE TWO MEN THAT BOTH PLANES CARRIED THE SAME LETTERS, WHICH MADE IDENTIFICATION SOMETHING OF A PROBLEM.

WE . . . WE'LL NEVER PROVE WHO WAS FLYING WHAT. WE'LL BE A LAUGHING STOCK!

BUNBURY . . . BAH! BEST FORGET IT, WHAT?

THE TWO PLANES JOINED UP AND FLEW OFF, THEIR RESPECTIVE PILOTS ROARING WITH LAUGHTER.

AS SOON AS WE LAND WE'LL ALTER THE LETTERING ON YOUR PLANE, FRANK. ONE B.T.'S ENOUGH FOR ANY SQUADRON.

AND ONE FEARLESS FREDDY IS MORE THAN ENOUGH.

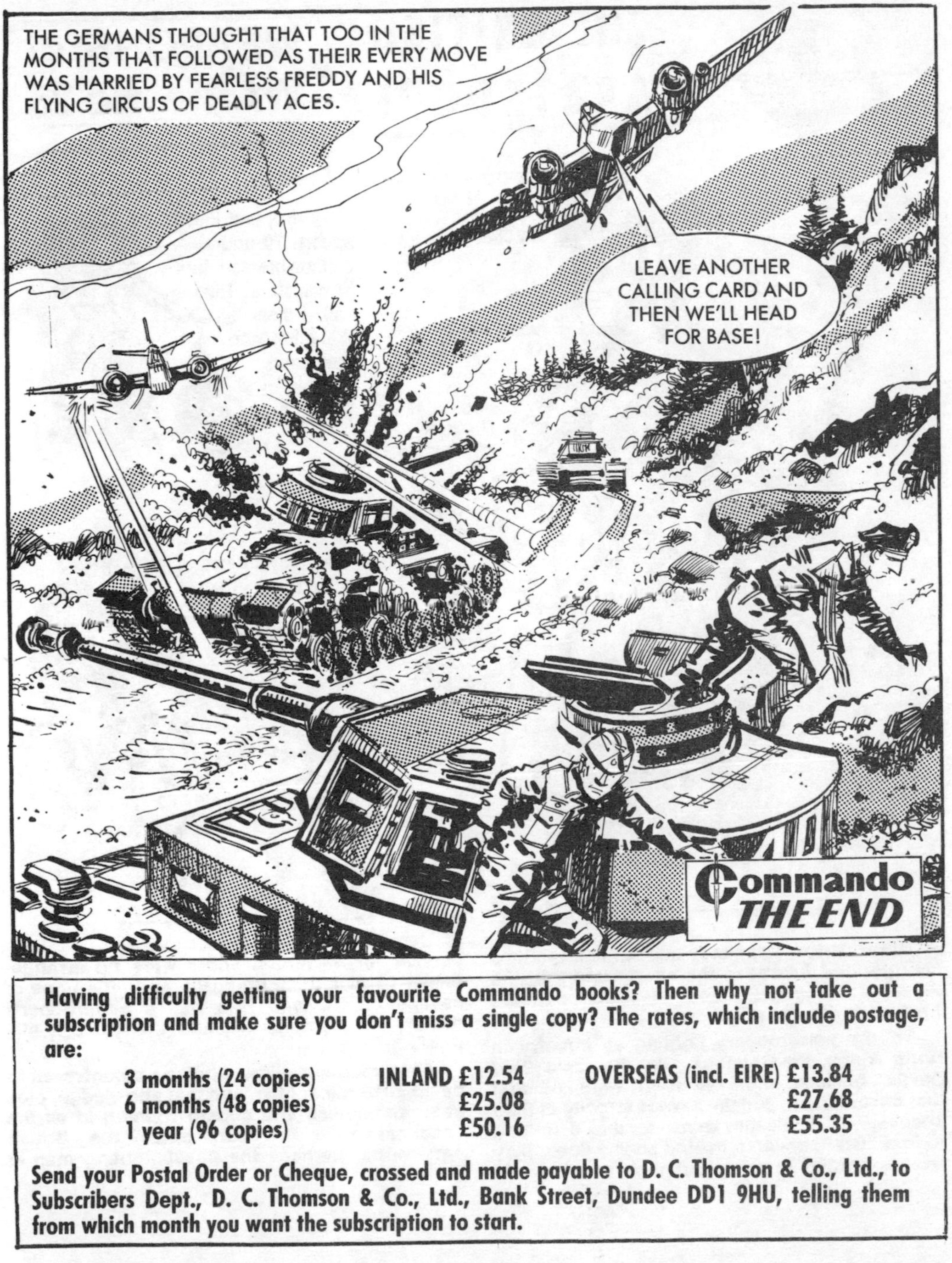
THE GERMANS THOUGHT THAT TOO IN THE MONTHS THAT FOLLOWED AS THEIR EVERY MOVE WAS HARRIED BY FEARLESS FREDDY AND HIS FLYING CIRCUS OF DEADLY ACES.
LEAVE ANOTHER CALLING CARD AND THEN WE'LL HEAD FOR BASE!
Commando
THE END

THE BRITISH PARATROOPER

WEAPONS of WAR — No 26

STEEL HELMET WITH INSIDE RUBBER PADDING AND SPECIAL CHIN-PIECE

TWO-INCH MORTAR

CAMOUFLAGE VEIL USED ALSO AS SCARF

STEN GUN WITH ANTI-BURN SLEEVE

BINOCULARS (officers and section leaders)

MORTAR-BOMB POUCHES

TRENCHING TOOL

ROPE WITH TOGGLE AT ONE END. LOOP AT OTHER. SEVERAL JOINED TOGETHER MAKING LONG ROPE

DENISON SMOCK WITH SIX LARGE POCKETS FOR STEN MAGAZINES 48-HOUR RATIONS ETC.

FIGHTING KNIFE.

They dropped these special 70 pound, collapsible scooters in canisters. They called them Wel-bikes and they were capable of 30 m.p.h.

This bicycle was folded in half when not in use, but it took only two wing-nuts to turn it into a handy means of transport for the paratrooper.

THE RED DEVILS

North Africa, Normandy and Arnhem—only a few glorious names in the short history of the Parachute Regiment, and of these, perhaps Arnhem is the most famous.

To the paratroopers fighting as infantry in North Africa, the Germans gave the name "Red Devils," because of the red desert sand and dust that coated them, and the savage ferocity of their attacks. And devils they were—for they'd nothing to lose. Dropped deep behind enemy lines, they were expected to carry out their mission and survive for 48 hours. There were no arrangements to pick them up again, and little hope of escape or survival. This was a paratrooper's destiny—to fight, to kill, and then to die, still fighting.

Each man knew this when he volunteered to be an airborne soldier, and that knowledge, plus strength, fitness and superb training in all the deadliest skills of war, made the British paratrooper perhaps the finest fighting man in the world.

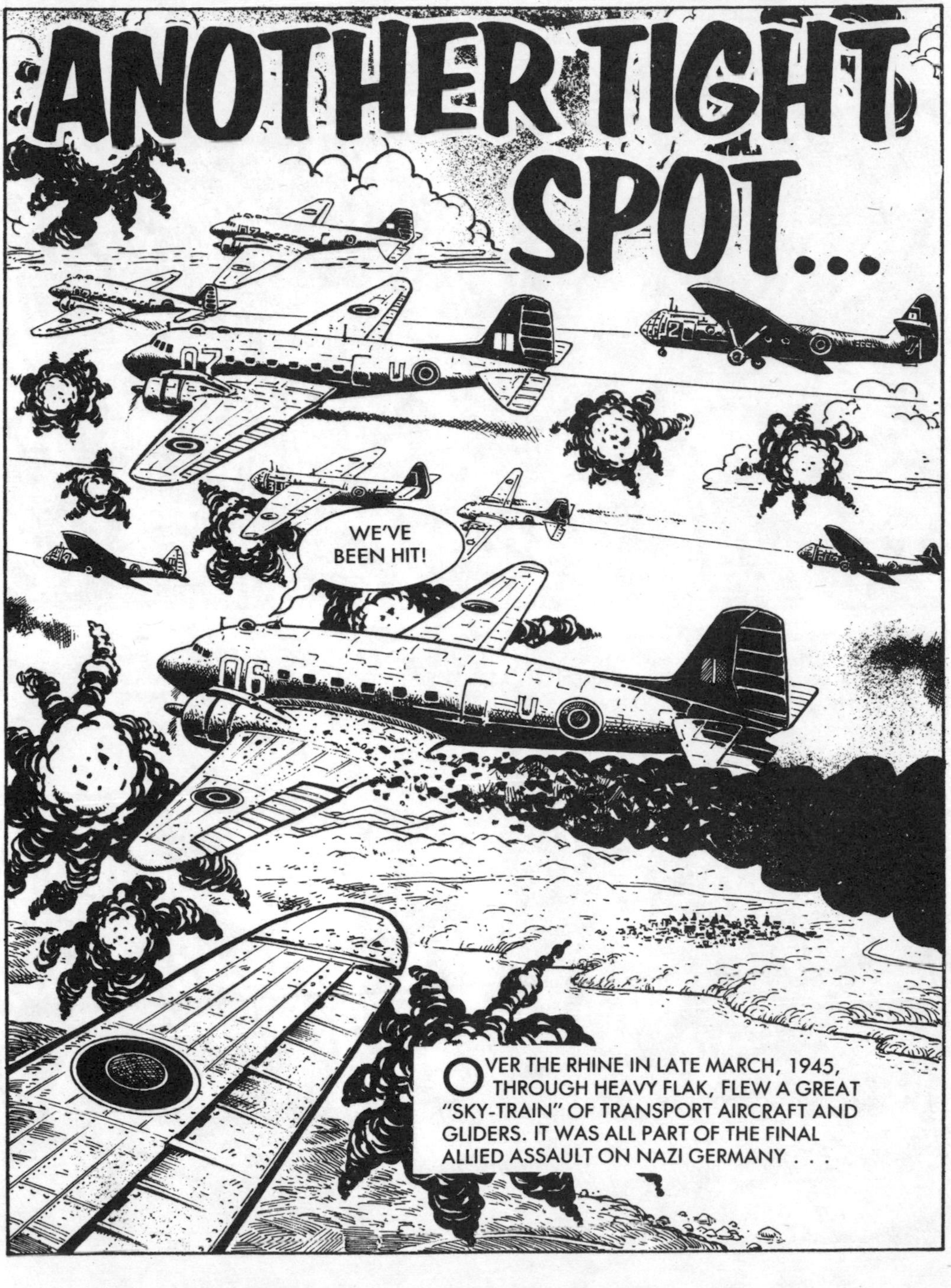
ANOTHER TIGHT SPOT...
WE'VE BEEN HIT!
OVER THE RHINE IN LATE MARCH, 1945, THROUGH HEAVY FLAK, FLEW A GREAT "SKY-TRAIN" OF TRANSPORT AIRCRAFT AND GLIDERS. IT WAS ALL PART OF THE FINAL ALLIED ASSAULT ON NAZI GERMANY . . .

THE DAMAGED C-47 TRANSPORT COMMENCED TO SIDE-SLIP OUT OF CONTROL. ABOARD WAS A PARATROOP RIFLE PLATOON, TWO SECTIONS OF WHICH WERE COMMANDED BY SERGEANT ANDY LESLIE.

SO THIS IS WHERE IT ENDS FOR ME . . .

WHERE IT HAD BEGUN WAS IN THE SCOTTISH HILLS. HIS FATHER WORKED ON A BIG ESTATE AND ANDY HAD BEEN TAKEN ON AS A SHEPHERD AND GAME BEATER AFTER LEAVING SCHOOL AT FOURTEEN.

THE SECOND WORLD WAR WAS IN ITS SECOND YEAR WHEN ANDY, NOW EIGHTEEN, MADE HIS WAY TO THE DEPOT OF THE HIGHLAND REGIMENT IN WHICH HIS FATHER HAD SERVED.

A VOLUNTEER, EH? GOOD LAD. TRUST A LESLIE NOT TO WAIT FOR THE CALL-UP.

ACCEPTED AND POSTED INTO THE TRAINING COMPANY, HE BEGAN TO LEARN THE MYSTERIES OF SOLDIERING.

LEFT! PICK UP THE STEP, THAT MAN. LEFT, LEFT!

IT WAS DURING THIS TRAINING THAT ANDY MADE A DISTURBING DISCOVERY ABOUT HIMSELF.

USE YOUR BAYONET! WHAT YOU WAITING FOR?

I CANNOT DO IT . . . I COULD NEVER KILL ANOTHER MAN, GERMAN OR NOT.

ALWAYS MUCH HAPPIER OBSERVING RATHER THAN HUNTING WILD LIFE, HE FOUND THAT HIS FEELING AGAINST TAKING HUMAN LIFE WAS EVEN STRONGER.

HE WAS GRANTED AN INTERVIEW WITH THE TRAINING COMPANY COMMANDER, HIS HONESTY IMPRESSING EVEN THE TOUGHEST OF THE INSTRUCTORS.

SIR, I DO NOT THINK I COULD KILL ANOTHER MAN.

WHICH MAKES YOU USELESS AS A SOLDIER, MY LAD.

ANDY WAS PUT ON FATIGUES WHILE HIS FUTURE WAS DISCUSSED.

I DON'T THINK HE IS A MALINGERER, SIR. AFTER ALL, HE DID VOLUNTEER TO JOIN UP.

TOO MUCH TROUBLE TO JUST TURF HIM OUT. I'LL HAVE TO THINK ABOUT IT.

WHAT FINALLY HAPPENED WAS THAT ANDY WAS TAKEN OFF FATIGUES TO ATTEND A MEDICAL ORDERLY COURSE AT A BASE OF THE ROYAL ARMY MEDICAL CORPS.

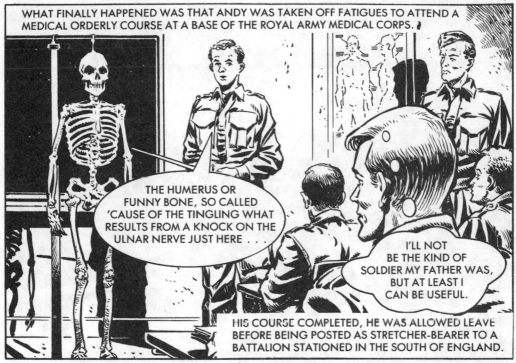

THE HUMERUS OR FUNNY BONE, SO CALLED 'CAUSE OF THE TINGLING WHAT RESULTS FROM A KNOCK ON THE ULNAR NERVE JUST HERE . . .

I'LL NOT BE THE KIND OF SOLDIER MY FATHER WAS, BUT AT LEAST I CAN BE USEFUL.

HIS COURSE COMPLETED, HE WAS ALLOWED LEAVE BEFORE BEING POSTED AS STRETCHER-BEARER TO A BATTALION STATIONED IN THE SOUTH OF ENGLAND.

ON A SPRING DAY IN 1942 A SUFFOLK VILLAGE WAS HIT BY TWO FIVE HUNDRED POUND BOMBS JETTISONED BY A GERMAN DORNIER BOMBER ON ITS HOMEWARD RUN.

NOW TURN ON COURSE ONE-FOUR . . .

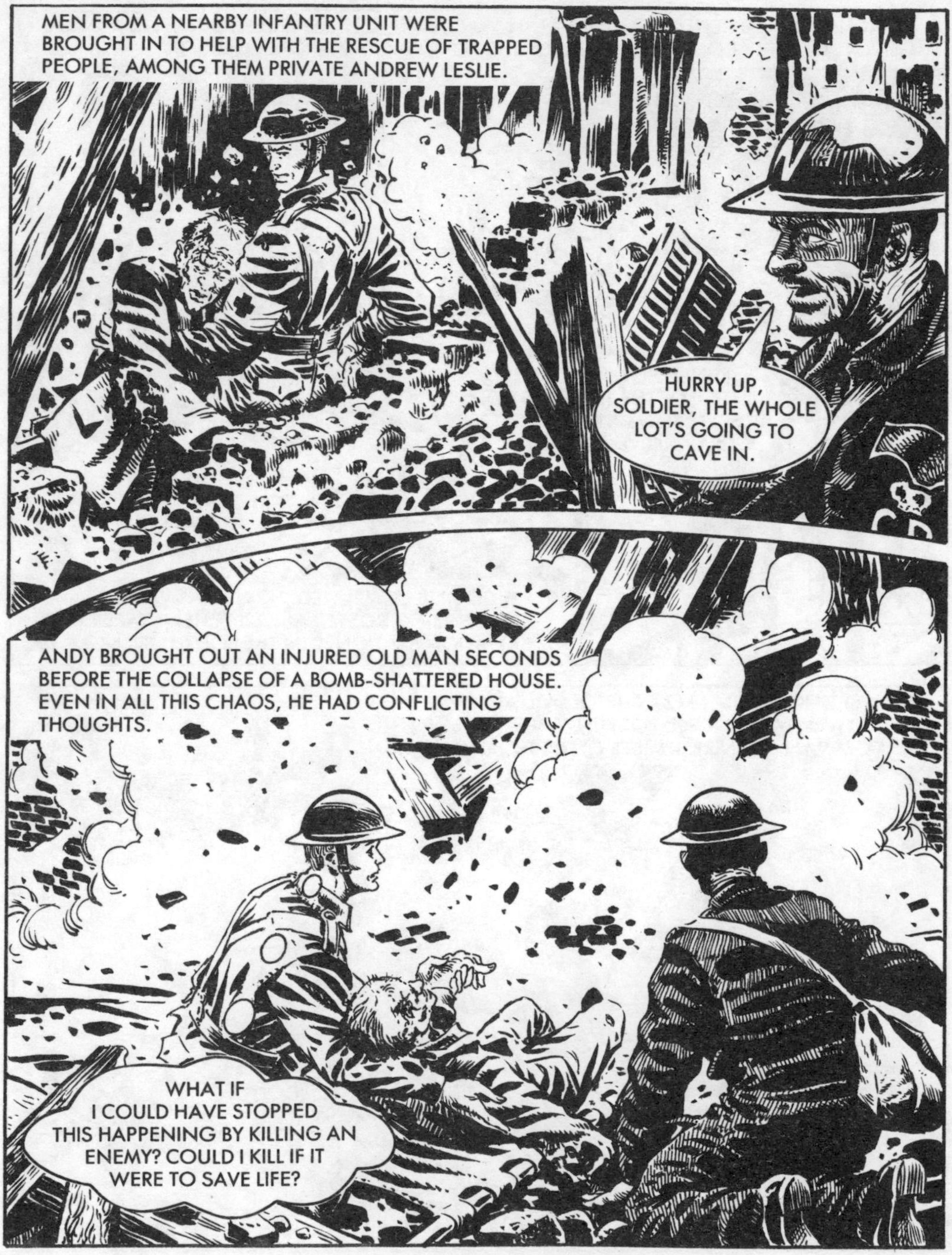
MEN FROM A NEARBY INFANTRY UNIT WERE BROUGHT IN TO HELP WITH THE RESCUE OF TRAPPED PEOPLE, AMONG THEM PRIVATE ANDREW LESLIE.
HURRY UP, SOLDIER, THE WHOLE LOT'S GOING TO CAVE IN.
ANDY BROUGHT OUT AN INJURED OLD MAN SECONDS BEFORE THE COLLAPSE OF A BOMB-SHATTERED HOUSE. EVEN IN ALL THIS CHAOS, HE HAD CONFLICTING THOUGHTS.
WHAT IF I COULD HAVE STOPPED THIS HAPPENING BY KILLING AN ENEMY? COULD I KILL IF IT WERE TO SAVE LIFE?

AN INNER STRUGGLE ENDED WITH HIM COMING TO A DECISION WHEN A POSTER FOR THE NEWLY-FORMED AIRBORNE FORCES APPEARED.

WHY SHOULD I STAND BY AND LET OTHER MEN DO THE KILLING THAT WILL PROTECT ME?

HE PUT IN A CAREFULLY WRITTEN APPLICATION THAT WAS READ BY THE ADJUTANT IN BATTALION HEADQUARTERS.

A STRETCHER-BEARER VOLUNTEERING FOR THE PARACHUTE BRIGADE? HE'LL BE WEEDED OUT IN THE FIRST FEW DAYS.

YES, SIR. ARMY ORDERS SAY WE HAVE TO ALLOW TEN VOLUNTEERS, THOUGH. MAKING THAT LAD ONE MEANS WE HANG ONTO A GOOD SOLDIER.

ANDY WAS SENT ON A SELECTION COURSE AT THE AIRBORNE FORCES DEPOT, JOINING A SQUAD OF OTHER HOPEFULS ON TWO WEEKS OF HARD TESTING.

EIGHTY! WHO SAID THAT MAN COULD TAKE A REST? DOWN AND UP — EIGHTY-ONE . . .

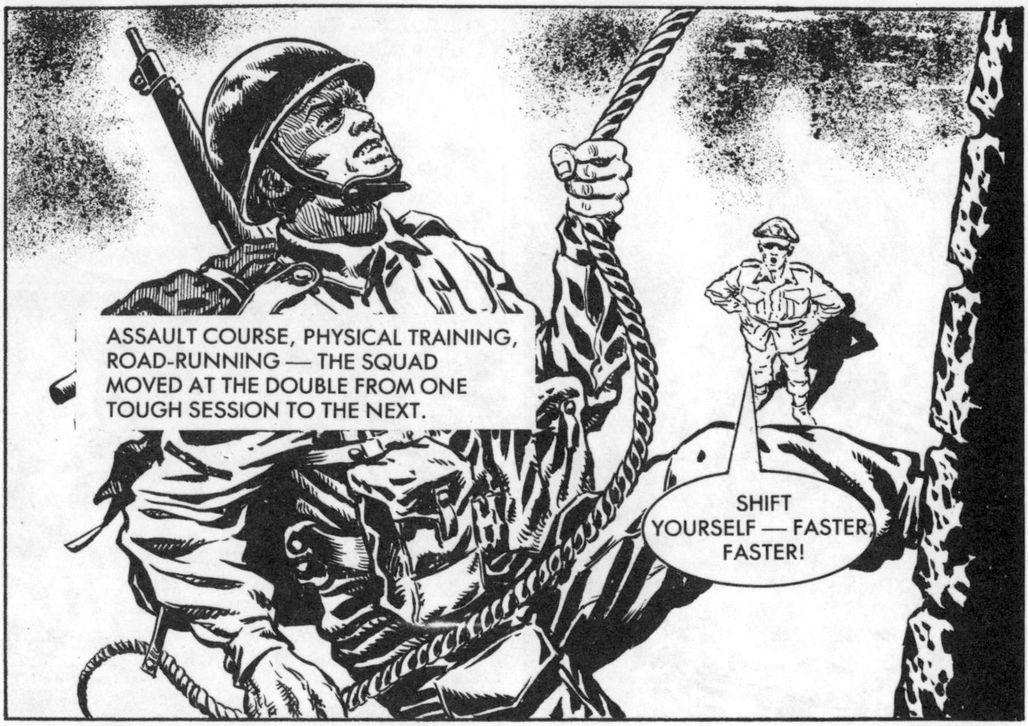
ASSAULT COURSE, PHYSICAL TRAINING, ROAD-RUNNING — THE SQUAD MOVED AT THE DOUBLE FROM ONE TOUGH SESSION TO THE NEXT.
SHIFT YOURSELF — FASTER, FASTER!

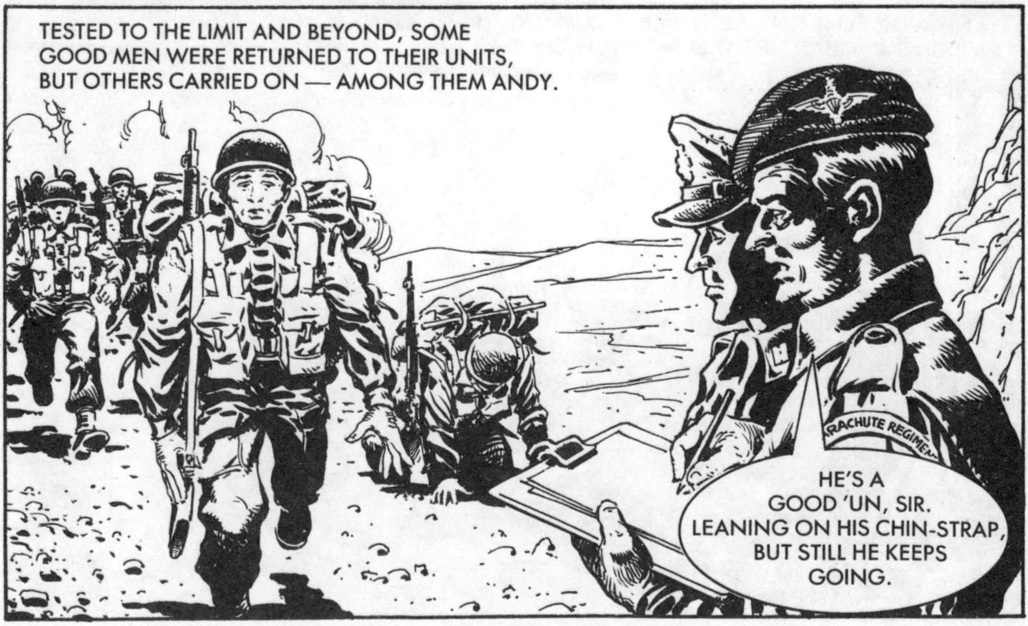
TESTED TO THE LIMIT AND BEYOND, SOME GOOD MEN WERE RETURNED TO THEIR UNITS, BUT OTHERS CARRIED ON — AMONG THEM ANDY.
HE'S A GOOD 'UN, SIR. LEANING ON HIS CHIN-STRAP, BUT STILL HE KEEPS GOING.

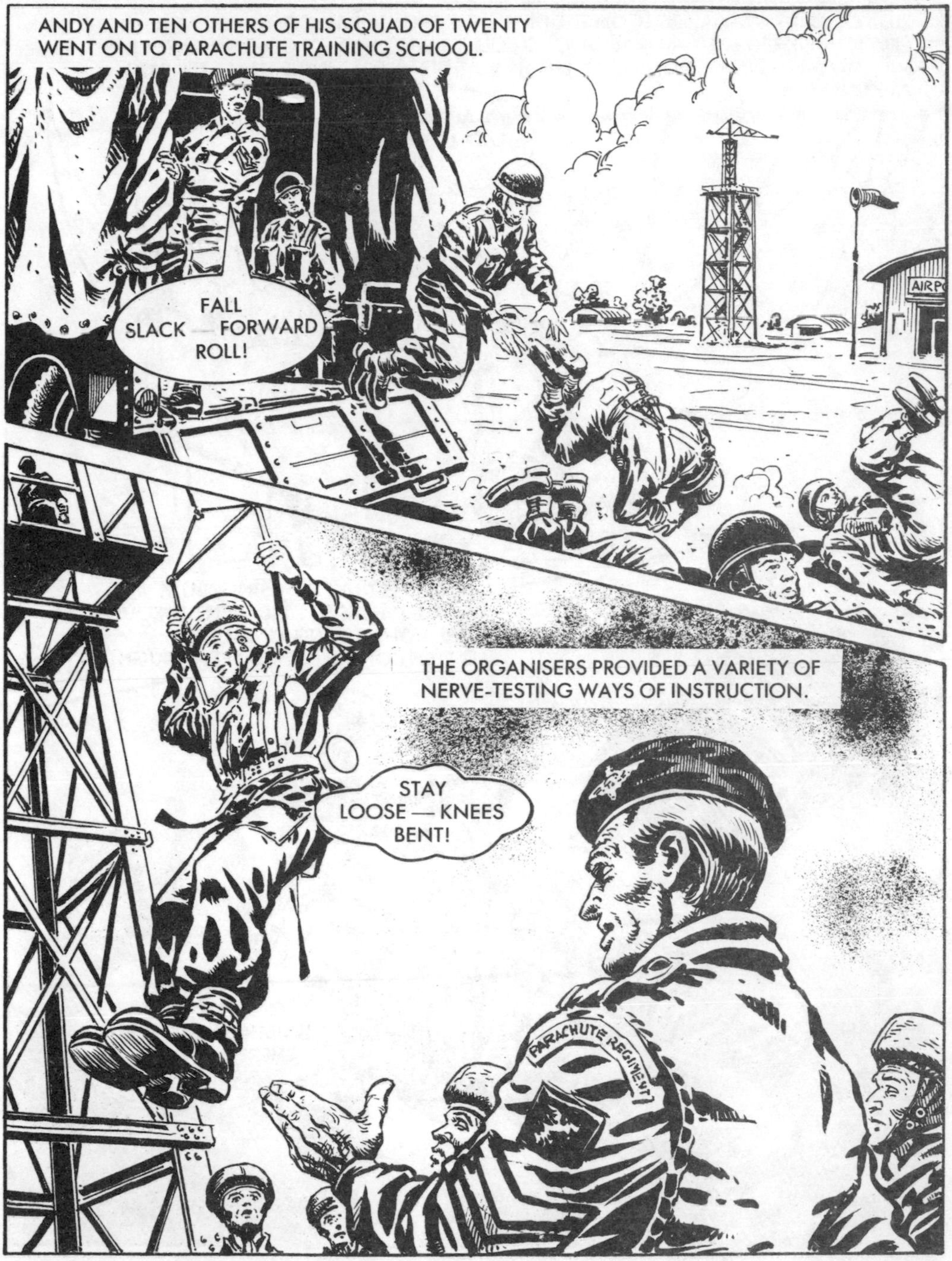
ANDY AND TEN OTHERS OF HIS SQUAD OF TWENTY WENT ON TO PARACHUTE TRAINING SCHOOL.
FALL SLACK — FORWARD ROLL!
THE ORGANISERS PROVIDED A VARIETY OF NERVE-TESTING WAYS OF INSTRUCTION.
STAY LOOSE — KNEES BENT!
PARACHUTE REGIMENT

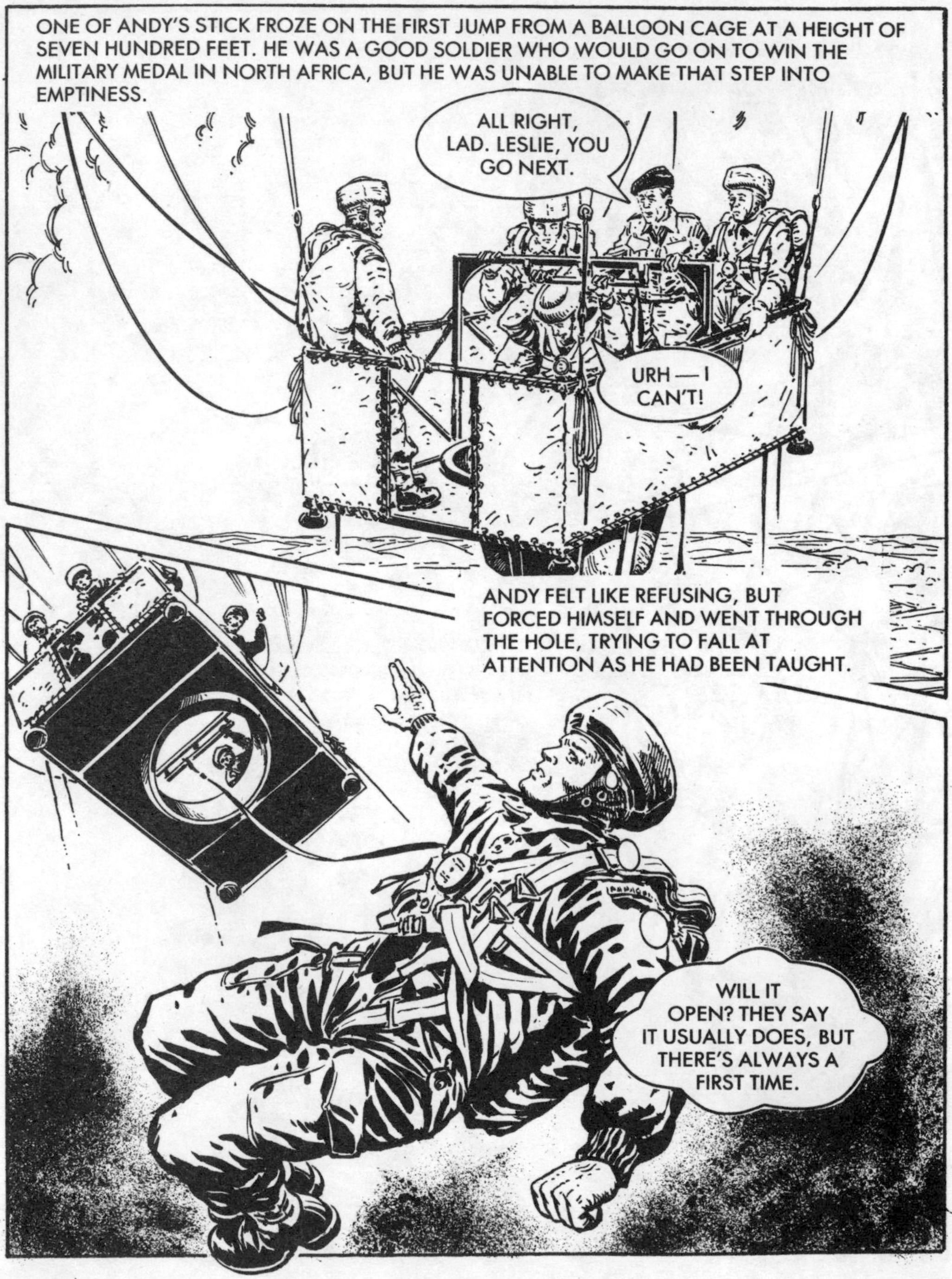
ONE OF ANDY'S STICK FROZE ON THE FIRST JUMP FROM A BALLOON CAGE AT A HEIGHT OF SEVEN HUNDRED FEET. HE WAS A GOOD SOLDIER WHO WOULD GO ON TO WIN THE MILITARY MEDAL IN NORTH AFRICA, BUT HE WAS UNABLE TO MAKE THAT STEP INTO EMPTINESS.
ALL RIGHT, LAD. LESLIE, YOU GO NEXT.
URH — I CAN'T!
ANDY FELT LIKE REFUSING, BUT FORCED HIMSELF AND WENT THROUGH THE HOLE, TRYING TO FALL AT ATTENTION AS HE HAD BEEN TAUGHT.
WILL IT OPEN? THEY SAY IT USUALLY DOES, BUT THERE'S ALWAYS A FIRST TIME.

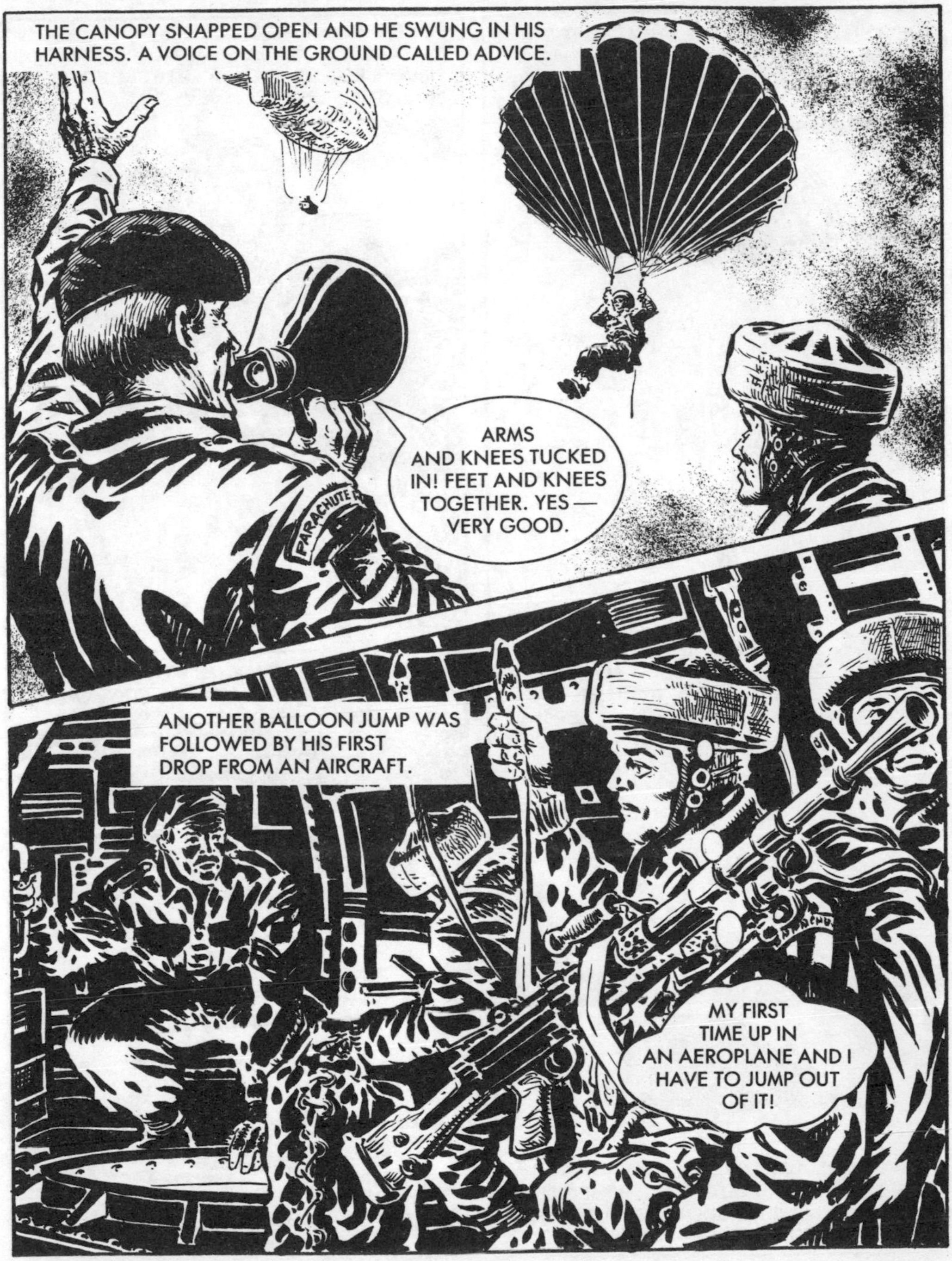
THE CANOPY SNAPPED OPEN AND HE SWUNG IN HIS HARNESS. A VOICE ON THE GROUND CALLED ADVICE.
ARMS AND KNEES TUCKED IN! FEET AND KNEES TOGETHER. YES — VERY GOOD.
PARACHUTE
ANOTHER BALLOON JUMP WAS FOLLOWED BY HIS FIRST DROP FROM AN AIRCRAFT.
MY FIRST TIME UP IN AN AEROPLANE AND I HAVE TO JUMP OUT OF IT!

HE WENT OUT THROUGH A HOLE IN THE FLOOR OF THE CONVERTED BOMBER. HE WORE BATTLE-ORDER, A BREN GUN THRUST THROUGH HIS HARNESS AND A SIXTY POUND KIT BAG ATTACHED TO HIM BY A TWENTY FOOT LINE.

ONE WAY OF MAKING SURE THE WIND DOESN'T BLOW ME OFF COURSE.

FIVE MORE JUMPS QUALIFIED WHAT WAS LEFT OF THE SQUAD TO WEAR WINGS SEWN BELOW THEIR RIGHT SHOULDER TITLE AND THE NEW RED BERET.

POSTED TO A PARACHUTE BRIGADE BATTALION, ANDY BECAME NUMBER TWO TO PRIVATE REG TODD ON A RIFLE SECTION'S BREN GUN.

TODDY'S A GOOD BLOKE TO BE WITH.

TRAINING WENT ON WITH LITTLE PAUSE, THE BATTALION HONING A BATTLE-EDGE ON ITS MEN WITH A VARIETY OF EXERCISES.

ARGH — A BLASTED DUCK POND!

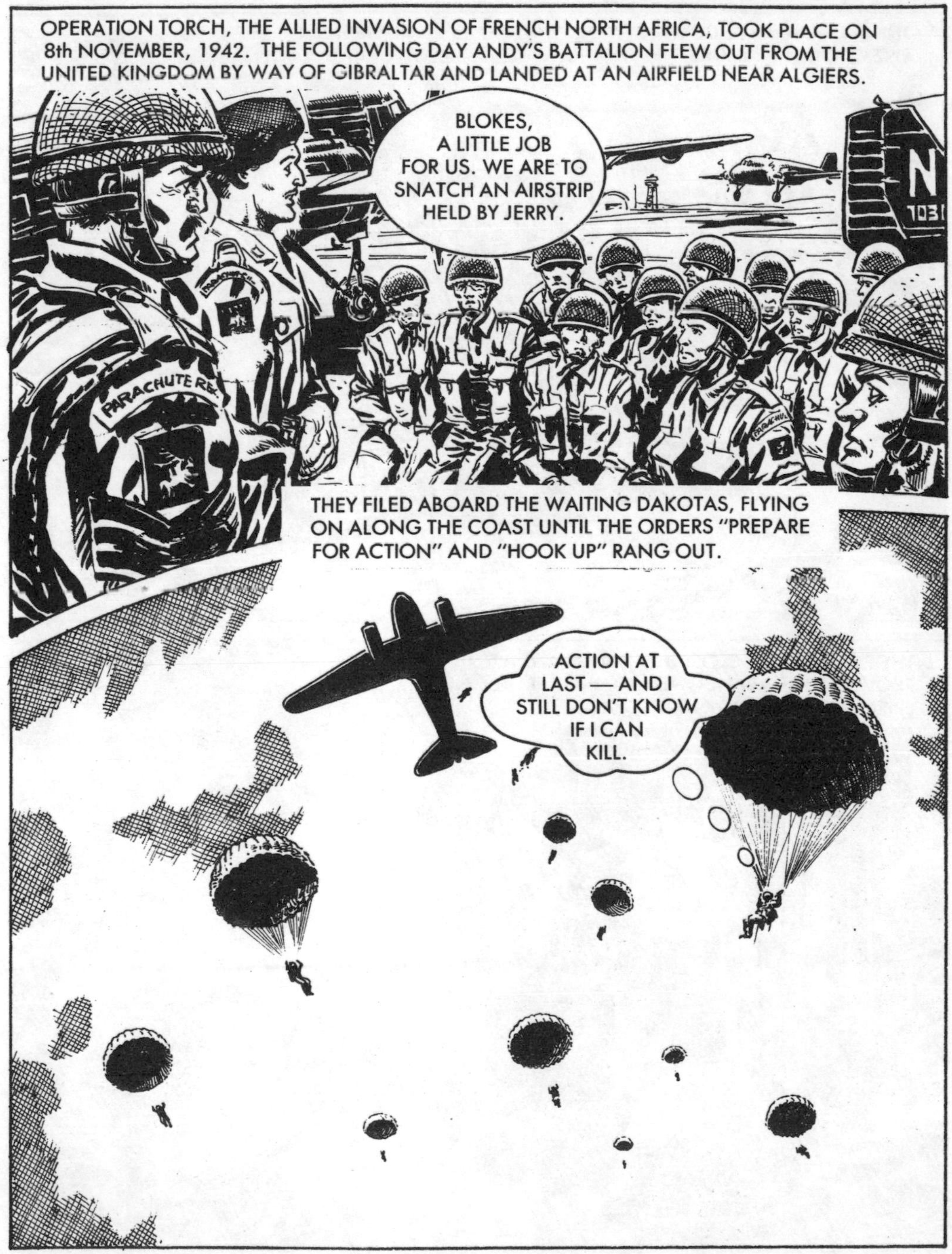
OPERATION TORCH, THE ALLIED INVASION OF FRENCH NORTH AFRICA, TOOK PLACE ON 8th NOVEMBER, 1942. THE FOLLOWING DAY ANDY'S BATTALION FLEW OUT FROM THE UNITED KINGDOM BY WAY OF GIBRALTAR AND LANDED AT AN AIRFIELD NEAR ALGIERS.
BLOKES, A LITTLE JOB FOR US. WE ARE TO SNATCH AN AIRSTRIP HELD BY JERRY.
PARACHUTE REG.
THEY FILED ABOARD THE WAITING DAKOTAS, FLYING ON ALONG THE COAST UNTIL THE ORDERS "PREPARE FOR ACTION" AND "HOOK UP" RANG OUT.
ACTION AT LAST — AND I STILL DON'T KNOW IF I CAN KILL.

THE SECTION CAME DOWN BEYOND THE SOUTHERN PERIMETER OF THE ENEMY-OCCUPIED AIRSTRIP. THERE WAS NO IMMEDIATE RETALIATION.

COME ON, LET'S GO.

THE PARATROOPS CLOSED IN ON AN AIRSTRIP THAT PROVED TO BE ABANDONED — APART FROM ONE FRIENDLY NATIVE PLYING HIS TRADE.

ICE-CREAM! YOU BUY?

OH, BLOOMIN' HECK!

REAL ACTION CAME DAYS LATER WHEN, AFTER A LONG MARCH, THEY SET UP AN AMBUSH OF AN ITALIAN ROAD COLUMN.

AAGH!

RIGHT IN THE BREAD BASKET!

A FEW BURSTS OF FIRE, A TRUCK IN FLAMES — AND THE COLUMN SURRENDERED. ANDY SAW HIS FIRST ENEMY DEAD AND FOUND HIMSELF WITH HIS OLD DOUBTS.

I STILL DON'T KNOW IF I COULD PULL THE TRIGGER WHEN IT COMES TO THIS.

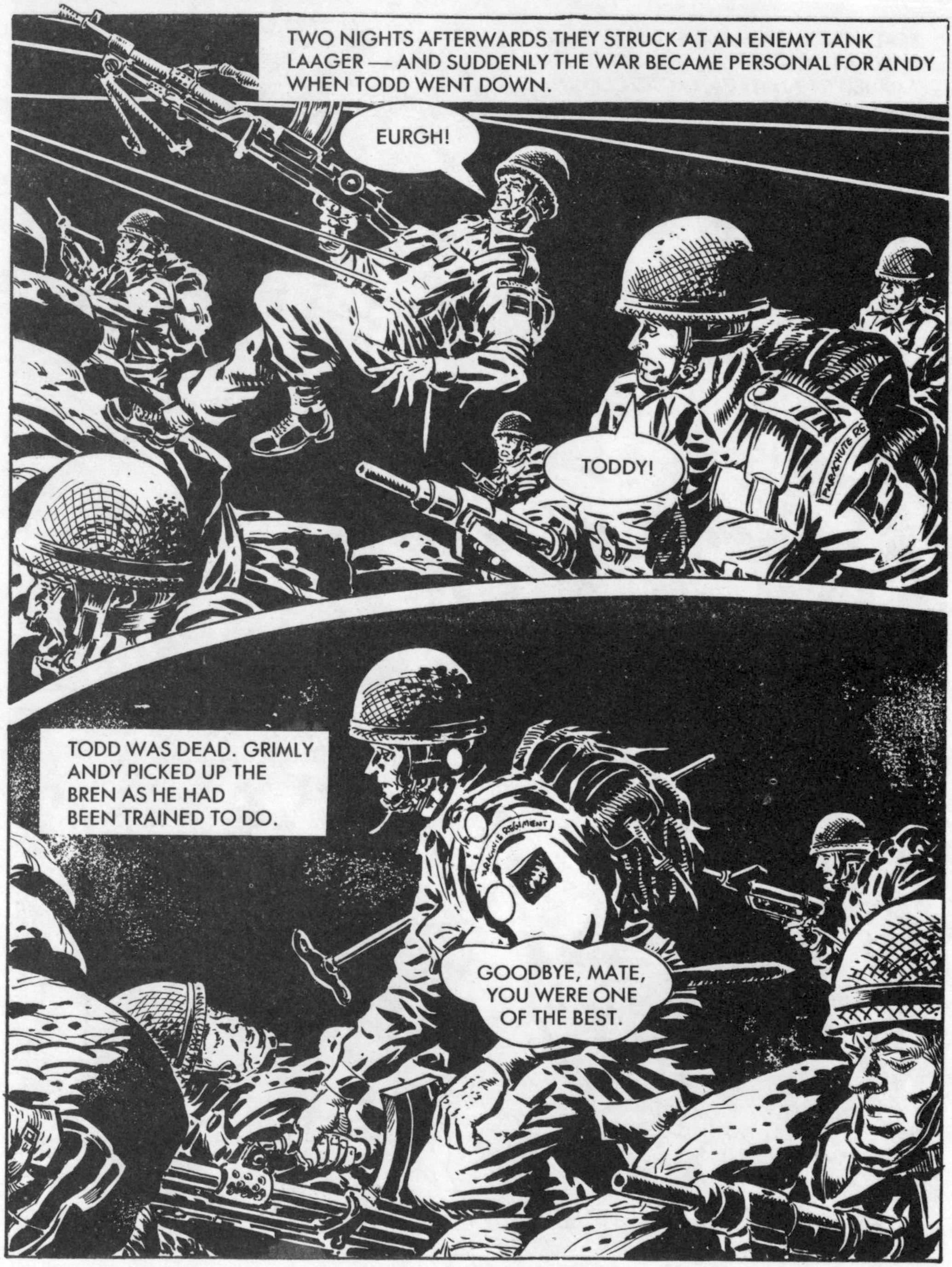
TWO NIGHTS AFTERWARDS THEY STRUCK AT AN ENEMY TANK LAAGER — AND SUDDENLY THE WAR BECAME PERSONAL FOR ANDY WHEN TODD WENT DOWN.
EURGH!
TODDY!
TODD WAS DEAD. GRIMLY ANDY PICKED UP THE BREN AS HE HAD BEEN TRAINED TO DO.
GOODBYE, MATE, YOU WERE ONE OF THE BEST.

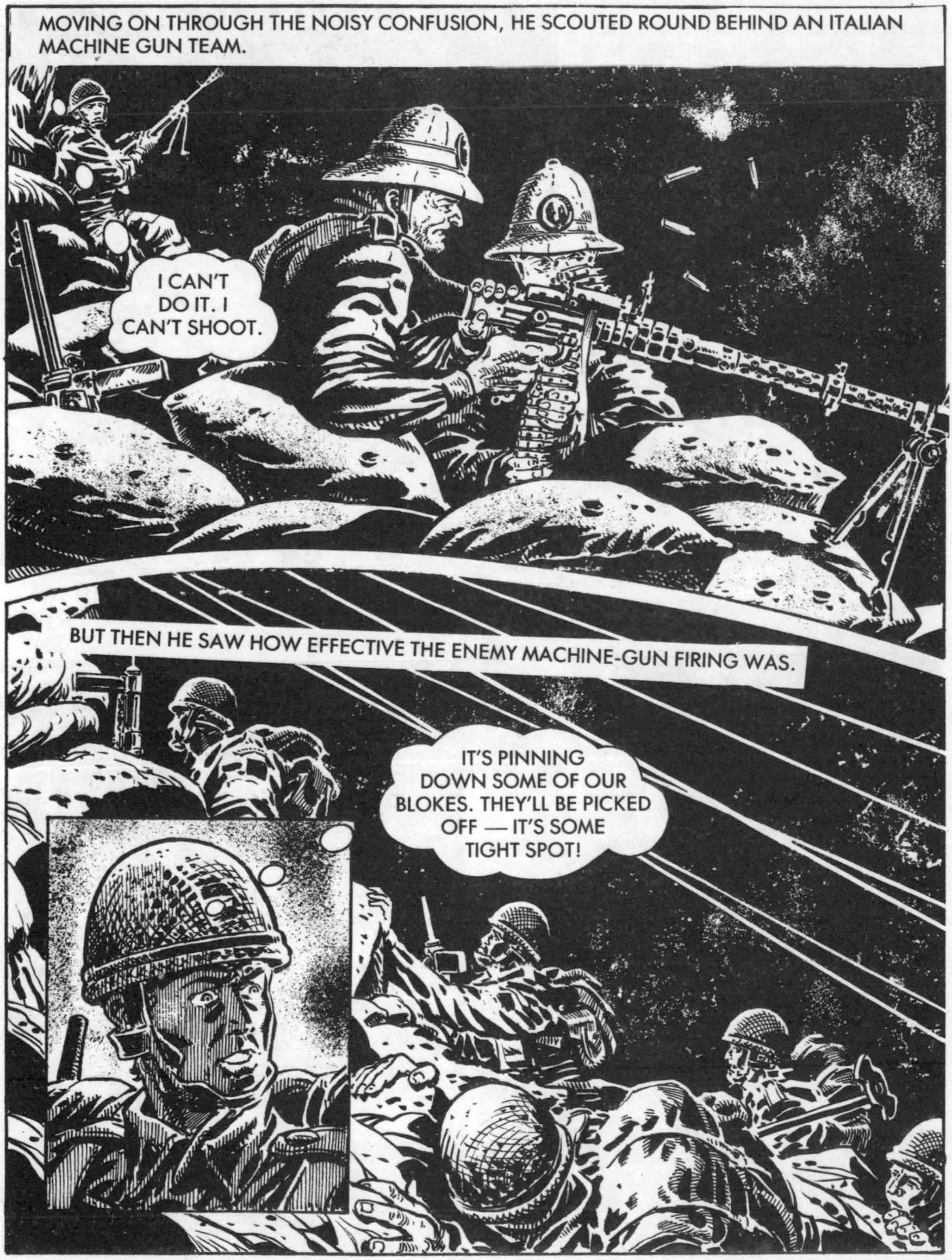
MOVING ON THROUGH THE NOISY CONFUSION, HE SCOUTED ROUND BEHIND AN ITALIAN MACHINE GUN TEAM.
I CAN'T DO IT. I CAN'T SHOOT.
BUT THEN HE SAW HOW EFFECTIVE THE ENEMY MACHINE-GUN FIRING WAS.
IT'S PINNING DOWN SOME OF OUR BLOKES. THEY'LL BE PICKED OFF — IT'S SOME TIGHT SPOT!

HE REACTED WITHOUT THINKING, CHARGING THE GUN POSITION, FIRING THE BREN FROM THE HIP.

AAGH!

FOR THE FIRST TIME HE LOOKED AT MEN WHOSE LIVES HE HAD TAKEN.

POOR BLIGHTERS, BUT IT WAS THEM OR MY MATES.

AN INSTANT LATER HE WAS STARTLED BY A RUSH OF AIR AND A NOISE LIKE THE PASSING OF AN EXPRESS TRAIN.

CRIPES! A HIGH VELOCITY SHELL.

THE DANGER CAME FROM A CLANKING PANZER WHICH MOVED INTO VIEW AS ANDY WAS JOINED BY TWO MEN OF HIS SECTION WITH THEIR TOUGH SERGEANT, SID STONE.

JERRY TANK, SARGE!

RATTLE A FEW MAGS OFF THE HULL. I'LL TRY WORKING IN CLOSE WITH A GAMMON BOMB.

WHILE SID STONE DODGED CLOSER, ROUNDS OF .303 HAMMERED ON ARMOUR-PLATE AS ANDY FIRED THE BREN IN SHORT BURSTS.

GOOD LAD, KEEP IT UP.

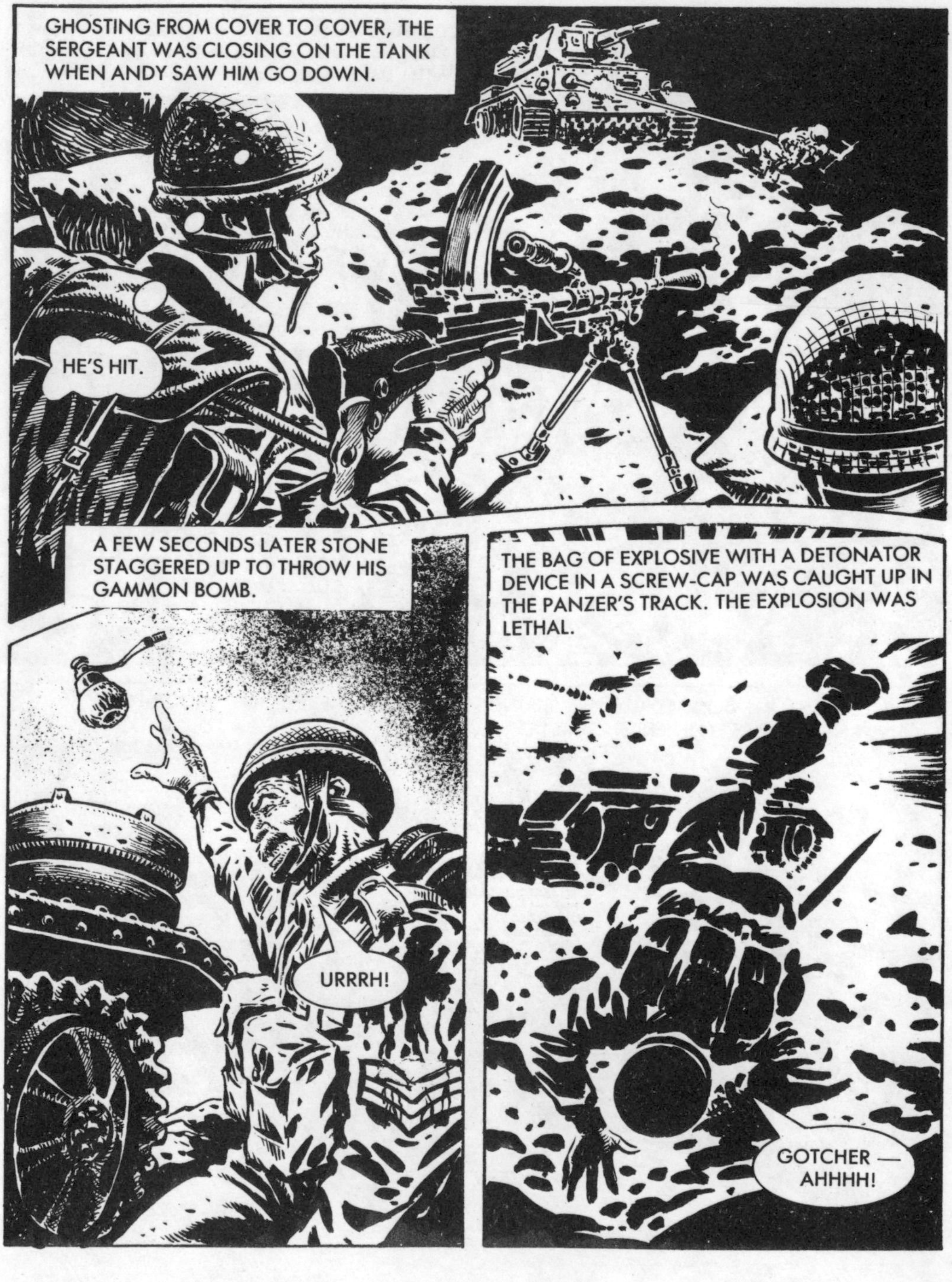
GHOSTING FROM COVER TO COVER, THE SERGEANT WAS CLOSING ON THE TANK WHEN ANDY SAW HIM GO DOWN.
HE'S HIT.
A FEW SECONDS LATER STONE STAGGERED UP TO THROW HIS GAMMON BOMB.
URRRH!
THE BAG OF EXPLOSIVE WITH A DETONATOR DEVICE IN A SCREW-CAP WAS CAUGHT UP IN THE PANZER'S TRACK. THE EXPLOSION WAS LETHAL.
GOTCHER — AHHHH!

TWO ARMED CREWMEN SCRAMBLED OUT OF THEIR SHATTERED TANK TO FIGHT ON — ONLY TO FALL TO FIRE FROM ONCOMING PARAS.

AAGHH!

QUICKLY THERE, ANDY CHECKED ON THE FALLEN SERGEANT STONE.

OLD SID LOOKS DONE FOR.

STRETCHER-BEARER!

THE PARAS STORMED THE CREST, OVER-RUNNING ENEMY POSITIONS IN A FURY OF SMALL-ARMS FIRE, RIFLE-BUTT AND BAYONET.

AAGH!

DAWN FOUND WEARY MEN VICTORIOUS ON A PATCH OF STONY, DUSTY GROUND. THE WOUNDED WERE CARRIED AWAY, SERGEANT STONE AMONG THEM.

I'M MAKING JACK WARD THE SECTION SERGEANT. ANDY, YOU STAY ON THE BREN AND PUT UP A STRIPE.

YESSIR.

NOVEMBER BROUGHT THE RAINS, MUDDY ROADS SLOWING THE ALLIED ADVANCE — ANDY'S BATTALION PREPARED FOR WHAT WAS TO BE THEIR LAST OPERATION IN NORTH AFRICA.

A SIMPLE JOB, FELLOWS — WE GRAB THIS AIRFIELD HERE AND HOLD IT UNTIL OUR PEOPLE ARRIVE IN A FEW DAYS.

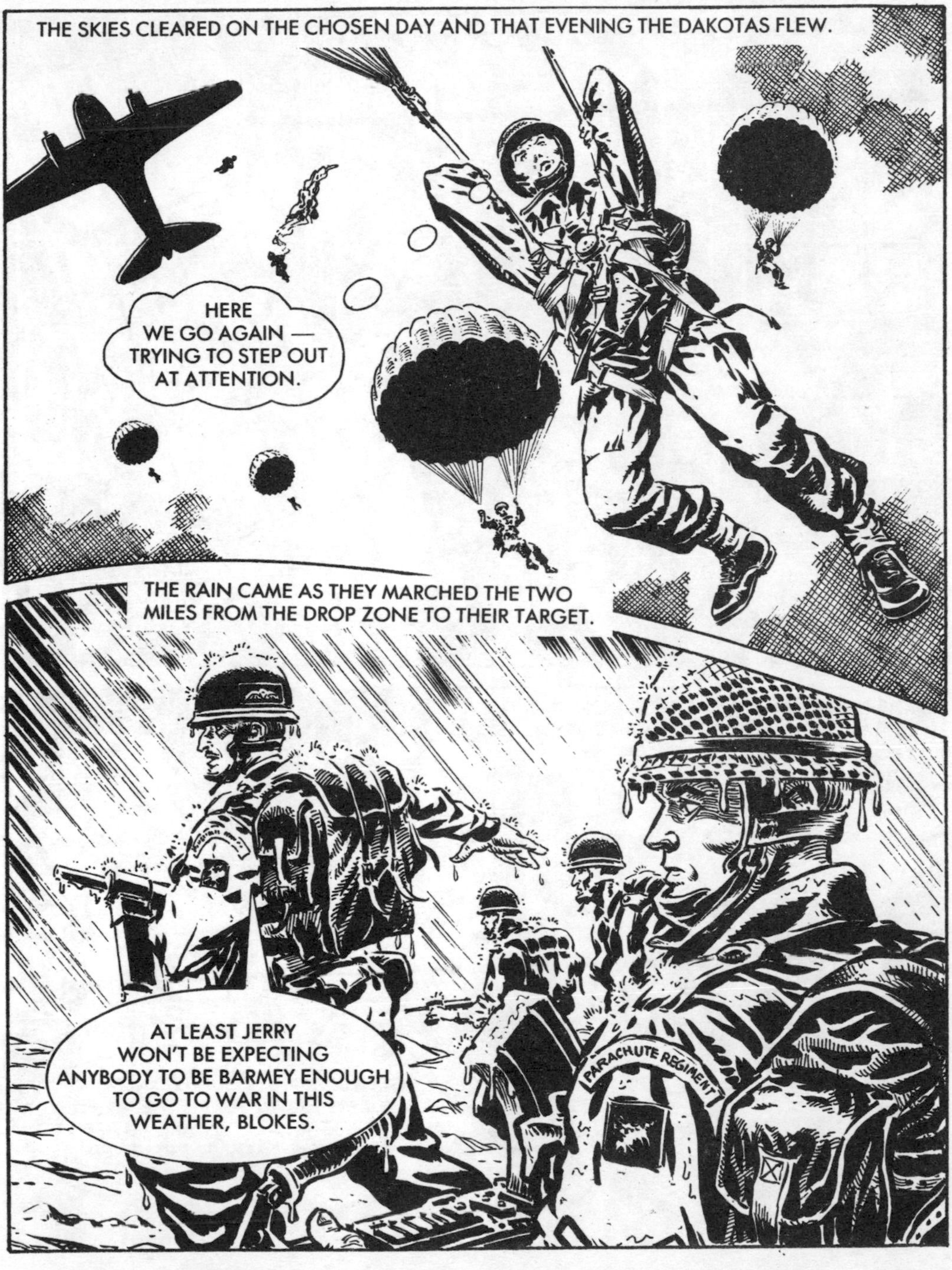
THE SKIES CLEARED ON THE CHOSEN DAY AND THAT EVENING THE DAKOTAS FLEW.
HERE WE GO AGAIN — TRYING TO STEP OUT AT ATTENTION.
THE RAIN CAME AS THEY MARCHED THE TWO MILES FROM THE DROP ZONE TO THEIR TARGET.
AT LEAST JERRY WON'T BE EXPECTING ANYBODY TO BE BARMEY ENOUGH TO GO TO WAR IN THIS WEATHER, BLOKES.
PARACHUTE REGIMENT

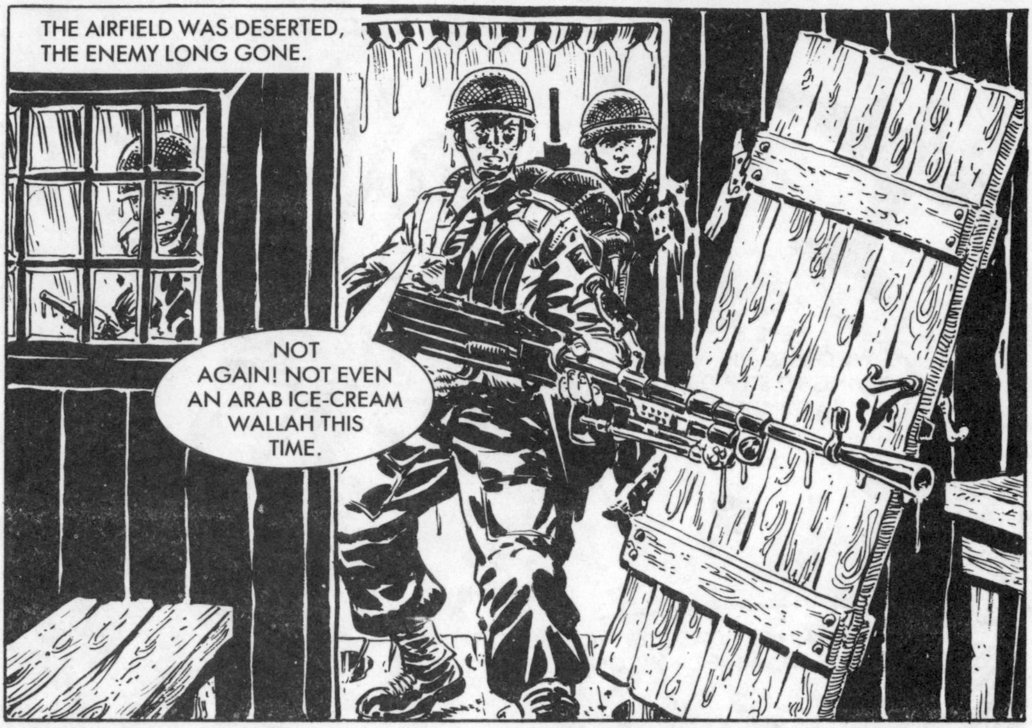
THE AIRFIELD WAS DESERTED, THE ENEMY LONG GONE.
NOT AGAIN! NOT EVEN AN ARAB ICE-CREAM WALLAH THIS TIME.

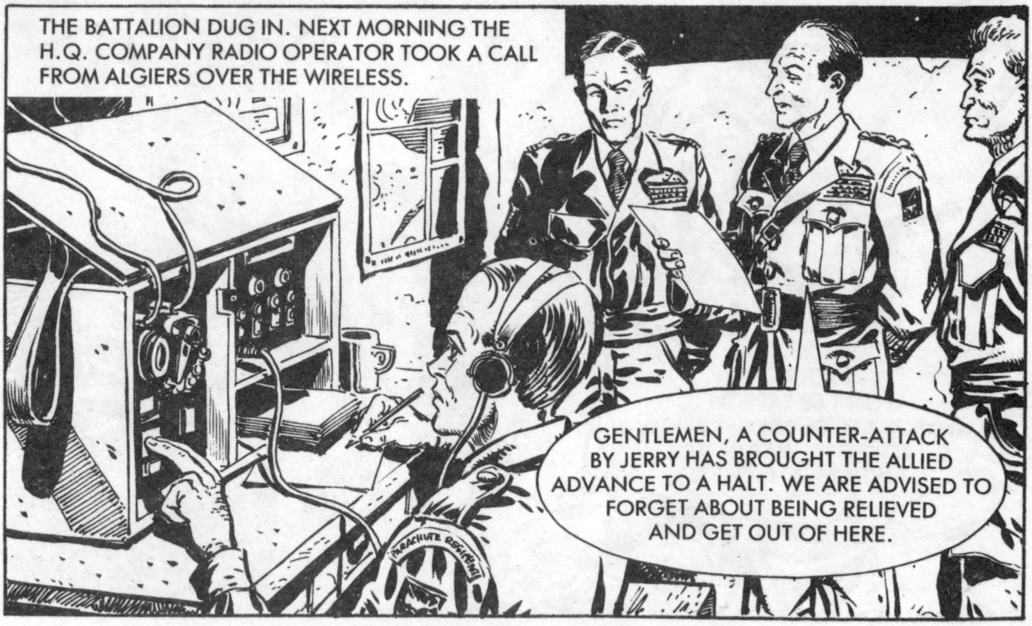
THE BATTALION DUG IN. NEXT MORNING THE H.Q. COMPANY RADIO OPERATOR TOOK A CALL FROM ALGIERS OVER THE WIRELESS.
GENTLEMEN, A COUNTER-ATTACK BY JERRY HAS BROUGHT THE ALLIED ADVANCE TO A HALT. WE ARE ADVISED TO FORGET ABOUT BEING RELIEVED AND GET OUT OF HERE.
PARACHUTE REGIMENT

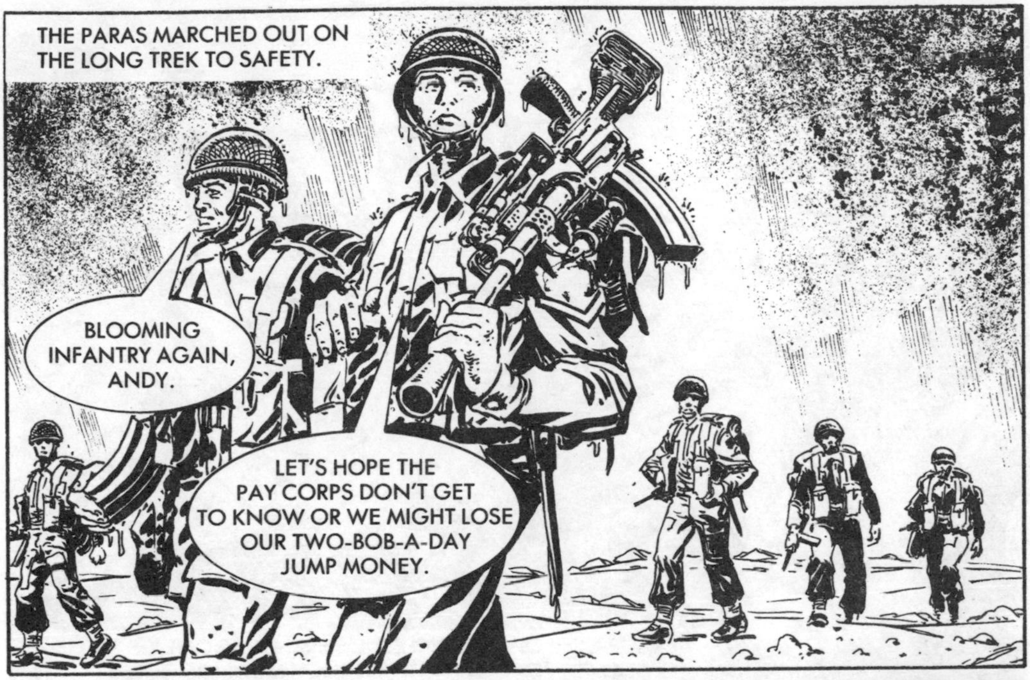
THE PARAS MARCHED OUT ON THE LONG TREK TO SAFETY.
BLOOMING INFANTRY AGAIN, ANDY.
LET'S HOPE THE PAY CORPS DON'T GET TO KNOW OR WE MIGHT LOSE OUR TWO-BOB-A-DAY JUMP MONEY.

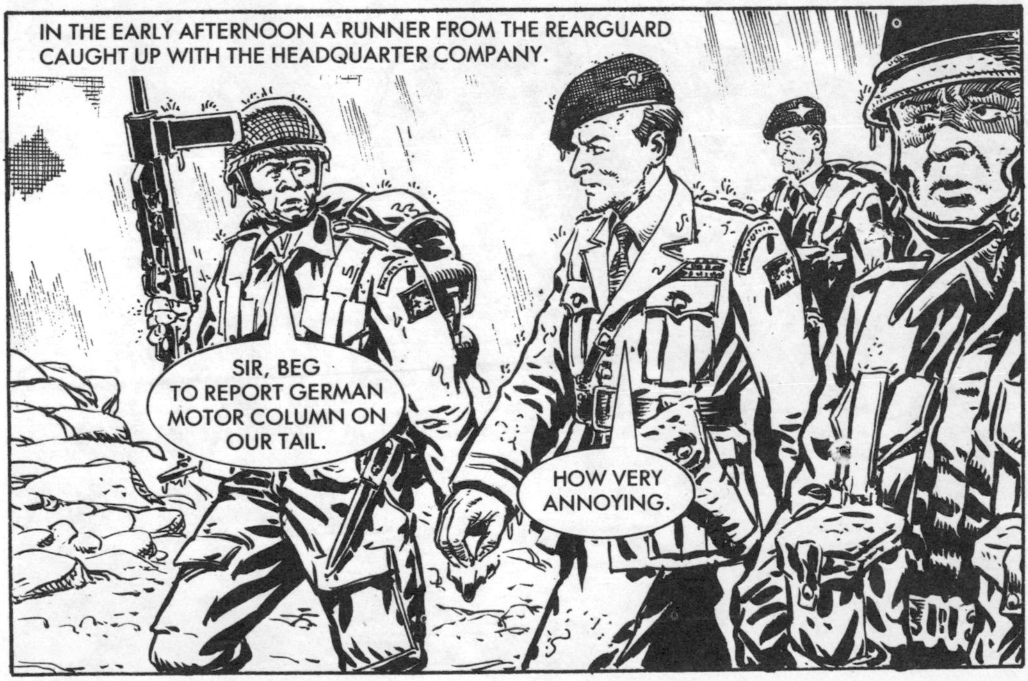
IN THE EARLY AFTERNOON A RUNNER FROM THE REARGUARD CAUGHT UP WITH THE HEADQUARTER COMPANY.
SIR, BEG TO REPORT GERMAN MOTOR COLUMN ON OUR TAIL.
HOW VERY ANNOYING.

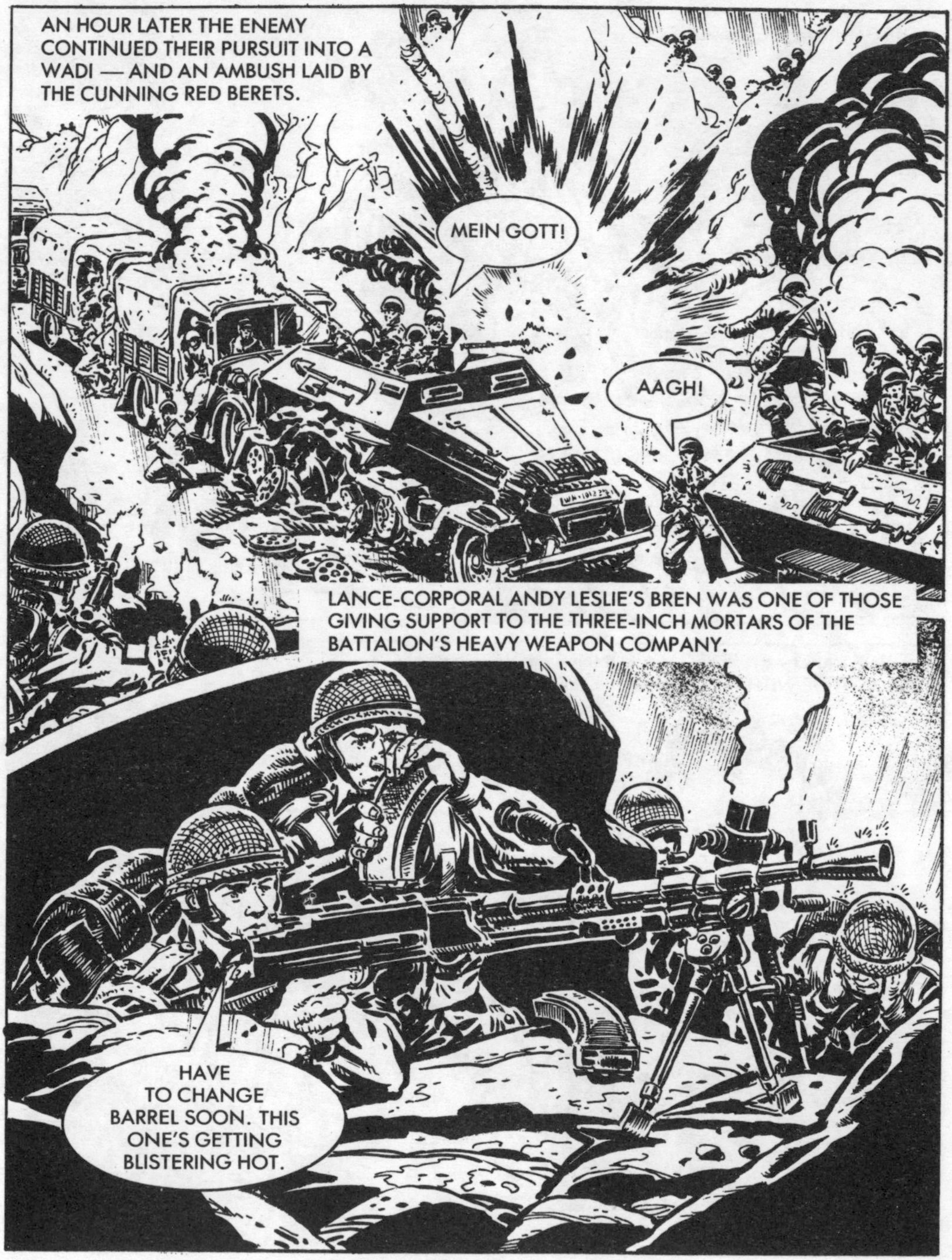
AN HOUR LATER THE ENEMY CONTINUED THEIR PURSUIT INTO A WADI — AND AN AMBUSH LAID BY THE CUNNING RED BERETS.
MEIN GOTT!
AAGH!
LANCE-CORPORAL ANDY LESLIE'S BREN WAS ONE OF THOSE GIVING SUPPORT TO THE THREE-INCH MORTARS OF THE BATTALION'S HEAVY WEAPON COMPANY.
HAVE TO CHANGE BARREL SOON. THIS ONE'S GETTING BLISTERING HOT.

LEAVING THE FOE SHATTERED, THE BATTALION RESUMED THE GRUELLING, STRENGTH-SAPPING MARCH.

IT COULD BE WORSE, ANDY. AT LEAST IT'S STOPPED RAINING

SSHH, DON'T TEMPT FATE, MATE.

NEXT MORNING ENEMY FORCES FORCED THE PARATROOPERS TO MAKE A STAND ON A HILL. ALL THAT DAY THEY ENDURED HEAVY BOMBARDMENT AND BEAT OFF REPEATED ATTACKS, TAKING MANY CASUALTIES.

ME AND ALL THE OTHER NONCOMS ARE OUT OF ACTION, ANDY. LOOKS LIKE YOU HAVE TO TAKE OVER THE PLATOON.

SOME PLATOON! ELEVEN MEN LEFT OUT OF THIRTY. WE ALWAYS SEEM TO END UP IN TIGHT SPOTS!

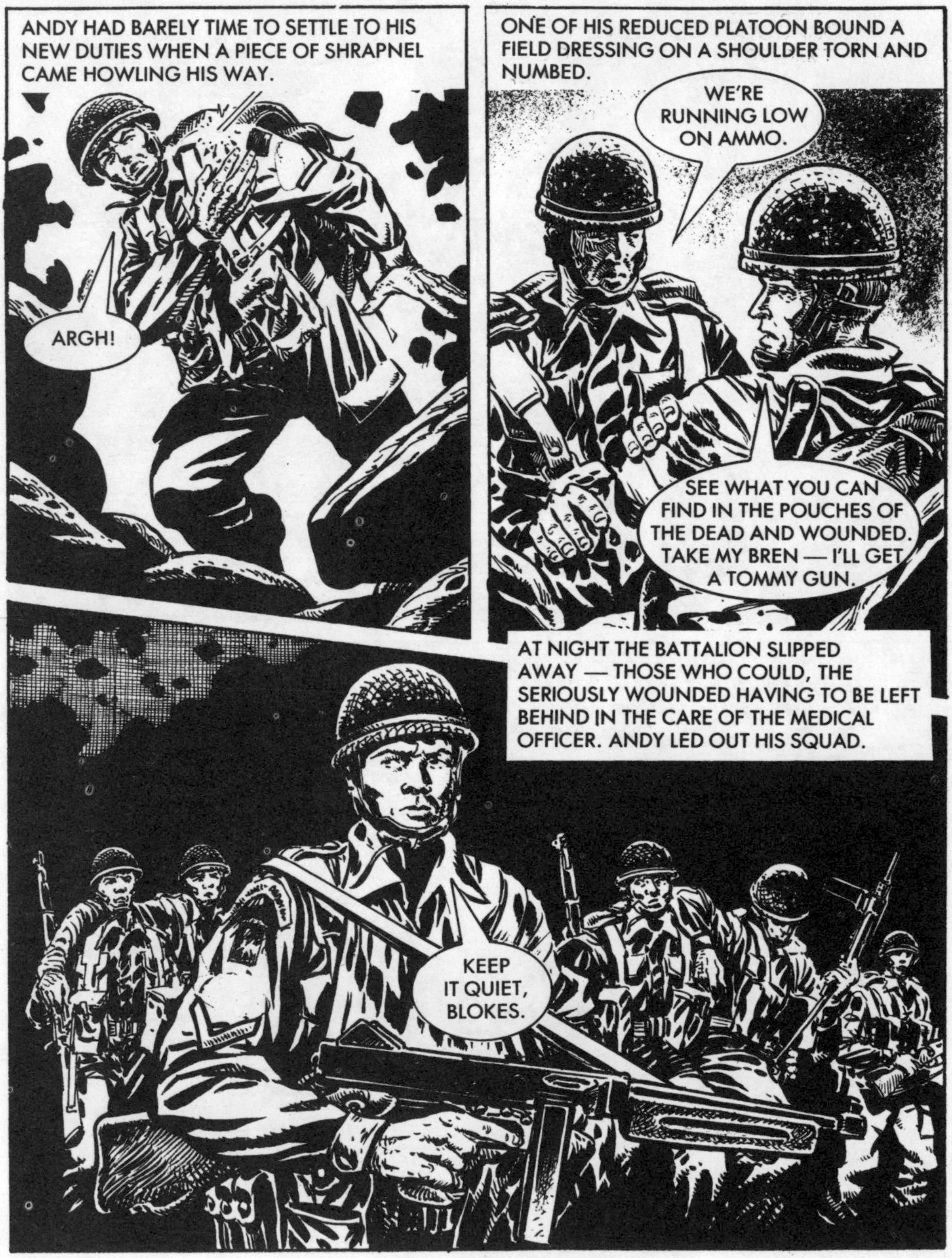
ANDY HAD BARELY TIME TO SETTLE TO HIS NEW DUTIES WHEN A PIECE OF SHRAPNEL CAME HOWLING HIS WAY.
ARGH!
ONE OF HIS REDUCED PLATOON BOUND A FIELD DRESSING ON A SHOULDER TORN AND NUMBED.
WE'RE RUNNING LOW ON AMMO.
SEE WHAT YOU CAN FIND IN THE POUCHES OF THE DEAD AND WOUNDED. TAKE MY BREN — I'LL GET A TOMMY GUN.
AT NIGHT THE BATTALION SLIPPED AWAY — THOSE WHO COULD, THE SERIOUSLY WOUNDED HAVING TO BE LEFT BEHIND IN THE CARE OF THE MEDICAL OFFICER. ANDY LED OUT HIS SQUAD.
KEEP IT QUIET, BLOKES.

TWO DAYS LATER AN EXHAUSTED, RAGGED, BUT STILL DEFIANT BAND OF MILITARY SCARE-CROWS MET AMERICAN SCOUT CARS THAT PROVIDED ESCORT TO THE ALLIED LINES.

BATTALION WILL MARCH TO ATTENTION.

THE TIRED, BATTLE-WEARY RED BERETS MARCHED IN AS IF THEY WERE ON SOME BRITISH PARADE GROUND. IT WAS A STIRRING SIGHT.

JUST LOOK AT THEM CRAZY LIMEYS.

I'M GLAD THEY'RE ON OUR SIDE!

ADMITTED TO BASE HOSPITAL IN ALGIERS FOR REMOVAL OF THE SHRAPNEL, ANDY MET AN OLD FRIEND — SERGEANT SID STONE, RECOVERING FROM HIS ATTACK ON THE TANK.

I THOUGHT YOU'D BE PUSHING UP THE DAISIES BY NOW, SID.

I SUPPOSE THAT MEANS YOU THIEVING VILLAINS HAVE SHARED OUT MY KIT.

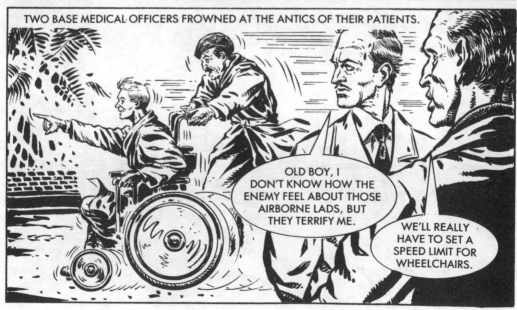

TWO BASE MEDICAL OFFICERS FROWNED AT THE ANTICS OF THEIR PATIENTS.

OLD BOY, I DON'T KNOW HOW THE ENEMY FEEL ABOUT THOSE AIRBORNE LADS, BUT THEY TERRIFY ME.

WE'LL REALLY HAVE TO SET A SPEED LIMIT FOR WHEELCHAIRS.

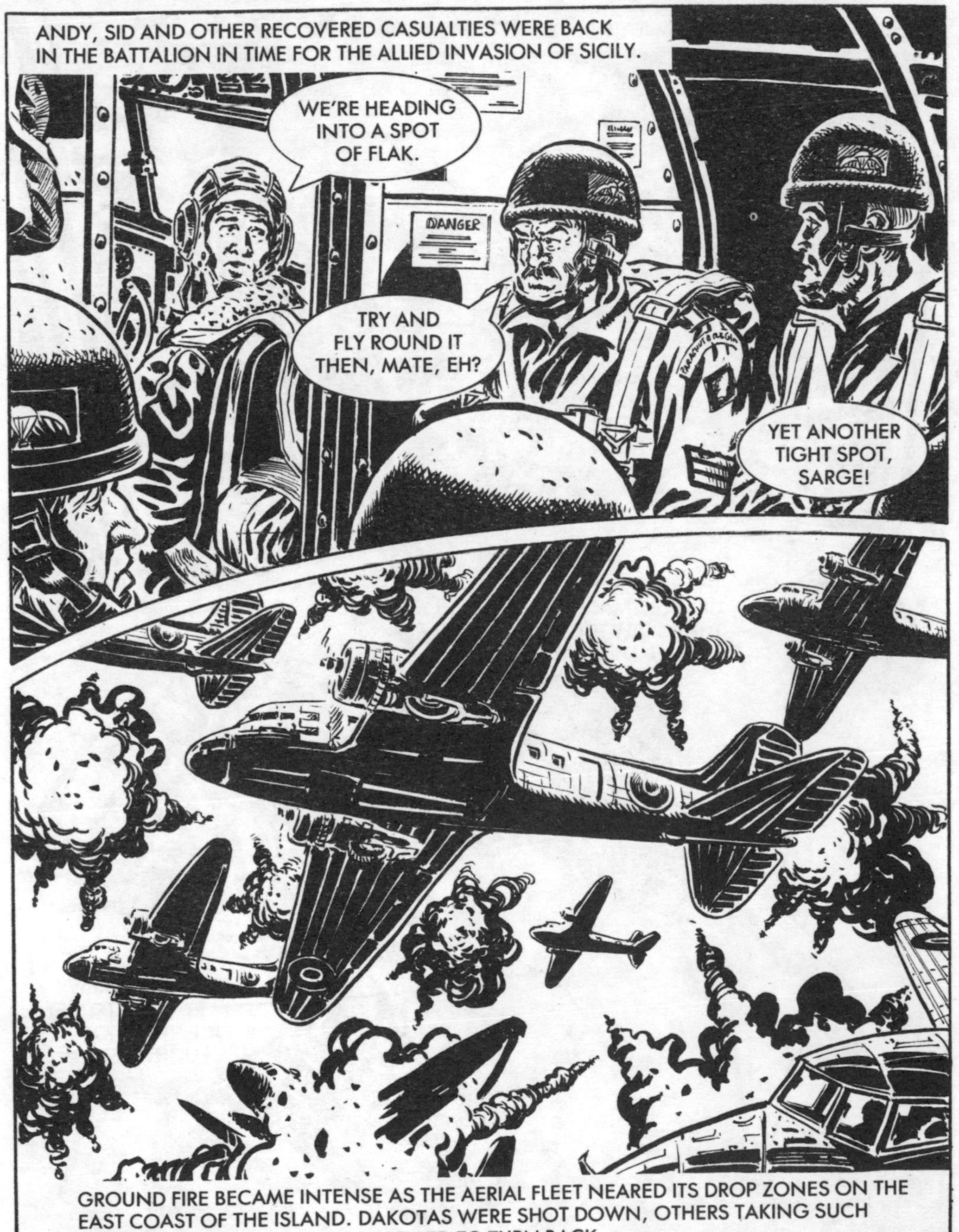
ANDY, SID AND OTHER RECOVERED CASUALTIES WERE BACK IN THE BATTALION IN TIME FOR THE ALLIED INVASION OF SICILY.
WE'RE HEADING INTO A SPOT OF FLAK.
TRY AND FLY ROUND IT THEN, MATE, EH?
YET ANOTHER TIGHT SPOT, SARGE!
DANGER
GROUND FIRE BECAME INTENSE AS THE AERIAL FLEET NEARED ITS DROP ZONES ON THE EAST COAST OF THE ISLAND. DAKOTAS WERE SHOT DOWN, OTHERS TAKING SUCH DAMAGE THAT THEY WERE COMPELLED TO TURN BACK.

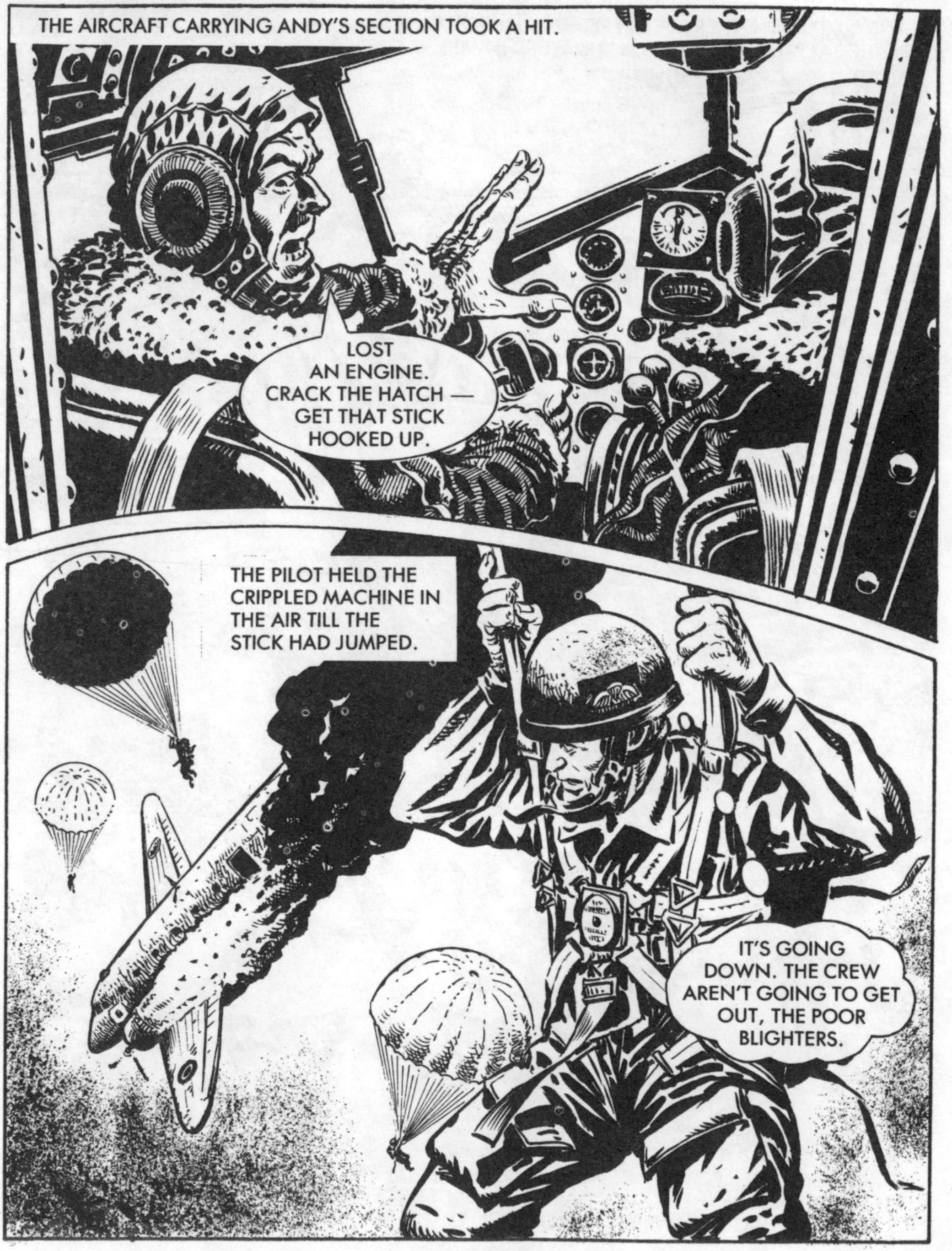
THE AIRCRAFT CARRYING ANDY'S SECTION TOOK A HIT.
LOST AN ENGINE. CRACK THE HATCH — GET THAT STICK HOOKED UP.
THE PILOT HELD THE CRIPPLED MACHINE IN THE AIR TILL THE STICK HAD JUMPED.
IT'S GOING DOWN. THE CREW AREN'T GOING TO GET OUT, THE POOR BLIGHTERS.

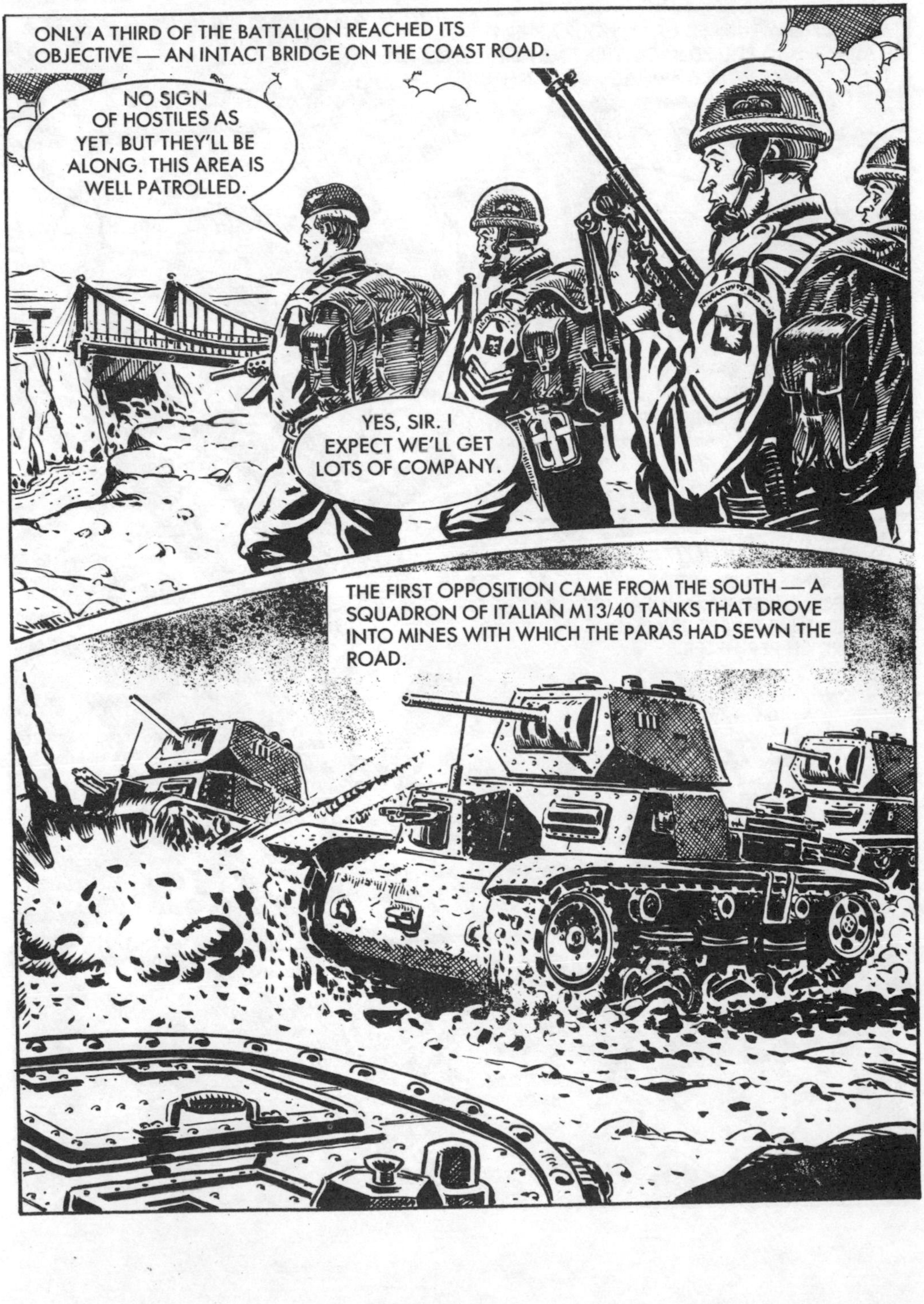
ONLY A THIRD OF THE BATTALION REACHED ITS OBJECTIVE — AN INTACT BRIDGE ON THE COAST ROAD.
NO SIGN OF HOSTILES AS YET, BUT THEY'LL BE ALONG. THIS AREA IS WELL PATROLLED.
YES, SIR. I EXPECT WE'LL GET LOTS OF COMPANY.
THE FIRST OPPOSITION CAME FROM THE SOUTH — A SQUADRON OF ITALIAN M13/40 TANKS THAT DROVE INTO MINES WITH WHICH THE PARAS HAD SEWN THE ROAD.

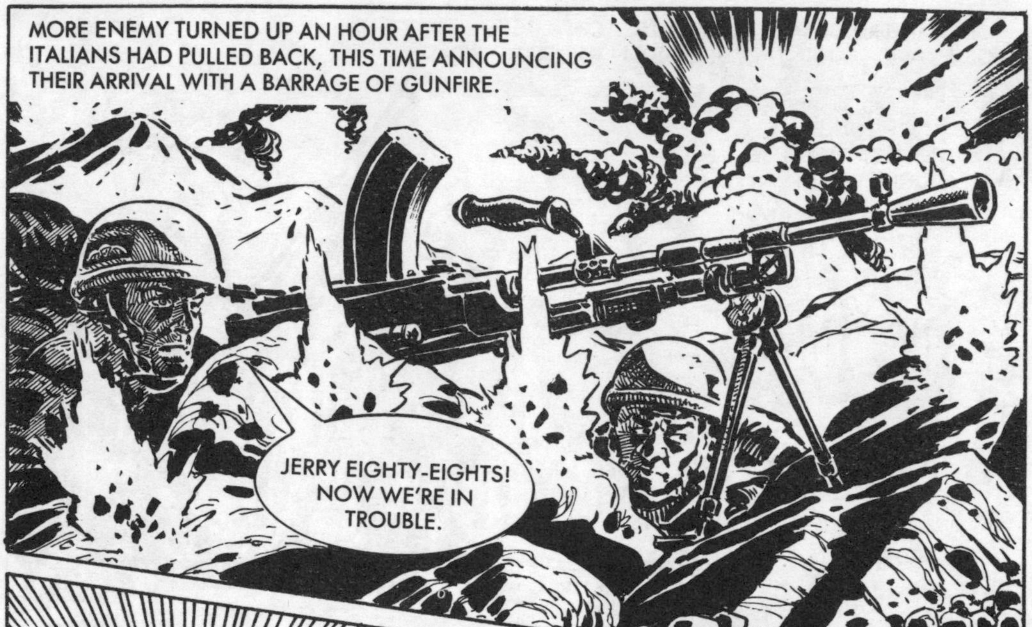
MORE ENEMY TURNED UP AN HOUR AFTER THE ITALIANS HAD PULLED BACK, THIS TIME ANNOUNCING THEIR ARRIVAL WITH A BARRAGE OF GUNFIRE.
JERRY EIGHTY-EIGHTS! NOW WE'RE IN TROUBLE.

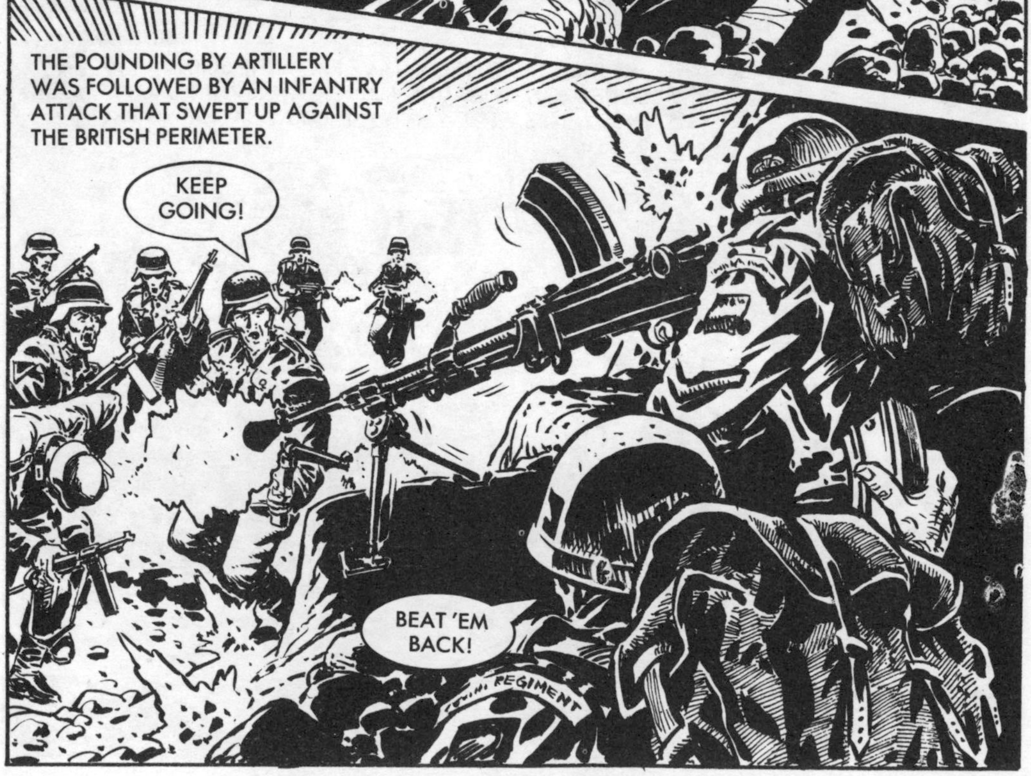
THE POUNDING BY ARTILLERY WAS FOLLOWED BY AN INFANTRY ATTACK THAT SWEPT UP AGAINST THE BRITISH PERIMETER.
KEEP GOING!
BEAT 'EM BACK!
REGIMENT

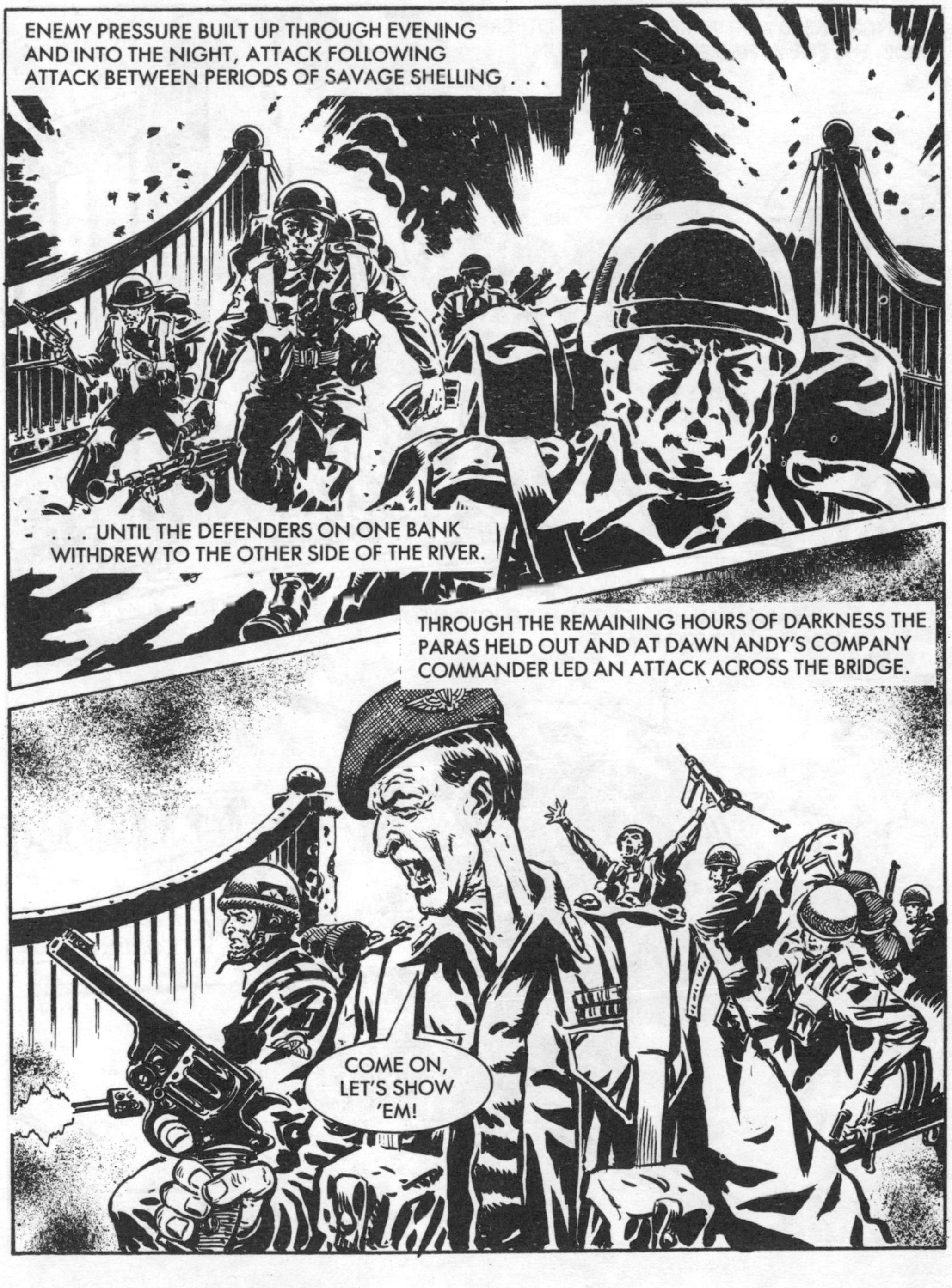
ENEMY PRESSURE BUILT UP THROUGH EVENING AND INTO THE NIGHT, ATTACK FOLLOWING ATTACK BETWEEN PERIODS OF SAVAGE SHELLING . . .
. . . UNTIL THE DEFENDERS ON ONE BANK WITHDREW TO THE OTHER SIDE OF THE RIVER.
THROUGH THE REMAINING HOURS OF DARKNESS THE PARAS HELD OUT AND AT DAWN ANDY'S COMPANY COMMANDER LED AN ATTACK ACROSS THE BRIDGE.
COME ON, LET'S SHOW 'EM!

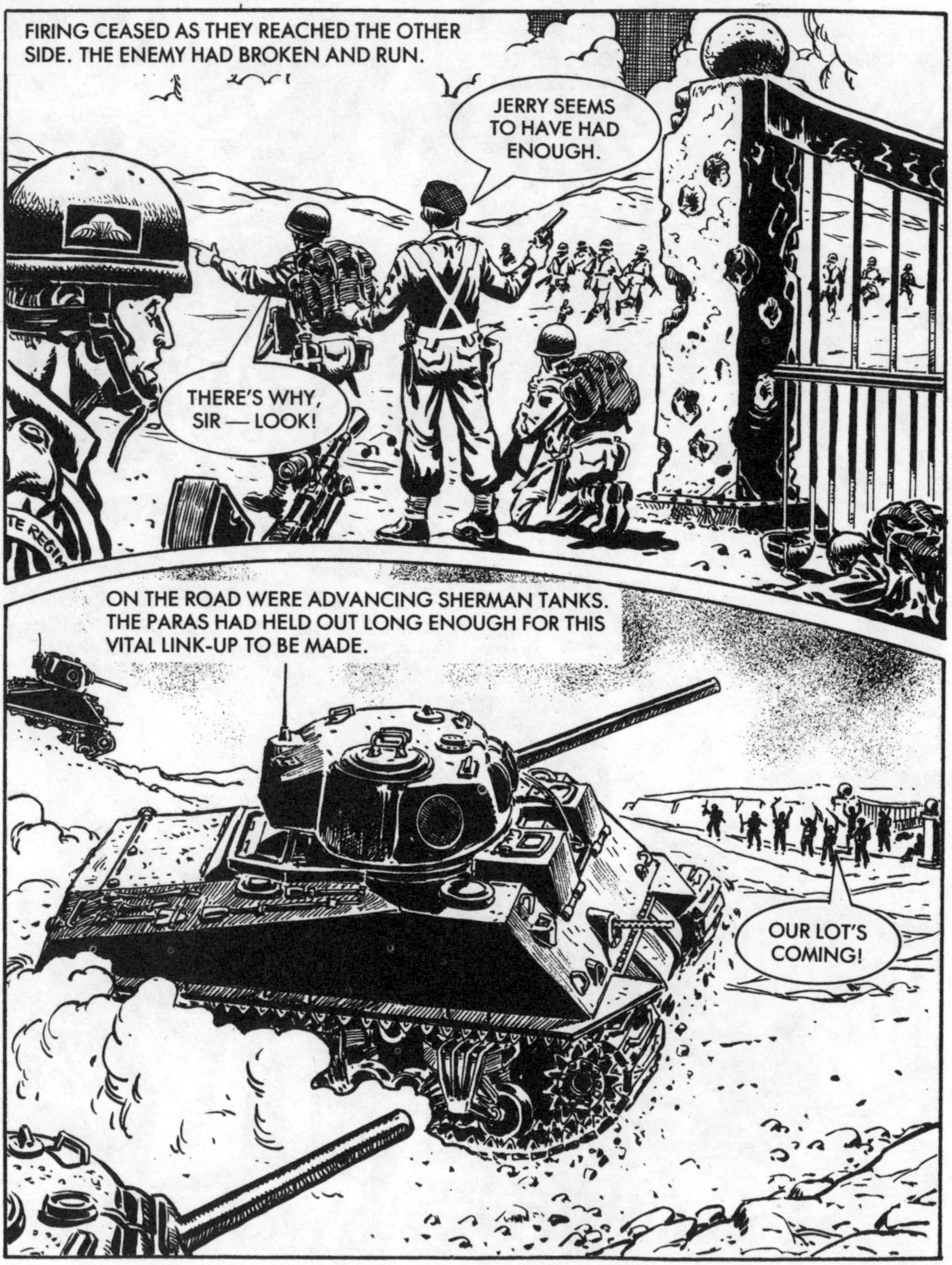
FIRING CEASED AS THEY REACHED THE OTHER SIDE. THE ENEMY HAD BROKEN AND RUN.
JERRY SEEMS TO HAVE HAD ENOUGH.
THERE'S WHY, SIR — LOOK!
ON THE ROAD WERE ADVANCING SHERMAN TANKS. THE PARAS HAD HELD OUT LONG ENOUGH FOR THIS VITAL LINK-UP TO BE MADE.
OUR LOT'S COMING!

ANDY HAD NOT MADE IT ACROSS THE BRIDGE, A NAZI BULLET SEARING INTO HIS LEG.

YOUR SECOND WOUND STRIPE, EH? COLLECT ANOTHER AND YOU GET FLOWN STRAIGHT BACK TO BLIGHTY.

I CAN HARDLY WAIT.

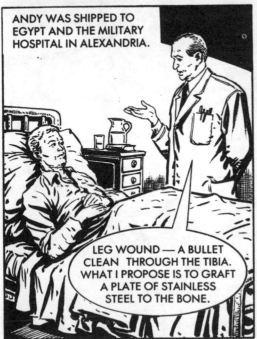

ANDY WAS SHIPPED TO EGYPT AND THE MILITARY HOSPITAL IN ALEXANDRIA.

LEG WOUND — A BULLET CLEAN THROUGH THE TIBIA. WHAT I PROPOSE IS TO GRAFT A PLATE OF STAINLESS STEEL TO THE BONE.

THREE MONTHS PASSED BEFORE HE WAS ABLE TO GET BACK TO THE BATTALION, BY THEN SERVING AS INFANTRY IN THE ADVANCE THROUGH ITALY.

NICE TIMING, LAD. NO NEED TO UNPACK — WE'RE HEADING BACK TO BLIGHTY!

WHAT, SARGE, ARE YOU JOKING?

SID WAS SERIOUS. THE RETURN TO THE UNITED KINGDOM WAS BY SHIP AND ANDY LEARNED THEN OF FURTHER PROMOTION.

BETTER PUT UP TWO STRIPES OR YOU'LL BE IMPROPERLY DRESSED AFTER THE NEXT DAILY ROUTINE ORDERS.

WHAT? ME A FULL CORPORAL?

HE WAS PUT ON A NON-COMMISSIONED OFFICER COURSE WHEN THEY ARRIVED AT THEIR DEPOT.

REPORTING BACK AT THE END OF THE COURSE, ANDY LEARNED THAT HIS FRIEND SID STONE HAD BEEN POSTED OUT.

WHICH LEAVES US SHORT OF A SECTION LEADER — A POSITION I WISH YOU TO TAKE UP. I NEED EXPERIENCED SOLDIERS TO BREAK IN OUR REPLACEMENTS.

SO NOW I'M A SERGEANT. WELL, AT LEAST I GET PAID FOR THREE STRIPES.

ANDY SET ABOUT HIS NEW DUTIES WITH A WILL, DRIVING THE NEW MEN HARD FOR THEIR OWN GOOD.

ENOUGH DIRT TO GROW CABBAGES AND THE BLOW-HOLE NEEDS POKING OUT, YOU GRUBBY PERSON. WHAT ARE YOU?

I AM A GRUBBY PERSON, SARN'T.

MONTHS OF TRAINING HARDENED THE UNIT FOR ACTION — WHICH CAME ONE EVENING EARLY IN JUNE, 1944, WHEN ONE BY ONE THEY BOARDED THE FAMILIAR DAKOTAS.

PASS! NEXT MAN.

THE INVASION OF FRANCE WAS WHAT IT WAS ALL ABOUT.

THE ARMADA THAT TOOK FLIGHT WAS AT THAT TIME THE LARGEST EVER ASSEMBLED FOR AN AIRBORNE OPERATION.

HOOK UP!

THEIR OFFICER, LIEUTENANT LAWSON, LED THE WAY WHILE ANDY BROUGHT UP THE REAR OF HIS JUMPING STICK.

THE DROPPING ZONE WAS SUPPOSED TO BE MARSHY GROUND . . . AND THAT WAS ONLY HALF THE STORY.

HERE WE GO AGAIN! HOW OFTEN HAVE I SAID THAT TO MYSELF.

WATER! THERE'S WATER EVERYWHERE.

SWIFTLY HE BEGAN TO UNBUCKLE HIS HARNESS TO FALL CLEAR OF IT.

TRYING TO STEER FOR A DIMLY GLIMPSED RIDGE OF DRY GROUND, HE LANDED SHORT IN A WATERY SPLASHDOWN.

URH! THE AREA MUST HAVE BEEN FLOODED.

ANDY AND OTHER PARAS WADED TO GATHER ON THE NEAREST PIECE OF HIGH GROUND.

HEY! HELP!

YOU LOT BRING IN THE CONTAINERS WHILE I GO OUT TO THAT BLOKE.

HE WADED OUT TO RESCUE THE MAN HOPELESSLY TANGLED IN HIS CANOPY AND RIGGING.

NOT SO MUCH OF THE YELLING, LAD. THERE'S SUPPOSED TO BE A WAR GOING ON.

SORRY, SARGE. NEXT TIME I'LL REMEMBER TO DROWN QUIETLY.

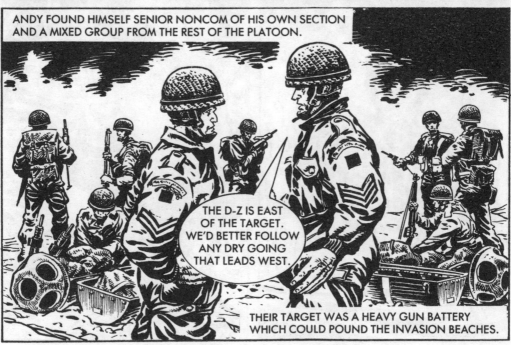

ANDY FOUND HIMSELF SENIOR NONCOM OF HIS OWN SECTION AND A MIXED GROUP FROM THE REST OF THE PLATOON.

THE D-Z IS EAST OF THE TARGET. WE'D BETTER FOLLOW ANY DRY GOING THAT LEADS WEST.

THEIR TARGET WAS A HEAVY GUN BATTERY WHICH COULD POUND THE INVASION BEACHES.

THEY MARCHED, THEIR NUMBER INCREASING AS OTHER PARAS CAME IN OFF OTHER TRACKS AND FLOODED GROUND, ONE OF THE NEWCOMERS BEING MAJOR SYKES, THE COMPANY COMMANDER.

YOU'VE DONE WELL, LESLIE, AND WE SHOULD BE COMING TO A CROSSROADS IF THIS IS THE RIGHT WAY.

THEIR STRENGTH HAD BUILT UP TO HALF THE BATTALION WHEN THEY CROSSED A JUNCTION AND MOVED ON ALONG ONE OF THE ROADS IT LINKED.

THE PERIMETER. THERE SHOULD BE AN INNER FENCE ABOUT TWENTY YARDS AWAY.

ENGINEERS CAME UP AND CHECKED THE LANE BETWEEN THE FENCES FOR ANTI-PERSONNEL MINES.

HOLD ON! SOMETHING HERE.

AS THE PARAS WAITED, THOUGHTS ON THE TARGET, THE HORIZON WAS LIT UP BY THE THUNDER OF ARTILLERY.

A BIT OF HATE GOING ON OVER THERE, SARGE.

DON'T GET IMPATIENT. OUR TURN WILL COME.

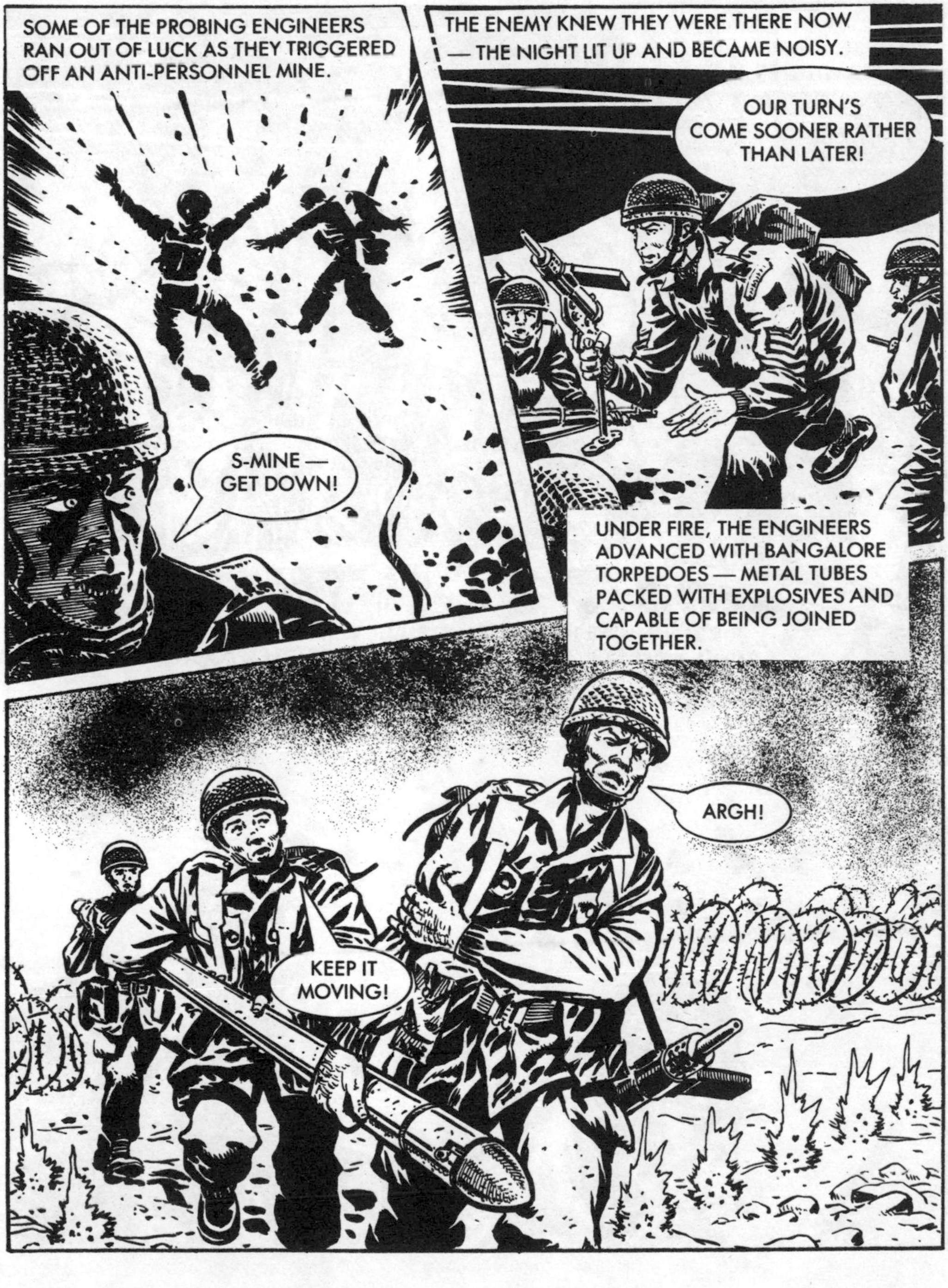
SOME OF THE PROBING ENGINEERS RAN OUT OF LUCK AS THEY TRIGGERED OFF AN ANTI-PERSONNEL MINE.
S-MINE — GET DOWN!
THE ENEMY KNEW THEY WERE THERE NOW — THE NIGHT LIT UP AND BECAME NOISY.
OUR TURN'S COME SOONER RATHER THAN LATER!
UNDER FIRE, THE ENGINEERS ADVANCED WITH BANGALORE TORPEDOES — METAL TUBES PACKED WITH EXPLOSIVES AND CAPABLE OF BEING JOINED TOGETHER.
ARGH!
KEEP IT MOVING!

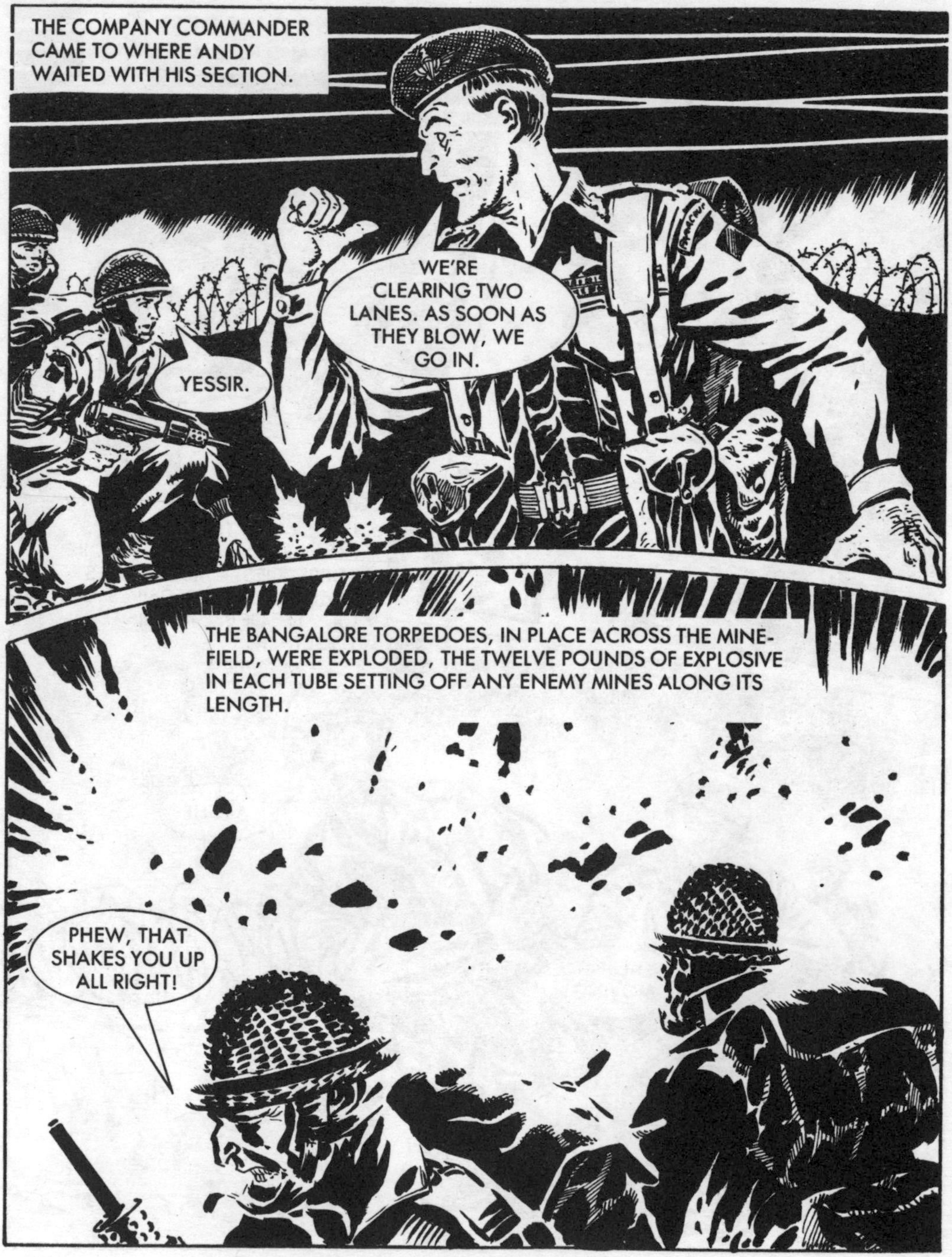
THE COMPANY COMMANDER CAME TO WHERE ANDY WAITED WITH HIS SECTION.
WE'RE CLEARING TWO LANES. AS SOON AS THEY BLOW, WE GO IN.
YESSIR.
THE BANGALORE TORPEDOES, IN PLACE ACROSS THE MINE-FIELD, WERE EXPLODED, THE TWELVE POUNDS OF EXPLOSIVE IN EACH TUBE SETTING OFF ANY ENEMY MINES ALONG ITS LENGTH.
PHEW, THAT SHAKES YOU UP ALL RIGHT!

THE PARAS WENT IN ALONG CRATERED LANES HURRIEDLY MARKED BY THE ENGINEERS.

KEEP TO THE LEFT OF THE TAPE.

THEY CAME UP AGAINST HEAVY FIRING FROM ENEMY DEFENCES, SUFFERING SEVERAL CASUALTIES.

TAKE COVER!

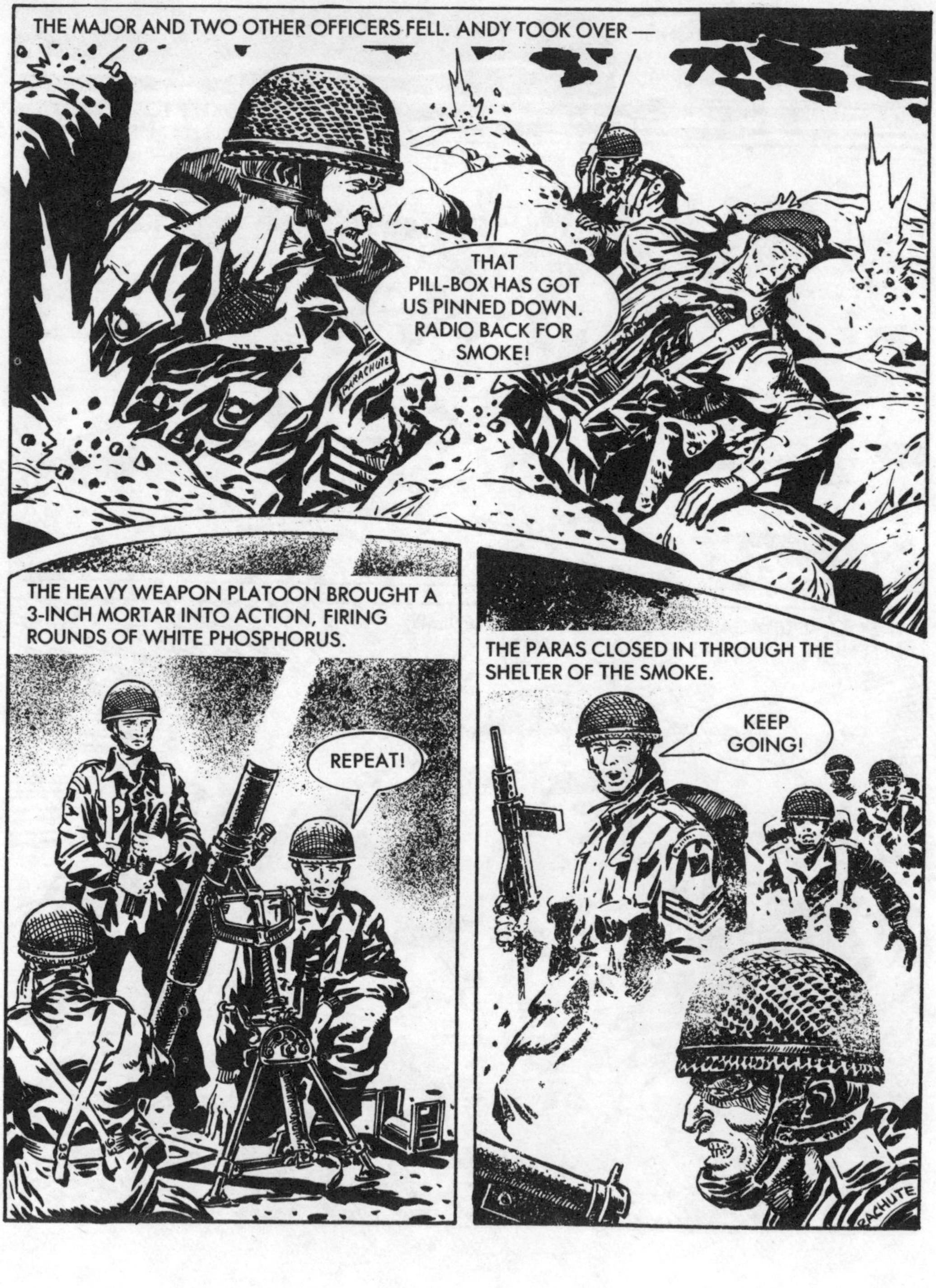
THE MAJOR AND TWO OTHER OFFICERS FELL. ANDY TOOK OVER —
THAT PILL-BOX HAS GOT US PINNED DOWN. RADIO BACK FOR SMOKE!
PARACHUTE
THE HEAVY WEAPON PLATOON BROUGHT A 3-INCH MORTAR INTO ACTION, FIRING ROUNDS OF WHITE PHOSPHORUS.
REPEAT!
THE PARAS CLOSED IN THROUGH THE SHELTER OF THE SMOKE.
KEEP GOING!

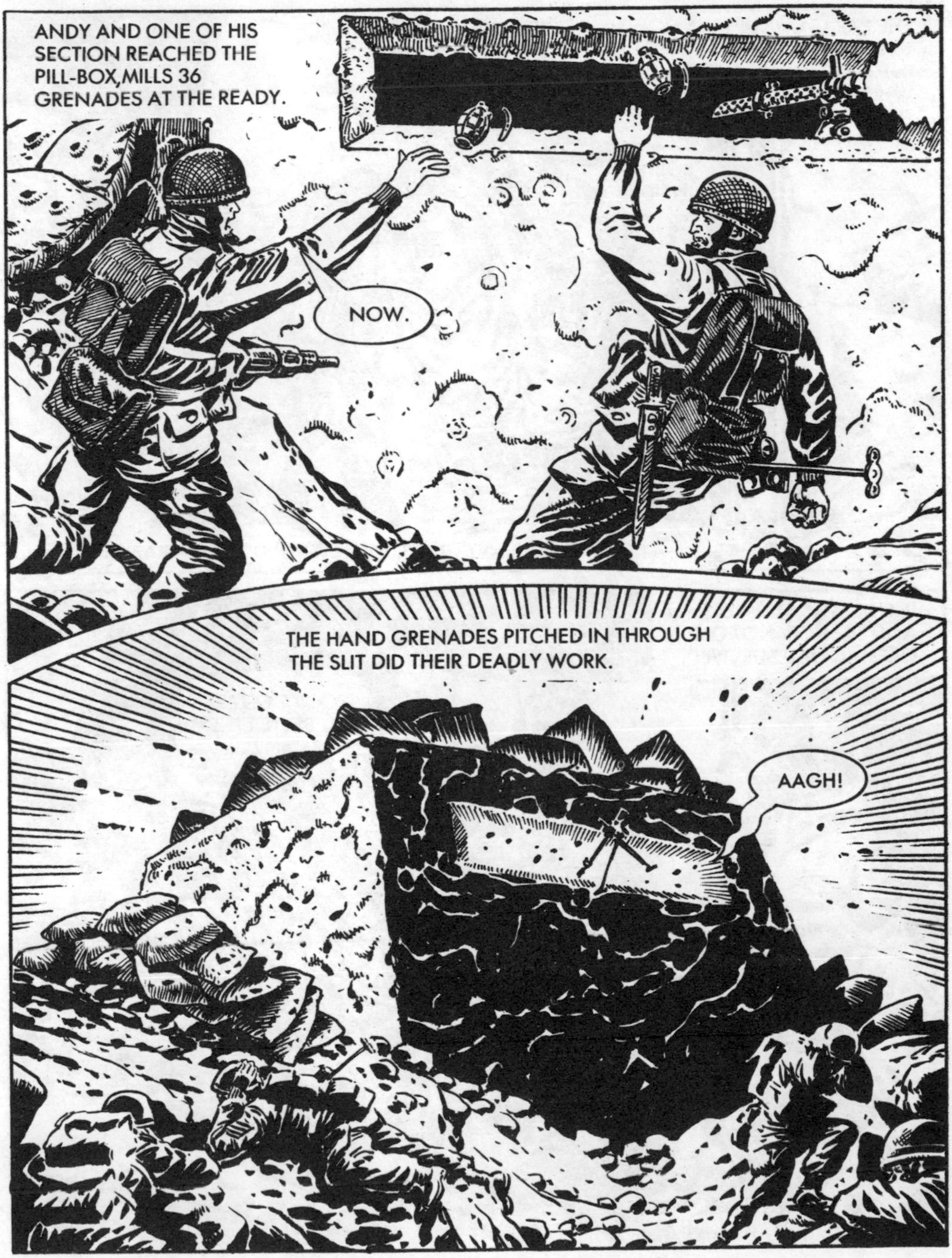
ANDY AND ONE OF HIS SECTION REACHED THE PILL-BOX, MILLS 36 GRENADES AT THE READY.
NOW.
THE HAND GRENADES PITCHED IN THROUGH THE SLIT DID THEIR DEADLY WORK.
AAGH!

THE PARAS CIRCLED THE NOW SILENT STRUCTURE AND DROPPED INTO A COMMUNICATION TRENCH WHICH LED TO A REAR STEEL DOOR.

BOLTED INSIDE.

ANYBODY GOT A CAN OPENER?

A CLUSTER OF HEAVY CHARGES SHATTERED THE ENTRANCE HATCH.

INSIDE WAS STILLNESS AND SILENCE. NOT ONE GERMAN HAD SURVIVED.

POOR GEEZERS, BUT BETTER THEM THAN US.

ANDY AND HIS LADS ROLLED UP THE ENEMY DEFENCES, CUTTING DOWN RESISTANCE, BLASTING THEIR WAY INTO BUNKERS.

ARGH!

BY DAWN THE BATTERY WAS TAKEN — THE DAWN OF THE SIXTH OF JUNE, D-DAY FOR THE ALLIED INVASION OF EUROPE.

UGLY BRUTE.

JUST A HARMLESS LUMP OF METAL THAT WON'T BE HAMMERING OUR LADS COMING ASHORE.

THE TROOPS FROM THE BEACHES LINKED WITH THEM. ANDY'S BRIGADE WENT ON TO SERVE AS INFANTRY IN THE BITTER NORMANDY FIGHTING THAT FOLLOWED.

SARGE, DOES ALL THIS HIKING MEAN WE LOSE OUR JUMP PAY?

LOOK, I'VE HEARD THAT ONE BEFORE — YOU'LL HAVE TO DO BETTER THAN THAT.

IN EARLY AUGUST THEY WERE RETURNED TO THE UNITED KINGDOM — THOSE WHO WERE LEFT.

LEAVE PASSES AND RAILWAY WARRANTS AT BATTALION OFFICE, LADS. THIS PLACE WILL BE FULL OF A NEW INTAKE WHEN WE GET BACK.

AMONG THE REINFORCEMENTS WAS A FAMILIAR FACE, THE OWNER SPORTING THE RANK OF SECOND LIEUTENANT.

SID — ER, SIR! SO YOU GOT YOUR PIP.

NOTHING ESCAPES YOUR EAGLE EYE, YOUNG ANDY. GOOD TO SEE YOU AGAIN.

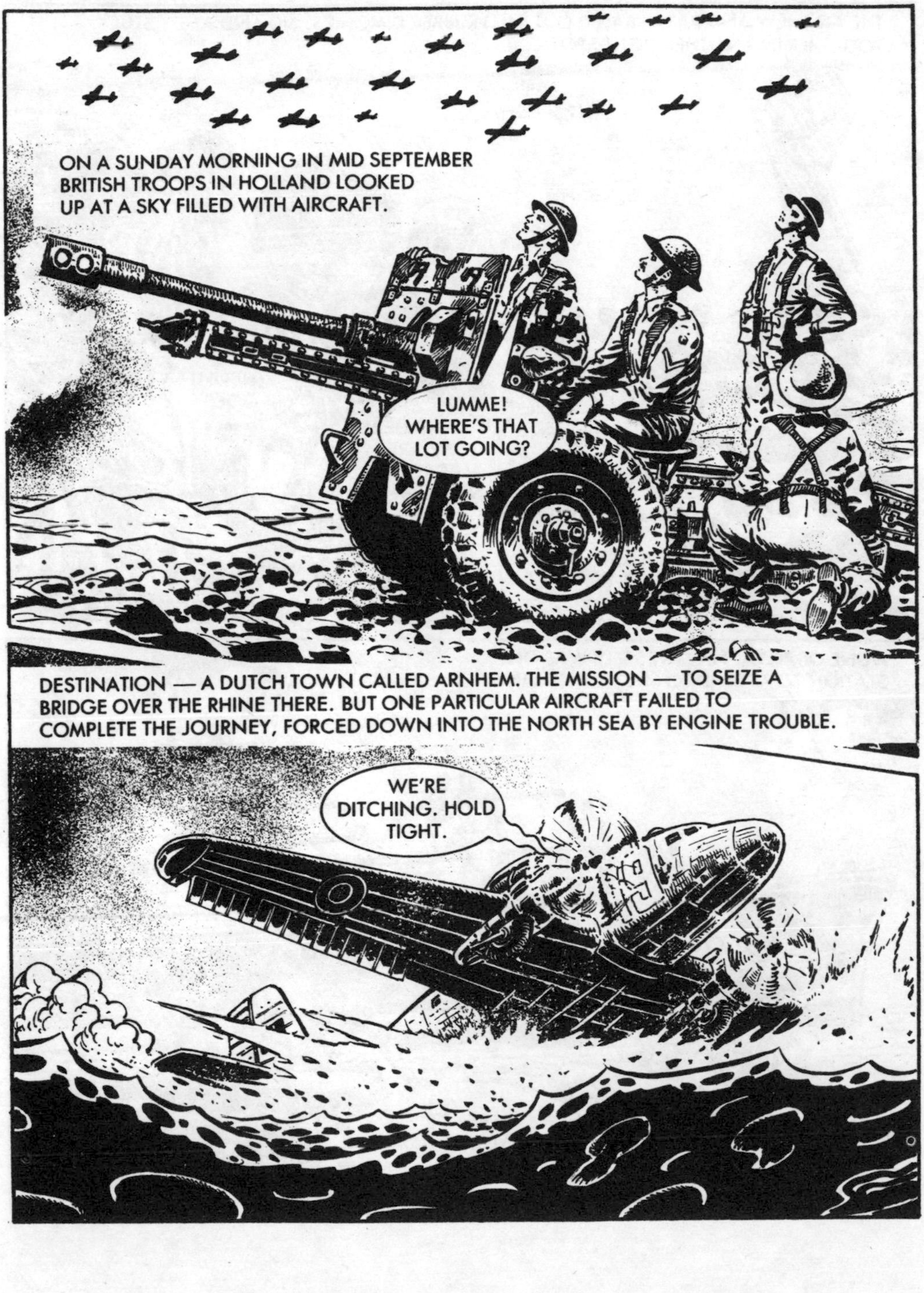
ON A SUNDAY MORNING IN MID SEPTEMBER BRITISH TROOPS IN HOLLAND LOOKED UP AT A SKY FILLED WITH AIRCRAFT.
LUMME! WHERE'S THAT LOT GOING?
DESTINATION — A DUTCH TOWN CALLED ARNHEM. THE MISSION — TO SEIZE A BRIDGE OVER THE RHINE THERE. BUT ONE PARTICULAR AIRCRAFT FAILED TO COMPLETE THE JOURNEY, FORCED DOWN INTO THE NORTH SEA BY ENGINE TROUBLE.
WE'RE DITCHING. HOLD TIGHT.

THE AIR CREW AND PARAS BALED OUT INTO RUBBER DINGHIES, SID AND ANDY STUCK TOGETHER IN ANOTHER TIGHT SPOT.

THERE IT GOES.

AND HERE WE ARE — ALL DRESSED UP AND NOWHERE TO GO.

A LINE OF ROYAL NAVY VESSELS WAS ON STATION TO ATTEND TO SUCH CASUALTIES.

WOULD YOU CHAPS CARE FOR A LIFT?

DEPENDS WHERE YOU'RE GOING, MATE.

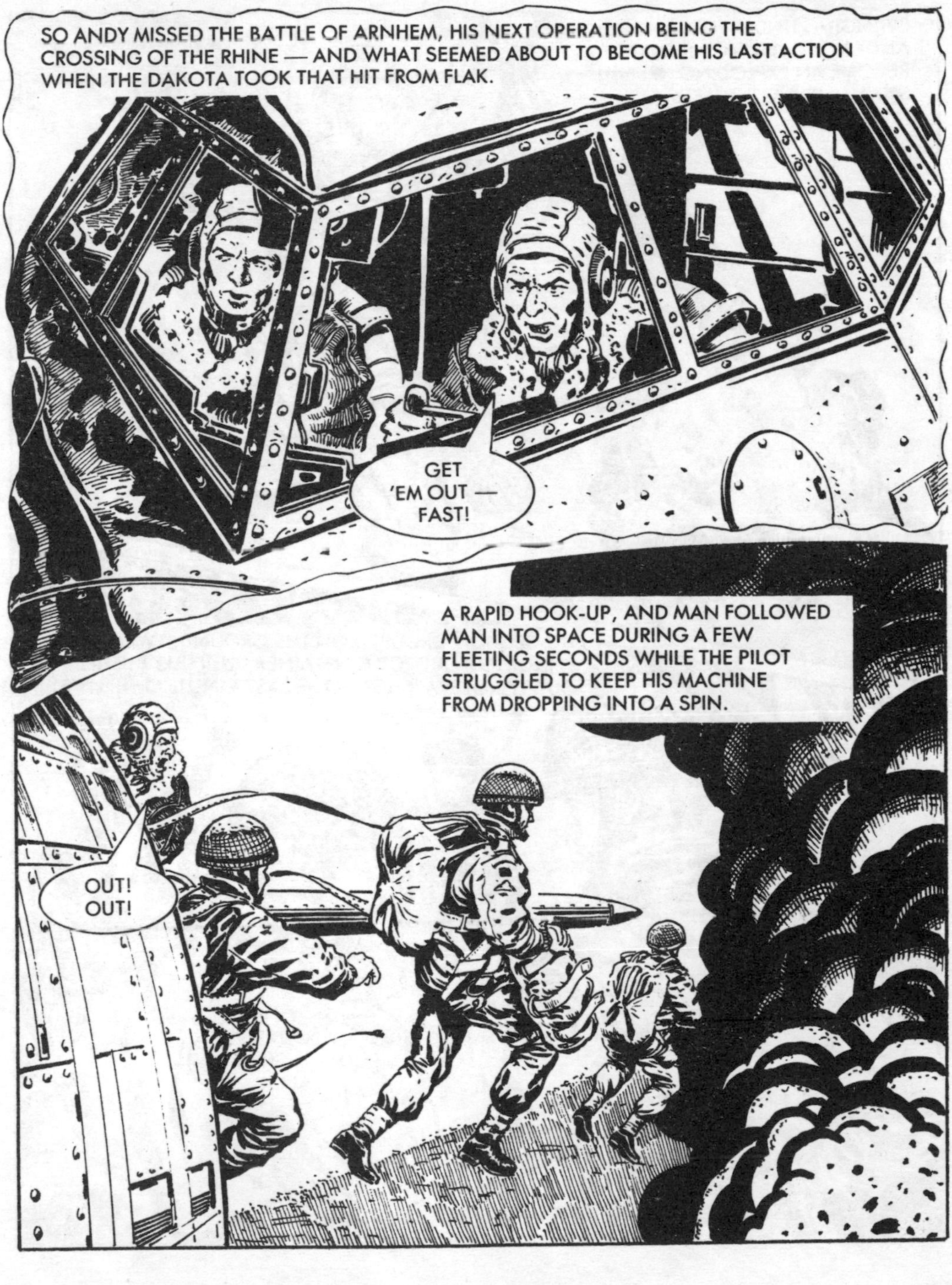
SO ANDY MISSED THE BATTLE OF ARNHEM, HIS NEXT OPERATION BEING THE CROSSING OF THE RHINE — AND WHAT SEEMED ABOUT TO BECOME HIS LAST ACTION WHEN THE DAKOTA TOOK THAT HIT FROM FLAK.
GET 'EM OUT — FAST!
A RAPID HOOK-UP, AND MAN FOLLOWED MAN INTO SPACE DURING A FEW FLEETING SECONDS WHILE THE PILOT STRUGGLED TO KEEP HIS MACHINE FROM DROPPING INTO A SPIN.
OUT! OUT!

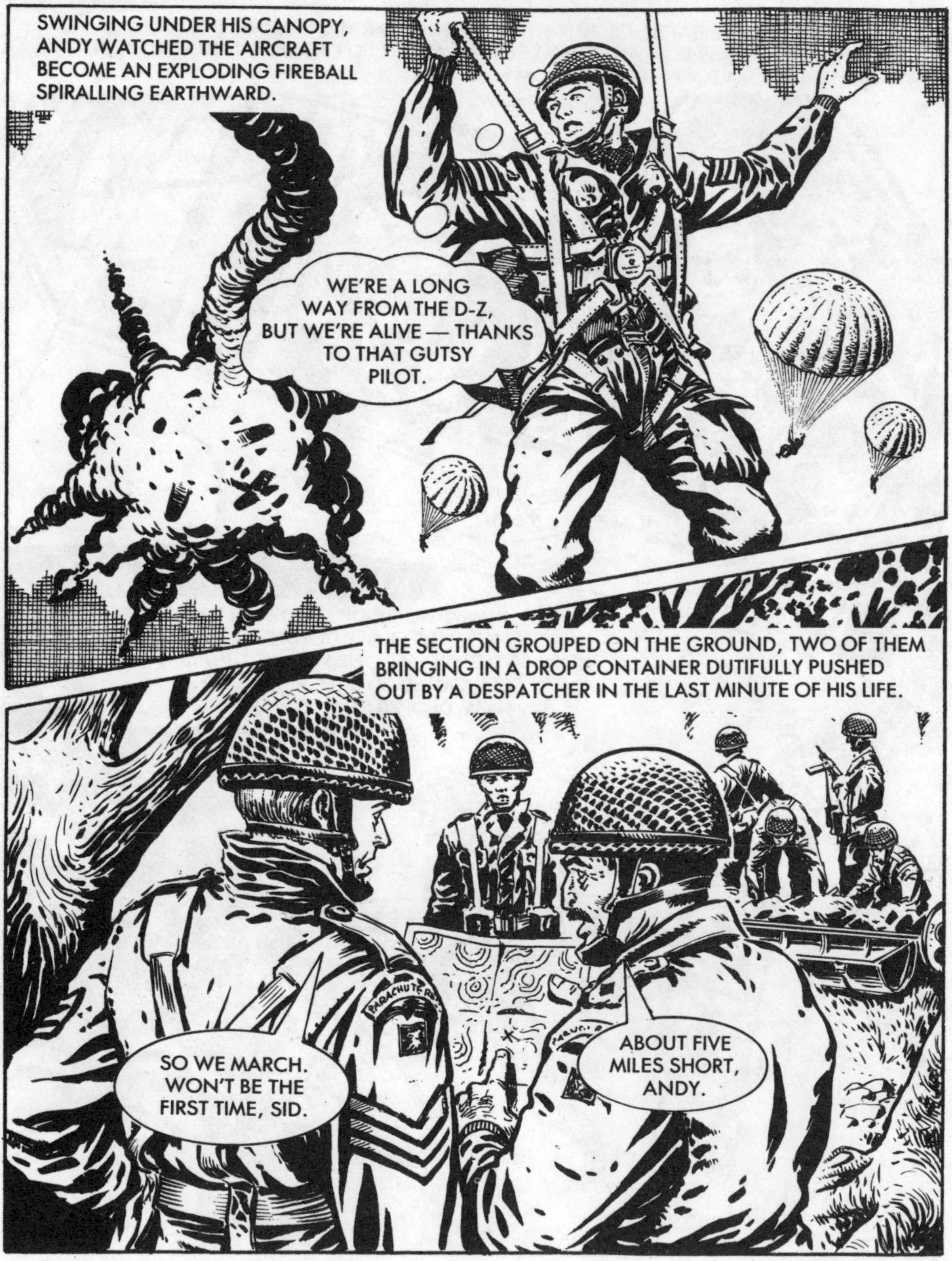
SWINGING UNDER HIS CANOPY, ANDY WATCHED THE AIRCRAFT BECOME AN EXPLODING FIREBALL SPIRALLING EARTHWARD.
WE'RE A LONG WAY FROM THE D-Z, BUT WE'RE ALIVE — THANKS TO THAT GUTSY PILOT.
THE SECTION GROUPED ON THE GROUND, TWO OF THEM BRINGING IN A DROP CONTAINER DUTIFULLY PUSHED OUT BY A DESPATCHER IN THE LAST MINUTE OF HIS LIFE.
ABOUT FIVE MILES SHORT, ANDY.
SO WE MARCH. WON'T BE THE FIRST TIME, SID.

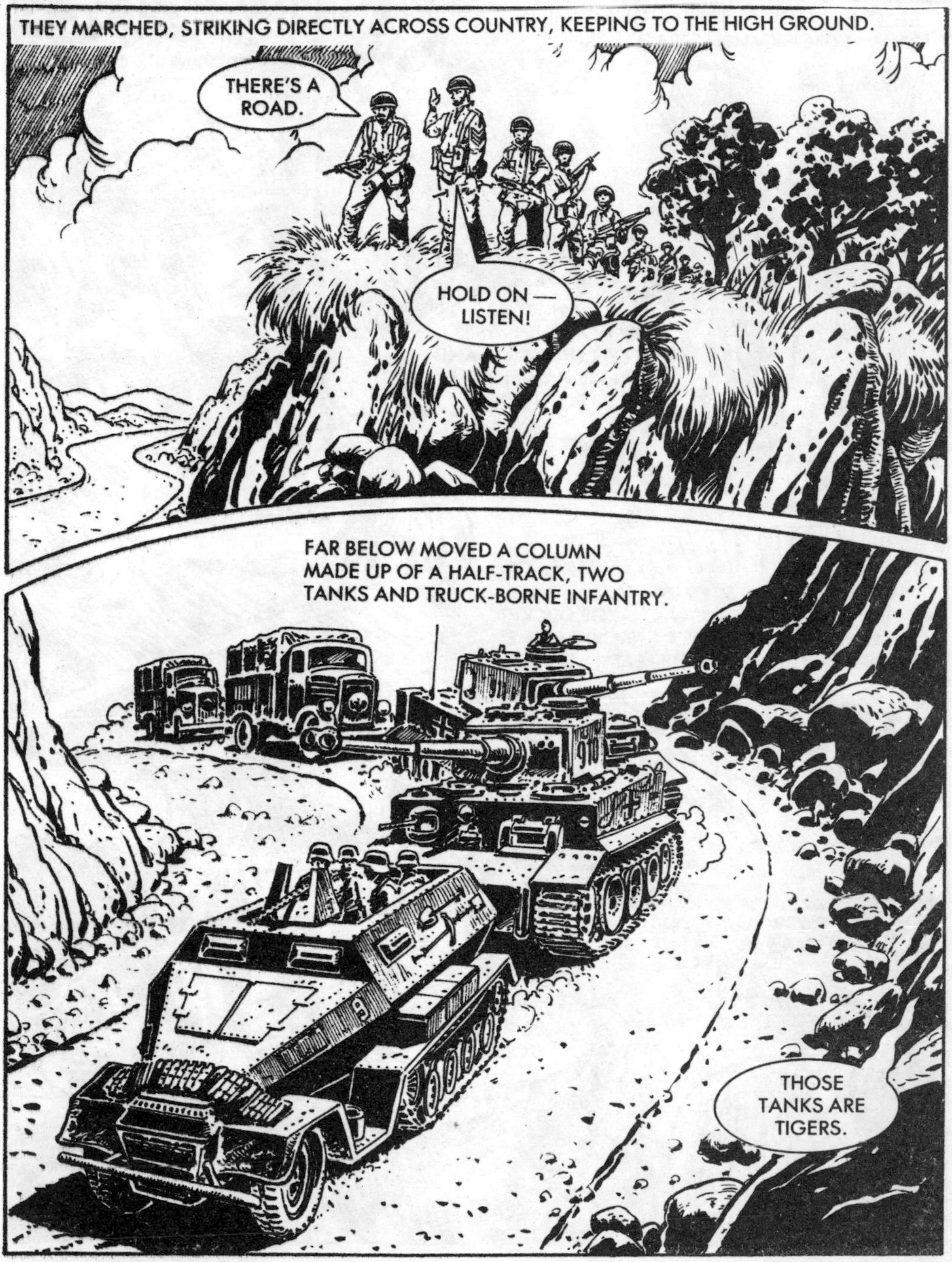
THEY MARCHED, STRIKING DIRECTLY ACROSS COUNTRY, KEEPING TO THE HIGH GROUND.
THERE'S A ROAD.
HOLD ON — LISTEN!
FAR BELOW MOVED A COLUMN MADE UP OF A HALF-TRACK, TWO TANKS AND TRUCK-BORNE INFANTRY.
THOSE TANKS ARE TIGERS.

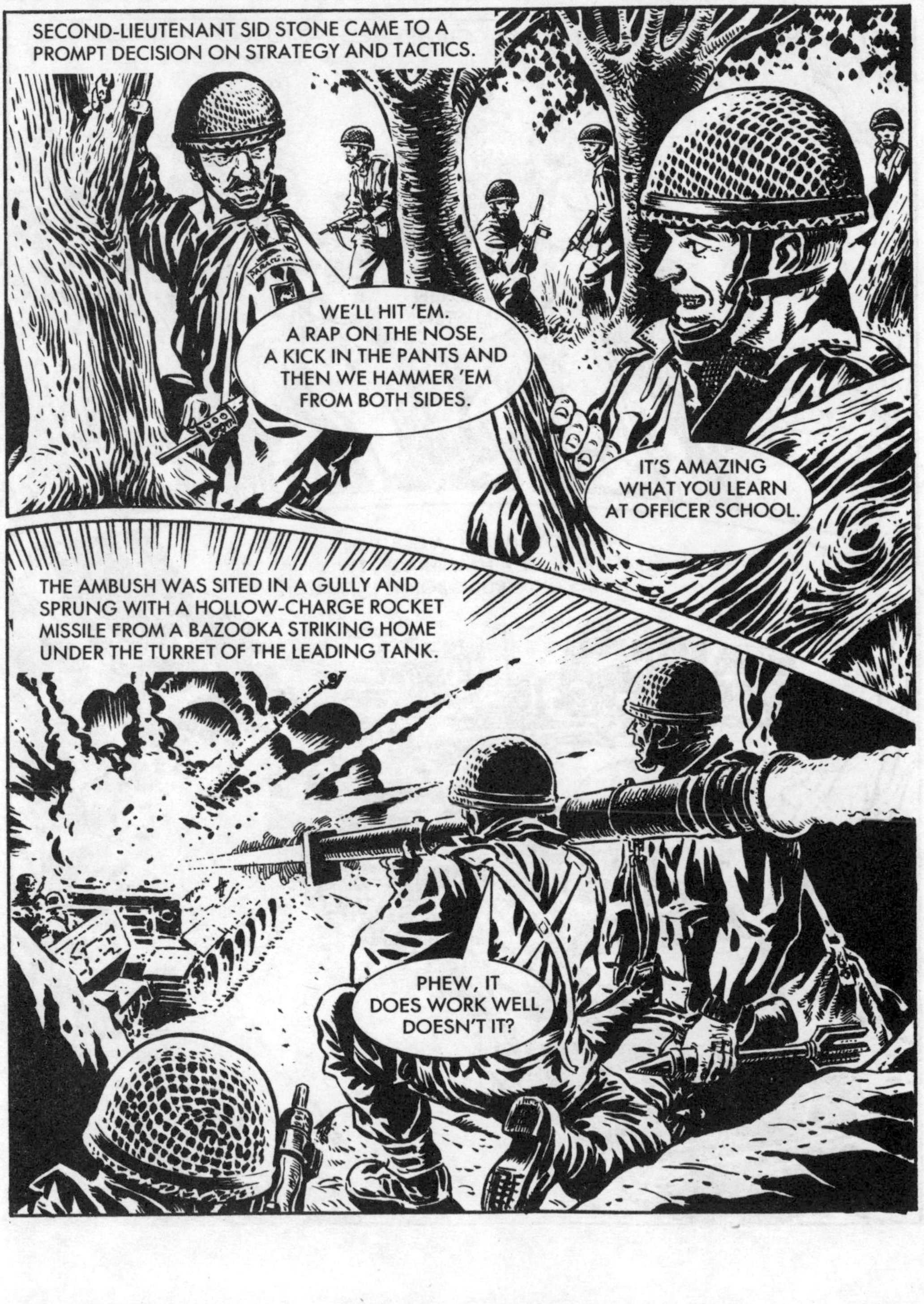
SECOND-LIEUTENANT SID STONE CAME TO A PROMPT DECISION ON STRATEGY AND TACTICS.
WE'LL HIT 'EM. A RAP ON THE NOSE, A KICK IN THE PANTS AND THEN WE HAMMER 'EM FROM BOTH SIDES.
IT'S AMAZING WHAT YOU LEARN AT OFFICER SCHOOL.
THE AMBUSH WAS SITED IN A GULLY AND SPRUNG WITH A HOLLOW-CHARGE ROCKET MISSILE FROM A BAZOOKA STRIKING HOME UNDER THE TURRET OF THE LEADING TANK.
PHEW, IT DOES WORK WELL, DOESN'T IT?

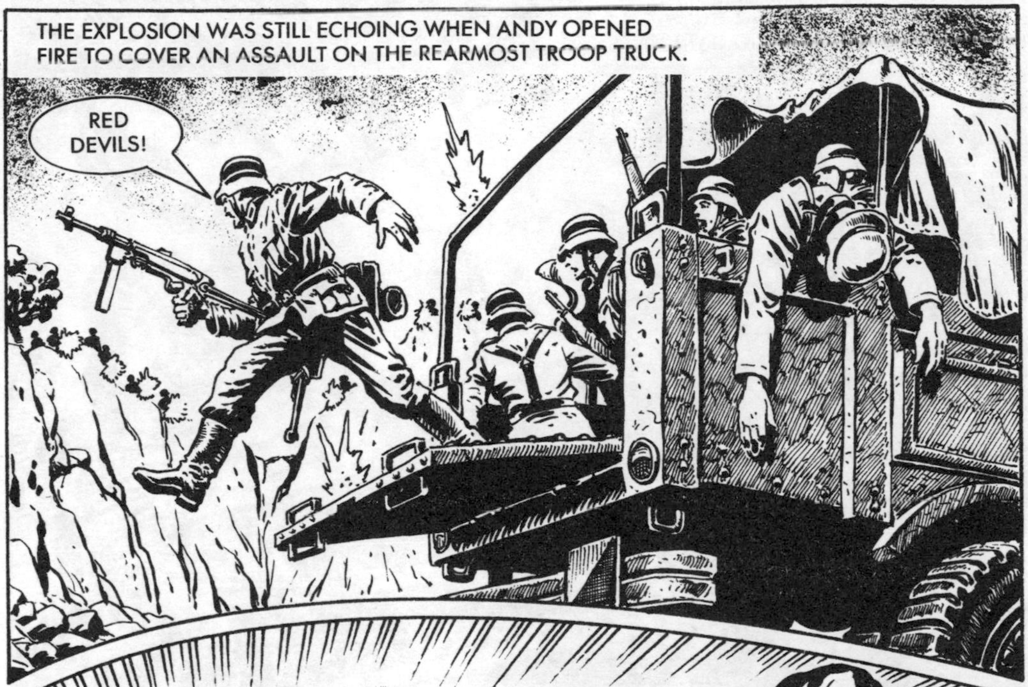
THE EXPLOSION WAS STILL ECHOING WHEN ANDY OPENED FIRE TO COVER AN ASSAULT ON THE REARMOST TROOP TRUCK.
RED DEVILS!

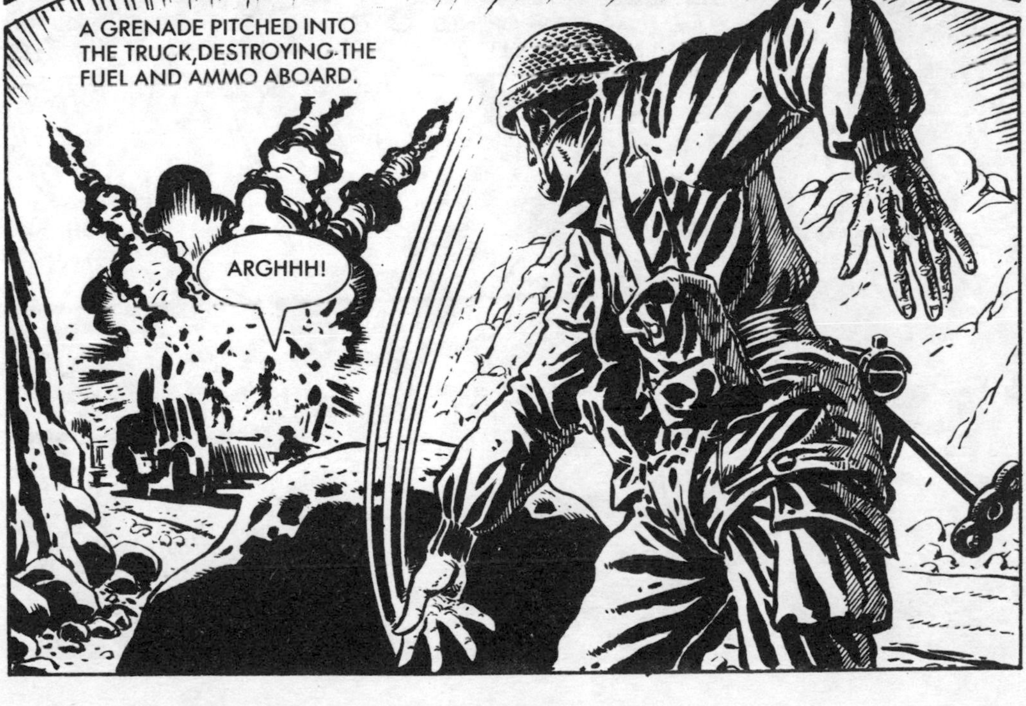
A GRENADE PITCHED INTO THE TRUCK,DESTROYING THE FUEL AND AMMO ABOARD.
ARGHHH!

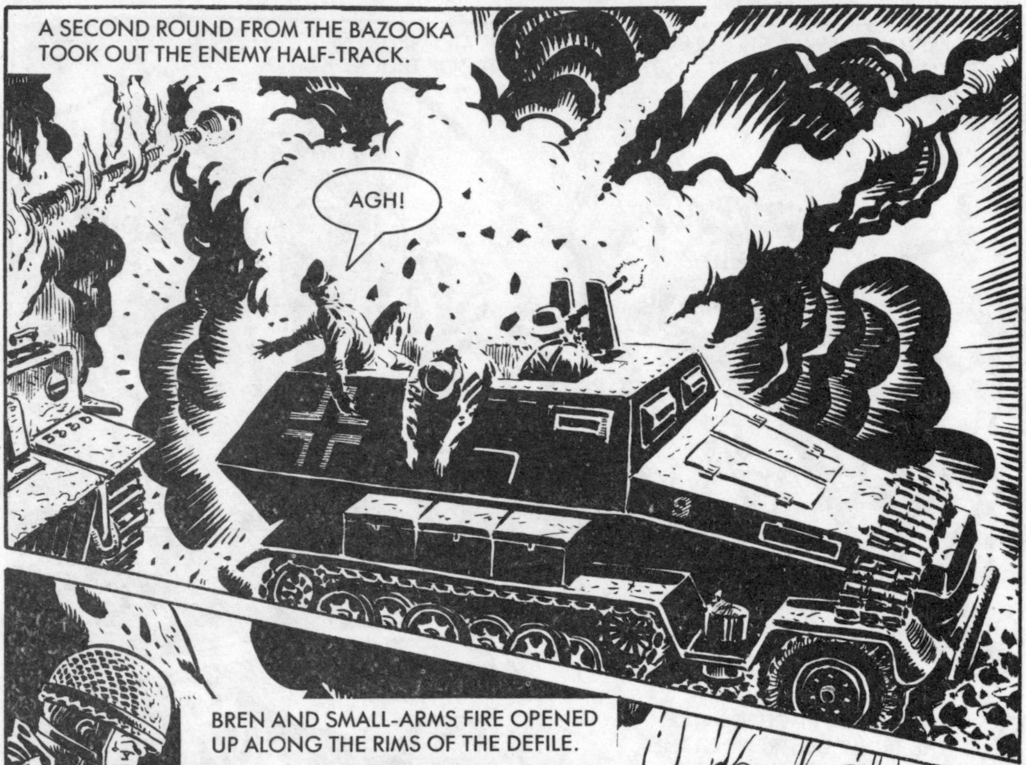
A SECOND ROUND FROM THE BAZOOKA TOOK OUT THE ENEMY HALF-TRACK.
AGH!

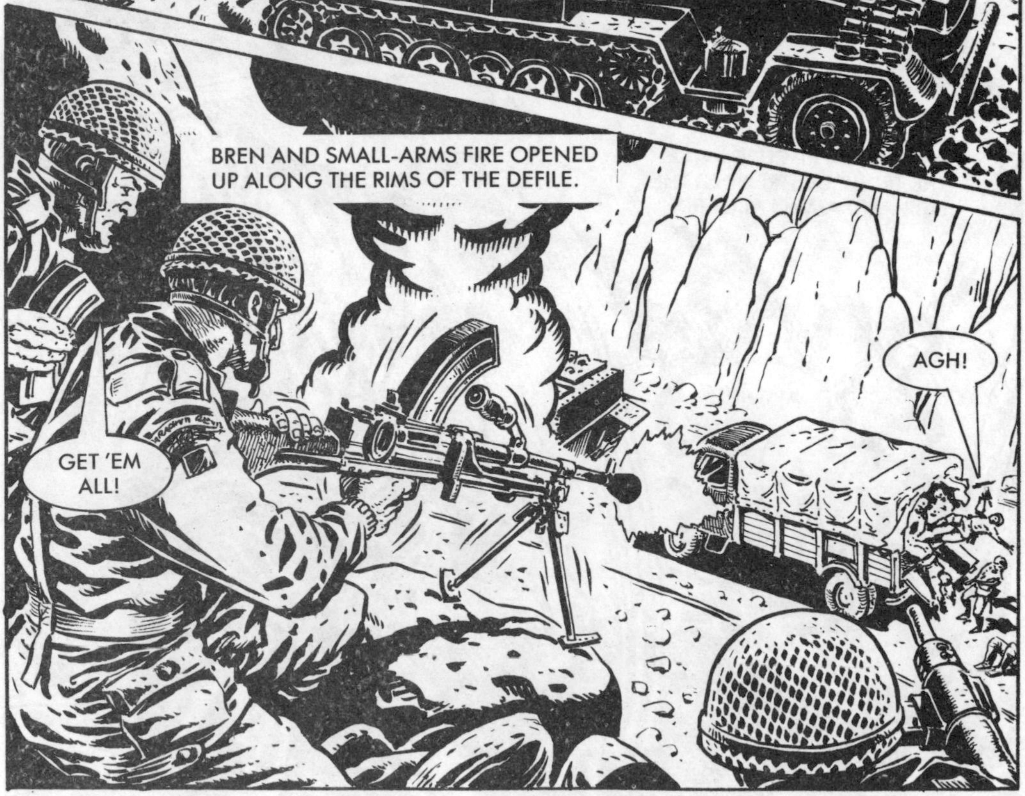
BREN AND SMALL-ARMS FIRE OPENED UP ALONG THE RIMS OF THE DEFILE.
GET 'EM ALL!
AGH!

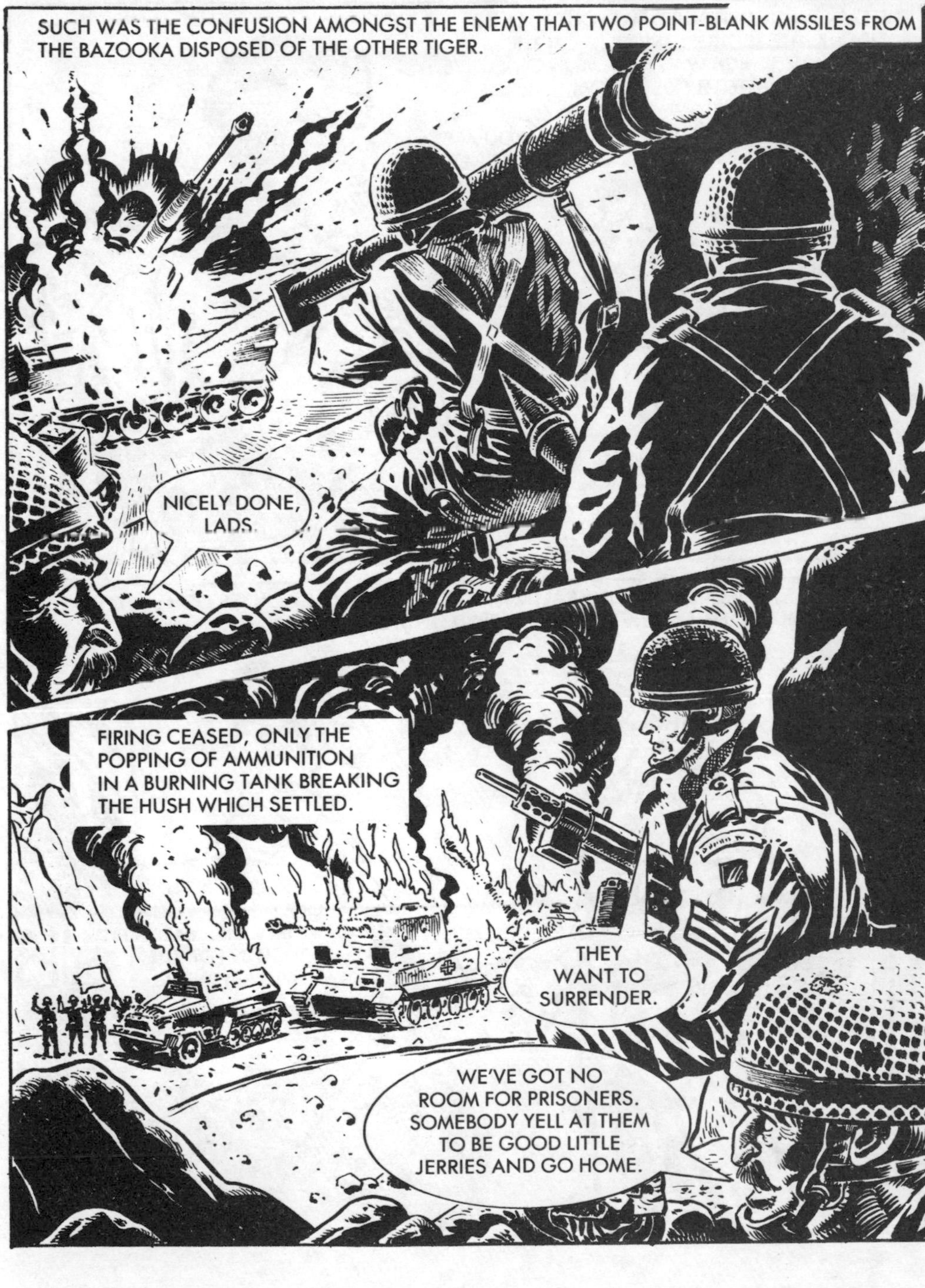
SUCH WAS THE CONFUSION AMONGST THE ENEMY THAT TWO POINT-BLANK MISSILES FROM THE BAZOOKA DISPOSED OF THE OTHER TIGER.
NICELY DONE, LADS.
FIRING CEASED, ONLY THE POPPING OF AMMUNITION IN A BURNING TANK BREAKING THE HUSH WHICH SETTLED.
THEY WANT TO SURRENDER.
WE'VE GOT NO ROOM FOR PRISONERS. SOMEBODY YELL AT THEM TO BE GOOD LITTLE JERRIES AND GO HOME.

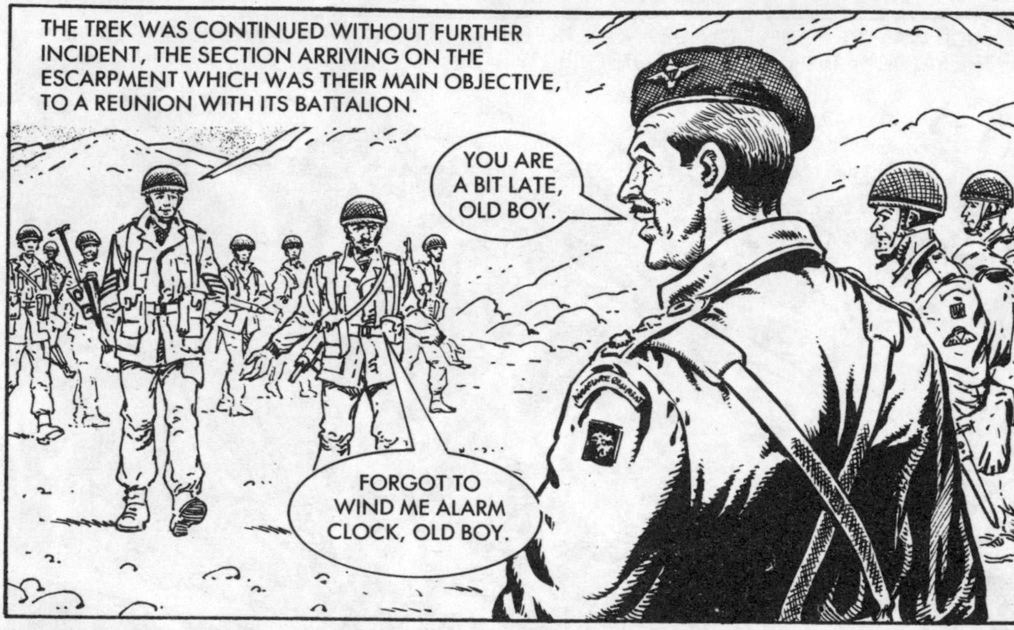
THE TREK WAS CONTINUED WITHOUT FURTHER INCIDENT, THE SECTION ARRIVING ON THE ESCARPMENT WHICH WAS THEIR MAIN OBJECTIVE, TO A REUNION WITH ITS BATTALION.
YOU ARE A BIT LATE, OLD BOY.
FORGOT TO WIND ME ALARM CLOCK, OLD BOY.

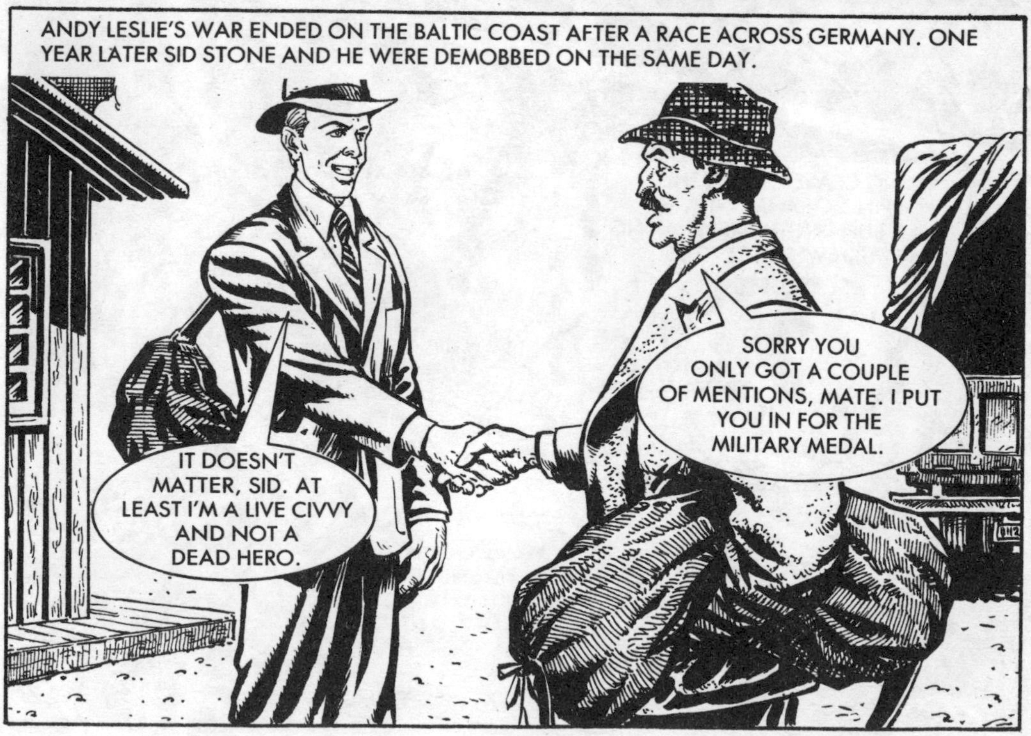
ANDY LESLIE'S WAR ENDED ON THE BALTIC COAST AFTER A RACE ACROSS GERMANY. ONE YEAR LATER SID STONE AND HE WERE DEMOBBED ON THE SAME DAY.
SORRY YOU ONLY GOT A COUPLE OF MENTIONS, MATE. I PUT YOU IN FOR THE MILITARY MEDAL.
IT DOESN'T MATTER, SID. AT LEAST I'M A LIVE CIVVY AND NOT A DEAD HERO.

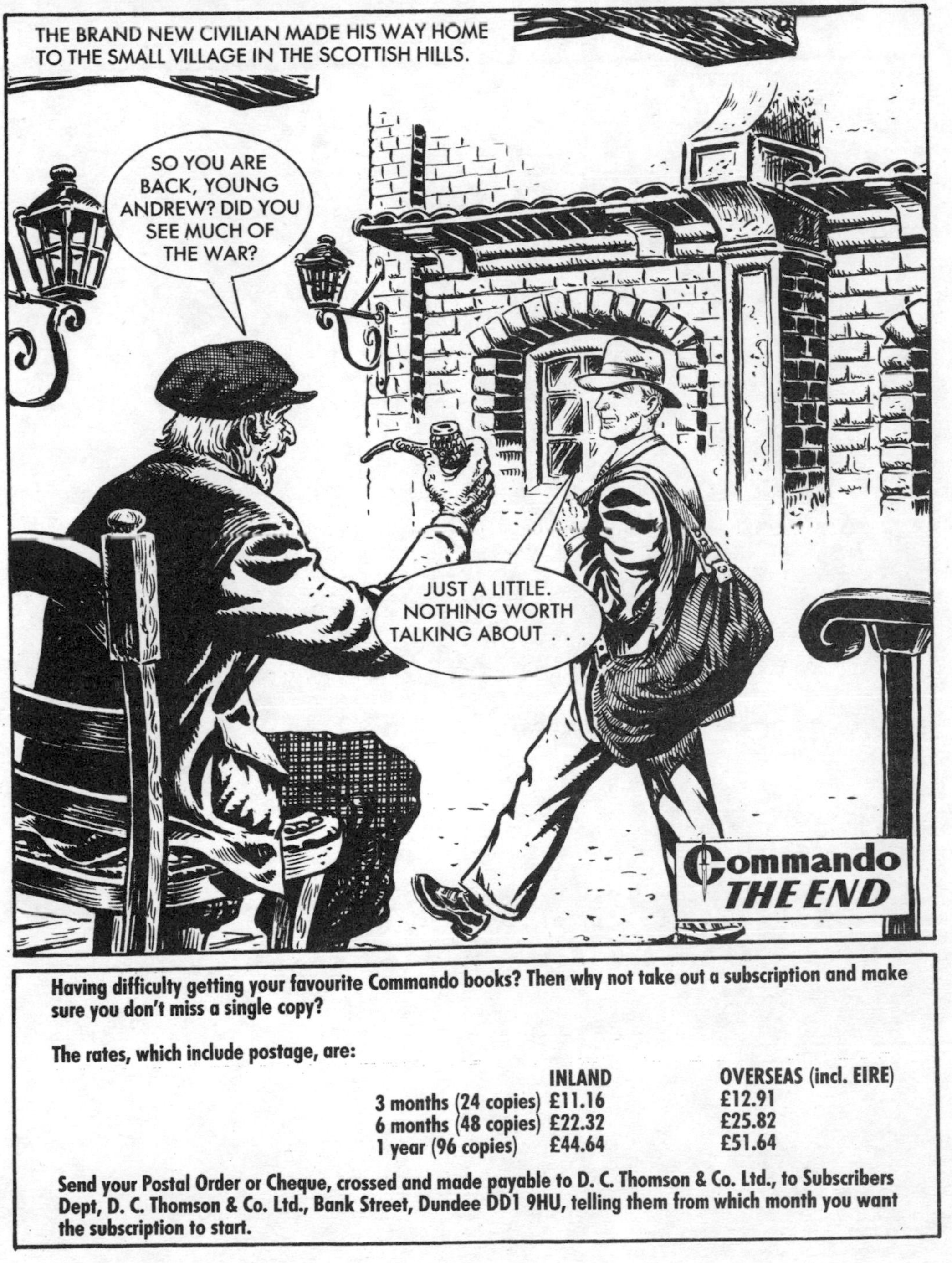
THE BRAND NEW CIVILIAN MADE HIS WAY HOME TO THE SMALL VILLAGE IN THE SCOTTISH HILLS.
SO YOU ARE BACK, YOUNG ANDREW? DID YOU SEE MUCH OF THE WAR?
JUST A LITTLE. NOTHING WORTH TALKING ABOUT . . .
Commando THE END

Commando

FOR ACTION AND ADVENTURE

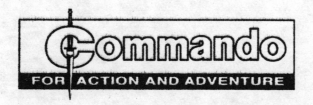

THE COVERS

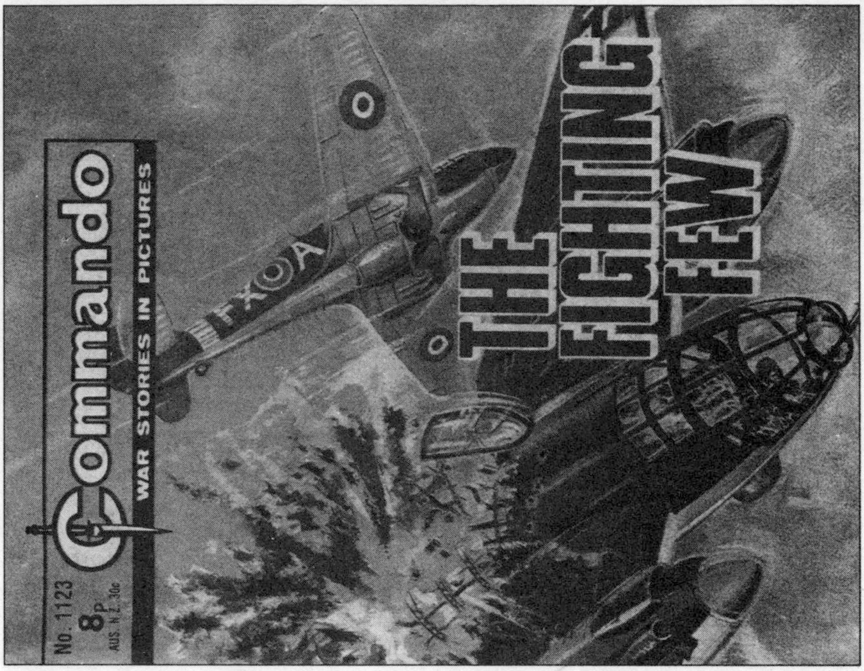
No. 1123
8p
AUS. N.Z. 30c
Commando
WAR STORIES IN PICTURES
THE FIGHTING FEW

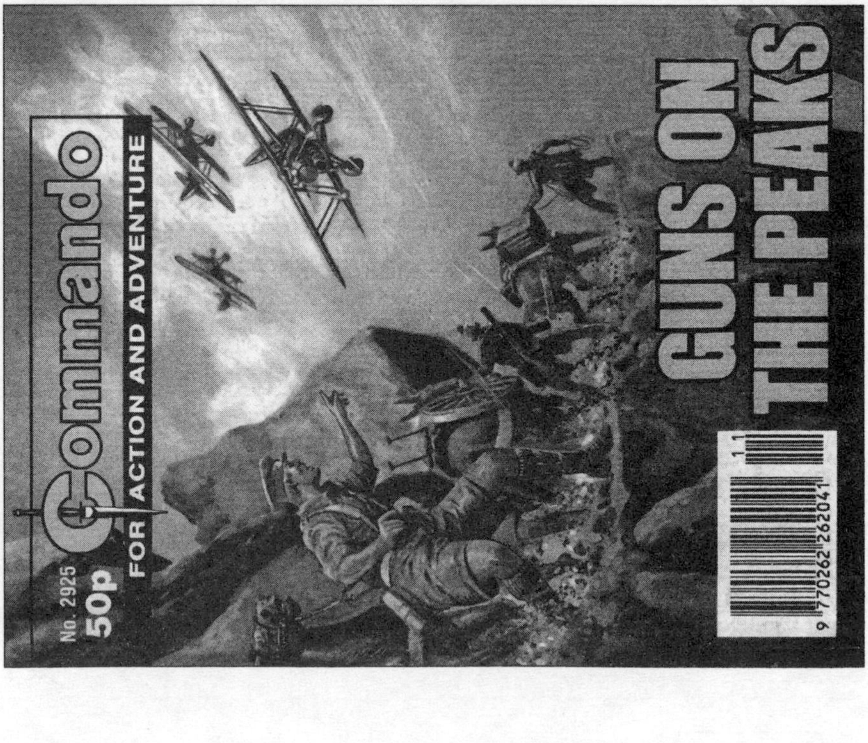
No. 2925
50p
Commando
FOR ACTION AND ADVENTURE
GUNS ON THE PEAKS
9 770262 262041

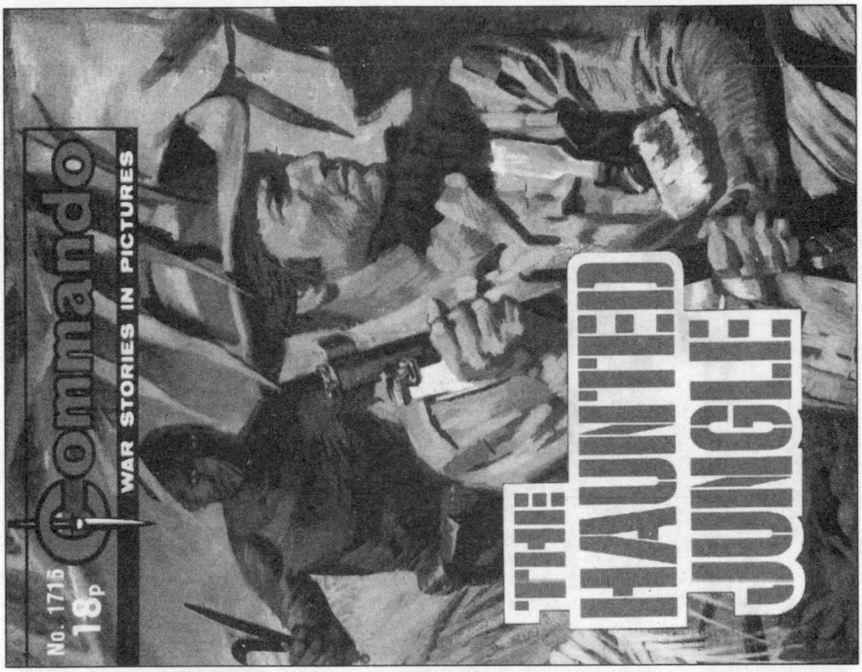
No. 1715
18p
Commando
WAR STORIES IN PICTURES
THE HAUNTED JUNGLE

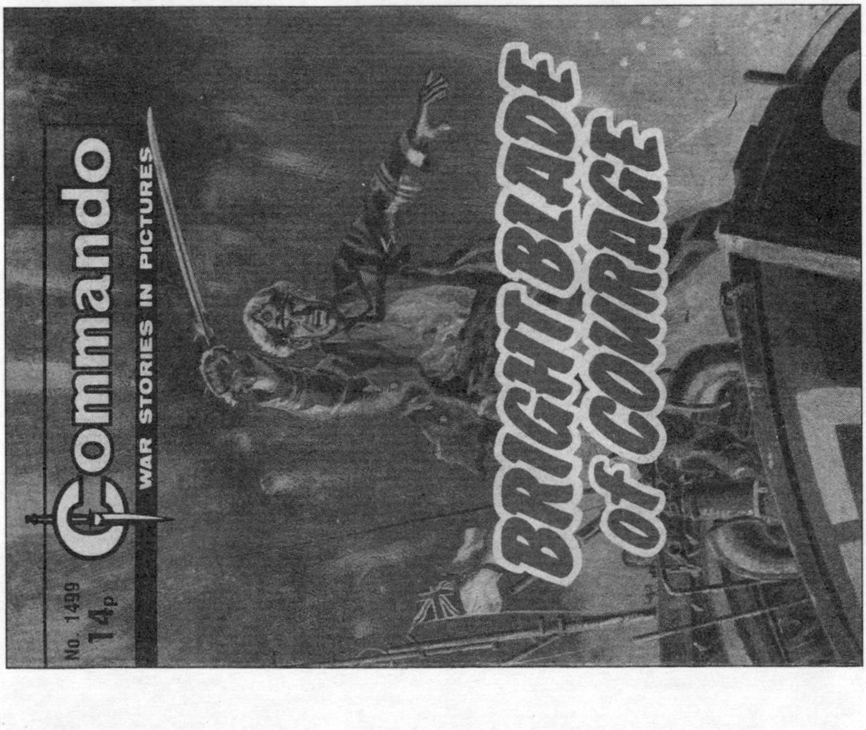
No. 1499
14p
Commando
WAR STORIES IN PICTURES
BRIGHT BLADE of COURAGE

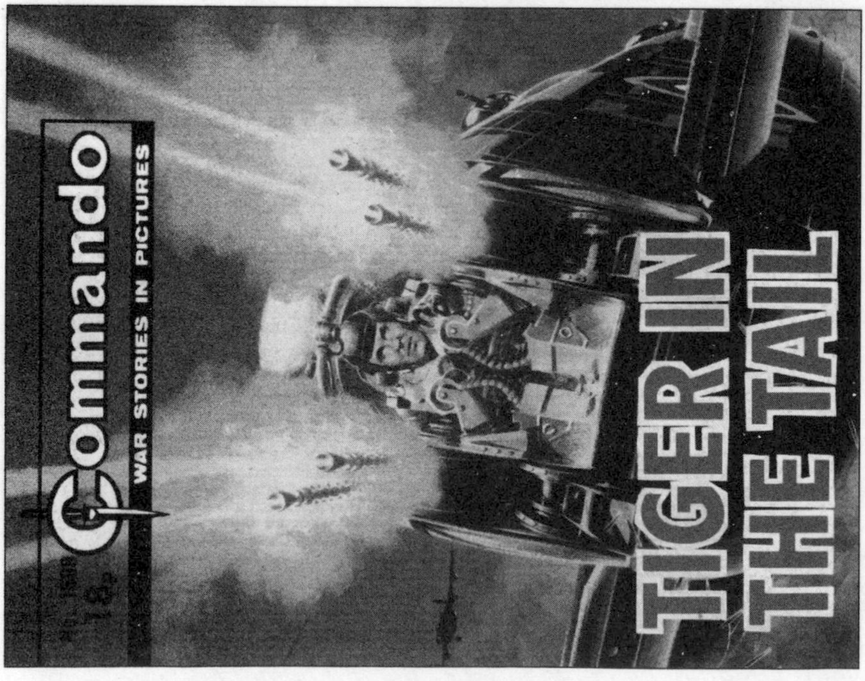
Commando
WAR STORIES IN PICTURES
TIGER IN THE TAIL

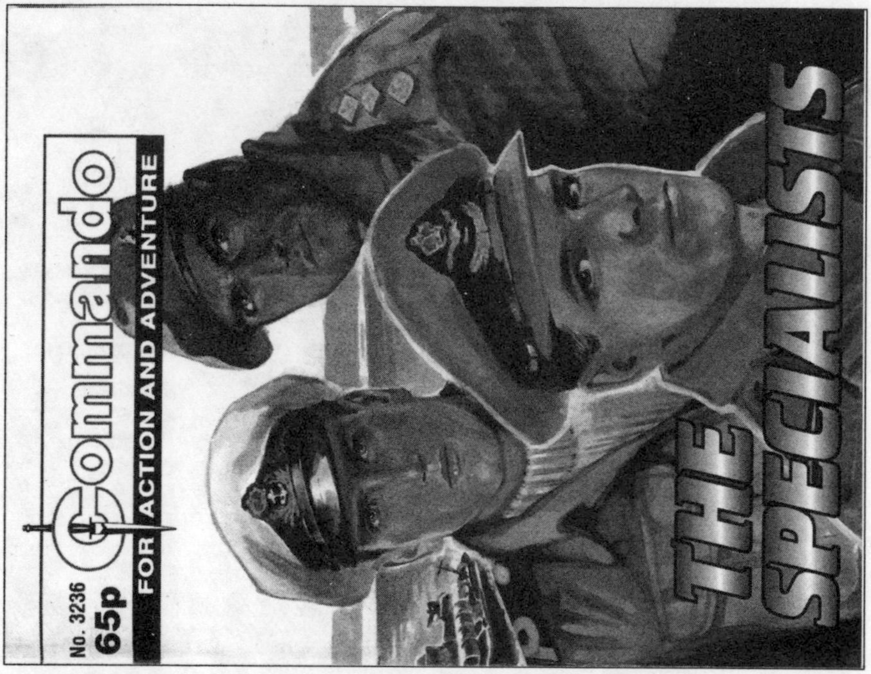
No. 3236
65p
Commando
FOR ACTION AND ADVENTURE
THE SPECIALISTS

Commando
No. 3603 90p
FOR ACTION AND ADVENTURE
VLR — VERY LONG RANGE

Commando
No. 1754 20p
WAR STORIES IN PICTURES
MIGHTY MIDGET

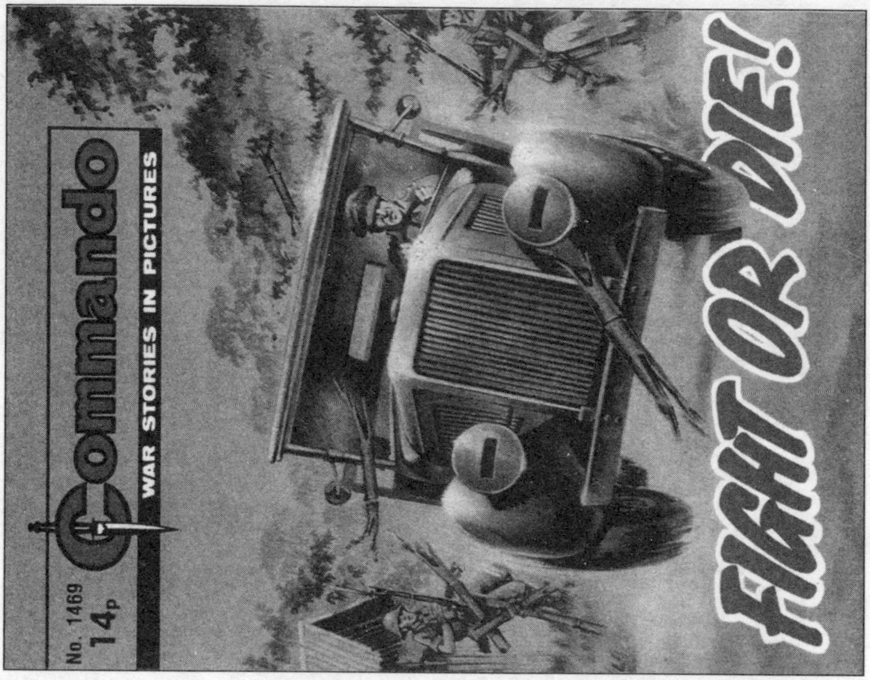
No. 1469
14p
Commando
WAR STORIES IN PICTURES
FIGHT OR DIE!

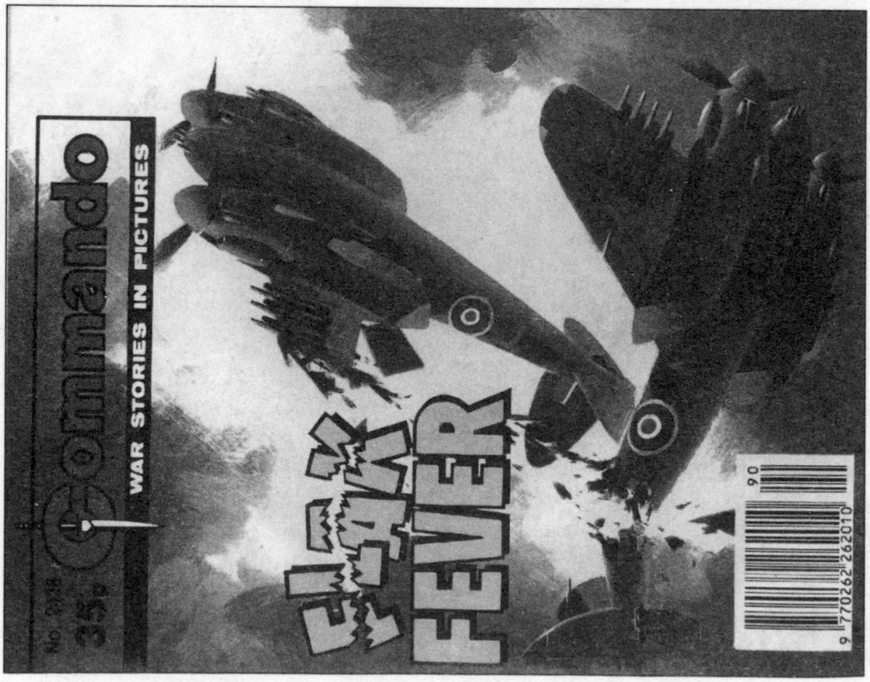
35p
Commando
WAR STORIES IN PICTURES
FLAK FEVER

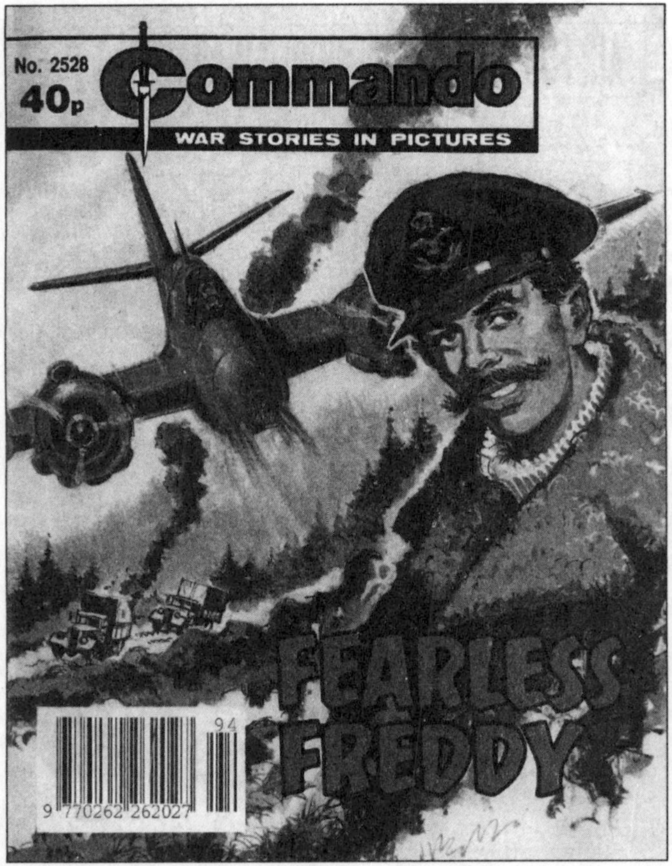
No. 2528
40p
Commando
WAR STORIES IN PICTURES
FEARLESS FREDDY
9 770262 262027 94

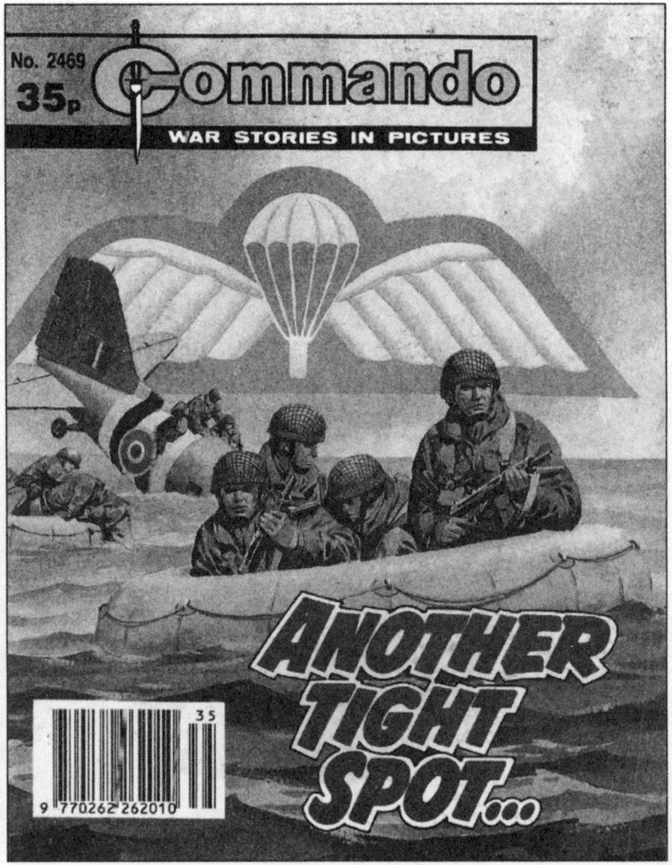
No. 2469
35p
Commando
WAR STORIES IN PICTURES
ANOTHER TIGHT SPOT...
9 770262 262010 35

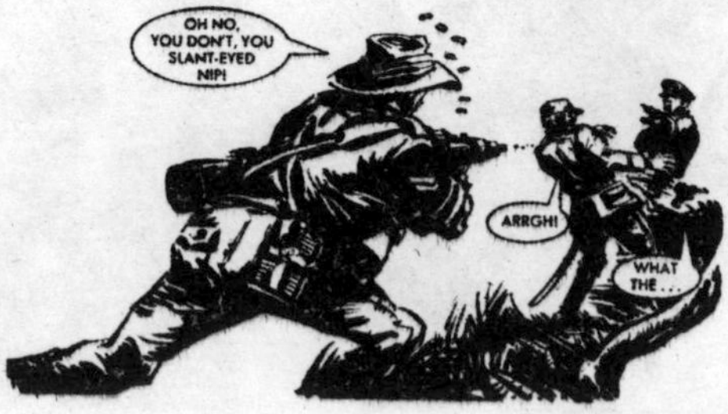
OH NO, YOU DON'T, YOU SLANT-EYED NIP!
ARRGH!
WHAT THE . . .

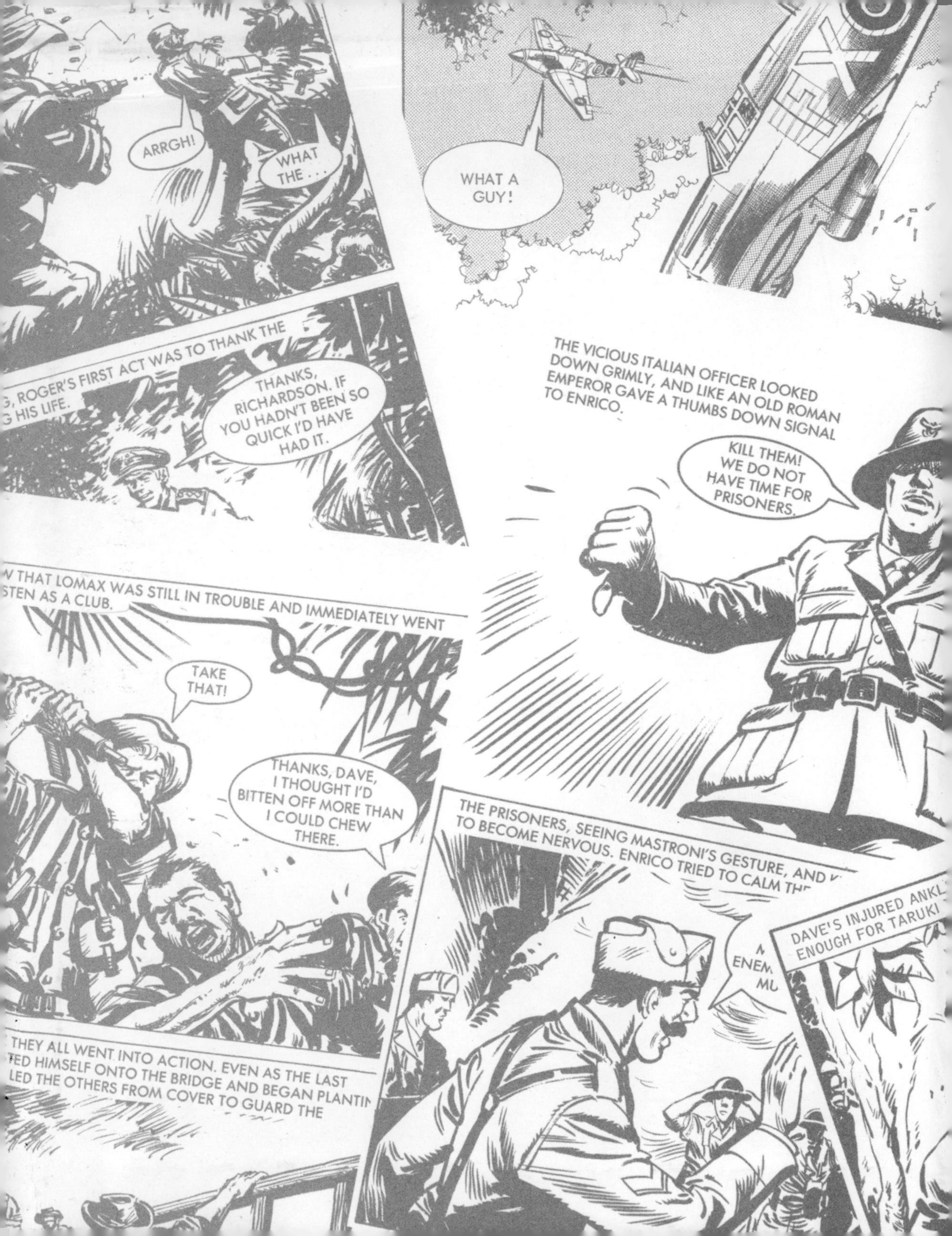
ARRGH!
WHAT THE . . .
WHAT A GUY!
G, ROGER'S FIRST ACT WAS TO THANK THE
G HIS LIFE.
THANKS, RICHARDSON. IF YOU HADN'T BEEN SO QUICK I'D HAVE HAD IT.
THE VICIOUS ITALIAN OFFICER LOOKED DOWN GRIMLY, AND LIKE AN OLD ROMAN EMPEROR GAVE A THUMBS DOWN SIGNAL TO ENRICO.
KILL THEM! WE DO NOT HAVE TIME FOR PRISONERS.
W THAT LOMAX WAS STILL IN TROUBLE AND IMMEDIATELY WENT
STEN AS A CLUB.
TAKE THAT!
THANKS, DAVE, I THOUGHT I'D BITTEN OFF MORE THAN I COULD CHEW THERE.
THE PRISONERS, SEEING MASTRONI'S GESTURE, AND
TO BECOME NERVOUS. ENRICO TRIED TO CALM TH
DAVE'S INJURED ANKL
ENOUGH FOR TARUKI
THEY ALL WENT INTO ACTION. EVEN AS THE LAST
FED HIMSELF ONTO THE BRIDGE AND BEGAN PLANTIN
LED THE OTHERS FROM COVER TO GUARD THE